4/13/98 B+T $55.00

AIDS Narratives

GENDER AND GENRE IN LITERATURE
VOLUME 7
GARLAND REFERENCE LIBRARY OF THE HUMANITIES
VOLUME 1628

Gender and Genre in Literature
Barbara E. Bowen, *Series Editor*

MOTHERS IN THE
ENGLISH NOVEL
From Stereotype to Archetype
by Marjorie McCormick

FEMALE HEROISM
IN THE PASTORAL
by Gail David

SOUTH AFRICAN FEMINISMS
*Writing, Theory, and Criticism,
1990–1994*
edited by M.J. Daymond

REDEFINING AUTOBIOGRAPHY
IN TWENTIETH-CENTURY
WOMEN'S FICTION
An Essay Collection
edited by Janice Morgan
and Colette T. Hall

AIDS NARRATIVES
*Gender and Sexuality,
Fiction and Science*
by Steven F. Kruger

GENDER IN THE THEATRE OF WAR
Shakespeare's Troilus and Cressida
by Barbara E. Bowen

THREE RADICAL WOMEN WRITERS
*Class and Gender in Meridel
Le Sueur, Tillie Olsen, and
Josephine Herbst*
by Nora Ruth Roberts

HOMEMAKING
*Women Writers and the
Politics and Poetics of Home*
edited by Catherine Wiley
and Fiona R. Barnes

AIDS Narratives
Gender and Sexuality, Fiction and Science

Steven F. Kruger

Garland Publishing, Inc.
New York and London
1996

Copyright © 1996 by Steven F. Kruger
All rights reserved

Library of Congress Cataloging-in-Publication Data

Kruger, Steven F.
  AIDS narratives : gender and sexuality, fiction and science / Steven F. Kruger.
      p.   cm. — (Gender and genre in literature ; v. 7) (Garland reference library of the humanities ; vol. 1628)
    Includes bibliographical references (p.   ) and index.
    ISBN 0-8153-0925-2 (alk. paper)
    1. American literature—20th century—History and criticism. 2. AIDS (Disease) in literature. 3. Literature and science—United States—History—20th century. 4. Gay men in literature. 5. Sex in literature. I. Title. II. Series. III. Series: Gender and genre in literature ; v. 7.
  PS169.A42K78   1996
  810.9'356—dc20   95-51014
                                                                        CIP

Cover design by Karin Badger.

Printed on acid-free, 250-year-life paper
Manufactured in the United States of America

Contents

Series Editor's Foreword — vii
Preface — xi
Acknowledgments — xv

Chapter 1: Is a Virus Language? — 3
  1. The Metaphors of Molecular Genetics — 5
  2. Virus As Language — 11
  3. Language As Virus — 15
  Notes — 24

Chapter 2: AIDS and the Battlefields of Masculinity — 33
  1. Sexualized Cells — 33
  2. Cells/Bodies/Populations — 42
  Notes — 61

Chapter 3: The Narratives of AIDS — 73
  1. Irreversible Decline and Uncontrollable Spread — 73
  2. *Facing It* — 81
  3. The Genre of the AIDS Novel: Frustrating Expectations — 88
  Notes — 105

Chapter 4: Gay and Other Subjects of AIDS — 111
  1. Heterosexual AIDS? — 111
  2. "Innocent Victims"/*At Risk* — 123
  3. Gay Subjects of AIDS, Homophobia, and Misogyny — 141
  Notes — 160

Chapter 5: John Weir's *The Irreversible Decline of Eddie Socket*   163
    1. Reforming Narrative   163
    2. Body and Voice: Narrative Delay, Closure, and Proliferation   177
    3. "Who Am I Quoting?": Citation, Narrative, and Identity   186
    Notes   202

Chapter 6: Apocalyptic Conspiracies: The "Epidemiological Narrative" of AIDS   205
    1. Ends and Origins   205
    2. Invoking History, Authenticating Fictions   226
    3. Fighting Back   234
    4. Avoiding AIDS   246
    Notes   252

Chapter 7: "But Then What?": Sarah Schulman's *People in Trouble*   259
    1. The Beginning of the End   259
    2. The Story of Justice   277
    3. Toward an Activist Aesthetic?   294
    Notes   301

Appendix: Bibliography of AIDS Literature   303
    Multi-Genre Anthologies   304
    Fiction   305
    Poetry   320
    Drama/Performance   327
    Nonfiction Narrative   334

Works Cited   355
Index   381

Series Editor's Foreword

The Gender and Genre in Literature series participates in what Eve Sedgwick has called one of the two great "heuristic leaps of feminism": the recognition that gender is a structuring force for "nodes of thought" that may have nothing explicitly to do with gender at all. Genre might be considered one of these nodes of thought, even though the word itself is simply a more direct importation from the French of the word "gender." The Gender and Genre in Literature series seeks to advance a discussion already under way within feminist criticism on the role of genre in enforcing the gender hierarchy: publication itself has historically been a gendering activity, as has been the choice, for instance, of epic over translation, drama over diaries.

But the discussion of gender and genre goes beyond these distinctions to investigate how the notion of genre itself is changing shape under pressure from feminist and other interventions in humanist epistemology. New categories of writing—letters, journals, popular fiction, travel narratives, advertising, science—are demanding attention as literary genres, while the traditional genres are being reanimated by efforts to disrupt their alignments with patriarchy, compulsory heterosexuality, and white supremacy. A painful history has already shown that any attempt to consider gender oppression in isolation from other forms of oppression just reinforces the hierarchies already in place, so deeply are they institutionalized in the late capitalist world. Thus the Gender and Genre in Literature series, while arguing for the importance of gender as a category of analysis, seeks to develop a complex and multiple understanding of gender with which to resee written culture.

The present volume, *AIDS Narratives: Gender and Sexuality, Fiction and Science*, demonstrates how serious the political implications of reconceptualizing literary genre can be. *AIDS Narratives* is a direct attempt to intervene in the cultural production of AIDS; it addresses itself as much to current agendas of AIDS activism as to questions within literary scholarship. Reading journalism with fiction, molecular biology texts with the *Congressional Record*,

Steven Kruger lays bare a political interconnectedness the rule of genre normally obscures; he shows that the metaphors available to immunologists in the late 1980s implied certain narratives, and that these narratives in turn structured journalistic, political, popular, and literary representations of AIDS. The narratives, of course, are not innocent: even at the level of the cell they are racialized, sexualized, gendered. One of the most influential sections of Kruger's book will be its analysis of how medical science unconsciously metaphorizes HIV infection—a microscopic process involving the virus and a single cell—as a kind of homosexual rape. Normative masculinity is consolidated through reference to the "queer" in a discourse that also focuses anxieties about gender, "foreignness" and race. The language of science, Kruger argues, simultaneously produces and reflects a larger cultural narrative that identifies gayness with disease, AIDS with gayness, and death with AIDS. Kruger's project is to rewrite this narrative; the book seeks to disengage queerness from death.

How, Kruger asks, does fiction, presumably more self-conscious about narrative than science, journalism or politics, position itself in relation to the prevailing AIDS narratives? Does American AIDS fiction in particular offer a counternarrative? The second part of the book is a study of this emerging literary genre in relation to what Kruger identifies as the two dominant narratives through which American culture understands AIDS: the first, "the narrative of irreversible decline," focuses on the story of an individual's discovery of and eventual death from AIDS; the second, "the narrative of uncontrollable spread," concentrates on the origins and the (usually apocalyptic) future of the epidemic. One is microcosmic, the other macrocosmic; one ostensibly private, the other public. Kruger's interest is in the way American AIDS fiction reinscribes, interrogates, and attempts to subvert these scripts. His discussion takes him from the earliest published AIDS novels, such as Paul Reed's *Facing It*, to such widely read works as Armistead Maupin's *Significant Others* and Alice Hoffman's *At Risk*, to the further reaches of apocalyptic AIDS fiction, and finally to two novels in which he finds achieved counternarratives.

The strength of Kruger's account lies not just in his encyclopedic command of the field (and it is encyclopedic—the book includes a bibliography of over a thousand fictional and nonfiction AIDS narratives), but in the intellectual authority his knowledge of the genre allows. *AIDS Narratives* is full of surprising, nuanced readings of works that have often received little formal criticism. At the same time it is a major reference source on a new literary genre. The book moves towards sustained readings of John Weir's *Irreversible Decline of Eddie Socket* (1989) and Sarah Schulman's *People in Trouble* (1990) as novels that see through the dominant cultural narratives and enable a radical reconception of AIDS and the identity categories on which current AIDS policy depends. Kruger contends that such a reconception through narrative, necessary for a transformation of U.S. AIDS policy, is in itself political praxis. *AIDS Narratives* stands in urgent relation to the present historical moment; offering a powerful analysis and calling for a critical, visionary fiction, the book contributes to the political transformation it demands.

Barbara Bowen
Queens College and The Graduate Center
City University of New York

Preface

Writing this book has been difficult, and possible only because of the many people supporting me in my work. The members of my family—Alice S. Kruger, Stanley I. Kruger, Susan D. Kruger, Jonathan Dull, Joshua D. Kruger, Diane Bassett, David M. Kruger—have shown a consistent interest in my (sometimes esoteric) writing, and have contributed to this particular project by keeping me apprised of developments in their own fields of interest—psychology, medicine, public health, history, popular culture. My colleagues at Queens College and at the Graduate School and University Center of the City University of New York have also provided much help. During the writing of this book, I had the pleasure of team-teaching with Joan Nestle, whose strong interest in the project helped sustain it. Estelle Raben, William Green, and Barbara Leavy gave me the opportunity to read their own work on AIDS drama, some of it while still in progress. Charles Molesworth, the Chair of my department at Queens, has in many ways supported the writing of this book, as has Joseph Wittreich, Executive Officer of the Ph.D. Program in English at CUNY. My medievalist colleagues in the City University, Bill McClellan, Catherine McKenna, Michael Sargent, Martin Stevens, Scott Westrem, and E. Gordon Whatley, have understood and supported my decision (temporarily) to abandon the Middle Ages. Patricia Clough, Nancy Comley, Janice Peritz, David Richter, and Amy Tucker have willingly listened to my complaints and provided advice. Tony O'Brien has been a true intellectual comrade. Bette Weidman has, in her constant generosity, made Queens College feel like a home.

Friends in the broader academic community have also given much support to this project. These include former teachers and current colleagues in medieval studies: Sherron Knopp, Rita Copeland (who heard and encouraged some of my earliest thinking about AIDS and narrative), David Wallace, George Brown, Mary Wack, Lisa Darien, John Kleiner, and Glenn Burger. Naomi Holoch gave me the opportunity to read a section of this book at

SUNY/Purchase; the comments I received from students and faculty on that occasion were enlightening. Alisa Solomon, Marina Heung, and Les Wright each made generous bibliographic contributions to this project. Jim Reilly has been a thoughtful and helpful correspondent. I was lucky to be able to participate in Dorothy Helly and Altagracia Ortiz's seminar on gender, race, ethnicity, and class while in the early stages of writing this book; the continuing support of the seminar members, especially Dorothy, has been remarkable. Through the seminar, I met Kathryn Katzman Rolland, Sarah Watstein, and José Hernandez, all of whom have taught the course on AIDS and Society at Hunter College; I have learned much from them.

When I began my obsessive reading about AIDS in the early 1980s, I did so largely in isolation. The first person with whom I shared ideas about that reading was Judith Raiskin, who has been, in more ways than I can enumerate, a guiding force for this work. She also was one of the first to encourage me to teach about AIDS, and I in many ways owe to her the remarkable experiences of that teaching, first as a graduate student at Stanford University and then at Queens College. The success of my class at Queens, "The Language and Literature of AIDS," has depended upon the unwavering institutional support of my departmental Curriculum Committee. During the Fall of 1993, a grant from the President of the College allowed me to bring several writers—David B. Feinberg, Tony Kushner, Sarah Schulman, and John Weir—into that class to discuss their past work and to read from new projects. All four authors were generous with their time and with their ideas.

Each of the many students who have participated in my classes on AIDS has made a mark on this book. The fact that I have taught both Sarah Schulman's *People in Trouble* and John Weir's *The Irreversible Decline of Eddie Socket* several times to outspoken classes partly explains my decision here to devote a whole chapter to each; my students' words are very much present in what I have written. In particular, I wish to thank Deneez Azeez, Yonina Borvick, Ava Chin, James Costas, Aviva Dreisinger, Trent Hamann, Cynthia Hanratty, Dana Kamins, Joseph (Mike) Labeck, John Muñoz, Carrette Perkins, Judy Rycar, and Tracy Steffy for their interest, energy, and honesty. Though Darrell Barnhill and Debi Share were not officially members of these classes, they were still in many ways important participants. And I would like to thank several other students who have taken an interest in, and helped with this project: Laura Ciraolo, Sharon Kraus, Christine Timm, Christopher F. Varga, and Meenakshi Venkatasubramanian of the CUNY Graduate School and Suzanne Kaebnick of SUNY/Stony Brook.

Deborah R. Geis was my collaborator in organizing a conference on AIDS and performance at Queens College in the Spring of 1991, and our collaboration continues in other exciting projects. John Weir, who spoke at that conference and who is now my colleague at Queens, has borne gracefully the burden of being written about in heavy academic prose, and he has told me (sometimes) whom he was quoting. Bob Tilton and Rita Connolly-Tilton have helped preserve the intellectual and social community of our days in California. Sara Blair, Susan Frye, Mary Favret, and Tom Moser, Jr., have done the same, though at the disadvantage of greater distance. Julee Raiskin, Mary Elene Wood, Eli Anthony Raiskin-Wood, Rebecca Mark, Jordana Raiskin, and Maria Damon have all remained integral to my extended community. Ron Scapp and Meryl Siegman provide me with the day-to-day support that makes work possible; Ron's incisive comments on much of the manuscript of this book helped me see my own work in ways that would not otherwise have been possible.

In completing this book, I have incurred an enormous debt to Barbara Bowen, the editor for the *Gender and Genre in Literature* series at Garland Publishing and my colleague at Queens College: she has read the whole manuscript with meticulous care and provided a thoroughgoing and lucid critique. Though, in revising the book, I have not always followed her suggestions, these have been always provocative and productive, and it is largely her encouragement that has allowed the book's completion. Kennie Lyman, Claudia Hirsch, and Phyllis Korper at Garland have also been helpful and generous with their time.

***

I dedicate this book to the memory of Tom Black, Melvin Dixon, David B. Feinberg, Arthur Hall, Donald R. Howard, Arturo Islas, Erika Jacobson, David Langworthy, Tom Mackey, Jack Winkler, and Greg Witcher, with sorrow for lost, and missed, connections.

Acknowledgments

The following material is used by permission:

Excerpts from *Genocide: The Anthology* by Tim Barrus. Copyright (c) 1988 by Tim Barrus. Reprinted by permission of Knights Press.

Excerpts from *Old Soldier* by Vance Bourjaily. Copyright (c) 1990 by Vance Bourjaily. Reprinted by permission of Donald I. Fine, Inc.

Excerpts from *A Cry in the Desert* by Jed A. Bryan. Copyright (c) 1987 by Jed A. Bryan. Reprinted by permission of Banned Books, Edward-William Publishing Company.

Excerpts from *Tangled Up in Blue* by Larry Duplechan. Copyright (c) 1989 by Larry Duplechan. Reprinted by permission of St. Martin's Press.

Excerpts from *At Risk* by Alice Hoffman. Copyright (c) 1988 by Alice Hoffman. Reprinted by permission of G. P. Putnam's Sons.

Excerpts from *Plague: A Novel about Healing* by Toby Johnson. Copyright (c) 1987 by Toby Johnson. Reprinted by permission of Alyson Publications, Inc., 40 Plympton Street, Boston, MA 02118.

Excerpts from *Gentle Warriors* by Geoff Mains. Copyright (c) 1989 by Geoff Mains. Reprinted by permission of Knights Press.

Excerpts from *Significant Others* by Armistead Maupin. Copyright (c) 1987 by Armistead Maupin. Reprinted by permission of HarperCollins Publishers, Inc.

Excerpts from *Sure of You* by Armistead Maupin. Copyright (c) 1989 by Armistead Maupin. Reprinted by permission of HarperCollins Publishers, Inc.

Excerpts from *Facing It: A Novel of A.I.D.S.* by Paul Reed. Copyright (c) 1984 by Paul Reed. Reprinted by permission of Paul Reed.

Excerpts from *The Boiled Frog Syndrome: A Novel of Love, Sex and Politics* by Marty Rubin. Copyright (c) 1987 by Marty Rubin. Reprinted by permission of Alyson Publications, Inc., 40 Plympton Street, Boston, MA 02118.

Excerpts from *People in Trouble* by Sarah Schulman. Copyright (c) 1990 by Sarah Schulman. Reprinted by permission of Dutton Signet, a division of Penguin Books USA Inc.

Excerpts from *The Irreversible Decline of Eddie Socket* by John Weir. Copyright (c) 1989 by John Weir. Reprinted by permission of John Weir.

AIDS Narratives

CHAPTER 1

Is a Virus Language?

Acquired immune deficiency syndrome (AIDS) and the human immunodeficiency virus (HIV) thought to cause it[1] occupy a curious and complex position in the metaphoric language of late twentieth-century Western culture, standing within a nexus of ideas linking linguistic coherence and incoherence to health and disease, life and death, the "natural" and the "artificial," control and chaos. Within such diverse discourses as those of biological science, information science, the mass media, popular culture, medicine, and politics, viruses, particularly HIV, are invoked simultaneously as linguistic entities with "meanings" of their own and as forces that confound linguistic process and intended meaning. Though AIDS comes for many reasons to be seen as an experience charged with and challenging meaning, one factor contributing importantly to such a construction is the consistent conscious and unconscious, subtle and blatant identification of the viral agent believed to cause AIDS as itself an *intentional* entity.

In this first chapter of my discussion, I will focus largely on the ways in which scientific discourse, and particularly the metaphoric language of science, portrays HIV as somehow intentional, and as perverse in its intentionality. I will then, in Chapter 2, examine how such a scientific depiction participates, along with journalistic and political discourses, in the construction of AIDS as a disease of gay men, part of a "battle" over masculinity, and how it thus largely excludes women with AIDS from public attention. In the remaining chapters of the book, I then move to consider the ways in which gendered and sexualized discourses of AIDS shape *narrative* understandings. On the one hand, AIDS is constructed as an invariably fatal weakening of an individual's bodily defenses, a depiction often used to reconfirm an identification between disease and a gayness imagined as itself always already weak and vulnerable. On the other hand, AIDS is understood in terms of the narrative of an epidemic "spread" largely attributable to gay "immorality" and "unnaturalness." Fictional writing about AIDS depends heavily upon these two large cultural narratives, with one major subgenre of the AIDS novel presenting accounts of personal illness, decline, and death, and a second focusing mainly on epidemic "spread." Novels about AIDS, however, also in many ways question, rewrite, and subvert the narrative structures upon which they thus depend, intervening particularly against the implicit and explicit homophobia of those structures. Examining a wide range of novels about AIDS, and focusing in greatest detail on John Weir's *The Irreversible Decline of Eddie Socket* and Sarah Schulman's *People in Trouble*, I am particularly concerned with exploring how literary genre has been shaped by the always politicized, gendered and sexualized, discourses and narratives of AIDS, and how such discourses and narratives may in turn be questioned, reconstructed, and undermined by fictional writing—how, in other words, novels themselves may help shape broader cultural understandings of the complex and conflicted phenomenon of AIDS.

In starting my discussion with a consideration of the somewhat esoteric languages of molecular biology and computer science rather than with the more clearly stigmatizing and politically inflected languages of the mass media or the Congressional Record, I do not intend to move this project away from an engagement with the political or toward some more abstract(ed) "theoretical" consideration of metaphoric language. On the contrary, by beginning with an examination of languages that claim for themselves a privileged position of abstraction and objectivity and that indeed are constructed as "the master discourse that administers all other discourses about AIDS,"[2] and by intervening against the "untenable, but politically manipulable, belief that we can separate biological science, and therefore the social policy based on that science, from the instability and duplicity that literary theory has increasingly identified as inherent in the operations of language,"[3] I hope to show the ways in which scientific discourses are in fact coopted for, implicated in, at the service of sexist, heterosexist, and racist representations, and ultimately thus to suggest how firmly entrenched in our culture are certain politically charged and potentially repressive ways of thinking about AIDS.[4] Doing away with the Jesse Helmses and Pat Buchanans of the world—admirable though that project might be[5]—would not do away with a certain complexly gendered, sexualized, and racialized depiction of HIV and AIDS that is deeply embedded in current discourses. My largest project here is to call such a depiction into question, interrogating its grounding in the language, metaphor, and narrative not just of the overtly political or public realm but also of realms like the scientific that are generally thought of, and present themselves, as value-neutral and apolitical.

1. THE METAPHORS OF MOLECULAR GENETICS

At the center of contemporary biology stands molecular genetics, a field that focuses on the molecular basis of inheritance in DNA or RNA, exploring how such molecules constitute a "blueprint" ultimately determining the full development of individual cells and whole organisms.[6] Examining as it does the originating molecule for that larger complex of molecules whose interactions and replication are defined as constituting life, molecular genetics, which developed as a field only as recently as the 1940s and 1950s,[7] has attained a remarkable position of prominence within modern biological science. Testifying to this prominence is the extraordinarily wide attention focused on "genetic engineering" from the 1970s to the present,[8] and the more recent publicity, energy, and funding given over to the "human genome project," an effort to elaborate a "map" of the whole sequence of human DNA. Despite some controversy over its true value, the latter project has often been presented as the search for a biological "holy grail" that holds the key to understanding and solving a wide range of biomedical problems, hereditary diseases and cancers chief among them.[9]

Research in molecular genetics has led to a reconceptualization of knowledge within many of the biological sciences, including fields crucial to our current understanding of HIV and AIDS—cell biology, virology, immunology. The study of viruses has in fact been intimately intertwined with molecular genetics throughout its history,[10] and much of our knowledge of the interactions between viruses and the cells they infect—the processes by which a virus may enter a cell, (sometimes) insert its DNA or a DNA copy of its RNA into its host's genetic material, "take over" molecular processes within the infected cell, and replicate itself—depends upon the work of molecular biology. Immunology, too, has relied significantly on the new genetics and its emphasis on molecular process. Thus, Stent and Calendar could claim in 1978 that "[o]ne special, and long-mysterious, instance of cell differentiation—the immune response of vertebrate animals—now seems close to being solved, thanks in part to the application of principles of molecular genetics";[11] and when Silverstein discusses "the renaissance of immunobiology," he notes that this has "depended . . . on participation in the modern revolution in molecular biology."[12]

Given the centrality of molecular genetics to contemporary biology, and more specifically to areas of study important in basic AIDS research, it is not surprising that the language of this field should especially pervade the scientific discourse on AIDS. Central to that language is a complex of metaphors that I will argue has been particularly important in shaping the understanding of HIV and AIDS, and that has had a broad influence beyond the strict realm of the biological sciences. Put most succinctly, at the core of molecular genetics stands a series of *linguistic* metaphors in which the processes of life are explained in terms of the functioning of language.[13]

Thus, the genetic material itself (DNA, or in organisms like the retroviruses, RNA) is described as genetic "information," and the essential task of molecular genetics involves explaining how such "information" is "expressed" in the establishment of a functional, self-replicating (living) unit.[14] The genetic "information" is, like language, thought of as representing in "coded" form a set of objects separate from itself—in this case, the proteins of the living organism: "successive groups of nucleotides along a DNA chain code for successive amino acids along a given polypeptide [protein] chain."[15] The individual molecular components of DNA (the nucleotides) are thus thought of as the basic semantic units of a language, and the "breaking" of the "genetic code" has been compared to the process of "cryptanalysis." More specifically, this important accomplishment of molecular genetics has been likened to the reading of ancient Egyptian hieroglyphs made possible by the discovery of the Rosetta Stone: "in the hands of Nirenberg, these artificial, random ribopolynucleotides synthesized by polynucleotide phosphorylase were to become a surrogate Rosetta Stone of the genetic code."[16]

The language of information, code, and expression is far-reaching in discussions of DNA and its functions:

> [T]he information content of any gene, and hence the actual *meaning* of the four-letter language recorded in the DNA, could not be anything but a representation of the primary structure of a given polypeptide.[17]
>
> Thus, as information-containing entities, DNA molecules were by then properly regarded as very long words (as we shall see later, they are now best considered very long sentences) built up from a four-letter alphabet (A, G, C, and T). Even with only four letters, the number of potential DNA sequences. . . is very very large for even the smallest of DNA molecules; a virtually infinite number of different genetic messages can exist.[18]

The representation of the four kinds of nucleotide making up DNA (adenine, guanine, cytosine, and thymine) as single letters, "A, G, C, and T," of course reinforces the understanding of these rather complex molecules as composing a "four-letter alphabet" or "four-letter language." DNA is in fact often represented on the written page as a "word" or "sentence" made up of these four letters: "GCTGGTGGAAAATGAGGAAATTCAAT."[19]

The notion of "coding" is further developed in descriptions of how precisely DNA "expresses" its "messages." The "meaningful" units of DNA (nucleotide-pair triplets) have been named "codons," and are sometimes also referred to as "sense words."[20] One of the early goals of molecular genetics was to determine "how . . . the 'reader' [is] supposed to know which of the triplets to 'read,'" a problem that involved determining whether some kind of molecular punctuation (a "comma") were present to guide the "reading" of the genetic code or, on the other hand, whether "a comma-less code," involving a limited "dictionary of sense words" with "no synonyms," existed.[21] Terms like "sense," "nonsense," "synonymous," and "ambiguous" codons have all been used in describing DNA,[22] and a new class of drugs, aimed at blocking the "expression" of specific DNA "messages," has been dubbed "anti-sense."[23] Recent work on DNA in fact has pushed the linguistic metaphor quite far, with one group of scientists explicitly "applying the techniques of linguistics to the study of DNA":

> [S]cientists are learning to categorize genetic sequences into categories like commands for protein subunits, commands for turning genes on and off, and the recipe for how the DNA can fit neatly into the cell—much as linguists divide words into nouns, verbs and modifiers. Using linguistic analysis, researchers say that they can examine a modest sample of DNA from any organism and quickly identify the creature of origin. "For example, if a virus integrated its genes into an animal, in principle you could detect that piece of DNA as foreign by saying its vocabulary is strange," said Dr. Trifonov.
> Scientists can even detect sequences that are the molecular version of curses, groupings of nucleotides that are only rarely encountered because they seem to jeopardize the structural integrity of the DNA molecule.[24]

In describing the multiple copying of DNA that characterizes some cancers and hereditary diseases—"when the body's genetic factory behaves like a broken copying machine"—a recent news report relies heavily and unselfconsciously on linguistic metaphors: "cancer, like some hereditary diseases, can be caused by a strange stuttering in the individual's DNA."[25]

The process of "gene expression" and the "control" of this process are now understood to be complex, involving enzymes, "repressors," "activators," structures like the ribosomes, and not involving the *direct* transfer of information from DNA to protein. Rather, DNA, lodged in the cell nucleus (in eucaryotic cells), works through an intermediary "information-carrying" molecule, "messenger RNA" (mRNA), which brings the "genetic information" (still expressed in "codons," though "written" in a somewhat different "four-letter alphabet"—A, G, C, and U [uracil]—from that of DNA) to the cytoplasm, where protein synthesis occurs. As such additional steps in the "information-transfer" from DNA to protein have been understood and characterized, they too have been described by means of the metaphors of "coding" and "reading," as the name "messenger RNA" itself suggests. The formation of mRNA from the DNA template is described as "transcription," understood as the "copying" of "information" from DNA into a complementary form in the nucleotides of RNA;[26] the subsequent production of proteins from the mRNA "transcript" is known as "translation" and is presented quite explicitly and elaborately as a process of "reading." As one textbook explains, "mRNA molecules are read in successive blocks of three nucleotides, called codons"; certain "codons" present "the signal for ribosomes to begin reading the mRNA molecule about to be translated into a protein. Since reading always begins at the appropriate AUG codon, the mRNA molecules are aligned on the ribosomes so that their messages are read in the correct **reading frame**."[27] Biochemical processes like "translation" are even described as involving "editing steps" to assure their "accuracy."[28] "Proofreading" is understood to occur at at least two separate points during "translation," when amino acids are bound to specific molecules of "transfer RNA" (tRNA),[29] and when an amino acid-tRNA complex binds to mRNA on the ribosome during protein synthesis.[30] Similarly, a "*proofreading* capability" has been identified in the "DNA polymerases," those enzymes responsible for DNA self-replication.[31]

The centrality of the linguistic metaphor in molecular genetics is especially emphasized by the fact that what has been called, since the late 1950s, the "central dogma" of the field is defined as the sequential and unidirectional "flow of genetic information"[32] from DNA to RNA to protein via the two processes of "transcription" and "translation."[33] While the 1970 discovery of "reverse transcriptase," an enzyme enabling "retroviruses" (like HIV) to produce DNA from an RNA template, showed that the unidirectionality of information flow claimed by the "central dogma" did not in fact hold, molecular geneticists have been loath to jettison the "central dogma" with its idea of sequential "transcription" and "translation":

> It is to be noted that the existence of reverse transcription in the life cycle of RNA tumor viruses does not really contravene the fundamental, dogmatic view of the nascent molecular genetics of the early 1950s that, in the heterocatalytic function of DNA, genetic information flows only from DNA to RNA. For the essence of that Central Dogma was that, since the transfer of genetic information depends on the formation of hydrogen bonds between complementary purine and pyrimidine bases of polynucleotide chains, there can be no reverse flow of genetic information *from proteins to nucleic acids*. But the Central Dogma did not foreclose the possibility of transfer of genetic information from RNA to DNA, via the Watson-Crick base-pairing mechanism.[34]

RNA chains sometimes do act as templates for DNA chains of complementary sequence. But such reversals of the normal flow of information are very rare events compared with the enormous number of RNA molecules made on DNA templates. Thus, the central dogma as originally proclaimed some 30 years ago still remains essentially valid.[35]

The reluctance of molecular geneticists to give up the "central dogma" suggests how strongly engrained are the ideas about information and the metaphors of language it embodies.[36] Certainly, the discovery of "reverse transcriptase" has not disturbed in any essential way the linguistic description of molecular process; as its name indicates, this enzyme has been understood as presiding over a process of "transcription" that simply "reverses" the "normal flow of information" between DNA and RNA.

In addition, other recent findings in molecular genetics that have had the potential to disrupt a linguistic model of genetic "expression" have, on the contrary, been assimilated to that model. Thus, a simply "representational" or "mimetic" understanding of the functioning of genetic information, with each gene "coding" a single polypeptide or protein—the "one gene-one enzyme" or "one gene-one polypeptide" hypothesis[37]—has been complicated by new understandings of DNA sequence and structure: the recognition of DNA regions that may never be "expressed" but whose existence may nonetheless play some role in the "control of gene expression," and the discovery of "jumping genes," whose movement on the chromosome may alter the way in which DNA is "expressed." In describing such phenomena, the linguistic metaphor has not been given up but rather extended and elaborated. Thus, "exons" (as opposed to "introns" or "intervening sequences") are regions of the DNA that are "*ex*pressed";[38] "moveable" pieces within the DNA are "transposable elements" and "transposons";[39] and DNA sequences "in which the same (or almost the same) sequence runs in opposite directions if one switches from one strand to its complement at the central axis of symmetry" have been dubbed "palindromes."[40] (One might say that the movement away from a straightforward "representational" model of gene expression mirrors a similar movement in linguistics itself toward more flexible, mutable, "postmodern" models of language.) In addition, the new technology of recombinant DNA continues to be thought of in linguistic terms: thus, this technology has enabled scientists to clone "all the DNA sequences from a given cell," and, revealingly, the collection of cloned sequences thus produced is spoken of as constituting a "gene library."[41]

The centrality of linguistic metaphors to the descriptive language of molecular biology is not of course inevitable. We can imagine (though perhaps only with some difficulty, given the coherence and pervasiveness of the current model) an alternative kind of description that, for instance, would emphasize the three-dimensional conformation of molecules more strongly than does a conception of linearly-coded information transferred through linguistic processes of transcription and translation from DNA to protein. The wholehearted adoption of the current model, along with the continued proliferation of linguistic metaphors in the explanation of newly discovered molecular phenomena, reflects and reinforces a certain persistent view of biological process as *intentional*.[42] How can we not see as somehow possessing intelligence the organism or cell described as a repository of "information," in which various processes "regulate" or "control" what is to be "expressed" by allowing or "repressing" the "transcription" and "translation" of certain parts of a "genetic code"? Other, non-linguistic metaphors are of course used to describe these same processes, but the most common of these tend to reinforce the picture of molecular activity as somehow involving intention. Thus, metaphors of production, in which the cell is envisioned as a microscopic factory, with a DNA "blueprint"[43] ultimately directing the "synthesis" of protein products, and related metaphors of gene expression as a function of "circuitry" and "switching,"[44] suggest, like the linguistic metaphor, a series of steps guided by some overarching intelligence.[45] Even the description of particular mechanical processes within the cell—for instance, the "splicing" together of pieces of RNA—often implies the presence of some kind of intentional agent—in this case, an "editor." (This is particularly true for "splicing" since the "splicing" of genes is now also something the biologist does rather routinely as part of the technology of "genetic engineering.")

While most molecular biologists would undoubtedly deny that they mean to impute intentionality at the level of DNA replication, RNA transcription, or protein synthesis, their language nonetheless consistently does so. I will give just one further example, from the description of a new theory developing within molecular genetics:

> Still, we cannot account for all the sequences that make up a eucaryotic genome nor do we understand the enormous variations in DNA amount that occur between closely related species. This has led some scientists to speculate that DNA is inherently "selfish," constantly endeavoring to expand itself to the limit tolerated by each organism. Surely transposons and *Alu* family sequences have properties most closely fitting what might be expected of **selfish DNA**: built-in mechanisms for reproduction and movement.[46]

In such language, and more generally in the linguistic metaphors of molecular biology, the human mind, with its intentionality and motivations, is strongly projected into biochemical process.

2. VIRUS AS LANGUAGE

Because of the simplicity of their structure, viruses are especially susceptible to being understood in terms of the linguistic metaphors of molecular genetics. Cellular organisms, even the most simple of them, contain complex structures that, while ultimately the "expression" of "information" encoded in their DNA, are not easily traceable back to the genetic template. But viruses can be much more simply described:

> A virus is essentially a packet of genetic information surrounded by a protein covering.[47]

> [A]ll viruses are small pieces of genetic material (DNA or RNA), each enclosed within a protective protein-rich coat that facilitates its transportation from one cell to another. . . . Viruses are no more alive than isolated chromosomes; both the chromosomes of cells and those of viruses can duplicate only in the complex environment of a living cell.[48]

> A virus particle is a structure that has evolved to transfer nucleic acid [either RNA or DNA] from one cell to another.[49]

Viral infection of cells is generally understood in terms of the linguistic metaphor: as the introduction into a host of parasitic genetic information capable of using the cellular apparatus of transcription and translation to further the expression of its own genome, directing the synthesis of new viral nucleic acids and proteins, and hence new viruses. As one general account of viral multiplication has it:

> [V]iruses have developed several strategies to deal with (a) encoding and organization of viral genes, (b) expression of viral genes, (c) the replication of viral genomes, and (d) assembly and maturation of viral progeny. . . . Irrespective of the size, composition, and organization of its genome, the virus must present to the eukaryotic cell protein-synthesizing machinery a messenger RNA that the cell can recognize as such and translate.[50]

Here, it is clear that the linguistic metaphor dominates the view of the virus's function, and also that the virus is seen as an intentional entity, capable of "developing strategies" for its survival and replication.[51]

The pervasiveness of the language of information, transcription, translation, and expression, and of the attendant language of intentionality, is clear as well in a more specific account of the molecular biology of HIV, written for a general scientific audience by two prominent researchers on retroviruses. Here, having described how "[i]nfection with the AIDS virus[52] takes many guises," the authors ask "[w]hat accounts for this diverse behavior and its destructive consequences?" and suggest that "[t]he answer is to be found in the life cycle of the virus, and in the tiny package of genetic instructions that controls it."[53] The detailed description of "life cycle" that follows this introduction reverts often to the language of information:

> Since 1984, when HIV became available in a workable form, the full power of contemporary molecular biology and genetic analysis has been turned on this scrap of genetic information.[54]

> To exert its effects the *tat* [regulatory] protein depends on a short sequence of nucleotides know as TAR (for *trans*-acting responsive sequence), which is found at the start of the viral genome and is included in the mRNA transcript of every HIV gene. . . . It has been proposed, variously, that *tat* and TAR increase the transcription of mRNA's from the viral DNA, the stability of completed mRNA's and the efficiency with which they are translated into proteins. The mechanism is not likely to be unique to HIV, and it is expected to shed light on the means by which higher organisms regulate gene expression.[55]

> The viral DNA polymerase lacks the error-correcting feature that analogous cellular enzymes have, and so the copying errors it makes in converting viral RNA into a single DNA strand and then synthesizing the complementary strand go uncorrected. The cellular RNA polymerase that makes the genetic material for new virions also does not correct its own errors.[56]

As these last citations make clear, even very specialized descriptions of viral function depend largely upon linguistic metaphors.

But the virus is usually not presented as precisely the same kind of information-containing and expressing entity as the procaryotic or eucaryotic cell with its DNA. Since the virus lacks much of the "machinery" of living cells, it must depend on a "host" to complete its own life cycle.[57] On the one hand, then, the simplicity of viral structure contributes to a view that would make the virus almost pure "genetic information" and hence a perfect model system for "unraveling the structure and function of genes."[58] On the other hand, the virus's parasitic nature—its need to replicate through a non-viral host—means that its "expressive" functions, the ways in which it uses its DNA or RNA, are somehow suspect, an arrogation of cellular processes not "properly" its own. Indeed, the virus is often described as not "truly" living;

unable to replicate outside a host, it is seen as standing somewhere between "true" living organisms and inanimate objects, "fill[ing] the gap between the chemist's molecule and the biologist's organism."[59]

Viruses are especially subject to suspicion, of course, when they harm or kill the host cell, or when they trigger cell "transformation" and oncogenesis. In such cases, though the virus is still conceived of in linguistic terms, it represents a suspect "foreign" language, a language in contest with the "proper" language of cells and cellular function:

> [I]f a virus integrated its genes into an animal, in principle you could detect that piece of DNA as foreign by saying its vocabulary is strange.[60]

> [T]he genetic material of the stripped-down virus enters the nucleus of the host cell and inserts its DNA into the DNA of the cell.
> Now controlled by the virus, the cell's DNA is *transcribed* into messenger RNA, which contains the virus's genetic material. The RNA "message" then returns to the cytoplasm, where it is *translated* into proteins dictated by the virus.[61]

> T7 [a bacteriophage infecting *E. coli*] makes proteins that redirect cellular transcription to viral DNA. . . . T7 makes an entirely new RNA polymerase (encoded by T7 gene *1*) that is highly specific for a set of distinct phage promoter sequences, the T7 late promoters. Of course, *E. coli* RNA polymerase must make the messenger RNA for gene *1* (as well as a few other early genes), but the new enzyme can then take over transcription of phage late genes.[62]

The language of a "strategic" linguistic "take-over," in which the virus "dictates" those functions proper to the cell, sometimes escalates so that it describes not just a contest between viral and cellular molecular processes, but a war:

> T7 encodes proteins that disable both host RNA and host DNA synthesis. The small . . . gene 2 protein binds and inactivates *E. coli* RNA polymerase, although this does not happen until enough early phage RNA has accumulated to ensure successful phage growth. . . .
> A drastic attack is reserved for components of cellular DNA synthesis. Here, T7 destroys the bacterial DNA by the combined effects of an endonuclease (encoded by gene *3*) and an exonuclease (encoded by gene *6*). In fact, the bacterial DNA is degraded to its nucleotide components, which provide the essential precursors for synthesis of T7

DNA. It is not clear why T7 DNA is not also destroyed by the nucleases, but one possibility is that phage DNA is repaired more efficiently after nuclease attack.

Bacteria defend themselves against phages and other foreign DNA with DNA restriction enzymes, against which cellular DNA is protected by methylation. . . . T7 evades the cellular restriction nucleases *Eco* B and *Eco* K with its gene *0.3* protein, a specific inhibitor that binds and inactivates the nucleases. . . .

Finally, T7 lysozyme destroys the bacterial cell wall and allows newly formed phage particles to escape and renew their growth cycle in other bacteria.[63]

One recent journalistic account suggests that some viruses do not simply "take over" cellular processes but may incorporate pieces of the host's genetic material into their own genome and then use that material as part of their own "invasion strategies." Here, the language becomes especially charged, with the virus's activity described as a criminally motivated and subtly violent betrayal of the host; the virus "fool[s] the cell into believing" something that is not true:

> Just when they thought they knew most of the nasty parasitic maneuvers of viruses, researchers are now finding a new and exceedingly devious way that the microbes exploit their hosts. They have discovered that viruses can pirate away copies of genes that control the health and well-being of the host and then turn those genes against the host species. . . .
>
> Scientists suspect that viruses have stolen many other genes and that the strategy is probably widespread throughout the viral kingdom. By studying the details of genetic embezzlement, scientists hope to develop approaches to treating viral illnesses. . . .
>
> "It's a rather clever trick," said Dr. Thomas Albrecht, a professor of microbiology at the University of Texas Medical Branch in Galveston. "The mammalian cell has an enormous number of genes compared to a virus, so the virus can choose what it needs from that large sample."[64] . . .
>
> Among the most important advantages that a virus can seek is protecting itself against the host's immune system. The AIDS virus manages that by killing key cells that can rally other warriors of the immune system. But in a paper that appeared several weeks ago in *Science*, scientists from DNAX described how the Epstein-Barr virus, which causes flu-like symptoms and other disorders, defeats the immune system with a far more subtle technique.[65]

The underhandedness of viral action that is especially emphasized here is also strikingly prominent in descriptions of *retro*viruses like HIV, which occupy a particularly problematic position vis-à-vis the linguistic metaphors of molecular genetics. Containing RNA rather than DNA as their genetic material and reversing the "normal flow of information" enshrined in the "central dogma," retroviruses contain in their very name the suggestion that their means of molecular "expression" are somehow abnormal, even perverse:

Retroviruses were so named because they reverse what seemed to be the normal flow of genetic information.[66]

In the absence of retrovirus infection, very little, if any, reverse transcriptase activity is present in normal cells; thus, under normal conditions, effectively very little DNA is made on RNA templates.[67]

The idea of a perverse take-over of "normal" biological process is one we find often associated with the description of HIV, and one that has far-reaching consequences for how we talk about AIDS.

3. LANGUAGE AS VIRUS

The idea that the virus is an informational (and intentional) entity has captured the popular imagination, as is indicated by the metaphoric ways in which viruses themselves have recently been used.[68] Thus, a recent book—*Media Virus!*—has identified the rapid dissemination of ideas and images through new technologies as "viral" in nature.[69] A television advertisement for the new computer videogame "Burn Cycle" boasts that "it's not just a game, it's an infection."[70] In both instances, there is a certain reversal of the metaphor of virus as language, with informational/computational processes coming to be seen as themselves viral.

Such an inversion of the linguistic metaphor of molecular genetics is examined by performance artist Laurie Anderson in her movie *Home of the Brave* (1986), where (quoting William S. Burroughs) she makes the claim that "language" itself "is a virus."[71] Beginning and ending with references to the binary language of computer science, Anderson's movie as a whole explores the connections (and tensions) between the biological and the technological. In this context, the phrase "language is a virus" suggests the problematic nature of the linguistic; a kind of organism, language is nonetheless foreign and invasive and also perhaps somehow technological ("a virus from outer space").[72] Indeed, Anderson suggests not only that "language is a virus" but also that it is a "magnet," a "charm," a "shipwreck," a "doghouse," an "iceberg." The progression of these identifications evokes—as does the projection of a different set of phrases, running from A to Z ("A FRAME / B

FLICK / C NOTE / D DAY / E COLI / F STOP / G MEN / H BOMB / I BEAM / J WALK . . . R SVP / S CURVE . . . Y ME? / ZZZZ"), on the screen behind the stage—the instability and fluidity of language as well as its complicated positioning among the categories of the natural (iceberg), the manmade (doghouse), the magical (charm), and entities (magnet, shipwreck) that themselves might be assigned to more than one of these categories.

The potential richness of "virus" as a metaphor for linguistic process (and my brief discussion has not exhausted the richness of Anderson's piece) derives at least partially from the ambivalences of biological science itself—the presentation of the virus as both participating in and confounding the "linguistic" processes of life. It also partly derives from another scientific realm, that of computer science (a realm of which Anderson is clearly aware, as her allusions to "binary code" make clear). The metaphoric reversal explicit in Anderson's performance—language as virus—has indeed in some sense been "performed" during the 1980s and 1990s within the "information sciences" themselves in the writing and dissemination of "computer viruses," and that "performance" has in turn enabled the further viral metaphorizing of information process ("media virus," the videogame as "infection").[73]

The phenomenon of the computer virus is particularly revealing of the close and complicated interconnections between the biological and informational that currently pertain in our culture, and of the larger issues those interconnections raise about the "intentionality" of biological process and the "naturalness" (or even "vitality") of language. The design of computer viruses comes at a moment in the development of computer science when the boundary between computer and human intelligence is increasingly challenged by the notion of "artificial intelligence," and when computer scientists are experimenting with what has been called "artificial life."[74] Biological and information sciences currently stand at a certain point of intersection: recently, in a particularly striking instance of their interpenetration, a computer scientist, Leonard Adleman (credited with the coinage of the term "computer virus" and himself involved in work on AIDS), "has used DNA, the genetic material, as a sort of personal computer," "translat[ing] a difficult mathematical problem into the language of molecular biology and solv[ing] it by carrying out a [biological] reaction" with DNA.[75] In the words of Donna Haraway: "Late twentieth-century machines have made thoroughly ambiguous the difference between natural and artificial, mind and body, self-developing and externally-designed, and many other distinctions that used to apply to organisms and machines. . . . [M]achine and organism [have been reconceived] as coded texts through which we engage in the play of writing and reading the world."[76] The biological virus, itself thought of as linguistic in nature and as standing at the boundary of life and non-life, is especially well-suited as metaphor for a non-biological (computational/informational) entity that seems nonetheless to mimic biology.

Of course, the correspondence between the biological virus and a certain kind of computer program "which makes copies of itself in such a way as to 'infect' parts of the operating system and/or application programs"[77] is not *simply* metaphoric.[78] That is, the term "computer virus" has not just been metaphorically applied to a pre-existing informational or computational phenomenon. Rather, "computer viruses" have been written, as well as named, by people who know what biological viruses are and at least the rudiments of how they function. Computer viruses, in other words, have been developed intentionally, at least in part, on the model of the biological viruses; they are not wholly independent phenomena described in comparison to the biological. Given that this is the case, a comparison of computer and biological viruses, and the languages used to describe them, reveals not only the similarities perceived to exist between two separate phenomenal realms but also the overlaps, close interactions, mutual influences of the two—the ways in which computer science has been shaped by an understanding and imitation of biology, and, on the other hand, the ways in which the conception of "computer viruses" might influence biology's own understanding and description of viral process.

The design of computer viruses echoes in many ways the structure and function of the biological viruses, and the language used to speak of computer viruses makes such echoes clearly audible. Of course, the computer virus is, literally speaking, a linguistic entity, written in a computer language and programmed to perform certain functions; not surprisingly, then, like the DNA or RNA core of a biological virus, it is conceived of as a piece of information or code. (Computer information more generally is sometimes compared to genetic information: "Normally the floppy disk feeds instructions to the computer; it's software. DNA is mostly software for the cell."[79]) But the computer virus does not exist as an independent program; rather, on the model of the biological viruses with their need for a "host," it must be inserted into another program in order to function and propagate:[80] "A virus is a code segment that has been incorporated into the body of another program, 'infecting' it."[81] In other words, like the biological virus, computer viruses are conceived of as "parasitic,"[82] dependent for their "expression" on residence in a "host." And like the biological virus, computer viruses are described as "self-replicating,"[83] though they depend on the function ("execution") of the "host" programs they have infected in order to "replicate":

> Viruses make copies of themselves, spreading across floppy disks, computer systems and networks. This similarity with their biological counterparts has given viruses their name.[84]

> Viral infections are spread by a virus (a small shell containing genetic material) injecting its contents into a far larger body cell. The cell then is infected and converted into a biological factory producing replicants of the virus.
>
> Similarly, a computer virus is a segment of machine code (typically 200-4000 bytes) that will copy its code into one or more larger "host" programs when it is activated. When these infected programs are run, the viral code is executed and the virus spreads further.[85]

In such statements, the biological analogy is made explicit, and that analogy is often intricately elaborated in the literature on computer viruses, with talk of the "three stages of a virus's life,"[86] viral "replication strategies" (recall the notion that biological viruses also have "strategies" for their reproduction),[87] "mutation,"[88] "evolution,"[89] "hybrids,"[90] and a "taxonomy" of computer viruses.[91]

The biological metaphor works especially to portray the computer virus as a disease entity—"infectious" and "spreading,"[92] causing "symptoms,"[93] demanding a "cure":

> Cure of viruses has been examined in some depth and appears to present little hope in a general sense. The tail-chasing problem indicates that the cure of viruses can be performed only while services are denied unless detection and cure are faster than infection. This is similar to illness in biological systems. In the real world, cure has often been far more difficult than detection because viruses get into the legitimate or illegitimate backup system.[94]

Writers speak of "outbreaks"[95] and "epidemics"[96] of computer viruses, of "exposure,"[97] "pollution,"[98] and "contamination,"[99] of a viral "scourge."[100] Here, the language often begins to evoke not just the general language of biology and medicine but the more specific discourse of AIDS. This is especially true in the description of computer viruses with a "latency" period—a lag between "infection" and the onset of "symptoms":

> Viruses use hiding mechanisms which allow them to replicate unnoticed before delivering the "payload." This time delay before discovery is analogous to the incubation period in a biological disease, when the carrier of the disease is infectious, but does not exhibit any symptoms.[101]

The notion of asymptomatic carriers is invoked in the discourse of computer viruses, as also in the discourse of AIDS, to emphasize deception, danger, even an apocalyptic threat, and to suggest that some infections occur more "innocently" than others:

> The trick is to write a bug—a "virus"—that spreads itself like an infection from program to program. The most devastating infections are those that do not affect their carriers—at least not immediately—but allow them to continue to live normally and in ignorance of their disease, innocently infecting others while going about their daily business. People who are obviously sick aren't nearly so effective at spreading disease as those who appear quite healthy! In the same way, program *A* can corrupt program *B* silently, unobtrusively, so that when *B* is invoked by an innocent and unsuspecting user it spreads the infection still further.[102]

> As an analogy to a computer virus, consider a biological disease that is 100% infectious, spreads whenever animals communicate, kills all infected animals instantly at a given moment, and has no detectable side effect until that moment. If a delay of even one week were used between the introduction of this disease and its effect, it would likely leave only a few people in remote villages alive, and would certainly wipe out the vast majority of modern society.[103] If a computer virus of this type spread throughout the computers of the world, it would likely stop most computer usage for a significant period of time and wreak havoc on modern government, financial, business, and academic institutions.[104]

When Hruska moves to summarize the threat of computer viruses, he does so in language that could be applied, with few changes, to the AIDS pandemic:

> The virus danger is here to stay. In the USA, the Far East and Africa it has already reached epidemic proportions and it is only a matter of time before it becomes more common in the rest of the world.[105]

The description of computer viruses—as "self-replicating" linguistic structures, as disease "organisms," as "epidemiological" phenomena—thus depends deeply on biological metaphors, many of which serve to evoke the most striking viral phenomenon of our era, HIV/AIDS. Such metaphors extend as well into a language of "prevention, detection, and cure"[106] common in the discussion of appropriate responses to the computer virus "threat." As with AIDS, certain behaviors (e.g., "shar[ing] diskettes promiscuously")[107] are defined as putting one at "high risk,"[108] and "user awareness and safe computing habits" (echoing "AIDS awareness" and the language of "safe[r] sex") are seen as "[t]he best defense against this contemporary threat":[109] "[P]ractice safe computing. . . . Do not exchange floppies with casual acquaintances. Even nice people get viruses."[110] A language of generalized suspicion—"Don't run programs you don't trust. / Don't trust a program unless you have to";[111] "You can't trust code that you did not totally create yourself"[112]—complemented by one of "digital hygiene";[113] talk of "false positives" and "negatives" in "testing" for the presence of a virus;[114] the invocation of "containment," "isolation," and "quarantine" as possible responses to infection;[115] and a heavily immunological discourse of "prevention" and "treatment"—with discussion of "immunity,"[116] an "immune system,"[117] "immunization schemes,"[118] "resistance,"[119] "inoculation,"[120] "vaccination,"[121] and "antibodies"[122]—all bring us close to the current discourse of AIDS. Hruska indeed describes the problems in "[c]reating user awareness" as "similar to the ones faced by the Government in persuading drug addicts not to share needles."[123] Elsewhere, "infected" users are urged to act "responsibly" and "notify other users with whom you may have shared infected diskettes so that they may check for infection on their systems,"[124] just as those testing positive for HIV are urged to notify their sexual "contacts." There has been talk of setting up a governmental "center for disease control for computer viruses."[125] And like HIV infection, infection with a computer virus is thought of as carrying "stigma":

> Virus attacks are rarely reported in the press, mainly because of the (legitimate) fear of bad publicity which an attack may bring to an organisation. . . .
> Organisations which have been affected by a virus usually prefer to lick their wounds alone. . . .
> As a result, it is impossible even to estimate how serious the virus problem is. . . .
> The reporting of an infection is entirely up to the organisation in question, and as long as a stigma remains attached to infection, and infection in turn is related to poor security measures, nothing will change.[126]

The deployment of computer viruses has been essentially simultaneous with the broad public awareness of AIDS. Though, as Peter J. Denning suggests, "the threat of such attacks had been known for many years earlier, the catch term 'virus' was applied by Fred Cohen in 1983";[127] Jan Hruska dates the first mention of "the possibility of computer viruses" to 1984.[128] Hruska further places "the first wide-scale computer virus infection" in 1986,[129] and Denning claims that "[t]he first viruses that attracted wide public attention appeared in 1987."[130] Even before the phrase "computer virus" had been coined, in the early 1980s, a virus-like program was written and named "Cyberaids,"[131] and later computer viruses have also been called "AIDS."[132] One "Trojan horse" ("a program . . . perform[ing] services beyond those stated in its specifications" and "often used as a means of infecting an unsuspecting user with a virus"),[133] "mailed to tens of thousands of users on a PC mailing list" in 1989, was also named after AIDS;[134] "pos[ing] as a legitimate program giving information on AIDS and assessing the user's risk group after asking him/her to fill in a questionnaire," the program in fact "encrypts" and "hides" "the names of the files on the [user's] hard disk" and then demands that money be sent in return for information that will allow proper computer functioning to be restored.[135] Significantly, it was early on suggested "that the hepatitis B virus may serve as a 'Trojan horse' within which the putative agent of acquired immunodeficiency syndrome [AIDS] is carried";[136] and the "endosomes" by which some viruses, including HIV, may enter host cells have more recently been compared to "Trojan horses."[137] In his "diary" *Mortal Embrace: Living with AIDS*, Emmanuel Dreuilhe develops this same metaphor in relation to both microscopic and social phenomena:

> The armed men of this Trojan horse are not only the sperm cells but also the many viruses that secretly enter the blood of Troy, a consenting and careless prey, bent on its own destruction. The oppression of the American homosexual community by the puritan majority had diminished somewhat over the past twenty years, and like the Trojans, overjoyed at what we thought to be the departure of the Greeks, we slowly let down our guard. But the sexual revolution (and the spread of drug addiction) was only a ruse. The soldiers were hidden in the womb of the horse, in the needle, in the phallus. No sooner had the homophobes lifted their siege than the massacre began.[138]

(That "Trojans" are condoms, and thus, in "safe[r] sex" practices, partly "responsible" for the prevention of HIV transmission, is a fact implicitly and complexly in play in metaphoric uses of the "Trojan horse"; the concealment of the penis by the Trojan is here both opposed to and associated with the concealment "in the womb of the horse" that figures, all at once, [biological and computer] viral action at the cellular level, infection at the level of the whole person, and the "attack" of AIDS on the "American homosexual community.") The evocation of the "Trojan horse" with respect to both computer and biological viruses, as well as, in Dreuilhe, the larger phenomenon of the HIV pandemic, suggests how intimately linked the metaphors of language and coding in both molecular genetics and information science are to thoughts of espionage and surreptitious attack, and how such thoughts might then lend force to certain "paranoid" fantasies about the origins and meanings of AIDS like those voiced by Dreuilhe.

The specific evocations of AIDS in the realm of the computer virus, along with the more general elaboration of biological/viral metaphors in computer science, suggest that, at least in part, the creation and "release" of viral programs has been a response to, even a mimicking of, the AIDS pandemic. Of course, such a response potentially acts out complicated, even contradictory, motives, especially since the "epidemic" of computer viruses is by no means an organized phenomenon but rather the result of the independent activity of diverse individuals. Perhaps the "spread" of computer viruses, because intentionally set in motion by human beings, in part counters the sense of powerlessness felt in the face of a natural disaster like the AIDS pandemic so clearly at this moment beyond human control. Or perhaps it plays out a certain fantasy that AIDS itself is somehow not "really" a natural phenomenon but rather something engineered more intentionally.[139] Such a fantasy, acted out through the parallel epidemic of computer viruses, reflects and magnifies a sense that intentionality somehow inheres in HIV and AIDS; it also gives voice to the complicated fears raised in response to the technology of genetic engineering seen as an ultimately transgressive and dangerous understanding and manipulation of biological "secrets."[140] The computer hacker, by enacting, within the realm of computer science, the fear of an intentionally created biological epidemic, perhaps again, at least imaginatively, asserts some control over what seems so fully out of control.[141]

In any case, the language used in discussing computer viruses, with its echoes of the biological, manifests complicated ideas about the nature, and particularly the meaningfulness, of the basic processes of life—and about how those processes might be related to human intentionality. The very choice of the biological metaphor to describe an intentionally crafted piece of computer language suggests how strongly engrained is the idea of virus as language and thus as intentional entity. Moreover, the strong threat to coherence associated with the computer virus seen as a program working through, but in opposition to, other programs—and a threat not just to the personal computer (so far the primary site of "viral infection") but also, on a grander scale, to the large computer networks that are more and more perceived as structuring the informational capacities of our "information society"—echoes the sense that the biological virus is not just another piece of information but one deeply inimical to "normal" cellular functioning, and one, for instance, in a syndrome like AIDS, affecting not just individual cells but complicated biological "networks" like the immune system.

Computer science thus adopts the language of biology at least in part because that language is rich in metaphors, suggesting its own appropriateness for describing informational entities and processes. In turn, the use of biological metaphors by the information sciences "feeds back" on an understanding of the biological systems that provide those metaphors to reinforce the sense that these involve intentionality—and, further, competition among different "meaningful" entities (cells and the viruses infecting them), even theft and warfare. That is, as the realm of the biological is mined for metaphors because it already tends, in its own metaphors, to depict life as at its core meaningful or intentional, that sense of meaning or intention is intensified by the very use of biological metaphors in describing processes that cannot be looked at as in any way *not* intentional. The metaphoric crossing of computational and biological realms tends to blur the distinction between a "natural" disease (or disaster) and an "artificial" (intentionally composed) challenge to coherence, so that, on the one hand, the computer virus is naturalized (gaining a life of its own) while, on the other, the biological virus is constructed as somehow artificial (in fact, in some theories about HIV, perhaps humanly constructed—and for very specific purposes of social control).

Those who write about computer viruses sometimes express anxiety about this crossing of the realms of biology and information science, attempting to make it clear that the computer virus is different from the biological by the very fact of the intentionality of its creation: "Virus mutations occur when a captured virus is modified in some way. This is done by intentional assembly programming and is quite distinct from biological mutations, which occur accidentally."[142] Such writers sometimes feel compelled to reassure their readers that computer viruses are not really natural, living entities: thus, Denning begins his book with an anecdote in which he, as expert, must answer and discredit the lay question, "[H]ow can a computer catch a virus? Does somebody sneeze on it?"[143] But the very need to make such clarifications points up how clearly the language of computer science itself in fact fails to distinguish the biological from the computational, the accidentally mutating virus from the one that undergoes "mutation" as an intentional process.

Diseases often, perhaps always, take on social and cultural meanings that make it possible for them to be seen not just as random events, but as part of some plan or meaningful pattern,[144] and the AIDS crisis, in what Paula Treichler calls "an epidemic of signification," has evoked an enormous range of such interpretations.[145] Though science might claim to have exorcised such "primitive" imputations of meaning from its own considerations of disease, the language we have been examining here would suggest otherwise. Molecular biology, in its most basic terms and concepts, metaphorizes its subject matter as language. And the virus is located at a point of particular significance—where the discourse of molecular "language" and "intentionality" intersects a computational discourse in which viruses themselves refer metaphorically to intentionally created informational entities. This guarantees that, at the current moment, a consideration of the virus will raise questions about intentionality and meaning, about how one ("parasitic") living process might (through the manipulation of "information" and, as it were, intentionally) undermine another. Further, the intersection of biology and computer science at the node of the virus focuses attention on the increasingly tenuous borderline between the natural and artificial, the living and the technologically engineered. The crossings that occur at that borderline are crucial to both technical and popular understandings (and fears) about HIV and AIDS. And as I will argue in the next section of my discussion, those understandings and fears are intimately tied up with broader social constructions of sexuality, gender, race, and class.

NOTES

1. Though most scientists actively involved in AIDS research have accepted that HIV is the prime causative agent of AIDS, there remains significant controversy over this claim. Scientists like Peter Duesberg have raised questions about the role HIV may or may not play in causing AIDS, and in the broader community of those concerned with AIDS, groups like HEAL (Health Education AIDS Liaison) have spent considerable energy challenging current understandings of the syndrome's etiology. See, for instance, HEAL's "Information Packet" (Spring 1991, updated Spring 1992), Section 2 ("The HIV/AZT Controversy"), which gathers together various material. For a refutation of Duesberg, and the suggestion that "the 'anti-HIV' theorists . . . consistently provide a gloss of scientific respectability to profoundly irrational and usually homophobic forces" (245), see Simon Watney, "Duesberg's Dangerous Dogma," *Practices of Freedom: Selected Writings on HIV/AIDS* (Durham: Duke University Press, 1994), 244-46; and see Jan Zita Grover, "Constitutional Symptoms," in Erica Carter and Simon Watney, eds., *Taking Liberties: AIDS and Cultural Politics* (London: Serpent's Tail, 1989), 150-51. I myself accept that HIV is importantly involved in causing AIDS, but identifying the syndrome's primary causative agent is not the same as fully understanding the processes of pathogenesis involved in it. The etiology of AIDS needs to be explored much more fully than it has yet been.

2. Cindy Patton, *Inventing AIDS* (New York and London: Routledge, 1990), 53.

3. Lee Edelman, "The Plague of Discourse: Politics, Literary Theory, and AIDS," in Ronald R. Butters, John M. Clum, and Michael Moon, eds., *Displacing Homophobia: Gay Male Perspectives in Literature and Culture* (Durham and London: Duke University Press, 1989), 290 [this volume was originally published as *South Atlantic Quarterly* 88:1].

4. For such a project, the work of cultural critics like Douglas Crimp, Cindy Patton, Paula A. Treichler, and Simon Watney provides a necessary starting point; see, for instance, Crimp, ed., *AIDS: Cultural Analysis/Cultural Activism* (Cambridge, MA, and London: The MIT Press, 1988) [originally published as a special issue of *October* 43 (Winter 1987)]; Patton, *Sex and Germs: The Politics of AIDS* (Boston: South End Press, 1985); Patton, *Inventing AIDS*; Patton, *Last Served? Gendering the HIV Pandemic*, Social Aspects of AIDS Series (London: Taylor & Francis, 1994); Treichler, "AIDS, Gender, and Biomedical Discourse: Current Contests for Meaning," in Elizabeth Fee and Daniel M. Fox, eds., *AIDS: The Burdens of History* (Berkeley, Los Angeles, and London: University of California Press, 1988), 190-266; Treichler and Lisa Cartwright, eds., *Imaging Technologies, Inscribing Science*, special issue of *Camera Obscura: A Journal of Feminism and Film Theory* 28 (January 1992); Watney, *Policing Desire: Pornography, AIDS and the Media*, 2nd ed. (Minneapolis: University of Minnesota Press, 1989); Carter and Watney, eds., *Taking Liberties*; and Watney, *Practices of Freedom*.

5. The fantasy of "fighting" AIDS through attacks on visible homophobes like Helms is frequently expressed in gay writing about AIDS. See, for instance, David B. Feinberg,

Queer and Loathing: Rants and Raves of a Raging AIDS Clone (New York: Viking, 1994), 102-8 ("100 Ways You Can Fight the AIDS Crisis"), and see the discussion in Chapter 6 below.

6. The recognition of the presence of genetic material within organelles like mitochondria and chloroplasts (in what has been called "maternal inheritance," since such organelles are present in eggs but not in sperm) complicates and challenges the idea that, given the nuclear DNA of any one of an organism's cells, the complete organism can be recreated ("cloned"); still, this idea persists and remains central to molecular genetics. On the genetics of mitochondria and chloroplasts, see Mark Carroll, *Organelles* (New York and London: The Guilford Press, 1989), 144-48 and 174-76.

7. Gunther S. Stent and Richard Calendar, *Molecular Genetics: An Introductory Narrative*, 2nd ed. (San Francisco: W. H. Freeman and Company, 1978), distinguish "molecular genetics" from its forebear, "classical genetics," as follows: "The fundamental unit of classical genetics is an indivisible and abstract gene. The fundamental unit of molecular genetics, by contrast, is a concrete chemical molecule, the DNA nucleotide, the gene being relegated to the role of a secondary-unit aggregate comprising hundreds or thousands of nucleotides" (23). On the origins of this new scientific field, see Stent and Calendar on "The Birth of Molecular Genetics" (24-29).

8. For a brief summary of the history of genetic engineering, see James D. Watson, John Tooze, and David T. Kurtz, *Recombinant DNA: A Short Course*, Scientific American Books (New York: W. H. Freeman and Company, 1983), 242-47.

9. On the "human genome project," see, for instance, Natalie Angier, "Gains Made in Effort to Map the Human Genetic Makeup," *New York Times* 1 Oct. 1992, A1, A22; and Angier, "Blueprint for a Human," *New York Times* 6 Oct. 1992, C6.

10. On the importance in early molecular biology of the study of bacterial viruses (bacteriophages) by the "Phage Group," see John Cairns, Gunther S. Stent, and James D. Watson, eds., *Phage and the Origins of Molecular Biology* (Cold Spring Harbor, NY: Cold Spring Harbor Laboratory of Quantitative Biology, 1966). Because the structure of viruses is much simpler than that of other organisms, often consisting simply of a DNA or RNA core surrounded by a protein coat, they have provided particularly useful systems in which to investigate the replication of DNA/RNA and the production of proteins from the DNA/RNA "template."

11. Stent and Calendar, *Molecular Genetics*, 749. Stent and Calendar present a brief discussion of the history of immunology, with special attention to the importance of molecular genetics in that history, 749-55.

12. Arthur M. Silverstein, *A History of Immunology* (San Diego: Academic Press, Inc., 1989), 330.

13. Donna J. Haraway, *Simians, Cyborgs, and Women: The Reinvention of Nature* (New York: Routledge, 1991), would see the development of a linguistically-tied genetics as part of a larger shift in twentieth-century biological science: "By the end of his career around 1940, Yerkes' science was already outmoded. It was being replaced by a different engineering perspective, based not on physiology, but on the physical sciences' analysis of information and energy in statistical assemblages. The physiology of sexual organisms gave way to biochemistry, structural analysis, and molecular genetics of information machines: integrons, replicators, self-assembling biological subsystems such as viruses and cell organelles and populations—the new books of nature to be read by mathematics. It is not an accident that modern genetics is pursued as a linguistic science, with attention to signs, punctuation, syntax, semiotics, machine read-out, directional information flow, codons, transcription, and so on. . . . The social goal of the new life science was clearly statistical control of the mass through sophisticated communications systems . . ." (46); "communications sciences and modern biologies are constructed by a common move—*the translation of the world into a problem of coding*. . . . In modern biologies, the translation of the world into a problem in coding can be illustrated by molecular genetics, ecology, sociobiological evolutionary theory, and immunobiology" (164).

14. "Gene expression" is the common term for the "transfer of information" from DNA "template" to protein "product."

15. James D. Watson, Nancy H. Hopkins, Jeffrey W. Roberts, Joan Argetsinger Steitz, and Alan W. Weiner, *Molecular Biology of the Gene*, 4th ed. (Menlo Park, CA: The Benjamin/Cummings Publishing Company, Inc., 1987), 1.86 [hereafter abbreviated as *MBG*].

16. The metaphor of "breaking the code" is used, for instance, by Stent and Calendar, *Molecular Genetics*, 541. The comparison to the Rosetta Stone occurs at 544-45. Earlier, however, Stent and Calendar recognize significant differences between deciphering the "genetic code" and reading hieroglyphics (540-41).

17. Stent and Calendar, *Molecular Genetics*, 221-22; emphasis in the original. Not surprisingly, the linguistic metaphor also pervades more popular scientific writing on DNA; see, for instance, Ann Giudici Fettner, *Viruses: Agents of Change* (New York: McGraw-Hill Publishing Company, 1990), 14-15, a book that grew out of Fettner's reporting on the AIDS crisis. See her earlier book, written with William A. Check, *The Truth About AIDS: Evolution of an Epidemic*, revised ed. (New York: Owl Book/Henry Holt and Company, 1985).

18. *MBG*, 1.78.

19. *MBG*, 1.457. Such a representation is useful in its simplicity, but moves us away from thinking of DNA as a complex, three-dimensional entity.

20. Stent and Calendar, *Molecular Genetics*, 224.

21. All the phrases quoted here are from Stent and Calendar, *Molecular Genetics*, 223-224. Similar metaphors can be found in other considerations of the same issues.

22. Stent and Calendar, *Molecular Genetics*, 222 ("synonymous"), 224 ("sense" and "nonsense"), 411 ("nonsense" and "synonymous"), 549 ("nonsense"), 554 ("synonymous"), 556 ("synonymous"), 558-66 ("nonsense"), 573 ("ambiguous").

23. Natalie Angier, "U.S. Clears Use of Gene Therapy Against a Form of Lung Cancer," *New York Times* 16 Sept. 1992, A20; and Lawrence M. Fisher, "Search Advances for 'Antisense' Drugs," *New York Times* 8 June 1993, C3. And see Flossie Wong-Staal, "Human Immunodeficiency Viruses and Their Replication," in Bernard N. Fields, David M. Knipe, Robert M. Chanock, Martin S. Hirsch, Joseph L. Melnick, Thomas P. Monath, and Bernard Roizman, eds., *Fundamental Virology*, 2nd ed. (New York: Raven Press, 1991 [1986]), 720 [*Fundamental Virology* will hereafter be abbreviated *FV*].

24. Natalie Angier, "Biologists Seek the Words in DNA's Unbroken Text," *New York Times* 9 July 1991, C11.

25. Gina Kolata, "Coincidence or Link Between Cancer and Hereditary Diseases?" *New York Times* 11 May 1993, C3.

26. For the metaphor of "copying," see, for instance, *MBG*, 1.363.

27. *MBG*, 1.228; emphasis in the original. For use of the metaphor of "reading frame" in discussing HIV, see, for instance, Wong-Staal, "Human Immunodeficiency Viruses," 713, 714, and 720.

28. *MBG*, 1.420.

29. *MBG*, 1.391-92.

30. *MBG*, 1.420.

31. *MBG*, 1.341; emphasis in the original. Also see 1.289-91 and 342.

32. *MBG*, 1.81.

33. F. H. C. Crick, "On Protein Synthesis," *Symposium of the Society for Experimental Biology* 12 (1958), 138-63.

34. Stent and Calendar, *Molecular Genetics*, 604.

35. *MBG*, 1.82.

36. For more on the central dogma's place in a biology dependent on information theory, see R. C. Lewontin, Steven Rose, and Leon J. Kamin, *Not in Our Genes:*

Biology, Ideology, and Human Nature (New York: Pantheon Books, 1984), 57-60; and see Chapter 2 below.

37. See *MBG*, 1.177 and 220.

38. *MBG*, 1.628. The formation of words like "codon," "exon," "intron," and "transposon" echoes the language of chemistry (ion, electron, neutron, proton) but also perhaps the newer language of computer science and cybernetics (automaton, etc.). For more on the connections between the linguistic metaphor in biology and the "information sciences," see below.

39. See *MBG*, 1.201-2. "Transposition," of course, has a broad range of meanings; still, especially given the extensive use of linguistic metaphors elsewhere within molecular genetics, one of the strong associations of the scientific term is with the *editorial* process.

40. On "palindromic sequences," the "significance" of which remains unclear, see *MBG*, 1.274-77; the quotation is from *MBG*, 1.274-75.

41. *MBG*, 1.273.

42. See Cindy Patton's brief but suggestive comments: "the media and the virus serve as mutual metaphors: scientists talk about messenger RNA and remark that the virus is 'trying to tell us something'" ("Visualizing Safe Sex: When Pedagogy and Pornography Collide," in Diana Fuss, ed., *Inside/Out: Lesbian Theories, Gay Theories* [New York and London: Routledge, 1991], 377); "And of course the virus itself becomes a character—the little hunk of protein that refuses to give up its secrets. 'Perhaps the virus is trying to tell us something,' both new right doomsday prophets and scientists have said. The virus is itself overlayed (*sic*) with communications language—messenger RNA, codes, evasion, changing its surface, transcription, long terminal repeats" (*Inventing AIDS*, 25-26).

43. For the metaphor of DNA as blueprint, see, for instance, Angier, "Blueprint," and Angier, "Keys Emerge to Mystery of 'Junk' DNA," *New York Times* 28 June 1994, C1, C3.

44. See, for instance, Wong-Staal, "Human Immunodeficiency Viruses," 715.

45. For images of the cell as factory, see Emily Martin, *The Woman in the Body: A Cultural Analysis of Reproduction* (Boston: Beacon Press, 1992 [1987]), 37-38 and 44-47. One depiction cited by Martin from *Time* magazine shows the "HTLV Virus" (i.e., HIV) "converting" the cellular "factory" into "its own genetic factory" (38).

46. *MBG*, 1.672; emphasis in the original. Interestingly, one influential statement in this area of speculation—Richard Dawkins's *The Selfish Gene* (New York: Oxford University Press, 1976)—simultaneously "humanizes" DNA and "mechanizes" living organisms: "We are survival machines—robot vehicles blindly programmed to preserve the selfish molecules known as genes" (ix). In such a description, intentionality at the molecular level, in its presumed primacy, essentially erases intentionality at the level of the whole organism.

47. Fettner, *Viruses*, 25. With the discovery of the "viroids," scientists now recognize the existence of infectious particles made up *only* of genetic information—in Fettner's term, "naked RNA" with no protein coat; see her account of viroids, 34-42.

48. *MBG*, 1.185.

49. Stephen C. Harrison, "Principles of Virus Structure," in *FV*, 37.

50. Bernard Roizman, "Multiplication of Viruses: An Overview," in *FV*, 89-90.

51. Roizman uses the metaphor of "strategy" throughout his article, entitling one of his major subdivisions "Strategies of Viral Multiplication" (89).

52. AIDS activists have strongly challenged the use of the term "AIDS virus"; see Jan Zita Grover, "AIDS: Keywords," in Crimp, ed., *AIDS: Cultural Analysis/Cultural Criticism*, 21: "A seemingly ineradicable term, *AIDS virus* is almost universally employed by the popular press and is increasingly used by physicians, scientists, and public health planners. The effect of this usage, which conflates HIV with a terminal phase of HIV infection—AIDS—is to equate infection with death. It also supposes that the invariable

outcome of HIV infection is death, whereas every other known virus's natural history suggests that a spectrum of outcomes is possible, ranging from quiescent, asymptomatic infection to symptomatic but subacute, to, in the case of HIV infection, immune exhaustion and subsequent infection by opportunistic infections and neoplasms; only the latter is clinically defined as AIDS. / *AIDS virus*, then, is a term more projective than descriptive. It imposes a mortal sentence on anyone infected with HIV, a projection of hostility and fear that bespeaks another's death in order to quell one's own anxieties."

53. William A. Haseltine and Flossie Wong-Staal, "The Molecular Biology of the AIDS Virus," in *The Science of AIDS: Readings from Scientific American Magazine* (New York: W. H. Freeman and Company, 1989 [1988]), 13.

54. Haseltine and Wong-Staal, "Molecular Biology," 14.

55. Haseltine and Wong-Staal, "Molecular Biology," 17.

56. Haseltine and Wong-Staal, "Molecular Biology," 24.

57. Viruses themselves do, however, often contain *some* of the enzymes (e.g., reverse transcriptase) necessary for their own perpetuation.

58. Bernard N. Fields and David M. Knipe, "Introduction," in *FV*, 3.

59. Wendell M. Stanley and Evans G. Valens, *Viruses and the Nature of Life* (New York: E. P. Dutton, 1961), 36. This view is a persistent one; see Francis Crick, *Life Itself: Its Origin and Nature* (New York: Simon & Schuster, 1981), 49: "With [viruses] we come near to the borderline between the living and the nonliving."

60. Angier, "Biologists," C11.

61. Fettner, *Viruses*, 28; emphasis in the original.

62. *MBG*, 1.514.

63. *MBG*, 1.516-17.

64. As the article itself must point out, the virus's "choice" occurs by "trial and error"—that is, it is not intentional in the way the verb "choose" here suggests.

65. Natalie Angier, "Viruses Said to Pirate Host's Genetic Material in Invasion Strategies," *New York Times* 3 July 1990, C3.

66. Haseltine and Wong-Staal, "Molecular Biology," 14.

67. *MBG*, 1.91.

68. The Latin "virus," from which the English word derives, means literally "slime" or "poison," but the history of its metaphoric moralizing uses is a lengthy one; thus, for instance, it refers to the "vitium contra naturam" [sin against nature] in Peter Damian's eleventh-century *Liber Gomorrhianus*, *Patrologia Latina* 145, col. 161. In English, the earliest uses correspond closely to the Latin literal senses, but the broad figurative use of "virus" to mean "a moral or intellectual poison, or poisonous influence" (*Oxford English Dictionary*, definition 3) predates more narrow scientific understandings of "virus" ("filtrable virus"). See Stent and Calendar, *Molecular Genetics*, 293-94, on the narrowing of the scientific term in the "first few decades of this century."

69. Douglas Rushkoff, *Media Virus! Hidden Agendas in Popular Culture* (New York: Ballantine, 1994). See Michiko Kakutani's review, "On the 'Datasphere' and a Generation Absorbed in It," *New York Times* 6 Dec. 1994, C19.

70. The language here plays on the military recruitment slogan, "it's not just a job, it's an adventure," and thus suggests a certain gendering prevalent more generally in videogame design and marketing: many of these games express violent militaristic fantasies and are importantly involved in certain current constructions of "masculinity."

71. Cindy Patton, "Visualizing Safe Sex," notes that "[p]ostmodern cultural criticism sees the intricacies of communication illustrated in the virus, as in minimalist musician Laurie Anderson's performance piece, 'language is a virus'" (377). The performance of "Language Is a Virus" that appears in *Home of the Brave* (A Talk Normal Production, 1986; Warner Reprise Video) follows the piece "Difficult Listening Hour," which concludes with the telling of a Red-Riding Hood-like story in which the wolfish inhabitant of the speaker's house says, "I'm the soul doctor, and you know, language is a virus from outer space, and hearing your name is better than seeing your face." The sentence

"Language is a virus from outer space," attributed to Burroughs, then appears projected behind the stage, and "Language is a Virus" itself begins.

For Burroughs's conception of the "viral" nature of language, see William S. Burroughs, "Ten Years and a Billion Dollars," *The Adding Machine: Selected Essays* (New York: Seaver Books, 1986), 48: "My general theory since 1971 has been that the Word is literally a virus, and that it has not been recognized as such because it has achieved a state of relatively stable symbiosis with its human host; that is to say, the Word Virus (the Other Half) has established itself so firmly as an accepted part of the human organism that it can now sneer at gangster viruses like smallpox and turn them in to the Pasteur Institute. But the Word clearly bears the single identifying feature of virus: it is an organism with no internal function other than to replicate itself."

72. Burroughs and Anderson perhaps echo here the biologist Francis Crick and his theory of "directed panspermia"—the idea that "life itself" arrived on earth from "outer space": "Leslie Orgel and I . . . had hit on the idea that perhaps life on Earth originated from microorganisms sent here, on an unmanned spaceship, by a higher civilization elsewhere" (Crick, *What Mad Pursuit: A Personal View of Scientific Discovery* [New York: Basic Books, 1988], 148). However, the "microorganisms" Crick refers to here are not viruses but rather procaryotic cells; see *Life Itself*, chapter 11 ("What Would They Have Sent?"), 117-29.

73. Computer science of course employs biological metaphors not only in its description of "viruses"; note, for instance, the common use of the language of "cloning" to describe the development of computer systems "compatible" with each other, and also the widespread description of problems in computer programs and operations as "bugs."

74. See, for instance, John Markoff, "Beyond Artificial Intelligence, A Search for Artificial Life," *New York Times* 25 Feb. 1990, E5; Malcolm W. Browne, "Lively Computer Creation Blurs Definition of Life," *New York Times* 27 Aug. 1991, C1, C8; and Browne, "Quest to Mimic Life Began in 1940's," *New York Times* 27 Aug. 1991, C8.

75. Gina Kolata, "Novel Kind of Computing: Calculation with DNA," *New York Times* 22 Nov. 1994, C1. And see Kolata, "Scientist at Work: Leonard Adleman: Hitting the High Spots of Computer Theory," *New York Times* 13 Dec. 1994, C1, C10; and "A Side Trip into AIDS Theory," *New York Times* 13 Dec. 1994, C11.

76. Haraway, *Simians, Cyborgs, and Women*, 152.

77. Jan Hruska, *Computer Viruses and Anti-Virus Warfare* (New York: Ellis Horwood, 1990), 120.

78. See Jacques Derrida's brief consideration of the question, "in the case of computers, is the use of the word 'virus' simply a metaphor?" (23), in "The Rhetoric of Drugs. An Interview," Michael Israel, trans., *Differences: A Journal of Feminist Cultural Studies* 5:1 (1993), 23-24.

79. Natalie Angier, "A First Step in Putting Genes into Action: Bend the DNA," *New York Times* 4 Aug. 1992, C7.

80. It is the virus's "parasitic" dependence on incorporation into other programs that distinguishes it from the computer "worm"; see Hruska, *Computer Viruses*: "Worms are similar to viruses, but unlike viruses (which need a carrier in order to replicate), worms replicate in their entirety, creating exact copies of themselves" (18). Also see Peter J. Denning, ed., *Computers Under Attack: Intruders, Worms, and Viruses* (New York: ACM Press, 1990; reprinted with corrections, Reading, MA: Addison-Wesley Publishing Company, 1991), xiv [hereafter abbreviated as *CUA*]; Denning, "The Internet Worm," in *CUA*, 197; and Eugene H. Spafford, Kathleen A. Heaphy, and David J. Ferbrache, "A Computer Virus Primer," in *CUA*, 317.

81. Denning, "Computer Viruses," in *CUA*, 288.

82. For use of this term, see, for instance, Hruska, *Computer Viruses*, 24.

83. See, for instance, Hruska, *Computer Viruses*, 31, and M. H. Brothers, "Computer Virus Protection Procedures," in *CUA*, 356.

84. Hruska, *Computer Viruses*, 17.
85. Spafford, Heaphy, and Ferbrache, "Computer Virus Primer," 316.
86. Spafford, Heaphy, and Ferbrache, "Computer Virus Primer," 312.
87. On computer viruses, see Stafford, Heaphy, and Ferbrache, "Computer Virus Primer," 328; on biological viruses, see Roizman, "Multiplication of Viruses," 89.
88. See, for instance, Hruska, *Computer Viruses*, 61-62. And see the following recent articles: Peter H. Lewis, "Personal Computers: The Virus: Threat or Menace?" *New York Times* 15 June 1993, C7; and Lewis, "The Executive Computer: Medicine, and Common Sense, for Virus Problems," *New York Times* 21 June 1992, F9.
89. See especially Fred Cohen, "Implications of Computer Viruses and Current Methods of Defense," in *CUA*, 381, 383, 390, and 393.
90. Hruska, *Computer Viruses*, 36.
91. Harold Joseph Highland, "Computer Viruses—A Post Mortem," in *CUA*, 307-8. Compare, for instance, Frederick A. Murphy and David W. Kingsbury, "Virus Taxonomy," in *FV*, 9-35.
92. See, in addition to the passages cited above, Hruska, *Computer Viruses*, 34-36; Denning, "Computer Viruses," 287-88; Harold Joseph Highland, "The BRAIN Virus: Fact and Fantasy," in *CUA*, 294-98; Spafford, Heaphy, and Ferbrache, "Computer Virus Primer," 321-31; and Cohen, "Implications of Computer Viruses," 382-84. Numerous other examples of the metaphors of "infection" and "spread" could be cited.
93. Spafford, Heaphy, and Ferbrache, "Computer Virus Primer," 333-34; and Brothers, "Computer Virus Protection Procedures," 358.
94. Cohen, "Implications of Computer Viruses," 396.
95. Hruska, *Computer Viruses*, 55.
96. Ian H. Witten, "Computer (In)security: Infiltrating Open Systems," in *CUA*, 128.
97. *CUA*, xiv.
98. Witten, "Computer (In)security," 126.
99. Brothers, "Computer Virus Protection Procedures," 370.
100. *CUA*, 283.
101. Hruska, *Computer Viruses*, 36.
102. Witten, "Computer (In)security," 123-24.
103. The biological disease Cohen here imagines of course does not correspond in its details with HIV infection; but the qualities of contagion, lethalness, and latency that Cohen gives his hypothetical disease do characterize commonly expressed fantasies and fears about HIV/AIDS.
104. Cohen, "Implications of Computer Viruses," 383-83.
105. Hruska, *Computer Viruses*, 13-14.
106. Cohen, "Implications of Computer Viruses," 384.
107. Lewis, "Personal Computers," C7.
108. For some uses of the language of risk, see Hruska, *Computer Viruses*, 26; Highland, "BRAIN," 294; Brothers, "Computer Virus Protection Procedures," 360; and Cohen, "Implications of Computer Viruses," 393.
109. Brothers, "Computer Virus Protection Procedures," 365. For other invocations of "user awareness," see Hruska, *Computer Viruses*, 65, and Cohen, "Implications of Computer Viruses," 391.
110. Lewis, "Personal Computers," C7.
111. Brothers, "Computer Virus Protection Procedures," 372.
112. Ken Thompson, "Reflections on Trusting Trust," in *CUA*, 103.
113. Denning, "Computer Viruses," 291. Also see Hruska, *Computer Viruses*, 65; and *CUA*, xiv.
114. Hruska, *Computer Viruses*, 75; and Cohen, "Implications of Computer Viruses," 392 and 394. Note the use of a language of innocence here in Hruska: "If a short pattern is used, the chances are that the scanning software will produce a number of false positives, finding the pattern in completely innocent software."

115. Hruska, *Computer Viruses*, 64 and 69; Spafford, Heaphy, and Ferbrache, "Computer Virus Primer," 332; and Brothers, "Computer Virus Protection Procedures," 361.

116. Highland, "Post Mortem," 307.

117. *CUA*, xiv.

118. Denning, "Computer Viruses," 290.

119. Brothers, "Computer Virus Protection Procedures," 372.

120. Hruska, *Computer Viruses*, 77; Denning, "Computer Viruses," 290-91; Spafford, Heaphy, and Ferbrache, "Computer Virus Primer," 329 and 338; and Brothers, "Computer Virus Protection Procedures," 366.

121. Brothers, "Computer Virus Protection Procedures," 364-65; and Cohen, "Implications of Computer Viruses," 390.

122. Witten, "Computer (In)security," 129; and Denning, "Computer Viruses," 291.

123. Hruska, *Computer Viruses*, 65.

124. Spafford, Heaphy, and Ferbrache, "Computer Virus Primer," 338.

125. Markoff, "Beyond Artificial Intelligence," E5.

126. Hruska, *Computer Viruses*, 62.

127. *CUA*, 283. Also see Spafford, Heaphy, and Ferbrache, "Computer Virus Primer," 328: "The first use of the term *virus* to refer to unwanted computer code occurred in 1972 in a science fiction novel, *When Harley Was One*, by David Gerrold. . . . The description of *virus* in that book did not fit the currently-accepted definition of computer virus—a program that alters other programs to include a copy of itself. Fred Cohen formally defined the term *computer virus* in 1983. . . . It appears, however, that computer viruses were being written by other individuals, although not named such, as early as 1981 on early Apple II computers." On the indebtedness of virus writing to the science fiction genre of "cyberpunk," see Paul Saffo, "Consensual Realities in Cyberspace," in *CUA*, 416-20.

128. Hruska, *Computer Viruses*, 13.

129. Hruska, *Computer Viruses*, 13.

130. *CUA*, 283.

131. Spafford, Heaphy, and Ferbrache, "Computer Virus Primer," 318.

132. Hruska, *Computer Viruses*, 49. Also see Spafford, Heaphy, and Ferbrache, "Computer Virus Primer," 342 and 351.

133. Hruska, *Computer Viruses*, 14.

134. Cohen, "Implications of Computer Viruses," 389.

135. Hruska, *Computer Viruses*, 15-16; and see "'Trojan Horse' Infects and Destroys Personal Computer Systems: AIDS Information Affected," *AIDS & Society: International Research and Policy Bulletin* 1:2 (Jan. 1990), 13.

136. Jerry Kolins, "On Trojan Horses and Surrogate Mothers" (letter), *NEJM* 311:1 (5 July 1984), 53; citing Malcolm I. McDonald, John D. Hamilton, and David T. Durack, "Hypothesis: Hepatitis B Surface Antigen Could Harbour the Infective Agent of AIDS," *Lancet* no. 8355 (13 Oct. 1983), 882-84. And see Paula A. Treichler, "AIDS, Homophobia, and Biomedical Discourse: An Epidemic of Signification," in Crimp, ed., *AIDS: Cultural Analysis/Cultural Activism*, 59, and the references cited there, n. 80.

137. See Warren E. Leary, "A Key to Flu Virus Infection Is Identified," *New York Times* 21 May 1993, A18.

138. Emmaneul Dreuilhe, *Mortal Embrace: Living with AIDS*, Linda Coverdale, trans. (New York: Hill and Wang, 1988), 115. For discussion of Dreuilhe, see David Wetsel, "The Best of Times, The Worst of Times: The Emerging Literature of AIDS in France," in Emmanuel S. Nelson, ed., *AIDS: The Literary Response* (New York: Twayne Publishers, 1992), 99-101, esp. 100 for a treatment of his use of "Trojan" metaphors; and Brian Patton, "Cell Wars: Military Metaphors and the Crisis of Authority in the AIDS Epidemic," in James Miller, ed., *Fluid Exchanges: Artists and Critics in the AIDS Crisis* (Toronto, Buffalo, and London: University of Toronto Press, 1992), 282-84.

139. The AIDS crisis has been an especially fertile ground for the proliferation of conspiracy theories that would make the pandemic either wholly intentional or the unintentional effect of a surreptitious experiment gone wrong. See the discussion of novels in which this is the case in Chapter 6 below.

140. See, most influentially, the series of books by Jeremy Rifkin: Ted Howard and Rifkin, *Who Should Play God? The Artificial Creation of Life and What It Means for the Future of the Human Race* (New York: Delacorte Press, 1977); Rifkin and Nicanor Perlas, *Algeny* (New York: Viking, 1983); and Rifkin, *Declaration of a Heretic* (Boston and London: Routledge and Kegan Paul, 1985).

141. We see such a dynamic played out in a movie like *War Games*, which involves illicit computer "hacking," though not computer viruses. The movie both expresses and masters a fear of nuclear war triggered by a computer technology that cannot be adequately controlled, though paradoxically it has been designed to ensure full control of the defense system.

142. Hruska, *Computer Viruses*, 61.

143. *CUA*, xi.

144. For one sustained argument about the ways in which diseases take on meaning, see Susan Sontag, *Illness as Metaphor* (New York: Farrar, Straus and Giroux, 1978) and *AIDS and Its Metaphors* (New York: Farrar, Straus and Giroux, 1989), later published in one volume (New York: Anchor Books/Doubleday, 1990).

145. Treichler, "AIDS, Homophobia, and Biomedical Discourse."

CHAPTER 2

AIDS and the Battlefields of Masculinity

1. SEXUALIZED CELLS

The metaphors of molecular biology and the scientific languages that have developed around AIDS are intimately articulated with gender ideology. In Western thought, femaleness has long been identified with matter and body, and with the passivity and weakness thought to inhere in body; by contrast, maleness is associated with form and idea, and with the active, shaping powers of mind.[1] While recent feminist work has presented strong deconstructions of such gendered oppositions, and while, as Donna Haraway suggests, "[t]he dichotomies between mind and body, animal and human, organism and machine, public and private, nature and culture, men and women, primitive and civilized are all in question ideologically," with "[h]igh-tech culture challeng[ing] these dualisms in intriguing ways,"[2] traditional dichotomies retain real power as organizing principles within Western culture. They have participated in the formation of contemporary science, and science still, if often obliquely and disguisedly, expresses and depends on them.[3]

The linguistic metaphors of molecular biology, in imputing intentionality to biochemical processes, enable the imposition of social and political ideas at cellular and subcellular levels. In the context of Western gender ideology, the very identification of DNA as an informational entity—as the carrier of the cell's "ideas"—suggests maleness. Indeed, as the Biology and Gender Study Group shows in an important article, biologists typically treat the cell nucleus, the holder of genetic "information," as "masculine," and the cell cytoplasm, where genetic "information" is ultimately "expressed," as "feminine":

> The nucleus came to be seen as the masculine ruler of the cell, the stable yet dynamic inheritance from former generations, the unmoved mover, the mind of the cell. The cytoplasm became the feminine body of the cell, the fluid, changeable partner of the marriage.[4]

As the Study Group goes on to suggest, twentieth-century models of relations between nucleus and cytoplasm have tended consistently and closely to reflect ideologies of marriage, and "[c]ontemporary biology, although aware of the interactions of the cytoplasm and nucleus, still tends to portray the nucleus as the head of the family's hierarchy" (180).

At the center of the centrally-located nucleus, at the pinnacle of the cell's "family hierarchy," stands DNA, "master molecule" (180) and, according to the "central dogma" of molecular genetics, point of origin for all cellular activity. In Evelyn Fox Keller's formulation:

> The central dogma is a good example of . . . master-molecule theories. . . .[5] In locating the seat of genetic control in a single molecule, it posits a structure of genetic organization that is essentially hierarchical, often illustrated in textbooks by organizational charts like those of corporate structures. In this model, genetic stability is ensured by the unidirectionality of information flow, much as political and social stability is assumed in many quarters to require the unidirectional exercise of authority.[6]

Keller's analysis makes clear that the hierarchical organization of the cell by biologists, in its separation of the cell into components distinctly responsible for control functions and for production, reflects capitalist structures, and structures that are themselves strongly gendered. As the Biology and Gender Study Group concludes:

> The master-molecule has become, in DNA, the unmoved mover of the changing cytoplasm. In this cellular version of the Aristotelian cosmos, the nucleus is the efficient cause (as Aristotle posited the sperm to be) while the cytoplasm (like Aristotle's conception of the female substrate) is merely the *material* cause. (181; emphasis in original).

We begin to see in such examples from cell biology that, when the metaphors of science are set in motion, becoming enmeshed in narrative, they tend particularly to do ideological work. In a culture where activity and passivity are consistently gendered and where positionality—inversion, relations between back and front, straightness and bending—is consistently associated with particular sexualized stances,[7] narrative often evokes gender roles and sexual identities. Not surprisingly, narratives of sexual reproduction tend to be especially "pregnant" in meaning, mirroring larger cultural expectations about gender and sexuality. Thus, as the Biology and Gender Study Group outlines, twentieth-century scientific narratives of the union of sperm and egg range from "a courtship analogy wherein the many spermatic suitors courted the egg in its ovarian parlour" (174), to an "epic of the heroic sperm struggling against the hostile uterus"[8] (174-75), to "more disturbing images" (175):

> In one image we see the fertilization as a kind of martial gang-rape, the members of the masculine army lying in wait for the passive egg. In another image, the egg is a whore, attracting the soldiers like a magnet, the classical seduction image and rationale for rape. The egg obviously wanted it. Yet, once *penetrated*, the egg becomes the virtuous lady, closing its door to the other *suitors*. Only then is the egg, because it has fused with a sperm, rescued from dormancy and becomes active. The fertilizing sperm is a hero who survives while others perish, a soldier, a shard of steel, a successful suitor, and the cause of movement in the egg. The ovum is a passive victim, a whore and finally, a proper lady whose fulfillment is attained. (176; emphasis in original)

In one recent news report, the discovery of "odor receptors" in sperm provides the opportunity for articulating a new, related cellular narrative of feminine seduction:

> Sperm cells possess the same sort of odor receptors that allow the nose to smell, suggesting that swimming sperm navigate toward a fertile egg by detecting its scent, scientists have found. . . . Last year, Dr. Garbers and his co-workers announced that fertile eggs secrete a compound that in test-tube experiments proved irresistible to sperm. Researchers speculate that the newly discovered receptors could be the sperm's machinery for recognizing those seductive molecules, but they do not yet have proof that the two findings are related.[9]

The relations of sperm and egg in such narratives have a clear connection to gendered depictions of nucleus and cytoplasm:

> The sperm, after all, is viewed as a motile nucleus while the cytoplasm of the zygote and its descendants is derived entirely from the ovum. . . . One might argue that the ovum provides a nuclear component equal to that of the sperm, but this is usually overlooked. . . . Even today among biologists, the term "maternal inheritance" is identical with "cytoplasmic inheritance." (Biology and Gender Study Group, 179)

And the gendered narratives of sperm and egg have a further crucial resonance. In modelling the fusion of gametes after the (active) male "penetration" of a (passive) female during procreative sex, such narratives provide a gendered and sexualized prototype for understanding other mergings that occur at the cellular level, including particularly the entry of viruses into their "host" cells. Like sperm, the virus—"a structure that has evolved to transfer nucleic acid from one cell to another"[10]—is conceived of as a package put together primarily to introduce genetic material into a cell. Also like sperm, the virus is much smaller than the cells it enters, and it is depicted as the active, energetic (male) partner in its interactions with those cells. In a recent report on "a spring-like mechanism on the surface of flu viruses that plays an important role in the viruses' infection of human cells" and that "may also be important in the infection of other viruses, including H.I.V.," the author makes the comparison of fertilization to infection explicit:

> Membrane fusion between and within cells is a vital natural process whereby chemicals and other materials carry messages and trigger reactions. In fertilization, Dr. Kim said, sperm fuse with eggs and at least one protein on the sperm surfaces has similarities in structure to the spring mechanism seen in viruses.[11]

The illustration accompanying this article makes the protein that contains this "spring-loaded infection mechanism" look like nothing so much as a bundle of dynamite. And a later report on the flu virus—again suggesting that "shedding light on [its] inner workings" "may also prove useful in understanding other viruses, including the one that causes AIDS"—makes even more explicit the phallic imagination at work in visualizing viral activity:

> You could think of this fusion peptide in the original molecule as the knife in a sheath tucked away somewhere. . . . The picture we now see is of the knife out of the sheath and extended completely overhead as though something had thrust it toward the cell membrane.[12]

Depictions of viral infection thus tend to invoke a gendered narrative of penetration; and since viral infection—and certainly infection by HIV—is understood as dangerous or fatal for the host cell, this is a narrative even more likely than that of fertilization to use the language of sexual *violence*. As Paula Treichler has shown, using the work of Haraway and a description from *National Geographic* of how "the AIDS virus" "attacks" the immune system, such narratives indeed often depend on the (still largely masculinized) "language of postmodern warfare: communication command control—coding, transmission, messages—interceptions, spies, lies."[13] In such accounts, HIV "penetrates" the cell membrane, "attacks" the nucleus, inserting copies of its own genetic information into the cell's DNA and "taking over" the "machinery" of "transcription" and "translation" by which the nucleus controls "expression" in the cytoplasm. In such narratives, we see the languages of linguistics, warfare, production, and sex (penetration/insertion) coming together in the description of a molecular process. And in such depictions, the virus itself, as penetrative agent, is unmistakably gendered male. The new particles of HIV that result from viral infection and replication, are, in most representations, remarkably phallic:

> Three of the segments collapse to form a bullet-shaped core surrounding the RNA and enzymes. . . . The [envelope] protein . . . juts from the membrane like a set of minute spikes. . . . Each spike is a complex of two or three identical units that in turn consist of two associated components. One component . . . rests outside the cell and the other . . . is embedded stemlike in the membrane. These glycoprotein complexes, swept up by the budding virus as it acquires its envelope, are crucial to HIV's ability to infect new cells.[14]

Treichler suggests that the most common graphic representations of HIV—"virus as grenade"—"encourage us to see the virus as a perfect inorganic military mechanism, primed for detonation";[15] these representations, however, do not simply evoke the inorganic, but, in both their sexual and military resonances, suggest a phallic masculinity.

HIV's "attack" on the cell, however, is not presented solely as the heterosexual ceding of a feminized cell to the violent advances of a phallic virus with its "bullet-shaped core" and "spikey" surface. The cell, after all, itself already represents a "marriage" of male and female, nucleus and cytoplasm, the "ideas" of DNA and the material products "coded" in those "ideas." "Take-over" of the cell by HIV involves not just the phallic "invasion" of the (feminized) cytoplasm in a kind of subcellular ejaculation or intravenous injection—"The cycle begins when an HIV particle binds to the outside of a cell and injects its core"[16]—but an "attack" on the (masculinized) nucleus and "usurpation" of the central, governing position of cellular DNA:

> The viral genetic information, now in the form of double-strand DNA (the same form in which the cell carries its own genes), migrates to the cell nucleus. A third viral enzyme, called an integrase, may then splice the HIV genome—its full complement of genetic information—into the host cell's DNA.[17]

Given the "maleness" of both cellular DNA and the "invading" retrovirus, the contest for control of the cell nucleus—and hence, as the "central dogma" would emphasize, for ultimate control of all the cell's "expressive" functions—is imagined in terms of male homosociality, with two differently "armed" male opponents battling for dominance. In some sense, the "territory" for which they battle is the feminized cytoplasm. But the "war" in the cell nucleus is depicted not only as a masculine struggle for dominance over feminized "land." Though in narratives of HIV infection both cellular DNA and viral genetic information are coded as male, these are not seen as equal or similar opponents; rather, they enact very different masculinities. Cellular DNA, after all, is the cell's "proper" genetic information, presiding over "normal" cellular processes of "expression." HIV is a "retrovirus" with an "alternative" kind of genetic information (RNA). While "viral genetic information" can be "convert[ed] . . . into DNA," and incorporated seamlessly into the cell's "proper" genome,[18] it remains essentially different from and foreign to its "host." As we have seen above, in its challenges to the "central dogma" and the "properly" unidirectional flow of information in the cell, the retrovirus—directing information *backward*—represents a perverse threat to the coherence of linguistic process imagined at the cellular level: "Its elaborate genetic regulation enables it to lie low, hidden from immune surveillance; to replicate slowly, possibly *deranging* the host cell's own genetic controls as it does so."[19] Cellular DNA—from which, in the ideology of the "central dogma," all information should flow, but which should itself remain unaffected by the "lower" forms of information contained in RNA and protein—receives an illegitimate supplement from the viral genome and is irrevocably tainted: "Once [spliced into the host cell's DNA] . . . the viral DNA (the 'provirus') will be duplicated together with the cell's own genes every time the cell divides. Thus established, infection is permanent."[20]

The perversity of HIV in such narratives of its action is clearly gendered and sexualized, presented as a debased but also threatening homosexual masculinity. When, in a recent news report discussing "promising new approaches for combating the AIDS virus," one scientist suggests that "[w]e should examine the idea that fighting the virus like gentlemen, facing it head on and attacking it directly, is not the way to go," the virus's own "indirectness," its failure to "attack head on," is seen to necessitate the adoption of an underhanded, "ungentlemanly," and thus somehow less than "masculine" posture on the part of its opponents.[21] Significantly, the process by which viral genetic information incorporates itself into cellular DNA has recently been explained as involving a kind of molecular "bending" that occurs as part of the cell's "normal" functioning but that has been turned by HIV and other viruses to "nefarious," "deadly," and "kinky" ends:

> The bending of DNA is also involved in more nefarious events, including the ability of a virus to invade a host's chromosomes. Researchers studying the complex interplay between a bacterial cell and its parasitic virus, the phage, have discovered that the virus gets into the host chromosome by exploiting the bacterium's own DNA bending

proteins, generating crimps in the DNA and then sneakily cutting and pasting its genetic information into the curled-over sequence.

Biologists believe that many human viruses, notably the one that causes AIDS, adopt a similar ruse, bending the DNA and then integrating permanently into the chromosomes. They suggest that by understanding normal DNA bending they may devise novel strategies to foil viruses before the deadly kinking and splicing occurs.[22]

In a geometry that evokes anal sex, cellular DNA is made to "bend over" so that the virus can "sneakily" insert itself into the host chromosome. And the "purposeful strategies for retaliation"[23] against such activity must somehow similarly attack the virus from behind; "new techniques" to "fight AIDS" have been described as "[a]iming to handcuff H.I.V. rather than going for a knockout."[24]

Presenting an alternative masculinity—a different and dangerous set of coded "ideas" that will disable the cell's normal functions, disrupting its expressive processes and turning the cellular machinery to a foreign and ultimately fatal agenda of production—the viral genome undermines, through a kind of homosexual rape, the gender hierarchy between nucleus and cytoplasm, DNA and the processes of expression and production, imagined at the cellular level. And just as anxieties about homosexual "recruitment" of ostensibly "straight" boys and men express a real uncertainty about the stability of "normal" male sexuality, its capacity for resisting "perverse" advances, so the sexualized accounts of viral "recruitment" of human cells suggest, at least for some of those cells, a dangerous predisposition toward "acquiescing" in the "perverse" takeover. Thus, in an account of viral action that Cindy Patton quotes from the "right-wing periodical *New Dimensions*":

> The mere presence of a virus does not necessitate infection because no virus can force itself onto a totally healthy cell. Some kind of receptivity on the part of the human cell is required to accept this kind of delivery. . . . It is an active process on the part of the recipient that is required before an infection can take place. It is not that we are innocent victims of a virus, but that we actively participate in acquiring a virus. It takes work and effort on the part of a living cell to absorb the inert, lifeless substance from within the wrappings of the virus.[25]

In such a view, as Patton suggests, only a cell that is somehow already "queer" can be transformed by HIV, an idea that reflects the broader, pervasive notion that only people (and communities) somehow already "sick" might be susceptible to the "queering" power of an agent like HIV, an idea expressed, for instance, from a position very different from that of *New Dimensions*, by the French feminist philosopher Luce Irigaray:

> Indeed, people don't just become ill out of the blue. For the whole of a body to be affected, its equilibrium must have already been disrupted. That's true for all illnesses. It's painfully obvious for illnesses said to be of the immune system. But all illnesses are, in fact, since being ill comes down to being unable to distance oneself from pathogenic agents.[26]

The cell, the gay man, the IV-drug user, "high-risk" communities show their true—"unbalanced," "perverse"—colors in being unable to separate themselves from the pathogenic.

The narrative of subcellular "battle" between conflicting systems of viral and cellular signification should not be read as enacting *only* tropes of gender and sexuality: in employing a language of foreignness and invasion, it also evokes a racism and xenophobia particularly resonant with American political discourses of a "general population" from which "high-risk groups"—gay men, African Americans and Latina/os, users of intravenous drugs (generally coded as "other" in terms of both race and class), prostitutes—are (more or less by definition) excluded,[27] and with American policies that, despite the promises of a new presidential administration, continue to bar immigration of those testing positive for HIV, policies represented most visibly by the only recently closed "H.I.V. prison camp" for Haitian refugees at Guantánamo Bay.[28] Haraway has suggested that

> Expansionist Western medical discourse in colonizing contexts has been obsessed with the notion of contagion and hostile penetration of the healthy body, as well as of terrorism and mutiny from within. This approach to disease involved a stunning reversal: the colonized was perceived as the invader.[29]

And political discourse, for instance, in the debate on immigration laws and HIV, amply demonstrates such xenophobic reactions. It has been suggested, on the floor of the United States House of Representatives, that "[i]ndividuals who are infected with the HIV virus, or already have AIDS, are constantly seeking entry into the United States," and that admitting them to this country would be "like throwing a bucket of gas on a building that is already on fire": "People will die if we allow folks to come into this country that are infected with the AIDS virus."[30] Such statements continue the tendency to distance AIDS geographically and racially, a tendency prevalent from the early (and stubborn) identification of Haitians as a "high-risk group" (the immigration debate continues to focus largely on Haitians) to the repeated emphasis on an "African origin" of AIDS.[31]

It is important, then, to recognize that a sexualized reading of the scientific narratives elaborated around HIV does not exhaust their possibilities. Still, despite marked shifts in the demographics of HIV infection in the United States and the recognition of the "heterosexuality" of AIDS in the worldwide context, HIV and AIDS in the American imagination continue to be intimately linked to ideas about gay men's sexuality, and particularly the practice of passive anal intercourse. As Cindy Patton has argued, "AIDS discourse has a curious retrograde motion" that she calls "the queer paradigm":

> [Y]ou can begin as a queer, and therefore as uniquely susceptible to AIDS, but whatever your cultural status, once you test positive for the HIV antibody, regardless of how you contracted the virus, you become nominally queer. . . . Queerness may be genetically determined, as in the much-hyped recent twin and hypothalamus studies, but if you weren't queer before, HIV will "alter your genetic identity," make you a "permanent, genetically-stamped AIDS-carrier."[32]

In part this paradigm depends upon "[t]he conviction that anal sex is at the root of AIDS," a belief that "enables heterosexuals to avoid thinking about making changes in their practice of vaginal intercourse."[33]

In the American context, which is also a prime locus for the production of scientific knowledge about HIV and AIDS, a sexualized reading of the scientific narratives of HIV infection—as representing a homophobic fantasy of viral activity that reflects and reinforces the close association of AIDS with gay men—is particularly evocative and powerful. In many ways, that narrative, even as it is elaborated in the most "objective" of scientific accounts, closely mirrors the structure of a homophobia that simultaneously and paradoxically constructs gay men as both abject weakness and powerful threat. On the one hand, the dangerous abnormality and perversity of gay men is projected onto HIV, itself depicted as a perverse agent able to "slip into cells," infiltrate the cellular DNA, and "remain there for life."[34] Just as gay men are feared as stealthy "recruiters" of "innocent" (presumably heterosexual or proto-heterosexual) boys, so HIV sneakily "recruits" the "normal" cell and its resources to perverse and dangerous ends. And just as homosexuality is often homophobically depicted as inimical to the very processes of life—stopping reproduction and the generations dead in their tracks—so, of course, HIV's "take-over" of cells is deadly. At the same time, however, other characteristics of a homophobically constructed male homosexuality are projected onto the "normal" cell and its DNA, which, in their "submission" to the perverse activity of HIV, become the object of sexual recruitment, of a perverse "bending," a stealthy, "backdoor" rape. The imagined "natural" passivity and weakness of gay men is transferred to the once-healthy cell and the homophobically imagined "disease" of gayness literalized in the disease processes of HIV illness and AIDS.

I want to emphasize here that I do not see scientists as consciously promulgating such a homophobic understanding of the molecular biology of HIV and AIDS. Indeed, most scientists would, I have no doubt, deny that what I have described as inherent in scientific accounts of HIV infection represents their own understanding of that subcellular process. Still, scientific descriptions of HIV infection and AIDS, articulated as they are in languages marked by ideologies of gender and sexuality, express and reinscribe those ideologies. Perhaps especially as they are popularized—put into a more "everyday" (and often more vividly metaphoric) language—such descriptions are available for the still-ongoing construction of AIDS as "the gay plague."[35]

2. CELLS/BODIES/POPULATIONS

Descriptions of cellular and subcellular process can thus be seen to mirror and evoke larger social forces—including sexism, racism, and homophobia. And this connection between the cellular and social is enabled not just by the sorts of analogical linkage so far discussed, with socially-resonant metaphors and language used by science to describe molecular events. Since HIV affects, as a privileged target, cells of the body's immune system, and since the immune system is conceived in contemporary biology as an immensely complicated network set up to "defend" the body as a whole, the scientific discourse makes a quite direct link between the cellular activity of HIV and the larger functioning of whole organisms. Like the individual cell, the body's immune system is conceived, in current biological theory, as a linguistic system—a "communications network"—that works through its ability to "recognize" or "read" the differences between "self" and "non-self" and thus police their boundaries.[36] The disruption of the cellular chain of signification by HIV, affecting as it does cells directly involved in the immune system, threatens linguistic competency not just for individual cells but for the body's whole "system of defense." The undermining of linguistic processes at the cellular level is seen as having a direct effect on similar linguistic processes at the level of the larger organism.

In a similar way, the challenge to gender hierarchy in the attack on "normal" masculinity that characterizes narratives of cellular HIV infection crosses over into depictions of the effects of HIV on immunity. As a "defense system" described in unequivocally military terms, in a culture where the military is still (if more and more problematically) envisioned as masculine and heterosexual, immune competence depends on the body's maintenance of a properly ordered, hierarchical, disciplined corps of cells:

In the bloodstreams of healthy individuals, there are white blood cells to seek out, locate, and destroy hostile invading germs. . . . One type, dendritic macrophages (radar) perform reconnaissance and early warning functions. . . . These reconnaissance cells . . . aggressively search for foreign germs. When they locate an invading microbe, they send out a chemical signal that acts as the first sign of trouble.

This signal is understood by the T-helper cells, the "field generals" making up the "field command structure" of the body's defense system. They sound a general alarm, launching a full-scale alert, mobilization, and attack. The T-helper cells send out the signal to the various units of the body's defense. Upon receiving this signal, the body's immune system begins to deploy T-killer cells (commandos) to locate the invaders and cause B-attack cells to manufacture and fire weapons (tanks, machine guns, planes, missiles) necessary to destroy the foreign germs. Phagocytic cells (infantry) are sent to devour and mop up the enemy.[37]

This enthusiastic elaboration of military metaphors is from a popularizing account by James I. Slaff and John K. Brubaker, and it develops the military analogy much more fully and explicitly than do most technical immunological texts. Still, it should be remembered that vocabulary like that of "killer," "helper," and "suppressor" T cells was developed within immunology proper, and Slaff and Brubaker's elaboration of such metaphoric language is not different in kind from what can be found in many other, more specialized texts.

As Cindy Patton suggests, "[r]apidly improving imaging technologies" in immunology have enabled people to "visualize their bodies as filled with tiny defending armies whose mission [is] to return the 'self' to the precarious balance of health," and "the metaphoric slippage between self-managament and military management" involved in such "visualizations" is importantly gendered: "both AIDS and the war are cast as masculine experiences in highly eroticized male-only zones."[38] Just as the perverse masculine challenge of HIV disrupts gender order within individual cells, so its challenge to the balance and integrity of the larger immunological system of defense undermines the body's normal (masculine) ability to respond to "challenge" or "attack," by (in different metaphoric constructions) sacking its "quarterback" or capturing its "general," the T-helper cell (Martin notes the more general depiction of T cells as "male" commanders of subordinate "female" B cells):[39]

The immune dysfunction . . . has long been known to result mainly from depletion of a specific set of white blood cells called *T*4 lymphocytes. The various parts of the immune system are highly interdependent, but if any one part can be called its quarterback, it is the *T*4 cell, also known as the helper *T* cell. . . . The loss of *T*4 cells seriously impairs the body's ability to fight most invaders . . .[40]

As soon as an AIDS virus enters a new bloodstream, it locates a specific T-helper cell. The virus has a method of incorporating itself within the genetic structure of a T-helper cell. . . . This process does not kill a T-helper cell, but renders it unable to perform its function as "field general" of the immune system. . . . One useful way of picturing this is that the "field general" has been "taken hostage" but not killed.[41]

Incredibly, the AIDS virus seems impervious to the antibodies that the body produces to combat it. The AIDS virus seems to be a killer with armor-plated protections against which the immune system's "bullets" have no effect. The AIDS virus has sheltered itself within the genetic structure of a T-helper cell and cannot be killed. It lurks in that form apparently indefinitely. There it remains, threatening to explode into an active phase of replication and to attack more T-helper cells.

The AIDS virus in a period of dormancy is holding one of the immune system's generals hostage with one hand on the throat and another with a gun held to the head. The general is not dead but is unable to perform traditional organizational functions. This period of dormancy ends when the "gun is fired." . . . When the AIDS virus explodes out of dormancy, it turns the host cell into a replicative factory. The AIDS virus uses the material of the invaded T-helper cell to manufacture millions of copies of itself during the six hours prior to the host cell's death. These newly created AIDS viruses can then swim freely in the bloodstream to locate other healthy T-helper cells to invade and destroy.[42]

The figures accompanying the account in Slaff and Brubaker make visible the military tropes elaborated in the text. Depicting the "capture" and ultimate "murder" of the T-helper cell, Slaff and Brubaker present graphically the connection often found in AIDS discourse between death of the individual cell and dissolution of the whole organism: The T-helper cell is depicted, in silhouette, as a human "general" who is gradually engulfed by an amorphous "AIDS virus" that first "turns the T-helper cell into a replicative factory" and finally obliterates it.[43]

In the militarized depictions of immune system "takeover" by HIV, the masculine defenses of the body, "taken hostage" and "disarmed," are no longer able to police the boundaries of self: "The AIDS virus achieves unilateral disarmament of the body's weapons against disease. An individual thus disarmed is an open invitation to microbial assault."[44] The language of the undefended body in such an account evokes not just medical and military but also sexual realms, reminding us that women's bodies, in Western culture, have typically been depicted as more permeable, open, undefended, "disarmed" than male bodies. Indeed, in rape defenses as in romance accounts of the male "protection" of women, women's bodies have often been constructed as themselves offering "an open invitation to . . . assault." And Western homophobia has consistently operated by associating gay men's bodies—as they open sexually in ways inimical to "real" masculinity—with the imagined fragmentation and permeability of the feminine.[45] The body of the person living with HIV or AIDS—its cells under "foreign attack" and then "control," its immune system "taken hostage"—becomes the body of a "victim," a body—weak, open to the attack of opportunistic infections, cancers, "dementia"—that has lost control over its internal systems of signification and of gender hierarchy, and that, in sustaining such losses, is consolidated to a misogynistically imagined female body and a homophobically imagined queer one.

Though the image of people living with HIV and AIDS as possessors of frail and perversely altered bodies is scrupulously maintained in media representations,[46] clear visual signs are in fact not necessary for the imaginative construction of "the body with AIDS." Whether or not symptoms of disease are "written" on the body, the person with HIV or AIDS immediately becomes "victim," a term that stubbornly persists despite repeated activist critiques of its implications: "We condemn attempts to label us as 'victims,' which implies defeat, and we are only occasionally 'patients,' which implies passivity, helplessness, and dependence upon the care of others. We are 'people with AIDS.'"[47]

Thus, for instance, as soon as Earvin "Magic" Johnson—a star athlete whose body, in its athleticism and despite its racial difference, had been constructed as the epitome of American masculinity—announced in 1991 that he was HIV-positive, even in the absence of disease symptoms or visual "proof" of illness, he was constructed as "AIDS victim." In the enormous media coverage of his announcement, the line between being HIV-positive but asymptomatic and having AIDS was quickly obfuscated, an obfuscation enabled by the general insistence of the media on calling HIV "the AIDS virus." And though much of this initial coverage praised Johnson's "courage" and "heroism" in declaring his HIV status,[48] there was a quick backlash against such valorization: "Johnson is a victim, not a hero. / Sympathize with him, as you would for anyone who has contracted the dreaded HIV virus."[49] Indeed, Johnson's retirement from basketball—the abdication of his public role as masculine icon in the face of his HIV status—was treated quite widely as a death, with Johnson often referred to in the past tense and "tributes" published—in both print and video media—that read like nothing other than obituaries:

> Uniform No. 32 hung limp in the locker, another of the weird sights that will, in time, become normal for the Lakers. . . .
> Last night, [Magic Johnson] wasn't there. He never will be again—not as a player.
> "It's going to be strange," said Terry Teagle, whose locker is next to Magic's. "Earv and I usually are the first ones here. I'm going to miss him. Usually, he's sitting here and I have to fight you guys [reporters] to get in my locker when you're talking to him."
> Gloom hung heavy in the room. . . .
> . . . Magic was bigger than the Lakers. He was as big as all of basketball. His loss has people close to him groping. . . .
> [Byron] Scott understands that not only those close to Magic are grieving. . . .
> It continues to be hard for the Lakers to accept that he's gone.
> "He's still with us," James Worthy said. "He's not in the locker room, but what he has done with the team and all the characteristics he has instilled in this team are still there."[50]

Even as Johnson emphasized his good health, rumors of serious illness surfaced, necessitating public appearances to confirm his continued strength.[51]

In all of this, HIV status and sexuality have been intimately tied up with each other; simultaneous with the construction of Johnson as "AIDS victim" have been persistent rumors about his homosexual or bisexual behavior:

> An old rumor about an involvement with another NBA player resurfaced the moment Johnson's press conference was announced and could be heard floating around the Garden at last Saturday's Knicks game.[52]

> Press room conversations returned to their normal noise level, including this exchange:
> First reporter: "They're saying he got it from a woman."
> Second reporter: "Stands to reason."
> First: "Not necessarily."
> Second: "Are you saying Magic got it *from a man*?"
> Yes, that was being said, though the denials were far more forceful, and they would carry the day.[53]

As Phillip Brian Harper suggests, Johnson's "public announcement of his HIV-seropositivity" has meant a retrospective rereading of Johnson's "sexual identity," making "the now-famous scene" in which he and Isaiah Thomas "kiss before a tip-off during the 1988 NBA finals" now readable as somehow gay where "prior to th[e] announcement . . . the kiss was never considered as having a properly *homosexual* import, or as indicating that Thomas and Johnson were themselves gay."[54] Having announced his HIV status, however, Johnson quickly felt the need to declare himself one hundred percent heterosexual[55]—most notably on the "Arsenio Hall Show" and in a widely quoted article written for *Sports Illustrated*[56]—and to make clear that he had been exposed to HIV in one of his frequent heterosexual experiences:

I'm far from being homosexual; you already know that.[57]

Magic told us, on the Arsenio Hall Show, that he caught AIDS the old-fashioned way, not from a blood transfusion or unprotected gay sex, but through plain old straight fooling around.[58]

But despite the normalizing language here and despite repeated claims that "the lesson of Magic Johnson is that AIDS can happen to any of us,"[59] what has been publicly declared and what is, secretly and not so secretly, imagined and believed are here in conflict. Johnson's "promiscuity," even if heterosexual, was described in language that clearly associated it with uncontrolled female and gay sexuality: "Magic Johnson was a slut";[60] "On *The McLaughlin Report*, Pat Buchanan proclaimed that Magic's condition 'is the result of perverted sex.'"[61] The language of blame here is fortified, if for the most part implicitly, by Johnson's being an African American. As bell hooks suggests, a persistent and pervasive American "portrait of black masculinity . . . perpetually constructs black men as 'failures' who are psychologically 'fucked up,' dangerous, violent, sex maniacs whose insanity is informed by their inability to fulfill their phallocentric masculine destiny in a racist context."[62] The stereotype of black men as hypermasculine and hypersexual, an image attached particularly to athletes like Johnson, but also as emasculated, infantilized and feminized, an image deployed, for instance, in a long series of television sitcom characters—*Webster*, the early "Duane Wayne" of *A Different World*, "Steve Erkel" of *Family Matters*—performs a simultaneous expression and allaying of anxiety about possible black challenges to "white supremacist capitalist patriarchy," in hooks's phrase.[63] A black athletic "hero" like Johnson, brought into dangerous proximity with the "queerness" of HIV, becomes particularly susceptible to the coercive force of such a double stereotype, coming to embody both the threat of the hypersexual and the abject weakness of the emasculated.

Even as Johnson went on to be named most valuable player in the NBA All Star Game,[64] to play successfully as a member of the Olympic "Dream Team,"[65] and to begin a "comeback" in the National Basketball Association, implicit and explicit doubts about his masculinity and sexuality continued to be displayed in the media. Such doubts were sometimes attached to and partly disguised by the valorizing language of male homosociality common in the world of American sports. Thus, for instance, Johnson's 1992 return to the Los Angeles Lakers was, at least in one account, described in strongly romantic terms: "Pat Riley visited with Magic Johnson last week in Los Angeles. There was no need to pop the question. The gleam in Johnson's eyes was a happy announcement that he would be returning to the Lakers."[66] And a similar homosocial/romantic moment between Johnson and Larry Bird is depicted in an account of the "retirement" of Bird's "number" by the Boston Celtics:

> Larry Bird was made into a lot of things by people who saw him as the torch carrier for his race in a sport dominated by blacks, but he was always his own, independent man. A year ago this month, he ignored team orders to rest his back and not attend the retiring of Magic's No. 32 in Los Angeles. Tonight, Bird and Magic hugged tight, with eyes misty all around.
> Larry asked Magic: "You're not coming back, are you?"
> Magic: "Noooo."
> Larry: "Then will you get the hell out of my dreams?"
> That said, they exchanged Olympic diamond commemorative rings and vowed they would be forever linked, that their's (*sic*) had been a great ride, and what a way to have gone out, with the Dream Team last summer in Barcelona, Spain.

The article was headed by a large photograph of Bird and Johnson staring raptly at Bird's ringed hand; the photo caption read, "Larry Bird showing his Olympic ring to Magic Johnson before they exchanged their rings during last night's ceremony."[67] Though these reports speak in the valorizing language of heterosexual marriage while carefully eschewing any *direct* imputation of the erotic, and though, as Harper suggests, "the extensive cultural sanctioning of professional sport's profoundly homosocial character actually serves to sublimate to a conventional hypermasculine significance whatever homoerotically inflected behavior takes place in that context,"[68] in the aftermath of Johnson's "coming out" as HIV-positive, such scenes are dangerously susceptible to homophobic readings. Indeed, strong rumors of homosexual behavior on Johnson's part have persisted, participating in his ultimate exclusion from professional basketball:

> It has been almost a year now since Magic Johnson announced to the world that he had tested HIV positive.
> He still hears the rumors, though, the rumors that he might have contracted the virus because of an alleged gay lifestyle. And he still denies those rumors.

Recently, however, after an unflattering column in *The Sporting News*, Magic confronted an unidentified NBA player who he said was spreading rumors that Magic's homosexual episodes led to his testing positive.

"If he [the player] is going to be a man, be a man," Johnson said . . .

"If you're going to say something behind my back," Johnson continued, his anger becoming more and more evident, "then when I come up to you, be a man and say you said it. . . .

"You backstab me, and I'm gone . . ."[69]

Significantly, the conflict here between Johnson and his unidentified "accuser" is couched in the terms of a contest of masculinity, with Johnson attributing "unmanly" behavior to his opponent and himself (twice) expressing fear of an attack from the "back." The rumors about Johnson's sexuality were, moreover, wrapped up with anxieties about the dangers of "playing with" him, as other basketball players expressed fear that HIV might, somehow, be transmitted on the basketball court:

It turns out that it was not just the issue of transmission that players have been whispering about these last several weeks. Several admitted that there had been widespread discussion on how Johnson may have contracted the virus in the first place.

"That's a lot of male egos out there not wanting to believe they can get this from a woman so they can go on doing what they want to do without having to worry," said the Nets' Sam Bowie.[70]

In the face both of the rumors and the fears—which, in retiring a second time, Johnson referred to obliquely as "the various controversies surrounding my return"[71]—Johnson decided not to pursue his "comeback," a decision that then itself raised speculations of failing health and that was described in language again associating him with homosexuality: "It's his life-style decision [i.e., not to play]."[72]

In the complicated treatment of "Magic" Johnson within the public spaces of the NBA and sports media, we see reenacted the homophobic pattern that continues to structure AIDS discourse in the American context, Patton's "queer paradigm." Just as gay men are constructed as simultaneously diseased and threatening in their sexuality, so people with HIV or AIDS, even when, as in the case of Johnson, it is publicly declared that they are not gay, are assimilated to gayness to be constructed both as "victim" (no longer physically *capable* of competing in the public arena of masculinity—even when there is manifest evidence to the contrary) and "threat" (no longer *allowed* to compete in the public arena of masculinity because threatening, through "contagion," others' masculinity).[73]

AIDS remains, in the American imagination, tied to homosexuality not just because of the historical accident of its being first recognized among gay men but also because such a connection is supported by, and itself buttresses, a whole homophobic system. One recent news story, identifying San Francisco, America's "gay mecca," as "the epicenter of the AIDS epidemic," depicts "[s]cores of gay men" gathering "to learn which drugs to use for suicide." The easy slippage from gayness to AIDS to death—with the evocation of earthquakes in the word "epicenter" perhaps suggesting the "naturalness" of all this—is only too evident in such a report.[74] In a chilling moment during the presentation of a case study in the *New England Journal of Medicine*, one of the doctors involved feels compelled to make the point "that homosexual men may have diseases unrelated to the AIDS virus."[75] The assumed identity of AIDS and gayness that is signalled here also informs the recent scientific work of Simon LeVay on the "homosexual brain": the population of gay men in LeVay's study consists wholly of those who have died of AIDS. Further, LeVay's work, in identifying structural differences between the brains of gay and straight men, and in suggesting that gay men's brains most resemble women's, stands all too readily available for the reconfirmation of gay men as medically anomalous and as "effeminate."[76] As Judith Butler suggests, "if homosexuality is pathological from the start, then any disease that homosexuals sometimes contract will be uneasily conflated with the disease that they already are."[77]

In literalizing the homophobic imagination of gayness as disease—expressed succinctly and frighteningly in one sign, "FAG = AIDS," held up by right-wing protestors at the 1993 March on Washington for Lesbian, Gay and Bi Equal Rights and Liberation—AIDS has become intimately, and for the moment inextricably, tied up with a deep anxiety about "normal" masculinity and with attempts to reconsolidate it. In 1987, Senator Jesse Helms, proposing an amendment to prohibit federal funding for "AIDS education, information, or prevention materials and activities that promote or encourage, directly or indirectly, homosexual sexual activities,"[78] could argue on the floor of the United States Senate, with little opposition (the amendment passed with only two senators, Weicker and Moynihan, voting against it), that "every case" of AIDS is traceable to "homosexual activity":

> Chuck Colson recently wrote something that I agree with. He said: "In all the recent attention focused on AIDS, one important fact seems to have been shoved into the closet." And that important fact to which Chuck Colson referred is the fact that "homosexual intercourse has been and remains the principal vehicle for the spread of the disease."[79]

Now we had all this mob here over the weekend which itself was a disheartening spectacle.[80] But I did not hear a single one of them deny what Chuck Colson said. They do not want us to think about it. They do not want society to think about it. They want to obscure the issue. But the fact is still there.

Monsignor Eugene Clark recently repeated the same message that Chuck Colson offered. Monsignor Clark wrote: "In fact, the virus-turned-plague has only one source—sodomy. Heterosexuals are infected only from homosexuals, or from heterosexuals infected by bisexuals."[81]

That is what Monsignor Eugene Clark said.

Now, I do not know whether Senators want to face up to the question of whether they agree to that or do not. It is easy to say, "Well, I will worry about that tomorrow." We cannot worry about it tomorrow. We have got to establish some priorities. Yes, I am old-fashioned enough to say moral priorities. We have got to call a spade a spade and a perverted human being a perverted human being,[82] not in anger, but in realism.

Think about it, Mr. President. Monsignor Clark was right. Every AIDS case can be traced back to a homosexual act. A hemophiliac who contracts AIDS from a blood bank has gotten it from a homosexual with AIDS who contributed blood or a heterosexual infected by an infected bisexual. For the prostitute, she got it from an infected man who had had sexual relations with a bisexual or a homosexual. For the drug addict, somewhere along the line the needle has been used by a homosexual or a bisexual man or a heterosexual woman infected by a bisexual or homosexual. Heterosexuals are infected only from bisexuals or other heterosexuals who have had sexual relations with bisexuals.[83]

Originally Helms's amendment had been directed against not just homosexuality but also intravenous drug use, prohibiting the funding of "AIDS education, information, or prevention materials and activities that promote, encourage, or condone sexual activity outside a sexually monogamous marriage (including homosexual sexual activities) or the use of illegal intravenous drugs."[84] But Senator Lawton Chiles of Florida argued against this provision in telling terms:

> I think that we recognize that right now the greatest risk of the spread into the heterosexual population is coming from the intravenous use of the needles—intravenous drugs used through a nonsterile needle. . . .
>
> . . . I think we have listened across the spectrum to the doctors and scientists and people and they say that that greatest risk, in many instances, is a drug user. Let us say it is a male and he uses an infected

needle. Perhaps in his normal relations with his wife he infects his wife; or in other relations.

Then a female partner is infected and then the disease begins to spread into the heterosexual population.[85] That seems to be the way that it is spreading and the greatest risk.

We have more—well, not more—we have a third of the children infected with AIDS in my State. If there is ever the innocent of the innocent it is these children that are infected. . . .

I do not think we are trying to condone the use of a needle, you know; or that you ought to take heroin or anything else. But I think we are trying to protect that mother and/or that innocent baby; and our general population.[86]

And much as I wish we could write down no one will use drugs, period; and no one will use drugs that are used by a needle, we just know that is going on. And now, as a side effect from that, if they are using that dirty needle, we know that that is the way that they are spreading this to the heterosexual population, to the population of males and females where it can mix and where it can spread.[87] And that appears to be the danger that you could really realize an epidemic in this country.

I guess you can say as long as this disease is confined among homosexuals, no real danger. It is bad, but they should realize this.

But now, when we are dealing with the other side of the coin, where children can catch it, where we know that the cases can multiply. The Senator from Connecticut has read these facts. Again, you have to look at them, in the face of the extramarital sex. They are out there. We know they are occurring.[88]

Chiles's homophobic "logic" here—that as long as AIDS is "confined among homosexuals, no real danger" and no real epidemic; that education for gay men (lesbians are completely ignored in this debate) is unnecessary since it would not affect the "general population"; that "they should realize this," that is, that gay men, somehow ("naturally"?) should realize the "danger" of their position, given what seems an identification (in Chiles's thinking) between homosexuality and AIDS—proved convincing enough to Helms:

[J]ust to assure my good faith to my friend from Florida, even though I do not agree with him that this amendment in any way purports, or, in fact, does inhibit education about the perils of drug use, I am going to send an amendment in the second-degree to the desk and I am going to strike everything about illegal drugs.[89]

In the final version of Helms's amendment—as in his own and Chiles's oral arguments—homosexuality is the privileged sphere of disease from which the healthy ("general population") must be protected, perversely, by a legislated silence in government-supported public health education that, in a circular movement, denying gay men the information they need for health, solidifies their identification with disease.

But Helms is, of course, not himself silent about homosexuality. While his legislation moves to silence AIDS education for gay men, his whole discourse on AIDS depends upon an obsessive speaking about homosexuality.[90] For Helms, the construction of a concept of health, both literal health and "healthy" (masculine) sexuality, depends upon its scrupulous segregation from a category of disease, both AIDS and "perverse" sexuality. For Helms, the suggestion that gay men might, through education, learn to practice "safe (healthy) sex," is self-contradictory: as long as sex is not heterosexual, it is by definition not healthy or safe. The possibility of healthy gay sex must, in fact, be foreclosed through legislation.

The dynamic that is enacted here is, unfortunately, a familiar one in American culture and not confined to the thinking of right-wing ideologues like Helms: the realm of the "healthy" depends for its construction upon the recognition and abjection of a realm of sickness or perversity. As Jonathan Dollimore has suggested, "dissidence may not only be repressed by the dominant (coercively and ideologically), but in a sense actually produced by it" in a move that "consolidat[es] the powers which it ostensibly challenges."[91] And as Judith Butler argues, the "construction" of what is admitted to be "human is a differential operation that produces the more and the less 'human,' the inhuman, the humanly unthinkable. These excluded sites come to bound the 'human' as its constitutive outside." Naturalized "normal" categories like "health" and "healthy sexuality" depend upon such excluded terms, but as Butler suggests the excluded also "haunt[s]" the "boundaries" of such categories "as the persistent possibility of their disruption and rearticulation."[92] The realm of the "sick" or "perverse" poses a frightening threat at the same time that it is understood to be a place for "victims," for the weak and powerless.[93] The discourse of AIDS recorded in the Congressional Record, and enacted differently in the media coverage of "Magic" Johnson, mirrors the homophobic ways in which "normal"/heterosexual American masculinity has constructed itself. As Eve Kosofsky Sedgwick has persuasively argued, that construction depends upon a category of the "queer," arbitrarily and shiftingly defined, whose existence as the fate of those transgressing the boundaries of the "properly" masculine is adumbrated even as it is kept closeted, secret, unspoken and unspeakable.[94] All men who have grown up under the threat of epithets like "fag," "queer," "sissy," "wimp," "cocksucker," "pansy," "homo," in the absence of any clear definition of those terms or public acknowledgment of the possibility of a healthy homosexuality—that is, essentially all American men—know, even if they would not acknowledge, the coerciveness of such a regime. Responding to a grant proposal put forward by "the so-called Gay Men's Health Crisis,"[95] Helms feels the need to reaffirm his own masculinity and consign the gay to the unspeakable, "obscene," and "revolting":[96]

> Mr. President, this Senator is not a goody-goody two-shoes. I have lived a long time. I have seen a lot of things. I served 4 years in the Navy. I have been around the track. But every Christian, religious, moral ethic within me cries out to do something. It is embarrassing to stand on the Senate floor and talk about the details of this travesty.
> And the subject matter is so obscene, so revolting, that I am embarrassed to try to discuss it in sufficient detail for Senators to understand that we have a problem here.[97]

While homosexuality must exist in order to secure heterosexuality, it must not be clearly defined, and it certainly must not be allowed to speak its own truths:

> Under the section entitled "Content," the session states that it was intended to dispel certain myths regarding mail (*sic*) and female sexuality and gender roles including "(a) heterosexuality is superior to homosexuality."
> That is what tax dollars are being spent for and no wonder the President of the United States hit his desk [upon being shown this material] and I hit this podium with the same feeling of revulsion and disgust.[98]

In Helms's rhetoric, such a ("revolting") self-speaking from within the realm of "disease" and "perversity" threatens physical illness to the "normal" listener.

As lesbian and gay experiences have begun, more and more publicly, to speak themselves, homophobic and heterosexist regimes have reacted, as did Helms with his 1987 amendment, not to deny the existence of homosexuality (which, after all, they depend upon for self-definition and the recent prominence of which has provided a rallying point for right-wing politics)[99] but to censor its particular voices. This is true, of course, of Helms's and others' moves against the National Endowment for the Arts.[100] It also characterizes the conservative movement against participation of lesbians and gay men in the St. Patrick's Day and Israel Day parades in New York City: organizers of both parades claimed that lesbian and gay individuals could march as long as it was not under a banner proclaiming their group identities; a compromise for the Israel Day parade, which would have allowed members of a gay and lesbian congregation to march along with another Jewish group (as members of the

Irish Lesbian and Gay Organization did in the 1991 St. Patrick's Day Parade), collapsed after the congregation's rabbi spoke publicly about the parade issue.[101] And in the debate over the service of lesbians and gay men in the military, the capacity of gay and lesbian soldiers for military service is no longer the central question; all parties now admit that lesbians and gay men have often in fact served with distinction, and the central issue has become whether they should be allowed to serve "openly." In fact, the "compromise" plan agreed upon—"don't ask, don't tell, don't pursue"—allows lesbians and gay men to serve only so long as they maintain silence about their sexuality.[102] The insistence on silence has recently reached a point of absurdity that emphasizes how truly dangerous the speaking of gayness is felt to be: Keith Meinhold, dismissed from the Navy "after he said in a television interview in 1992 that he is gay," and recently reinstated by the courts, has been told "that he would not be disciplined under the new policy [of "don't ask, don't tell, don't pursue"] so long as he did not repeat his earlier statement that he is gay." This warning is reported in an article headlined "U.S. Drops Effort to Oust a Gay Sailor"; though, as the headline suggests, "everyone now knows" Keith Meinhold's sexual identity, Meinhold himself must not be allowed to speak that identity.[103]

The insistent definition of AIDS as essentially gay, and as a failure of "proper" masculinity, serves to consolidate the view of gayness as disease. It also serves to push AIDS into a position that, like gayness, demands silence. Witness the enormous tensions around the public revelation of AIDS (whether or not that revelation also seemed to contain the revelation of gayness) in the cases of Rock Hudson, Liberace, Brad Davis, Max Robinson,[104] Congressman Steward McKinney, Rudolf Nureyev, and Arthur Ashe (who compared the pressure to reveal that he had AIDS to "outing").[105] And witness the history of reticence in government-sponsored AIDS education, which extends beyond the explicit constraints imposed by Helms's legislative efforts: under pressure from conservatives, the distribution of an informational pamphlet originally intended to be sent to all American households was significantly delayed;[106] the "America Responds to AIDS" television campaign, though it has occasionally flirted with more direct messages about safer sex, has almost completely satisfied itself with portraying AIDS as an awful and amorphous threat about which Americans should educate themselves, and can educate themselves if only they call a toll-free number.[107] In such an "educational" effort, AIDS remains a largely undefined danger against which "normality" defines itself; it should come as no surprise that most Americans believe in their own "normality" and refuse to recognize, even in actual risk behaviors that they practice, the possibility that they themselves are at risk for HIV transmission.

In addition to reconfirming homophobic and heterosexist definitions of the "normal" over against the "queer" and "sick," and in addition to working against a particularized speaking about HIV and AIDS that would detail "risky" acts of drug use and sex, the continued structuring of AIDS in terms dictated by discourses of masculinity serves to erase or obfuscate much of importance. Thus, the roles of class and race in the AIDS crisis—their central part in determining whom education and prevention efforts are *least* likely to reach; in creating underclasses of homeless people and people in prison who encounter special difficulties in relation to HIV and AIDS; in limiting access to health care, to experimental and alternative treatments, to research protocols—tend to be pushed aside, despite repeated activist efforts to call attention to just these issues.[108]

When race and class *are* raised within discussion of the AIDS crisis, it is often with ambiguous effect: while to be effective education efforts must target specific African American, Latina/o, and poorer communities, emphasizing to people within those communities the real risks associated with HIV, the process of singling out "minority groups" for HIV education may also threaten a certain stigmatization. Like the association of AIDS and gayness, attention to racial and class differences in populations at risk for HIV can become a way to distance AIDS, in the popular imagination, from white, middle-class heterosexuals. The construction of whole "minority communities" as "high-risk groups" operates to consolidate the dangerous sense that HIV and AIDS "belong" to someone else, with sexual, racial, and economic differences invoked together as "proof" of the abnormality, perversity, otherness of AIDS. In response to just such stigmatizing moves, there has been, as Harlon Dalton, Ana Maria Alonso and Maria Teresa Koreck have pointed out, some reluctance from within both African American and Latino/a communities to admit that AIDS is a pertinent issue and thus to mobilize community-based education efforts.[109]

A mutual reinforcement of racist, classist, and homophobic/heterosexist discourses indeed characterizes the construction of intravenous drug users as the second major "HIV risk group" after gay men. Racial and class differences operate importantly in this construction, with users of drugs almost universally constructed as African Americans and Latina/os of the "lower" classes; they are indeed often thought of as homeless and always (by virtue of their use of drugs) as "criminal." It becomes almost impossible to place someone like Brad Davis—white, successful actor—in a "risk group" so constituted in the public imagination, though, upon his death from AIDS-related causes, it was reported that Davis "had contracted the disease from his use of drugs when he was younger."[110] Along with race and class, gender and sexuality are also involved in the construction of the category of "intravenous drug user": "drug addicts" are largely conceived of as male, as in the comments quoted from Senator Chiles above, and as the common phrase "iv-drug users [implicitly male] and their sexual partners [implicitly female]" suggests. Drug use itself is described in terms easily assimilated to the homophobic conception of gayness and AIDS as aberrations of masculinity. Thus, the title of one recent story on drug-related crimes in Yosemite National Park, "Crimes Against Nature," performs a conflation of drug use, homosexuality, and ecological threat.[111] The use of drugs, as an "unnatural" act, as an "addiction" and a debilitating illness perhaps associated with "brain irregularities,"[112] comes to be closely identified with HIV and AIDS—just as, for gay men, HIV illness and sexuality (again, perhaps linked to the structure of the brain)[113] have been conflated. Much educational material aimed at reducing HIV transmission among injecting drug users revealingly emphasizes not the avoidance of particular risk behaviors (the sharing of needles and works) but the generalized danger of drug use itself and, in a more stigmatizing mode, the "sickness" of belonging to the identity category "drug addict."

Like "queerness," "drug addiction" can be seen to play an oppositional but constitutive role in relation to contemporary American "normality": seen as a state endemic to racial otherness and to an underclass, thought to be inimical to (masculine and productive) work and a prime source of criminal behavior, it has become the object of a "war" whose goal is as much the reinforcement of authoritarian social structures as it is the actual diminishment of crime.[114] The "war on drugs" provides a wealth of media images in which to view Blacks and Latinos being arrested. And as "war," it presents a particularly masculine space; the presence of an epidemic of HIV infection and AIDS in the midst of that war reconfirms the homophobic projection of AIDS onto a perverse (unemployed, unproductive, addicted, criminal) other to "normal" masculinity. A related discourse emphasizes the lack of adult "male role models" in the contemporary African American family.[115]

As we see both in this construction of drug users in relation to HIV and AIDS and in the stubborn association of AIDS with gay men, the largest exclusion that results from defining AIDS in the terms of a male homosocial contest within a contemporary crisis of masculinity involves women; indeed, there has been a consistent erasure of women from the public discourse on AIDS.[116] Even as the demographics of the epidemic have shifted to include more and more women, AIDS continues to be imaged primarily in relation to masculinity, with the bodily "norm" of health imagined as a masculine one, and the body of the person with AIDS "feminized" in relation to that "norm." Women, of course, are always already "feminized," and they are largely thought to stand apart from an HIV illness conceived of as a fall out of masculinity into the weak, "effeminate," and queer.

The exclusion of women from the ground upon which the AIDS crisis is imagined to occur has had enormous practical consequences in both health care and medical research: until recently, the official (Centers for Disease Control [CDC]) definition of AIDS, because it was based largely on early studies of gay men, excluded many women with HIV illness, with awful practical consequences—for instance, the denial of Social Security disability benefits.[117] This of course also meant that women were much less likely to be selected for research projects and experimental drug protocols than were men whose syndromes more easily fit the definition of AIDS. Moreover, many such projects and protocols, in their conception, excluded women, choosing to work with as homogeneous a group of subjects as possible, usually a group of white men, and excluding women "to avoid liability for a drug's potential damage to her reproductive capacity or, if she were pregnant, to a fetus."[118] This reflects of course not just the definition of AIDS in relation to a masculine norm, but our culture's more general tendency to think of an "abstract" body that is male; specifically female physiology—menstruation, ovulation, pregnancy, menopause—is treated in relation to that body as anomalous or supplementary.

This kind of exclusion is supported by the language used to talk about HIV and AIDS, and most strikingly by the common use of the metaphors of war in AIDS discourses.[119] Such language tends to exclude women, particularly at a moment in the contemporary crisis of American masculinity when there is an active public debate on the "suitability" of women for combat, and when those who argue for the importance of traditional gender roles have chosen the military as a privileged site for the defense of "manhood" against both feminist and queer challenges. Such an exclusion occurs not just in the rhetoric of the right, but also in voices opposed to such rhetoric that nonetheless adopt the metaphor of AIDS as battlefield. Thus, for instance, Paul Monette, in his memoir *Borrowed Time* and in his elegiac *Love Alone*, repeatedly evokes a brotherhood of "warriors" fighting AIDS: "Then someone you know goes into the hospital, and suddenly you are at high noon in full battle gear. They have neglected to tell you that you will be issued no weapons of any sort. So you cobble together a weapon out of anything that lies at hand, like a prisoner honing a spoon handle into a stiletto. You fight tough, you fight dirty, but you cannot fight dirtier than it."[120] While Monette's construction of a community of gay men taking strength from each other and from a history of gay men's struggle and self-assertion is often quite powerful, it is also disturbing in its reinforcement of the notion of AIDS as masculine war and its more than partial erasure of the involvement of women in the AIDS crisis.

Given the general exclusion of women from the structures of language and thought within which American culture has tended to construct HIV and AIDS, when women have entered AIDS discourse, it has usually been under the sign of something other than their being women, as "exceptions."[121] In part, they have served as auxiliary players in the contest of masculinity to which AIDS has been so intimately linked. Thus, in relation to heterosexual men—as often in the past with sexually transmitted diseases[122]—prostitutes, "promiscuous" women, women not conforming to social expectations have been portrayed as dangerous, as "AIDS carriers," as repositories of disease. Thus, in the fall of

1991, it was readily believed that "Dallas faced a threat known only as C.J., a woman who claimed to be spreading the AIDS virus in revenge on the man who had infected her"; even in announcing that "there is no C.J. as purported to be," the police suggested that "there are lots of C.J.'s out there, either knowingly or unintentionally spreading HIV. That's why we haven't called it a hoax."[123] And in a *New York Times Magazine* article on AIDS in Thailand, headed by a photograph of six prostitutes on display in a window, we are told that "[i]n this area, in this kind of brothel, four of five women carry the AIDS virus," that "the disease [is] spread by the brothels," and that "the sexual and commercial transactions in this brothel, common throughout Thai society at every level, are a form of indirect murder or suicide": "More than 75 percent of Thai males have been to prostitutes, and 75 percent of them go to the cheapest brothels, where the AIDS infection is most prevalent. Then they spread it to their lovers, wives and unborn children."[124]

As in depictions of gay men and users of intravenous drugs, descriptions of "dangerous" women—as deceptive (because not visibly ill) sources of pollution—mirror descriptions of HIV itself. Women with HIV or AIDS are often in fact depicted in language that suggests they *are* their illness, and they are often treated as vectors of disease, infectious agents endangering their sexual partners and babies.[125] Like gay men, these women embody a "feminizing" threat to "normal" masculinity, all the more frightening because of their positioning within heterosexuality itself. And this female threat to masculinity is reinforced by linking women who are "at risk" explicitly to an anomalous *male* sexuality: it is, as in the "analysis" of routes of HIV transmission given by Helms, largely through "bisexuals" (almost always meaning *male* bisexuals) that such women are themselves thought of as having been exposed to HIV. In such an "analysis," women provide a conduit for the corruption of "straight" masculinity by the queer.

Indicating the strength of a fantasmatic identification of HIV and AIDS with "anomalies" of gender and sexuality is the fact that—despite manifest evidence to the contrary in the low incidence of HIV in lesbian populations—lesbians along with gay men have been identified in the popular imagination with the threat of AIDS (as they are also clearly seen as a threat to masculinity).[126] Thus, in the San Francisco Bay area, in New York City, and in England there have been more and less official moves to prohibit not just gay men but lesbians from donating blood, despite a complete lack of evidence linking lesbians to an increased rate of HIV transmission.[127]

When women living with HIV or AIDS are not perceived as fitting into categories threatening to masculinity, when they are not lesbians or prostitutes or "promiscuous," public discourse seems to have difficulty placing them, and they tend to be treated as individual "anomalies," standing outside the usual understandings of HIV and AIDS. This occurs despite there being perfectly understandable routes of transmission for the virus (except in the case of Kimberly Bergalis, where the exact means of transmission is still controversial).[128] We choose to think of women whose sexual behavior does not transgress accepted norms as at "low risk," a kind of thinking that operates to reassure heterosexual men about their own safety; women like Elizabeth Glaser, Mary Fisher, Alison Gertz, whether infected through sex or the exchange of blood, largely remain, in the eye of the media, individuals, unassimilated to any sense of a larger "risk community."[129] Even while such women are presented as embodying "a message for heterosexuals who could make a potentially fatal mistake if they dismiss the threat of AIDS," the unexpected, surprising, anomalous nature of their diagnosis is most emphasized:

> Alison Gertz wasn't supposed to get AIDS.
> She has never injected drugs or had a blood transfusion, and she describes herself as "not at all promiscuous." But she does say she had a single sexual encounter—seven years ago—with a male acquaintance who, she has since learned, has died of AIDS.
> Though AIDS has hit hardest among gay men and poor intravenous drug users, it also affects people like Ms. Gertz.
> "People think this can't happen to them," she said in an interview at her Manhattan apartment. "I never thought I could have AIDS."
> She is 23 years old, affluent, college-educated and a professional from a prominent family. She grew up on Park Avenue.[130]

This is clearly very different from the treatment of gay men and injecting drug users living with HIV or AIDS; here, all gay men and drug users tend to be assimilated into their respective "high-risk groups" and thus treated as anything but individuals. When in fact a gay man, because of prior fame, has come to prominence in the AIDS crisis, either his gayness or his AIDS (or both) is ignored or concealed, and he continues, in large part, to be treated as an individual whom we "know"; witness the examples of Rock Hudson, Liberace, Robert Reed, Rudolf Nureyev. It seems difficult for us to see members of "high-risk groups" as individuals or, conversely, those we know "individually" as properly placed within a "high-risk group"; this of course reflects the continuing construction of "high-risk groups" as radically abnormal, perverse, other.

As I hope to have shown in this chapter, the languages of AIDS—from the most scientifically abstruse and "objective" to the journalistic to the more manifestly political—are deeply implicated in cultural stereotypes about gender, sexuality, race, and class, and these languages work forcefully to maintain the view of AIDS as a disease primarily of gay and otherwise anomalous "victims" posed against "healthy," "normal" men. When women are included in the discourse on AIDS, it is often only out of a concern for their role in the "spread" of disease, for the threat they might pose to heterosexual men.

Understanding the disturbing logic of such patterns, we can perhaps move more forcefully to intervene against them. AIDS activists have in fact repeatedly made such interventions, insisting that "SILENCE = DEATH" as a first step in resisting the silences and erasures that close around AIDS;[131] challenging the "victim" label and the invidious distinction of "innocent" and "guilty victims"; trying to reconstruct a "general population" that includes gay men and lesbians, people of color, the poor and homeless, and users of IV-drugs; moving to change the official CDC definition of AIDS so that it includes women affected by HIV. These efforts have had real success, but still, despite the emphasis that activists and public health authorities have given to the changing demographics of HIV and AIDS in the United States, the implication of HIV and AIDS in discourses concerned largely with masculinity has been deeply resistant to change. Much political work remains to be done to extricate HIV and AIDS from their position at a node of heterosexual male anxiety, while not erasing the important continuing needs of gay men in the AIDS crisis; to recognize the importance of race and class as factors in determining vulnerability to HIV, and to include women and women's bodies in the scientific and political discourses of HIV and AIDS, while resisting the stigmatization of people living with HIV and AIDS based on factors of class, race, gender, and sexuality. As I hope the above discussion has persuasively shown, and as AIDS activism has itself recognized, such urgent work is deeply involved with questions of representation and language, with the discourses of AIDS and depictions of people living with HIV and AIDS. The central question of the remainder of this book will be how *fictional* narratives have responded to and participated in broader cultural constructions of HIV and AIDS—and whether we can see such narratives, and particularly the novel, intervening politically to challenge such constructions and their many dangerous (mis)understandings.

NOTES

1. For the classic formulation, see Aristotle, *Generation of Animals*, A. L. Peck, ed. and trans., Loeb Classical Library (Cambridge, MA: Harvard University Press; London: Heinemann, 1953), 2.4.738b20-30 and 2.2.716a5-7.

2. Haraway, *Simians, Cyborgs, and Women*, 163 and 177.

3. For some of the important feminist work on science, and for further bibliography, see Sandra Harding and Merrill B. Hintikka, eds., *Discovering Reality: Feminist Perspectives on Epistemology, Metaphysics, Methodology, and Philosophy of Science* (Dordrecht: D. Reidel, 1983); Ruth Bleier, *Science and Gender: A Critique of Biology and Its Theories on Women* (New York: Pergamon, 1984); Evelyn Fox Keller, *Reflections on Gender and Science* (New Haven: Yale University Press, 1985); Anne Fausto-Sterling, *Myths of Gender: Biological Theories About Women and Men* (New York: Basic Books, 1985); Sandra Harding, *The Science Question in Feminism* (Ithaca:

Cornell University Press, 1986); Susan Bordo, "The Cartesian Masculinization of Thought," *Signs* 11:3 (1986), 439-55; Bleier, ed., *Feminist Approaches to Science* (New York: Pergamon, 1986); Martin, *The Woman in the Body*; Nancy Tuana, ed., *Feminism and Science* (Bloomington: Indiana University Press, 1989); Donna J. Haraway, *Primate Visions: Gender, Race, and Nature in the World of Modern Science* (New York: Routledge, 1989); Ludmilla Jordanova, *Sexual Visions: Images of Gender in Science and Medicine between the Eighteenth and Twentieth Centuries* (Madison: University of Wisconsin Press, 1989); Helen E. Longino and Evelynn Hammonds, "Conflicts and Tensions in the Feminist Study of Gender and Science," in Marianne Hirsch and Evelyn Fox Keller, eds., *Conflicts in Feminism* (New York and London: Routledge, 1990), 164-83; and Haraway, *Simians, Cyborgs, and Women*.

4. The Biology and Gender Study Group (Athena Beldecos, Sarah Bailey, Scott Gilbert, Karen Hicks, Lori Kenschaft, Nancy Niemczyk, Rebecca Rosenberg, Stephanie Schaettel, and Andrew Wedel), "The Importance of Feminist Critique for Contemporary Cell Biology," in Tuana, ed., *Feminism and Science*, 172-87; the passage cited is on 179. Further references are given parenthetically in my text.

5. Here Keller cites David L. Nanney, "The Role of the Cytoplasm in Heredity," in William D. McElroy and Bentley Glass, eds., *A Symposium on the Chemical Basis of Heredity* (Baltimore: Johns Hopkins University Press, 1957), 134-66, and Evelyn Fox Keller, "Feminism and Science," *Signs* 7:3 (1982), 589-602. The language of DNA as "master molecule," with the gendering implicit in the phrase, persists in both technical and popularizing scientific writing; see, for one instance, Angier, "Keys Emerge," C1.

6. Keller, *Reflections*, 170-71. See also Haraway's comments on the central dogma, *Simians, Cyborgs, and Women*, 206.

7. For one particularly suggestive reading of such positionalities, see Lee Edelman, "Seeing Things: Representation, the Scene of Surveillance, and the Spectacle of Gay Male Sex," in Fuss, ed., *Inside/Out*, 93-116.

8. The idea of a "hostile uterus" participates in an ambivalent discourse about women in which femininity is conceived as weak and passive at the same time that female sexuality is depicted as threatening and voracious. A related discourse arose in the early years of the AIDS epidemic in which the "rugged vagina" was opposed to the "vulnerable anus" and "fragile urethra" in an attempt to explain the incorrect conclusion that "AIDS is likely to remain largely a gay disease." See Treichler, "AIDS, Homophobia, and Biomedical Discourse," 37-39 [the citation is from the illustration on 38]; Treichler, "AIDS, Gender, and Biomedical Discourse," 206; and Treichler, "Beyond *Cosmo*: AIDS, Identity, and Inscriptions of Gender," *Camera Obscura: A Journal of Feminism and Film Theory* 28 (1992), 25-28.

9. Natalie Angier, "Odor Receptors Discovered in Sperm Cells," *New York Times* 30 Jan. 1992, A19.

10. Harrison, "Principles of Virus Structure," 27.

11. Leary, "Key to Flu Virus Infection," A18.

12. Tim Hilchey, "How a Flu Molecule Stands on Its Head to Infect Human Cells," *New York Times* 6 Sept. 1994, C3.

13. Treichler, "AIDS, Homophobia, and Biomedical Discourse," 59. Also see Haraway, *Simians, Cyborgs, and Women*, 224-25.

14. Haseltine and Wong-Staal, "Molecular Biology," 14-15.

15. Treichler, "AIDS, Homophobia, and Biomedical Discourse," 61. Also see the illustration from *Time* magazine reprinted in Martin, *The Woman in the Body*, 38, in which the "HTLV virus" (i.e., HIV) is depicted as a tank.

16. Haseltine and Wong-Staal, "Molecular Biology," 14.

17. Haseltine and Wong-Staal, "Molecular Biology," 14.

18. Haseltine and Wong-Staal, "Molecular Biology," 14.

19. Haseltine and Wong-Staal, "Molecular Biology," 25; my emphasis.

20. Haseltine and Wong-Staal, "Molecular Biology," 14.

21. Warren E. Leary, "New Techniques Hold Promise in Fighting AIDS," *New York Times* 8 Nov. 1994, C5.

22. Angier, "First Step," C1, C7.

23. The phrase is from Wong-Staal, "Human Immunodeficiency Viruses," 720.

24. Leary, "New Techniques," C5.

25. Cindy Patton, "Tremble, Hetero Swine!" in Michael Warner, ed. (for the Social Text Collective), *Fear of a Queer Planet: Queer Politics and Social Theory* (Minneapolis and London: University of Minnesota Press, 1993), 143 and 154; Patton here cites Paul Bahder and Teresa Bahder, "The Spiritual Significance of Viral Infection," *New Dimensions* (1989).

26. Luce Irigaray, "'I Won't Get AIDS,'" *Je, Tu, Nous: Toward a Culture of Difference*, Alison Martin, trans. (New York and London: Routledge, 1993), 62.

27. On the discourse of the "general population," see, for instance, Grover, "AIDS: Keywords," 23-24; and Patton, *Inventing AIDS*, 99 and *passim*. On the use of the category "high-risk group" rather than "high-risk act," see Grover, "AIDS: Keywords," 27-28; and Patton, *Inventing AIDS*, 103 and *passim*.

28. The phrase "H.I.V. prison camp" is from the recent ruling by Judge Sterling Johnson, Jr., ordering the camp's closing; quoted in Mary B. W. Tabor, "Judge Orders the Release of Haitians," *New York Times* 9 June 1993, B4.

29. Haraway, *Simians, Cyborgs, and Women*, 223.

30. *Congressional Record—House* [Debate on Immigration Provisions], 11 March 1993, H1207, H1209; the first statement was made by Representative Stearns of Florida, the last two by Representative Cunningham of California.

31. On the large issues raised here, see Renée Sabatier, *Blaming Others: Prejudice, Race and Worldwide AIDS* (Washington: The Panos Institute; Philadelphia: New Society Publishers, 1988), and Paul Farmer, *AIDS and Accusation: Haiti and the Geography of Blame* (Berkeley, Los Angeles, and Oxford: University of California Press, 1992). For one example of the scientific discourse of an African viral origin, see Max Essex and Phyllis J. Kanki, "The Origins of the AIDS Virus," in *The Science of AIDS*, 26-37. For analyses of the discourses of "African AIDS," see Sabatier, *Blaming Others*; Patton, *Inventing AIDS*, chapter 6 ("Inventing 'African AIDS'"), 77-97; Patton, *Last Served?* chapters 2 ("The Gendered Geopolitics of Space") and 4 ("Women's Health in a Global Perspective"), 21-47 and 77-96; Patton, "From Nation to Family: Containing African AIDS," in Henry Abelove, Michèle Aina Barale, and David M. Halperin, eds., *The Lesbian and Gay Studies Reader* (New York and London: Routledge, 1993), 127-38 [an earlier version of this essay appears as "Containing 'African AIDS': The Bourgeois Family as Safe Sex," in Andrew Parker, Mary Russo, Doris Sommer, and Patricia Yaeger, eds., *Nationalisms and Sexualities* (New York and London: Routledge, 1992), 265-84; Watney, "Missionary Positions: AIDS, 'Africa,' and Race," *Practices of Freedom*, 103-23; Treichler, "AIDS and HIV Infection in the Third World: A First World Chronicle," in Elizabeth Fee and Daniel M. Fox, eds., *AIDS: The Making of a Chronic Disease* (Berkeley, Los Angeles, and Oxford: University of California Press, 1992), 377-412; Jeff O'Malley, "The Representation of AIDS in Third World Development Discourse," in Miller, ed., *Fluid Exchanges*, 169-76; Randall M. Packard and Paul Epstein, "Medical Research on AIDS in Africa: A Historical Perspective," in Fee and Fox, eds., *AIDS: The Making of a Chronic Disease*, 346-76; and Barbara O. de Zalduondo, Gernard I. Msamanga, and Lincoln C. Chen, "AIDS in Africa: Diversity in the Global Pandemic," in Stephen R. Graubard, ed., *Living with AIDS* (Cambridge, MA, and London: The MIT Press, 1990), 423-63 [originally published as *Daedalus* 118:2-3 (1989)].

32. Patton, "Tremble, Hetero Swine!" 154; the material cited by Patton is from Gene Antonio, "AIDS: The Real Dangers of Casual Transmission" (interview with David Kupelian), *New Dimensions* (1989).

33. Patton, *Inventing AIDS*, 117; and see the broader discussion, 116-19. Also see Patton, *Sex and Germs*, 95, and *Last Served?* 19, 99-100, and 105-6.

34. Haseltine and Wong-Staal, "Molecular Biology," 24-25.

35. Michael VerMeulen, "The Gay Plague," *New York* 31 May 1982, 52-62.

36. For a full treatment of media, scientific, and popular "visions of the immune system," see the excellent discussion in Emily Martin, *Flexible Bodies: Tracking Immunity in American Culture—From the Days of Polio to the Age of AIDS* (Boston: Beacon Press, 1994), esp. Part 3. On the larger implication of "immune system discourse" in postmodern "constitutions of self," see Haraway, "The Biopolitics of Postmodern Bodies: Constitutions of Self in Immune System Discourse," *Simians, Cyborgs, and Women*, 203-30.

37. James I. Slaff and John K. Brubaker, *The AIDS Epidemic: How You Can Protect Yourself and Your Family—Why You Must* (New York: Warner Books, 1985), 13.

38. Patton, *Inventing AIDS*, 60-61; also see Brian Patton, "Cell Wars."

39. Martin, *Flexible Bodies*, 102-3.

40. Robert R. Redfield and Donald S. Burke, "HIV Infection: The Clinical Picture," in *The Science of AIDS*, 64.

41. Slaff and Brubaker, *The AIDS Epidemic*, 13-14.

42. Slaff and Brubaker, *The AIDS Epidemic*, 16-17.

43. Slaff and Brubaker, *The AIDS Epidemic*, 14-15.

44. Slaff and Brubaker, *The AIDS Epidemic*, 17-18. The language here of course echoes the cold war language of an arms race and of nuclear disarmament.

45. For a provocative and problematic consideration of how gay men might intervene in the homophobic construction of anal sex as "a self-annihilation originally and primarily identified with the fantasmatic mystery of an insatiable, unstoppable female sexuality," while not denying "the risk of the sexual itself as the risk of self-dismissal, of *losing sight of the self*" (222; emphasis in the original), see Leo Bersani, "Is the Rectum a Grave?" in Crimp, ed., *AIDS: Cultural Analysis/Cultural Activism*, 197-222. For a partial response to Bersani, which sees his account as itself "indulg[ing] in misogyny" (38), see Carole-Anne Tyler, "Boys Will Be Girls: The Politics of Gay Drag," in Fuss, ed., *Inside/Out*, 32-70, esp. 38-40. And see Eve Kosofsky Sedgwick's reading of Bersani—"Gender Criticism," in Stephen Greenblatt and Giles Gunn, eds., *Redrawing the Boundaries: The Transformation of English and American Literary Studies* (New York: The Modern Language Association of America, 1992), 288-91.

46. For consideration of such representations, see Jan Zita Grover, "Visible Lesions: Images of the PWA in America," in Miller, ed., *Fluid Exchanges*, 23-51 (illustrations following 51); Monika Gagnon, "A Convergence of Stakes: Photography, Feminism, and AIDS," in Miller, ed., *Fluid Exchanges*, 53-64; Douglas Crimp, "Portraits of People with AIDS," in Domna C. Stanton, ed., *Discourses of Sexuality: From Aristotle to AIDS* (Ann Arbor: The University of Michigan Press, 1992), 362-88; Simon Watney, "The Spectacle of AIDS," in Crimp, ed., *AIDS: Cultural Analysis/Cultural Activism*, 71-86; Sander L. Gilman, "AIDS and Syphilis: The Iconography of Disease," in Crimp, ed., *AIDS: Cultural Analysis/Cultural Activism*, 87-107; Martha Gever, "Pictures of Sickness: Stuart Marshall's *Bright Eyes*," in Crimp, ed., *AIDS: Cultural Analysis/Cultural Activism*, 108-26; and Stuart Marshall, "Picturing Deviancy," in Tessa Boffin and Sunil Gupta, eds., *Ecstatic Antibodies: Resisting the AIDS Mythology* (London: Rivers Oram Press, 1990), 19-36.

47. People With AIDS Coalition, "Founding Statement of People with AIDS/ARC (The Denver Principles)," in Crimp, ed., *AIDS: Cultural Analysis/Cultural Activism*, 148. On the language of "victim," also see Grover, "AIDS: Keywords," 26-27, 28-30; and the articles contained in Miller, ed., *Fluid Exchanges*, under the heading "Media and Mediation," 222-56.

48. See, for instance, the cover headlines, "Courage," *New York Post* 8 Nov. 1991, and "Magic's Brave New World," *New York Newsday* 9 Nov. 1991; Curtis G. Bunn,

"Courage Praised By Riley," *New York Newsday* 9 Nov. 1991, 158; Michael Specter, "When AIDS Taps Hero, His 'Children' Feel Pain," *New York Times* 9 Nov. 1991, 1, 32; and Fred Bruning and Laurie Garrett, "Stunned Nation Reacts to Hero's Illness," *New York Newsday* 9 Nov. 1991, 6, 12.

49. Dave Anderson, "Sorry, But Magic Isn't a Hero," *New York Times* 14 Nov. 1991, B19. Also see Bill Reel, "What Magic Did Isn't Really So Heroic," *New York Newsday* 13 Nov. 1991, and the letters in response to that article, *New York Newsday* 23 Nov. 1991, 16. For a more complicated (queer) reaction against the heroizing coverage of Johnson, see the series of articles in *NYQ* no. 5 (24 Nov. 1991), an issue that proclaims on its cover, "Magic Johnson Is Not *Our* Hero": Avram Finkelstein, "It Has Been a Week of Magic," 27; David Robinson, "An Open Letter to Newscasters," 27-31; Sara Simmons, "A Community Responds," 28-29; and Anonymous Queers, "It Is Too Late for Heroes," 30-31.

50. Jan Hubbard, "A Strange Homecoming," *New York Newsday* 11 Nov. 1991, 92, 80. For other examples of memorializing language, see Ira Berkow, "Magic Johnson's Legacy," *New York Times* 8 Nov. 1991, B11; Clifton Brown, "A Career of Impact, A Player with Heart," *New York Times* 8 Nov. 1991, B11, B13; "Fellow Players Stunned," *New York Newsday* 8 Nov. 1991, 158, 157; Bob Herzog, "Hall of Fame Says Magic Must Wait," *New York Newsday* 9 Nov. 1991, 86; Harvey Araton, "Keep Magic in the Mainstream," *New York Times* 13 Nov. 1991, B7; Doug Simmons, "Magic's Manhood," *Village Voice* 19 Nov. 1991, 37, 156; and Nelson George, "The Magic Touch," *Village Voice* 19 Nov. 1991, 37, 156.

51. See, for instance, Joe Gergen, "'See? I'm Not Sick,'" *New York Newsday* 12 Dec. 1991, 157.

52. George, "The Magic Touch," 156.

53. Simmons, "Magic's Manhood," 37; emphasis in the original.

54. Phillip Brian Harper, "Private Affairs: Race, Sex, Property, and Persons," *GLQ* 1:2 (1994), 125-26; emphasis in original.

55. This has been a concern for other celebrities as well. From a recent review of Arthur Ashe's autobiographical *Days of Grace* (New York: Knopf, 1993): "[H]e was concerned about his reputation; he wanted it clear that he had been infected with HIV from a blood transfusion during coronary bypass surgery in 1983" (Christopher Lehmann-Haupt, "The Art of Going Gentle into That Good Night," *New York Times* 10 June 1993, C17); Ashe, however, wanted to make clear that, in his case, the exposure to HIV occurred neither homosexually nor heterosexually.

56. Earvin Johnson, Roy S. Johnson, ed., "I'll Deal with It," *Sports Illustrated* 78 (18 Nov. 1991), 16-27.

57. Richard W. Stevenson, "Johnson's Frankness Continues," *New York Times* 9 Nov. 1991, 33; also see "Magic Starts New Chapter: Teacher: On 'Arsenio' Touts Safe Sex," *New York Newsday* 9 Nov. 1991, 5. Further "proof" of Johnson's heterosexuality was provided by the much reproduced photograph of his recent wedding; see, for instance, Marianne Goldstein and Florence Anthony, "Magic is HIV Positive," *New York Post* 8 Nov. 1991, 5; Bruning and Garrett, "Stunned Nation," 6.

58. Sheryl McCarthy, "Magic Conjures Up What's Real," *New York Newsday* 11 Nov. 1991, 14.

59. McCarthy, "Magic Conjures," 14. This is a "lesson," of course, that has now been proclaimed many times but never really learned.

60. B. D. Colen, "What Magic Might Say Now," *New York Newsday* 3 Dec. 1991, 67.

61. Simmons, "Magic's Manhood," 156.

62. bell hooks, "Reconstructing Black Masculinity," *Black Looks: Race and Representation* (Boston: South End Press, 1992), 89.

63. hooks, "Reconstructing Black Masculinity," 89.

64. See Clifton Brown, "For One Stirring Afternoon, Magic Johnson Dazzles Again," *New York Times* 10 Feb. 1992, A1, C4; and George Vecsey, "Magic Makes Highlights for His Tape," *New York Times* 10 Feb. 1992, C1, C4.

65. See the sports coverage for the summer of 1992.

66. Harvey Araton, "Johnson Goes from Dream Ride to the Rat Race," *New York Times* 30 Sept. 1992, B9.

67. Harvey Araton, "A Worthy Bird Has an Unlikely Night," *New York Times* 5 Feb. 1993, B7-8,

68. Harper, "Private Affairs," 126.

69. Fred Kerber, "Magic Slam Dunks Story," *New York Post* 22 Oct. 1992, 69; this story was announced on the front page of the *Post* by the headline, "Magic Slam Dunks Rumors He's Gay." Also see Clifton Brown, "Johnson Delights and Earns a Night Off," *New York Times* 22 Oct. 1992, B20.

70. Harvey Araton, "N.B.A. Finds It Can't Overleap Reality," *New York Times* 3 Nov. 1992, B11.

71. Michael Martinez, "Citing 'Controversies,' Johnson Retires Again," *New York Times* 3 Nov. 1992, B9.

72. Martinez, "Citing 'Controversies,'" B9; the remark was attributed to Dr. Michael Mellman, Johnson's physician. For more on the forces involved in Johnson's second retirement, see "'Not the Same As No Risk,'" *New York Times* 3 Nov. 1992, B11; "The Talk About Magic," *New York Times* 3 Nov. 1992, B11; Tom Friend, "Just Like Starting over for Lakers," *New York Times* 3 Nov. 1992, B11; Clifton Brown, "Decision Shocks Riley and Players," *New York Times* 3 Nov. 1992, B11; Lawrence K. Altman, "Decision Disappoints AIDS Experts," *New York Times* 3 Nov. 1992, B11; Araton, "N.B.A. Finds It Can't Overleap Reality"; Ira Berkow, "Magic's Collision Course," *New York Times* 3 Nov. 1992, B9; William C. Rhodes, "Magic, Not AIDS, Leaves Stage," *New York Times* 4 Nov. 1992, B21; Tom Friend, "No Anger by Johnson on Malone's Remarks," *New York Times* 4 Nov. 1992, B22; and Jeffrey Schmalz, "Call Him Earvin: 'I Can't Be Magic,'" *New York Times* 19 Nov. 1992, C1, C10. Fears about playing with Johnson were raised as early as his participation in the 1992 All-Star Game; note the romantic metaphor used to express these anxieties in the title of the following article: Ira Berkow, "All-Stars to Give Magic a Nervous Embrace," *New York Times* 7 Feb. 1992, B9, B11. The threat of HIV transmission was also raised, if at first largely dismissed, in reports that came out at the beginning of Johnson's "comeback": George Vecsey, "Magic Words for Earvin: 'Go for It,'" *New York Times* 30 Sept. 1992, B9; Clifton Brown, "Johnson, Unbowed by H.I.V., Will Return to Pro Basketball," *New York Times* 30 Sept. 1992, A1, B14; and "Best Wishes from Bird," *New York Times* 30 Sept. 1992, B14.

73. Note the similarity here to the current debate over lesbians and gay men serving in the military: on the one hand, gay men especially are depicted as not "masculine" enough to serve; on the other, they are seen as threatening military order.

74. Jane Gross, "At AIDS Epicenter, Seeking Swift, Sure Death," *New York Times* 20 June 1993, 16.

75. "Case Records of the Massachusetts General Hospital: Weekly Clinicopathological Exercises: Case 51-1986," *NEJM* 315:26 (25 Dec. 1986), 1660-68; passage quoted from 1667.

76. Simon LeVay, "A Difference in Hypothalamic Structure Between Heterosexual and Homosexual Men," *Science* 253 (30 Aug. 1991), 1034-37, and *The Sexual Brain* (Cambridge, MA: The MIT Press, 1993). For some of the media response to LeVay's work, see Robert Massa, "The Way We Wear Our Genes," *Village Voice* 24 Dec. 1991, 49; Gabriel Rotello, "Do Gays Really Have a Nerve?" *New York Newsday* 13 Aug. 1992, 48, 90; and Darrell Yates Rist, "Are Homosexuals Born That Way?" *The Nation* 19 Oct. 1992, 424-29.

77. Judith Butler, "Sexual Inversions," in Stanton, ed., *Discourses of Sexuality*, 357.

78. Amendment no. 963; *Congressional Record—Senate* [Debate on Helms Amendments], 14 Oct. 1987, S14216. The language here alters that of an earlier amendment (no. 957)—"AIDS education, information, or prevention materials and activities that promote, encourage, or condone homosexual sexual activities" (S14211)—which was itself an amendment of an amendment (no. 956) with a quite different thrust (S14204; cited below).

79. That a criminal like Colson here becomes "moral" authority is a subject all its own. That Colson's language here is of the "closet," claiming to reveal what has been perversely and dangerously hidden, is no mistake. The "closet" of homosexuality is here identified with the dirty and deadly "secret" of AIDS. For the fullest treatment of discourses of the "closet" in contemporary American culture, see Eve Kosofsky Sedgwick, *Epistemology of the Closet* (Berkeley and Los Angeles: University of California Press, 1990).

80. Helms here refers to the 1987 March on Washington for Lesbian and Gay Rights.

81. The Monsignor's idea of routes of transmission is rather hazy, but Helms will "clarify."

82. Helms chooses language here that suggests a link between his homophobia and his racism.

83. *Congressional Record—Senate*, 14 Oct. 1987, S14204. Compare, with Helms's "epidemiology" here, the "genealogical narrative" cited by Lee Edelman, "The Mirror and the Tank: 'AIDS,' Subjectivity, and the Rhetoric of Activism," in Timothy F. Murphy and Suzanne Poirier, eds., *Writing AIDS: Gay Literature, Language, and Analysis* (New York: Columbia University Press, 1993), 14, from a 1991 editorial in the *Manchester Union Leader*. For a partial analysis of the Senate debate over the Helms Amendment, see Douglas Crimp, "How to Have Promiscuity in an Epidemic," in Crimp, ed., *AIDS: Cultural Analysis/Cultural Activism*, 256-65; Watney, "The Possibilities of Permutation: Pleasure, Proliferation, and the Politics of Gay Identity in the Age of AIDS," in Miller, ed., *Fluid Exchanges*, 358-59; James Morrison, "The Repression of the Returned: AIDS and Allegory," in Nelson, ed., *AIDS: The Literary Response*, 167-68; and Peter M. Bowen, "AIDS 101," in Murphy and Poirier, eds., *Writing AIDS*, 151-52.

84. *Congressional Record—Senate*, 14 Oct. 1987, S14204.

85. It is revealing that Chiles chooses to mark the "beginning" of the "spread into the heterosexual population" at the point when "a female partner is infected," rather than when the (heterosexual) male "drug user" is infected. This reflects the tendency, commented on more fully below, to exclude intravenous drug users from the "general (heterosexual) population" and to see women as "vectors" of HIV/AIDS rather than as themselves "subjects" of infection and illness.

86. *Congressional Record—Senate*, 14 Oct. 1987, S14205.

87. Some strange conflation of the virus's "spread" and ideas of heterosexual reproduction seems to be at work here and below.

88. *Congressional Record—Senate*, 14 Oct. 1987, S14210.

89. *Congressional Record—Senate*, 14 Oct. 1987, S14211. This was, however, not Helms's final effort to limit education and prevention efforts aimed at intravenous drug users. In October of 1989, he introduced an amendment that would ban the use of government funds to provide sterile needles to those using drugs; see "Murderous Mischief on AIDS," *New York Times* 23 Oct. 1989, A18.

90. In other of Helms's legislative moves (e.g., against the National Endowment for the Arts) there is a similar obsessive return to homosexuality. And see his recent opposition to the nomination of Roberta Achtenberg as Assistant Secretary of Housing and Urban Development; Clifford Krauss, "Housing Nominee Is Attacked," *New York Times* 21 May 1993, A12.

91. Jonathan Dollimore, *Sexual Dissidence: Augustine to Wilde, Freud to Foucault* (Oxford: Clarendon Press, 1991), 26-27.

92. Judith Butler, *Bodies That Matter: On the Discursive Limits of "Sex"* (New York and London: Routledge, 1993), 8.

93. The character of Roy Cohn in Tony Kushner's *Angels in America* makes explicit how homosexuality and AIDS are constructed as sites excluded from power; Kushner, *Angels in America: A Gay Fantasia on National Themes: Part One: Millennium Approaches* (New York: Theatre Communications Group, 1993), 45-46.

94. See especially Sedgwick's discussion of "homosexual panic" in *Between Men: English Literature and Male Homosocial Desire* (New York: Columbia University Press, 1985), 83-96, and then, more completely and complexly, in *Epistemology of the Closet*, 19-21 and 182-212.

95. *Congressional Record—Senate*, 14 Oct. 1987, S14203.

96. Helms plays over and over on the trope of "revolt," both political and visceral; this occurs repeatedly in the context of gay unspeakability: "I am restraining myself in describing it [GMHC's "Safer Sex Comix"]. I believe that if the American people saw these books, they would be on the verge of revolt. / I obtained one copy of this book and I had photostats made for about 15 or 20 Senators. I sent each of the Senators a copy—if you will forgive the expression—in a brown envelope marked 'Personal and Confidential, for Senator's Eyes Only.' Without exception, the Senators were revolted"; "Good Lord, Mr. President, I may throw up"; "I will not consume the Senate's time reading the details of this revolting project. But, Mr. President, you know those little bags they have on airlines when it gets bumpy. If I were to read the sickening details to you, Mr. President, you would need one" (*Congressional Record—Senate*, 14 Oct. 1987, S14203).

97. *Congressional Record—Senate*, 14 Oct. 1987, S14203.

98. *Congressional Record—Senate*, 14 Oct. 1987, S14203.

99. For one complex consideration of a certain mutual dependence between the Christian right and gay political movements, see John Weir, "In God's Country," *Details* 12:12 (May 1994), 116-21, 175-76.

100. See, for instance, Michael Oreskes, "Senate Votes to Bar U.S. Support of 'Obscene or Indecent' Artwork," *New York Times* 27 July 1989, A1, C18; Grace Glueck, "Senate Vote Prompts Anger, But Some Approval in the Art World," *New York Times* 28 July 1989, B6; Glenn Collins, "On Helms and Grants with Poison Pills," *New York Times* 7 Aug. 1989, C11, C14; Glueck, "Border Skirmish: Art and Politics," *New York Times* 19 Nov. 1989, Section 2, 1, 5; Erika Munk, "The Arts Act Up: Can We Save the National Endowment?" *Village Voice* 3 April 1990, 57-59; Holly Hughes and Richard Elovich, "Homophobia at the N.E.A.," *New York Times* 28 July 1990, 21; and Gwen Ifill, "Senate Votes to Limit Arts Grants," *New York Times* 20 Sept. 1991, C3.

101. On the St. Patrick's Day Parade controversy, see the extensive coverage in the *New York Times*, including Jerry Gray, "Gay Group Rebuffed in Bid to Join St. Patrick's Parade," *New York Times* 8 March 1991, B3; Gray, "Longer St. Patrick's Parade May Allow Gay Irish Group," *New York Times* 9 March 1991, A27; Todd S. Purdum, "New York Sets Out on Legal Path to Allow Gay Irish Unit in Parade," *New York Times* 25 Jan. 1992, 1, 26; Bruce Weber, "Gay Irish Group Sues to March in Parade," *New York Times* 3 March 1992, B3; Bruce Weber, "Judge Permits Parade Ban of Gay Group," *New York Times* 14 March 1992, 27-28; Bruce Weber, "Judge Refuses to Order Gay Group Admitted to St. Patrick's Parade," *New York Times* 17 March 1992, A1, B2; Dennis Hevesi, "Gay Irish Win Right to March in a Parade That Might Die," *New York Times* 29 Oct. 1992, B1, B4; James C. McKinley, Jr., "Parade Permit Will Benefit Gay Marchers," *New York Times* 9 Jan. 1993, 25, 28; Richard Pérez-Peña, "Irish Groups Expect Unity on Parade," *New York Times* 30 Jan. 1993, 25; James C. McKinley, Jr., "St. Patrick's Standoff: Gay Issue Still Unresolved," *New York Times* 12 Feb. 1993, 25; Joseph P. Fried, "O'Connor Says Catholic Groups May Shun St. Patrick's Parade," *New York Times* 16 Feb. 1993, B5; Richard Pérez-Peña, "Judge Allows Group to Bar Gay Marchers," *New York Times* 27 Feb. 1993, 21, 25; Francis X. Clines, "To Be Irish, Gay and on the Outside, Once Again," *New York Times* 13 March 1993, 23, 26; Joseph J.

Sullivan, Jr., "St. Patrick's Parade Organizers Don't Bar Gays from Marching" (letter), *New York Times* 15 March 1993, A18; Doreen Carvajal, "Cardinal to Be Marshal for St. Patrick's Parade," *New York Times* 15 Dec. 1994, B3; and Jane H. Lii, "Judge Says Gay Group Can't March," *New York Times* 16 March 1995, B3.

On the Israel Day Parade, see Shawn G. Kennedy, "Israel Parade to Include a Gay Group," *New York Times* 21 April 1993, B3; and Jacques Steinberg, "Gay Dispute Fails to Disrupt Israel Day March," *New York Times* 10 May 1993, B1, B3.

102. See, for instance, Michael R. Gordon, "Hints of Gay-Ban Compromise in Senate," *New York Times* 30 March 1993, A18; Eric Schmitt, "Compromise on Military Ban Gaining Support Among Senators," *New York Times* 12 May 1993, A1, A16; Eric Schmitt, "Gay Congressman Offers a Plan on Homosexuals in the Military," *New York Times* 19 May 1993, A14; Jeffrey Schmalz, "Split on Gay Tactics for Military Ban," *New York Times* 23 May 1993, 18; Richard L. Berke, "President Backs a Gay Compromise," *New York Times* 28 May 1993, A2, A14; Eric Schmitt, "Joint Chiefs to Get 2 Options on Homosexuals," *New York Times* 29 May 1993, 8; Justin Richardson, "Uncle Sam Wants You to Live a Lie" (letter), *New York Times* 10 June 1993, A26; and Melinda J. Byrne, "Don't Give Up" (letter), *New York Times* 10 June 1993, A26.

103. Stephen Labaton, "U.S. Drops Effort to Oust a Gay Sailor," *New York Times* 29 Nov. 1994, A20.

104. See the fine analysis by Phillip Brian Harper, "Eloquence and Epitaph: Black Nationalism and the Homophobic Impulse in Responses to the Death of Max Robinson," in Murphy and Poirier, eds., *Writing AIDS*, 117-39; also printed in Abelove, Barale, and Halperin, eds., *The Lesbian and Gay Studies Reader*, 159-75.

105. The metaphor of "coming out of the closet" has, as Sedgwick suggests in *Epistemology of the Closet*, begun to float free "from its gay origins" (72); it is now commonly and easily applied to revealing one's HIV status. More jarringly, in a recent newspaper report on "an abstinence program developed by the Southern Baptist Convention," it is used to refer to *virginity*: "I feel there's a lot of people that are virgins . . . but they're afraid to come out"; "I have so much fun saying no. . . . So many of us are coming out of the closet. I'm a virgin and proud of it" ("'True Love Waits' for Some Teen-Agers," *New York Times* 21 June 1993, A12). As Sedgwick argues, such usages, rather than suggest that "coming out" has been "evacuated of its historical gay specificity," suggest "that exactly the opposite is true": "I think that a whole cluster of the most crucial sites for the contestation of meaning in twentieth-century Western culture are consequentially and quite indelibly marked with the historical specificity of homosocial/homosexual definition, notably but not exclusively male, from around the turn of the century" (72).

106. See Lowell Weicker's comments in the *Congressional Record—Senate*, 14 Oct. 1987, S14206.

107. See Philip J. Hilts, "U.S. Agency Is Criticized for Dropping AIDS Ads," *New York Times* 1 July 1992, A10.

108. ACT UP has been especially vocal around questions of race and class—see the section "Race, Women, and AIDS" in The ACT UP/New York Women and AIDS Book Group, *Women, AIDS, and Activism* (Boston: South End Press, 1990), 81-111—though it has also been criticized as exclusionary, as a group dominated by middle-class gay white men. Groups specifically addressing HIV/AIDS and racial concerns include the Minority Task Force on AIDS (NYC); the Upper Manhattan Task Force on AIDS; the New York City Commission on Human Rights, AIDS Discrimination Unit; the Chinatown Health Clinic (NYC); the South Carolina AIDS Education Network (SCAEN); COSSMHO, the National Coalition of Hispanic Health and Human Services Organizations; the Haitian Coalition on AIDS (Brooklyn); the Minnesota American Indian AIDS Task Force (Minneapolis); and the National Native American AIDS Prevention Center (Oakland and Minneapolis). Groups like Housing Works (NYC) have focused attention on homeless people and HIV/AIDS, and organizations like the ACLU National Prison

Project and AIDS Counseling and Education (ACE) at Bedford Hills Correctional Facility (NY) have addressed the concerns of prisoners living with HIV and AIDS.

109. Harlon Dalton, "AIDS in Blackface," in Graubard, ed., *Living with AIDS*, 237-59; and Ana Maria Alonso and Maria Teresa Koreck, "Silences: 'Hispanics,' AIDS, and Sexual Practices," in Abelove, Barale, and Halperin, eds., *The Lesbian and Gay Studies Reader*, 110-26 [originally published in *Differences: A Journal of Feminist Cultural Studies* 1:1 (1989), 101-24].

110. Glenn Collins, "Brad Davis, 41, a Leading Actor in 'Normal Heart' and 'Querelle,'" *New York Times* 10 Sept. 1991, B5.

111. Alexandra Bandon, "Crimes Against Nature," *New York Times Magazine* 24 July 1994, 30-31.

112. Daniel Goleman, "Scientists Pinpoint Brain Irregularities in Drug Addicts," *New York Times* 26 June 1990, C1, C7.

113. See LeVay, "Difference in Hypothalamic Structure," and *The Sexual Brain*.

114. For evidence of how the trampling of civil rights is currently glorified in the name of the "war against drugs," see almost any episode of the television series *Cops*.

115. On the complex history of conceptions of black masculinity, see hooks, "Reconstructing Black Masculinity."

116. On women in the AIDS crisis, and for further bibliography, see Diane Richardson, *Women and AIDS* (New York: Routledge, 1989 [1988]); Ines Rieder and Patricia Ruppelt, eds., *AIDS: The Women* (San Francisco and Pittsburgh: Cleis Press, 1988); the ACT UP/NY Women and AIDS Book Group, *Women, AIDS, and Activism*; Andrea Rudd and Darien Taylor, *Positive Women: Voices of Women Living with AIDS* (Toronto: Second Story Press, 1992); Treichler, "AIDS, Homophobia, and Biomedical Discourse"; Treichler, "AIDS, Gender, and Biomedical Discourse"; Treichler, "Beyond Cosmo"; Gena Corea, *The Invisible Epidemic: The Story of Women and AIDS* (New York: HarperCollins, 1992); Leslie Doyal, Jennie Naidoo, and Tamsin Wilson, eds., *AIDS: Setting a Feminist Agenda* (London: Taylor & Francis, 1994); and Cindy Patton, *Last Served?*

117. See Risa Denenberg, "What the Numbers Mean," in ACT UP/NY, *Women, AIDS, and Activism*, 1-4, esp. 3-4; Denenberg, "Unique Aspects of HIV Infection in Women," in ACT UP/NY, *Women, AIDS, and Activism*, 31-43, esp. 32-33; Denenberg, "Treatment and Trials," in ACT UP/NY, *Women, AIDS, and Activism*, 69-79, esp. 72; Sunny Rumsey, "AIDS Issues for African-American and African-Caribbean Women," in ACT UP/NY, *Women, AIDS, and Activism*, 103-6, esp. 105-6; Jean Carlomusto, "Focusing on Women: Video as Activism," in ACT UP/NY, *Women, AIDS, and Activism*, 215-18, esp. 217-18; Corea, *Invisible Epidemic*, 210-12, 259-68, 276-82, 288, and 295; Mireya Navarro, "Dated AIDS Definition Keeps Benefits from Many Patients," *New York Times* 8 July 1991, A1, B5; B. D. Colen, "CDC Wants to Broaden the Definition of AIDS," *New York Newsday* 15 Nov. 1991, 17; Robert Pear, "U.S. Alters Rules on People with H.I.V.," *New York Times* 17 Dec. 1991, A16; Mireya Navarro, "Agencies Slowed in Effort to Widen Definitions of AIDS," *New York Times* 10 Feb. 1992, A1, B11; "U.S. to Weigh Female Illness in Defining AIDS," *New York Times* 3 Sept. 1992, A16; Lawrence K. Altman, "Federal Health Officials Propose an Expanded Definition of AIDS," *New York Times* 28 Oct. 1992, B9; Mireya Navarro, "More Cases, Costs and Fears Under Wider AIDS Umbrella," *New York Times* 29 Oct. 1992, A1, B2; Mireya Navarro, "New Definition for AIDS Arrives, Bringing New Concerns," *New York Times* 6 Jan. 1993, B3; Mireya Navarro, "AIDS Numbers Increase Under New Federal Rules," *New York Times* 22 March 1993, B3; and Lawrence K. Altman, "Widened Definition of AIDS Leads to More Reports of It," *New York Times* 30 April 1993, A18.

118. Denenberg, "Treatment and Trials," 73. Also see Gina Kolata, "N.I.H. Neglects Women, Study Says," *New York Times* 19 June 1990, C6.

119. For discussion of the uses of military language in relation to AIDS, see Sontag, *AIDS and Its Metaphors*; Michael S. Sherry, "The Language of War in AIDS Discourse," in Murphy and Poirier, eds., *Writing AIDS*, 39-53; and Patton, "Cell Wars," with a discussion of Sontag at 272-73.

120. Paul Monette, *Borrowed Time: An AIDS Memoir* (San Diego, New York, and London: Harcourt Brace Jovanovich, 1988), 2; and see the poems in *Love Alone: Eighteen Elegies for Rog* (New York: St. Martin's Press, 1988). Sherry, "The Language of War," also comments on Monette's use of war language in these works and in the novel *Afterlife* (43); and see Edelman's comments on *Love Alone* in "The Mirror and the Tank," 22-25.

121. See Treichler, "AIDS, Homophobia, and Biomedical Discourse," 45-46, and Patton, *Last Served?* 10-13 and 48-76.

122. See Allan M. Brandt, *No Magic Bullet: A Social History of Venereal Disease in the United States Since 1880*, expanded ed. [with a new chapter on AIDS] (New York and Oxford: Oxford University Press, 1987).

123. "Dallas Police Discount AIDS Revenge Tale," *New York Times* 23 Oct. 1991, A14.

124. Steven Erlanger, "A Plague Awaits," *New York Times Magazine* 14 July 1991, 24, 26, 49, 53; passages cited from 24 and 26.

125. For one particularly striking instance, see the picture of the Burk family accompanying Redfield and Burke's "HIV Infection," 62, in the caption of which, as Treichler points out, the deaths of both Patrick (husband/father) and Dwight (son) are noted, but in which the fate of Lauren (wife/mother), "who . . . transmitted [HIV] to their son" (Redfield and Burke, 63) remains unstated; Treichler, "Beyond *Cosmo*," 34-35.

126. See Terry Castle, *The Apparitional Lesbian: Female Homosexuality and Modern Culture* (New York: Columbia University Press, 1993), 12, for one example. And see Sander L. Gilman's analysis of Peter Zingler's 1989 novel *Die Seuche*, in which a lesbian character "becomes the image of the person with AIDS"; "Plague in Germany, 1939/1989: Cultural Images of Race, Space, and Disease," in Murphy and Poirier, eds., *Writing AIDS*, 72.

127. See, for some examples, Richardson, *Women and AIDS*, 88.

128. See, for instance, Lawrence K. Altman, "AIDS and a Dentist's Secrets," *New York Times* 6 June 1993, Section 4, 1, 3.

129. Note that, in Elizabeth Cox's memoir *Thanksgiving: An AIDS Journal* (New York: Harper & Row, 1990), the question of her own (negative) HIV status is long deferred. See the comments on Cox in John M. Clum, "'And Once I Had It All': AIDS Narratives and Memories of an American Dream," in Murphy and Poirier, eds., *Writing AIDS*, 204-7, and Timothy F. Murphy, "Testimony," in Murphy and Poirier, eds., *Writing AIDS*, 311 and 313-14.

130. Bruce Lambert, "Unlikely AIDS Sufferer's Message: Even You Can Get It," *New York Times* 11 March 1989, 29, 32; passages cited from 29.

131. On "SILENCE = DEATH," see Douglas Crimp, with Adam Rolston, *AIDS Demo Graphics* (Seattle: Bay Press, 1990), 14-15; Crimp, "AIDS: Cultural Analysis/Cultural Activism," in Crimp, ed., *AIDS: Cultural Analysis/Cultural Activism*, 3-16, esp. 7-12. For critical readings of the rhetoric of "SILENCE = DEATH," see Edelman, "The Plague of Discourse," and Richard D. Mohr, "On Some Words from ACT UP: Doing and Being Done," *Gay Ideas: Outing and Other Controversies* (Boston: Beacon Press, 1992), 49-52.

CHAPTER 3
The Narratives of AIDS

1. IRREVERSIBLE DECLINE AND UNCONTROLLABLE SPREAD

At the current moment, two narratives, one "microcosmic" and the other "macrocosmic," structure American scientific, journalistic, and popular depictions of AIDS, and it is in relation to these two large cultural narratives that AIDS fictions take up position.[1] The first structuring narrative tells the story of an individual, charting the "course" of his or her HIV illness: coming into contact with HIV through sex or intravenous drug use or a blood transfusion, one tests positive for antibody to the virus, develops symptoms (lymphadenopathy, thrush, night sweats, the lesions of Kaposi's sarcoma, "HIV wasting syndrome," opportunistic infections), is diagnosed as having AIDS, or "full-blown" AIDS, and dies. Passivity is imputed at all stages in this narrative, except the initial stage, where, too often, a certain "culpable" activity is associated with the exposure to HIV. The vocabulary of "progress," of travel ("the long road from HIV to AIDS"),[2] of "decline," of "inexorable suffering and death,"[3] characterizes versions of this narrative. Thus, for example, in one influential medical schema, "the course of HIV infection" is defined in six "progressive" stages:

> The Walter Reed classification system . . . begins with stage zero: exposure to the virus through any of the known transmission routes. . . . Once the presence of HIV has been documented by any reliable test, patients are said to be in Walter Reed stage one. . . . For the majority of patients the first sign that something is amiss in the immune system is the development of chronically swollen lymph nodes. With the appearance of this chronic lymphadenopathy a patient moves into stage 2. . . . Stage 2 typically lasts for from three to five years, and patients still feel well even when it ends. The beginning of stage 3 is defined by a persistent drop in the $T4$-cell count to less than 400, which is a harbinger of a decline in immune functioning. Patients remain in

this stage, however, until direct evidence of an impairment in cell-mediated immunity is discovered—usually about 18 months later—at which point they enter stage 4. . . . Progression to stage 5 is usually determined on the basis of the development of anergy [failure to mount an immune response to antigens]. . . . Some time later the first overt symptom of a breakdown in cell-mediated immunity arises: the development of thrush, a fungal infection of the mucous membranes of the tongue or the oral cavity. . . . Many people develop chronic or disseminated opportunistic infections at sites beyond the skin and mucous membranes within a year or two after entering stage 5. The emergence of these infections reflects an extremely severe decline in immune function and constitutes progression to stage 6, or what is also called opportunistic-infection-defined AIDS. . . . Most patients enter stage 6 with a T-cell count of 100 or less and most, unfortunately, die within two years.[4]

The "decline" associated with HIV illness is often represented graphically, as, for instance, by Mills and Masur, who chart the "progress" of disease in terms of increasingly severe opportunistic infections and a decreasing number of CD4+ lymphocytes.[5]

Of course, the "progression" of HIV illness is in fact interrupted in many and various ways—by its long and variable latency period and by remissions; by preventive measures and treatments (AZT, ddI, ddC, aerosolized pentamidine, foscarnet, radiation and chemotherapies, holistic and alternative approaches) that may be directed against HIV itself, against opportunistic infections and HIV-associated neoplasms, or intended to support the immune system and the general state of health. Indeed, some have moved, "as the armamentarium of anti-HIV drugs increases," to reconstruct AIDS not as a virulent plague but as a "manageable chronic disease."[6] Fee and Fox suggest that, "by June 1989, the idea that AIDS should be regarded as a chronic illness was widely accepted," noting that "Samuel Broder, head of the National Cancer Institute, publicly declared [at the international AIDS meeting in Montreal] that AIDS is a chronic disease and cancer the appropriate analogue for therapy."[7] Though there have been strong objections to a "cancer model" of AIDS, since this seems to reject hope for a cure and replace it with "early detection, followed by toxic treatments, with 'survival' defined as two more years of life,"[8] such a model does at least interrupt the facile equation of AIDS and death.

The experience of "long-term survivors" of AIDS like Michael Callen provides the most powerful counter-testimony to the pervasive cultural narrative of inexorable decline and death:

I was momentarily paralyzed by the insight that here in America, the one essential fact about AIDS—a notion so simple as to be accessible to a six-year-old—is that everyone who gets it dies. Or in the words of the surgeon general, everyone with AIDS is *"expected . . . to die."*[9]

I did a quick reality check: I have AIDS, but as far as I could tell, I was not dead.

Later that week, I read an article that said that AIDS is invariably fatal—that there are no known survivors. As I sat holding the newspaper in my hands, it dawned on me that I was alive five years after my AIDS diagnosis—several years after I was supposed to be dead. I realized that I could name a half-dozen other friends, many of whom were diagnosed before me, who were surviving and thriving with AIDS.

I got furious! How did the myth get started that everyone who gets AIDS dies, and what were the consequences of this lie? How many other long-term survivors were out there? Why have we survived?

I resolved then to write about the best-kept secret of the epidemic: Not everyone dies from AIDS.[10]

Still, the emphasis in most depictions of AIDS remains on the disease's incurability, on the inevitability of the narrative's final stages. This emphasis is reinforced by the growing insistence that HIV infection necessarily leads to the development of AIDS, that there will not be, as was originally thought and hoped, a large number of asymptomatic "carriers" who, though infected, would never develop "full-blown" AIDS, or a large number of people with the milder symptoms of "AIDS-related complex" (ARC) who would not "progress" to AIDS. When, in 1986, they first presented their "staging classification for HTLV-III/LAV infection," Redfield, Wright, and Tramont stressed "that the use of the word 'stage' does not imply that all patients . . . will have progressive disease. Many questions about clinical progression are currently unanswered";[11] two years later, however, Redfield and Burke emphasized a different conclusion: "These findings underscore the grim reality that, in the absence of a scientific solution to HIV, most (and perhaps all) people who are infected with HIV will eventually develop end-stage disease and will die prematurely."[12]

The second major narrative of AIDS—which might be called an epidemiological or population narrative—involves not the individual person living with HIV or AIDS but the historical trajectory of the epidemic. Here, in the most common forms of the narrative, an "origin" for AIDS is posited (usually in Africa and usually involving the transmutation of a less virulent animal virus into a more virulent human one);[13] the "progress" of the epidemic—the "spread of the disease," the "explosion of cases"—is then traced in particular populations until it reaches (in the narrative's projection) an unmanageable "caseload." The "worst-case scenario" (which is generally the one presented) shows an apocalyptic spread of disease depicted as especially disturbing in its abandonment of particular "risk groups" (gay men, intravenous drug users, hemophiliacs, blood transfusion recipients, "minority" communities, sex workers) for the "general population," with the assumption being, of course, that gay men, drug users, African Americans, Caribbeans, and Latina/os, and poor men and women do not belong to that "general population." This narrative often appears in the summary form of a graph that depicts not only the past and present situation but also a projection of future infection and mortality.[14] As with the first, personal, narrative, the population narrative is susceptible to interruptions: the slowing of infection rates attendant upon education and altered behavior, existing treatments that may delay the onset of disease, possible future treatments and vaccines. But it is the apocalyptic completion of the narrative that the public language of AIDS most commonly emphasizes. Rather than stress the slowing rates of new infection within communities of gay men, for instance, the epidemiological narrative focuses with fear (and fascination) on the "rapid" spread of the disease into new communities more and more closely attached to a conception of the "general population":

> Most of those affected in the near future will be either homosexual men or IV drug abusers, and a significant proportion of them will be blacks and Hispanics. Yet, given the fact that the virus is transmitted through sexual contact, through the traces of blood in needles and other drug paraphernalia and from mother to newborn infant, one can envision many possible chains of infection, which leave no segment of the U.S. population unaffected by the threat of AIDS.[15]

At particular historical moments, this narrative has played an especially dangerous, panic-inducing role—for instance, in 1983, when reports of "infants and children with syndromes of severe cellular immune deficiency . . . born into families with well-recognized risks for AIDS"[16] led some scientists to conclude too hastily that AIDS might be spread through "household exposure."[17] An editorial by Anthony Fauci of the National Institutes of Health emphasized the dire epidemiological consequences of such a (false) conclusion:

> It took some time for people to believe that AIDS was indeed transmissible. Then it was assumed that it could only be transmitted by sexual contact among homosexuals and by blood products. Recently, the CDC has reported AIDS among the female sex partners of IV drug users, and others have reported AIDS among female prostitutes. The finding of

AIDS in infants and children who are household contacts of patients with AIDS or persons with risks for AIDS has enormous implications with regard to ultimate transmissibility of this syndrome. First, it is possible that AIDS can be vertically transmitted.[18] Perhaps even more important is the possibility that routine close contact, as within a family household, can spread the disease. If, indeed, the latter is true, then AIDS takes on an entirely new dimension. Given the fact that the incubation period for adults is believed to be longer than one year, the full impact of the syndrome among sexual contacts and recipients of potentially infective transfusions is uncertain at present. If we add to this the possibility that nonsexual, non-blood-borne transmission is possible, the scope of the syndrome may be enormous.[19]

Significantly, "[n]ewspaper and TV stations that had ignored the epidemic before suddenly took notice when word came over the AP wires that the disease might be spreading easily": "as one midwestern editor put it, with the report by AP and UPI on the casual contact story, 'now this disease seemed to be creeping toward "average" Americans.'"[20] A moment like this one in the history of the AIDS crisis emphasizes how close to the surface lies the fantasy of AIDS as unstoppable plague; and such a fantasy is strongly supported by narratives of the spread of HIV even when these are accompanied by accurate information on possible routes of HIV infection.

Personal and epidemiological narratives complement each other: the personal narrative traces the individual illnesses and deaths that make up the population narrative, which itself traces the spread of the agent of disease and death. One represents a pattern of inexorable individual decay, the other a pattern of ravenous, uncontrolled growth attendant upon that decay. In their mutual dependence, the two narratives echo scientific accounts of the life-cycle of HIV wherein the deaths of individual immune system cells are correlated to the replication and spread of the viral agent. In the personal narrative, as in the narrative of cellular death, the central figure is the passive sufferer (the "patient" or infected cell), the "victim" of invading forces; on the other hand, central to the population narrative, as to the narrative of HIV's replication and dispersion within the human body, is the disease agent, the active "killer," the viral force that cannot be resisted.

Population and personal narratives come together in a particularly disturbing way when the agent of the epidemic's spread is identified with the body of the "infectious" patient him- or herself. In such depictions, the person with AIDS, seen as irremediably given over to death, becomes the source of others' deaths; he or she is, simultaneously and paradoxically, the active bearer of disease and its passive sufferer. This dangerous conflation of individual illness with the larger growth of the AIDS epidemic is perhaps most famously illustrated by Randy Shilts's depiction of Gaetan Dugas ("Patient Zero"), whom he closely identifies with the origins of AIDS in North America:

> The morning newspapers on Monday, March 26, [1984,] carried stories of a study about to be published in the *Journal of American Medicine* (*sic*).[21] News of this formal publication of the cluster study, two years after the CDC's Bill Darrow had pieced the tale together, was accompanied by complicated diagrams, with all the arrows and circles centered on one person—the now-famous Patient Zero. The study and the news stories, of course, did not name Gaetan Dugas, although they did allude to the fact that researchers believed he was still alive.
>   Gaetan had survived his fourth bout with *Pneumocystis* and appeared to be on his way to recovery. . . . As always, Gaetan had managed to nurture a torrid love affair . . . with a handsome male model. By the end of March, he persuaded the model to fly to Quebec and accompany him back to British Columbia.
>   The model was on the plane east when Gaetan died in Quebec City. It was March 30, a month past Gaetan's thirty-first birthday, and it had been nearly four years since he first had gone to see the doctor in Toronto about the purple spot near his ear. In the end, it wasn't an AIDS disease that killed Gaetan—his kidneys, strained by the years of infection, simply gave out.
>   Whether Gaetan Dugas actually was the person who brought AIDS to North America remains a question of debate and is ultimately unanswerable. The fact that the first cases in both New York City and Los Angeles could be linked to Gaetan, who himself was one of the first half-dozen or so patients on the continent, gives weight to that theory. Gaetan traveled frequently to France, the western nation where the disease was most widespread before 1980. In any event, there's no doubt that Gaetan played a key role in spreading the new virus from one end of the United States to the other. The bathhouse controversy, peaking so dramatically in San Francisco on the morning of his death, was also linked directly to Gaetan's own exploits in those sex palaces and his recalcitrance in changing his ways. At one time, Gaetan had been what every man wanted from gay life; by the time he died, he had become what every man feared.[22]

Such a depiction, of course, reflects the phobic, and particularly homophobic, movement in which gay desire is equated with an impulse toward death and the person with HIV or AIDS is seen simultaneously as weakened (queer) "victim" and powerful (queer) "threat."

Introducing a collection of articles reprinted from *Scientific American* and designed to present the "extraordinary achievement" of science in response to the AIDS crisis, Jonathan Piel begins with an explicit appeal to fictional narratives: "Had a novelist sought a plot device that would lay bare the strengths, weaknesses and contradictions in the social fabric, the policy-making institutions and the moral vision of contemporary humanity, he or she could not have hit upon a better one than the AIDS epidemic."[23] Having thus suggested the epidemic's kinship with the intentional narratives of the novelist, Piel goes on to describe AIDS in terms strongly evocative of both personal and population narratives:

> A blood-borne pathogen spread by sexual contact, drug abuse and advanced techniques of medical therapy leaps oceans, aided by a network of rapid convenient air travel. It quietly gains footholds in both the northern and southern hemispheres, in market economies and planned economies. The virus attacks, cripples and destroys the body's only defense against disease: the immune system.[24]

The progress of illness at the level of the individual is sketched with economy in the sequence of verbs, "attacks, cripples, destroys"; the body becomes a besieged citadel, and though the narrative of siege is not carried to its conclusion, we see "the body's only defense" irreparably breached. The larger narrative by which the pattern of epidemic spread is suggested is also set forth metaphorically, by personification of the "pathogen," which boldly "leaps oceans" (like some superhero or monster) and underhandedly "gains footholds" (like a network of spies or revolutionaries).[25] In this last image, the AIDS epidemic becomes more than the "plot device" of Piel's hypothesized "novelist" but also a sinister "plot" that must be uncovered.[26]

Of course, there is a certain truth in the AIDS narratives thus evoked: HIV is spreading in epidemic fashion; it does cause immune deficiency and, often, death. Still, many dangers inhere in our most common narrative understandings of HIV and AIDS and in the ways these structure responses to the AIDS crisis. The narrative of inexorable individual disease encourages the view of people with AIDS as passive victims, helpless in the face of an implacable enemy; it reconfirms the homophobic construction of people with AIDS as, like the gay men with whom they are conflated, the possessors of weak, degenerate, and degenerating bodies. It also, by depicting the person affected by HIV or AIDS as irremediably given over to disease and death, reinforces the imagination of a strict separation between the "diseased" and the "healthy," encouraging the uninfected to see those infected as essentially "other." In part, the epidemiological narrative, by depicting the epidemic's uncontrolled growth, works in an opposite direction, undermining a sense of separation between infected and uninfected. Insofar as this leads people to see AIDS as affecting "us" and not just "them," this may have positive results: the threat of the spread of AIDS may be met by reasonable and productive measures, education, the practice of safe(r) sex, the use of "universal precautions" by health care workers. It may also, however, be used as an excuse for unreasonable and repressive measures: the forced segregation of the infected, the isolation or persecution of "high-risk" groups, the ban on travel or immigration for people testing HIV-positive—attempts to make real, tangible, and permanent the perceived and hoped-for distinction of "diseased" and "healthy." Furthermore, the epidemiological narrative, by focusing its attention not on individuals but on populations, by looking at "risk groups" rather than "risk behaviors" and at the overall pattern of infection and disease instead of at individual cases, allows, even when it does not actively encourage, the dehumanization of the person with AIDS, the replacing of the individual by a statistic, the subordination of individual behavior to membership in a community "at risk." In an effect that is perhaps more subtle, the tracing out of an epidemiological narrative tends to posit not only a future moment of apocalypse but also a past moment, a "ground zero" or "Patient Zero," at which the origin of AIDS is thought to occur. In the imagination of this past moment of "causation," the epidemic's origin is often identified with foreignness—Africa not the United States, the United States not Russia, "promiscuous" gay men not heterosexuals—in a process that easily leads to the scapegoating of those thought to participate in that origin (in the United States context, most often men like Shilts's Gaetan Dugas depicted as leading the "fast-lane" life of 1970s gay sex).[27]

Both narratives present the picture of a "battle" already lost: individuals and populations affected by HIV and AIDS are irretrievable. In part, the reliance on such narratives may explain why efforts to "combat" AIDS have been so heavily concentrated on methods designed to protect the uninfected and have addressed themselves so slowly to issues of treatment: "people with AIDS are being written off as 'unsaveable,' as if all the predictions for future mortality were somehow set in stone, as if nothing could be done to reverse the course of the epidemic with the imperfect knowledge we do have."[28] The main thrust toward improving and extending the life of people with AIDS has come from within communities themselves perceived to be at "high risk" for the disease, especially from AIDS treatment activists within such organizations as ACT UP, TAG, and CRIA; other communities, the "general population," too often seem content to let the disease "run its course" as long as they themselves remain more or less unaffected.

Cultural narratives of AIDS play a crucial role in attempts to understand the past, present, and future of the epidemic, providing a stabilizing framework within which to place unpredictable, disturbing, world-threatening events so that these seem to make sense as part of a coherent story. Such narratives allow an ordering of events that gives them "meaning"; metaphorically containing them in narrative provides a sense of control, even if (paradoxically) the narratives in which they are contained assert the resistance of illness and pandemic to containment and control. And narratives such as these serve not only to describe "reality," nor only to provide evidence of its coherence, but also to shape it, helping to determine treatment protocols, research agendas, educational and political priorities. Thus, understanding AIDS through the kinds of coherent narrative usually attributed to the intentions of an author encourages the treatment of the pandemic as though it were authored and as though its cause and ultimate reason for being might be uncovered, and such a belief in the intentionality of AIDS in turn allows for moralized understandings—the religious right's claim that AIDS is somehow a divine punishment, "God's magic bullet" to do away with homosexuality, "promiscuity," drug use[29]—that provide the rationale for plans of action like Helms's blocking of federally-funded education for gay men that themselves push toward those ends (the death of individuals with AIDS, the devastation of particular communities) that personal and population narratives seem to intend.

2. FACING IT

For the author who wishes to write about AIDS, the narrative structures already present in the broader culture pose particular problems. The personal narrative threatens to reduce any story about someone with AIDS to the same story of decay and death. For the gay or anti-homophobic author writing about a gay experience of AIDS, the problem is even more pointed. How not to reproduce a "death driven narrative as the definition of the gay subject," a kind of narrative whose history, as Jeff Nunokawa has suggested, stretches from *The Picture of Dorian Gray* to Shilts's account of Gaetan Dugas?[30] How to intervene against what Paul Morrison identifies as "[t]he cultural function of AIDS"—"to stabilize, through a specifically narrative or novelistic logic, the truth of gay identity as death or death wish," a logic that arrives at the "clear" conclusion that "homosexuality = death"?[31] As the fiction writer Adam Mars-Jones has recently suggested:

> At a time when media coverage tends to push the issues of Aids (*sic*) and homosexuality closer and closer together, as if epidemic and orientation were synonymous, how can you justify writing fiction that brings this spurious couple together all over again? Surely the truly responsible thing to do now would be to write sexy nostalgic fiction set in the period before the epidemic, safe-guarding if only in fantasy the endangered gains of gay liberation?[32]

But Mars-Jones answers his own question in the negative:

Well, no. Even when I thought that the problems of writing about Aids (*sic*) satisfactorily were insurmountable, for me at any rate, I still felt that it would be a good thing, even politically, if the trick could be managed. Fiction might create a psychological space in which the epidemic could be contemplated, with detachment rather than denial or apocalyptic fear.[33]

Might narrative in fact be used to challenge, to subvert, to rewrite the common equations of gayness and disease, gayness and AIDS, AIDS and death?[34]

The impulse of many writers has been to frustrate the narrative of personal decline, to complicate it, to refuse to carry it through to its conclusion. Thus, in a novel like John D'Hondt's *The Bunny Book*, the narrative of Peter's illness and death, though present, is almost unreadable amidst a proliferation of other material—the story of the bunny Amber and his human contacts; myths about rabbits from many cultures—that often relates only very obliquely to the story of Peter and his lover, the narrator.[35] In a similar, if more sophisticated, move into myth and history, Geoff Ryman in his novel *Was* interweaves Jonathan's illness with a century-old story of the supposed "real-life" model for L. Frank Baum's Dorothy and with other "Oz-related" narratives. The novel's central interest shifts to Jonathan and his "decline" only as it draws to its conclusion, and even then Ryman scrupulously avoids depicting Jonathan's death:

> Bill looked around him, shouting "Jonathan!"
> On the right, bare and harvested, there was no one.
> "Where are you?" Bill started to run across the fields, toward Dorothy's farm and then stopped. This is crazy, he thought. There's nowhere to hide. If Jonathan was ahead of him, he would see him running. If he had fallen over, he would still see him, there was no cover, Bill could see every clump of dirt. . . .
> It was crazy, but Jonathan had gone.[36]
>
> You can't just disappear, Bill told himself. The dogs will find him somewhere. He felt humbled by the world, by Jonathan himself. This was what Jonathan wanted, Bill told the fiery light on the hillside. He wanted to stay here. He wanted to disappear. He wanted to find Oz.[37]

Other interesting (and powerful) avoidances of death occur, for instance, at the conclusion of Robert Ferro's novel *Second Son*,[38] and in the final scene of Norman René and Craig Lucas's film *Longtime Companion*, where, if only imaginatively and for a moment, those who have died are resurrected.[39]

A refusal of the narrative of disease and death, however, bears its own dangers. It can be read as a failure to face the realities of illness, as a denial of the possibility of death; in writing about AIDS in the 1980s and 1990s, experiences of illness, death, and loss are crucial to what must be expressed. Nor can writers simply reject the population narrative: it is important not to cover over the devastating effects of AIDS on gay, African American, and Latina/o communities, on the poor and the homeless, as it is important to recognize the realities of the continued spread of HIV. But the population narrative as it is usually deployed leaves little room for intervention; insofar as it depicts certain communities as helpless in the face of an inexorable "plague," it must be challenged by writers who do not wish simply to throw their hands up in despair.

Most fictional treatments of AIDS do not rely completely or straightforwardly on either the population or personal narrative, though almost all evoke such narratives, if sometimes mainly to reject them. Because the novel at the current moment, especially the novel that does not self-consciously define itself as "experimental," remains most often a form centered on the development of character and on actions of a largely "private" nature, the personal narrative has so far been most important in shaping the genre of the AIDS novel. Even if one has never before read a fictional account of AIDS, one "knows," from broader cultural experience, and in particular from familiarity with the narrative of individual illness, what such an account might entail: readers have certain generic expectations even before their first encounter with a novel about AIDS.[40] Thus, when one of the earliest AIDS novels,[41] Paul Reed's *Facing It* (1984), opens in a Manhattan hospital with an evocation of "the hospital morgue" (9), and, a few pages later, introduces a young, usually healthy, gay man,[42] Andy, who is inexplicably ill, the reader can already predict much of the ensuing novel's narrative pattern.[43] The earliest readers of the novel, of course, would have known less about AIDS than do readers a decade later, and one can imagine those for whom the novel itself provided a first encounter with AIDS. Novels like *Facing It*, and popularizing nonfiction accounts like Randy Shilts's *And the Band Played On*, have indeed themselves played important roles in establishing and reinforcing larger cultural narratives about AIDS. Still, the novel's presumed primary audience, urban gay men like Andy himself,[44] would, in 1984, already have been all too familiar with AIDS and its manifestations, and much of the novel's power derives from a discrepancy between what its characters (living in the period between June 1981 and February 1982) know and what readers might know in 1984. As soon as Andy's symptoms—fatigue and weakness, pallor, weight-loss, swollen lymph glands, an unexplained staph infection (11-14)—are described, the well-informed reader may deduce that he has AIDS, and can project the course of his illness. Poignantly, neither Andy nor David his lover, nor Dr. Branch his physician, can yet know what the reader might three years later, and as these characters are swept up in the mysterious details of Andy's disease, their helplessness is mirrored in the reader's own sense of helplessness, unable to use what he or she knows about AIDS except to predict a hopeless conclusion. As each stage of the illness unfolds, the reader's expectations are disturbingly confirmed: the disease "progresses" just as we "know" it will, while simultaneously the characters in the novel grope to understand what they face. As they gain insight into Andy's illness, and the similar illnesses being experienced by other gay men, the characters slowly construct in their own minds the narrative of a disease that leads inexorably to death, a narrative already accessible to readers.

Just at the moment in the novel when Dr. Branch's initial diagnosis (hepatitis) is proven wrong, a possible alternative explanation of Andy's illness arises: an article in *Morbidity and Mortality Weekly Report* (what in retrospect we know to be one of the first scientific accounts of AIDS)[45] shows that gay men other than Andy have been inexplicably ill, diagnosed with "Kaposi's sarcoma, *Pneumocystis* pneumonia, and other opportunistic infections associated with immunosuppression" (44). The characters of the novel have their first inkling of a pattern into which Andy's strange situation might fit, a pattern already potentially fixed in the reader's mind. As the novel progresses—with Dr. Branch gaining medical knowledge, Andy gaining the knowledge of experience, and David, a journalist, beginning to research the illness and its manifestations—the characters' expectations become bleaker and bleaker, approaching congruence with the informed reader's. Early on, Dr. Branch realizes that what the *Morbidity and Mortality* report "seems to suggest . . . is that by the time of detection, it's already too late" (49). Andy is diagnosed with Kaposi's sarcoma (59, 69), which unambiguously connects his illness to the other cases among gay men. Before receiving that diagnosis, Andy still believes (or hopes) that his disease will pass—"He wasn't dying, at least not yet" (66)—but his hope for survival quickly dissipates:

> Never in his life had he felt such real terror, such horror that his body was diseased and that he would, most likely, die. . . . He was afraid to die. Even though he had known that the biopsy would prove positive, he had not yet received the death sentence—as he now thought of it—until the words were out of Dr. Branch's mouth. Now he knew; now it was certain. So, "I am to have my own death," Andy said aloud as he walked along, quoting a line from May Sarton. Now the moment was here, and the prospect of having his own death, no matter how well or poorly he might face it, terrified and infuriated him. (79-80)

Andy's fears are as yet not fully confirmed: the characters in the novel still know too little about his illness to be sure of its outcome. But as the story progresses, deterioration and death seem more and more inescapable. Andy's physical condition continues to worsen: "He was very thin now, very pale. It was difficult to recognize that this was the same young man who, just months before, had been strong, muscular, exercising with weights regularly at the gym, avidly pursuing his job at City Hall" (121). Furthermore, as we follow Andy's illness and treatment, we meet another patient, Patrick Ross, whose illness serves to parallel and predict the course of Andy's. Patrick's situation drives home to Andy in the strongest possible way what he himself can expect. At Dr. Branch's suggestion, Andy first meets Patrick when both are to undergo chemotherapy for Kaposi's sarcoma: "I just thought it might be helpful to you to meet someone else who'll be going through the same thing you will" (109). The two talk briefly and plan to meet again, but are prevented from doing so by Patrick's deteriorating condition: "within a week of commencing chemotherapy, the young man had taken a serious turn for the worse and been hospitalized in isolation. Knowing that Patrick had done so badly did not reassure Andy about his own progress. He remained scared and doubtful" (121). Andy continues to think about Patrick; he suspects that Patrick is dying and feels "compelled" to visit him (128). Finding Patrick "in critical condition," "blind" (129) and suffering from what Andy sees as dementia, "Andy realized that they could not have carried on a decent conversation after all. Patrick was too ill, too far gone. . . . in a state somewhere between sleep, madness and death" (130).

But while the auxiliary narrative of Patrick's illness clearly prefigures the more central story of Andy's decline and death, Andy himself works to defeat any strict parallel between his own situation and what he observes in Patrick:

> For a long time, Andy just sat there and stared at Patrick, sick with the image of a bright young man dying in such misery and wildness. It had a profound effect on Andy at that moment, and Andy felt that he had, somehow, not tried hard enough; he had conceded to the cancer too soon.
>
> And as he sat there, holding Patrick's thin, weak hand in his own, Andy decided that he would either beat this thing or go with dignity. After all, he told himself, remembering that day two months earlier, "I am to have my own death."
>
> Finally, when Patrick had slipped into sleep, Andy let go his hand, let if fall gently on the sheet, and then left. (130-31)

Andy cannot in fact fully separate himself from Patrick—he cannot "beat this thing"—but, as the novel traces the last few months of his life, it shows Andy following through on his resolve to end in a different place than did Patrick. Though Patrick's dementia is at one point explained physiologically— "[t]he worst of it struck his nervous system" (129)—the novel ultimately treats it as mainly a psychological, almost a moral, failing: Patrick has "conceded too soon," "not tried hard enough." Neither Andy nor Patrick escapes the inexorable physical decline of AIDS, but Andy, unlike Patrick, struggles to face his illness with "dignity," to "have his own death":

> It was his dignity they witnessed, the resolute and abrupt decision on his part that morning that he would face the cancer and his death with dignity, with strength. It wasn't that the fear and anxiety were gone; it was that he perceived it as solely his burden, that he would shoulder as he could. He would not end it in madness and confusion. (131)

While Patrick dies an object of homophobic ridicule—"Dr. Irving Krantz had, the day before, made some joking wager about 'how long that crazy fag in room 217 would last'" (189)—Reed shows Andy, as his death approaches, "facing it" with remarkable clarity and serenity. David returns from a trip to San Francisco, investigating the AIDS research being done there, to find that "Andy had worsened, terribly" (196):

> There had been a new and sudden proliferation of KS lesions all over his body, and the staph infection had broken out again in his groin. Andy showed the red, pustular sores and the KS lesions to David the evening he returned from San Francisco. David had looked, reluctantly; it was approaching overload. (196)

David has difficulty facing what he now "knows" will happen: "Andy would go fast now; David knew the pattern. The onset of a serious decline in the condition signaled the start of what David knew to be a death sentence for Andy, for all so far. He would have to face it, somehow" (197). Andy, however, responds with strength:

> "David!" It was Andy shouting, standing before David and yelling his name. "David? Snap out of it! Lord knows I never expected to have to be the strong one at this point . . ." He didn't finish the sentence. David looked up at his lover, so pale and thin, so dignified as he faced the severity of his illness. And David realized that he had no right to behave as he was, to draw away into his own world of selfish cares and fears.
>
> That he should be the strong one, David said to himself. That he should be the strong one . . . David was filled with a sudden strength, a vitality borrowed from Andy's dignity. What had seemed so pathetic only a moment before—Andy's ghastly gray pallor, his thinning hair,

the hideous lesions on his skin—what had seemed so pathetic now seemed the inverted symbol of Andy's strength.

He *has* stuck it out! David told himself. He's been strong and faced it at every turn, while I ran and hid in my fucking press coverage of the damned crisis. It was nothing new, really, but it was, for David, one of those rare and triumphant moments of crystal clarity, when the tragedies, as well as victories, of the world somehow fit, a moment when David saw that what had already been accomplished had been good, had been real.

He stood and held Andy close, saying nothing. It was a moment when the whole of Andy's illness became a true reality, when both of them saw together that they had weathered a storm, and, moreover, that there was more to come: they accepted Andy's illness. And they gathered their strength for what was left. (197)

The morning after this scene, Andy cannot be awakened and is rushed to the hospital (198), now suffering from *Pneumocystis* pneumonia; his imminent death is repeatedly evoked: "It doesn't look good. This is the pattern too often" (214); "he's really too weak to hold out this time" (214); "He knew that it was most likely that Andy would succumb to the pneumonia, probably that night. None of the KS patients in a similar condition had survived it yet" (214). The last paragraph of the novel depicts what all this has pointed to, following Andy to his very last moment of consciousness:

It's all so simple, so plain, Andy thought to himself. He watched David looking at him, wondered what he might be thinking. He saw David's lips moving, forming the words "I love you." That's good, Andy thought, but he couldn't answer. He was ready to open his mouth and whisper the same, but something small and magnificent deep inside him had loosened itself, was growing larger, expanding, releasing itself. Andy could hear David crying, but it didn't matter. It was done. (217)

Unwilling to intervene in the narrative of physical decline, wanting, in this early, self-proclaimed "novel of A.I.D.S.," to show the full, horrible extent of Andy's illness, Reed nonetheless interrupts narrative expectations to the extent that he maintains Andy's strength of mind and "magnificent" humanity to the very end, refusing to cast him as the abject, powerless victim seen over and over again in media representations—though, in posing Andy against the less "dignified" Patrick, Reed does include such a figure in the novel. *Facing It* depicts AIDS as inexorable illness, as entailing a clear trajectory toward death, but it struggles against what might, in such a narrative, make the person with AIDS simply a victim, a dead man who hasn't yet quite died.

3. THE GENRE OF THE AIDS NOVEL: FRUSTRATING EXPECTATIONS

Just as Patrick's disease and death adumbrate (with a difference) the pattern of Andy's illness, so that pattern suggests, to Andy's lover David, a possible future trajectory for his own life:

> There was in that moment a great selfishness, something David had denied in his focus on Andy's sickness. But now, his mind grasped the fear and made a panic of it. How the hell was he to go on, not knowing if he had AIDS or would get it? Had he somehow given the virus to Andy? Or had Andy given it to him, and now, at this very moment as his heart beat and his cheeks flushed, the virus was incubating, ticking away in his system like a time-bomb, working its devastation on him as well? Or was he now immune and thus safe? Or could he pass it to someone new? He felt a palpable terror at the sudden onset of reality, for he had only once before considered a remaining life of solitude—no one willing to take him, or he himself unwilling to risk the chance. The prospect made chaos of all he knew; in that moment his world, his entire cognitive framework turned to dust. He could nearly feel the particles of that destruction settling around him, for it seemed that there was nothing more appealing at that moment than death itself. He looked at Andy, now stirring and opening his eyes, and felt a great wave of jealousy that it was *his* turn, *his* dignity that was facing death. David wanted it then, wanted to go with Andy. (176)

The potential, anticipated reiteration of the narrative of illness begins to move *Facing It* into a larger social realm, away from the account of one illness and toward a consideration of epidemic spread (what I have called the population narrative). Along with this movement comes a kind of psychologized epidemiology, David's obsessions about who has "given" the virus to whom, and whether in fact he himself can now "pass it to someone else."

The narrative of spread, however, remains in the background of Reed's novel, expressed only on the edge of the personal narrative, suggesting only vaguely the ways in which individual illness fits into larger social patterns. In many other of the novels that have thus far been written about AIDS, the focus remains on individual health and sickness, and on the "private" emotions involved with these. While David's thoughts about the future connect him strongly to a larger community of gay men affected by AIDS, these thoughts remain couched in mainly personal terms—as private, internal fears.

Indeed, in gay men's fiction, the kind of fear that David expresses, drawn from the anxious experience of watching the epidemic grow through the early and mid-1980s, most typically provides a starting point for narratives of individual illness rather than a way to move out of the personal and into the population narrative. When, near the beginning of Larry Duplechan's *Tangled Up in Blue*, a young gay man, Crockett, speaking on the phone with a friend, "sound[s] a little down" (20) and, to another friend, seems "thinner than she remembered, his ribs just a bit more apparent than usual beneath his *Born to Run* T-shirt" (41), the narrative pattern traced out in Andy's illness immediately comes to mind (even for a reader who has not previously encountered a novel about AIDS like *Facing It*, since, as I have suggested above, such a narrative pattern is very much present outside the world of fiction—in scientific understandings of AIDS, in the mass media, in everyday conversation).[46] When Crockett responds defensively to the question "Have you lost weight?" (41) and the conversation turns quickly to AIDS, such expectations are strengthened; and when Crockett himself admits concern for his condition—worrying about his weariness ("How could I possibly be this tired?" [48]), thinking about the "slight but insistent swelling of the glands in his throat and under his arms" (56), and concluding that "[s]omething was wrong with him—he was almost sure of it" (55)—the story that is to follow seems predetermined. Indeed, the reader's fears, and Crockett's, soon gain a strong confirmation:

> He was drying his right leg with a second towel (thinking how thin his calf felt), when he first noticed the spot on his foot. Purple and ugly, like a bruise.
> He sat down hard on the toilet seat, his wet legs soaking the rug. This time the tears came. He wept into the towel he was using to dry his legs, crying aloud until his throat hurt, until there were no tears left. (57)
>
> Crockett had been reasonably sure what he was up against from the first swelling of his lymph glands. He had recognized the ugly sore on his foot on sight; he knew the story it was bound to tell. (62-63)

There is one crucial difference between Crockett's situation and Andy's: Crockett's story begins in 1985, at the time of Rock Hudson's illness (16-18, 41-44, 197-98), and the characters of the novel know as well as its readers the facts of AIDS, "the story" a discovery like Crockett's is "bound to tell":

> Gay men were dropping like flies from a disease that looked like something out of a cheap horror flick, a disease nobody could even *talk* about curing, and two of Daniel's closest friends were gay men. What kind of fool wouldn't be worried?
> A fast, ugly image splattered against Daniel's mind, like a big bug against a windshield: a picture of an AIDS victim glimpsed in some

magazine, a young man with thin blond hair, his face skeletal and disfigured with illness, a face very like Crockett's face. (19)

In much fiction about AIDS, as here, the discovery of what seems to be a Kaposi's sarcoma lesion (or some other clear "sign" of AIDS) contains within it, for the character as for the reader, the promise of a whole devastating narrative. Indeed, the complete story of discovery, diagnosis, disease, and death can be telescoped into a very brief space, as in Jameson Currier's short story "Montebello View": "Two years ago, Matt made a doctor's appointment when he noticed a bruise near his ankle. Ten months later he was dead."[47] Later in the same story, such a telescoping of narrative recurs, though now rather than summarize the past it projects the future: "In a few weeks Mrs. Moeller would find out Ethan was sick. In a year she would bury him beside her two husbands."[48]

Like Crockett's or Matt's discovery of "a bruise," Michael's bout of diarrhea (163-67) in Armistead Maupin's *Sure of You*, the final novel in the six-part *Tales of the City* series, threatens with terrible economy to transform comedy into tragedy:[49] "For a moment, perversely, Brian's imagination went berserk. He saw Michael at ninety pounds, the way Jon had been, an old man at thirty-two" (166). Later on, Michael himself—HIV-positive (as is revealed early in Maupin's previous novel, *Significant Others* [22]) but not diagnosed with AIDS—discovers a "purplish inflammation" (200) that he fears signals Kaposi's sarcoma; when a nurse practitioner tentatively confirms this self-diagnosis, he imagines himself moving further down the road he has seen others (including his lover Jon)[50] travel:

> Three years of daily fretting had left him overrehearsed for this moment, but it still seemed completely unreal. He had vowed not to rail against the universe when his time came. Too many people had died, too many he had loved, for "Why me?" to be a reasonable response. "Why not?" was more to the point.
>
> And there were lots worse things than KS. Pneumocystis, for one, which could finish you off in a matter of days. August had assured him the pentamidine would prevent that, if he did it faithfully. And KS had been known to disappear completely with the proper treatment. Unless it spread, unless it got inside you.
>
> He remembered Charlie Rubin when the lesions moved to his face, how he'd joked about the one on his nose that made him look like Pluto. They had covered him eventually, forming great purple continents. Charlie was blind by that time, of course, so at least he was spared the sight of them.

He sat on a bench and began to cry. It wasn't major grief at all, just another pit stop in the Grand Prix of HIV. He still felt fine, didn't he? He still had Thack and a home. And Brian and Shawna. And Harry. And Mrs. Madrigal, wherever she might be.

He tilted his head and let the sun dry his tears. The air smelled of new-mown grass, while what he could see of the air seemed ridiculously blue. The birds in the trees were as fat and chirpy as the ones in the cartoons. (225-26)

Even as Michael's thoughts here evoke for him a familiar narrative of decline and death—and one, as in *Facing It*, observed previously in the experience of others (here, explicitly, Charlie Rubin and, implicitly, Jon)[51]— these thoughts also show an awareness of that narrative's fictive quality (just as the world itself, in its burgeoning life, seems more a "cartoon" than "real"). Reflecting on his situation during an earlier phone conversation with his mother, Michael recognizes both his deep implication in the experience of AIDS and the unpredictable nature of that implication: "How could he ever explain to her that he had had 'it'—or it had had him—from the very moment he learned of Jon's diagnosis, over seven years earlier? Most people thought you got this thing and died. In truth, you got this thing and waited" (176). All does not lead inexorably to death, though that is in part what Michael fears; there are "pit stops" in this "Grand Prix of HIV."

Indeed, in a reversal that emphasizes the failures of a narrative that would admit only the possibility of decline, Michael returns to the doctor's office to find that what at first had seemed a clear "diagnosis" of Kaposi's sarcoma was incorrect; Michael has not "progressed" to AIDS, after all, despite what seemed the obvious signs, and he leaves the doctor's office, as after "the other false alarms he'd experienced over the years, with a noticeable spring in his step" (227). Similarly, in *Tangled Up in Blue*, Crockett's self-diagnosis, about which he at first has "no doubt" (62), turns out to be a "false alarm." A visit to the doctor shows that the spot is just a bruise (67), and Crockett must revise his earlier dire expectation: "I thought I was a goner" (67).

In their characters' discovery of the "stigmata" of Kaposi's sarcoma, which, in their very visibility, seem particularly reliable "signs" of AIDS, both Maupin and Duplechan thus evoke the narrative of AIDS as inexorable decline. Both, however, also move almost immediately to negate the "signs" of illness and thus derail expectations of a narrative whose course is predetermined by the nature of HIV illness. Already in an early novel like *Facing It*, despite its carrying through of the personal narrative to the moment of Andy's death, the need for some questioning of this narrative is recognized. The "course" of Andy's illness does not simply follow the model provided for it by Patrick's, and the story of that illness is supplemented by a whole series of (partly competing or opposed) narratives: the tracing of Andy's and David's psychological responses, which, though deeply affected by Andy's steady decline, do not simply follow or replicate it; a narrative of gay pride especially emphatic in the novel's final pages, where Andy wonders if, by some "conscious decision to be more conforming," he might have avoided AIDS, and decides that, "no, I wouldn't have chosen not to be gay" (216); Dr. Branch's fight for funding of his research on AIDS; accounts of increasing knowledge about AIDS in the realms of science (represented by Dr. Branch) and journalism (represented by David); inklings of a political response to the AIDS crisis, for instance, around the dropping of the name "GRIDS" (gay related immune deficiency syndrome) in favor of AIDS (141). None of these other narratives can stay the "progress" of Andy's illness, and certain subplots—for instance, the account of Andy's relation to his homophobic and rejecting parents—indeed work to consolidate that narrative, with Andy's mother, under pressure from her husband, turning unambiguously away from her son shortly before his death: "she realized as she nodded her head and capitulated, that she would never see Andy again" (204). Still, the novel does admit, in its narrative complexity, certain counterpressures to the account of illness, decline, and death.

Maupin and Duplechan go further, challenging the personal narrative even as they deploy it. But in both *Sure of You* and *Tangled Up in Blue*, at the same time that relief and hope are provided by narrative interventions—and particularly by the reversal of seemingly unambiguous diagnoses of AIDS—the narrative of decline and death remains present and pervasive. Waiting in the doctor's office before his self-diagnosis is contradicted, Crockett recalls his own first awareness of "GRID" and how "[h]e watched a mental line graph slope dangerously upward as the diagnosed cases increased from a handful to hundreds, to thousands" (63). Having thus reminded himself of the epidemic spread of AIDS, mentally resketching the population narrative in its graphic form, Crockett encounters more immediately two individual figures whose imagined experiences of AIDS—like those of Patrick in *Facing It* or Jon and Charlie Rubin in the Maupin novels—seem to predict the course of his own story:

> He sat across from a man who was probably about Crockett's age, but who looked lifetimes older, so thin his wrist bones stood out and the joints of his fingers looked like tiny knobs. The man was reading a magazine with Rock Hudson's face on the cover. Crockett looked from the man's impossibly thin fingers to the picture of Rock's impossibly thin face, and felt an ache in the pit of his stomach like a boxing glove with a horseshoe in it. Crockett heard his writer's voice, narrating

again: "He looked at the picture. He stared into the frightening funhouse mirror of his future." (64)

Though, when he is finally examined by the doctor, Crockett discovers that he does not have AIDS, his classic symptoms—the lymphadenopathy, persistent cold, weight loss, occasional diarrhea (66)—don't add up to nothing:

> Crockett sat up, wrapped his arms around his bent knees. "So I don't have it?"
> "Kaposi's sarcoma? Definitely not."
> "I mean AIDS."
> "Well . . ." Crockett's heart sank like lead. "Between what I can see and what you've told me, I'd say you're looking a lot like ARC. That's AIDS-related complex, which is—"
> "Thank you," Crockett said quickly, "I know what it is."
> "Well, excuse me for breathing." Dr. Walden raised one eyebrow. "In that case, Doctor, I probably don't have to tell you that ARC may never erupt into full-blown AIDS."
> "But it may." Crockett's voice was almost a whisper. The doctor nodded slowly.
> "Yes. It may." (67)

Later, as he drives home from the doctor's office, considering his situation, Crockett feels a deep ambivalence in response to the ambivalent position in which he finds himself, caught in the diagnosis of ARC somewhere between health and disease. Sexually attracted to a boy he sees from his car, "Crockett felt something bubble up inside of him, working its way up. . . . It was a real good feeling. It felt juicy and nasty. It felt like life. Crockett smiled. He didn't feel much like a dying man at the moment" (70-71). Feeling alive, refusing the conclusion that he is now somehow given over to death, Crockett nonetheless thinks of himself as though he is, despite his momentary feelings, "a dying man." As he later explains to his friend Daniel,

> I *am* sick. . . . I don't have AIDS, not full-blown AIDS anyway, not yet. This, this AIDS-related complex, it's like the preliminaries, it's like the overture, it's pre-AIDS. I don't have any of the things that'll kill you, yet, but I am infected with the virus and it's like, chipping away at my immune system. Sometimes I swear I can hear it. (77)

A moment later, however, in a contradictory movement, Crockett suggests that perhaps things are not so bleak: "Hey, who knows? This could be as bad as it gets for me. They say not everybody who gets ARC will get AIDS. Maybe I'll be lucky" (78). Such ambivalent self-descriptions recur throughout the novel:

> It's funny. . . . I feel good today. Really good. I feel like I'm in the best shape of my life. . . . It's hard to believe that . . . within a year, two years . . . I could be dead. (231)

> I'm still symptomatic of ARC. I haven't been hit by any of the big ones. . . . Some days, today for instance, I can hardly believe I'm even sick. Other days, it's a lot easier to believe. (257)

The ambiguous movement thus initiated around Crockett's (false) self-diagnosis of AIDS and (true) diagnosis of ARC—later confirmed by an antibody test, "Positive. . . . Of course" (139)—permeates the novel. Though Crockett's life has not, in any measurable way, changed in response to his diagnosis, he and his friends repeatedly imagine him as on the way to "a slow, ghastly death" (151). Crockett dreams that "[h]e is being pursued by a beast, possibly The Beast" (171). Daniel thinks of ARC as "this horror, this goddamned disease" that has "come in from out of the stage left wings, reducing Crockett's life to rubble" (130). And Daniel's dream of "a ghastly spectre of Crockett" presents the novel's fullest imagination of its protagonist's projected future:

> He was naked and emaciated, his eyes sunken, only the odd wisp of hair clinging to his flaking scalp, his face and body spotted with ugly purple sores. Daniel reached out one hand toward the waste that was his friend, while the rest of his body recoiled from the sight. He hid his eyes with his other arm, and cried out, his scream echoing back and forth off the walls of the dream. (132)

At one point, the novel in fact suggests, in the story of an acquaintance's reaction to his own AIDS diagnosis, that the imagination of a future of illness is horrible enough to move one to suicide:

> "Snookie found out he had it; decided he'd rather die all at once than . . . you know. He'd never been sick in his whole life. So he killed himself. Swallowed most of a bottle of, um"—Johnnie laughed, almost a cough—"Sominex. Sominex, for God's sake!" He looked down at the floor. "After he was out cold, his body tried to . . . eject the stuff and he, um, choked to death on his own vomit. . . ." (183)

In such a story, the association of AIDS and death is confirmed and intensified; while the diagnosis of AIDS or ARC elsewhere predicts "a slow, ghastly death," here, illness becomes unspeakable (". . . you know") and diagnosis and death collapse into almost the same moment.[52]

Crockett himself, however, keeps being pulled back from full implication in a narrative of decline and death. The ex-lover, Johnnie,[53] who narrates Snookie's suicide makes clear that he does not intend this story to be exemplary, quite the opposite—"Don't you ever try anything like that. Don't you even think it, you hear me? Just don't!" (183)—though Crockett himself, "while he had no immediate plans involving lethal overdose, . . . could certainly understand the attraction a bottle of an over-the-counter sleeping aid might hold" (184). While the novel's other characters repeatedly imagine a future of illness for Crockett, they also repeatedly check the impulse to make that his only possible future. When Daniel points out to Maggie that time is "the one thing Crockett hasn't got" and that "[w]e're talking about a guy who's *sick* here"—"He's got AIDS, remember?"—she responds with an angry corrective: "Oh, he's got ARC, mister expert. . . . Not AIDS. ARC! He may never get AIDS. He could bury us all" (235). Crockett himself objects quite directly to the tendency in others to push him toward death—"you thought, 'Oh, shit, the boy's gonna die, better make my peace'" (240); "Jesus fuck, Harold . . . I'm not dead yet" (251)—recognizing a "tone of voice" that suggests "he were some sort of bomb that could explode at any moment" (251).

The novel in addition sets up, as it approaches its end, an explicitly hopeful countermovement to the imagination of "progressive" disease and death. Even as it acknowledges that "[f]ear had come to be the overall theme of Crockett's existence" (186)—"Afraid of the seemingly inevitable breakdown of his immune system, of the ever-encroaching incapacitating illness, of a death worthy of a Stephen King novel" (186)—*Tangled Up in Blue* suggests that there might be constructive ways to respond to fear. In a moment of physical closeness with Johnnie, Crockett "manage[s] to forget just how scared he [is]" (186), and Johnnie gives Crockett a massage that he later reveals to be a "healing. Of the holistic variety" (188) and that allows Crockett to sleep well and to awaken "amazed at the clearness of his head," "unusually wide-awake," and "feeling . . . good" (187). In this scene, Johnnie points Crockett toward a new kind of care for his body:

> See, there are these energy centers at various points in the body, called chakras. Sickness, disease, illness is often the result of energy imbalances among the various chakras. What I did, after relaxing you with a good old-fashioned back rub, was basically to help clear and balance your chakras, freeing up those energy centers to assist your

body's natural healing processes. So you feel better today than you did yesterday, when your chakras were totally out of balance. (189)

Though Crockett responds to Johnnie's explanation with skepticism, he also attends to his body—"it hardly seemed coincidental that Crockett felt better than he had in weeks" (189)—and follows up on the recommendation that he seek out Theo, the woman "who brought out [Johnnie's] gift" for healing (189), a woman who, following the example of Louise Hay and "us[ing] meditations, affirmations, macrobiotic diet" (194), "healed her own breast cancer" (189). Theo herself offers Crockett a qualified promise of better health:

> [Y]ou should understand from the get-go that I'm not a medical doctor and I'm not a witch doctor. What I deal in, mostly, is the strengthening of the body's immune system through the reduction of stress, which even the medical establishment is coming to acknowledge as a factor in the strength and weakness of the immune system. Also positive affirmations, and creative visualizations, in which we attempt to change the state of the body by changing the state of mind. . . . I might also give you some nutritional advice if you want. . . . I don't claim to work miracles, and I don't claim to have a cure. But I do think I can help you help yourself. Keep you stronger. (191-92)

While Crockett here again responds skeptically, the next day he finds himself "refreshed" and able to work in an "unusually productive" way: "Just how much the previous day's visit from Theo Davis had to do with this resurgence of energy, Crockett didn't even care to conjecture—he felt good and he wasn't arguing with it" (197). Though neither the novel nor Crockett ever draws a clear conclusion about the value of Theo's "holistic" practices—"I don't know if it's helping or what, not yet. I don't even know if I believe in it myself" (204)—these do seem to make a difference in Crockett's well-being:

> There was, it seemed, something different about Crockett. Daniel couldn't put his finger on it—maybe it was his coloring, or maybe it was just Daniel's own imagination—but he could swear Crockett looked healthier. It was the only word he could think of: healthier. (203)

Later, Crockett also involves himself in a medically-sanctioned "experimental AIDS treatment" (231, 237) "supposed to stimulate the thymus and strengthen the immune system" (245). Here, too, Crockett is skeptical about the actual health benefits: "I don't even know if I'm getting the real drug or not. I might be in the control group that's getting a placebo" (245). But as the novel moves toward its close, both the drug trial and the episodes with Johnnie and Theo provide an alternative to the imagination of Crockett as deathly ill, bespeaking an attention to his body and its health clearly opposed to the idea that HIV has somehow "reduc[ed] Crockett's life to rubble" (130).

Tangled Up in Blue concludes on a decidedly upbeat note, with Crockett reconciled to his good friend Maggie, perhaps beginning a new romantic relationship, considering the possibility of renewed contact with his long estranged mother, nearing the completion of the romance novel he has been writing and ready to "get a good start on his real novel" (264). His ability to continue working represents a real psychological stride—"He'd been so afraid he might never finish it, might never be able to even make a good start on any real writing; but for now things weren't quite so grim as that" (262-63)—and Duplechan's novel significantly ends with the line, "For the moment, he had work to do" (264). Without denying the provisional, momentary nature of his "happy ending" ("for now," "for the moment"), Duplechan concludes Crockett's story at a moment in which both work and relationships are in the process of initiation or reinitiation, thus setting in motion the imagination of a life still full of possibilities, a narrative counter to the story of slow and ghastly death that haunts the novel from its first intimation of Crockett's illness.

Maupin's *Sure of You* resists the narrative of inexorable decline even more powerfully than does *Tangled Up in Blue*: Michael's false diagnosis of KS comes in the midst of a novel throughout which his HIV-positive status is known and during which his good health remains unchanged. Still, the novel is deeply concerned with the possibility of future illness, a concern evinced not only in a major episode like that of Michael's false diagnosis, but also in the depiction of the smallest, most everyday details of his life. From the first chapter on, the beeper that "[e]very four hours" (7) reminds Michael to take his AZT is a constant presence. It interrupts his and his business partner Brian's work, having become "a fixture in both their lives" (7). It interrupts sleep—"At eleven o'clock he was jolted awake by his beeper, prickly as a needle in the darkness" (32). It interrupts his getting dressed just a moment before the discovery of the "purplish inflammation" that he reads as a sign of AIDS (200). At a bar, where, "[a]s providence would have it, his beeper went off just as his Calistoga arrived," it signals to the bartender and a customer that Michael is "[a]nother bionic man" (62). It marks his relationship with friends: the little girl Shawna asks if he is "gonna make that noise [Beep, beep] tonight" (93). And in its last appearance, near the end of the novel, it helps explain Michael's new-found "stridency": when Mary Ann asks, "what's gotten into you?" the beeper goes off, "answering her question more eloquently than anything he might have said" (219-20).

Others' attitudes toward Michael—particularly their solicitude about his health—similarly serve as reminders of a certain precariousness in Michael's situation, projecting, in their worry, a future of disease and decline. This is clear in Brian's "imagination" of "Michael at ninety pounds" (166); in Mona's musings, "he could be [sick]. No, he would be. That was what they said now, wasn't it?" (153); in Michael's mother's direct question, "You haven't got it, though, have you?" to which Michael responds, "No, Mama, . . . I have the virus. I'm O.K. now, but I could get it eventually. I probably will" (176); and in Shawna's worried question, "Does Michael have AIDS now?" to which her father Brian responds, "No. . . . Michael is just HIV positive" (193). Worry and fear are also apparent in more everyday and subtle interactions, when, for instance, in a quiet, domestic moment following Michael's "false alarm" (227), his lover Thack says, "I want you to stick around, O.K.?" (230), or when the novel's reigning (unorthodox) mother figure, Anna Madrigal, inquires obliquely about Michael's health before leaving on a month's vacation—"if everything's not all right with you . . ."—only to apologize as obliquely for asking—"I know it's irrational, but it's all I've thought about ever since . . ." (47). Though she herself emphasizes to others that "[h]e wasn't sick. . . . He might have the virus, but he wasn't sick" (153), Anna's continuing worries play an important role in her own decision not to pursue a love interest in Greece (191, 242-43); in the book's final chapter, her concern about Michael's health remains strong: "How is Michael, by the way? . . . He had strep throat the last time I talked to him" (257).

Though, like Mrs. Madrigal, Michael's friend Mary Ann understands his situation quite clearly—"He's got the virus, but so far he's been fine" (38)—throughout the novel, she has trouble believing in Michael's good health. When she greets Michael and Thack by exclaiming, "You guys both look *wonderful*!" (86), a comment later reiterated more privately to Michael—"I can't get over how good you look" (87)—Michael himself feels that "[i]t was a little too gushy. Michael hated it when she overcompensated like this. What state of deterioration had she expected to find him in, anyway?" (86), and he responds to her with a simple "I feel good" (87). Later in the novel, he confronts her more directly:

> "I wish there was some way to convince you that I'm not dead yet."
> She gazed at him, blinking.
> "That's the way you've acted," he added. "Ever since I told you I was positive." (220)

The reminders of possible future illness, however, like this last encounter, tend to function ambivalently, expressing a fear of "deterioration" at the same time that they assert its absence. Even the beeper's constant interruptions, reminding Michael over and over again that all is not right with his health, are nonetheless seen as instrumental to his continued good health, reminding him to take the AZT that, in "his first six weeks" of treatment, caused "his T-cells

[to] soar to six hundred" (228). Similarly, his regular visits to the doctor for pentamidine both interrupt and enable everyday functioning: "August had assured him the pentamidine would prevent [Pneumocystis pneumonia], if he did it faithfully" (226).

Even Michael's most morbid thoughts, and his most disturbing encounters with others who are ill, do not function uncomplicatedly to prefigure a bleak or irremediable future. From the beginning of the novel, Michael is concerned with the house next door, whose owner, "a bachelor," has died, and which now stands "empty . . . with its streaky windows and cardboard boxes, the fading beefcake pinup taped to the refrigerator door": "The sight of the place always made him shiver a little, like a deserted hamster cage with the straw still in it" (25). In the midst of a harsh drought, he waters the tree fern that is "the last patch of green in sight" in the neighboring yard (24), but ultimately to no avail: "[T]he garden of his dead neighbor told the truth [about the drought], its ravaged tree fern blunt as a crucifix in the amber light of morning" (107). Even as Michael assesses the devastation of the drought, however, "[s]uddenly, a flock of parrots—forty strong, at least—landed in the fruitless fig tree . . . next door" (107-8); their "beautiful" apparition (108)—which "[y]ou can't be sure of" but which is "more special when it's a surprise. When they just swoop down out of nowhere" (257)—stands in clear contrast to the parched landscape. And the drought itself does finally come to an end: "huge flannel-gray clouds appeared over the city like dirigibles, hovering there forever, it seemed, before dumping their cargo on a grateful population. The rain came with sweet vengeance, making things clean again" (250). What might easily become an emblem of Michael's bleak future—the dried out yard, the deserted and doomed house of a dead gay neighbor ("the new owners are gonna level the place. . . . The foundation's bad" [25])—instead becomes part of a complex pattern of events in which there is both rain and drought and in which a flock of parrots can suddenly and remarkably appear.

In a similar way, Michael's encounters with people who are sick do not serve to predict a future that is without hope. Meeting a man who has "the sweet E.T.ish quality Michael had come to associate with guys who'd been sick for a long time" (62) and who reveals that he has "six T-cells" ("I'm feeling real possessive about them. . . . I may start giving them names" [63]), Michael first responds by "count[ing] his own blessings in silence": "The last time he checked, he had three hundred and ten" (63). But this encounter does not just provide Michael with a point of comparison, nor represent a more advanced version of Michael's own condition. The man's situation has itself been unpredictable: "[My mother] came out here five years ago. . . . When I got sick. . . . I guess she thought I didn't have too long, but . . . surprise, surprise" (63). He cannot serve in any easy way to predict Michael's future. When he reappears near the end of the novel, his health essentially unchanged, he indeed represents not some inevitable future state of disease but rather the active pursuit of health:

> "I was just down at the Buyer's Club."
> "The one on Church?"
> "Yeah."
> "What did you get?"
> "Dextran. Some freeze-dried herbs."
> Michael nodded. "I did Dextran for a while."
> "No good?"
> "Well, I heard your body can't absorb enough to make any difference."
> "I heard that too." The man shrugged. "Can't hurt. The Japanese take it like aspirin."
> "Yeah."
> "Have you heard about this new thing? Compound Q?"
> Michael hadn't.
> "It's been killing the virus in lab tests. Without damaging the other cells."
> "Oh, yeah?"
> "They haven't tried it on people yet, but there's a lot of . . . you know."
> "Cautious optimism."
> "Right."
> Michael nodded. "Wouldn't that be something?"
> "Yeah."
> "What is it? A chemical?"
> "That's the amazing part. It comes from the root of some Chinese cucumber."
> "No shit."
> "It's a natural thing. It's right here on earth." The man gazed out over the valley for a while, then looked back at Michael. "I try not to get too hopeful."
> "Why the hell not?"
> "I guess you're right," said the man. (251-52)

Similarly, a man "with dementia" (133) whom Michael helps near the middle of the novel serves not only to present a picture of illness and a kind of warning—"'You know,' he yelled down, 'you don't get points for this. Nobody's keeping score in heaven. If you get it, you get it'" (137)—but also to provide Michael with some valuable advice about living:

> "*It's time to get mad, Michael. Niceness doesn't count for shit!*"
> "Believe it or not," said Ramon, "he has moments when he's really clear."
> Michael had the creepy feeling that this was one of them. (138)

Ultimately, Maupin makes Michael's story the account of someone who comes to live with a strong sense of his own mortality and of future limitations, but who also makes a real life for himself, learning to "get mad" in ways that help enable that life. One story line concerns Michael's accepting his mother's concern for him at the same time that he comes to terms with his anger at her, especially for how she treated Jon: "[she] had never spoken to his first lover— not even when she knew he was dying" (27). Michael's movement here is measured by how he responds to his mother's hints that, when he dies, he be buried back in the family plot in Florida. At first, Michael lets the hints "pass without comment, knowing she meant well, the way she had years before when she'd lobbied annually for him to spend Christmas 'with the family' in Orlando. It had never even occurred to her that his family might be elsewhere" (177-78). But ultimately Michael responds in a way that is more effective and satisfying than silence. In a letter to which Maupin devotes a full chapter, Michael confronts his mother, refusing "the idea of Christian burial . . . as unnecessary and a little ghoulish" (248) and emphasizing that San Francisco is now his home and Thack the appropriate one "to make arrangements for [his] cremation" (249). In doing so, he addresses what he sees as the underlying problem in his mother's attitudes, her refusal to recognize the life and family he has in San Francisco: "This wouldn't be so important to me if I didn't believe in families just as much as you do. I have one of my own, and it means the world to me. If there are goodbyes to be said, I want them to be here, and I want Thack to be in charge" (249). Importantly, however, Michael doesn't simply assert his own wishes and reject his mother's; he has come to a point where he can see her worry about him as real concern, where he wants to connect with her (promising to "try to call more often" [249]), and where he can make certain concessions:

> If you still want to do a memorial service in Orlando (assuming you can't come here), Thack can send you part of the ashes. I think you know I'd prefer not to have a preacher involved, but do whatever makes you comfortable. Just make sure he doesn't pray for my soul or ask the Lord's forgiveness or anything like that. (249)

It is largely Thack who pushes Michael to reconsider his relationship with his mother—"You treat her like shit, Michael" (26)—and it is also Thack who enables the biggest change Michael undergoes in the course of the novel. Like the man with dementia, Thack urges Michael toward anger and toward a more political stance in the world. He repeatedly brings the political into their everyday life, suggesting that they "go to an ACT-UP meeting" (31); insisting, despite Michael's reluctance, on building a trellis in the shape of a pink triangle to "deliver a political message" (69; the trellis is a theme to which the novel often recurs—see 113, 124, 174, 253); challenging a news reporter's claim that the seventies were "a great big blank" by reminding him of "gay liberation," "marches and political action, a new literature, marching bands, choruses . . . a whole new culture" (91); confronting two homophobic teenagers on a city bus who have declared "You catch AIDS and die like a fuckin' dog" (83); making "a parlor game out of spotting the secret AIDS deaths in the obituary columns . . . draw[ing] his own conclusions and fly[ing] into a towering rage" (85)—"This is why people don't give a shit about AIDS! Because cowardly pricks like this make it seem like it's not really happening!" (85). Mary Ann feels that Thack is "forever grinding his axes in public" (97), and at first Michael seems largely to concur: "Michael . . . found his lover's anger exhausting. Now, more than ever, he needed time for the other emotions as well. So what if the world was fucked? There were ways to get around that, if you didn't make yourself a total slave to rage" (31-32). The political conflict between the two comes to a head around the figure of Russell Rand, a designer who, in Thack's words, "was famous for being gay" but who has now married and is "out selling wedding rings and singing the praises of heterosexual love": "He needs to be surrounded by fags and told what a fucking hypocrite he is" (109). Michael, attracted by Rand's celebrity, at first strongly resists this view, arguing that perhaps Rand's marriage is not hypocritical ("Maybe he really loves her" [109]) and that, after all, he and his wife Chloe are "doing an AIDS benefit in L.A." (110);[54] Michael in fact is willing to sit through Rand's defense of Nancy Reagan without saying a word (106). As Thack comments to Brian: "The trouble is he wants everyone to like him. He works at it way too hard. He's spent so much time being a good little boy that he's never figured out which people aren't worth it" (207).

Michael, however, comes to a point where he does speak up; when Rand propositions him sexually, he responds, after an initial hesitation, in a way that is uncharacteristically confrontational:

> Michael stared at the ground for a while, then said: "You're really amazing, you know."
> The designer's brow furrowed.
> "How can you live with yourself?"
> "Look, if you mean Chloe . . ."
> "No, I mean your own self-worth. What do your friends think when you start spouting that crap?"

"What crap?"

"You know. About the love of a good woman. The joys of being straight. I saw you on the *Today* show last week. I've never heard such a line of shit in my life. You're not fooling half as many people as you think."

Even in the fog, and under a pink light, Rand colored noticeably. "Look, you don't know me . . ."

"I know you're a hypocrite."

Rand took a long time to react. "You run a nursery, for Christ's sake. Nobody expects you to be straight."

"You think they expect dress designers to be?"

Rand nodded dolefully. "The world doesn't want to know. Trust me."

"Who cares?"

"I do. I have to."

"No you don't. You're just greedy. Keeping up a front while your friends drop dead."

Rand gave him a flinty glare. "I've raised more money for AIDS than you'll ever see."

"And that lets you off the hook? Entitles you to lie?"

"I think it entitles me to . . ."

"You had a chance to make a real difference, you know. You could've shown people that gay people are everywhere, that we're no different from . . ."

"Oh, get real!"

"Why not? Are you that disgusted by yourself?"

"Why should the public know about my private life?"

"We sure as hell know about Chloe, don't we?" (216-17)

Soon after, Michael also confronts Mary Ann, the one of his friends herself most implicated in the glitzy world of the Rands:

"He's a liar, Mary Ann."

"He's a public figure."

"Oh, I see. Can't have Amurrica knowing he's queer.[55] Anything but that, God knows."

"There are practical considerations," she said. "You're not being at all reasonable."

"I haven't got time for people who don't like themselves."

He peered sullenly out the window. . . . It made him sad to realize that she hadn't grasped this fundamental concept in all their years of knowing each other. If she, of all people, didn't get it, was there any hope for the serious bigots?

She turned and looked at him. "You sound so strident. It isn't very becoming."

He kept quiet. (219)

After each of these encounters comes a reminder of Michael's health status: in the latter, his beeper goes off; in the former, he "remember[s] suddenly . . . the purple spot" on his leg, which, at this point in the story, he still believes is a sign of AIDS (218). Michael's state of health, impressing on him life's urgency, pushes him to live more actively, to speak up, express his anger, learn not to waste time on "people who don't like themselves." He builds with Thack a strong relationship in which the awareness of the possible shortness of time serves not so much to limit their lives as to urge them both toward full enjoyment: "Without ever stating it, they both seemed to realize the same thing: If there was nesting to be done, it had better be done now" (24). When Brian and Thack talk about Michael, Thack expresses a strong sense of the ways in which AIDS has affected their lives—"We talk about dead guys all the time. . . . It's just the way it is" (206)—but also a strong sense of the full life he is determined to have with Michael:

> Brian asked: "Doesn't it scare you?"
> "What? Michael?"
> "Yeah."
> Thack seemed to sort something out for a moment. "Sometimes I watch him when he's playing with Harry or digging in the yard. And I think: This is it, this is the guy I've waited for all my life. Then this other voice tells me not to get used to it, that it'll only hurt more later. It's funny. You're feeling this enormous good fortune and waiting for it to be over at the same time."
> "You seem happy," Brian ventured.
> "I am."
> "Well . . . that's a lot. I envy you that."
> Thack shrugged. "All we've got is now, I guess. But that's all anybody gets. If we wasted time being scared . . ."
> "Absolutely." (207-8)

Ultimately, *Sure of You* depicts Michael as someone living and changing and not as someone given over to disease; though HIV and the future possibility of AIDS are never forgotten in the course of the novel, neither do they so constrain our expectations that all we can imagine about Michael's life is an inexorable death.

NOTES

1. For various approaches to exploring how "AIDS takes its place within the narrative systems along whose tracks events seem to glide quite naturally, whether in news reports, movie plots, or everyday explanations" (Williamson, 69-70), see Judith Williamson, "Every Virus Tells a Story," in Carter and Watney, eds., *Taking Liberties*, 69-80; Watney, "Short-Term Companions: AIDS and 'Popular' Entertainment," *Practices of Freedom*, 197-220; Paul Morrison, "End Pleasure," *GLQ* 1:1 (1993), 53-78; Julia Epstein, "AIDS, Stigma, and Narratives of Containment," *American Imago* 49:3 (1992), 293-310; Jamie Feldman, "Gallo, Montagnier, and the Debate over HIV: A Narrative Analysis," *Camera Obscura: A Journal of Feminism and Film Theory* 28 (1992), 100-33; and Mandy Merck, "A Case of AIDS," in Boffin and Gupta, eds., *Ecstatic Antibodies*, 44-53.

2. "The Long Road from HIV to AIDS," *New York Times* 17 Nov. 1991, Section 4, 1.

3. Barbara R. Jasny, "Editorial: AIDS 1993: Unanswered Questions," *Science* 260 (28 May 1993), 1219.

4. Redfield and Burke, "HIV Infection," 65-68. Also see Robert R. Redfield, D. Craig Wright, and Edmund C. Tramont, "The Walter Reed Staging Classification for HTLV-III/LAV Infection," *NEJM* 314:2 (9 Jan. 1986), 131-32.

5. John Mills and Henry Masur, "AIDS-Related Infections," *Scientific American* 263 (Aug. 1990), 52-53.

6. Jon Cohen, "How Can HIV Replication Be Controlled?" *Science* 260 (28 May 1993), 1257.

7. Elizabeth Fee and Daniel M. Fox, "Introduction: The Contemporary Historiography of AIDS," in Fee and Fox, eds., *AIDS: The Making of a Chronic Disease*, 5.

8. ACT UP/New York, The McClintock Project Working Group, *The Barbara McClintock Project to Cure AIDS* (undated); quotation from 9. On the "contradictory but stable definitions of AIDS as being at the same time curable and incurable" (xi), see John Nguyet Erni, *Unstable Frontiers: Technomedicine and the Cultural Politics of "Curing" AIDS* (Minneapolis and London: University of Minnesota Press, 1994).

9. Callen here quotes C. Everett Koop, "Surgeon General's Report on Acquired Immune Deficiency Syndrome," U.S. Department of Health and Human Services [1987], 12.

10. Michael Callen, *Surviving AIDS* (New York: HarperCollins, 1990), 19.

11. Redfield, Wright, and Tramont, "The Walter Reed Staging Classification," 132.

12. Redfield and Burke, "HIV Infection," 71. Also see Robert C. Gallo, "The AIDS Virus," *Scientific American* 256 (Jan. 1987), 47-56, esp. 55-56. For a sense of the changing and uncertain nature of widely-disseminated information on the "progression" of HIV infection to AIDS, see John Preston's "Introduction" to *Personal Dispatches: Writers Confront AIDS* (New York: St. Martin's Press, 1989), xxi-xxii. And see Stuart Marshall, "Picturing Deviancy," 32-33, for one critique of the conclusion that HIV infection inevitably leads to AIDS.

13. See, for instance, Essex and Kanki, "The Origins of the AIDS Virus." For a critical reading of such theories of origin, see Sabatier, *Blaming Others*, 35-67 (chapter 4, "Origins of AIDS: Origins of Blame"; chapter 5, "Green Monkeys and Germ Warfare").

14. VerMeulen, "The Gay Plague," 52, shows an early representation of this sort. Also see the cover of *AIDS: The State Response*, Proceedings of a Conference for the Illinois General Assembly (April 1986); the cover of *U.S. News and World Report* (12 Jan. 1987), reproduced in Treichler, "AIDS, Homophobia, and Biomedical Discourse," 41; the Winter 1989 *AIDS Quarterly with Peter Jennings* (WGBH Educational Foundation), where the volume of news reports on AIDS is plotted in parallel to, and lagging behind, the incidence of AIDS; Jonathan M. Mann, James Chin, Peter Piot, and Thomas Quinn, "The International Epidemiology of AIDS," in *The Science of AIDS*, 55;

and William L. Heyward and James W. Curran, "The Epidemiology of AIDS in the U.S.," in *The Science of AIDS*, 41 and 48.

15. Heyward and Curran, "The Epidemiology of AIDS in the U.S.," 39.

16. Anthony S. Fauci, "The Acquired Immune Deficiency Syndrome: The Ever-Broadening Clinical Spectrum," *JAMA* 249:17 (6 May 1983), 2375-76; quotation from 2375.

17. James Oleske, Anthony Minnefor, Roger Cooper, Jr., Kathleen Thomas, Antonio dela Cruz, Houman Ahdieh, Isabel Guerrero, Vijay J. Joshi, and Franklin Desposito, "Immune Deficiency Syndrome in Children," *JAMA* 249:17 (6 May 1983), 2345-49; quotation from 2348. As Patton, *Sex and Germs*, 40, points out, early epidemiological data from Africa were also wrongly interpreted as "proof that 'household contact causes AIDS.'"

18. Vertical transmission from mother to child *in utero* or upon birth is indeed the means of HIV transmission in cases like those reported by Oleske, et al., and this possibility was supported by a report published in the same issue of *JAMA*: Arye Rubinstein, Marc Sicklick, Asha Gupta, Larry Bernstein, Norman Klein, Ethan Rubinstein, Ilya Spigland, Lazar Fruchter, Nathan Litman, Haesoon Lee, and Melvin Hollander, "Acquired Immunodeficiency with Reversed T4/T6 Ratios in Infants Born to Promiscuous and Drug-Addicted Mothers," *JAMA* 249:17 (6 May 1983), 2350-56. According to Randy Shilts, however, Fauci, in writing his editorial, only had access to Oleske's paper, which favored the "household contact" hypothesis (*And the Band Played On: Politics, People, and the AIDS Epidemic* [New York: Penguin, 1988 (1987)], 300).

19. Fauci, "The Ever-Broadening Clinical Spectrum," 2375-76.

20. James Kinsella, *Covering the Plague: AIDS and the American Media* (New Brunswick and London: Rutgers University Press, 1989), 58 and 74. For more on the panicked reporting of this story, see Kinsella, 56-58, 73-74, and 106-7; and Shilts, *And the Band Played On*, 299-302. As John S. James has recently noted, in a discussion of media coverage of recent International Conferences on AIDS, a story still tends to receive "media attention because of the possibility that it could affect people who considered themselves removed from AIDS" ("Berlin Conference Overview," *AIDS Treatment News* 177 [18 June 1993], 2).

21. The paper Shilts refers to here is D. M. Auerbach, W. W. Darrow, W. W. Jaffe, and J. W. Curran, "Cluster of Cases of the Acquired Immune Deficiency Syndrome," *American Journal of Medicine* 76 (1984), 487-92.

22. Shilts, *And the Band Played On*, 438-39. On Shilts's depiction of Dugas, see, for instance, Crimp, "How to Have Promiscuity in an Epidemic," 238-46; Jeff Nunokawa, "'All the Sad Young Men': AIDS and the Work of Mourning," in Fuss, ed., *Inside/Out*, 312-13; Ellis Hanson, "Undead," in Fuss, ed., *Inside/Out*, 331-33; Watney, "Politics, People and the AIDS Epidemic: *And the Band Played On*," *Practices of Freedom*, 98-100; Morrison, "End Pleasure," 69; Williamson, "Every Virus Tells a Story," 72-73; and James Miller, "AIDS in the Novel: Getting It Straight," in Miller, ed., *Fluid Exchanges*, 257-65, esp. 258.

23. Jonathan Piel, "Foreword," in *The Science of AIDS*, vii.

24. Piel, "Foreword," vii.

25. See Treichler, "AIDS, Homophobia, and Biomedical Discourse," 59-60, citing Haraway, *Simians, Cyborgs, and Women*, 43-68 and 149-81, on the (postmodern) replacement of combat metaphors with metaphors of code and espionage in the realm of immunology.

26. We could multiply examples of scientific appeals to both personal and population narratives. For a simultaneous appeal to both, see Jasny, "Editorial," introducing a special issue of *Science* devoted to "AIDS: The Unanswered Questions." The personal narrative is especially likely to be central in case studies of people with HIV and AIDS, though here the larger narrative of decline is also often interrupted by the detailed presentation of treatments and of changes, including improvements, in the patient's

condition; see, for instance, "Case Records of the Massachusetts General Hospital: Weekly Clinicopathological Exercises: Case 46-1984," *NEJM* 311:20 (15 Nov. 1984), 1303-10; "Case Records of the Massachusetts General Hospital: Weekly Clinicopathological Exercises: Case 9-1986," *NEJM* 314:10 (6 March 1986), 629-40; "Case Records of the Massachusetts General Hospital: Weekly Clinicopathological Exercises: Case 51-1986"; and Robert R. Redfield, D. Craig Wright, William D. James, T. Stephen Jones, Charles Brown, and Donald S. Burke, "Medical Intelligence: Disseminated Vaccinia in a Military Recruit with Human Immunodeficiency Virus (HIV) Disease," *NEJM* 316:11 (12 March 1987), 673-76. For an appeal like Piel's (if one less flamboyantly metaphorical) to the population narrative, see Gallo, "The AIDS Virus," 47. In scientific treatments, the narrative of the epidemic's spread is often shown to parallel another narrative, that of scientific progress in understanding AIDS: see, Gallo, "The AIDS Virus," 47; and Lewis Thomas, "Epilogue: AIDS: An Unknown Distance Still to Go," in *The Science of AIDS*, 123-24.

27. See, for just one instance, Vincent Coppola, Richard West, and Janet Huck, "The AIDS Epidemic: The Change in Gay Life-Style," *Newsweek* 18 April 1983, 80.

28. ACT UP/New York, Treatment & Data Committee, *The Countdown 18 Months Plan*, Nov. 1990, 1. Also see such ACT UP/New York documents as *A National AIDS Treatment Research Agenda*, V International Conference on AIDS, Montreal (June 1989; revised Sept. 1989); *AIDS Research Agenda 1991*, June 1991; and *The Barbara McClintock Project to Cure AIDS*.

29. The phrase "God's magic bullet" is from Geoff Mains's novel *Gentle Warriors* (Stamford, CT: Knights Press, 1989).

30. Nunokawa, "'All the Sad Young Men,'" 313.

31. Morrison, "End Pleasure," 54 and 62.

32. Adam Mars-Jones, "Introduction: Monopolies of Loss," *Monopolies of Loss* (New York: Knopf, 1993), 2.

33. Mars-Jones, *Monopolies of Loss*, 2.

34. For other considerations of the operation of, and resistance to, such equations in works of fiction, see Clum, "'And Once I Had It All,'" and James W. Jones, "Refusing the Name: The Absence of AIDS in Recent American Gay Fiction," in Murphy and Poirier, eds., *Writing AIDS*, 225-43.

35. John D'Hondt, *The Bunny Book: A Novel for Anyone Who Believes Life & Death Are, After All, a Wonder* (San Francisco: GLB Publishers, 1991). In some ways, the obliqueness of D'Hondt's approach to Peter's illness is effective; when we do focus directly on Peter, the rareness of the moment tends to make it especially powerful. Still, the overall effect of D'Hondt's book, and its engagement with the narratives of "Bunnyland," is of a certain avoidance of illness and death.

36. Geoff Ryman, *Was* (New York: Penguin, 1993 [1992]), 347-48.

37. Ryman, *Was*, 360.

38. Robert Ferro, *Second Son* (New York: Crown, 1988). On Ferro's novel, see Jones, "Refusing the Name," 228, 233-35, 238-39; James Miller, "Dante on Fire Island: Reinventing Heaven in the AIDS Elegy," in Murphy and Poirier, eds., *Writing AIDS*, 295-97; and Miller, "AIDS in the Novel," 268-69.

39. Norman René, director, Craig Lucas, writer, *Longtime Companion*, American Playhouse for PBS, 1990. See discussion of the ending of *Longtime Companion* in Watney, "Short-Term Companions," *Practices of Freedom*, 205-13, esp. 211-12; Bert Beaty, "The Syndrome Is the System: A Political Reading of *Longtime Companion*," in Miller, ed., *Fluid Exchanges*, 111-21, esp. 119-21; Kevin J. Harty, "'All the Elements of a Good Movie': Cinematic Responses to the AIDS Pandemic," in Nelson, ed., *AIDS: The Literary Response*, 127-29; Gregory Woods, "AIDS to Remembrance: The Uses of Elegy," in Nelson, ed., *AIDS: The Literary Response*, 165; Bowen, "AIDS 101," 145; Clum, "'And Once I Had It All,'" 207-8; and Miller, "Dante on Fire Island," 297-303.

40. See Williamson, "Every Virus Tells a Story."

41. Dennis Altman, *AIDS and the New Puritanism* [= *AIDS in the Mind of America*] (London: Pluto Press, 1986), 22-23, briefly discusses the earliest fictional responses to AIDS, calling *Facing It* "the first novel centered on AIDS"; Emmanuel S. Nelson, "AIDS and the American Novel," *Journal of American Culture* 13:1 (1990), 47-53, identifies it as "the first major work of fiction in the AIDS genre" (47). See the brief essay by Reed himself, "Early AIDS Fiction," in Judith Laurence Pastore, ed., *Confronting AIDS through Literature: The Responsibilities of Representation* (Urbana and Chicago: University of Illinois Press, 1993), 91-94. In an earlier novel like Andrew Holleran's *Nights in Aruba* (New York: Plume, 1984 [1983]), there is a strong awareness of AIDS, without the novel being "centered on AIDS"; see, for instance, 120, 182, 184, 231, and 233. The same is true of Armistead Maupin's *Babycakes* (New York: Harper & Row, 1984). At least one novel concerned with illnesses in the gay community, Dorothy Bryant's *A Day in San Francisco* (Berkeley: Ata Books, 1982) predates the official "discovery" of AIDS in 1981; though published in 1982, it concerns events occurring in 1980 and does not seem aware of the category of "acquired immune deficiency" first named GRID (gay related immune deficiency) and later CAIDS (community acquired immune deficiency syndrome) and AIDS. Health concerns in the gay community significantly predated the 1981 CDC "discovery" of AIDS; see, for instance, the interview with Arthur Felson in Lon G. Nungesser, *Epidemic of Courage: Facing AIDS in America* (New York: St. Martin's Press, 1986), 3-22. Early plays like William M. Hoffman's *As Is* (New York: Vintage/Random House, 1985) and Larry Kramer's *The Normal Heart* (New York: Plume, 1985) were first produced and published in 1985, though productions of several less visible shows preceded these; see Joel Shatzky, "AIDS Enters the American Theater: *As Is* and *The Normal Heart*," in Nelson, ed., *AIDS: The Literary Response*, 131-39.

42. We first discover Andy's gayness somewhat obliquely: "'By the way,' Branch said, continuing to feel Andy's neck, 'how is David doing these days, anyway?' / 'He's fine,' Andy answered. 'A little frustrated about his career, though. . . . He keeps working at the part-time copy-editing jobs from different publishing houses, though, and he *is* turning out a fair number of free-lance features for the gay press'" (12-13).

43. Paul Reed, *Facing It: A Novel of A.I.D.S.* (San Francisco: Gay Sunshine Press, 1984); citations are given parenthetically in my text. For brief critical treatments of the novel, see Nelson, "AIDS and the American Novel," 51; and Miller, "AIDS in the Novel," 266-67. Reed is also the author of the novel *Longing* (Berkeley: Celestial Arts, 1988), a gay coming-of-age novel set in the years immediately preceding the AIDS epidemic; the knowledge of AIDS, and of the changes it will bring, haunts the book. See, for instance, 123-24, and the brief discussion in Nelson, "AIDS and the American Novel," 49. Reed has also written nonfiction dealing with AIDS: with Patti Breitman and Kim Knutson, *How to Persuade Your Lover to Use a Condom . . . And Why You Should* (Rocklin, CA: Prima Publishing, 1987); *Serenity: Support and Guidance for People with HIV, Their Families, Friends, and Caregivers*, 2nd ed. (Berkeley: Celestial Arts, 1990 [1987]); and the autobiographical *The Q Journal: A Treatment Diary* (Berkeley: Celestial Arts, 1991) and *Savage Garden: A Journal* (San Francisco: House of Lillian, 1994). Under the pseudonym Max Exander, he has also published (safer sex) erotica: *ManSex* (San Francisco: Gay Sunshine Press, 1985), *SafeStud* (Boston: Alyson, 1985), *LoveSex* (Boston: Alyson, 1986), and *Leathersex* (New York: Badboy/Masquerade Books, 1994).

44. Published by Gay Sunshine Press (San Francisco), the novel concentrates its attention on gay communities in New York City and San Francisco.

45. Reed quotes the 3 July 1981 report ("Kaposi's Sarcoma and *Pneumocystis* Pneumonia Among Homosexual Men—New York City and California," *MMWR* 30:25, 305-7), which received the first mainstream media coverage, for instance in the *New York Times* article (Lawrence K. Altman, "Rare Cancer Seen in 41 Homosexuals," 3 July 1981, A20) that is used as the starting point of the movie *Longtime Companion*. There had been an earlier brief report, "*Pneumocystis* Pneumonia—Los Angeles," *MMWR* 30:21

(5 June 1981), 250-52, that received less extensive press coverage. But see "A Pneumonia That Strikes Gay Males," *San Francisco Chronicle* 6 June 1981, 4.

46. Larry Duplechan, *Tangled Up in Blue* (New York: St. Martin's Press, 1989); citations are given parenthetically in my text. Duplechan's novel is briefly discussed by Nelson, "AIDS and the American Novel," 52. Duplechan is also the author of two earlier novels, *Eight Days a Week* (Boston: Alyson, 1985) and *Blackbird* (New York: St. Martin's Press, 1986), and one more recent novel *Captain Swing: A Love Story* (Boston: Alyson, 1993). Neither of the earlier novels deals with AIDS, and each depicts a period prior to the epidemic; as Duplechan writes, in a prefatory note to *Eight Days a Week*: "*Eight Days a Week* is a period piece. The bulk of the story is set in 1979, which, while not so very many years ago, was nonetheless a very different time. Jimmy Carter was still President; John Lennon was still alive. Dance music was called 'disco' then. And nobody had ever heard of AIDS. / *Eight Days a Week* is also a love story. The story includes vivid descriptions . . . of acts of gay love that have, in light of the current gay health crisis, been termed unsafe according to recent safe sex guidelines. It is my feeling that to impose a 1985 AIDS consciousness upon 1979 gay characters would be like writing a Civil War epic and refusing to mention slavery, because the majority of Americans no longer hold slaves. / I would, however, like it understood that we at *Eight Days a Week* neither advocate nor encourage slavery. / Neither do we advocate or encourage unsafe sex" (7). *Captain Swing*, on the other hand, postdates *Tangled Up in Blue* and reveals the ultimate fate of Crockett Miller, "whom AIDS reduced to a sixty-some-odd-pound skeleton with skin before finally finishing him off at the age of thirty-two" (43); AIDS, however, remains largely tangential to *Captain Swing*.

47. Jameson Currier, *Dancing on the Moon: Short Stories About AIDS* (New York: Viking, 1993), 78.

48. Currier, *Dancing on the Moon*, 84.

49. Armistead Maupin, *Tales of the City* (New York: Harper & Row, 1978); *More Tales of the City* (1980); *Further Tales of the City* (1982); *Babycakes* (1984); *Significant Others* (1987); and *Sure of You* (1989); citations from *Sure of You* are given parenthetically in my text. AIDS is first introduced as a concern in *Babycakes*, and continues to be important in each of the last three books. For a brief critical discussion of the depiction of AIDS in *Babycakes* and *Significant Others*, see Miller, "AIDS in the Novel," 268-69.

50. Maupin does not depict Jon's illness and death directly. *Further Tales of the City* ends with Jon alive and well, while the next novel in the series, *Babycakes*, opens with him already dead (see 15-16). Michael's response to his death is one of the central concerns of *Babycakes*, and remains important in both *Significant Others* and *Sure of You*.

51. Charlie Rubin is an important minor character in *Significant Others*, at the beginning of which he is already living with AIDS. Like Jon, he dies in the gap between two of Maupin's novels; see *Sure of You*, 22.

52. A similar movement occurs in Currier's story, "Ghosts," *Dancing on the Moon*, 147-88.

53. In Johnnie Ray Rousseau and Theo Davis, Duplechan introduces important African American characters, but racial questions remain largely peripheral to *Tangled Up in Blue*, unlike in Duplechan's other novels. Johnnie Ray Rousseau is the central figure in each of those other novels.

54. The Rands' AIDS benefit comes up repeatedly in the novel—see also 73, 97, 209, 217. Thack argues that this political work still falls under the shadow of hypocrisy— "A nice liberal married couple helping out the poor sick gay boys. Only you can be damn sure they won't be mentioning the G-word" (110)—a view which Maupin seems to support, when he shows Chloe Rand, asked "How was the benefit?" at first having difficulty remembering it at all (209).

55. Here, Michael echoes Thack's earlier words about Rand: "Can't have America knowing he's a pervert" (110).

CHAPTER 4
Gay and Other Subjects of AIDS

1. HETEROSEXUAL AIDS?

In their novels, Duplechan and Maupin move not only to frustrate the easy, straightforward progress of a narrative of decline and death but also to distance AIDS from a simple, naturalized association with gay men. Each invokes the population narrative, with its depiction of the spread of AIDS beyond strictly delimited "risk groups," as a way of challenging the notion that AIDS is "the gay plague." The population narrative, however, has a certain homophobic potential—as the Senate arguments of Helms and Chiles make clear—and its invocation, even by anti-homophobic writers, runs certain risks. While both Maupin and Duplechan, by moving to broaden the purview of AIDS to heterosexuals, partly call into question the equation "FAG = AIDS," they also partly reinscribe that equation. Even as these novels raise the possibility of "heterosexual AIDS," they, through certain contradictory impulses, reinforce the idea that gay men are somehow most firmly and genuinely bound to AIDS and its origins.

In *Tangled Up in Blue*, the gradual discovery of Crockett's illness parallels another discovery dependent on the reader's access to a familiar cultural narrative: Maggie's morning sickness, with which the novel opens, points clearly to her pregnancy (1-9, 46-48). And the narratives of illness and pregnancy do not just echo each other, but rather converge in a surprising way, with Crockett's ARC presenting a certain threat to Maggie and her fetus. Maggie is married to Daniel, who, unbeknownst to her, is Crockett's ex-lover. Here, the population narrative functions alongside the personal narrative, with the gay man Crockett presenting a (past but only recently discovered) risk of infection for the bisexual (but now heterosexually married) Daniel. With Crockett's diagnosis, a whole chain of possible viral transmissions falls into place:

> Daniel, you have to get tested, for the AIDS virus. Right away. . . . Look: you probably aren't infected; but if you *are* infected, you could be infecting Maggie every time you make love to her. Wouldn't you rather be sure? . . . If Maggie's carrying the virus, your baby could be born with it. (78-79)

As Maggie herself later imagines, just before Daniel reveals his antibody status to her: "He's got it. He's infected. I'm infected, and the baby, too. We're all going to die" (143).

This plot does much to destabilize the identification of AIDS with gay men that is made by certain of Duplechan's characters. Thus, early in the novel, as Daniel worries about Crockett's health, he observes that "[g]ay men were dropping like flies" (19); but, though he is Crockett's ex-lover, the confidently "not gay" and only reluctantly bisexual Daniel (145) refuses to extend worry to his own situation. Even when Crockett reveals that he has been diagnosed with ARC, Daniel cannot imagine himself implicated in the same realm of illness; it is up to Crockett to make explicit Daniel's risk and urge him "to get tested" (78): "It took Daniel entirely by surprise. It just hadn't occurred to him. 'Really? But that . . . it was years ago'" (79).

Duplechan's deployment of the population narrative thus successfully reveals and challenges the non-gay world's self-confidently imagined "immunity" from HIV and AIDS, breaching the protective wall that would confine the epidemic to gay men. Since the proposed source of infection for Daniel and his family is the gay relationship he had with Crockett, however, a homophobic conception of the transmission of HIV, not wholly unlike that enunciated by Helms—"Every AIDS case can be traced back to a homosexual act"[1]—is still potentially at work. Daniel responds to Crockett's revelation and the concern for Daniel's well-being that it expresses as to an act of hostility; though he does not explicitly blame Crockett for what is happening, he comes close to identifying Crockett, the gay source of "risk," as an intentional agent of violence:

> Daniel felt as if he'd been bludgeoned mercilessly with a large baseball bat, and not allowed to fall down. He felt emptied; split like a side of beef; cored like an apple. Strange, he thought, how life can be. There you sit, in the middle of a perfectly ordinary crazy workday, in the middle of a perfectly ordinary Century City restaurant with your best friend and a martini, thoughts of your newly pregnant wife at the back of your mind; when suddenly some guy in battle fatigues and an old beret storms in with a chip on his shoulder and an Uzi submachine tucked into his armpit and paints the room red; or an 8.5 Richter quake drops twenty-two floors of office building into your lap; or the Russians

decide to drop the Big One on Los Angeles and vicinity. Or maybe your friend drops the news that he's infected with the twentieth-century edition of the Black Death. And maybe, hey just maybe you are, too. And that newly pregnant wife of yours, and your unborn firstborn, to boot. Ain't life a bitch? (79-80)

Structurally at least, the gay man Crockett stands here with the Russians, the treacherous earth, and the terrorist; though he is Daniel's "best friend" and sits beside him during the imagined attacks, he also "drops the news" that, like "the Big One," threatens to destroy life as Daniel knows it.

Later in the novel, too, "anomalous" sexuality—Daniel's past flirtation with gay life—is intimately wrapped up with AIDS. The revelation that Daniel makes to Maggie—that he has been tested for HIV—is simultaneous with, almost identical to, the revelation that he has had a gay affair (143-44): if he had never "fallen" into gayness, he would never have needed the test. For Maggie, shocked by the simultaneous revelations, disease and Daniel's "bisexuality" become inextricably linked:

> Only during her lunch break . . . did Maggie allow herself to dwell on It: Daniel's confession of his affair with Crockett, the truly disturbing concept of being married to a bisexual, her sudden and unexpected confrontation with the *fact* of being married to a bisexual, and her own sloppy goulash of emotions in the face of both concept and fact—all this Maggie had already begun to think of as It. She wished she had never learned about It. She wished It didn't bother her so much. She wished she could snatch back the past twenty-four hours, along with her old happy life, a life without It.
>
> Inevitably connected to It, though separate from It, was the horrible fact of Crockett's illness. He had the *real* It. (157-58)

As AIDS becomes real and present for the "straight" characters of Duplechan's novel, they feel the strict "straightness" of their world called into question. The two "It"'s of bisexuality and "horrible" illness are "inevitably connected," reinforcing each other in their "disturbance" of an "old happy life" from which sexual "anomaly" and the threat of AIDS were excluded, if only, in Daniel's case, by an act of willful ignorance.

In Maupin, as in Duplechan, AIDS comes to pose a threat for the heterosexual nuclear family, with Brian—the only straight man among the figures who appear in all six of Maupin's novels—having possibly been exposed to HIV. This plot is developed in *Significant Others*, the novel that precedes *Sure of You* in Maupin's series. Like Duplechan, Maupin here evokes the population narrative of epidemic spread: Brian has been sexually involved with a woman named Geordie Davies, whose male lover "[i]s a junkie or something";[2] now, both she and her lover have AIDS, and she confronts Brian with this information. The chain of infection that stretches from drug-using man to Geordie and (perhaps) to Brian also potentially extends to Brian's wife Mary Ann. And though Brian and Mary Ann's daughter, Shawna, is adopted, and thus separate from this chain, Brian's own worried (and ambiguous) words suggest that, in his mind, she is also somehow at risk: "Michael, there are innocents involved here. . . . Mary Ann . . . Shawna, for Christ's sake" (68). In one important way, of course, the chain of transmission imagined here differs from that in *Tangled Up in Blue*: it is unambiguously heterosexual. There is no causal connection like that in Duplechan between a gay man's HIV infection and a straight man's possible infection; nor does Maupin here evoke "the bisexual" as transfer point between a gay realm of disease and a healthy heterosexuality. Though the plot involving Brian's fear of AIDS *is* interwoven with Michael's (gay) experience of HIV—his memories of Jon, his friendship with Charlie Rubin, his own positive antibody status and the ways in which this affects his new relationship with Thack—the account of Brian's possible exposure to HIV occurs in *Significant Others* rather than in *Sure of You*—that is, before Maupin comes to explore most fully Michael's own health situation.

In Maupin, heterosexual exposure to HIV is thus effectively delinked from an association with gayness in a way that is not true in *Tangled Up in Blue*; as a result, *Significant Others* presents a more unambiguous challenge to the identification of gayness and AIDS than does Duplechan's novel. In fact, speaking through Michael, Maupin explicitly recognizes the dangers of the homophobic construction of AIDS as gay:

> When Jon got sick, I was so angry, because nobody really gave a fuck. They pretended to be concerned, but these were just faggots dying. They were sick to begin with. I remember thinking . . . that nothing would ever happen, no one would ever care until straight people started getting it. (204)

And, again through Michael, the novel directly challenges any attempt to reify a difference between "homosexual" and "heterosexual AIDS" or "guilty" and "innocent victims":

> [Michael:] "You're gonna be all right."
> [Brian:] "I've never been so damn scared. . . ."
> "I know. I've been through this, remember?"
> "Yeah, but . . . this is different."
> "Why?"
> "Michael, there are innocents involved here."

"What?"
"Mary Ann . . . Shawna, for Christ's sake."
"Innocents, huh? Not like me. Not like Jon. Not like the fags."
"I didn't mean that."
"Well, lay off the innocent shit. It's a virus. Everybody is innocent." (68)

Still, the treatment of Brian's encounter with HIV does contain suggestions that a not perfectly "straight" sexuality is somehow integral to AIDS. The meeting in which Geordie informs Brian of her illness, and his risk, has been set up by Brian so that he can ask Geordie to "initiate" his nephew into sex: "The defloration of his nephew became Brian's pet project" (49). Though Brian's wished for participation here in a homosocial/heterosexual "traffic in women," his desire to "share" Geordie with his nephew, is not explicitly homoerotic, it does evoke a certain male-male sexual connection at the very moment when Brian himself becomes subject to the threat of HIV. Later, telling Michael that Geordie has AIDS and is "really sick," Brian focuses attention not just on the fact that he has had sex with her "[s]ix or seven times. Eight tops," but also on the particular kind of sex they had and, by implication, on its particular relation to male homosexuality: "We did anal stuff" (67). The gender ambiguity of Geordie Davies's name, as well as her status as "a true bachelor girl" (49), bolsters the homoerotic implications of her connection to Brian.

In the "[t]en non-fucking days" (74) between Brian's visit to the clinic to have his blood drawn and his return for the antibody test results, he has to decide either to tell Mary Ann what is happening or find a way not to have sex with her, and during this period, Brian's sexuality is, in several ways, brought into question. When Michael suggests that he just use "rubbers"—"Tell her you think they're a safer form of birth control"—Brian has to remind him of his own "sterility" (75), a characteristic elsewhere depicted as in conflict with heterosexuality (understood as procreative sexuality), even as it is seen finally not to stand in the way of Brian's thorough "straightness": "Sterile or not, this man was a breeder through and through" (101). In bed with Mary Ann during the period of abstinence, Brian has to claim not to be "up to" having sex (78). Finally, he decides that he can't stay in town, and he proposes a trip with Michael that will, in Michael's words, be "[j]ust you and me" (79). Brian's retreat into male homosociality places him as well in proximity with male homosexuality; not only does he travel with his gay friend, but they go to the Russian River, "our humble tribute to Fire Island" (101), with its town "too much like Castro Street" (102). The trip comes to include not just Michael but also his new acquaintance and love interest, Thack, and Brian finds himself repeatedly implicated in a gay world that is not genuinely his but into which his encounter with the possibility of HIV has insistently thrust him. Despite its more explicit use of Brian to undermine an identification of AIDS and gayness, the novel thus, in subtle, largely implicit ways, turns back toward such an identification.

On the trip, Thack at first thinks that Brian is Michael's "date," and Michael must reassure him that Brian is "just an old friend" and "straight" (93). Brian himself expresses regret to Michael that the trip hasn't turned out to be "[j]ust you and me"—"This was gonna be our time, man" (100)—and later, when Thack comments that Brian is "[h]ot," Michael finds himself feeling "jealous" of his "straight" friend (104). Though Brian's presence in this world of gay men is ultimately taken care of by connecting him to a woman, Wren Douglas, even this clearly heterosexual relation has its sexually "anomalous" implications. Wren's name, like Geordie's, is ambiguously gendered and Wren, though a sex symbol, is famous for her unconventional attractiveness; she is, in her own words, "*the World's Most Beautiful Fat Woman*" (2). Brian's first encounter with her serves only to implicate him more fully in a realm outside strict heterosexuality. When Brian reveals that he is travelling with his "buddies" and ignores Wren's seductive approach (106), an approach that she later admits is an attempt "to pick him up" (127), she perhaps concludes that he is gay: "Without actually smiling, her full mouth registered amusement at some private joke" (106). Later, Michael must reveal to her that Brian "is straight" (127). And though Brian recognizes Wren's seductiveness, because of his uncertain HIV status, he now stands in a sexual position different from any he has previously occupied; he cannot respond sexually to Wren: "There was flirtation in her tone, but he pretended not to notice. What was left of his libido had been beaten into cowering submission. He had never gone for such a long time without being horny" (106).

The changes in Brian's sexual stance are accompanied throughout by his anxious involvement with HIV—not just the fear of infection but also actual physical symptoms. When Geordie makes her revelation, Brian has been feeling "kind of funky," as though he had "the flu" (68), and he continues to feel strange after giving blood for the HIV test:

> [H]e stood stock still and tried to read his body's signals. There was a heaviness in his limbs which may or may not have been there earlier. Some of the soreness seemed localized, a dim ember of pain lodged in a corner of his gut. (75)

The night he refuses to have sex with Mary Ann, his muscles ache, he has a fever, and he experiences night sweats (78-79). Such symptoms continue at the Russian River: "The headache that had nagged him on the road had subsided somewhat, but the spot in his gut was still burning. He was hot all over, in fact, and his mouth tasted foul" (105); "Brian held up a corner of his sheet. 'Look at this,' he said. It was drenched with sweat" (109).

The feared decline into illness parallels Brian's movement into proximity with homosexuality. Thus, his second bout of night sweats occasions an especially close physical moment with Michael: "Brian lay on his stomach. Michael blotted his back with the wet sheet, then kneaded the knotty muscles above his shoulder blades. There was a moment of deceptive quiet before Brian began to sob into the cushions" (109). Inversely, the possibility of a return to good health is intimately linked with a return to heterosexuality. When Michael informs Wren that Brian "[ha]s been kind of under the weather lately," she responds by thinking, "I could cure him" (127). Brian indeed begins to move back into heterosexuality—turning to Wren for sex, comfort, and company (221)—at the same time that he returns to apparent good health, though the results of his antibody test remain unknown.[3] Wren replaces Michael as Brian's physical comforter: "When his tears surfaced, she began to rock him gently" (208).

In *Tangled Up in Blue*, Daniel finds himself in a situation strictly parallel to Brian's—awaiting the results of his antibody test, reluctant to tell his wife that he has perhaps been exposed to HIV, needing to decide what to do about sex in the interim—and he too experiences a certain challenge to his sexuality. Unlike Brian, he decides not to abstain from sex:

> [H]e could think of no way to suddenly stop making love with Maggie—or even to introduce condoms into their lovemaking, a course of action he'd also considered—without arousing his wife's suspicion, without having to lie, perhaps elaborately. The possibility that he might be infecting Maggie with AIDS every time he made love with her was beyond frightening, but Daniel did consider it a very remote possibility. Besides, he and Maggie had been making love, regularly and often, for over a year. Would another two weeks or so really make a difference? (130-31)

At first, as Daniel intends, the couple's sex life remains unchanged: "For the few days between that fateful lunch date with Crockett and the morning he was tested, Daniel and Maggie had made love at least once each evening, and it was good, as it nearly always was" (131). But on the day of his test, as the threat of HIV becomes more real and as Daniel moves into greater proximity with the gay world—the test takes place at "the clinic adjacent to the Gay Center" (141) and while there Daniel is propositioned by a male nurse—things do change:

> Then he went to the clinic in West Hollywood, and cute little nurse Andy drew blood from Daniel's arm. And that night, Daniel couldn't come.
>
> It wasn't that Daniel was impotent. Indeed, he had barely slipped his arms around Maggie's waist and hugged her close before he was hard enough to cut glass. He just couldn't come. He thrust into Maggie until his arms buckled and his abdominal muscles cramped; until Maggie had come and come and come again and finally slapped wearily at his shoulders and begged him to stop. He used his hands; then Maggie used hers. Maggie used her lips and tongue, and while it wasn't exactly her forte—it made her jaw hurt—she did give it the old college try. And he couldn't come. (131)

On succeeding nights, the problem continues and escalates—"A couple of nights later, it wasn't happening for Maggie, either. . . . The following night, Maggie had a little headache, and Daniel was tired. / The following night, he faked it" (131).

Accompanying Daniel's sexual problems is a nightmare that "began the night after his orgasms stopped" (132) and that clearly links sexual dysfunction to the danger of AIDS, a danger identified in the dream as originating with the gay Crockett and then extending to Daniel and his family:

> Daniel was moving—half running, half flying—through a long, winding, maze-like corridor with no doors. He felt worried and frightened. He was looking for Maggie. He called out her name, as loudly as he could, but the sound of his voice seemed to stop inches from his lips and then evaporate. Still he ran, searched, and called.
>
> And then the corridor stopped, and Crockett was there against the sudden wall, a ghastly spectre of Crockett. He was naked and emaciated, his eyes sunken, only the odd wisp of hair clinging to his flaking scalp, his face and body spotted with ugly purple sores. Daniel reached out one hand toward the waste that was his friend, while the rest of his body recoiled from the sight. He hid his eyes with his other arm, and cried out, his scream echoing back and forth off the walls of the dream.
>
> He turned back and Crockett was gone, and in his place was Maggie: a skeletal, spotted figure bent into a corner, barely recognizable as Daniel's wife, but doubtlessly she. In her lap lay a baby. Little more than bone, curled and twisted into itself, barely alive, spotted with purple. Daniel stretched out his arms toward the hideous figures, and suddenly saw his own hands and arms, bony and gnarled, covered with sores.

Daniel's scream came from all around him, entered his body through every pore, then flew from his mouth, and he was screaming and screaming, and he was the scream. (132)

While under the threat of HIV and AIDS, waiting for their test results, both Brian and Daniel are thus removed from their "healthy" (married) sexuality at the same time that they come into a closer relation with gay men. In an affiliated movement, HIV in each of these novels threatens the stability of the heterosexual nuclear family, and its disruptions are again often tied to gayness. Brian is separated, by his own decision to retreat with Michael, from his wife and child; while away from home, he begins to rethink his family life: "I take care of our daughter. I manage the house. . . . It's not enough. . . . It's not . . . a manhood thing with me. It just isn't enough. It used to be all I ever wanted . . . having a kid, being a husband" (223-24). This rethinking leads ultimately to his becoming Michael's business partner, a partnership posed (jokingly) in the terms of marriage (257-28, 273); though in one sense this is a conservative move, repositioning Brian in the traditional role of "breadwinner," it also represents a recognition that family roles—"having a kid, being a husband"—are not self-complete. It is, of course, a breaking out of such roles—Brian's extramarital sex with Geordie—that leads to his possible exposure to HIV; while the relationship here is heterosexual, it is noteworthy for its experimental quality ("We did anal stuff") and for its distance from the commitments of family: "Neither her lover nor his wife had intruded on their lovemaking, which was refreshingly devoid of romance. Geordie was a true bachelor girl" (49). Brian himself regards his possible exposure to HIV as an act of hostility toward Mary Ann—"Does a nice guy do this to his wife?" (207)—and later, even as his brief relationship with Wren helps bring him back into the fold of heterosexuality, it perpetuates the kind of wandering from marriage represented by the earlier involvement with Geordie.

Here, however, the damage ultimately done to marriage and family is relatively minor. Brian's return to Mary Ann, with his decision to tell her that he has been tested for HIV, even before he has received the test results, signals the repair of their marriage (see 260, 270, 273). In *Tangled Up in Blue*, on the other hand, the disruption of Daniel and Maggie's household is more far-reaching. When Maggie accidentally discovers a slip of paper indicating that Daniel has visited the AIDS clinic, and Daniel is forced to reveal both that he has been tested for HIV and that he was once involved with Crockett, their family quickly begins to disintegrate. Maggie's first impulse is to separate herself from Daniel:

Daniel watched the door close, and stared blankly at it—like the lead actor in an amateur production of Ibsen—for a length of time he could not have estimated. He suddenly felt, if not lost exactly, then at least strangely dislocated. Maggie had closed herself off from him, physically and otherwise, leaving him with a feeling of aloneness infinitely deeper than the mere absence of her company. . . . As it was, Daniel wasn't sure he had a wife anymore. (152-53)

Maggie intensifies the separation a day later, deciding that she "need[s] to get away for a while": "There was some small doubt in her mind that she could go on as Daniel Sullivan's wife: this was, in fact, her primary reason for wanting to lay a few miles of physical distance between herself and Daniel" (170). Going to her mother's house, Maggie stays away for six days (218); in a concomitant movement, Daniel draws closer to Crockett:

> Daniel held him close, stroking his back, enjoying the feeling of the sweater on Crockett, and the feeling of Crockett beneath the sweater. He had all but forgotten just how good Crockett could feel in his arms. Almost before he knew it, he was beginning to grow hard. Crockett pulled away before Daniel could, stepping back quickly, an odd smile on his face. (204)

Nor is it only Maggie and Daniel's marriage that is implicated in the plot of familial breakdown. Maggie's first angry outburst at Daniel involves her pregnancy—"If I could rip it out of me right now, I'd do it" (147)—and just when she seems ready to return to Daniel, repairing the rift in their family, that rift is intensified through her experience of a miscarriage (228-31). When husband and wife are in fact reunited, in the hospital, the reunion focuses not so much on the making whole of the family but on the acknowledgment of a loss for which Maggie feels culpable—"I lost the *baby*, Daniel. . . . I didn't mean to!" (230). In fact, in the logic of the narrative, it is not so much Maggie's angry retreat from the family that has led to the loss of her child, since that retreat itself responds to disruptions stemming from Daniel's affair with Crockett. The gay affair and the threat of HIV are both made somehow real, present, and permanent in the couple's loss of their child.

The plot of familial breakdown in *Tangled Up in Blue* is indelibly marked by the sense that somehow gay men are culpable for AIDS. Maggie's retreat from both Daniel and Crockett isolates those who, in their relationship with each other, have put her at risk. After the miscarriage, she returns to them, but does so slowly, tracing the imagined chain of HIV transmission in reverse. She moves first to reunite with Daniel, restoring the heterosexual couple. Initially, however, and for a significant amount of time, she refuses to have contact with Crockett, enacting his "isolation" as danger or threat, as gay man and person living with HIV: "I just don't want to talk to him. I don't want to see him. . . .

I don't want him in this house" (234). Though Maggie ultimately does "return" to Crockett, the distance that separates him from Daniel and Maggie is never really forgotten. While the novel does conclude with Crockett in many ways reintegrated into a social world—not just Maggie and Daniel's family, with whom he agrees to have Thanksgiving dinner (264), but also, possibly, his birth family and a new romantic relation—the novel's final scene depicts him alone. In any case, he remains the only major figure in the novel, despite the threats posed to Daniel and Maggie, living with HIV.

In fact, in neither novel does the chain of HIV transmission that threatens the heterosexual heroes and their wives prove to have operated; in each, even as, on the one hand, the plot argues that all are susceptible to HIV, on the other, it differentiates between the straight and gay man at risk. Crockett and Daniel go together to be tested, and Duplechan develops a careful parallel between the two. After both have given blood, when Crockett says, "Funny thing is: I'm ninety-nine percent sure of the outcome, and I'm still scared," Daniel responds, "Same here" (126). Ironically, however, the two men are "sure of the outcome" in diametrically opposed ways: Crockett has already been diagnosed with ARC and is taking the antibody test simply to confirm that diagnosis; for Daniel, the assumption is quite the reverse, with Crockett himself, as soon as he raises the possibility of Daniel's infection, reassuring him that he "probably [is]n't infected" (79). After the two receive their test results, the difference between them is spelled out and any parallels collapse:

> Crockett was waiting outside the door, just as Daniel had left him. "You done?" Daniel asked.
> "Uh-huh," Crockett said. He got up from his chair, and Daniel set the brisk pace as they walked through the waiting room and out the double doors. Once in the parking lot, Crockett stopped. He looked up at Daniel's smiling face and said, "Negative?"
> Daniel nodded. "Yeah. Jesus, what a relief!" He gave his whole body a vigorous shake. "You?" Crockett's face had already told him everything, but he asked anyway.
> "Positive," Crockett said. "Of course." He squinted in the bright sunlight, patted down his pockets in search of his sunglasses, which he was not carrying.
> Daniel's smile fell slightly but refused to go away. Because he wanted so much to comfort his friend, and so that Crockett wouldn't see him smiling, Daniel took Crockett by the shoulders and pulled him into a hug. "Jesus, Crockett," he said. "I'm sorry."
> Crockett said, "Yeah, me too," into the front of Daniel's polo shirt. (139)

In *Significant Others*, the movement toward Brian's negative test result is similar. Michael, known to be HIV-positive from the beginning of the novel, repeatedly invokes his own experiences as providing a potential model for Brian, and Brian as insistently resists the parallel:

> Michael gave him a dim smile. "Sooner or later, it's a question of how you want to spend your time."
> "I'm sorry," said Brian. "That's too pat."
> Michael regarded him for a moment, then said: "My mother gave me a new address book last Christmas. I haven't written in it yet, because I can't make myself leave out the people who are dead. I can't even cross out their names."
> Brian nodded.
> "How pat is that? There's one on every page. All of the *H*'s are gone, except you."
> It felt a lot like a punch in the gut. "Thanks for telling me," he said.
> "Oh, right," said Michael, rolling his eyes impatiently. "Homosexuals, Haitians, hemophiliacs and people whose name begins with H."
> "Look, if you're gonna . . ."
> "It's O.K. to be afraid, Brian."
> "I know that."
> "It's also exhausting, and I'm tired of it. So I don't do it anymore. It's probably that way with your friend. There's nothing particularly noble about it. It just happens."
> "So that's it, huh? Just don't be afraid. That's your advice."
> "You can do what you want to do," said Michael. (256-57)

When Michael directly reminds Brian that "I've been through this," Brian responds, "Yeah, but . . . this is different" (68), and even as Michael explicitly objects to Brian's suggestion of "difference," Michael himself participates in a certain confirmation of difference, reassuring Brian that "it's not that easy for a woman to give it to a man" (67) and insisting that "[y]ou're gonna be all right" (68):

> "You're gonna be all right. I know it. You're feeling guilty right now and that makes it worse."
> "Maybe."
> "That's most of it, Brian. I can tell."
> "What about . . . you know, the night sweats?"
> "It only happened once," said Michael.
> "Twice."
> "O.K., twice. Your mind can cook up all sorts of ugly stuff."

"You think my mind did that?"
"It could have."
"I dunno."
"Your headaches are gone, aren't they? Your sluggishness."
They were, he had to admit.
"You're not gonna die," said Michael. "Somebody's gotta take care of me."
"Hey." Brian looked across at him. "Shut the fuck up."
"O.K., O.K. . . . So nobody's gonna die." (257)

The ultimate instantiation of difference, of course, occurs with the findings of Brian's antibody test—"[i]t came back negative" (273). Ultimately, though each novel brings its straight characters into a certain proximity with HIV, Maggie and Daniel, Brian and Mary Ann stand beyond its reach; in the two novels, "heterosexual AIDS" is represented directly only in the minor figures of Geordie and her lover. Threatened by HIV, the major heterosexual characters of these novels nonetheless remain immune to its effects. And the marital and familial structures of heterosexuality, though deformed momentarily by "queer" pressures that the novels associate with HIV, are at last fully recuperated, perhaps even strengthened by having been tested against the sexually "anomalous" and the "unhealthy." While the move toward broadening the cast of characters susceptible to HIV so that it is not exclusively composed of gay men does work in part to undermine the homophobic imagination of AIDS as "the gay plague," each novel ultimately shifts its focus back to the gay man with HIV as the center of the plot of illness. Crockett, readmitted to Daniel's and Maggie's lives and family, still remains isolated from them in his experience of illness. Geordie's illness is explored to some extent in *Significant Others*, but by the time we get to the final novel in Maupin's series, *Sure of You*, Michael and the plot of AIDS in the gay community have returned to the forefront. The flirtation between heterosexuality and HIV in these novels leaves the heterosexual finally reconfirmed in its health, still standing largely opposed to the "queer"—both queer sexuality and the realm of illness so closely associated with it.

2. "INNOCENT VICTIMS"/*AT RISK*

The move to reiterate the definition of AIDS as somehow "homosexual" tends to characterize even works whose explicit agenda would challenge that definition. Thus, for instance, while the made-for-television movie *Roommates* (1994) is clearly intended to posit a certain equivalence between a gay and straight man living as roommates in a group home for people with AIDS,[4] it differentiates the two in a variety of revealing ways. Each is ill, but not similarly so. The gay man, played by Eric Stoltz, comes from a privileged, upper-class family, is physically small and delicate in his sensibility, and suffers a generalized debility in the aftermath of *Pneumocystis* pneumonia. His roommate, on the other hand, played by Randy Quaid, is a physically-powerful man from a tough, working-class background; he is diagnosed with brain tumors that cause intense headaches and lead him not into a weakened state but into behavior that is erratic, self-destructive, and (at least in the perceptions of most of those around him) threatening and violent. In the course of the movie, both men end up in the hospital, but for very different reasons: the straight man steals a car and crashes it, while the gay man suffers a recurrence of *Pneumocystis*. One hospital stay thus has no direct relation to HIV infection, while the other has everything to do with it. At the end of the movie, indeed, the gay man with AIDS has died, while his straight counterpart, recovered from the accident, lives on with little apparent change: his continued life is emblematized, in the movie's final scene, by his taking on of a new (gay) roommate.

Such a plot, despite its good intentions, operates in many ways to reconfirm a homophobic construction of AIDS: the gay man is the "real" AIDS "victim" here, his straight friend—in his physical vigor, his coarseness, his continued life—failing quite to fit the "victim" stereotype. Such an atypical depiction of a person with AIDS might indeed have provided a real challenge to that stereotype were it not that the depiction depends so strongly upon, and so strongly reinforces by contrast, the image of "gay AIDS" as debility.

Homophobia need not, of course, be the sole root of reassertions of a close association between AIDS and gayness. Thus, the (non)depiction of "heterosexual AIDS" in writers like Duplechan and Maupin, while it does participate in broader homophobic constructions of AIDS as gay, also reflects a deep ambivalence among many gay men concerning our relationship to AIDS. While an organization like Gay Men's Health Crisis has changed with the demographics of HIV and AIDS to respond to the needs of non-gay and gay people alike, it has maintained its name—as a sign of its history and of the deep and continued involvement of gay men in the AIDS crisis. While Maupin and Duplechan do move to emphasize that it is not only gay men who should be concerned with HIV and AIDS, they themselves are most engaged with depicting certain real and common gay experiences of the 1980s—gay men getting sick and dying, gay men caring for each other, gay men fearing for ourselves. Even as the identification of gayness with AIDS is recognized as wrong and dangerous, we gay men feel a need to claim AIDS as ours, our own intense experience, not to be given over to some abstract concern for "everyone" that might erase our real presence, that might allow for a willful forgetting of gay communities. After all, in the history of American representations of AIDS, the move to show that AIDS affects "everyone" has often involved the elision of sexual, racial, and class differences, and the ignoring of "marginal" populations—including intravenous drug users, the homeless, and prisoners.[5] While the most common media image of the horrors or dangers of AIDS remains the ailing "homosexual body,"[6] the media largely avoid images of gay men when the aim is to reach a presumed "general population" with the message that it too is "at risk." Lurking here, of course, is the distinction between "innocent" and "guilty victims," and part of gay writers' reluctance to depict AIDS as reaching beyond the boundaries of the gay community may arise from a sense that the depiction of so-called "average Americans" with HIV and AIDS has too often manifested an impulse to ignore gay men's lives and, worse, to distinguish such lives from those of the "innocent."

The history of such depictions necessarily informs the reception of fiction about AIDS, and it contributed, as David Leavitt suggests, to a real nervousness among at least some gay readers concerning the publication of Alice Hoffman's *At Risk*,[7] one of the earliest novels about AIDS to be presented by a major American publishing house and perhaps the only such novel yet marketed with full energy:

> Every A[merican] B[ooksellers] A[ssociation convention] has its "big books," and that year [1988], one of the biggest was a novel called "At Risk" by Alice Hoffman. . . . I was just one of many gay men at the A.B.A. that year, and looking back, I think we were all a little frightened by the brouhaha about "At Risk"—the huge pyramids of glossy readers' copies, the enormous advertising budget, the "six-figure paperback floor."[8]

"The story of an American family, as ordinary and as special as your own,"[9] *At Risk* depicts Amanda Farrell, "an eleven-year-old who contracts a disease that no one ever thought would touch the small New England town where her family lives, a disease that throws her parents and brother, their friends and neighbors into a terrible struggle to come to terms with it."[10] Such a story has the potential to mobilize not just "sympathy" for people with AIDS but also a homophobic and scapegoating sympathy like that expressed by Chiles on the floor of the Senate—"If there is ever the innocent of the innocent it is these children that are affected."[11] As Leavitt remembers his own reaction upon the appearance of Hoffman's novel:

> [W]e sensed, in some deep way, that this was going to be bad for us. After all, "At Risk" was the story of a child, one of the so-called innocent victims of AIDS whose stories—because they escape our society's prejudices against gay men and drug users—are deemed more palatable to a "general" audience. What made me nervous was the implication, inherent in the phrase "innocent victim," that the majority

of people with AIDS are "guilty" victims, who had brought the disease on themselves by engaging in homosexual sex or shooting drugs. Wasn't it those people, after all, who had donated the tainted blood in the first place? Weren't they on some level responsible for the plight of the child, the children?[12]

The central premise of Hoffman's novel—Amanda's transfusion-related AIDS—might, of course, be taken in other directions than that envisioned here by Leavitt. Rather than use the mode of her character's HIV transmission to distinguish an "innocent victim" from the "guilty," Hoffman might, by depicting AIDS in a preadolescent girl, challenge the reflexive identification of AIDS with gay men. The novel might work to emphasize that "AIDS can happen to anyone," that we are "all innocent" in the face of illness.

At least in its explicit agenda, *At Risk* is in fact careful to avoid the invidious distinction between guilty and innocent that Leavitt fears. The novel takes on questions of culpability and blame directly, with one of its central concerns being the stigmatizing behavior of the community that surrounds Amanda and her family. A group calling itself the Community Action Coalition forms to try to keep Amanda out of school, "distribut[ing] fliers warning parents of the consequences of having an AIDS patient in a public elementary school" (95/112);[13] Amanda's brother Charlie is no longer allowed to play with his best friend Sevrin, and Sevrin's parents transfer him to a new school; children are afraid to use the school bathroom—"Do you think she sat on one of the toilets? I'll never, ever use them again" (123/149); her orthodontist refuses to remove Amanda's braces; and Amanda is prevented from competing on the gymnastics team "[b]ecause the parents of one of her teammates have a credible medical report that allows that there is a slight chance of infection to her teammates if her blisters bleed while she's on the uneven parallel bars and another girl with open blisters immediately follows her onto that piece of equipment" (147/182). Amanda thus becomes the focal point for strong communal fear and anger:

> The school board members ask Ed Reardon [Amanda's doctor] what will happen if Amanda cuts herself and bleeds on another child; they want to know if her saliva is dangerous. Not one of them is really listening when Ed explains that siblings of children with AIDS have shared toothbrushes and not come down with the virus. They don't hear him when he insists their children are more likely to be run down by a truck in their own backyard than to contract AIDS from Amanda. Now Polly [Amanda's mother] knows why she, Ivan [Amanda's father], and Ed Reardon have all chosen to sit together on one side of the table. The accused. (92/108-9)

Hoffman's novel does depict the social formation of categories of "guilt" and "innocence" around AIDS, but Amanda and her family, despite her "innocent" exposure to HIV, are placed firmly on the side of "the accused." Here, the novel does not position Amanda, as Leavitt fears, against those exposed to HIV through drug use or sex.

Under the pressure of Amanda's illness and the surrounding community's scapegoating, the Farrell family itself internalizes the process of stigmatization and develops its own economy of blame. Charlie several times expresses anger toward his sister for how her situation has affected him: "Something inside him is exploding with little pops of fury. He'd like to strangle Amanda. He knows this is all her fault. She's the reason why everyone was staring at him, and he didn't even do anything; she's the sick one" (132/160; also see 131/159). Charlie also, however, feels guilt over Amanda's illness; he "wonder[s] if there's been some mistake"—"Maybe it should have happened to him" (70/79). In fact, in a movement that clearly echoes the broader community impulse toward "accusation," each member of the family in part blames her- or himself. Polly feels that "someone, something, must be to blame" (61/69) and she and Ivan "both have this horrible feeling of culpability, as if there must have been something they could have done to prevent this, if only they'd been better parents" (56/62): "[I]n spite of herself, Polly feels as if she is guilty of something, as if she somehow let her daughter get sick" (91/107). What might be expressed as anger toward the outside world is instead turned inward. Though "Polly hates her neighbors" for their treatment of Amanda, "it's herself she blames" (190/241):

> She's guilty even in her dreams. . . . It's as if the idea of a plague can unlock a terrible, deep panic that no one can stop, not with hard facts or with dreams. More than ever, Polly is convinced that she did not protect her baby, she could not stop this from happening to her little girl. (190-91/241-42)

And as Polly comes to recognize, her own emotional reactions are not so distinct from those of her panicked neighbors. Though she has a dream in which she cares for a woman no one else will touch, she also sees herself recoiling from the woman's kiss: "She knew that the minute everyone's back was turned, she would find some running water, the hotter the better, and wash away that kiss" (191/242). When Charlie exhibits symptoms similar to those that first signaled Amanda's illness, Polly panics, like the townspeople making her daughter into a dangerous source of infection: "He's got it. . . . He got it from her" (176/222). Amanda, too, participates in self-accusation. Having been mistreated by "[t]wo girls [she] sincerely hates" (122/148), recognizing that they "hate her," Amanda nonetheless cannot "blame them": "she hates herself too, not all of her, just this thing that's inside her" (123/149). The impulse here to identify the "thing that's inside her" with "herself" replicates the communal move to construct Amanda as a threat, an agent of disease.

Through all of this, Hoffman makes it clear that the impulse to find someone to blame, while psychologically real, is "irrational" (93/110); it leads people to ignore well-attested facts, drives them to "protect" themselves in ways that offer no actual "protection." One major movement in *At Risk* thus shows the person with AIDS—and in this case, one of Senator Chiles's "innocent of the innocent"[14]—scapegoated, stigmatized, conceived of as guilty and threatening, a "risk" for others.

Still, there are moments in the novel when Amanda is in fact thought of as somehow more "innocent" than other people with AIDS, when the "responsibility" for her illness is projected away from her and onto the others who have supposedly "given" her HIV. This occurs mainly in Ivan's thinking. Ed Reardon chooses to reveal Amanda's diagnosis to "Ivan alone, without Polly," believing that "a scientist could better accept the random path of a virus" (52/56). But though Ivan does immediately focus attention on the "path" of viral transmission, he does so with no sense of its randomness, with no "accept[ance of] the indiscriminate order of cruelty" (53/56):

> It crosses his mind that he should kill Ed Reardon. Ed is the one who diagnosed Amanda's appendicitis. There was unexpected bleeding during her surgery; Ivan remembers being told she needed a transfusion. That was when she was given the contaminated blood. (54/57-58)

Ivan imagines the chain of infection as fully as he can in an attempt to specify, and (were it possible) punish, whoever "caused" Amanda's illness:

> He has already told Polly that, as far as he's concerned, Amanda's been murdered. He is looking for suspects; if he could ever find out who donated the blood Amanda got, he would break that person's neck, he would listen to the bones snap. He'll never find that person, but from the way he was acting, it appeared that Ed Reardon was the next best thing. (58/65)

It is here that the novel moves closest to the distinction of "guilty" and "innocent" people with AIDS that Leavitt expresses as his main fear about *At Risk*. Though Ivan never specifies whom he imagines as the probable "suspects" in Amanda's "murder," readers most likely fill in this gap with familiar images of "guilty victims"—those "who had brought the disease on themselves by engaging in homosexual sex or shooting drugs. . . . [those] who had donated the tainted blood in the first place."[15]

Ivan's sketchy, and angry, evocation of "others" with AIDS, however, does not stand unqualified in Hoffman's novel. A gay (or bisexual) man and intravenous drug user living with AIDS is also introduced explicitly into *At Risk*; significantly, he stands in particularly close relation to Ivan and participates in a countermovement to Ivan's angry search for "suspects." Obsessed with Amanda's illness—"all he can think about is blood and bones and antibodies" (99/116)—but unable to talk with those around him, Ivan calls "an AIDS hotline in Boston, sponsored by a gay organization Ivan's never heard of" and begins to speak regularly with "a man named Brian, who staffs the phone two nights a week" (100/118). Brian is a decidedly minor character in Hoffman's novel—he only makes one bodily appearance; the rest of the time, he is a voice on the phone—but he plays an important role in the novel's development of ideas about AIDS.

All the family members in *At Risk* respond to Amanda's illness with a certain moving out of the nuclear family. Amanda dedicates herself all the more forcefully to gymnastics and develops a friendship with the psychic Laurel Smith, to whom she can speak as she can't with her mother. Charlie, in many ways ignored by his parents in their concern for his sister, withdraws into an internal world of scientific fantasy, becoming a dinosaur in a striking series of dreams. Polly puts all her trust in Ed Reardon—"She believes him. That is why Ed Reardon feels married to her" (156/195)—and the two almost become romantically involved. And Ivan's attachment to Brian participates in the same movement out of a family in perpetual tension:

> [Amanda's] words fall across the table like splinters of glass. They should be eating chocolate cake, instead they are bleeding from their souls. Ivan closes his eyes and immediately wishes he could talk to Brian; the thought startles him and then he thinks, Of course. He wants to telephone a hotline and speak to a stranger because there is no one he can talk to in this house anymore, there aren't even words to use. (116/140-41)

The breakdown of the nuclear family in such scenes participates in the novel's broader depiction of a disintegration of social bonds in the wake of Amanda's illness: Polly moves toward adultery; many of Ivan's most intense emotions become focused on a gay man. AIDS leads not only to the isolation of the Farrell family from its community but to deep stress within the family itself, and AIDS is thus confirmed as a force deeply disruptive to the "normal." But the familial strains here do not simply participate in a disintegrative process: each member of the family (except perhaps Charlie) finds support in unaccustomed *social* relations—Amanda from her "mean" gymnastics coach (106/127) and from the marginal, asocial figure of Laurel Smith; Polly from

Ed Reardon; Ivan from a gay organization's hotline and from Brian. Even as the need for support from outside the family calls attention to the deficiencies of the "normal," new social bonds resist the communal push toward ostracism and stigmatization. When Amanda's orthodontist refuses to see "patients with AIDS" (194/245), and when Polly is unable to find someone to take his place (196/247), Brian needs only a few minutes to find a willing replacement through his connections at the hotline (196-97/248-49).

Brian thus participates in an *ad hoc* social network that forms around the Farrells and that helps connect them to an organized system of AIDS services and information. Through Brian, Ivan involves himself in Amanda's care in ways otherwise not possible. He imitates for Amanda the "sweet mixture of spring water and honey and liquid protein" that Brian himself drinks (187/237; see 139/170). Ivan consults Brian on "Amanda's vitamin therapy" (141/172), and calls him "to ask . . . more about interferon, a drug Brian used to go to Mexico for when he was in California" (135-36/166). Ivan's whole approach to Amanda's illness is deeply influenced by Brian; moving away from "his faith in science, in medicine, in tested and proven remedies," Ivan comes to focus instead on "alternative therapies," prescribing "a strict regimen of folic acid and vitamin C" and a "high-fiber diet" (102/122).

The only one of Hoffman's characters other than Amanda to have AIDS, Brian is overdetermined as a representative of all the most common modes of HIV transmission:

> In the beginning he made charts and lists, he was obsessed with figuring out how he got AIDS, he has been in love only with men, but he has slept with both men and women, and years ago he shot cocaine all through a tour of the South without ever thinking twice when he shared someone's needle. (138/169)

Where Amanda's exposure to HIV can only have occurred in one way, and in a situation over which she has no control and in which she remains completely passive, Brian's "risk factors" are multiple and all somehow "intentional," dependent upon his own decisions and behaviors. Still, rather than present the novel (and Ivan) with a "suspect" in Amanda's "murder," Brian does quite the opposite, becoming part of the team that supports Amanda's continued life. Despite his own poor health, he is perhaps the only character in the novel to suggest that Amanda might have some real future ahead of her: "Kids are funny. . . . They can be stronger than we are. Don't give up on her. . . . Don't listen to doctors. They told me I'd be dead months ago" (142/173).

Brian replaces Ivan's imagination of a shadowy murderous blood donor with a reassuringly familiar "human voice" (100/118):

The odd thing is, he doesn't even sound like a stranger, and maybe that's why it gets easier and easier for Ivan to call him, so that by the following week Ivan doesn't have to look for the paper with the hotline number.

He knows it by heart. (100/118)

The "other" with AIDS, perceived, in Ivan's first response to Amanda's diagnosis, as an outside threat, becomes, in Brian, not only human and approachable but helpful and nurturing. In turn, where Ivan's imaginative move outward toward people with AIDS other than Amanda is initially suspicious and angry, his actual encounters with Brian push in an opposite direction, turning a vengeful, murderous impulse around into intense and gentle attachment. From the first phone call to the hotline, Brian gives Ivan the opportunity to express emotions he can't otherwise:

Ivan's throat is so tight that what comes out doesn't sound like any recognizable language. But the voice on the other end of the line keeps talking, telling Ivan it's all right, he doesn't have to say anything right away, he can just go on crying. (100/118)

When Brian has "a recurrence of pneumocystis" (136/166) and can no longer work at the hotline, Ivan goes to visit him, bringing him flowers (137/167). And several times Ivan's feelings toward Brian are explicitly compared to the tenderness he feels for his own children:

Ivan begins to talk about the stars. He tells Brian the stories he used to tell the children, stories of mythical heroes plucked from death and set into the sky. (141/172)

For an instant, when he looks at Charlie, Ivan imagines he's seeing Brian. They both sit hunched over, they're both so young. (168/211)

Though Hoffman provides herself with the perfect set-up for distinguishing a "guilty" Brian from an "innocent" Amanda, she refuses to follow through with that distinction, and indeed shows Ivan, the one character who tries to identify Amanda's illness as a "murder," turning fully away from his initial accusatory stance. Further, Hoffman subtly ties Brian and Amanda to each other from the outset of the novel, with Brian making his first appearance in relation to Amanda (not Ivan), just when the seriousness of her illness is about to become clear: "Both she [Amanda's friend Jessie] and Amanda are in love with some singer in a rock group, whom they refer to by his first name, Brian, as though they were on intimate terms with him" (29/24). While Brian, a public figure, is forced by the stigma of his illness into privacy—"He keeps [a collection of songs he's written in the past few months] in a folder; no one will ever hear them" (137-38/168)—and stigma operates in reverse for Amanda, thrusting her from obscurity into the spotlight, Hoffman shows the two, in the deep disturbance of their accustomed lives, sharing similar experiences. Brian, like Amanda, suffers the consequences of others' ignorance and fear. When Reggie, a member of his former band, comes to visit, he is "so uncomfortable that Brian [is] doubly glad he hasn't told his family in New Hampshire": "Reggie didn't touch anything in the apartment; he had a blank, startled look on his face, and Brian realized Reggie had never seen the welts of Kaposi's sarcoma on his face before" (138-39/169). Without Brian, the band has fallen on hard times, and Reggie explicitly blames Brian and his illness for their difficulties: "'Man,' Reggie said without ever facing Brian again. 'Why did you do this to us?'" (139/170).

At Risk—through its depiction of both the pressures of scapegoating and ostracism and the ways in which communities resist those pressures—successfully challenges certain phobic responses to AIDS. As Pastore suggests in her reading of the novel, *At Risk* "creates enough compassion to make people angry about AIDS prejudice generally,"[16] and the novel's "compassion" extends not only to "the known" (Amanda) but to "the 'Other'" (Brian): it thus allows "the dominant middle class" to "know the realities of AIDS so that they can cultivate empathy and compassion instead of fearing the leprous 'Other.'"[17] But in reading *At Risk*, one must wonder whether the evocation of "empathy and compassion" is a sufficient intervention against hostile understandings of people with AIDS. Hoffman's novel is deeply sympathetic to Amanda and her family, as also to Brian; in extending this sympathy to all with AIDS, not just to the "innocent" child, Hoffman clearly avoids the kind of pitfall identified by Leavitt. But the novel's emphatic and repeated moves into *pathos* and sympathy do leave unquestioned certain ideas about AIDS and people with AIDS that are part and parcel of the phobic, stigmatizing processes that the novel depicts and disapproves. That is, while *At Risk* critiques the attacks made against Amanda and Brian, in its own depiction of AIDS and people with AIDS—indeed, in some of its most affecting and sympathetic passages—it replicates important features of those constructions of AIDS that underpin the deployment of social stigma.

Making an eleven-year-old girl the center of *At Risk*—decoupling AIDS from its familiar "risk groups"—provides Hoffman the opportunity to intervene in, or even to deconstruct, the personal narrative of decline and death that, as we have seen, dominates cultural (including fictional) representations of AIDS. If it were, for instance, a gay man experiencing the symptoms Amanda has early in the novel—as in Reed, Maupin, and Duplechan—readers could quickly and easily construct a whole narrative of fatal illness—even if, as in Maupin and Duplechan, their readerly expectations were ultimately frustrated. But given who we know Amanda to be at the beginning of the novel—with no indications of "risk factors" and no suggestion of a possible route of HIV transmission until the very moment of diagnosis, when Ed Reardon recalls her "worrisome appendectomy" (50/53)—Amanda's experience of a lingering "summer cold" (13/5), sore throat (13/5, 39/39), fever (13/5, 38/38), night sweats (23/17), vomiting (29/25), chills (30/26, 39/39), swollen joints (30/26) and lymph nodes (40/41), weight loss (40/41), and "disturbingly low white blood count" (49/51) will not so easily lead readers to construct that same narrative. In the novel itself, Ed Reardon is the first to recognize the seriousness of Amanda's condition, but "the first thing he thinks of . . . is cancer" (41/41), not AIDS. It is only when lab results indicate "[a]n organism called cryptosporidium," "an opportunistic disease," "in Amanda's stool sample" (50/52) that the thought of AIDS and its attendant narratives enters the novel: "[Ed] feels dizzy even before he's told that Amanda Farrell, whom he has seen through chicken pox, ear infections, and inoculations, as well as a broken arm and a worrisome appendectomy, has tested positive for AIDS" (50/52-53).

But while Amanda's status outside any "risk group" thus allows the reader to experience her first symptoms without thought of AIDS, Hoffman uses the delay in specifying Amanda's illness not to mitigate but to strengthen the narrative of inexorable decline and thus to intensify the sympathetic possibilities in the situation of an eleven-year-old girl "given over" to death. In the novel's first three chapters, while the nature of Amanda's illness remains uncertain, Hoffman projects a strong sense of the future, of her characters' hopes and expectations, of their implication in a variety of life-narratives; at the same time, she suggests, ominously, the interruption of those narratives and even an impending death.

The novel begins with an evocation of the season—late summer—and a strong sense of the changes, the decline toward winter, that the season holds in store: "Already, the sparrows in the chestnut tree are restless. They're not fooled by the pure yellow light any more than they're fooled by this last burst of August heat" (11/3). The Keatsian awareness that the fullness of the season contains the seeds of its own decline, which participates in a theme of seasonal change pursued throughout the novel,[18] occurs alongside an explicit appeal to the future: "By dusk there will be a storm, with raindrops that are surprisingly cold, but of course by then the birds in the backyards and out on the marsh will have taken flight" (11/3). Hoffman returns to this opening at the end of the first chapter,[19] reinvoking the novel's prediction of "a storm" now in direct connection to Amanda's illness:

> "You'll be better in the morning," Polly says.
> It's what she always says when the children are sick, and they always believe her. But this time Polly is wrong. Just after dusk the rain will begin, but it won't bring any relief. In the morning, the last day of August and the hottest on record, Amanda will still be shivering beneath two cotton quilts. (30/26)

With the future tense constructions that thus frame the novel's opening chapter,[20] Hoffman puts simultaneously into play a sense of narrative inevitability—the change of seasons, the storm that *will* come—and a sense that such inevitable events necessarily override other narrative expectations, no matter how habitual or seemingly certain these may be ("It's what she always says").

Future tense constructions in the novel's opening chapters in fact reveal a whole tissue of expectations and hopes, from the most trivial to the most grand:

> By the time Amanda is fourteen, Polly will be lucky if her daughter speaks to her, never mind listens to her. . . . Sooner or later, she'll have to hate her mother, and all Polly can hope for is that this break will be temporary, that it won't cause any permanent damage. (16-17/9-10)

> Polly has decided, they will definitely have fried clams tonight. (28/23)

> [Amanda] can't wait for school to start; she's been looking forward to sixth grade all summer. With Helen Cross graduated and Evelyn Crowley getting sloppy, Amanda will be the best gymnast on the team. (39-40/40)

Each of these predictions, springing from the characters' sense of the progress of their own lives, is "destined" to be, like Polly's assurance that Amanda will "be better in the morning," derailed by illness. The dinner of fried clams is forgotten. Amanda's year in school will be far different from what she expects. She will never be fourteen. From the retrospect of Amanda's diagnosis, the characters' expectations are all rewritten with a certain irony. Polly and Ivan "find themselves wishing they could stop time and keep Amanda and Charlie children forever" (18/12), but even keeping them children will not avert what is already happening to Amanda. "Polly knows Amanda hopes she won't grow any more; the smaller the gymnast is, the better her chances of staying in the sport" (25/19); Amanda will not in fact "grow any more," but neither will she have the "chance" to fulfill those ambitions that she imagines such an arrested development would enable.

In these opening chapters, Hoffman reinforces the strong sense that something inevitable and disturbing is about to enter her characters' lives by focusing explicit attention on predictions of the future and on death and dying. The very name of the town in which the Farrells live, Morrow, evokes futurity, and the brief account Hoffman gives of its "wicked history" (17/10), with occult touches later emphasized in the treatment of Laurel Smith, intensifies the novel's heavily anticipatory opening, specifically preparing for the introduction of Amanda's illness (and for the town's fear of "plague" and its potential for scapegoating):

> Whether or not two witches were drowned in the pond in the center of the common is uncertain. . . . What nearly turned Morrow into a ghost town was the influenza epidemic after World War I. Whole families perished in single rooms. Children were lost one after another, wives locked themselves in attics so they would not infect their husbands. (17/11)

Polly, a photographer, has herself recently worked on "an in-depth study of coping with death": "After photographing her first terminal patient, Polly spent half an hour throwing up by the side of the road. . . . Only two of the people she photographed have not yet died" (21/15-16). And she is now involved in "what the children have dubbed the Casper Project: photographing the seances of a local medium" (15/8), Laurel Smith.

Hoffman gives the novel's second chapter over to Laurel, who, at the age of twelve, foresaw her grandmother's death, and who then continued to "receive messages" (32-33/30-31). A connection between Laurel and Amanda is drawn early in the novel—"She has long blond hair like Amanda's" (22/16)—and Laurel's intimate involvement with death, and a death linked specifically to youth, is emphasized:

> [Her former husband] insisted that she was in love with death. He was more wrong about this than anything else; Laurel is, and always has been, terrified by death. When a baby cries, she hears a death rattle. The branches of a white birch are crossbones. She cannot look at spaded earth, even if it is only a corner of a suburban lawn dug up for a new rhododendron. (32/30)

> While other girls her age were thinking about shades of lipstick and Saturday nights, Laurel could not stop thinking about the brevity of a human lifespan. At night her dreams were terrifying things filled with cemeteries, silence, full white moons. (33/31)

While in some sense Amanda's AIDS diagnosis comes as a "surprise" in *At Risk*, the groundwork for it is thus carefully laid, and in such a way that the quick association between AIDS and death that Ivan makes has been well prepared:

> For five years Ivan has been losing [Amanda] without knowing it. Every time he has sent her to her room for being fresh, every time he missed a gymnastics meet, every hour he has spent looking at dead stars, he has been losing her.
> And now, on Thursday morning, as blackbirds light on the brambles that grow alongside the road, he has lost her. (54/58)

In retrospect, the "normal" actions of everyday life are all ("every time"/ "every hour") rewritten as part of a narrative of "loss," a narrative that, even in the moment of its becoming present to consciousness, is already somehow complete. Similar narrative effects characterize the moment when Ivan finds out about Brian's illness:

> It's only when Ivan refuses to get off the phone that he's told how sick Brian's been all along. For the past few weeks he brought a canister of oxygen with him when he answered phones, and over the weekend, while Ivan was fixing the broken radiator in the living room, Brian had a recurrence of pneumocystis. He is not coming back. (136/166)

The diagnosis of AIDS again wholly changes the past, giving Ivan's prior conversations with Brian a different meaning and making the trivial action of fixing the radiator seem to have some strong meaning in (ironic) relation to Brian's life-threatening situation. The revelation of AIDS also again forecloses the future: "He is not coming back."

Ivan's "loss" of Amanda, in effect his giving her over to death, occurs remarkably early in a novel in which she never in fact dies. (Several critics suggest that both Amanda and Brian do die within the novel; this is not the case, but the misreading shows how strongly Hoffman, while avoiding a direct depiction of their deaths, in fact dedicates her characters with AIDS to an inexorable decline.[21]) While, as we have seen, one of the novel's main actions involves the fight to have Amanda continue as "normal" a life as possible—for instance, by keeping her in school—from the point of diagnosis on, another, equally crucial action concerns the reconciliation of Amanda, her family, and friends to her death, a death depicted as inevitable and, in some sense, felt as having already occurred. A similarly double movement characterizes the depiction of Brian: even as his survival is emphasized, he is seen as already gone. His caretaker Adelle remarks that he's "too mean and stubborn to die fast" (141/172), but having said this, "as soon as he turns away, she looks as if she might burst into tears" (141/173). When Brian cites his own situation to urge Ivan not to "listen to doctors" ("They told me I'd be dead months ago") Ivan's equivocal response—"And here you are" (142/173)—marks both Brian's real presence and the extreme tenuousness of that presence. Ivan has, after all, just strongly felt Brian's impending absence: "What the hell is he [Ivan] supposed to do without Brian? Who will there be for him to talk to?" (141/173).

Several interlocking movements in the narrative of *At Risk* operate to reconfirm—to crystallize as a reality—the sense of loss present already at the moment of Amanda's diagnosis. Each of the novel's main characters moves through a process of accepting that loss. Ed Reardon must come to admit that there is nothing he as a doctor can do to save Amanda: "I've been lying to you. . . . I've been letting you think that there were possibilities, that this wasn't terminal. I can't lie to you anymore" (161/200). Ivan's attachment to Brian provides him with a way of confronting—though also, at moments, of avoiding (see 163-64/205-6)—what is happening to his daughter. Polly becomes intensely aware of what Amanda will never experience:

> She can't listen to Madonna singing over and over again, "True love, oh baby," when she knows that her daughter will never stand in the dark on a summer night and, more aware of her own heart beating than of the mosquitoes circling the porch light, lean her head upward, toward her first kiss. (89/104)

(A similar moment of nostalgic regret for a future that will never be occurs in *Amanda's* own thinking, after her "last wish" [192/243], the removal of her braces, is fulfilled: "[S]he's still smiling when she walks out into the waiting room because now she knows. She would have been beautiful" [202/254].) Polly's own attraction to Ed Reardon is explained at least in part as her attempt to compensate for her daughter's losses: as she kisses Ed, the narrator comments (or Polly herself thinks), "This is the kiss Amanda will never have" (162/201). Charlie is several times involved in explicit conversations about Amanda's possible death (see 73/83, 167-68/210-11, 211/267), in one of which he concludes that, if a cure "won't be in time for Amanda," "I wish she'd just die" (168/211). He also works out his response to death through the dreams in which he becomes the last *Tyrannosaurus rex*: here, having lost "the thing that was like him but bigger" (70/79), a figure of both parent and older sibling, he himself faces extinction (see 70-71/79-81 and 168-69/211-13).

The struggle for a reconciliation to death is most strongly dramatized in Amanda herself. At first, given her diagnosis, she responds with strong denial—"I can't be sick! . . . Don't you understand anything! I can't miss school!" (57/63; also see 75/85)—and continues to project an unimpeded future for herself: "Someday she'll drink beer, she'll have a scarlet dress with a wide silver belt, and earrings so long they'll brush her shoulders" (64/71-72). But she quickly begins to think of herself as dying:

> It's strange but even when she laughs she feels something hot behind her eyes. Sometimes she holds her breath and tries to imagine what it's like to be dead. How would it be to leave her body behind? She has never believed in heaven. . . . It's easier to think about becoming one with the earth. She could believe that; out of her body will come grass, roses, black-eyed Susans. She could almost believe that, if it weren't happening to her. (104/124)

> Stupid, but it was only at the dinner table that she realized in order to die of a disease you really have to die and not come back. (117/141)

> Now, every night before she goes to sleep she tells herself that she's going to die. She repeats it to herself, calmly, carefully, rolling the words on her tongue. (123/149)

The change in Amanda's thinking is shown in a particularly strong way in her shifting expectations about gymnastics. Initially, despite her illness, she approaches the sport with full confidence: "Not only does Amanda believe she'll be in the finals, she's certain she'll win" (80/92). But this gives way to more and more limited hopes: though "[s]he has been thinking all summer about the meet next June, because it would help rank her in junior high" and help her become "Bela Karolyi['s] . . . student," "[s]he has stopped thinking about trying to get Bela to be her coach, she has stopped thinking about junior high school. She wants to win the meet at the end of the term just to win it" (106/127). And soon afterward, she realizes that even this diminished expectation is unrealistic: "Today when she woke up she thought to herself, I'm not going to be in the finals, and as soon as she thought it she knew it was true. She doesn't have the strength or the stamina" (120/145). All she wants now is "to make it to the last meet in June. . . . She thinks no further than that" (123/150), but her final performance in fact occurs much sooner: "From now on she'll be sitting on this bench watching her teammates compete, instead of waiting for her turn. She's had her turn" (151/186).

Amanda, having "learn[ed] to accept her approaching death with touching nobility,"[22] self-consciously begins to withdraw herself from life, and particularly to mark the limits of her close relationships with others. She begins "to wonder what would happen to Jessie if Amanda suddenly disappeared" (124/151), and she emphasizes to Jessie that she "won't be around forever," urging her "to start making other friends now" (152/188): "[Amanda]'s already started spending less time with her mother. Now it's time to do the same with Jessie" (152/187). Concomitant with the movement away from both her mother and her best friend is Amanda's increasing closeness to Laurel Smith, but this is facilitated particularly by Laurel's associations with death. (Polly greets Laurel's overtures to Amanda as in fact threatening because of Laurel's proximity to death: "She figures she has a right to be suspicious when a woman who communes with spirits wants to brush her daughter's hair" [121/146-47; also see 119/144].) Laurel provides Amanda someone with whom she can talk "about death," something she can't do with others like her mother "because she's afraid she'll hurt" them (146/181). And even the relation with Laurel ultimately leads Amanda further into a sense of isolation. When she expresses the wish that Laurel, as a medium, communicate with her after her death, Laurel must reply that she "can't do that"; she can only promise to "dream about" Amanda "[a]lways" (180/227-28). Amanda's withdrawal from the world is completed when, just before she enters the hospital at the end of the novel, she insists on making out her will (214-15/270-71).

As all of this happens, the novel carefully traces the course of Amanda's illness, documenting her weight loss (120/145, 187/238), night sweats and fevers (136/166, 155/193, 206/260), diarrhea (141/172), lassitude (187/237), and nausea (187/237). It focuses attention on pneumonia as "[t]he biggest threat" to Amanda (79/92), shows her undergoing prophylaxis for *Pneumocystis* (155/193) and developing, nonetheless, the "difficulty breathing" (156/194) and other symptoms that signal to Ed Reardon "*Pneumocystis carinii* pneumonia as soon as he sees her" (157/195). While the narrative of Amanda's illness allows for a remission—her release from one hospital stay and her return to school— during that remission her general condition is shown to deteriorate further (187-88/237-39) and the possibility of "another bout with pneumonia" (178/225) is kept constantly in mind. The "recurrence" Ed Reardon has "been afraid of all along" (207/261)—"Amanda's temperature doesn't begin to rise until midnight. Once it begins, her fever keeps on climbing until the following afternoon . . . when it reaches 103" (206/260)—in fact occurs with a certain sense of inevitability emphasized by present tense verbs that refer to a deferred (future) moment ("[not] until midnight") that nonetheless has already passed. The last we see of Amanda, she is being taken off to the hospital: "After she'd been carried into the Blazer, Amanda looked out her window and waved to them. Charlie can't stop remembering that, the way her hand moved like a piece of white paper" (215/271-72).

This final image of Amanda caps a movement in the novel that serves to isolate the person with AIDS as she approaches her "inevitable" death, attenuating and blotting clean her presence. This movement applies as much to Brian as to Amanda: Isolated in his illness, Brian "spends a great deal of time looking out his window, which has black iron bars" (137/168). Ivan's visit to him provides an unusual moment of sociality—"God, he's actually excited to have company" (139/170)—but that visit ends with an eerie dissolution of Brian's body:

> It's late now, and the sunlight is fading. Adelle coughs and goes to the windows to lift the shades higher. When the light fills the room, Ivan swears he can see all the bones in Brian's body rising to the surface like fish. He can see Brian dissolving, and in this instant Ivan realizes that Brian is barely here, he is already looking at something far away, something in another dimension no one else can see. (142/173)

When Ivan leaves, Brian sinks back into the shadowy realm he has occupied throughout the novel, reappearing, as he has appeared previously, only as a voice on the telephone.

In a parallel moment at the end of the following chapter,[23] Amanda undergoes a similar transformation in Polly's eyes:

> Polly wants to call Amanda back, but she doesn't. Amanda will always be her daughter, now and forever. That's why she can stand and watch as Amanda runs outside so quickly you'd think she was weightless, you'd think she was flying straight into the sun. (153/189)

Though Amanda here shows more energy than Brian, she (like him) seems to be already far away, not just looking at "something in another dimension no one else can see" but already in that other zone.

In the course of but a few pages toward the end of *At Risk*, Amanda is reduced three times to a two-dimensional sheet of paper: first, in Polly's photographing of her (213-14/268-70); next, in the making of her will (214-15/270-71); and finally, in the narrator's (or Charlie's) evocation of her "hand like a piece of white paper." All three moments are memorializing ones. Charlie "can't stop remembering" Amanda's hand. As Polly decides to take the photograph, she asks, "What if it was happening, and I didn't have a picture of her?" to which Ivan responds, "It is happening" (213/268). And though Polly at first resists Amanda's making of the will, she finally insists on witnessing it: "Polly turns to look, so she can always remember Amanda as she is right now, straining to sign over everything she owns, still finding something worth giving" (215/271). Though Amanda remains alive at the novel's conclusion, her bodily presence has been erased, replaced by mementos. The novel's final scene shows us not Amanda struggling in the hospital to live, or even Amanda dying, but rather Charlie determined never to forget her:

No matter what, there will always be two kids in their family. Even if everything she owned is thrown away, even if her closets are empty, her room will always belong to her, and whenever he's asked, at school or by a stranger he meets, he'll always say, "I have one sister, Amanda," because he always will. He'll have her long after his parents have grown old and died, and if he ever has children of his own he'll tell them everything about her, what her favorite music was, the names she used to call him, everything, so they'll remember her, too. (217/ 273; also see 219/275)

All of this is a logical conclusion to the novel's identification of AIDS as immediate loss, its vision of the body of the person living with AIDS as given over already to an unearthly realm. I should emphasize that what I see as problematic in *At Risk* is not the novel's concern with death or with how people prepare themselves for (their own and others') deaths; such a concern responds to the real pressures of an illness that so often includes death. Rather, to my mind, the problem lies in the novel's too easy acceptance of a narrative of illness whose endpoint is predetermined, and a narrative itself fully shaped by the expectation of that endpoint. Such a narrative participates strongly in the cordoning off of people with AIDS, defining them as irretrievably "lost" to life's mainstream, so that, while the explicit agenda of *At Risk* is to challenge a process of stigmatization, its own depictions contribute to that very process. When "empathy and compassion" are evoked for Amanda and Brian, it is not so much because "they" are "like us," but rather because "they," who *may once have been* "like us," are now seen to be *no longer so*; "they" have entered another realm, a realm in which "their" death is seen to be inevitable in a way that "ours" is not.

3. GAY SUBJECTS OF AIDS, HOMOPHOBIA, AND MISOGYNY

Like *At Risk*, Vance Bourjaily's *Old Soldier* has as an explicit project the challenging of phobic responses to AIDS.[24] Unlike Hoffman, however, Bourjaily chooses not to explore AIDS within the daily world of his characters, but instead situates the most intense confrontation with AIDS at a campground on a river in the Maine woods, where Joe McKay, the "old soldier" of the book's title, has gone to fish. Six other men—Joe's old friend Arnie, the "gatekeeper and campground manager" (92); twenty-six-year-old Carl Shumaker, his father John, and his uncle Doc Miles; and Brad and Grady, "a couple of lean country boys from Pennsylvania who'd migrated to Pittsburgh and become steel workers" (104)—at first inhabit the campground, and the seven are later joined by Joe's brother Tommy. A gay musician who has just found out that he has AIDS, Tommy arrives at night, while all the campground guests are gathered around Joe's radio listening to a Boston Celtics game.

When the game is over, despite "seem[ing] tired" (126), he joins the group with some enthusiasm: "It wasn't in him, Joe knew, to be anything less than the gladdest hand in town in a situation like this, no matter how tired from a long, bumpy motorcycle ride the man might be" (127). But when the others leave the two brothers alone, "Tommy deflate[s]" (127) and reveals that he hasn't been able to play in the bagpiping contest he just attended:

> "I'd have run out of breath."
> . . .
> "I don't like telling you what being short of wind means in my world these days." . . .
> . . . "It's one of the early symptoms," Tommy said.
> "Where do we go to get you tested?"
> "It's been done. In Cambridge last weekend. Heard the results day before yesterday. Had to get examined some more. That's what made me late. I've got it, Joe, the fairy-killer. God who loves us found a way to slap the wrists of bad little fairy boys, only the way he slaps, it breaks off your hand and the rest of you goes pouring out the stump. What's the dirty new four-letter word?"
> By the time he'd finished speaking, Joe was down beside him with an arm around Tommy's shoulders. "AIDS? What are we going to do about it, Tom?" (128-29)

Tommy's punitive language here is jokingly, if bitterly, meant. It echoes an earlier, less personal discussion between the two brothers where Tommy defines AIDS as "[d]ear old God's final solution to the sodomy problem. He's been working on it for centuries" (50). In the later scene, Tommy goes on to use this same sort of language to make a political point: "Joe, I know how you feel about the President. No matter what sorry specimen's in there, he's your commander-in-chief. I just wish Wrinkle Dick and Nancy didn't take the same attitude as God who loves us" (130).

But while Tommy himself thus attempts to turn homophobic moralizing back against itself, the punitive force of his language is about to be mobilized in ways he cannot yet envision. Carl Shumaker has overheard the conversation between the two brothers, and his father appears at the McKay campsite the next morning to report that he has "a scared boy down there" and to ask whether Tommy "used the outhouse when he came in last night" (132). Tommy must embark on a crash course in HIV transmission, emphasizing that "you can't get AIDS from a toilet seat" and that, despite his having shaken hands with everyone, his "hand wasn't bleeding": "There's no way any of you folks could have got infected" (132). When Shumaker leaves, having arranged for a further meeting, Joe himself asks for confirmation of what Tommy has said—

"Is that right, Tommy? About the blood? ... We hear all sorts of junk" (133)—and Tommy continues providing information: "It's a lazy goddamn virus, AIDS. It only gets into your bloodstream where the skin's broken. Or with a needle" (133). In the later meeting with John Shumaker and Doc Miles, a chiropractor, Tommy confronts a variety of misconceptions about AIDS. Miles claims that "it's a highly infectious disease, with one hundred percent fatalities," and when Tommy tries to give him "a pamphlet about AIDS and how it's transmitted" (136), Miles is at first afraid even to touch it. Instead, Tommy must read the information aloud (137), finally getting Miles to agree at least to "think about it" (138).

In the meantime, however, "[t]here's kind of a panic on" (135), and though Doc Miles is ultimately persuaded by the information Tommy provides (142), this happens too late to derail events already set in motion. Carl is convinced that he has been infected and has run "off into the bushes" (135). "The boys from Pennsylvania are packed up, talking about leaving" (135), but before they leave, Brad and Grady torch Joe's camper, and Joe is injured: "As he ran to it, the glass in the door shattered, and he had hot glass shards in his face" (139). Later, Carl flattens all four tires on Joe's truck—"to keep [him] from getting over to Tommy" (148)—and Carl begins to stalk Tommy. The only way for Joe to reach and help his brother is to run his canoe, with Arnie, through a stretch of dangerous rapids (149-51), and when Joe and Arnie arrive back at the campsite, they find both tires on Tommy's motorcycle flattened and Tommy gone (151). Joe searches for his brother, and for Carl, in the woods; hearing two shots (152), he sneaks up on and captures Carl, but a moment too late, just after Tommy has been shot in the ankle (153-54). Though in some sense the dangers put in motion by the news of Tommy's AIDS have now run their course—Brad and Grady are gone, pursued by the state police; Joe puts Carl into a bear trap for safekeeping (156-57)—Tommy's wound must still be attended to and Joe must figure out a way to transport his brother from the woods. And of course what has happened has deeply disturbed Tommy and Joe's lives—as the novel's surprise ending makes especially clear.

Presenting the plot of AIDSphobia under the special stress of an isolation from "civilization," a separation from the characters' wonted social worlds—Tommy's cosmopolitan New York, Joe's suburban Connecticut—allows Bourjaily to bring an intense concentration, and also simplicity, to his novel's final scenes. The events that unfold in response to Tommy's arrival occur in rapid succession, with little opportunity for other concerns to direct attention away from them. The only lull in the action comes when, after the camper fire and before Carl's hostile intentions become clear, Joe goes on one last fishing outing, but this interruption itself sets up the novel's climactic events: it separates Joe from Tommy and thus allows both for the confrontation between Tommy and Carl and for Joe and Arnie's frantic and exciting canoe run through the rapids. Setting the response to Tommy's AIDS in the Maine woods also permits Bourjaily to present his novel's final conflicts as the simple clash of two well-defined groups of men—good and bad, reasonable and unreasonable, Joe, Arnie, and Tommy, on the one hand, and the Shumakers and Brad and Grady, on the other. The only complication of this simple schema comes from Doc Miles, who switches sides midstream, persuaded by Tommy's educational pamphlet. Bourjaily thus avoids confronting, in the depiction of responses to Tommy's AIDS, the messiness of the social world, a messiness that stands at the center of the very different treatment of phobic responses in *At Risk*, where Hoffman considers how not just individuals but organizations—for instance, the school board—may both participate in and resist the deployment of social stigma. In *Old Soldier*, the conflict over AIDS remains very much outside clearly organized social institutions. When John Shumaker suggests that Joe's having hurt Carl and imprisoned him is "a police matter," Joe responds, "What's shooting people? A boy scout matter?" (159), but there is ultimately no sense that the authorities intervene or need intervene in the events at the campground. It is in fact only with some reluctance that Joe gives up his personal pursuit of Brad and Grady when Arnie informs him that he has already called "the cops" (140-41). Very early in the novel, Joe advises an AWOL soldier, travelling to confront his sister's husband, who has beaten her, to "[g]o after him": "There's things we don't call cops for when we can take care of them ourselves" (15).

The concluding scenes of *Old Soldier* thus occur in a world outside the usual social constraints and, significantly, in an all-male world. This gender exclusivity has generic as well as thematic importance, marking a shift in the novel from its earlier, socially implicated explorations—of Joe's ending marriage, of Tommy's life in New York—toward more exclusively "masculine" genres: *Old Soldier* takes its place, for instance, in the "growing canon of angling fiction"[25] and in the literature of wilderness adventure that includes, as a clear precursor, James Dickey's *Deliverance*, advertised in its first paperback incarnation as "about four men caught in a primitive and violent test of manhood,"[26] and containing, of course, homosexual acts as a central element of that test. *Old Soldier* similarly depicts a "test of manhood," with Bourjaily shaping the novel's confrontation between good and bad as a conflict between two different sorts of (straight) masculinity set off by the queer presence of Tommy.

From the outset, Carl Shumaker is depicted as somehow deficient in the codes of masculine behavior, though he strives hard to demonstrate his mastery of these. When Joe has a flat tire approaching the campground and Carl stops to help him, Joe, who "had dealt with a lot of young men, trained them" (91) as an army sergeant, "Automatically . . . found himself noting about this one: *Couple of degrees off plumb*" (91). Carl, to Joe's mind, isn't quite "straight," though Joe intends nothing explicitly about sexuality in this judgment. While Joe several times refuses help with the tire, Carl insists, only then to demonstrate his own ineptitude:

> "Let me take this lug wrench a second." Joe came out from under the truck to see young Shumaker struggling to loosen first one wheel lug, then another.
> "Someone must have put these on with an air wrench," Carl said.
> "Shit, I can't budge the damn things, Joe. Boy, I'd like to get the guy who put these on with an air wrench . . ."
> "You start 'em with your foot, Carl," Joe said, and showed him how. It didn't take more than a few minutes longer to change the tire with Carl's help than Joe would've spent doing it by himself. (93)

Elsewhere, as in this entry into the novel, Carl repeatedly misunderstands masculine skills and behaviors. Seeing Joe and Arnie kidding with each other, he is convinced that they are fighting over camping fees, and he offers Joe money: "Joe didn't know whether to hoot or get pissed" (95). He repeatedly invades Joe's privacy (101-3, 103-4, 114, 118), and what at first looks to Joe like Carl's coming to respect that privacy—his vacating the campsite next to Joe's (131)—turns out instead to be the beginning of his panicked response to the brothers' conversation about AIDS.

Brad and Grady, while more confident than Carl in their own masculinity, nonetheless also fail to live up to Joe's standards. Listening to the basketball game with the other men, they behave in an "unsportsmanlike" manner, hoping, for instance, that one injured player has hurt himself "good" (125; also see 104). And they mistreat Carl in ways that Joe clearly does not sanction (118, 120-21). Joe, in addition, is critical of John Shumaker, recognizing Carl's manner in his father—"The words spilled out as they did when this guy's son talked, tumbled over each other" (132)—and openly questioning the way he is raising (or not raising) his son: "Why do you call Carl a boy? . . . He's twenty-six. If you'd treat him like a man, he might just make one someday" (132; also see 122). Joe himself, if somewhat reluctantly, takes on Carl's "training," teaching him the masculine pursuit of fishing in a clear compensation for John's fatherly deficiencies; John, indeed, thanks Joe "[f]or taking an interest in my boy" (122).

Joe's own masculinity rests at least in part on his willingness to tolerate others' sometimes bothersome behavior, though this tolerance does not include a willingness to sacrifice his own standards; when he takes on the task of "training" Carl, subjecting himself to Carl's annoyances, he does so because he clearly feels that his efforts might help "make a man." Joe has a clear sense of his place in the world in ways that Carl and John, Brad and Grady repeatedly fail to display. The distinction here of course is most salient in the different characters' reactions to Tommy. While Joe himself is not necessarily more certain of the facts about HIV than are the others, he is secure in feeling a particular kind of homosocial trust; he knows that his brother would not put him at risk. When Tommy remarks that Joe "didn't hesitate to hug" him despite not being sure of the modes of HIV transmission, Joe replies, "Come on, peckerbrain. If there was any reason not to, you'd have said so" (134). Arnie, who stands with Joe against the other campers, takes a similar stance: when Joe advises him that Tommy has AIDS and asks if he's "sure [he] want[s] to ride" with the two brothers, Arnie responds, "Well, he can't give it to me, can he? Notice you're riding with him" (141).

HIV transmission does become a real possibility in the novel, but significantly, this occurs only through the breakdown of trusting male alliances, only (ironically) because of Carl, Brad, and Grady's irrational fears of transmission. After he is shot by Carl, Tommy bleeds profusely, and he warns his brother, when Joe attempts to dress the wound, not to get blood on himself: "He was getting some blood on him, of course, but he had no wound or sore on his hand, and he wasn't going to worry, either" (154). When the bleeding has stopped and Joe goes off to find "some morphine or something" (155) so that Tommy can make it back to camp, Tommy warns him again:

"Joe, your face. Where the glass got you. Don't wipe your face till your hands are clean."
Joe grunted. Wiping his face was just what he'd been about to do. Wiped his hands hard on his pants instead. (155; also see 163-64)

The violently phobic reactions of Brad and Grady, causing Joe's cuts through the burning of the camper, and of Carl, wounding Tommy, come together here to create a real risk; these men, in their dysfunctional masculinity—their panicked reaction to a situation that, as Joe and Arnie recognize, in fact offers nothing to fear—cause, for others, the very dangers they intend to ward off. And it is only the trusting and caring relations among men—Tommy's warnings to Joe as well as Joe's willingness to brave the possibility of infection in caring for his brother—that minimize the damage done by a hostile and panicky masculinity.

The novel's final scenes thus pit against each other, on the one hand, a macho posturing that hides deep insecurities easily evoked by AIDS, and, on the other, a "true" masculinity that can accept AIDS for what it is, and even put itself "at risk" when the situation demands such "heroism." That the novel becomes a contest of masculinities set off by the fear of HIV transmission is revealing of the kind of ideological position that AIDS—as a threat to masculinity, as a sign of all that endangers the masculine—continues to occupy in American culture. Bourjaily, to his credit, tries to rewrite the ideology so that "true" masculinity is able calmly to confront AIDS and the sexual difference that Tommy represents in the economy of the novel and that, in the wilderness scenes, is conflated with his AIDS diagnosis. Bourjaily poses, against a homophobic, AIDSphobic masculinity, a more "genuine" and secure masculine stance. Earlier, the novel makes a point of showing Joe's (successful?) struggle to come to terms with his brother's sexuality:

> One of Joe's most troubling memories . . . was of being nineteen, home on leave from the big war. . . . Standing in the crowd, Joe heard a man say, "I hear that pretty blond one sucks a sweet dick."
> Joe had whirled, looking for the guy to hit, thought he saw who it was, but couldn't get to him. Joe had to get older, before he learned to live with Tommy's being gay. Joe had had to serve with homosexual guys in the wars, and learn that some of them could soldier, to get his head straight about the matter. (10)

But while the sanctioned masculinity embodied in Joe thus eschews an explicit homophobia as well as the irrational fear of AIDS, its operations—Joe's "getting his head *straight*"—remain clearly differentiated from the homosexual and from an AIDS closely identified with homosexuality. Just before reflecting on the process by which he "unlearned" homophobia, Joe engages in a homophobic imagining of how Tommy might have avoided becoming gay:

> Joe tried to think whether he and Tommy had ever gone fishing together, and decided they probably hadn't. By the time Tommy was fishing age, Joe was already in the army. Maybe Tom[27] would have turned out different if he'd had a big brother at home. (10)

And while, in the first conversation Joe and Tommy have about AIDS, the heterosexual Joe is momentarily implicated as a potential subject of HIV, Joe quickly turns the conversation away from himself, and the possibility of "heterosexual AIDS" never reappears in the novel:

> "You had yourself tested, Tommy?"
> "No, goddamn it, have you?"
> "Me?"
> "You've been sleeping with Deedee. She's been partying with Victor. How do you know who else big Vic parties with?"
> Joe seemed about to say something, changed his mind and kept it simple.

"Life in the minefields." (49-50)

Joe's final response here is typical, moving the discussion, at least metaphorically, toward the male homosocial pursuits, sports, fishing, the army, by which his masculinity is repeatedly defined. In the course of the novel, we see Joe bonding with a radio salesman over basketball (3-7); picking up a young hitchhiker who, it turns out, is AWOL from the army (7-17); negotiating a reprieve for the soldier with his sergeant (17-19); managing a truck stop (36); dreaming himself in the midst of an air raid (63); tossing the caber with other "muscular jocks" (this occurs "thirty-five years ago," in Tommy's memory) (78); and, of course, retreating to the all-male world of the campground and fishing. From its beginning, the novel's picturesque language is marked by Joe's status as "old warrior" (80)—"The Boston Celtics were a lost squad of walking wounded. The Milwaukee Bucks were fresh, dug-in and loaded" (4)— by his particular, heavy investment in the worlds of male homosociality.

Those worlds may sometimes admit "homosexual guys"—"*some* of them could soldier" (10)—but, in the novel, Tommy (and other gay men) are in fact quite consistently excluded from them. Tommy and Joe do share a familial history and an ethnic identification that provide common ground for their respective masculinities. They both voice a certain racism—particularly in relation to Victor, the Latino man for whom Joe's wife is leaving him—and a racism that at least partly bases itself in a denigration of the other's masculinity:

> [Tommy] found himself talking to a remarkably thick-skulled Latino who insisted that if Tommy wanted to take modellink lesson, Tommy mus' calm to de skull for inderfew his personal self, it did not make different whose brudd-in-law.
> How much dumb shit must a man endure? Tommy said, slowly and distinctly that he vass brudd-in-law Khadafy, and vould one car bomb send to these modellink skull, salaam aleikum, and hung up. (31; also see 3, 26-27, 32-33, 36, 66)

The two brothers bond more positively over their own Scottishness. Joe has experimented with the bagpipe that Tommy is expert at and Tommy has "fooled around with" the caber toss, though "it was Joe who had the strength and the knack" (78). Both show a particular emotional attachment to the pibroch "Lament for the Children," which Tommy plays on the bagpipe and which, as Joe explains, was perhaps composed by Patrick Mor MacCrimmon who "went to church one Sunday in 1610, accompanied by eight strong sons. Before the year was over, seven of the boys were dead of the plague" (12). The song, in Joe's words, "has all the tears in it a brave man could ever allow himself to cry" (14) and Tommy intends to play it "for the friends [he's] lost" to AIDS—"Bruno. Fletcher. Gary. I wanted the audience to mourn them with me, even if they didn't know they were doing it" (130). Both brothers associate the "Lament" with male homosocial losses, and elsewhere Tommy's losses stand explicitly parallel to Joe's:

> "Maybe I'm starting to know how you felt in the war."
> . . .
> . . . "How long's your casualty list? People you've known?"
> "Three cities full. New York, New Orleans, San Francisco. Guys I've been close to? Seven so far. Some of them going way back. Every month or two you hear another name. Frank tested positive, Gary's gone to bed and won't get up again."
> "Yep." (47, 49)

In these moments of masculine connection between the two brothers, however, the novel also underlines the distinctions between them: Tommy's "war," of course, is not the same as Joe's. Their ethnically-marked accomplishments at the "Highland Games in Florida thirty-five years ago" are differently gendered: "Joe won everything—the caber, the weight toss, weight throw, sheaf throw and hammer—while Tommy swept the solo piping events. They'd come away with six hundred bucks in prize money, Tommy in his kilt, Joe in uniform" (78).

When Bourjaily moves to depict Tommy's urban gay life, he does so in terms that clearly differentiate Tommy from Joe and that replicate much homophobic thinking. The language here, in contrast to Joe's colorfully gruff, and often obscene, masculine metaphorics, becomes cutesy: "Out on West 88th Street, Tommy thought of flagging a dear little taxi because the drivers had such a marvelous assortment of accents these days, but decided it would be funnier to ride Joe across town on the Honda" (43). Tommy's friends call him "Dog," an acronym for "Dean of Gays" (43; also see 33, 37, 39, 42, 57, 71, 76), and Tommy refers to other gay men as "dear boys" (see 33, 34, 57, 69). Clearly, Bourjaily is reaching for a certain camp voice here, which he successfully captures only in a funny monologue Tommy delivers as part of his nightclub act—"Now, it's a nationally known fact that thirty-four percent of all truck drivers are gay . . ." (60); the monologue, though it reconfirms a variety of stereotypes about gay men and lesbians, is also the novel's only depiction of a real, energetic defiance of straight norms. Elsewhere, in representing Tommy's life, Bourjaily is busy describing an "epicene" (33) world. Tommy includes his "shiny $385 espresso machine . . . as a piece of living room furniture, because he love[s] the way it look[s]" (33); he rides a motorcycle as "[p]art of [his] image"—"[h]e love[s] the looks of the machine the way he love[s] the looks of his big espresso maker" (44). This aestheticized relation to his possessions stands in implicit contrast to the practical value Joe places on his unpretty but reliable camping gear:

> The locomotive was a big, red, 4-wheel-drive Chevy pickup with a black camper top, all fresh-waxed, and with a bashed-up aluminum canoe strapped to the roof, proud of its scars. The caboose was a fifteen-year-old, pop-up camper, a little lopsided, but scrubbed up clean the day before. (7)

Though Bourjaily makes Tommy the center of an extensive network of gay men, providing aid (lodging, money, advice) for his "dear boys," when we actually see him helping two friends negotiate a conflict, it is over a remarkably trivial matter:

> You see, you're not fighting about money, you're fighting about manners, and Peter's apologized for his, which were atrocious. On the other hand, he had shared his stash with you that the nice man gave him, so he felt entitled to take a bottle of your single keg to the party. (42)

Again, this stands in strong contrast to Joe's more consequential conflict resolution, the help he provides the AWOL soldier in negotiating conflicting family and military obligations. Not surprisingly, the language of Bourjaily's characters repeatedly slips into the homophobic, with, for instance, Arnie referring to Brad and Grady as "sorry cocksuckers" (148). Even Tommy makes homophobic judgments: "[H]e had to stop to shake hands with the tall headmaster and the giggly guy who taught music. . . . Giggly made a rather fruity introduction" (73).

Though *Old Soldier* leaves it largely to the reader to compare its very different presentations of straight and gay masculinity, Bourjaily does provide at least one situation in which a more direct comparison of male sexualities is made. In some ways, this comparison reverses expectations: Joe, "the childless macho man" (55), though he has been married twice, has no children, while Tommy, "the family man, Dean of Gays" (55), through a brief marriage in his youth to Holly, has a son. Ultimately, though, the reversal here serves mainly to reconfirm Joe's "real" masculinity over against Tommy's. In his own thinking about his marriage, Tommy recognizes that Joe was somehow the more appropriate husband for Holly—"Holly was queer for muscles, of which Tommy'd even had a few himself back in those years, though never like Joe's" (52)—a recognition that brings "to mind a question Tommy'd always wanted to ask" (52), and which finally he does: "Joe, did you ever fuck Holly?" (53).

The answer is yes—"After you broke up, I hope I don't need to add" (53)—and in one of the novel's most fully developed sexual descriptions, Tommy himself speaks the affair between his brother and ex-wife:

> "I can do the rest myself," he said. "Small, dirty blonde with dirty eyes, and those lovely teats pretty near falling out. The nighties were always loose up top. That beautiful little flat ass. She said, 'Gawd, I'm one hungover girl,' and slipped her bare feet over yours, and there was just enough vulnerability in the way she did it to make you grab everything she had, top and bottom. She turned around and sagged back into you, and you played with her stuff a minute and goosed her into the bedroom."
> "No," Joe said slowly. "We hit the kitchen floor. Neither one of us could wait." (54-55)

Though the paternity of Tommy's son is explicitly reconfirmed in this scene—"Little Joe's your kid all the way, Tommy" (53)—the novel's implications push in an opposite direction. Little Joe is, after all, named for his uncle, and he has followed in his uncle's, much more than in his father's, footsteps: "Little Joe was a basketball hotshot at a New England prep school that favored jocks. Come to remember, it was Uncle Joe who started the kiddo playing the game" (52). Little Joe "look[s] more like [his] idiot uncle every day" (72; also see 53). The partial subversion of expectations in giving the gay brother a son is disarmed by the consistent move to make that son more properly "belong" to his uncle than his father. And of course, the revelation of Joe's affair with Holly serves to "unman" Tommy and "masculinize" Joe.

Joe's masculinity in fact depends upon a certain heterosexual prowess, but it also represents itself through a strong misogyny. While, to Joe's mind, men should protect women against violence, and while Joe himself is able to be friendly with women (especially when sex is out of the question; see 88-89), he also sees women as posing a strong threat to the independence that he values and that enables his masculine presence in the world. *Old Soldier* begins, "Joe McKay got what he wanted for his sixtieth birthday in April, a request for a divorce from the lady he had dumbass married five years earlier" (3), and Joe explicitly connects the prospect of divorce to "a freedom he'd never considered seeking that began to excite him" (29). Indeed, all the novel's major female characters are manipulative and controlling. Irene, Tommy's neighbor, closes a business deal by having sex with her client (see 41, 56, 62-63). Attracted to Joe, she brings the brothers back together after a fight, but only by tricking Tommy:

[I]t wasn't until they were halfway to New Haven that he tumbled to what the sly and slimy bitch was doing to him. . . .

He . . . said in his smoothest, most caressing voice, "You are a totally horrid cunt."

. . .

. . . "You're taking me to see Joe, aren't you?" (65-66).

Deedee, Joe's most recent wife, is a storehouse of misogynistic stereotypes. She can't control her shopping: "In her fifteen Pan-Am stewardess years, Joe imagined, there must have been bazaars all over the world that closed to celebrate the day after her crew left town" (22). She and Joe have an intense fight on the night of Joe's sixtieth birthday during which Deedee reveals that she has been sleeping with her co-worker Victor and wants a divorce. Both Deedee and Irene are identified repeatedly with a physicality that, while it may attract Joe, also seems a bit repugnant to him: "[Deedee] was a tall, reckless, forty-three-year-old blonde, with a slim, seductive figure and an American-girl, bob-nose face" (19); "[Irene] was a rather raunchily attractive lady, with big brown eyes and jiggly skin" (39). Irene comes to be identified as "the jiggly, tearass lady" (56).

Just as homophobic language is used to disparage male characters in the novel, so is the language of misogyny: Brad and Grady are "cuntheads" (140) as well as "cocksuckers." When Tommy fights with Joe, he calls him "pig's cunt" alongside "prick" (64) and "all cock and no balls" (63). The AWOL soldier is, in the words of his first sergeant, both a "freckle-prick deserter" and a "little cunt sniffer" (18). Affiliation with the female is, in all these cases, distance from a proper masculinity, and in fact is tied up, in a complex way, with gayness.

Revealingly, Bourjaily often pits women against gay men, while both stand in significant opposition to male heterosexuals. Some of the novel's most virulent misogyny comes from Tommy—usually directed against Deedee—and some of its most virulent homophobia from Deedee—directed against Tommy: "With Deedee and Tommy it had been disgust at first sight" (26; also see 7, 27, 31-32, 47). While Deedee and Tommy attack each other, Joe can stand securely aside, his gender and sexual position solidified by the insecurity of its mutually destabilizing "opposites."

As D. A. Miller suggests in his psychoanalytic reading of the construction of male heterosexuality, straight masculinity depends upon a fantasmatic casting out of both the female and the homosexual:

The same reason . . . that qualifies the anus to provoke castration anxiety in the male subject, as evincing on his own body anatomo-fantasmatic potential for his being—even anatomo-fantasmatic proof of his having been—in the mother's place, keeps such anxiety from being altogether controlled in the classic recognized manner, namely, by means of a fantasy about the body of what the subject is comforted to construe as the *opposite* sex. For even if his success in confining this sex (socially as well as psychically) to the castration attributed to it in the primal scene were far less problematic than is ever demonstrably the case, his anus would remain to raise, on his own male person, the very possibility (of being fucked and so forth) that, with all the force of binary opposition, he had projected onto *her* vagina. Accordingly, he requires another binarism to police the difference between man and woman as, by the back door, it reenters to make a difference within men. So it is that, with a frequency long outlasting the formative years, however particularly striking then, straight men unabashedly *need* gay men, whom they forcibly recruit (as the object of their blows, or, in better circles, just their jokes) to enter into a polarization that exorcizes the "woman" in man through assigning it to a class of man who may be considered no "man" at all. Only between the woman and the homosexual together may the normal male subject imagine himself covered front and back.[28]

In *Old Soldier*, Joe consistently navigates a ground of masculinity and heterosexuality defined in contradistinction to the female and the queer, and moreover a ground largely "covered," protected from attack, by the mutual sniping of gay men and women, a specifically gay misogyny and female homophobia. Even when Joe falls into a direct confrontation with Deedee, and even in Tommy's absence, the marital conflict is played out at least in part between the gay man and woman: As part of her final battle with Joe, Deedee "smashe[s] a forty-year-old framed photograph of Joe's brother, Tommy, as a blond boy in his parade kilt" (7): "She'd driven a shard into the kid's handsome face, laughed like a maniac when she saw it, and shrieked: / 'The big fat faggot's got a hole in his head'" (7; also see 27). Joe responds with a parallel gesture, taking "a poster photo, made in her modelling days, of Deedee" and passing it "through the flame to blister it" (27). The woman's image and that of the homosexual are both marred (but not destroyed) in a battle that leaves Joe's own sense of self relatively unchanged, or indeed with a certain self, taken away by marriage, returned to him. Though the fight makes Joe feel, by turns, "angry," "lustful," "weary," "sorrowful" (28), "pained," and "distant" (29), it leaves him feeling "on the brink of exhilaration," anticipating the "freedom" of divorce (29). The fight, with its emblematic violence against both women and gay men, enables Joe's escape from marriage figured as a clear deviation from "straightness"—"Living alone became his habit until Deedee came along and knocked him for a loop" (30)—a marriage whose end promises an end to "looping," a return to "straight and level flight" (30).

Joe's "confident" masculinity depends not only upon a strong male homosociality but also upon a rejection of both femaleness/femininity and male homosexuality, and a pitting of the two against each other that facilitates the more confident assertion of the straight and male. It is no surprise, then, that, when the novel puts "manhood" to its test in the wilderness, women are rigorously excluded. And while Tommy is, of course, present at and central to the wilderness scenes, the "test of manhood" still excludes homosexuality in a particular way. Gayness is never explicitly at issue in the novel's final scenes, and, in fact, Tommy himself is careful not to introduce it in any direct way: when he teaches the others about HIV transmission, he talks only about blood, not "other body fluids I didn't think I needed to mention under the circumstances" (133). In the all-male milieu of the woods, Tommy's homosexuality remains unspoken, pushed in some sense in the wide open spaces back into the space of the closet. It is "present" only in Tommy's self-censoring person and to the extent that the other characters perform an identification between (the named) AIDS and (the unnamed) gayness. Tommy himself has made just that identification earlier, at the Gathering of the Clans he attends immediately after receiving his AIDS diagnosis; there, under the influence of Dexamil, his imagination moves between the current moment and his youth, and between the two "secrets" of homosexuality and AIDS: "He was seventeen, a secretly troubled boy with a smile that fooled 'em all, but he went back and forth from that to his real age of fifty-five, and to knowing what the secret was this time" (78).

While homosexuality is unspoken in the novel's final scenes, Tommy's AIDS thus allows for a certain phobic representation of sexual difference. And while he is closely allied with Joe and Arnie, Tommy, as the main target of violence, unschooled in the ways of the wilderness, remains somehow distant from their masculinity. When Joe goes fishing, Tommy, despite having been invited several times to join him, remains at the camp, to sleep. Tommy provides his "side" in the wilderness conflict with its only weapon, a gun he carries with him, but this is a decidedly unmanly weapon, not at all like the hunting rifle that Carl carries for the other "side":

> Tommy went over to the Honda and unlocked the tool box. What he came back with was a .25 caliber, pearlhandled automatic, which Joe recognized immediately though it must have been forty-five years since he'd last seen it. Joe took it, hefted it. It practically disappeared in a hand as big as his.

"Lemme see, Top," Arnie said, and took possession. "Yep. What they used to call a ladies' gun. Guys bought 'em for their wives back in that Depression."

"There were a lot of hungry bums around," Joe remembered. "Mom used to keep this in the glove compartment, but I'm sure she never fired it except when Dad made her practice."

"She gave it to me when I went to New Orleans," Tommy said. "She thought it was a rough place, and it was, but I never fired the gun, either." (144)

When Joe is searching for Tommy and Carl in the woods, he "tr[ies] to imagine . . . Tommy, armed with his little lady's gun, trying to evade and maybe get the drop on a nut with a rifle": though Joe himself knows that "[t]he smart thing would be to go left, into deeper cover," he "doubt[s] Tommy kn[ows] how to think that way" (152). Tommy has in fact followed the less "smart" (and less "masculine"?) course of action, and he is wounded; incapacitated, he now depends wholly on the other men, and primarily Joe, for rescue.

Tommy serves as an irritant to the all-male scene, the motive force that will allow for the testing of masculinity, but he himself is not one of the subjects of that test. Arriving while the others are listening to a basketball game, he does not make his presence known until their (masculine) enjoyment is over— "I've been sitting by the camper, waiting for your game to end" (126). Tommy himself somehow knows that his presence will interrupt the scene at the campground, though clearly he does not foresee its full disruptive power.

In some sense, indeed, both homosexuality and AIDS—in the person of Tommy—exist in the novel only to catalyze the test of masculinity; both disappear once that test is complete. Not surprisingly, this disappearance is linked closely to the belief that AIDS involves an inevitable trajectory toward death. The novel's first explicit mention of AIDS evokes death—"he'd been celibate for all fourteen of the months that had passed since he'd sat with a young man named Bruno through the final weeks of Bruno's death from AIDS" (38)—and the first discussion of AIDS, in which Tommy explains why he has chosen not to be tested, sketches a "sure" linkage between HIV positivity and death: "So what's your preference? You want to know for sure you're strapped onto a self-propelled stretcher, moving slowly onto a mine? I'll take as much ignorance as I can get, for as long as I can have it" (50). Here, knowledge of one's HIV status is linked immediately to a "self-propelled" narrative whose movement may be "slow" but is also inevitable and fatal. Joe asks whether anyone "recovers," and Tommy answers, "I've heard rumors of remissions, but I think it's drumming on the tombstone. I don't know of any. I'm going to say nobody recovers" (50).

Tommy reconfirms this sense of the narrative of AIDS after his own diagnosis:

[I]f you test positive for AIDS, and you've already got this PCP, the barn door's open and you're not going to see the horses anymore. (129)

He also, however, expresses his understanding of AIDS as a "terminal" illness more temperately, recognizing here that his diagnosis does not in fact mean immediate death:

The only difference between you and us terminals is that we know what's going to get us, and more or less when. If somebody doesn't squish me under a truck or drown me in the river first, I've got about three years. That's a lot of time, Joe. (129-30)

The force of the novel, however, works against the "slow" version of AIDS that Tommy narrates here; indeed, it enacts, in Tommy's own person, a clear identification between diagnosis and death. Though there are several indications early in the novel that Tommy's health may not be all that it once was—he "needs some rest" (11), he "look[s] kind of tired" (38)—it is not until he is playing a long solo on the clarinet that he realizes something is wrong:

He started playing the great, nonstop line of music and, toward the end, caught himself cheating, cutting it into phrases, about to run out of breath. Puzzling.
Managed to finish it strong, hoping he didn't show the fear that had begun to chill him. His legs felt wavery, and his feet were ice cold. His stomach was heaving, not violently but deeply. He sat down, letting the applause buy him recovery time, but he wasn't really recovering, only holding on. (74)

Tommy . . . hop[ed] the infinity of sadness that he felt didn't show on his face or sound in his voice. Shortness of breath, dear Jesus, was often the first symptom of the onset. He didn't want to think the word AIDS with Joe there, and kept pushing it away.
"Dad, you must be tired after putting on a show like that," Little Joe said. (75)

Though the doctor assures Tommy that "You can run short of breath for a lot of reasons other than PCP" (75), in the days that follow—while he attends the Gathering of the Clans and waits for his official test results—Tommy has no doubt that he has AIDS, and the novel moves economically to suggest his approaching death. Helped by the Dexamils and Quaaludes the doctor prescribes (76), the days intervening between the initial suspicion of AIDS and its confirmation are a hallucinatory period characterized by a collapsing of Tommy's life history into the present: he confronts his own youth (78-80) and helps an Indian woman who, in his imagination, becomes also his great-grandmother (105-10). These retreats into the past enable Tommy "to lose himself . . . in the sense of living at a different, far-back time of his life" (80), but they also respond to, and reconfirm, the "[r]eality and foreboding" (80) Tommy feels: "So he took another Dexamil to get rid of the feeling that he was already dear old dead" (78).

"Forebodings" indeed fill the days before his unambiguous diagnosis. Tommy imagines "quit[ting] the music business and mov[ing] to Scotland"—"To go gently" (81). Watching the tides at the Bay of Fundy from his motorcycle, he hallucinates his own death:

[H]e could see, out there on the flat, a man on a motorcycle, with that crushing first wave coming towards him, trying to ride away from it. A fat man. The wheel was spinning, digging into the mud, deeper and deeper, until the bike disappeared and the man turned toward the incoming rush of tide, walked toward it, and he disappeared, too. (77)

Rather than play the "Lament for the Children" at the Gathering of the Clans as originally planned, Tommy plays it in isolation, at a place known as "Hippie Joe's castle," the strange seaside house of a "Yank [who] ran off from that war" (81) and "[s]tarved himself to death" (82); Tommy's incomplete performance, played "with no listeners except the ghost of Hippie Joe" (82), marks a break with his prior life:

Somewhere, no more than halfway through and just as he'd expected, he ran out of breath. He didn't try to force it. He let the music sound out, diminish, whisper out over the sea, and now it was time to start back to whatever word was waiting for him. (82-83)

Deciding not to return to the Gathering of the Clans, Tommy recognizes that he has somehow become a different person than he was a few hours earlier:

He'd started back thinking he'd look up the pipe majors for another familiar evening of booze and shop talk, but as he thought more about it, it seemed as if the Tommy who would have relished that might have drifted off with the pipe music over the cliff and into the sea in front of Hippie Joe's castle. (95-96)

In a comic version of his Bay of Fundy vision, Tommy here again imagines his (former) self disappearing into the sea: "He . . . let himself grin, thinking of that fat Tommy, swimming into the surf now, on his whale's way to Newfoundland" (96).

Of course, Carl's phobic response to hearing of Tommy's AIDS expresses in its murderous impulse the identification of AIDS and death. But Carl's attempt fails fully to secure that identification, and it is left to Tommy, and the novel itself, to finish that work. Wounded in the woods, though not in a life-threatening manner, left alone while Joe goes off to figure out a way to transport his brother to safety, Tommy reflects on the situation:

> Now he started thinking about Joe. And Little Joe. The two people he loved in this world. Wondering about staying in Joe's house as he got sicker. Not liking that much. How messy he'd be. Hating the idea of telling Little Joe. Feeling a lot of fear. A lot of it, and not just for when the painkiller would wear off. (162)

Strangely, this is the last we see of Tommy. When Joe and Doc Miles return to the log where they have left Tommy, ready to take him out of the woods, he is gone, disappeared:

> "Jesus," Joe said. "It's the right log, isn't it?" It wasn't really a question. There was blood on it and around it. "Tommy," he shouted. "Tommy."
> "He can't be gone," Doc Miles said.
> "He could have dragged himself," Joe said. There was a trail of disturbed leaves on the forest floor. They followed it to the river. There was blood on an exposed rock three feet out in the water.
> "Tommy," Joe yelled. "Tommy," and splashed out into the river, looking wildly downstream. There was nothing he could see downstream but water, and this time the tug of it against his legs was something fearful.
> "Oh, God," he said, turned, splashed back. "God, Tommy."
> Joe McKay slipped, fell to his knees on the riverbank, and wept.
> Then he stood up and said, "I'm going back for a paddle. I'm going to take this canoe down the river."
> "No, Joe," Doc Miles said, putting a hand on his arm. "No, there isn't any sense in that. Look at that water move."
> Joe looked, and let Miles put an arm around his shoulder. There was nothing he could do. He knew the river. Nothing. (164-65)

Given the choice between the "three years" he himself figures he has left and the option of being "drown[ed] . . . in the river first" (130), Tommy chooses the latter, chooses to literalize the fantasies of disappearing into the water that earlier express his fear of AIDS, chooses to confirm, in the most immediate way possible, the identification of himself as given over to death.

Joe memorializes Tommy immediately after his death in an action that echoes both the death itself and Tommy's premonitions of it:

> [Joe] waded into the river a few steps, set the bagpipe down in the water and watched the red-plaid bugger turn on its lazy side and float jauntily away, like some kind of goofy, Scotch, freshwater octopus, with half its legs sticking up in the air. (166)

But the novel shows no real mourning for Tommy back in "civilization": in Bourjaily's final chapter, a kind of coda to the wilderness adventure, when Joe asks Tommy's son, Little Joe (Joker), if he "miss[es his] Dad," Little Joe answers, "I never saw that much of him. Only in the last year or two—but I was starting to like him a lot. Sure I miss him. I wish he was here with us" (168). The reunion of Joe and Little Joe in this final chapter in fact fulfills the movement set up much earlier to ally Little Joe more with his straight uncle than with his gay father. Little Joe has had "reservations about his father for obvious enough reasons" (72), that is, because of his father's homosexuality. Tommy's "[h]ating the idea of telling Little Joe" (162) about his AIDS, part of the reflection that leads to his suicide, takes its place alongside a long-lived discomfort between father and son about the father's sexuality. And the discomfort of sexual difference has now, through Tommy's own action, been erased from the novel. Joe's "fatherly" relationship with Little Joe, indicated as "proper" even in the characters' names, is enabled by Tommy's removal of himself, his making way for Joe to play the role of "raiser of men" that we have seen him so adept at throughout the novel.

The erasure of the homosexual that Tommy's death effects is underlined in the novel's final chapter, even as Joe and Little Joe remember Tommy. They are playing basketball together, Joe's not Tommy's game, a fact that is made explicit in their conversation:

> "Did you and Dad play one-on-one when you were kids?"
> "Not much. Horse was his game. He was okay from the line."
> "What was his shot like?"
> "Kind of off-balance, from the chest, but it went in a lot." (168)

And what his son remembers about Tommy reaffirms his absence (his death) as perhaps a good thing in contrast to his presence (his life):

"He died a clean death, didn't he?"
"Yes."
"His life wasn't all that clean, though."
"Shut up, Joker. He had a lot of fun. He helped a lot of people. And people are going to be listening to his records for a while."
"And then they won't."
"Go take that run, mousebrain. Sweat that kind of crap out of yourself." (169)

Despite the largely "liberal" impulse of *Old Soldier*, the novel ends up strongly reinforcing an identification of gayness with weakness, disease, and death. The conclusion to Tommy's (brief) illness succeeds not only in constructing AIDS as somehow properly equivalent to death, but also in removing the homosexual from the novel and thus allowing the triumphant reaffirmation of a straight male homosociality unimpeded by both the female and the homosexual: as the novel ends, Little Joe's father has been replaced by a more appropriate role model; his mother is six time zones away (169). As the publicity for *Old Soldier* makes explicit, Tommy's "love" for Little Joe is that "of a father for a son he can only die for;"[29] his death functions as a "cleansing" of what "wasn't all that clean" from the novel, a removal of both AIDS and homosexuality. In the wake of that death, we are left with the "healthy" scene of straight male homosociality, freed of the queer presence that has disturbed it. The abjection, the casting out, of homosexuality and of the illness condensed with it, allows the reaffirmation of an undisturbed, male, heterosexual space, where young men can be raised into "true" masculinity.

NOTES

1. *Congressional Record—Senate*, 14 Oct. 1987, S14204.

2. Maupin, *Significant Others*, 67. Unless otherwise noted, all further references to Maupin in this chapter will be to *Significant Others* and will be given parenthetically in my text.

3. For the progress of Brian's narrative away from illness and toward heterosexuality, see 141, 192-93, 205-8, 221-24, 232-34, and 238.

4. *Roommates* was first broadcast on 30 May 1994, on NBC.

5. For just one instance, see Barbara Kantrowitz, with Mary Hager, Geoffrey Cowley, Lucille Beachy, Melissa Rossi, Brynn Craffey, Peter Annin, and Rebecca Crandall, "Teenagers and AIDS," *Newsweek* 3 Aug. 1992, 44-49.

6. The phrase is Watney's, "The Spectacle of AIDS," esp. 78-83.

7. Alice Hoffman, *At Risk* (New York: G. P. Putnam's Sons, 1988). For critical discussion of *At Risk*, see Nelson, "AIDS and the American Novel," 47-48; Judith Laurence Pastore, "Suburban AIDS: Alice Hoffman's *At Risk*," in Nelson, ed., *AIDS: The Literary Response*, 39-49; and Joseph Dewey, "Music for a Closing: Responses to AIDS in Three American Novels," in Nelson, ed., *AIDS: The Literary Response*, 23-38, esp. 27-29. Pastore briefly discusses *At Risk* in relation to Hoffman's other fiction.

8. David Leavitt, "The Way I Live Now," *New York Times Magazine* 9 July 1989, 28. Pastore, "Suburban AIDS," 39-40, also uses Leavitt's reactions as a starting point for her discussion of *At Risk*.

9. Back cover of the paperback edition (New York: Berkley Books, 1989).

10. Book jacket of the hardcover edition; nowhere in the framing of either hardcover or paperback editions is AIDS mentioned explicitly.

11. *Congressional Record—Senate*, 14 Oct. 1987, S14205.

12. Leavitt, "The Way I Live Now," 28.

13. Parenthetical citations give page numbers from the hardcover and paperback editions of Hoffman's novel respectively.

14. *Congressional Record—Senate*, 14 Oct. 1987, S14205.

15. Leavitt, "The Way I Live Now," 28.

16. Pastore, "Suburban AIDS," 47.

17. Pastore, "Suburban AIDS," 49.

18. For the development of this theme of seasonal change, see 15/7, 63/71, 74/84, 76/86, 94/110-11, 108-9/130, 113/137, 137/167, 171-72/217-18, 174/220, 195/247, and 200/261.

19. There is another rainstorm in the novel's final chapter; see 206/261.

20. Chapter 2, which focuses on Laurel Smith, is similarly framed by evocations of the future; see 31/29 and 35/34.

21. See Dewey, "Music for a Closing," 28, where Charlie is said to have "received news that his sister is dead"; and Pastore, "Suburban AIDS," 42 ("Amanda pulls through the first bout of PCP but dies after the second bout"), 46, and 47 (on Brian's "death").

22. Pastore, "Suburban AIDS," 47.

23. Hoffman several times uses the ends of chapters to present similar moments experienced by different characters. See, for instance, the concluding passages in chapters 5, 6, and 7.

24. Vance Bourjaily, *Old Soldier* (New York: Donald I. Fine, 1990). References to the novel are given parenthetically in my text.

25. Howard Frank Mosher, "Adventures in the Maine Woods," *New York Times Book Review* 28 Oct. 1990, 15.

26. James Dickey, *Deliverance* (New York: Dell, 1971 [1970]), 1.

27. The use here of the less diminutive nickname "Tom" in place of the much more common "Tommy" reinforces Joe's imaginative, wishful conjuring up of an alternative sexual identity for his brother.

28. D. A. Miller, "Anal Rope," in Fuss, ed., *Inside/Out*, 135.

29. This phrase is contained in both the synopsis provided on the inside book jacket of *Old Soldier* and in the publisher's pre-publication press release.

CHAPTER 5

John Weir's *The Irreversible Decline of Eddie Socket*

1. REFORMING NARRATIVE

In certain clear ways, John Weir's *The Irreversible Decline of Eddie Socket* belongs to the genre of AIDS novel exemplified by Paul Reed's *Facing It*:[1] the narrative of "irreversible decline" is, as its title declares, at the center of the story, and AIDS is here explored largely as an experience of white, urban (New York) gay men. At the same time, however, Weir's novel calls into question both the narrative it deploys and the identification of AIDS with gayness that it may at first seem to ratify. It does so not by constructing an account of illness alternative to the narrative of inexorable decline and death, the sort of redescription involved, for instance, in making AIDS a "chronic disease" and in emphasizing the possibility of "surviving and thriving" with AIDS.[2] Nor does it extend the reach of AIDS beyond gay men, as occurs in Hoffman's *At Risk* and (more tentatively) in Duplechan's *Tangled Up in Blue* and Maupin's *Significant Others*. Weir's questioning in fact proceeds in a more radical manner. Even as he depicts a particularly gay experience of AIDS, he interrogates the very identity categories that make possible the conflation of AIDS and gayness, destabilizing those categories and thus also that conflation. And even as Weir's novel represents AIDS through the "personal narrative" of illness, it intertwines that narrative with a variety of others, sometimes complementary, sometimes competing, and refuses to accept that narrative as the one "true" account of AIDS. How precisely to understand the several trajectories of Eddie's life and death becomes an active and explicit question in the novel, and Weir further asks what it means even to try to comprehend a life in narrative terms, according to particular histories of the self. In the process, all the novel's own narrative constructions become objects of inquiry. *The Irreversible Decline of Eddie Socket* thus simultaneously puts into play and puts in question some of our most common ways of understanding AIDS.

Weir's presentation of the narrative of "irreversible decline" in *Eddie Socket* is decidedly eccentric. While the novel's title declares Eddie himself as

163

the subject of decline, and while AIDS is first introduced into the novel in relation to Eddie—with "the pig, the punishing voice inside Eddie's head" (4), declaring, "I can't wait until you [arty little homosexual(s), faggot(s)] all get AIDS and die" (14)—for the first third of the tripartite novel, AIDS in fact seems more distant from Eddie than from any of the other major characters, except his parents. Eddie himself doesn't appear to know people with AIDS, in contrast to his boss Saul and Saul's (and Eddie's) lover Merrit Mather, who seem to know almost only people with AIDS: "Mark nods at me now, and I smile. He has AIDS, and so does his lover. Claudio is dead and his lover, diagnosed a year ago, is in the hospital" (29). When first introduced to the novel, Saul and Merrit have in fact "just come from [Claudio's] viewing"—"As in, dead body. Not that it's such an unusual thing. Actually, it would be unusual if we had not just come from a viewing, these-days-wise" (16). AIDS-related deaths, and their attendant rituals, have reformed Saul and Merrit's life together, structuring it in new, but already familiar ways:[3]

> So anyway, the phone rings, six o'clock this morning, cold Friday morning late in March. Merrit picks it up, he blinks, he looks at me and frowns. He doesn't have to say a thing. Right away I know another person died. It's the wake-up call. It always comes at six o'clock. . . . It can only mean death, and I don't have to hear it to know how it goes. "Hello, Merrit? This is Tom: I just got a call from Jim who spoke to Richard, who just talked to Luis who was in the room with Peter when Claudio—" and it's the whole gay community inside your telephone receiver at dawn, rehearsing the chorus that begins, "I just got a call," and ends with a pause, a dash, the word left out, the crucial word. That's the space for you to fill in yourself, to tell yourself the words in whatever way you prefer—he died, or he expired, or he smoked his last, or crossed the River Styx to meet Saint Peter at the pearly gate. (23)

In the first section of the novel, the insistent presence of AIDS for Saul and Merrit is concretized in the figure of Horatio, a friend whose ashes, unclaimed for seven months, Saul is carrying when he and Merrit first encounter Eddie (18, 26-27). Horatio, with all the losses he represents, is at the center of Merrit and Saul's tense relationship, participating intimately, and messily, in their lives:

> So what do I do? It's shameful, but I have to admit, and don't pretend you haven't committed similar acts, with someone, your mother, your lover, assuming there's a difference. I knock Horatio on the floor. I was aiming for the salad bowl, except my aim was never very good. I

do knock some carrots off the table, but also, alas, poor Horatio. His canister shatters everywhere, and the bag he was in bursts open, spilling brittle bits of bone and powdery ash on the floor, and his remains get mixed with round bits of carrot.

Merrit says, "Oh Christ."

I say, "That's what you've done to my heart."

. . .

. . . Then Larry [Merrit's dog] walks into the room, with ash on his nose. He comes for a kiss, and lays a sooty slop of drool on each of our laps. (62, 64)

Saul "env[ies] Eddie what appears to be his ignorance of this: that my marriage is to me a series of funerals, and wake-up calls" (29). And while Eddie does confront AIDS in certain ways—Horatio "accompanies" Eddie and Merrit on their first date, with Merrit asking Eddie to "take charge" of him (19)—Eddie's main response to the epidemic has been a withdrawal: "He had stopped having sex two years earlier" (5). He puts AIDS aside in a way that the other characters—Merrit and Saul; Eddie's roommate Polly Plugg and her boyfriend Brag, with their concern for safer sex (see 34, 42, 52-55, 114)—do not. When Merrit returns to Eddie's apartment with him, Eddie realizes that he is completely unprepared for a sexual encounter: "he had nothing in the house like condoms, or lubrication" (42).

While Weir's novel makes clear early on that it will in part be about AIDS, its first third shows Eddie himself concerned primarily with other matters. The initial disjunction between AIDS and Eddie renders uncertain the meaning of his promised "irreversible decline," which we might indeed come to imagine as involving not AIDS but rather the general malaise that affects Eddie from the beginning of the novel:

That his life was filled with despair he never questioned: the despair of loneliness or the despair of boredom, the despair of having had too much of what he nominally wanted, yet nothing of what he yearned for truly in his heart of hearts, the despair of being white and guilty about it, and of being generally gifted, but not specifically motivated, just inert. (5)

In not immediately specifying the referent of its title, the novel undermines any easy assumption that an "irreversible decline" and gay man together *must* mean AIDS. Nevertheless, the novel does come finally to implicate Eddie in a narrative of "irreversible decline" defined by AIDS, and thus in some sense to reaffirm the collocation of gay men, AIDS, and "irreversible decline" that it has earlier called into question. The disjunction of "irreversible decline" from the "obvious" referent of AIDS is ultimately shown to be not a true disjunction but a deferral, and a deferral that in fact makes the ultimate linkage of Eddie to AIDS all the more powerful. The first line of the novel's second section—"Eddie Socket got it. AIDS" (99)—hits with particular force for the very reason that, to this point, Eddie has remained at a distance from the experience of AIDS. The chapter that contains the revelation of Eddie's AIDS is called "It Never Entered My Mind," and Eddie here "gets it" in a double sense, along with his diagnosis coming to understand something of the force of AIDS that he has so far tried to avoid.

The belated entry of AIDS into Eddie's narrative thus enacts a complex, and partly self-contradictory, movement—a questioning of the *necessity* of "the irreversible decline of Eddie Socket" *as* AIDS followed by the powerful deployment of AIDS as, in fact, "irreversible decline." But while Eddie is here in some sense "turned over" to AIDS and the novel itself "turned over" to a narrative of "irreversible decline," Weir continues to rewrite that narrative, calling its invariable structure and its inevitability into question even as these are evoked. The blunt announcement of Eddie's "getting" AIDS launches the "personal narrative" of illness, but at the same time represents a significant departure from that narrative. Writers like Reed, Duplechan, Maupin, Hoffman, and Bourjaily never announce an AIDS diagnosis without preparation, without presenting signs and symptoms of illness that often lead to a self-diagnosis only later confirmed by a physician. Weir, to the contrary, carefully avoids any intimation of Eddie's illness in the first third of his novel, so that the announcement of diagnosis comes with no preparation. The gradual discovery of illness, so important in other AIDS novels, is not, however, erased from Weir's narrative; rather, it is postponed, presented retroactively:

> The lesion on his foot had shown up a few days after that [Eddie and Merrit's last weekend together]. At least, that was the first time he noticed it, and for two days he pretended that it wasn't there. Anyway, it could have been a long-forgotten smudge of tar from childhood, off the streets of Flemington, or indelible ink—his pens leaked, everywhere. The refrigerator door was stained; why not his heel? But the second lesion, a reddish-purple almond-shaped blister on the vulnerable, livid flesh of his inner thigh, was harder to ignore. Could it have been a kiss? A lover who had come to him when he was sleeping, dreaming? Merrit's tooth marks? Eddie thought not. Was it really just a bruise, then? A blood clot? Well, the one on his heel itched. Poison ivy? He bathed in scalding hot water and baking powder, but it didn't go away. At the end of the week, he found Dr. Fillgrave, who did a biopsy. They sent away to Kansas, or Lincoln, Nebraska, somewhere like that,

for the lab results. Eddie had gotten AIDS from Nebraska, he thought, trying to laugh. But his customary defenses were failing him. (100)

This passage covers all the "stages" that characterize an approaching AIDS diagnosis in more straightforward narrative presentations—the lesions (and their fantasmatic denial), the trip to the doctor, the biopsy, the lab results. As Eddie sees the "signs" more and more clearly, the imaginative transformations of their meaning—a smudge, a stain, a kiss, a bite, a bruise, a clot, poison—approach identity with the very illness (conceived as sexual "stain" and as injury) that they try to conceal. And this replacement of denial by discovery is in some way identified with the action of AIDS itself. Eddie's "customary defenses fail him" in a double sense: even as he can no longer "defend" himself from illness through denial, illness—AIDS as a failure of the body's "customary defenses"—manifests itself.

But while Weir thus brings Eddie step by step to his "getting it/AIDS," it is not insignificant that this occurs retroactively, as a "filling in" postponed until after the sudden and stark announcement of diagnosis. The more usual sequence of intimation, suspicion, perhaps denial, confirmation takes characters and readers together through a process of discovery that moves "forward" with what seems ineluctable force: How could the lesion not evoke thoughts of AIDS? How could those thoughts not be confirmed by testing? It is of course such a logic of narrative necessity against which authors like Maupin and Duplechan intervene by showing their characters confronting "signs" of AIDS that turn out not to be "true." Weir also intervenes against this logic, but in a different way, reversing the order of narrative so that the confirmation of illness precedes its intimation. The sudden announcement of Eddie's "getting" AIDS comes not as the endpoint of some orderly, necessary process. Rather, *here it is*, a sudden, unpredictable, perhaps even unthinkable rupture in Eddie's life and in Weir's storytelling, presented, after all, under the heading "It Never Entered My Mind" (99). That Eddie and Weir retrospectively reconstruct the narrative of "discovery" may in part repair that rupture, but it does not fully cover it over.

Indeed, this retroactive "filling in" of the narrative is presented as part of Eddie's complex reactions to his diagnosis, and it takes its place within a retrospective and prospective (re)reading of events rather than a "progressive" account of them. The story of how Eddie "discovers" that he has AIDS, marked throughout by what Eddie "notices," "pretends," "ignores," "thinks," stands amidst a proliferation of narratives stretching backwards and forwards in time, all occurring as Eddie—"barricaded" (100) "in the bathroom just outside the doctor's office where he was diagnosed" (99), recognizing as "the facts" that "[h]e was a man, not a boy, alone in a bathroom, which was painted aqua blue, and made of cinder blocks, and he had AIDS" (100)—tries "to determine how all this made him feel" (100). His first thoughts are prospective, engaging the idea of AIDS as death, though only obliquely:

> Eddie Socket got it. AIDS.
> "America is dying slowly," he said, sitting on the lid of a toilet seat and staring into a mirror. . . . He folded and refolded a postcard he had gotten that morning from his father, which was inscribed with more of the quotation by Saint Cyril his father had been running past him for weeks like a miniseries. "We go to the father of souls," it said, "but it is necessary to pass by the dragon."[4] (99)

While Eddie here confronts his father's Christian moralizing about the "path" toward death, and while we might expect Eddie now to figure himself and not just "America" as "dying slowly," he presents instead a countertext and countermovement, a comic response written against the heavy "morality" of the postcard:

> Eddie wrote a lyric on his father's postcard, which he softly sang to the tune of "Frère Jacques":
> Purple lesions, purple lesions
> On my foot, on my thigh,
> Slowly multiplying.
> Does this mean I'm dying?
> No, not I. No, not I. (99)

From here, Eddie moves into a mixture of retrospective and prospective thinking, reviewing the doctor's visit that has just been completed and that includes, alongside the diagnosis, a prognosis:

> Dr. Fillgrave had a fixed, bland expression beneath which percolated a bilious loathing, and he treated Eddie as if he were just another cadaver. "You'll last a good two weeks, don't worry, two years, maybe six years if you're lucky," he offered, helpfully, when all the blood rushed out of Eddie's face and he thought he was going to faint, "unless of course you don't have health insurance, in which case, the quicker the better, eh?" He actually said that, like a bad stand-up comic doing "the doctor from hell." But doctors, Eddie thought, if they didn't kill you with their ignorance, they would surely try to kill you with their knowledge. That he, indeed, did not have medical insurance seemed to him merely an additional argument in favor of alternative treatments, like suicide, perhaps, or—what? "Douche with Borax," the doctor suggested, flatly, when Eddie asked him what to do about sex. For his

first concern was still Merrit. He didn't know if this was a way to hang on to him, or to drive him, irrevocably, away. Though it seemed he had already lost him, for Merrit hadn't called since their last weekend together. (100)

The thought of the weekend with Merrit leads to the reconstruction of the narrative of discovery (quoted above), and, as Eddie feels his "defenses failing him," the retrospective movement continues with evocations of a more and more distant past. "[L]ook[ing] in the mirror," Eddie confronts his "pig" and speaks both his homophobic imaginings about the "causes" of AIDS and his resistance to these:

"That's some pair of lesions you've got there," said the pig. "Kind of a nice shade, just this side of rigor mortis."
"I don't need you."
"How come you got sick?"
"Bad luck," Eddie said. "I haven't had sex in two years. And Merrit tested negative."
"Yeah, right, and the check's in the mail, and I won't come in your mouth if you don't want me to. Took those drivers up the dirt path once too often, huh?"[5]
"Listen, I've been perfectly abstemious for two years," he said, stuffing his father's postcard into his pocket. "K. S.," he said.
"Kill Sodomites." (101)

While Eddie recognizes that what is called for is not an addressing of the question "how come you got sick?"—"bad luck" is an answer that denies the force of the question "how come?"—he still cannot help speculating about the origins of his illness: "all he could think apart from the pig, were stupid things, like wishing that he had finished reading *War and Peace*, and wondering which dick it was, which dicks (there hadn't been so many), which dollop of semen, or blood" (101). He thinks back to "[t]he first time he had had sex" (102), reflecting on what sex has meant or failed to mean to him, and he moves to connect the sexual past to his current situation in a way that both asserts a causal link between sex and illness and questions the moralizing reading that would attribute AIDS to a particular kind of ("promiscuous") sex life: "And it [sex] had not even occurred, not to Eddie, as often as (probably) anyone else would have thought it had (his mother, his father, Polly, Merrit Mather), considering he had gotten AIDS. If he had known he was going to get sick anyway, he would have tried to enjoy it more" (102).

In the brief scene that opens the second section of Weir's novel, a whole complex of narratives thus arises from the rupture that is Eddie's diagnosis.

These include the harshest possible version of a moralized narrative of "irreversible decline" that stretches backward and forward in time and links "sodomitical" sex in some essential way with AIDS and AIDS itself with an unavoidable death. At the same time, this narrative is recognized explicitly as a homophobic construction—of the Christian "morality" Eddie's father sends him in bits and pieces; of "the pig, the punishing voice inside Eddie's head" (4); of the "Fillgraves" who will try to "kill you" with both "their ignorance" and "their knowledge"—and, in counterpoise to such voices, the scene posits other possible constructions. The "abstemious" life that Eddie has prescribed for himself, and that "moralists" like his father and Saint Cyril would also insist on, has no consequence for his situation, which can in fact be seen as arising from "bad luck." And while Eddie's thoughts are filled with premonitions of death—"suicide, perhaps, or—what?"; "two weeks, . . . two years, maybe six years if you're lucky"—the future is itself subject to "luck," by no means clearly or completely laid out: "Does this mean I'm dying? / No, not I." Eddie's "first concern," after all, is not death but the possibility of continuing his relationship with Merrit.

The complications that thus attend the introduction of Eddie's illness into the novel do not challenge the "reality" of AIDS, declared strongly as what Eddie "got." Nor do they deny the narrative of "irreversible decline" real power as a means for understanding AIDS, its "causes" and "effects." But the complicated deployment of the narrative does suggest that it is a *means* of understanding, one among several ways of thinking about Eddie's situation, and not a necessary or "natural" account of the "course" of illness.

Weir chooses—unlike Reed or Hoffman or Bourjaily—not to make the narrative of "irreversible decline" the *sole* way of putting together the story of AIDS. This narrative is central to the novel, with Eddie moving from diagnosis to a display of symptoms to the hospital and finally to death. But at no stage does the narrative become the smooth, uninterrupted account of decline and death that its synopsis would make it: Eddie's illness involves instead multiple punctuations and interruptions. Though, after his diagnosis, Eddie almost immediately begins exhibiting what may be read as symptoms, these are explained, by Eddie himself, but by the narrator too, as primarily meaningful in ways unconnected to illness. On the morning when Eddie plans to travel, with Polly, to visit his mother and reveal to both women that he has AIDS, an intention ultimately unfulfilled, he "woke up early feeling sick to his stomach, slightly headachy, and dry at the back of the throat" (121). This feeling, however, is explicitly connected not to his illness but to "what it meant to visit Mom, and Flemington, New Jersey"; he is "not ill, but nervous, like a boy in grammar school on his way to a spelling bee in which he would be tested on words that had, for him, uncomfortable meanings, words like Sally, faggot, homo, queer, all the words that had been used against him in grade school and high school" (121). Similarly, when Eddie meets with Merrit to tell him that he is sick—an enterprise only marginally more successful than the earlier attempt to tell his mother and Polly—Eddie feels symptoms ostensibly connected not to AIDS but to what is happening with Merrit: "Merrit was treating him like a trick; Eddie had the awful, dry-mouthed, headachy feeling of having awakened in a stranger's bedroom at dawn, and been offered coffee, rather diffidently" (136). Later still, in a phone call to his mother, Eddie "sound[s] out of breath" (180), but why this is is never specified.

Eddie's diagnosis in fact leads to a long sequence in the book, almost the whole of its middle third, where, despite such suggestions, the "progress" of illness is essentially suspended while at the center of attention stand other matters—Eddie's "failure to confess to anyone he truly cared about" (149) that he has AIDS, the trip he takes to California "with an itinerant drag queen from Staten Island named Eulene" whom he meets on the bus (152). AIDS is by no means forgotten in this suspension of the narrative of illness. The California trip is motivated by Eddie's sense that "[h]e had . . . three choices: he could sleep away the rest of his life, he could find a miracle cure, or he could leave" (149); as he begins the trip, Eddie "packed what he wanted to die with" (150). But though AIDS remains significant in the account of Eddie's actions—and not least as an absent presence, creating tension over when and how it might actively reappear—the novel follows its powerful announcement of diagnosis *not* by giving Eddie over to a separate realm of disease and death but rather by continuing to examine the ways in which he leads his life. Even if Eddie becomes sicker and sicker during the period depicted in the novel's second section, the "progression" of illness is not where Eddie, or Weir, chooses to focus attention.

In its putting aside of the narrative of "irreversible decline," this second part of the book, like its first, engages in a deferral. As in the novel's earlier refusal to define the referent of Eddie's "irreversible decline," where Eddie's own avoidance of AIDS and the novel's distancing of him from it reflect each other, the suspension of the narrative of illness in the novel's second section is at least in part a function of Eddie's psychology: it enacts, in its silence about changes in his health, a certain denial of illness foregrounded in Eddie's inability to "confess to" friends and family and dramatized by his trip to California. The "runaway kid" he has internalized advises him to "[f]lee, all is discovered" (149).[6] And the novel's eventual return to a charting of illness— as its second section draws to a close—is explicitly linked to Eddie's beginning awareness that he "was starting to get sick, though he hadn't quite acknowledged it," that "[t]he only people who" know this are "Dr. Fillgrave and a couple of lab technicians in Nebraska," and "that the time had probably come to tell someone that he had AIDS" (183). As in the account of diagnosis and the events preceding it, the novel moves here in part to conflate Eddie's willingness to admit illness with the manifestation of symptoms. Eddie tells Eulene that he is sick, "but obliquely" (189), making sure she "figure[s] this out" herself (190) before he says "directly" (189), "I was diagnosed in, I don't know, April or May or June" (190); correlated with this "oblique" revelation is an increasing clarity in the outward signs of his illness. Eddie at first "look[s] pale" and "tired" (185) to Eulene; later, she discovers that his hands are "sweaty and cold" (189). And she ends up checking "his forehead . . . for fever" (189). As Eddie's resistance to "acknowledging" his illness wanes, the narrative of that illness returns; or, in the converse formulation, as illness intensifies, his "customary defenses fail him" once again and he is forced to recognize that he is really sick.

While from this point on the narrative of illness remains central to the novel, it still does not show a smooth, uninterrupted "decline." The transition from the end of the novel's second part to the start of its third mirrors, in its sudden acceleration of narrative, the earlier jump between first and second sections. Having told Eulene of his illness, having decided to "go home" (190), and having called his mother from the airport to tell her "I have a terminal disease" (192), Eddie returns to New York in a way that, dramatically, continues the process of revelation: appearing ill on Saul's doorstep (195), he also almost immediately insists on seeing Polly (196). A striking escalation in illness again mirrors the drive toward revelation: before his departure from San Francisco, Eddie's illness was just "starting" to manifest itself—"I really didn't get sick until the plane," he says to Saul (196)—but that sickness has become far "advanced" by the time of his arrival in New York. In the opening words of the novel's final section, spoken by Saul:

> "You lean," he says to me. All right? "You lean." Shocked the hell out of the doorman, let me tell you. "I had stepped outside," the doorman says, his eyebrows radically arched, discreetly signaling distress, "to hail a cab for a lady. The young man was waiting here when I returned, asking for you." And I mean, let me tell you now, you have to understand, this description of Eddie as a "young man waiting," well, it's rather a circumspect depiction. If I didn't know my doorman better, I would suspect him of irony. Because we're talking scrambled eggs here on the floor of the Prasada, scrambled Eddie, who looks like nothing so much this morning as the prone, lamenting personification of AIDS. I mean, of course it's AIDS, what else could it be, I ought to know by now the look of someone dying from AIDS—for he's come to my lobby to die. This is my call, my wake-up call for Eddie. And I have to give him credit, it's a very dramatic variation on a tiresome theme, Eddie collapsed on the white marble floor, at eight o'clock in the morning, asking for me, no kidding, not Merrit, but me. (195)

Like the sudden announcement of Eddie's diagnosis, the rapid acceleration of illness here, at the same time that it participates in returning the narrative of "irreversible decline" to prominence, constitutes a rupture in that narrative; in one quick movement, Eddie is sped from his adventure on the West Coast back to New York and into the hospital. The sense of disruption here is intensified not only by the long period in which Eddie's symptoms have remained unrecognized but also by the gradual way in which those symptoms enter the novel in the scene with Eulene; we might expect a similarly gradual "progress" of illness in later scenes. And in addition to disturbing a sense of predictability, the narrative acceleration here threatens to catapult Eddie out of narrative—"he's come to my lobby to die"—and thus to confirm a strong identification of AIDS with quick, inexorable death. Saul stresses a prognosis for Eddie that is not good:

> I can tell you that Eddie is going to go right away. Some people hold on for months, some for years, some even forget that they're sick, then, bang, one morning they're gone. But some fall apart in a week. Eddie's one of those. I can tell. I'm writing his eulogy now in my head. (195-96)

Certainly, the novel has moved at many points toward the identification of AIDS with death—in Saul and Merrit's experience of AIDS as unremitting loss; in Eddie's naming of Dr. Fillgrave; in Fillgrave's prognosis for Eddie; in Eddie's own anticipations of death (he spends the evening of his diagnosis "making a will" and "choosing a cemetery plot" in Woodlawn Cemetery "next to Herman Melville" [116]), and in his recognition that even the most reflexive anticipations of the future must be rethought:

> "Sometime when I'm sixty and she [Eddie's mother] [i]s dead, I'll hear 'Musetta's Waltz' in some disgusting bar somewhere miles away, and weep. Except, oops—"
> "Except what?" Polly said.
> He was going to say, "Oops, except I forgot she's the one who's going to be weeping at sixty for me," but it seemed wrong to say, even if Polly had known he was sick. It was just too sentimental. Early death? Judith Traherne, in *Dark Victory*? *Not my scenario*, he thought . . . (129-30)[7]

Part of Weir's clear agenda is to face Eddie's death squarely and in so doing to confront what he calls in another context "the foolish American faith that nobody dies"; he wants vividly to show "what death feels like . . . its monotony, its repetitiveness, the slow accretion of losses."[8] From the point of

Eddie's return to New York, beginning with Saul's observations in the lobby of his apartment house, the novel focuses in very closely on what happens to Eddie as he becomes sicker, and through this whole process, the anticipated endpoint of Eddie's illness, his death, impends. Trying to impress the hospital receptionist with the urgency of Eddie's need for a bed, Saul says, "He's terminally ill. . . . Terminal, as in train station, as in last stop" (198). Looking over at Eddie in the emergency room, Saul imagines that he can see HIV at work: "Eddie . . . looks as if the last eleven of his red blood cells are about to be devoured, tasty morsels, by the killer virus" (198). When finally Eddie is "tuck[ed] . . . neatly into his rollaway bed like an oversized shoe tree," Saul observes that "he's there to keep the shape and stiffness of his sheets, though considering how thin he's gotten in the past few weeks—the past few hours, for all I know—he's not going to keep much of anybody's shape for long" (198). "Personifying" AIDS for Saul (195), Eddie also comes for both Saul and Polly to represent death and dying: "I think, I want to look at death, I'll visit Eddie" (225); "*no one is busy dying quite as rapidly, as unexpectedly, as my friend Eddie Socket*" (213). Eddie himself, as he receives visitors in the hospital—where he realizes he will "be living . . . from now on" (206; also see 229 and 238)—feels "like Rudolph Valentino in a casket, surrounded by aggrieved, adoring fans" (205); "his life passed in and out of his room, ominously, portentously, a daily procession of luminaries emerging from out of his past, bearing gifts, like the Magi" (206).

The novel carefully follows the manifestations of Eddie's illness: his shingles (214); the problems with his spleen, "growing like the Blob, subsuming unsuspecting red cells into its spongy, vascular walls" (230; also see 235 and 245); the thrush, "[j]ust some foam around the edges of his mouth, like a sink regurgitating" (236); the "PCP, pneumonia" (237); his "coughing blood" (238). He is seen depending sporadically upon an oxygen mask (216, 236, 237). And Eddie himself details other aspects of his treatment:

> "I don't want to give them my spleen," Eddie said. . . .
> "You're on medication?" his father asked.
> "Oh, yeah, a lot of stuff."
> "What stuff?"
> "I don't know. Percodan mostly, as far as I know, and mists and sprays, and hourly injections, and little red pills, and big blue pills. I've got a chart in the drawer, I have to mark down what I take, when I take it. That's all. I don't have to say how I like it, or why it's good for me. It's pretty easy to be dying, I guess, you lie here and no one ever asks you to explain yourself, they just say 'Roll up your sleeve.' Or 'Stick out your tongue.' Or 'Don't bleed on me.'" (231)

> [T]he doctors contemplate which of my organs are dispensable, and remove them. They want to open up my scrotum, take away my balls, and stuff white bits of Styrofoam in there to soak up the blood. What blood? I ask. The blood from the incision in your scrotum. Now is this Catch-Twenty-two or is this Nazi doctor school or what? Because, if they consider me an organ bank, they ought to know that I don't have so many organs I can spare. (239)

At the same time, however, that the novel so closely examines Eddie's decline, so clearly presents his treatment as ineffectual or even injurious, and so directly portends his death, it also shows Eddie's illness to be not fully predictable, to admit contingency. As noted above, Eddie's first responses to AIDS both grapple with a sense of unavoidable death and question whether death is the necessary end of AIDS: "Was he dying? People lasted longer lately, but then sometimes they didn't. How long would he last? He needed time, to do a lot of things" (102). Even as Eddie reveals to his mother that he has "a terminal disease," his thoughts move in a contrary direction:

> I'm thinking that I want my life. I want it whole, and I want it complete, I want its texture and its spirit, I want its internal rhythms and its external shape, I want it all at once and forever, and I want it now. I want it now that it's going, Mom, and that's the final reversal. "The tables have turned with a vengeance." That's Tennessee Williams.[9] (192)

A certain sense of teleological uncertainty inheres in Eddie's story even as he becomes sicker and sicker. Despite Saul's seeming certainty about Eddie's prognosis, in the first hospital scenes he works intently against his own presumption of a sure, quick death:

> We get him plugged into an IV and a TV, and I scream for blood (literally), and we sit with him through the transfusions, which lethally indifferent nurses administer. Then I scream some more and get sedatives, which another nurse injects into one of Eddie's pale, almost fleshless buttocks, while a doctor stands by, ineffectually. (198)

Saul is anything but "lethally indifferent" or "ineffectual" here, and his own prediction that "Eddie is going to go right away" (195)—accompanied as it is by the qualification that this is a pattern *not* followed by many others—in fact turns out to be untrue, in part thwarted by his own efforts in getting Eddie to the hospital, setting him up in a room, starting his treatment, and negotiating the "truly, truly Kafkaesque absurdity and circularity with the world of health insurance, forms inside of forms inside of forms" to get Eddie "Medicaid coverage, and insurance benefits, and a larger room" (205). Eddie survives much longer than Saul at first predicts, and Saul himself comes to a new assessment of Eddie's future prospects: "Eddie is what you'd call a scrapper, a term reserved for underdog political candidates and losing pitchers. They're going to take out all his organs one by one until there's nothing left" (238). While this is, of course, not a *hopeful* assessment, it does emphasize survival in a way Saul's earlier prognosis does not. And throughout the account of Eddie's illness vicissitudes rather than certainties are stressed: twice an operation to remove Eddie's spleen is scheduled, and twice it is postponed (238, 239). Saul, even while he repeatedly expresses a knowledge of Eddie's impending death, acts to care for and comfort him in ways that assert his continued, wished for—if painful and precarious—life: "I put my hand on his back, I can feel his spine. I want my cells to drain from my palm to his marrow" (226). Similarly, Polly, visiting Eddie as he is about to die, expresses how she feels things *should* be: "People are not supposed to get worse in hospitals. They're supposed to get better" (245). While the wish may be futile—Eddie responds, "I guess it hasn't worked for me" (245)—she does her best to fulfill it in caring for Eddie as none of his professional nurses will:

> Neither one of them spoke as she washed his hair. The showerhead had a long attachment, the tip of which she held close to his head, and wet and lathered and rinsed and lathered and rinsed Eddie's hair, which had turned thin and soft with his sickness, almost textureless. She soaped his arms and chest, and legs, and his back, very gently, and she drained the tub and rinsed him everywhere, between his toes, his pubic hair, the backs of his legs. He watched her hands when he could, and grunted softly. Then when they were done, she helped him again to his feet, and wrapped him in a towel, and he sat on the john while she went back into his room and finished cleaning the floor. She changed his linen, dropping the sheets and soiled towels in the corner, with his soiled shift. She helped him walk out of the john, but he had to be lifted into his bed, where he pulled the fresh white sheet across his legs, and held Polly's hand. She sat beside him on the bed; he didn't want to let her go. (247)

Though, in the novel's final section, the account of Eddie's illness moves forcefully toward the closure of death, the narrative of "irreversible decline"— evoked in the novel's title; set in motion only when its first third is already complete; suspended for almost the whole of the novel's second third; and even in its final, strong impetus toward closure involved in particularities of illness and treatment that, while part of Eddie's "course" toward death, also constitute the not wholly predictable details of his life—never becomes one monolithic, overpowering force, sweeping away, unalterably, all other thoughts and expectations; rather, this narrative is repeatedly deployed, derailed, fragmented, redeployed, reconfigured.

2. BODY AND VOICE: NARRATIVE DELAY, CLOSURE, AND PROLIFERATION

Despite the drive toward death in the "personal narrative" of AIDS, none of the novels earlier discussed except *Facing It*—in which Reed follows Andy, in the last moment of the novel, to his last moment of consciousness—actually brings its protagonist to death in full view of other characters and of the reader. Maupin and Duplechan maintain Michael and Crockett living more or less normal lives with HIV; when people with AIDS (Jon, Charlie Rubin) die in Maupin's *Tales of the City* series, they tend to do so in the interstices between novels. In Hoffman's *At Risk*, Amanda doesn't die, but her physical presence is erased, and memorials erected in its place. Tommy's death in Bourjaily's *Old Soldier* is literally a disappearance, occurring offstage, with Tommy's bulky body finally replaced by the bagpipes that Joe, *in memoriam*, sends downstream after him. In *The Irreversible Decline of Eddie Socket*, however, Weir follows Eddie to his death, keeping him constantly in view, focusing close attention on his body and its decay: "Eddie was falling apart magnificently" (219); "He has the dignity of falling apart spectacularly, in a way I wouldn't have thought possible" (241). In a remarkable sequence of scenes, Eddie's body is displayed—to Saul, to Polly, to his mother and father, to Eddie himself, and of course, over and over again, to the reader. Following the advice that he has Saul give Merrit in preparation for his (never achieved) visit to Eddie in the hospital—"Look at him squarely, and flinch if you want, and let him know that you see. Don't pretend he's not there" (254)—Weir insists on looking at Eddie, on not having him simply disappear, whisked away, replaced by more comfortable, controllable memories or mementos.[10]

Indeed, the display of Eddie's ailing body is intensified, not replaced, by memories. Immediately after Saul and Polly have taken Eddie to the hospital, just as the specularizing of his body begins, Polly remembers a prior image of that body:

> His belly . . . is, or rather, was, slightly distended, outwardly sloping, curving roundly over his cock, which is inset deeply, almost feminine the way he carries it, his hips highly arched, his pubic hair growing thickly, and his penis held within, protected. (200)

Polly here imaginatively reconstructs a lost corporeality, the image of a now impossible fullness that condenses "[w]hat [she] really like[s] about [Eddie]" (200) and that runs counter to both traditional straight and gay imagings of the male body. Eddie's "distended" belly and "inset" penis stand separate from typical representations of the "invulnerable" (heroic, athletic, gym-toned) "masculine" body, and yet the "almost feminine" stance is presented as not vulnerable but "protected," an image of safety and health. This image of the full, protected, remembered body will hang over all the scenes that follow, as the "progressive" failure of Eddie's bodily "defenses"—the loss of the protectedness that Polly holds firmly in her memory—appears graphically in description after description:

> [H]e's a sour-smelling, emaciated, pigeon-breasted, dying little boy, with too much to think about and not a lot to do, and a scruffy growth of beard now, since the hospital, and big blue eyes, and long, skinny legs, and bedsores, and a hopeless expression, a collapsed expression, a decided, given-up expression, and a mask these days he uses off and on for oxygen and long, long beautiful eyelashes, and thrush. (236)

> I can see the balls in the joints of his elbows, all this skin collapsed around them. He groans a little as he tries to lift himself. His ass is missing. He doesn't have buttocks anymore, just skin there, hanging on his bones like a bad fit. His anus hangs out naked down below, like a monkey's. (241)

In part such descriptive passages objectify Eddie, keeping him at a distance; at the same time, however, in bringing his body so vividly into focus, they collapse distance, thrusting Eddie into an intense intimacy with other characters and with the reader:[11] "[Polly] had never felt, not with him or anyone, the terrible hush and hotness of intimacy that she now felt, looking at his ruined body" (247). Over and over the display of Eddie's body in fact leads in the novel to a physical and emotional closeness nowhere else achieved. It is as Eddie's body is made present to his father, as the two compare the width of their arms—"'Of course, it used to be thicker,' [Eddie] said" (232)—that they approach their one moment of (near) connection: though Eddie concludes, from the comparison, that "[w]e're nothing alike," the two men do touch, and Eddie remembers when, as a child, "[he] sat up on his [father's] knees, on the bed, and reached out for a hug, which his father supplied" (232). A fuller vision of the changes in Eddie's body, shared with his mother, leads similarly to a moment of real, if fleeting, intimacy:

> [H]e was naked long enough for them to see, concretely, what had happened to him. His legs were pale and bluish in spots, and covered with lesions that multiplied daily. His feet were scaly and dry. His hips were stretched with skin that sagged and bunched almost like the

hospital shift. His penis hung sadly, grotesquely flaccid, and brown. His ribs were like the cartoon carcass of a fish, licked clean of flesh. He rearranged his legs, and stretched the shift until it covered his genitals. But quickly, before he covered himself, he looked in his mother's eyes. He knew that she saw. For in the instant he was naked, he could see her recoiling as if she had been shot. He felt her intake of breath, saw the childish look of disbelief that flickered across her face. She held her arms to her sides and straightened her back. He had caught her sharp look of pain and incredulity. (211-12)

The "pain" of intense vision here, while it may lead to a "recoiling" from what seems "grotesque," even inhuman, also brings the two together, in a "brief exchange, lasting no more than an instant—the sizzling tip of a match, just extinguished, against her wrist, or fingertip," allowing for the common experience of not just pain but love: "[S]he said, so delicately that both of them were uncertain afterward whether it had been an echo in their own heads, or something projected into the silence between them, briefly, 'I love you'" (212).

Even after observing Eddie with a certain clinical detachment bordering on disgust—"his color is definitely missing something. Or maybe it's the smell. I don't know if it's death smell or hospital smell or unwashed Eddie smell, but it's sweet and it's ammoniac, vaguely urinous but also the smell of overripe fruit, and faintly the smell of old, dried shit" (238)—Saul, at Eddie's request, ends up in bed with him:

It isn't very easy with the tubes, the IV, but I find a spot. I lie down with my back to Eddie, watching out the door. He folds his arm around my chest, adjusting all the tubes. He finds my hand and grabs it. Then he buries his head in my shoulder blades and cries, and slowly falls asleep. (239)

Where the body of the person with AIDS, in Hoffman's *At Risk*, "is barely here," "dissolving" (142/173), Eddie's body, no matter how transformed—"no longer close to resembling the body [Polly] had known since college," having "assumed a shape that represented something else, she couldn't say what" (244)—never loses its powerful materiality. That materiality often forces a certain pulling back and disavowal, as in the scene with Polly where Eddie ultimately dies:

He lay splattered on the floor now, like a bird thrown up against the windshield of a car, not reduced to his essential humanity, but transformed to something messy, and pathetic. She could hardly think that this was what she had in common with everyone, the way the body falls apart with sickness and disease. It would never happen to her. (244)

He was naked now, but Polly didn't like to think of what she saw as Eddie's body. She gave it other properties, in her imagination, endowed it with a particular volume and weight, as if it were something familiar to her, if not exactly human. The voice coming out was Eddie's but that was coincidental. The body was like something she had known about, but never discussed. (246)

At the same time, however, the body *is* Eddie's and its demands for support and care enmesh Polly, much as she may wish to flee:

At first, she had wanted to run, then to take him in her arms, then to break a flowerpot over his head, and bring it all to an end. She had wanted all these things in quick succession. She had wanted to escape the smell of his room, of plastic fitted sheets and shit, and HandiWipes. But her need to go made her guiltily loving. Then she was angry, then sad. But when she stopped responding, and decided just to clean him up off the floor, she felt relieved, and knew she could stay. (246)

He took her hand again and squeezed, and Polly wanted something— wanted to embrace him, hold him, stand him up, dismiss him, tie him down and shoot him full of drugs to make him better, or to make him go away. She didn't want to touch him. She didn't want to need him, or to have to wonder how it would feel when at last she lost him. (248)

The complex emotional responses here reflect the simultaneous distance and closeness of Eddie's body, Polly's desire both to consign that grotesquely transformed body to another realm and to embrace it, to hold what is, after all, Eddie. His illness, his bodily disintegration, his impending death are all things that Polly may not want to identify with Eddie, or with "his essential humanity" (244). But if Polly is to have Eddie now in any way it must be along with illness, disintegration, impending death. And as Eddie's body approaches death, its final distancing from those who remain alive, it most insistently pushes toward intimacy:

He lifted his legs across her knees slowly, and she put her hand around his ankle. That was all she could think to do. Most of him was spread across her lap—there wasn't much of him. She stroked his ankle.[12] . . . [He] relax[ed] more and more of his weight onto her lap, into her arms. (248-49)

Polly holds Eddie during his last moments, and though she may not "want to feel what was happening to her"—"She didn't want to understand the connection between them. She felt herself watching. She felt herself suddenly watching"—"Eddie's ramblings, even his presence in the room, his weight in her arms, felt real to her, perhaps too real" (250).

Throughout, Polly maintains both an intense connection to Eddie and a wishful withdrawal from him:[13]

> As Eddie reached to her, as she hugged him to her chest and tangled in his bedclothes, inextricably, as at last she felt the kind of connection she had wanted with a man, with someone, it frightened her, and she withdrew. (250)

When Eddie does finally die—though his body is still the same "splayed and still," "splattered" (244) body that Polly discovers at the beginning of the scene, and though Polly tries to maintain her distance, "look[ing] only at the appearance of things" (250)—she is in intimate, indissoluble connection with him:

> He lay on Polly's lap and turned his head away from her and draped his legs and dropped his arm, and he died. She held him, and she had the appearance of things. And the appearance was this: she sat very still, supporting him. She was tangled in his bedclothes. She tipped her face to his and watched him. He was very thin, and with his dying breath his soft white body and the muscles of his stomach and his chest, pigeon-breasted with his reddish nipples, and his naked arms, quite long, and thin, his boy's knees and his slender calves, and feet, second toes longer than the first, and narrow shoulders, ample hips, and vulnerable belly crumpled, bent in the middle, and his fingers clutched the bed sheets at her knees. She watched him, held him, tenderly. His last hot breath condensed like steam upon her cheek. (251-52)

The careful account of Eddie's "falling apart"—attending, as it does, to the "exact sequence of motion and fact," "the appearance of things" (250)—impels the narrative toward closure, toward death, toward the moment in which Eddie is unambiguously gone, when his mother "sprinkles him into the Hudson, to float downstream to the bay with all the turds from Yonkers and the old Chevrolet submerged in the water just below the bank and the tugboats and the catfish and the bass" (274). Though something of Eddie remains even here— "some of the ash gets under her nails, where it will linger for days" (274)—the "loss" felt is, in Saul's words, "the worst kind" (274), "absolute" (275), "the aching up-all-night cavernous feeling of emptiness. Not even pain" (275). The impetus toward a narrative closure that is "absolute loss" and "emptiness," however, is also resisted by the insistent specularizing of Eddie's body, an attending to Eddie that keeps him present—"grotesquely," and in a form that we, like Polly, may not want to identify with Eddie and his humanity—but intensely present nonetheless. There is, in the scenes leading up to Eddie's death, a certain "fullness" of physicality—*not* Polly's remembered, "protected" body; rather, a "ruined body," but one that still resists the impulse toward "emptiness."

In these scenes, moreover, Eddie's presence persists not only in his physicality but also in the maintenance of his intelligence, his memories, and particularly his voice: "But Eddie kept talking" (251). Until the very end, he participates actively in the assessment of his own "magnificent falling apart," instigating the comparison of his body with his father's; experiencing simultaneously with his mother the vision of his ailing body; speaking his discomfort—"I'm wet. And where I'm not wet, I'm sore. And where I'm not sore, I'm numb. And where I'm not numb—which is a lot more of me than if I had my way—I itch. And where I don't itch—" (246); and insisting, in the scene where he dies, on looking at himself in the mirror—"He held it at arm's length at first, then closer, looking at his face in bits and pieces: his teeth, then his chin, then his nose, his forehead, finally his eyes" (248). And Eddie manifests his presence not just in an awareness of his own body and illness. Just as Eddie earlier responds to his diagnosis with a complex (internal) movement back and forth in time, so here, even as he dies, Eddie introduces to the scene a proliferation of narratives, giving present voice to various stories, historical and imagined. Some of these narratives—for instance, an account of the stigma attached to him by the hospital staff ("they don't even like to take away my tray when I've finished eating" [245-46])—are intimately linked to his illness;[14] others, however, move counter to the narrative of "irreversible decline." Talking with Polly, Eddie embarks on a long, complex and conflicted, reconsideration of his relation to sex—how he was "never really very good at it" (248), how he "[n]ever really even did it very much" (249), and yet "[h]ow almost nice it sometimes was to be a body wanting only pleasure, and to have it gratified" (249). He recounts how, "[f]or a time," he had sex only with "Jersey dudes" and how this made him feel "that [he] belonged" (249), compensating for the homophobic abuses of his childhood: "These gorgeous, butch Jersey voices, only they were not abusing me, not 'Easy out,' but giving pleasure. 'Great butt,' they said, and 'beautiful skin'" (249). He recalls how sex with Merrit was special (250). And finally he reflects at length on a much earlier sexual encounter, reliving a moment of partial connection, and imagining how having lived that moment differently might have changed his life:

"Patrick was beautiful, and he believed in God. Do you remember? He was beautiful and he believed in God, and he was gay, I know that because I slept with him that night before we left Oberlin. I never told you, Polly. Do you know why I slept with him? Because very late one night, in his room, he quoted poetry to me. Is that too queer? It was something from Yeats, I didn't recognize it then, he didn't know the title. He lay on his bed and said he wanted me to be his lover, but that God would not approve or something, and he said, I swear, he lay down on his bed, his room had sayings from the Gospels written on construction paper circling the walls, he took my hand and said, 'Tread softly because you tread on my dreams.' Which meant, 'I'd sleep with you if I were not so scared, and don't be angry.' I found the poem the next day, wrote it down, and left it under his door, and we didn't speak the rest of the year. Until the night before I left. And then I went to his room. He insisted I stay in his bed while he slept on the floor. We held hands across the space between us. Then he asked for a back rub. A back rub! Then he said I gave a lousy back rub, and he got into bed with me and showed me how. Then we lay together, Polly, then he took me in his arms. Then I tried to kiss him, and he wouldn't be kissed. Then we jerked each other off. He got back into his sleeping bag after that. Our semen dried against my stomach. I think he went to Haiti after graduation. I hugged him once the next day. I wonder where I'd be right now if Patrick Dean and I had not been so afraid. Would it have made any difference? Polly? Do you think? The poem went like this: 'Had I the heavens' embroidered cloths, enwrought with gold and silver light, something something half-light, I would spread them under your feet.'" He closed his eyes. "'But being poor I have only my dreams; I have spread my dreams under your feet,'"[15] he said, but that was as far as he got. (251)

It is here that Eddie dies, speaking until the end.

Eddie's final reflections function not just as nostalgic reminiscence and not just as a poignant way of setting Eddie's death against the life that has preceded it. They also make real and present Eddie's lasting search to live his life with some sense of connection to others. Though that search is cut short, it continues to the end, and resists the end even in approaching it. While Eddie cannot escape death, certain important changes, not part of the narrative of death, occur to him even as he dies: When Polly discovers Eddie at the beginning of this scene, she finds that "[h]is voice had changed, too, aged, perhaps mellowed. The whine was gone. He sounded almost wise, almost forgiving, if not self-forgiving" (244). And when Eddie looks in the mirror, he discovers a change that might in fact show a certain "self-forgiveness":

"No pig," he said, softly.
"I'm sorry?"
"I'm not. I said I think my pig is dead."
"I can't tell when you're talking nonsense," Polly said.
"African swine flu virus, maybe," Eddie muttered. (248)

Even as Eddie dies, he moves the story elsewhere, to "a barroom in the back somewhere, or . . . the piers, or . . . the park" (249), to Merrit, to Oberlin and Patrick Dean, to moments of vitality, if also of pain and missed opportunity. Even as he looks at himself one last time in the mirror, he sees a death that runs counter to the physical death he himself is about to experience; "the punishing voice inside [his] head" (4), with him since the start of the novel, disappears in an overcoming of self-hatred.

Not even as he dies is Eddie's story reduced just to the narrative of "irreversible decline," though that narrative, of course, is devastatingly at work, the source of a powerful sense of "loss" and "emptiness." Never in the novel is his illness Eddie's only story; intertwined with it, complicating it, sometimes reinforcing it, sometimes competing with it are a variety of other stories—the failure of "his real life to begin" (3); the homophobic abuses he has endured; his complex relationships with his mother and father, with Saul, with Polly, with Merrit; the trip to California and his friendship with Eulene; his "yearn[ing] . . . for New York," the city to which he feels he has "given his life" (105). Further, Weir places all of Eddie's stories in a rich and complex social context, detailing a particular kind of 1980s life: a life of Bloomingdale's and D'Agostino's bags, the latter containing the ashes of Horatio; a political scene that includes Polly's Jesse Jackson button, left over from 1984 (46), and Eddie's "Reagan Youth" button (see 14, 43, 73-75), the wearing of which encapsulates a particular cynicism about politics alongside a strong, but only implicit political claim (Reagan = Hitler);[16] a New York that includes "the nineteenth-century city, represented by the [Williamsburg] bridge, with its charming amenities, its walkway and midpoint way stations," alongside "the modernist world of New York, which aged badly, turned to slums or just industrial waste" (104), a city "falling apart, magnificently" (219), like Eddie himself; the particular devastation of gay communities by AIDS and a particular sense of hopelessness at a time before the rise of a full-fledged AIDS activism.[17]

Within Eddie's broader social world, of course, stand Polly, Saul, Merrit, Eddie's mother and father, Brag, all of whom have their own stories, intersecting more or less closely with Eddie's. Polly's beginning love affair with Brag parallels Eddie's with Merrit,[18] and Eddie's weekend with Merrit ("A Weekend in the Country," 78-88) replicates an earlier weekend shared by Merrit with Saul (24). Brag's later "betrayal" of Polly (with Merrit) parallels

Merrit's "betrayal" of Saul (with both Eddie and Brag), a complicated set of plots that come together most fully in the scene where Polly and Saul, having taken Eddie to the hospital, realize that their respective men are together in Europe.[19] Eddie's trip to California is the mirror image of his mother's earlier trip, from California to New Jersey, narrated in bits and pieces throughout the novel,[20] and in turn it is echoed by Merrit's trip to Europe with Brag (see especially "The Egoist," 168-74). Saul's story particularly focuses on how he might lead his life without Merrit, a theme introduced in the first chapter narrated by Saul ("Scenes from a Marriage," 21-29), continuing to the novel's final chapter, also in Saul's voice ("The Art of Losing," 268-76), and including Saul's experiments with finding a substitute for Merrit, both his sexual encounter in the park ("Dreams About Clothes," 142-48) and his visits to Eddie in the hospital: "Eddie is what I've given myself, instead of Merrit. That's what I'm doing here, replacing Merrit, finding someone else to love" (226). And of course the various viewings and funerals Saul and Merrit attend prepare for the (much different) disposal of Eddie's remains.

When Eddie has died, though the plot of "irreversible decline" has come to closure, the novel cannot in fact yet end; too much remains unresolved. Merrit's failure to confront Eddie before he dies; Polly's response to Eddie's death, and the way in which she intends now to continue her life; Saul's final escape from the relationship with Merrit, which is both an escape and one more loss—all still need to be, and are, explored.

In its density of narrative material, in the sheer complexity of its plot, *The Irreversible Decline of Eddie Socket*, from among the works so far discussed, most closely resembles the Maupin *Tales of the City* novels, in which narratives of illness also take their place within a complex network of other stories. But while Maupin's novels interweave a variety of plots, they are much more loosely structured than Weir's novel, their episodes strung together in a manner not unlike the interlacing of separate plots in the medieval romance. Weir's novel, on the surface, may give the sense of a proliferation of material almost out of control; as Richard Hall comments, with *Eddie Socket* partly in mind:

> Something is happening to the surfaces of the new novels. Thoughts, events, relationships are speeding up. Time, a sense of leisure and the inevitable, the only protection we have against everything happening at once, is disappearing. . . . The words spin by, a few daubs in the darkness, which we collect and reformulate to produce mental images, connections. Ezra Pound's remark, "Narrative is a form cut into time," no longer holds. Narrative is condensing; simultaneity is desired.[21]

But in fact Weir's novel is highly structured and very much under control. The parallels I have begun to note among various events that occur widely separated from each other are one means of providing such structure. The novel's three parts, titled "Perhaps," "Alas," and "Indeed," each divided into ten chapters, also provide the novel with a larger, architectonic structure that, on the one hand, may be seen as reinforcing the narrative of "irreversible decline"—the "perhaps" of the novel's opening uncertainty concerning Eddie and AIDS, the "alas" of his diagnosis, the "indeed" of his decline and death—but that, on the other, might also sketch competing narrative patterns—for just one possible instance, the "perhaps" of various developing relationships (Eddie and Merrit, Polly and Brag), the "alas" of their failure, the "indeed" nonetheless of a certain affirmation of human connectedness and community.

3. "WHO AM I QUOTING?": CITATION, NARRATIVE, AND IDENTITY

Further complicating the already complex structure of *Eddie Socket* is what may be the novel's most striking stylistic feature, its reliance on a prolific and dense network of allusion, typified by (but not limited to) its widely allusive chapter headings. John M. Clum reads the novel's allusiveness as a recuperative gesture, partially repairing the novel's "overwhelming sense of loss":

> *The Irreversible Decline of Eddie Socket* is also a celebration of the remnants of gay culture and imagination in its playfulness and sense of irony; chapter titles that echo opera, Sondheim, and Lorenz Hart lyrics; and Eddie's and Saul's camp sense of humor. In chronicling the loss of culture, the novel evokes that lost gay world and fixes it.[22]

Weir's allusions do often function within a specifically gay tradition of camp, helping preserve a "gay world" in danger of being lost:

> Merritt's more like Alma Winemiller [than like dainty Blanche DuBois], terminally virginal or rather, sporadically virginal depending on whom she's with and whether she's angry with her father at the moment, or—no, who Merrit is, he's Mary Tyrone, as long as we're doing women of the American stage, he's a nun. He's not addicted to morphine, but he's a nun. "You mustn't touch me when I'm going to be a nun." That's Merrit. (57)[23]

But Weir's allusions operate in more diverse and complex ways than Clum's assessment suggests. Thus, for instance, the novel's final intertextuality—the dependence of its last chapter, "The Art of Losing," on Elizabeth Bishop's elegiac villanelle "One Art"[24]—intensifies a sense of loss, gathering the power of Bishop's forcefully understated poem into its own quiet, regretful, enumerative conclusion:

So many things are lost, I think. Door keys are lost, and wallets are lost, and houses and cities are lost. Friends are lost, too, eleven in the past nine months, and lovers are lost. Even grief is lost, finally, and then you mourn the loss of that. I pull my hand away from Merrit's neck, and walk around the room, touching everything. The clocks, the pinewood cabinets. The old white china, and the pantry door. The floor creaks comfortably under my feet. I move around and around the room, as if to memorize the final setting, the placement of objects, Merrit's arrangement of all the things of his life. Even losing Merrit, I think, is easy enough, if only I put him in his place in the room, among the fixtures of a life that I no longer lead, there at the table, preserved, wearing a sweater that doesn't belong, nursing a tooth, and drinking heated milk. (275-76)

Citation in *Eddie Socket* serves multiple functions. The novel's many cultural references partly detail its social world, like shopping bags and political buttons helping to situate the characters' various stories in a particularized context. Allusions also work, as in the use of Bishop's poem, to call forth complex texts that might intensify, elucidate, comment on the novel's primary actions. When, on his way with Polly to his mother's house in New Jersey, Eddie quotes the first lines of William Carlos Williams's "To Elsie"— "Yeah, well, the pure products of America go crazy. Who am I quoting?" (123)—this does not have the effect so much of characterizing Eddie's social world (though it does let us know whom he has read) as of bringing Williams's great, disturbing Jersey poem into the novel. If we recognize the quotation, we might go to the poem, (re)read it, and ask how its vision—"No one / to witness / and adjust, no one to drive the car"[25]—connects to Eddie's various narratives (his illness, his relationships with Polly and with his mother) and to the stories Eddie himself tells as Polly and he drive along: "All right, now we're passing a famous bar, the one with the antlers on top of the roof, The Hunter's Rest, where all the high school boys hung out, the ones who called me faggot, with their chicks" (123-24).

Of course, the effects of Weir's allusiveness in large part depend upon his audience. Only the perfect "Weirian" reader will catch all the references, which range from the Bible, Dante, and Shakespeare, to *All About Eve* and *Since You Went Away*, to Sondheim and Rodgers and Hart, Judy Collins, the Rolling Stones, and the Beatles, to Yeats and Eliot, Faulkner, Flannery O'Connor, and Gore Vidal. What for one reader will be a richly evocative intertext may remain for another unidentified or only vaguely recognized, adding a certain flavor to the moment but nothing more. Still, whether or not the full implications of each reference are grasped by individual readers, the novel's rich allusiveness has a larger, cumulative effect. Time after time, citations introduce new narrative material into *Eddie Socket*, so that, if the narratives of the novel itself may be thought of as proliferating, the material imported into the text through citation constitutes a virtual narrative explosion.

Sometimes allusion introduces a narrative significant for the novel in an extended way, as, for instance, when Eddie uses the plot of *Since You Went Away* to reveal to both Eulene and his mother that he has AIDS (189-92), or when, in the account of Eddie's illness, Christological traditions are repeatedly evoked—"He stretched his arms out and hung his head, and said, 'I thirst. Who am I quoting?'" (104); his death in Polly's arms, "posed as if in pity" (251), visually echoes the Pietà ("pity").[26] Such extended citations may serve simultaneously to reinforce and to complicate the novel's own narrative constructions: though the Christological material, presenting the model of a death not to be escaped, may fortify the narrative of "irreversible decline," it also stands in contrast to it, since nothing in Weir's novel suggests a true Christological significance to Eddie's demise— "posed as if in pity, but only 'as if'" (251).

The bulk of Weir's allusions function more locally, providing momentary intrusions that again may support or intensify what is happening in the novel— "repeating in her head," as Polly thinks of Eddie's illness, "is a queer line from an old Bob Dylan song," "He who is not busy being born is busy dying" (213)—but may also work against or deflect its main narrative lines, as when Saul, in the scene of Eddie's return to New York, trying to sort out Eddie's account of his situation, comments, "All right, I'm thinking, Dr. Fillgrave, Doris Day, Eulene, and Polly Plugg, he's living in an Archie comic strip" (196). In either case, however, the allusion is an interruption. The more fully we dwell on it, even if it serves to confirm or intensify something happening in the novel, the more the progress of reading is disturbed; another text, another set of actions, another story enters into the experience of the novel.

This effect of allusive interruption echoes other narrative effects that dilate or deflect the reading process and that thus help prevent the novel's narratives from proceeding smoothly, as if inevitably and naturally. The reliance upon citation also serves to call narrative into question in other, perhaps more basic ways. While the novel's intertextual evocations may support the shape of its own stories by signaling parallels in more familiar, culturally canonical narratives, the very process of citation serves to undermine the authority of the novel's narratives insofar as these might claim to be mimetic, fictions that, while creating characters and events, somehow also "imitate" a particular social world, particular kinds of "realistic" action, particular historically grounded conflicts. Do narrative attempts to comprehend a life present "the exact sequence of motion and fact carefully recreated" (5) that Eddie himself repeatedly evokes as a model for understanding the shape of events in the world, or are we to read any account of events as somehow already citational, not simply mimetic but always a shaping of events according to prior scripts and models? When, at the beginning of the novel, Eddie examines his own failure to "emerge" by appealing to Shakespearean authority—"I was thinking of Richard the Second. He was the king who couldn't emerge. He couldn't decide. But then it was time for him to be deposed. He had had a life, after all. He called for a mirror, and said, 'How can I have been alive so long, how can I be important enough for such an event, and still look seventeen?'[27] I just turned twenty-eight" (4)—are we to understand the citation as simply analogical, a way comparatively to clarify the shape of Eddie's life, or, on the other hand, as suggesting that that shape in fact depends on other, prior texts, texts that inform from the beginning both the characters' understanding of what it means to live a life and the novel's sense of narrative possibility? When Eddie, like Richard II, "calls for a mirror" in the face of death (247-28), it indeed seems that the Shakespearean precedent at least in part determines (and does not simply reflect) Eddie's story.

The very structure of citation, its reliance upon prior texts, stands in tension with the usual claim of realist fiction to be a primary (original) account. Weir not only exploits that structure but also explicitly thematizes the ways in which citationality might challenge certain common understandings of narrative. After all, even the novel's strongest statement of a realist aesthetic— "Eddie's 'exact sequence of motion and fact,'" cited by Polly as she "look[s] only at the appearance of things"—is itself cited, "a quote from someone, though now she would never know whom" (250).[28] Repeatedly, events in the novel are understood as quoted, determined by prior texts. Eddie sees himself leading "[a] life in quotes" (105)—that is, both a life not "in earnest" (see 5, 8, 17, 24) but rather distanced by ironic "devices" from "the world" (4), and a life modeled on others, quoted from authoritative versions of "a life": "[H]e had learned to be aloof and sophisticated, in an East Village way, part Gertrude Stein, part Charlie Chaplin, part Jean-Paul Belmondo in *Breathless*" (4-5). Though the novel's other characters may be less conscious than Eddie of their own citationality, even the most "earnest" of them cite prior narratives in their actions. The marriage of Eddie's parents is repetitive and self-quoting—"five or six times a year, [Eddie's father] went out to the family home in Flemington . . . and each time he stayed longer than he intended, to 'give it another try.' Invariably, two weeks later, he went hopelessly back to the city in silence. . . . Then six months later, they did it all again" (13)—as is the relationship between Saul and Merrit:

> Merrit is never gone. We can't let go. We have to turn and linger, we have to hold on to each other. It happens every time we say good-bye, leaving the church this afternoon, we turn, to wave. He walks a little farther down the street, he turns to me, I turn, we wave. It's very

queer. We keep on walking, then again I turn, he turns, we wave. It
goes on just like this, until we're out of sight of each other finally, even
after the worst fights. It's our version of never going to bed angry, I
guess. Of never letting go. I turn, and Merrit turns. We wave and
wave. (226-27)

Merrit replays in his weekend with Eddie the script of past weekends with
"former lovers" (85): sex with Eddie "among a bunch of white narcissi" (87)
replicates sex with Saul "in a patch of pink narcissus—I think it was white, but
I remember it somehow as pink" (24). And, as Eddie's observations suggest,
both experiences have broader extratextual resonances: "You're D. H.
Lawrence" (87); "He said, 'For God's sake let me live, and have my love!' He
said, 'I'm quoting John Donne'" (88).[29] Polly finds herself, in her relationship
with Brag, also quoting earlier moments of her life that are themselves
citational:

> Then she remembered, of course, who it was she had been here with
> before. It was another William, her first New York lover, Brag's
> namesake. She remembered that it had been the end of a terrible
> evening in which they had gone to see *Persona* or *The Silence*, or
> maybe it was *Winter Light*. . . . Perhaps he was not unaware of staging
> a suitably Bergmanesque scene afterward, between the two of them, in
> this patisserie, with her tears, and his cold withdrawal. That made him
> Max von Sydow, which wasn't right—he was terribly callow and
> terribly clever, and anyway, she never cast people as effectively as
> Eddie did. She didn't have the right sensibility. Though she could see
> now where it would be helpful to think of her life as a Bergman film—
> then she could laugh at her own pretension, and walk away from the
> current encounter, with William the Second, comparatively unscathed.
> (110-11)

The novel's characters sometimes try to escape the prescriptedness of their
lives in a desire for more immediate experience. Eddie, responding to his
diagnosis, "saw that he had buried all his feelings underneath a glossy sheen
of easy alienation. He had taken snapshots of his life, pictures in his head of
Eddie Socket posing for the magazine spread, the Oscar acceptance speech, the
close-up" (100-101), and he decides that he needs "to get beneath the surface
of things" (103). He doesn't, however, get very far:

> Because his head was stuffed with advertising slogans and images, big
> blocks of solid colors shaped to suggest penises, Merrit's actual penis
> shaped to suggest Eddie's yearning, television jingles, "Lost in Space,"

and literary references, and Bette Davis draining a martini and saying, "Fasten your seat belts, it's going to be a bumpy night," he didn't know how to think, or feel, but only how to avoid thinking, or feeling. (102-3)

When he tries to strip away the quotations—"there he was quoting again, the whole fucking world was in quotes. Was death going to be in quotes, too? Something had to matter, and if death didn't matter either, why be disaffected at all?" (106)—what is left, death, the end of narrative, is itself somehow already "in quotes," "cliché": "He suddenly wanted to die, to feel something that mattered. And that seemed to him the most fucked-up thing of all. It was the worst kind of cliché. But it scared him" (106).

If the novel's characters are never quite capable of escaping citation, the novel as a whole displays itself to be composed citationally, its surface peppered with quotations, its many narratives paralleling each other and evoking an enormously wide range of outside texts. Among the novel's other narratives, that of "irreversible decline" can be recognized as not a "primary" telling of events, not an account of some "natural" sequence of bodily diminishments, but rather as an account predetermined, overdetermined by a whole series of prior texts, fictional and otherwise: "Eddie dropped his head quickly in silent tribute to Rock [Hudson], who wouldn't have done the wild thing with Doris [Day], anyway. All that chastity for nothing" (66); "It was spring, and Eddie was dying, which sounded like the plot for a movie starring Jane Wyman and Rock Hudson. *Magnificent Obsession*" (102). Eddie's story of course is not identical to the narratives thus cited, and some of the prior texts evoked define Eddie's story as much by discrepancy as correspondence:

> I'm trying to remember the clinical definition of tragedy. I think if I can find the right combination of words to describe Eddie's situation, everybody's situation, that would help, you know, a timely utterance to give my thoughts relief.[30] So, what I'm thinking is hubris, pity, and catharsis, and the oldest who have borne the most, such that we who are young shall never see so much, nor live so long.[31] . . .
> . . . [I]t's not convincing, not dramatically, it doesn't play for all these twenty-eight-year olds to die. . . . [I]f you're learning wisdom from a tragedy, what happens when you suffer terminal disease and death, and all you learn is that you're falling in a dream?
> So I guess that makes this comedy. Or maybe a tragedy reframed? A crisis at the center of an unflappable world, a hot subject in a cold frame?[32] Or the other way around, a cold subject in a hot frame. (199)

Still, even if no prior narrative understanding is wholly adequate to the depiction of Eddie's illness, that depiction, over and over again, relies upon the citation of prior texts.

Particularly significant for a reading of the narrative of "irreversible decline," with its impetus toward the closure of death, are Weir's several evocations of texts in which the homophobic identification of homosexuality with death determines the shape of the story:

> [Merrit] was impatient, patronizing, and homophobic. Not kiss in the street? Did he think he was trapped in *The Well of Loneliness*, or what? In the story of his life, he probably killed himself in the end, like something out of Gore Vidal. (80)

Watching *Rebel Without a Cause*, Saul observes, in a passage that resonates with the insights of queer theory, how normative heterosexual narratives depend upon the expulsion, the death, of the queer:

> [T]onight, I'm connecting with the film because of Dean's jacket. . . . It gets passed around. . . . Jimmy Dean is promiscuous with his jacket. It's the mantle of his budding masculinity, which everybody wants. . . . It ends up finally on Mineo, who, after he declares his love for Jimmy Dean (not in so many words, of course), pathetically dies. In fact, he's assassinated, but he's got the jacket, which Dean, having had *his* rite of passage (he gets to knock nipples with Natalie, whose breasts look surgically pointed), has cast aside. Sal gets the coat, and dies, and Jimmy gets the girl, and they procreate. The jacket has become a shroud, it clothes the dead, Sal Mineo, the homosexual.
>
> So Jimmy Dean becomes a man, at Mineo's expense. Why couldn't he have made it up with Sal, adopted him or something, saved him, rescued him, made love to him, moved in with him and Natalie? I wanted that, I wanted Sal to live. But then there was this sacrifice, it shocked me. Why couldn't Natalie have died? Or Dad? Or Mom, who is, predictably, the real villain of the film? Or the chief of police, for God's sake? No, the faggot had to die, he died with Jimmy's coat, and Dean reached down to him, the corpse, and put his shoe in place, his penny loafer.[33] And he turned, and there was Natalie, and two years later he was working in a corporation, probably, and she was vacuuming. (145-46)

While the precise relation between such a narrative and the novel's account of AIDS is never fully specified, the reader is here explicitly alerted to the homophobic possibilities in narratives of homosexual death; Weir in some sense calls on readers to interrogate his own novel as Saul interrogates *Rebel*, urging us to ask "why the faggot has to die?"

Of course, by calling explicit attention to the homophobia of narratives that demand the death of "the faggot," Weir makes possible within his own text an intervention against such narratives that, with a text like *Rebel*, can occur only through a resistant, critical reading like Saul's. Weir forces us to consider whether the narrative of AIDS as "irreversible decline"—and not just that narrative's deployment in the novel but its underwriting of a broader cultural understanding of AIDS—is itself constructed out of, cited from, a larger set of heterosexual norms established upon the bodies of dead queers. All of the novel's self-conscious interventions—deferrals, reformulations, interruptions—in the narrative of "irreversible decline" may, in fact, be read as sabotagings of the juggernaut that pushes toward gay death as the proper end of narrative, repeated reminders of how the narrative of AIDS as "irreversible decline" represents a particular construction dependent upon the citation of homophobic precedents.

At the same time, of course, Weir does allow the narrative juggernaut to reach its end, Eddie's death; he refuses to cover over the historical fact of gay men's deaths in the AIDS pandemic. While a conception of AIDS as "irreversible decline" may arise from, and reify, homophobia, the deaths of gay men are real, partly the result of homophobic refusals to attend to AIDS in the early years of the crisis, and in any case central to what the novel wishes to display to its readers. Eddie clearly comes to stand for a whole series of deaths, "the droplet of red blood . . . from his anus" (241) completely coloring Saul's field of vision: "who is getting out of this? is anybody getting out of this? the widening red circle, everywhere I looked in that hospital room I saw it, that deepening, widening red circle. I still see it" (243).

But the novel also resists the homophobia of narratives of "irreversible decline" precisely by questioning a logic that would enable Eddie or anyone to become representative of a whole group of people. The understanding of AIDS as "gay plague," the genocidal imagination of AIDS as wiping out homosexuality, depends, of course, on a stable sense of gayness that would enable the strict separation of gay from straight. While some sense of a common gay identity is present in Weir's novel—Saul refers to the "gay community" (23) and clearly identifies himself with that community; both Eddie and Saul "come out" as gay to their parents (13, 91)—this identity is not stable or unified in a way that could make "gay man" an ontological category somehow "naturally" (or "unnaturally") more implicated in disease and death than any other. The range of "gay man" in the novel includes Saul, who came out to his family at the age of seventeen, but who was "practically still a virgin" at the age of twenty-nine (91), and who is now, along with Merrit, firmly placed in a particular community of gay men; Eddie, whose claimings of gayness are decidedly ambivalent—"I don't like the word 'homosexual.' . . . We prefer 'gay.' . . . All I mean is everybody's gay to some degree. . . . It's just what I'm doing right now" (74-75); Merrit, who has been "married to a woman" (22, 42) and whose family doesn't "know he's gay" (27); Eulene, a "drag queen" (152) who speaks of her experience with men as similar to Eddie's (154-55); Brag (and here we reach what some might define as a limit to gayness), who enters the novel as Polly's boyfriend and exits it as Merrit's (his sexual performances with the two are decidedly similar to each other [compare 53-55 and 171]); and perhaps Eddie's father (Eddie's mother recalls an old friend of his and comments, "Sometimes I suspected they were having an affair" [71]).

The destabilization of identity categories like "gayness" indeed occurs throughout *Eddie Socket*, intersecting with and reinforcing the novel's questioning of narrative. The existence of a particular identity category, like that of a particular narrative pattern, does not imply the "naturalness" or even the firm, unambiguously-defined quality of that category. Just as the life histories of Weir's characters depend on the citation of other narratives for their shape, so those characters' "selves," rather than bodying forth some essential core of identity, are shown to be, at least in large part, the effects of citation. This is true even (or especially) for celebrities who constitute iconic models to be cited by others:

> They discuss Michael Jackson's latest surgery. "What about his nose," Eddie says, "you think it's Diana Ross?" "Actually," Polly says, "I think he passed right through Diana Ross, and now he's on to Eartha Kitt." "I think his nose is Candice Bergen," Eddie says. "What about his helper cells?" I want to scream. "What about his spleen? Who do you think his spleen is? Perry Ellis?" (197).

Judith Butler's recent, influential work on identity as "performative" and "citational" is helpful in thinking through the operations of Weir's conception of identity.[34] As Butler emphasizes, claiming that identity is "performative" does not mean that it is to be seen as pure "performance," put on or off like a costume and under the full control of volition. Rather, in a formulation dependent upon a Derridean reading of speech act theory, she posits that "performative" identity comes into being through the repeated reiteration of particular behaviors that may in fact be tightly constrained by social norms. One is not "male" in some essential way at the core of one's being; rather, it is one's continuing, repetitive participation in actions understood as "male" that calls up a sense of stable "male" identity, just as the "performative" speech act—"Let there be light"—in being spoken calls into being what it speaks. "Being" a particular identity is always *repetitive* and never settled; one never ceases to perform the claim "I am this gender." And the performative depends for its power on citation: performing "maleness" requires the quotation of some prior, normative sense of the "male," a quotation that, persuasively performed, will project a sexed identity. A sense of self, of oneself as a stable subject, depends upon the success of such citations, and, further, upon a concealment of the process of citation so that the self will seem self-sufficient, an entity in and of itself. It depends as well upon the exclusion of alternative, not-to-be-admitted identities: "whiteness," "maleness," "heterosexuality" depend upon the exclusion, the abjection, of "blackness," "femaleness," "homosexuality." But the repetitive, performative, citational features of identity formation also constantly threaten the self's stability; in the act of repetition, there is always the possibility of variation, divergence from the norm. And since the norm depends upon certain exclusions, the excluded is always available for a return that can challenge or subvert that from which it is anxiously cast out.

While Weir does not cite Butler in *Eddie Socket*, something like her postmodern conception of identity is performed in the novel. Among the "texts" cited (and interrogated) by Weir's characters are those normative categories of identity that Butler would claim are produced performatively and citationally, that depend upon particular, socially-determined exclusions, and that, even as they are so produced, disguise themselves as "natural," stably-existing determinants of being. For instance, Weir makes racial identity an issue from the first sentence of his novel, where Eddie's "standard white American features" are noticed (3); soon afterward, Weir suggests how racial identity affects Eddie's sense of self: "He was a white boy, after all, an American, and he secretly had the greatest expectations" (4). Marking "whiteness" as a racial category in a culture where it is usually only the departure from "whiteness" that is thought of as constituting "race"—along with Weir's deferral of an assignment of race to the novel's one African American character, Eulene (introduced "on the bus outside Erie" [152], it is only in St. Louis that Eulene identifies herself as "black" [157])—brings racial questions to the foreground of the novel, something rare in American novels where the central problematic is not a racial one. Several times the novel moves to note and destabilize common conceptions of racial difference:

> Horatio was from Argentinian aristocracy, a son of coffee growers, while Claudio grew up poor on West 106th Street, went to Vietnam, and put himself through school. . . . They didn't get along, and what made it worse was that it couldn't matter less to any of their Anglo friends whether they came from Harlem or Honduras, because Spanish-speaking, in racist New York, is Spanish-speaking; as far as white people bother to know, they all come from just one massive country somewhere off Florida with a colony in Yonkers. (28)[35]

The novel's white characters perform their racial identities in a variety of ways: Merrit is unself-conscious about the privileges race confers on him. For Saul and Polly, "whiteness" is complicated by a Jewish ethnicity. And while Eddie does recognize the ways in which being white allows him privilege, he also moves sometimes too easily to deny that privilege: "[Eddie] had a rather naive, perhaps even racist faith in Jews as uniformly intellectual and self-examining, and being gay he felt an affinity for anyone who had been discriminated against, historically or personally" (7). When Eddie moves to distance himself from "whiteness" and its privileges, Eulene calls upon him to recognize that, while he may wish to disavow his racial identity, it nonetheless remains formative of his being in the world:

". . . I'm a big black drag queen, honey, and you're a sculpted little white boy, and you probably don't even shit."
"I'm not a white boy."
"What do you call it, then?"
"What do you mean, what do I call it?"
"I mean the color of your skin. Faded Nancy Reagan red? Plantation peach?"
"I don't think of myself as white."
"Think harder." (157)

Just as the novel thus foregrounds how broad cultural understandings of race call into being subjects with a sense of racial identity that may simply be accepted as "natural," that may be conflicted, that may be challenged by others and by themselves, but that may never be wholly escaped, so it focuses attention on the ways in which other cultural constructions—of class, sexuality, and gender—participate in identity formation. Class in part differentiates Merrit from Saul and from Eddie. While Eulene has to recall to Eddie the force of race, Eddie, in turn, reminds her of the ways in which race may be complicated by class:

"Sure, you've got a mansion back there somewhere, you don't have to worry about nothing. They let you out on the road without your chauffeur?"
"Just because I'm white," Eddie said, "doesn't mean I'm rich." (157-58)

Though Saul, Eddie, and Merrit all identify themselves as gay, each negotiates the sense of sexual difference in his own way. And just as the novel marks "whiteness," and not just "blackness," as a racial category, so it focuses attention on "heterosexuality"—the strange marriage arrangement of Eddie's parents; Polly's sexual dissatisfactions—alongside "homosexuality," and on "maleness" alongside "femaleness." While Eddie sees "straight men" as "not just the opposite sex . . . [but] a separate race" and claims to have "modeled himself after women," he still is "a man, and so he felt better than women and worse than men, and that made him—what? Kind of confused" (230-31). Polly sees Eddie's maleness less conflictedly:

> The problem was, she kept on meeting men like Eddie. Whether they were straight or gay, they were all men; they were all more interested in dicks, she suspected, than anything else. What was a straight banker, after all, other than the flip side of Eddie Socket, played fast and turned up high, with drums? (33)

It is not just the "other" sexuality or gender that is implicated in the novel's attention to sexual and gender difference but the whole process of sexual and gender identity formation.

Throughout, the novel makes it clear that no matter how much one might attempt to escape certain constricting, socially-demanded identities, these are never fully escapable. Each of Weir's major characters struggles with a self-constitution felt to be, on the one hand, internal, "natural," inescapable, and, on the other, imposed from outside by forces constraining or even hostile to the self, but still constitutive of it. Saul hears "[o]ptimistic voices, rabbinical voices, short, clipped, satirical, sounding like the voices of the fathers, or the received community of guilt; sounding like my uncle Shmoi when I was twelve, on Holy Days" (95); a set of patriarchal norms speaks to him from within. Merrit encounters "ghosts" that seem to demand something of him, though he can't quite figure out what:

> [T]here would be someone he knew, from the past, sometimes a death from AIDS, sometimes an old high school crush. They all looked wounded, and vengeful, and pathetic. . . . They turned up, glaring, everywhere. . . . He was followed around by accusing memories. He didn't know what they wanted. (170)

Polly encounters her own set of "ghosts," assessing her own life against the imagined lives of her "peripheral people," "half a dozen . . . people, mostly women, but a few men, too," "all about her age," who "had come to the city around the same time she had. At least, she assumed they had": "They formed a comfortable background, against which she measured herself. How was she doing?" (111-12). And Eddie, of course, lives his life in negotiation with the internalized, hostile figure of "the pig." He may choose a "Bohemian" life (the novel's first chapter is titled "La Bohème"), and he may identify himself as gay, but he also must confront a certain homophobia within himself. And while he may cite his gayness as a means of identifying with all the oppressed of the world, sexual difference cannot simply erase white and male privilege. Certain of the self's performances of identity may resist hegemonic norms, but others may be "straight" citations of them.

Eddie tries in various ways to intervene against the identities demanded by his society, attempting, for instance, to disturb patriarchal practices of naming that, in Butler's terms, "fix the object," "initiating" it "into the patronymic lineage of authority."[36] Eddie reverses those practices, renaming his own parents, his father "Joseph Stalin"—since he feels "as if he had been purged from his father's life" (13)—and his mother "Doris Day": "She was blond and freckled. She loved dogs. When she got drunk at dinner parties she would wrap herself in a tablecloth (preferably checkered) and sing 'It's Magic'" (66). He recognizes that his own given name, Waldo Jeffers, also his father's real name, calls him into being in particular ways that he must resist:

> All my life, I grew up male, white, American. I believed that I could make such big, romantic gestures. But Saul? Americans have totally lost the talent to affect reality at all, except destructively. I won't be American like that. I won't be Waldo Jeffers, he's a Jersey boy. My name is Montgomery Clift. My name is Lorenz Hart. My name is Michelangelo Buonaroti. I'm Italian, I'm in love with Pope Julius the Second, I am working on a tomb for him. When I receive the papal semen, it is bloody, very bitter, and he utters phrases affectionately in Latin. "Agnus Dei." (240)

In an act of resistance, he changes his name to Eddie Socket, parodying and reversing the process that would make men's names stable and unchanging and women's names dependent upon men's, a process that would also insist on the man being the "plug" and the woman the "socket":[37] "Eddie had met [Polly Plugg][38] at the end of their last semester of college, and had instantly changed his name to go with hers" (7). Eulene's self-namings similarly intervene against a patriarchal logic, with her first chosen (feminine, geographical) drag name precipitating a parallel (masculine) one:

> I grew up in the Kill Van Kull, in Staten Island . . . and when I started doing drag routines, I used that name, I called myself Miss Kill Van Kull. . . . [O]ne night after my number, a gorgeous man with aluminum teeth came up to me and introduced himself as Arthur Kill. (154)

But renaming does not erase Eddie's given name: his mother refuses to call him anything but "Wally" throughout the novel. And Eddie himself wishes sometimes for a name that would not at all resist societal, and particularly gender, expectations:

> I think it would be great if my name actually were Guy. It would be like never being alone. I could go into a delicatessen anywhere in the country, and the man behind the counter would say, "What'll you have, guy?" And I would wonder how I had made all these friends, without having to be a movie star, or something. (184)

The novel does not simply make the recognition of the self's citationality a liberatory one. Knowing that the self is not self-contained means recognizing that it is in many ways constituted by citations not of *chosen* texts but of societally-defined and confining norms of race, gender, sexuality, class. Still, the recognition of the self's dependence on citation also enables it to be seen as not natural and stable, as capable of citations that will resist given societal norms, work against heterosexism and racism, cross or confuse the boundaries of gender identification. Saul, commiserating with Polly about the infidelity of men, while still implicated in the male infidelity he rejects, can explore alternative identifications:

> I bury my cheek in her breast. I can hear her heartbeat. She is suddenly warmer, and closer, and more reassuring than all the men I have pursued in order to work out my anger with Merrit. I fall asleep in her arms, wondering, if I'm not a straight man, and I'm not a gay man, what does that make me? Maybe, I think, nearly asleep, my face to her chest, maybe I'm really a lesbian. (204)

The recognition that the self is somehow performed and cited rather than stable and self-identical can be the source, in Weir's novel, of a certain self-assertive pleasure, an enjoyment of performative self-formation. It is in the actual context of performance—doing "a combination lost object-preoccupation-fourth wall-phone call exercise" (262) in her acting class—that Polly realizes her closest approach to a confident sense of self: "I'm beautiful, and sensual, and intelligent, and I know who I am in the world" (267). Eulene, whose life Eddie reads as a series of gender, race, and class performances—she looks simultaneously like "Olivia de Havilland in *The Heiress*" and James Earl Jones, and sounds like "Blanche du Bois, or one of the Dead End Kids, though her middle range . . . Eulene in repose—moved and sounded like a coupon-clipping mom from Todt Hill, slightly fussy, chatty but preoccupied, and, despite the occasional queeny grandeur (or, perhaps, because of it), deeply conventional" (152)—has one of the novel's strongest moments of self-assertion, a moment that simultaneously embraces a certain kind of transgressive performance:

"Eulene," Eddie said, "can I ask you a personal question?"
"I wish you would."
"Why are you wearing a dress?"
"Because," she said, turning around, throwing out her arms, and tipping her head to the sky, "because I look goddamn good in chiffon." (159)

While a certain resistant power is thus recognized in a conception of the self as the fragmented effect of citational performances, Weir's novel and its characters still express nostalgia for the unified, "whole" subject. Polly at first is attracted to Brag because "he was the sort of person to whom the business of being an adult came otherwise quite naturally. . . . [S]he could never wholly manage the willing suspension of disbelief that projected him and others like him credulously into the world" (30-31). Eddie's attraction to Merrit is similarly based on a sense of his wholeness and self-possession: "[he], unlike [Eddie], was three-dimensional—not really Montgomery Clift, not flat like an image on the screen, but someone whose actions reverberated in the actual world. Eddie keenly felt his own flatness in comparison" (19).

Eddie himself is ultimately unmasked, at least in Polly's mind, as "not 'in quotes'. . . at all": "there was no getting around his sentimentality" (217); "He was romantic, he was sentimental, he was Rodgers and Hart" (220). Eddie yearns for "wholeness," a desire that is "sentimental" and "romantic" because it does not correspond to the fragmented, incomplete life and world that confront him. Such "wholeness" is available only in fantasies like that of a "three-dimensional" Merrit that are ultimately exploded: "Merrit was nothing more than the neat result of the way that light came down on the surface of things, an atmospheric trick, a mirage. . . . Merrit was a smooth, flat, white, glossy surface, onto which Eddie could project whatever yearning he liked" (103).[39] Eddie "had been promised a whole world" but "had found himself living in a shattered one." "Wholeness" may sometimes seem to present itself, but only in forms that may, like Merrit, be illusory: "maybe being an adult was just learning to pick up the pieces that seemed to apply, and go with little bits, and don't disdain wholeness when it offers itself, even if it comes in the guise of a church" (167).

When Saul finds himself sitting next to Elizabeth Taylor on the "crosstown bus" (241), having just visited Eddie in the hospital, she seems absolutely real, unartificial, and her body particularly miraculous in contrast to Eddie's:

[Her eyes are] every bit as blue, as violet, as you would think, and she is just as beautiful as I expected. Even more. She's sitting perfectly straight . . . and she isn't coarse, and she isn't loud, and she isn't fat. . . . [A]nd she smells terrific, and she isn't wearing any makeup and her skin is smooth and clear, and her breasts are warm against my arm. . . . I cry and cry and cry. Elizabeth Taylor takes my head into her arms and presses it to her bosom. I'm vaguely aware that I'm getting snot all over her Technicolor breasts, but it doesn't matter, not to her, she's real. (241-42)

As soon, however, as the Technicolor image is made "real," it deconstructs itself, shows itself in fact not to be so distinct from Eddie's "tired," "ruined" physicality:

I look up into her beautiful eyes, and I say, "I want to be the color of your eyes." She giggles lightly and says, "It's contact lenses."
"I don't believe you," I say.
"No, it is," she says, still gently, "Look."
Well, I look, but I don't see, and then she—laughing, she pokes her fingers in her face and pulls her lenses out. I sit up then, and look again. And she's right—really, she has the plainest, steel-gray, boring eyes you ever saw. Tired, hopeless eyes, like Eddie's.
She says, "You think the rest is real?" and she slowly starts to pull herself apart. Her chin, her cheeks, her breasts. Her breasts, where I have only just now lain. Her left buttock, her right kneecap. Piece by piece she pulls herself apart. She's a walking prosthesis, everything is rubber and it comes off in her hands. (242)

In this remarkable, surreal scene, the artifice of self is first taken at face value—as bodying forth a "whole" identity—then shockingly revealed for the artifice it is. This, and the novel's other explorations of the complex processes by which "whole" selves are constructed—out of "bits" and "pieces," "prostheses," citations, performances, poses—render impossible, for the novel, any conception of identity that would support the claim that "person with AIDS" (or "AIDS victim") constitutes a stable identity clearly to be associated with the (also destabilized) category of "gay man," or, more broadly, "other." "Self" in Weir's novel is always already "other" in that it is never simply self-identical but always the performed effect of identifications and desires partly dictated by prescribed norms, partly arising from a resistance to or transgression of those norms. The deconstruction of Elizabeth Taylor's body, coming, as it does, in the midst of the novel's close inspection of Eddie's body and its transformations, suggests that what all human beings share is not some stability of self nor even a solid, material body, but something quite other than stability, solidity, "wholeness." Far from being the embodiment of a radical "other" to be repudiated, Elizabeth Taylor's deconstructed body, Eddie's body in distress, in their frangibility, their fragmentation, their mortality—"the way the body falls apart with sickness and disease"—represent, despite Polly's resistance to the idea, "what she had in common with everyone" (244).

NOTES

1. John Weir, *The Irreversible Decline of Eddie Socket* (New York: HarperCollins, 1991 [1989]). Citations are given parenthetically in the text. In addition to his novel, Weir has published much journalism about AIDS, including "AIDS Stories," *Harper's* 273:1636 (Sept. 1986), 22, 24, 26; "There Goes the Neighborhood . . .," *VOX* (Winter 1991), 16-19; "Homo in Heteroland," *QW* no. 41 (16 Aug. 1992), 22-25 [reprinted in Ethan Mordden, ed., *Waves: An Anthology of New Gay Fiction* (New York: Vintage/Random House, 1994), 3-12]; "Death Becomes Him (Not)," *QW* no. 44 (6 Sept. 1992), 38-39; "NWA's [Novels with AIDS]" [review of Jim Oliver, *Closing Distance*], *QW* no. 50 (18 Oct. 1992), 42-43; "Getting a Life," *Details* 11:8 (Jan. 1993), 20-21, 23, 25-28; "Bent out of Shape" [review of *Philadelphia, Savage Nights*, and *Totally F***ed Up*], *Details* 12:9 (Feb. 1994), 131-33; "In God's Country"; and "After You've Gone: Rage, Rage," *New Republic* 13 Feb. 1995, 11-12.

2. See chapter 3 above.

3. Also see Saul's discussion of the "three types" of "AIDS funeral"—"Orthodox," "Conservative," and "Reform"—later in the novel (221-25).

4. Weir quotes St. Cyril from Flannery O'Connor's epigraph to *A Good Man Is Hard to Find*. See *Three by Flannery O'Connor* (New York: Signet, 1962), 128 (note both that the epigraph does not appear in other editions of O'Connor's *A Good Man Is Hard to Find* and that *Three by Flannery O'Connor* has been reissued by Signet with *Everything That Rises Must Converge* replacing *A Good Man Is Hard to Find*). Also see O'Connor's brief comments on the passage from St. Cyril in her "The Fiction Writer and His Country," *Mystery and Manners: Occasional Prose*, Sally Fitzgerald and Robert Fitzgerald, eds. (New York: Farrar, Straus and Giroux, 1969), 35.

5. The force of the desire to identify the precise "cause" of HIV infection—and thus to be able to plot the narrative of illness from the moment of its inception—is reflected in the number of readers (among my students) drawn to the suggestion that Merrit "gave" Eddie HIV, even despite everything in the novel that would militate against such a possibility.

6. Weir here cites Robert Penn Warren, *All the King's Men* (San Diego, New York, and London: Harcourt Brace Jovanovich, 1982 [1946]), 270: "West is where we all plan to go some day. It is where you go when the land gives out and the old-field pines encroach. It is where you go when you get the letter saying: *Flee, all is discovered*."

7. This is echoed in a later moment when Eddie's mother, visiting him in the hospital, does not stop herself from imagining his future despite her recognition that he is "going to die": "'You'll see what happens when you start to get old, past forty-five, your parents are dying, and your kids are fucking up, and generally speaking you're done with the great themes of your life, you've gotten over the pain. And then you can't afford to fight anymore, or be uncommitted, or whine, or complain. Because the real things have started to happen.' / 'I think this is real,' Eddie said, quietly" (211).

8. John Weir, "Homo in Heteroland," 25.

9. Tennessee Williams, *Summer and Smoke*, Part Two, scene 11, in *Four Plays* (New York: Signet, 1976 [1948]), 119.

10. Joseph Cady's distinction between "immersive" and "counterimmersive" AIDS writing is useful in thinking through the differences among the various novels' depictions of people with AIDS (though Cady's own way of divvying up works between his two categories is, to my mind, sometimes debatable). See "Immersive and Counterimmersive Writing About AIDS: The Achievement of Paul Monette's *Love Alone*," in Murphy and Poirier, eds., *Writing AIDS*, 244-64; and "Teaching About AIDS through Literature in a Medical School Curriculum," in Pastore, ed., *Confronting AIDS*, 233-48.

11. A similarly intense and complex specularizing of the body occurs in Tom Joslin and Peter Friedman's video *Silverlake Life: The View from Here* (Zeitgeist Films, 1993).

12. The focusing on Eddie's ankle here echoes earlier moments of intimacy mixed with distance; see 93-94 and 130-31.

13. Polly's ambivalence is prepared for earlier in the novel; see, for instance, 214 and 220. And the final scenes of the novel, after Eddie's death, work in part to resolve Polly's ambivalences, to place Eddie, lost but not lost, in her life; see 262-67.

14. Weir several times focuses attention on the ways in which Eddie is stigmatized in the hospital. See, for instance, 229-30 and 239.

15. William Butler Yeats, "He Wishes for the Cloths of Heaven" [the title Weir gives this chapter in his novel], in *Selected Poems and Two Plays of William Butler Yeats*, updated edition, M. L. Rosenthal, ed. (New York: Collier, 1966), 27.

16. Larry Kramer made the claim explicitly in his June 9, 1987, speech to the Boston Lesbian and Gay Town Meeting: "AIDS is our holocaust and Reagan is our Hitler" (*Reports from the Holocaust: The Making of an AIDS Activist* [New York: St. Martin's Press, 1989], 173).

17. Weir, writing in 1985-1988, would have just witnessed the formation of ACT UP (1987-1988), in which he was to become an active participant.

18. Compare, for instance, the novel's fifth chapter, "Tea and Sympathy," with its sixth, "The Man in the Brooks Brothers Suit," and the second chapter of the second part, "The Gentleman Is a Dope," with the fourth, "On the Waterfront."

19. See the first chapter of the third part, "The Return of the Native."

20. See 150: "He was going to find northern California, as his mother had hoped to find it in New Jersey. He was going to take her journey, but he was going to get it right."

21. Richard Hall, "From the Guest Prose Editor: The High-Tech Gay Novel," *The James White Review* 8:3 (Spring 1991), 3.

22. Clum, "'And Once I Had It All,'" 218.

23. The camp allusiveness and strong irony of Weir's book have made its tone difficult for critics to read. While Clum sees the novel's "playfulness" as secondary to its overall bleakness—"[its] world . . . offers loss for the older generation, and, for Eddie and his peers, a tangential link to a world never really experienced" (217)—Daniel Harris reads the novel's sense of the "tragic" as obfuscated by its irony, placing it with a "contemporary literature . . . in many ways immune to the tragedy of AIDS, inoculated against it by a tendency toward flippant ironizing, like the compulsive jocularity found in John Weir's *The Irreversible Decline of Eddie Socket*" ("Making Kitsch from AIDS: A Disease with a Gift Shop of Its Own," *Harper's* 289:1730 [July 1994], 59).

24. Elizabeth Bishop, "One Art," *The Complete Poems 1927-1979* (New York: The Noonday Press/Farrar, Straus and Giroux, 1983).

25. William Carlos Williams, *Selected Poems* (New York: New Directions, 1968), 30. Other aspects of the poem—including its misogyny and its heterosexism—are pertinent to the moment of its evocation in Weir's novel.

26. Also see 106, 206, 219, 228-29, and 240.

27. See William Shakespeare, *Richard II* IV.1.277-92; *The Complete Works of Shakespeare*, 3rd ed., David Bevington, ed. (Glenview, IL: Scott, Foresman & Co., 1980).

28. See Ernest Hemingway, *Death in the Afternoon* (New York: P. F. Collier & Son, 1932), 2: "[B]ut the real thing, the sequence of motion and fact which made the emotion and which would be as valid in a year or in ten years, or, with luck and if you stated it purely enough, always, was beyond me and I was working very hard to get it."

29. Eddie here conflates the first lines of Donne's "The Canonization" and "The Baite," and through the latter also evokes Marlowe's "The Passionate Shepherd to His Love" and Ralegh's "The Nymph's Reply to the Shepherd." See John Donne, *Poetry and Prose*, Frank J. Warnke, ed. (New York: Modern Library, 1967), 13-14 and 39-40; and

Alexander W. Allison, Herbert Barrows, Caesar R. Blake, Arthur J. Carr, Arthur M. Eastman, and Hubert M. English, Jr., eds., *The Norton Anthology of Poetry*, 3rd ed. (New York and London: W. W. Norton, 1983), 105-6 and 185-86.

30. Quoted from William Wordsworth, "Ode: Intimations of Immortality from Recollections of Early Childhood," line 23; see Allison, et al., eds., *The Norton Anthology of Poetry*, 552.

31. The references here are to Aristotle's *Poetics* (see the translation by Gerald F. Else [Ann Arbor: University of Michigan Press, 1967]) and the conclusion of Shakespeare's *King Lear* (V.3.330-31; in *The Complete Works of Shakespeare*, Bevington, ed.).

32. Weir here quotes Susan Sontag, "Spiritual Style in the Films of Robert Bresson," *Against Interpretation and Other Essays* (New York: Anchor Books/Doubleday, 1990 [1966]), 180: "Sometimes the most beautiful effects are gained when the material and the form are at cross purposes. Brecht does this often: placing a hot subject in a cold frame."

33. The action here echoes Merrit's straightening of Claudio's shoe at his viewing, early in the novel (28-29).

34. See, in particular, Butler, *Gender Trouble: Feminism and the Subversion of Identity* (New York and London: Routledge, 1990), 1-34 and 134-41; and *Bodies That Matter* (New York and London: Routledge, 1993), 1-23, 93-119, and 223-42.

35. Also see Eddie's observations about Merrit's racism (80).

36. Butler, *Bodies That Matter*, 215. Interestingly, in Weir's novel, Saul's full name—"Saul Isenberg, Saul Isenberg"—is only invoked by his internalized, patriarchal voices (95).

37. See Eddie's comment: "All I have is my dick, and my mouth. A hole, and a plug. If I could stretch far enough, I'd have a solution" (210).

38. Polly's name, while "actually Polly Plugg," is at the same time the effect of a citation that demonstrates the force of particular American ethnic scripts: "'Maybe once it was Pflug,' she had said, 'or maybe Rabinowitz. I have no idea. Plugg is something my grandfather saw on the side of a milk truck in lower Manhattan when he got off the boat in 1902'" (7).

39. Also see Saul's description of Merrit as "two-dimensional"—"It is possible to see Merrit only in profile; from the front, he disappears" (89).

CHAPTER 6

Apocalyptic Conspiracies: The "Epidemiological Narrative" of AIDS

1. ENDS AND ORIGINS

Most narratives about AIDS focus on individuals, on their lives, illnesses, and deaths. Even a sweeping historical treatment like Shilts's *And the Band Played On*, while it examines larger political and epidemiological trends, recurs repeatedly to the terms of the "personal narrative."[1] The vast preponderance of nonfictional narrative writing about AIDS has indeed been not historical but (auto)biographical—testimonial and memorial.[2] In fictional narrative, similar impulses are at work, with many novels and short stories taking the form of memoir and testimony.[3] The tendency of fiction to focus on the stories of individuals reflects in addition the common consignment of the "mainstream" American novel to a largely "private" realm. Though novelists may experiment with forms that allow a direct addressing of political questions, such fictions are always under the threat of being dismissed as "propaganda," as not "real" literature. The main "political" forms in American fiction remain "unserious," "popular" genres like the spy thriller, where in fact the political content most often serves primarily as excuse for action and adventure. "Mainstream" American novels continue to be defined by psychologizing, personalized genres like *Bildungsroman*, romantic comedy, and family drama; it is not surprising that, in the last decade, David Leavitt, whose work—even his recent historical novel *While England Sleeps*[4]—belongs largely to such genres, has been the most visibly successful gay American novelist. In American gay men's fiction, the pressure away from an explicit concern with the political is also reflected in the career of a major writer like John Rechy, whose writing moves from "public," "experimental," "documentary" works like *City of Night* and *The Sexual Outlaw* toward individual- and family-centered novels like *Marilyn's Daughter*. Even the more politicized *The Miraculous Day of Amalia Gómez*, Rechy's most recent novel, shies away from the broad public realm of the earlier work to focus most intently on one family.[5]

I do not mean to suggest that AIDS novels that focus on individual stories, novels like those already discussed, do not have important "public" and political dimensions; they do, of course, in the very decisions they make concerning how to depict the individual "course" of illness. And none of these novels in fact confines its attention exclusively to "personal narrative"; all confront, in one way or another, the realm of "epidemiology," examining the fear of epidemic "spread" (as in *Facing It, Significant Others*, and *Tangled Up in Blue*), the broader effects of AIDS on communities (as in *Sure of You* and *The Irreversible Decline of Eddie Socket*), the social and political operations of stigma (as in *At Risk* and *Old Soldier*). The personal, however, remains primary to each, the center of the story and its concerns.

In contrast, another subgenre of AIDS fiction takes the "epidemiological" or "population narrative" as its starting point and relegates the "personal narrative" more or less fully to the background. As Shaun O'Connell suggests, next to "documentary, largely autobiographical records of case histories of persons with AIDS" stands a second category of AIDS fiction:

> horrific cautionary tales of fascist responses to the AIDS crisis: dystopias, in the manner of *1984*, in which writers posit scenarios of massive retaliation against homosexuals by a society—set some time in the near future, or in the reconfigured immediate past—which seeks a Final Solution to the plague.[6]

Novels like Jed A. Bryan's *A Cry in the Desert*,[7] Toby Johnson's *Plague: A Novel about Healing*,[8] Marty Rubin's *The Boiled Frog Syndrome: A Novel of Love, Sex and Politics*,[9] Tim Barrus's *Genocide: The Anthology*,[10] and Geoff Mains's *Gentle Warriors*,[11] while they sometimes focus partly on individuals living with AIDS, make their center the larger story of "plague": the "spread of disease" and efforts at its "containment"; political consequences of the epidemic, including the workings of panic and stigma.[12] Such novels stand largely outside "mainstream" American fiction. They have been published for the most part by small gay presses, though several novels that have appeared from larger publishers—for instance, Sarah Schulman's *People in Trouble*, Paul Monette's *Afterlife*, and James Robert Baker's *Tim and Pete*—share certain features with books of this subgenre. And such works mainly ally themselves not with the "serious" fictional genres but with more marginal, and also often more "popular," sorts of "genre fiction"—(dystopian/utopian) science fiction, political thrillers, detective stories, erotica and pornography—genres where the emphasis is less on psychology or carefully drawn characters and more on plot, action, and intrigue. O'Connell associates Bryan's and Johnson's novels specifically with "the suspense fiction of Robert Ludlum, Ken Follett, or Tom

Clancy"[13]—though, in taking on gayness and AIDS as central concerns, these novels also move to the margins of "suspense fiction."

The five novels I will discuss here are very different from each other, but they still cohere generically. Most significantly, all depend upon, and develop, certain central features of the "epidemiological narrative" of AIDS. All are projective narratives, working from the "current" situation of the AIDS crisis (different in each novel, since, for each, the fictional "now" is a somewhat different moment in the 1980s) to predict the effects of the "spread" of illness. All are also, to a greater or lesser extent, retrospective, extrapolating backward from "now" to speculate on the origins of AIDS. Some of these novels construct a very particularized future while only sketchily considering the past (e.g., *Genocide: The Anthology*); some more fully map out the past and only glance toward the future (e.g., *Gentle Warriors*). But each of these novels depends crucially upon an "epidemiology" of AIDS—a narrative of origin, transmission, "risk groups," accelerating "spread," epidemic, pandemic, and "plague," and of the social and political consequences of epidemic. Each novel moves toward an ending that is definitively an end—of gay men, of the world as we know it—even as each, more or less pessimistically, explores possible ways of intervening against, resisting, the epidemic and its effects, ways of derailing the narrative to avert its projected end.

These novels, then, are all "apocalyptic," in the popular sense of "apocalypse" as a cataclysmic interruption and end to "normal" life: the possibility of "apocalypse soon" hangs over even those novels that predict an avoidance of the worst possible ending.[14] The "epidemiological" subgenre is also "apocalyptic" in the stricter sense of the word as involving a process of uncovering or revelation. The "truths" revealed in these fictions pertain not only to a projected, world-threatening future but also to the present and past of the AIDS crisis. While beginning from and tracing the familiar "epidemiological narrative" of AIDS, each novel also claims to reveal essential features of that narrative that have been ignored, obfuscated, or actively concealed, and thus to unveil the "real" meaning of the AIDS crisis. As I will argue more fully below, in their belief in such a hidden significance, and in the discovery of that significance within an account of AIDS *as epidemic*, these novels express and illuminate ideas that more generally inform narrative understandings (like medical epidemiology itself) that, on the one hand, work to identify a point of origin for HIV and, on the other, project its continued, uncontrolled, and perhaps uncontrollable "spread."

Of the five novels that I here group together as representative of an "epidemiological" subgenre of AIDS fiction, *Plague* and *Gentle Warriors* stand closest to narratives of personal illness. None of the major characters in *A Cry in the Desert* or *The Boiled Frog Syndrome* has AIDS. In *Genocide*, while several important figures—for instance, Star and Adonais in the chapter "THE

FOREST AND THE ECHO"—are ill, their illness is not AIDS, nor is Barrus mainly concerned with tracing the "progress" of individual disease. *Plague* and *Gentle Warriors*, on the other hand, develop more particularly and fully the "personal narrative" of AIDS. Gregg, one of the protagonists of *Gentle Warriors*, belongs to a group of gay men with AIDS central to the novel's action; illness is a real presence in the book, and Gregg's death is one of its crucial final events. In *Plague*, one major storyline follows Jon Stiers, a psychiatrist, as he responds to the illness and death of his former lover Ted, and as he counsels the members of a PWA support group, particularly Pat Stratford, whose experience of illness the novel depicts in a fairly detailed manner. Pat's decision to commit suicide, and the aftermath of his suicide, figure prominently in the novel's larger plot. Still, despite such presentations of individuals' experiences with AIDS, in neither *Plague* nor *Gentle Warriors* is the "personal narrative" the real point. Gregg and the other men with AIDS in Mains's novel—Jim, Sam, Tom—figure most importantly in a story of political intrigue. Pat Stratford dies before *Plague* is half complete, and the remainder of Johnson's novel concerns less and less individual people with AIDS, and more and more the broader scene of epidemic.

Johnson's *Plague* functions most consistently as a detective story. The novel's "Prolog," set in "the recent past" (7), presents a radio communication from "[a] research station near Ilebo," "east of Kinshasa. . . . Zaire. . . . Central Africa" (8), that makes the reader aware of a mystery to be uncovered:

> "(static) . . . the thing got out of control. . ." a strained voice blared into the room a moment later. ". . . can't stop it. I'm about done for . . . only one left here . . . the animals broke out . . . Oh God, a whole wall of 'em came at me . . . (sobs) . . . attacked us . . . everybody exposed . . . went rabid . . . Oh God, all dead now, all dead . . . except me . . . Animals escaped. . .
>
> ". . . You've got to bomb the whole area . . . it's the only chance, I tell you!" the voice began to scream.
>
> Then suddenly the speaker composed himself, "Believe me, I've been thinking about this. This thing could destroy the world. I don't think there's any other way. And there isn't much time. I mean it. It'd be worth it. An atom bomb—like the one we dropped on Hiroshima—that's about the only thing that can stop this . . . this . . . (silence)" (8-9; ellipses in original)

The African setting,[15] the suggestions of medical research out of control, of a world-threatening contagion, and the association between "this thing" and the apocalyptic power of the atom bomb—"The world's a powder keg. What that guy's talking about could trigger a nuclear war" (9)—all echo certain real-world "scientific" suggestions about the origins of HIV that have, in the words of Mirko D. Grmek, "seduced the imagination by coupling disasters symbolizing today's twin peaks of horror," AIDS and nuclear destruction:

> One American scientist, Ernest Stirnglass, maintained that the AIDS virus arose from a mutation stimulated by—the experimental atomic explosions! According to him, the beginning of the epidemic in central Africa and the recent prevalence of AIDS in that part of the world were due to the increase in radioactivity in the equatorial zone, from the fallout of strontium-90, the radioactive element brought by wind and rain from the Saharan sites of French nuclear tests.[16]

The details of Johnson's opening passage thus point toward a theory of origin for AIDS (though AIDS has not yet been mentioned explicitly), an origin linked from the very first with a vision of world calamity; the main narrative of *Plague* serves to unearth the suppressed truth of the disastrous origin thus evoked. In a complicated plot that involves chance and coincidence, computer espionage, a chase through a house filled with secret passageways, what at first appears to be murder (but is later discovered to be "just a fluke accident" [248]), drugging, kidnapping, and interrogation, Jon Stiers, his boyfriend Mark Hartman, Billy DePalma, a bisexual computer hacker who is HIV-positive, and his girlfriend Lynn Graves, who works for the right-wing Liberty Bell Foundation (a group whose chief executives, Edward Buchanan and George Wilson, were privy to the mysterious emergency radio transmission from Ilebo), uncover the truth behind the AIDS epidemic:

> "Are you saying that you consciously planned how AIDS would spread?" Jon asked.
> . . .
> "I [George Wilson] *tracked* the spread, if that's what you mean, after it was clear that a new disease was showing up among homosexuals and I began to suspect that this might be related to the Ilebo Station project."
> . . .
> "Are you suggesting they created HIV?"
> "Who knows? The reports we'd found said they developed a virus that targeted immune cells and was concentrated primarily in blood and semen—it was designed to attack males.[17] It was aimed at soldiers, after all. We researched other blood-borne viruses, like Hepatitis-B," Wilson calmed down a little as he struggled to explain himself. "We saw that the risk groups were homosexuals, drug abusers, and hospital workers. We really worried about the doctors and nurses. We didn't want to hurt

them. But the African research had shown one of the advantages of this particular weapon was that, since it required large inoculations, it wasn't likely to get out of control: accidental needle-sticks didn't seem to carry enough of the virus to transmit it. But it did get out of control." Wilson's voice broke. "That was supposed to be my job: to determine when to release the antidote."

. . .

. . . "Edward said we had an obligation to stop the spread of sexual perversion. Even though it turned out that the virus wasn't specific enough to do that, it looked like the social backlash would. By that time we'd delayed announcing what we had so long already, we decided to wait for public pressure to restore morality." (177-78)

Though the novel does cast some doubt on whether Wilson's story here is to be believed—"Looks like George Wilson had, uh, gone off the deep end and was imagining things" (239)—it presents without question the events at Ilebo Station, and most of its details in fact tend to confirm Wilson's construction of the origin of AIDS. Presenting HIV as intentionally "created" and allowed to "spread," the novel also strongly suggests that, for such a biological weapon, there should be an engineered "antidote": though this is never presented as certain, and though it is never absolutely clear that Jon Stiers successfully forces Edward Buchanan to release the "antidote," as he attempts to do, much evidence points toward confirming this possibility: Buchanan dies in the crash of a plane equipped with "a crop spraying device" (247), and Stiers concludes that "maybe Buchanan did indeed spread that antidote virus of his around New York City, so all of a sudden a lot of New Yorkers showed up with what seemed like naturally occurring retraclone" (246), "an immune enzyme called Reverse-Transcriptase Receptor Antagonist [RTRA] which prevents retroviruses . . . from replicating" (245). In any case, by the end of the novel, significant advances have been made in curtailing the "spread" of AIDS: "the epidemic's under control" (246).

While *Plague* leaves open the possibility that its narrative constructions about AIDS might, even in its own fictional terms, not be "true," it nonetheless presents a coherent account of the AIDS epidemic that would make intentional all stages in its history—the African origin of HIV in scientific research; Buchanan and Wilson's decision to allow the virus to "spread" for the express purpose of stopping "the spread of sexual perversion"; the "collateral casualties" to "innocent civilians" (66) that, while unplanned, still result from the anti-homosexual plot; Wilson's second thoughts about his involvement in that plot, brought about by the realization that he and Buchanan, "[a]re going to kill off far too many collaterals and maybe never succeed at neutralizing the targets" (66); his resulting decision to leak crucial information about the "project"—reliable "evidence of the paranoid fantasy most homosexuals in this country had entertained at one time or another" (169)—to Stiers; the confrontation between Stiers and Buchanan that (probably) results in the release and "spread" of an "antidote virus"; the ultimate "control" of the epidemic "thanks to safe sex and nation-wide education about sex and the research that discovered RTRA" as well as the (probable) effects of the "antidote" itself. Johnson lays out a complete narrative of "plague"—from the appearance of HIV and AIDS, to the threat of gay genocide and world "destruction" (9), to the defusing of that threat—in which, even when things "get out of control" (177), all stages result from human decisions and actions. In Johnson's novel, the "authors" of the "plague" are clearly identifiable.

The "history of AIDS" thus presented in *Plague* is quite similar to that posited by Mains in *Gentle Warriors*, though the latter novel is less concerned with the process by which that "history" is discovered, operating not as a detective story but as a consideration of the political events that follow a revelation of the truth about AIDS. The group of gay men upon which the novel focuses has long suspected (from as early as 1980 [248]) that AIDS is not simply a natural phenomenon and the epidemic not just the result of government inattention to the earliest cases of illness. Though one character, Sam, at first argues that rumors of an intentional origin to AIDS are simply rumors, proposing instead an explanation that would still assign blame for the "spread" of illness and still place the origin of AIDS in Africa—"The North American spread of the AIDS virus was caused by negligence and greed in the blood-products industry. . . . The AIDS virus was in the general U.S. blood pool long before it hit us. It got there because the conglomerates bought cheap blood in Central Africa and distributed plasma products in America without adequate testing" (11-12)—he does so not out of conviction but to help conceal his own involvement in a counterplot directed against the presumed originators of HIV. Indeed, the novel moves quickly to confirm what one skeptic calls "those crazy rumors," the "[c]laims that our fine government planted the seeds of this disease" (29):

> Tonight, it all came out. The secret behind the rumors that have been circulating for several months. In Baltimore, a CIA agent stepped forward to confirm the rumors are true. Mr. Edward Stevens told a press conference that the AIDS virus was created and then tested by the CIA in Central Africa before being planted in the American homosexual population. (34)

Stevens, a member of a Christian fundamentalist group, the New Covenant Fellowship, "that held the Last Judgment was imminent" (48), makes explicit the genocidal intentions of the CIA plot:

"I want to make it very clear that we carried out our experiments with a great deal of care. We were, you could say, creating God's magic bullet. Contrary to some elements of public opinion, the general American population is not at risk. Innocent Americans will not die from this disease. We chose our target population because it is a major threat to national security, to the moral fabric of American life, and to the ideals of the American Dream."

. . .

"Mr. Stevens, can we hold out any hope to your victims? Is there a known cure to the AIDS virus? Surely you people wouldn't release a killer virus without a cure?"

They waited, expectantly. This was the least good that could possibly come out of this nightmare.

"A cure," Stevens drawled, as if fielding a misguided question. "Now that's just something about which I can't say. Homos and druggies. They deserve what they get." (37-39)

While the CIA and the American government deny what Stevens has revealed, labelling the revelation itself "a vicious and evil plot . . . perpetrated against this administration and the people of the United States of America" (160) and Stevens "a double agent for the Soviet Union" (161); while the novel elsewhere raises the question (like that in *Plague* concerning George Wilson's reliability) of whether Stevens is just "a right-wing crazy . . . who would like to take credit for something over which he had no control" (11),[18] his story is strongly supported by further revelations:

The devious means by which the virus was alleged to have reached the New York gay community. Two homo agents who had unknowingly been pumped full of it and sent to pig out at the Mineshaft and the St. Marks Baths in the guise of checking national security. (89; also see 112).

Evidence the CIA had run a supersecret genetic engineering lab near Port-au-Prince. The name of a retired biologist, USO, who had supervised the Zaire experiments known by their official name: OPERATION MACACQUE. (156)

Everyone in the novel—from the gay men who conspire to infect the President with HIV and thus force the release of a cure, if one exists (81 and 202),[19] to the government of San Francisco, which issues a warrant for the President's arrest—operates on the assumption that Stevens is telling the truth. As does *Plague*, then, *Gentle Warriors* presents a history of AIDS in which the development of HIV is intentional, its deployment specifically motivated by a genocidal homophobia, and its future wrapped up with an impending apocalypse, resisted by Gregg and his friends, wished for by fundamentalist Christians, and voiced by a "TV evangelist":

> This is their Last Judgment. . . . There will be no calling back to the throne of God, no opening of the graves for these people. They will suffer no hope as their souls find torment in hell. . . . Whether or not the Soviets had anything to do with AIDS, we know one thing. It was ultimately the work of God. It was God's statement to the despicable. And it was to the greatness of this country. (191-92)

In both *Plague* and *Gentle Warriors*, despite the devastating effects that HIV itself has, the AIDS "apocalypse" is imagined as consisting of not just a coherent plan of biological warfare but also a marshalling of social forces to stigmatize and help eliminate those with AIDS and all homosexuals. In *Plague*, when Wilson and Buchanan recognize that AIDS alone will not be capable to "stop the spread of sexual perversion," they count on the "social backlash" to do the job (178). Right-wing Senator Charles Wanamaker from Orange County (based loosely on California Congressman William E. Dannemeyer) proposes that "public funds for medical treatment for people with AIDS" be cut off "after their second bout with a major opportunistic infection" (128), and he "call[s] for all PWAs to be rounded up and moved out to one of those camps they built for the Japanese in World War II," with funding for these "concentration camps" to be provided by "a special surtax on homosexuals" (62). Similar measures pose a threat in *Gentle Warriors*. The federal government has already passed "the Quarantine Laws" (28, 30)—measures that, in the view of their proponents, "give American cities and counties like San Francisco the real means to control the AIDS threat" (28)—and these have been implemented in Chicago, Salt Lake City, and "dozens of cities and counties, mostly in the South and Midwest" (80):

> Whole populations had been tested. Everyone carried with them a plastic identification card; cards for those positive to HIV were striped with a red band across the bottom edge. Thousands of individuals were under partial or strict security, as they euphemistically referred to detainment. Job restrictions were applied to the red-striped. And under pressure from the Catholic church and the Sally Ann, a majority coalition of Chicago City Council had declared that AIDS, homosexuality and evil were one and the same and had no rights except to be discouraged by the strongest means possible. (79)

Walter Harrison (a right-wing, black candidate for District Attorney whose campaign, it is revealed, has been partly funded by the Ku Klux Klan) calls strongly for the implementation of such measures in San Francisco, and it is suggested that he would really like to see people with AIDS confined to "death camps" (72). Indeed, an "octongenerian (*sic*) senator from North Carolina" (clearly modeled after Jesse Helms) has "proposed legislation [that] would root out all homosexuals and put them in camps" (158).

Such ideas of direct and overt political oppression are, in *Plague* and *Gentle Warriors*, largely supplementary to the surreptitious biological warfare that the heroes of these novels confront and combat; in other novels of the "epidemiological" subgenre, however, this relationship is reversed, with the (un)natural history of HIV made secondary to the imagination of a dystopian future in which detention, quarantine, concentration camps, and genocide are the rule. *A Cry in the Desert* and *The Boiled Frog Syndrome*, however, still concern themselves in part with uncovering the origin and past history of HIV. Speculations on such matters in Rubin's *The Boiled Frog Syndrome* follow a familiar pattern: the novel's protagonist, Stephen Ashcroft, documenting events that have led to a Christian fundamentalist government in the United States, internment camps for gay men and lesbians, and a resistance movement in European exile of which Ashcroft himself is an important part, "start[s] where it all began" (50), with the intentional origin of AIDS:

> [W]e suspected very early on that AIDS, the so-called Gay Plague, was somebody's attempt at germ warfare that had gone amok. We almost had it documented, but then *they* killed a few key people. Of course, in the beginning, most people outside the gay community didn't regard AIDS as a problem; they regarded it as a solution, just as most white Americans, I'm ashamed to say, in their secret hearts regarded black poverty and sickle-cell anemia as solutions, not problems.
>
> We knew for a fact that our American germ warfare people had been working since the end of World War II on ethno-specific viruses that would wipe out certain populations and not touch others; I think that at one time they wanted to destroy the Chinese. Of course, none of these viruses worked outside of the laboratory, for the simple reason that in only a very few remote places on earth do you have an isolated population with a pure, unadulterated gene pool. So who knows what sort of bizarre madness could have made them think that the AIDS virus, a mutation of a Central African virus that had been endemic in the straight population for decades, would have remained confined within the gay community? (50)

When, according to Ashcroft, "[t]he original mutated African virus seemed to be losing its punch," "[t]he only thing that kept the plague going on was that new mutations of the virus kept appearing, or, as I frequently claimed in my writing, kept being introduced" (110-11). Ashcroft's friend Aristophanes Brent gathers proof of such suspicions—"They started it, obviously, in order to kill off the gay population of the United States, and eventually, they hoped, the entire world" (113)—but Brent disappears before he can provide Ashcroft the documentation of his claims (115).

The reconstructed history of HIV in Bryan's *A Cry in the Desert* is less fully conspiratorial than that in *Plague*, *Gentle Warriors*, or *The Boiled Frog Syndrome*, with the virus apparently arising and spreading without direct human intervention:

> From what we can determine, it may be an African disease brought to Haiti and Florida by mercenaries during the war in Angola. Haitians of both sexes have been reported victims as well as some African emigres in Belgium. It's also been tied to dope mainliners and prostitutes. The hotspots are still New York and the West Coast, but as reporting improves, new cases are cropping up in Chicago, Houston, New Orleans. And now here [Las Vegas]. Transient cities as well as ghettoes are the worst risks. We're a prime target, although we've been ignoring the fact far too long. (10)

But if, in Bryan's history, HIV was not engineered by human beings, its action *has*, from the beginning of the epidemic, been manipulated in ways actively concealed from the public:

> We have an AIDS serum now. Have had for some time. Completely effective if the secondary infections aren't too far advanced. (193)

> Stakl's people in St. Louis and other places have been working on the problem since 1979. They had developed a satisfactory vaccine before the quarantine law went into effect. . . . Now, however, we can produce as many cases as you like, advanced ones, in short order. Or we can eliminate the disease altogether. (205; see also 217-18)

While AIDS might thus have been prevented from becoming an epidemic, and while it might be eliminated at any moment, considered inaction has led to its perpetuation, with one central goal being, again, gay genocide.

In both *A Cry in the Desert* and *The Boiled Frog Syndrome*, however, speculations about the origins of HIV are ultimately overshadowed by the consideration of oppressive political responses to AIDS, with Bryan and Rubin both focusing their attention less on the past and more on a dystopian future. *A Cry in the Desert* starts at a moment relatively early in the epidemic—the novel's main action occurs in 1983—when the first case of AIDS appears in Las Vegas (5, 10, 24). From here, the novel traces the expansion of the epidemic—other local AIDS cases soon follow (35, 75)—and a parallel political "epidemic" of panic, vigilantism, and concerted oppression. These two movements are intimately linked in the novel not just because, as AIDS appears to "spread," so too does panic, but also because those who would like to see homosexuality done away with consciously manipulate the health crisis to that end. The novel's main villain, Alfred Botts, a deeply homophobic scientist for the CDC, has a dream "the very night after having read the first bulletin from CDC headquarters in Atlanta regarding what would come to be called AIDS" through which he recognizes that "the gay plague" is "the scourge of God" and the appropriate "catalyst" (19) for a plan to eliminate homosexuality: "Homosexuals are a blight on society, on humanity in general. . . . They are genetic mistakes, parasites on a species that can little afford debilitating effects. For the good of mankind, they must be eliminated" (206). To put his plan into action, Botts not only exploits existing cases of AIDS, but fabricates cases, both through a testing program that falsely identifies many as infected—"the actual test results were a hoax" (98)—and through the intentional exposure of others to the virus. In his attempt to stir public panic, Botts is particularly concerned to demonstrate that one can "contract AIDS through a . . . mucus transmission link" (79), and he does so by fabricating data, transfusing "two patients, a mother and child" with "contaminated blood" (67). Though neither patient actually becomes ill, Botts has them both killed and announces that they died of AIDS and that the only possible risk factor was non-sexual contact: "The young woman was allegedly a prostitute often seen in the company of homosexuals but not sexually involved with them" (79). (Bryan echoes here early fears of transmission through "routine contact," referring to the May 6, 1983, *JAMA* article and editorial that bolstered such fears [89; in the novel, however, the *JAMA* findings are presented in a news report dated June 10, 1983].) Near the novel's conclusion, Botts admits that his "research" facility has in fact only "dealt with fifteen actual cases of AIDS" (205).

Botts and his allies, however, successfully manipulate public information so that AIDS in Nevada truly appears to have reached epidemic proportions and to demand radical action. As early as 1981, when "the first cases [of AIDS] were recognized in New York" (5), Botts "panicked his local assemblyman . . . into proposing" (9) "the Emergency Quarantine Act [EQA]" (5), "a bill that would legally quarantine all known homosexuals should an epidemic threaten the general populace" (9). Though that original bill was passed by the Nevada legislature, Botts comes to recognize it as inadequate—"[t]he main problem . . . was its vague wording" (25)—and he uses the occasion of the first local AIDS case to push for a new, more effective EQA and a whole program of quarantine and research called ERAD, "Emergency Research and Development," the full nature of which the novel only gradually reveals. The passage of the new quarantine act (59) and construction of the ERAD facility proceed simultaneously, and a connection between the two quickly becomes clear: the quarantining instituted under the EQA will provide inmates for ERAD.

With the complicity of the media (41, 85-86) and the support of one particularly vociferous fundamentalist preacher, the Reverend Theophilus Stokeswood (38-39, 86), a gradual plan to identify and incarcerate all homosexuals goes into effect. First, gay men are urged to test themselves for infection through a "do-it-yourself kit" that, while "totally anonymous" (71), secretly marks the testee with a "small bluish dot" (91) and a "radioactive pellet" "[t]rackable at twenty feet with a sensitive counter" (94). This is followed by a call for "voluntary quarantining" (125), which at first has little effect. Simultaneously, however, the public panic brought on by reports of "mucus transmission" and by other attempts to stir up homophobia—Botts, for instance, stages a political assassination that he can then pin on a gay man (128-29)—leads both to official measures against gay men and lesbians, with the city government passing ordinances that "den[y] the right of homosexuals to prepare or serve food or drink in public places with other than a strictly gay clientele" (113), and to a strong vigilante movement: gay hustlers are beaten to death (116-21); a gay teacher is crucified and burned (131-34); a lesbian couple is raped and beaten, and one of the two dies as a result (141-43). Vigilante groups draw up "[c]rude, unsubstantiated lists of suspected homosexuals" (131), and people begin to feel that they might in fact be safer if incarcerated: "a person might as well leave town or go into hiding if his or her name appeared on such a list. Thousands did. The exodus to ERAD had begun" (131).

Botts quickly follows up the voluntary "exodus" with an involuntary "roundup" (151): state borders are closed to anyone who has been tested and thus carries the "radioactive tatoo" (*sic*) (149). Those intercepted trying to escape are handcuffed and transported to ERAD on buses (147-49). "Hunters," with "geiger counters and clubs" ferret out people in hiding (182). Others are captured by "[a] hundred different methods":

> Lists. Vigilante lists. Tax lists for two men or women who own a house or car together. Health department records. Military records. School records. Police records. Credit card applications and accounts records. Psychiatrists' reports. Business and military personality profiles. Employers, neighbors, friends, family. They drew from the obvious places, bars and baths, until they closed down. Including out-of-staters. Now they haunt stores and churches. They're even canvassing private

homes with concealed counters to get anyone they might have missed. After that, people just disappear. (182)

Transported to ERAD, the inmates find that, though the facility is "on the books as an emergency research hospital dedicated solely to the eradication of the disease" (26), it is in reality "an immense isolation compound" (30), cordoned off by "chain link fences, some electrified," "guards," "dogs" (168), and "electronic" devices (184), and controlled by a powerful computer—"Greta . . . the most advanced entity of her type" (202)—with a complex system of high-security access. Both inmates and project employees are "watched constantly" (203). Though the part of the facility shown to the public features "luxurious accoutrements," enabling "every conceivable activity from reading and lounging in modern overstuffed chairs to weight lifting and playing video games" (201), this is just a facade covering the institution's real identity as a "concentration camp" (177). Many of those incarcerated in ERAD become the subjects of medical research (see, e.g., 66 and 207). All are ultimately to die, but in a cost effective way, organs and other materials carefully "extracted": "With proper care and distribution, a good corpse might be worth from $500,000 upwards" (194). Though one of the novel's gay heroes, Carl, is ultimately successful in transferring evidence of the real goings on at ERAD to the outside world and in himself escaping incarceration to rejoin his lover Larry, the novel offers little hope that Botts's plans can be effectively interrupted. From its beginning, the novel has invoked apocalyptic language to describe the current state of the world—"Civilization, as we know it, is dying. Not with the cataclysmic force of an atomic blast but with the tenacious inevitability of a cancer so far advanced that no power can halt its progress" (3)—and its final plot twist threatens to transform Botts's genocidal plan into something even more broadly devastating, the plot of his associate Stakl "to take over the world": "He's going to blackmail the government out of existence. . . . Those mega-virus gene-fusing experiments have been all too successful. Right now he can wipe out Los Angeles or the whole fucking country if he wants to" (227-28). Though Botts apparently short-circuits Stakl's plan (235), his own continues unimpeded. At the novel's conclusion, a second confinement facility like ERAD opens (235), and "blood testing via the successful home test kit was to begin shortly in eight of the western states" (214): "It was apparent that Botts' plans to exterminate all of the gays in the country were more than delusions" (214). As the only two survivors of a large cast of gay characters, Carl and Larry, suggest at the end of the book: "'. . . Nothing short of a well-placed atom bomb is going to stop this.' / 'If that's true, then we are doomed. All of us. Gays, straights, the whole damned human race'" (234).

Though the details of its plot are different, and though its scope, national and international from the outset, is broader than that of Bryan's Nevada-centered novel, Marty Rubin's *The Boiled Frog Syndrome* tells much the same story of an oppressive regime bent on the destruction of gay men and lesbians. The novel retrospectively recounts, in the documentation—interviews, letters, journal entries—gathered together by Stephen Ashcroft, the history of a fundamentalist takeover of the Unites States that is intimately tied up with a plan to intern all gay men and lesbians. The whole process—gradual, seeming at first not to disturb daily life too radically—is analogized by the "boiled frog syndrome" of the novel's title:

If you take a frog and put him in a pot of boiling water, he will, quite naturally, try to leap out and save himself. But if you put him in a pot of cold water, and then heat the water very, very gradually, one tiny half-degree at a time, the frog will continue to sit there in that pot until he boils to death. (52)

The beginning point of the "boiling" is a moment in the 1980s when, in the view of the novel's protagonists, the United States is already deeply troubled—by diminished cultural expectations and educational standards ("What in the hell have we raised here, with our television and our dumbed-down textbooks? A generation of retards?" [93]), and by governmental corruptions and bankrupt policies ("our human rights violations in Central America, our economic injustices at home, and the crippling national debt caused by the scandalous waste and outright criminal fraud of our bloated military procurement" [97-98]). Against this background, Rubin develops the recent history of the lesbian and gay movement, reviewing its past successes—in particular, the Dade County Referendum campaign of 1977, when, despite the nullification of a county gay rights ordinance, the losing side wins "a moral victory," demonstrating "that here was a bloc of votes and an affluent minority group that needed to be wooed" (61)—and staging AIDS-era lesbian and gay politics as a confrontation with resurgent "militant radical religious right-wing crazies" (84). While the lesbian and gay movement is powerful enough to field, as its candidate for governor of Florida, Doug McKittrick, a charismatic, intelligent gay man with a good chance of winning election, reactionary forces simultaneously make gains. They succeed, in 1985, in silencing press coverage of South Florida's Gay Pride Festival (62-67), and they more generally "slowly but surely tak[e] over the media" (50). In 1986, "[w]ith diabolical timing, probably to prevent a nationwide rash of violent incidents at various Gay Pride Celebrations across the country, . . . on the very Monday following Gay Pride Day . . . the United States Supreme Court announced its infamous [Bowers v. Hardwick] decision in the Georgia sodomy case" (94). Under the pressure of "so-called 'Christian' picketers and hooligans" (85), censorship is instituted (85, 106-7)—PBS is "forced . . . to shut down" (106)—and the system of higher education is attacked (107-10). Individuals who know too much of governmental corruptions or who oppose the moves of the religious right disappear (115), have their careers destroyed (110) and their memories erased (106).

The political tensions of this era are particularly focused in the conflict between gubernatorial candidate McKittrick and a "crazy television evangelist" (134), the Reverend Peter Joshua Wickerly, who campaigns for McKittrick's opponent:

> When Wickerly raved about the accursed sodomite who was running for office, Doug discussed fiscal sanity in the state's budget. When Wickerly talked about the Word of God, Doug quoted Biblical passages about good government and the obligations of rulers. (136-37)

But while, for a time, things thus seem balanced between the two sides, and McKittrick's approach indeed appeals to a broad-based electorate, the gubernatorial campaign ultimately serves as the site for the lesbian and gay movement's failure. At one of McKittrick's campaign appearances, "they" (139)—"this mysterious *they*" (145) later identified as a conglomeration of "the military/industrial complex," "the Religious Right" and "The Mob" (146)—"struck" (139):

> [T]he crazed, wild-eyed man somehow managed to break through the cordon of police that surrounded the speakers' platform. Screaming "Filthy sodomite! Queer son of Satan!" he pulled out an enormous pistol that looked like a World War II Luger and pumped three shots into Douglas McKittrick at close range. (141)

McKittrick dies, and with him the momentum of the gay movement.

Wickerly's movement on the other hand continues to build on its successes and is "able to accomplish the final take-over with Machiavellian brilliance and simplicity" (147). In the harsh repressions that accompany this "take-over," AIDS plays an intimate part. Though Rubin imagines "the number of cases reach[ing] a plateau and then start[ing] to drop off" once the originators of AIDS discontinue "their program of grotesque experiments," by then it is "too late for us politically": "we gay people had been relegated to the status of lepers, rather like the caste of Untouchables in India" (20). Gay bars are raided in "a coordinated pattern . . . all across the country" (153); people "open" about their gayness at work are "summarily fired" (153); "all gay organizations" are labeled "subversive" by "[a]n Executive Order from the White

House" that allows them to be "disbanded" and their "records and assets" seized (153). An actual "take-over" of the federal government follows: first, the Vice President dies in a plane crash, and Wickerly is named in his place; then, the President "claim[s] severe ill-health," and "resign[s] in favor of the Reverend Vice President, who in turn appoint[s] the most reactionary right-wing Senator then in office, a Southern Baptist and homophobic fag-basher, to be his Vice President" (154). With the religious right thus firmly in control, anti-gay violence increases, culminating in a night explicitly compared to *Kristallnacht*:

> [M]obs of religious fanatics attacked the gay communities from Portland, Maine to San Diego, California. . . .
> . . .
> When morning came, seven hundred and sixty-three gay men and women had been brutally killed. Eleven thousand more of us had been beated (*sic*) or otherwise injured. . . . There was not a gay business that had survived until now that was left standing, anywhere in the United States. Every one of our newspapers and other periodicals—the few that were still publishing—had been destroyed. . . . As for the twenty million of us, approximately, who survived, all we could do was lick our wounds and slink back into the closet; this time, it seemed, for keeps. (155-56)

But a return to the closet in fact offers gay men and lesbians no security. Wickerly's administration has "pushed through their docile and compliant Congress . . . legislation that made possible the detention and quarantine of a wide variety of social undesirables," including "homosexuals, astrologers, iconoclastic writers, dissident intellectuals, and organizers of all political movements outside of the two-party mainstream" (123). And the government soon institutes the computer-based "DIVAF program," designed to root out gay men and lesbians for incarceration:

> DIVAF stands for *Discriminant Inferential Variant Analysis Factor*. A nice sounding piece of gobbledygook which basically means, How Is Your Neighbor Different?
> . . .
> . . . Nowadays, the government can scan through tax records, medical records, insurance records, occupational license records, credit records, bank records and, of course, the latest census records.
> Now whether we like it or not, homosexuals do have a spiked profile pattern against which the DIVAF program can compare records. (121)

Identifying gay men and lesbians by their "spiked profiles," the government rounds them up into "concentration camps" (210). Though conditions in the camps are generally good, many books are banned (28), "[a]ny expression of sexuality" is prohibited (28), only "the religious channel" is available on television (28), men and women are segregated (29), and "[a]lmost every day, one of us falls ill and . . . we never see him again" (28):

> There are a lot of men dying. . . . If there's an outbreak of influenza, for example, the medicine never seems to arrive in time. Or all of a sudden the food trays give an entire camp food poisoning or dysentery. Most of our people survive it, but always a few more die. The suicide rate is high, too. (19-20)

In fact, it turns out that not everyone who disappears from the camps dies: the government also uses the inmates of the camps for "revenue enhancement," "sell[ing]" inmates to surviving family and friends who can be "bled . . . for ransom money" (210). The failure of those on the outside to ransom an inmate results in his or her death (212).

In the vision of a possible future that Rubin thus presents, the American landscape has become wholly inhospitable to gay men and lesbians. The country is "[a] great big prison camp where everyone does as they're told" (209); for those who don't, actual prison camps await. Though there is an active resistance movement in exile, this in fact offers only the slightest of hopes. When Stephen Ashcroft's lover Troy Anderson, ransomed from the camps, asks, "Do you think we'll ever be able to go back to the United States?" Ashcroft can only respond: "I rather doubt it. . . It [all that Stephen and Troy had in their former lives] ended the night Doug McKittrick was assassinated" (230).

Rubin and Bryan thus both envision a future in which political freedom—particularly for gay men and lesbians but also more generally—disappears in movements motivated by homophobia and directed toward gay genocide. A similar imagination of the future characterizes Tim Barrus's *Genocide: The Anthology*, though this novel in certain ways stands apart from all the others. It is even more future-oriented than Bryan's and Rubin's works, often standing in close relation to science fiction genres; it speculates in no extended way on the origins of HIV and AIDS, though it does posit an intentionality at the root of genocidal epidemics—"FIRST the Native American was quarantined/detained AND THEN he was infected" (44)—that resonates obliquely and analogically with the history of AIDS. In general, Barrus is less concerned than the other writers considered here with developing a coherent, fully elaborated "epidemiological narrative." As its full title suggests, *Genocide* is not a traditional, narratively-unified novel, but an "anthology," of alternating prose and poetry,[20] and of prose that moves back and forth between the clearly fictional and the presumably autobiographical and nonfictional; at least one chapter, "TRESPASS," is closer in form to the essay than it is to the short story or novel. Still, *Genocide* does develop certain more extended narratives—for instance, the story of the brothers Star and Adonais central to three of the anthology's units ("CHINATOWN CHINATOWN," "DEMONIC BAPTISM," and "THE FOREST AND THE ECHO") and connected, through the last of these, with an earlier story ("WARRIOR"). A narrator, "Tim," appears at several different points. Recurring patterns of image and language connect the book's disparate sections. And all the narrative material Barrus "anthologizes" coheres in its vision of the more or less proximate future consequences of a current political moment dominated by AIDS. Despite its anti-narrative impulses, then, the novel does develop a certain progressive narrative beginning with a "now" of "friends dying ever-so-gracefully elegantly shitting in hospital beds" (130) and projecting a variety of future moments that lead ultimately to the edge of apocalypse.

Such a narrative, however, must be reconstructed by the reader since the novel proceeds without respect for chronology. *Genocide* begins with the end, opening with that chapter ("THE DEPENDENCY OF VARIABLES") most advanced in time, depicting a moment when the universe itself—what Barrus calls the "virus universe"—has come to be defined by an inescapable disease: "Jia's people had left planet after planet to escape the virus in a universe where the virus seemed to thrive with its incredible focus—to feed, to survive. Genocide" (8). Trying to "outrun the virus," "vanish[ing] from the known universe" (9), the spaceship OMICRON and its crew find themselves "well beyond the point where" it was "believed the virus universe might end—the place where it might bend back on itself" (5). In fact, however, that universe and the hegemony of "virus" go on and on, and Barrus concludes this opening story by suggesting the inevitability of the future it sketches: "The variables had evolved past dependency into the lavish variables of infatuated fate. It had all been envisioned" (16).

From this starting point, Barrus moves to depict more proximate moments: the novel's second, sixth, seventh, and eleventh chapters present a view of the future in which the earth has been devastated by a variety of disasters; the remaining six chapters depict a more "realistic" landscape closer to the "present" moment of the 1980s. All of these show, in place of the rather abstract "virus universe" of the novel's opening chapter, an often gruesomely particularized world of illness, destruction, and oppression. The stories most proximate in time ("TRESPASS," "PULL," "MIDNIGHT'S KNOCK ON THE MADNESS DOOR," "A FAREWELL TO LOVE," "RENEGADE," and "RAINFUCK") are also most "realist" in mode. Haunted by "the not-so-gay history of quarantine/detention in the United States" (43) and international political oppression like that in Chile and El Salvador (see 75-86), these stories detail the effects of AIDS on the narrator's community:

> [M]y ex-lovers and ex-obsessions . . . were all quietly dying and needed me. . . . I was only able to see so many of them die, only able to hold so many of them, one-friend-lover-at-a-time, in my suffocating arms. I only had so many tears, and my arms ached. (131)

And they begin to show the deployment of a repressive political apparatus linked to the AIDS epidemic. That apparatus at first remains rumored rather than confirmed:

> It was the summer of rumor. . . . Stories about camps, stories about those who had disappeared, stories; they were only stories. . . . No one knew, really, if there was any truth to the stories. Truth. Most people thought the stories were true. Most people knew someone who knew someone who had disappeared. . . . It was the summer of quarantine. (60-61)

The rumors indeed prove to be true: "And then the serious talk of the quarantine became serious real" (132). "Health papers" must be carried (130). A man is "escorted away . . . by officials wearing rubber gloves" (141); another "narrowly avoid[s] French quarantine" by entering a different "sort of quarantine" (172), exile on an Indonesian island; yet another must leave his lover in order to avoid capture and incarceration (145-58):

> It was a time of roundups and trains and the sick stink from ovens at the edge of town—any town would do, and quarantines and horror and let's-go-quietly arrests in the hushed bloodless faggot night. It was a time of fear and piles of bodies and queers and brothers who died faggotnaked thin thin diarrhea emaciated in your arms, in camps, in trains, in ditches dug into the ground by the men buried there, men who were buried by men who would be buried elsewhere themselves. (149-50)

Not only do the purges arise from AIDSphobia and homophobia, they also express racism: "Moses was black. . . . And there it was: he could not be hidden" (153); "Jimmy Dog would never see his home again; Jimmy Dog was a faggot, and not only that, but he was an Indian faggot. / He could not be hidden" (157). And illness and quarantine are worldwide phenomena: "even this part of the earth contained those poor souls now referred to as—the infected. . . . The proposed quarantine camp would be constructed in the Australian outback" (186).

The anthology's remaining four chapters—"CHINATOWN CHINATOWN," "WARRIOR," "DEMONIC BAPTISM," "THE FOREST AND THE ECHO"—set in a more futuristic landscape, trace a similar history of oppression—of "quarantine trains" (20) filled with "detainees," "the infected" (24; see also 95, 101, 196)—and show its horrific future developments: a state run according to the "Official Policy of Self-Destruction" (22), the "State Policy of Relocation" (24), and the "Official State Policy of Coexistent Deterioration" (33); "the bluish tattoo" of the camps (100); "the quarantine's ovens" (96); a surreal, Dantesque [21] amusement-park ("Karnival") death camp ("Chinatown Chinatown") in which those who are "INCAMP" (21) kill themselves by "rid[ing] the rides tilt[ing] the tilt" (23)—"such places had once (there were many legends) been simply referred to as 'health camps,' now they were just called 'extinction camps'" (26).[22] The central figures of these stories are Star and Adonais, "assigned the INCAMP position of bodyscraper" (28): "You climbed down into the semidark hellhole space underneath the rides and you picked up the dripping pieces, you slushed your arms into the mass of wet human bloody garbage and you disposed of whatever you found" (29).

The landscape of these stories is devastated not just by AIDS, and not just by the camps and their violence, but by ecological disaster:

[T]he earth had for some time sweated with poison. . . . The venom of civilization was hauled to this desert spot and dumped into the same desert pits that the human death waste from Chinatown Chinatown was poured into. Benzene. Tetrachloroethylene. Polychlorinated biphenyls. Polyvinyl-chloride. (33)

While Star and Adonais may escape the camp, and others may avoid quarantine to form renegade bands, a kind of "resistance" (94-96, 102) movement engaged in war against "those who hunted them" (95), no one is able to escape the earth's own barrenness.

Barrus imagines a time after the virus and the quarantine, a post-AIDS world:

There were no more quarantines, quite simply because there were no more traces of non-heroin virus left in this place that had once been choked with virus. . . . There had been a war, a quarantine, a time of general terror and madness and burning of the planet—to get at the accumulation of viral horror which was eating the earth. Hosts became rare. Quarantines had not worked, and in his panic man turned against man in his fear, in his panic, in his ignorance, in his unfathomable stupidity, in his disconnectedness, in his faithlessness in himself. The planet was radiated. Virus burned for ten war-like years. (110-11)

But the world left in the wake of the "burning" of "virus" is a desert as ruined and inhospitable as the camps:

Those who survived referred to the earth as Demonic Baptism. It had been an age of genocide and survival. The earth itself turned demonaic (*sic*) and had baptised it (*sic*) creatures with horror and death and war and virus and starvation and plague and INCAMP quarantine until the earth itself was INCAMP quarantine, until the earth was desert. (108)

In this landscape, political oppression continues. There is slavery (see, e.g., 111, 117, 195), now also practiced by the "resistance" bands themselves (202-11). The "resistance" still confronts its enemies: "Captured enemy soldiers—sad downcast eyes who had quarantined those who had now returned the favor—were torn limb from bloody limb and fed to street dogs" (209). "Genocide" continues: "although the time of genocide was supposedly over . . . nothing was over and anything was possible" (111-12).

Like Bryan and Rubin, Barrus thus presents a view of the future—whether the future of a barren "post-virus" earth, or that of a "virus universe" inescapably enmeshed in disease—approaching apocalypse. *A Cry in the Desert*, *The Boiled Frog Syndrome*, and *Genocide* all push toward ends hinted at but not fully developed in *Plague* and *Gentle Warriors*, a future that fulfills (and sometimes exceeds) the genocidal dreams of Buchanan and Wilson in *Plague*, of Ed Stevens, the New Fellowship Covenant, and the CIA in *Gentle Warriors*. Each novel reads out of the current moment of the AIDS crisis a future of political repression whose end will be, at the very least, the destruction of lesbian and gay communities, and, at the most, the ruin of earth itself.

2. INVOKING HISTORY, AUTHENTICATING FICTIONS

Having developed a very bleak view of the future in *Genocide*, Barrus steps outside his own fiction to emphasize, in what might be read as combined prologue and epilogue to the "anthology," that he does not regard his book as just an exercise in fantastic dystopian writing. On the back cover of *Genocide*, immediately following a blurb that emphasizes the book's simultaneous "imagination" and "realness" ("This is a vision of hell that somehow feels real as you venture into Barrus' imagination") and that suggests a possible aversion of the future envisioned by Barrus ("Is it real? Does it have to be this way?"), a statement attributed to "Tim Barrus" intervenes, as a kind of answer to such questions:

The only hope gay men have rests in the connections which bind them together; and in my subjective opinion, this is not enough . . . my concept is one of irreversible annihilation. If you see hope in this work, that's your stuff, not mine. (ellipsis in original)

Connecting the fictional work and its apocalyptic constructions strongly to the "real" world, Barrus here suggests that, in his own view, it does indeed "have to be this way."

Both Bryan's and Johnson's novels are prefaced by statements that similarly position them in direct, even urgent, relation to the current moment, moving to authenticate their visions of the future. On the copyright page of *A Cry in the Desert* is what amounts to a rationale for the publication of a book that, as Bryan himself elsewhere suggests, many publishers saw as "too strong, too militant, too graphic, too unsettling,"[23] and, one might add, too alarmist:

> The people and events in this book are fictitious. . . .
>
> The devasting (*sic*) effect that AIDS has had on its victims, however, is very real. Apart from the obvious ravages the disease extracts from its victims, there is the toll taken by the fear and hatred that have too often surrounded this disease. It is the hope of the publishers that this book will in some way help the understanding of its readers for the dangers of a disease such as AIDS. The potential for hysteria is a real and present danger that could conceivably be worse than the disease itself.
>
> The message is clear. AIDS is not a *gay plague*. It is a very real danger to us all.
>
> A portion of the profits from the sale of this book will be dedicated to helping AIDS victims. The publishers would like to urge that the readers of this book join in the fight against this deadly killer.

Facing the copyright page in *Plague*, and preceding the novel's dedication, is a similar statement:

> For a significant segment of the American population, the 1980s has been dominated by a health crisis of proportions rivaling the plagues of old. Politicians, public officials, medical personnel, and health activists have recognized that education represents the major bulwark against the spread of the disease.
>
> . . .
>
> The following is a work of fiction. The plot and the characters are imaginary. The names of medical treatments and drugs have frequently been altered. The social problems created by this disease and the plight

of people with HIV infection, however, as well as the instructions about risk reduction and the teachings about attitudinal healing are accurate. The projections for the resolution of the plague that haunts us in 1987 are reasonable extrapolations of current medical fact. (3)

Such attempts at self-authentication, at placing the "fictitious," "imaginary" constructions of these novels in intimate relation to the "real and present dangers" of "disease" and "plague," of "hysteria" and "the social problems created by this disease," clearly display a certain nervousness about the novels' "projections" and "extrapolations," a fear that these will not be taken seriously, credited as "reasonable" responses to the here and now of AIDS. At the same time, of course, in anticipating and proactively addressing potential criticisms— and in Barrus's case, "hope"-filled misreadings—the authors and publishers show a strong commitment to having these works read seriously, as real warnings of dangerous future possibilities, and furthermore as calls to action, to "join in the fight."

While the generic affiliations of these five works—with novels of mystery and suspense, spy thrillers, science fiction, erotica and pornography—might lead us to see them as primarily geared to entertainment and diversion, the novels in fact belie these affiliations with an earnestness of mission clear in the prefatory material just cited and confirmed over and over within the novels themselves. Appealing to plot-oriented readers through the density of action and event in their convoluted, conspiracy-ridden plots, focusing luridly on violence (for instance, in the crucifixion/burning scene of *A Cry in the Desert*), and sometimes introducing sex in only tangential connection to other, more central concerns, each of these works nonetheless repeatedly claims for itself the status of a serious political treatment of, and intervention in, the AIDS crisis. All five novels are sensitive to the possible charge that they represent alarmist, "paranoid" overreactions, and each moves to authenticate its version of the history and possible future of AIDS, primarily by appealing to historical precedent. Anticipating, and indeed often thematizing, the response that "it can't happen here"—"these are . . . people who basically believed in America; who thought that this could never happen in our country" (Rubin 20)—the novels repeatedly show how it has happened here and elsewhere, and thus might again.

As Les Wright suggests in his excellent discussion of *The Boiled Frog Syndrome* and *Gentle Warriors*, the novels of "gay genocide" rely most heavily upon historical parallels to Nazi Germany.[24] The very language of "genocide" and "holocaust" is, in the second half of the twentieth century, inseparably tied to the history of Nazism. The "camps" of each novel, the knock on the door (Barrus 75-86), the transport "trains" (Barrus 20, 149, and *passim*), the "roundup" of people (Barrus 151-52; Bryan 151), "tattoos" (Barrus 100, 117,

198, 208; Bryan 149, 182), the numbering of prisoners (Barrus 100, 198; Bryan 201), "barbed wire" (Bryan 84; Rubin 156), the "ovens" (Barrus 96, 149), all evoke the Nazi Holocaust without the need for any more direct allusion to it. Each novel, however, also moves to tie the history of AIDS and the prediction of its political consequences more explicitly to the Holocaust. The names of the German concentration camps—Dachau and Auschwitz (Johnson 190; Bryan 207; Rubin 29, 200; Barrus 49, 56), Bergen-Belsen (Rubin 200), Treblinka (Mains 181)—appear repeatedly in these novels. In *Genocide*, Barrus evokes "dead jews and queers dead" (86), and he makes clear the central place of the "German concentration camps" in his broader history of "quarantine/detention" (43-44). Rubin introduces "a Holocaust survivor," Aaron Ten Eyck (17), into *The Boiled Frog Syndrome*; Ten Eyck's experience in World War II, recounted at length (167-200), makes him the perfect interlocutor for Stephen Ashcroft in the development of parallels between Hitler's regime and the "Wickerly holocaust" (147) (see, for instance, 20-21). Ashcroft's own status as a refugee "resistance" fighter in Amsterdam of course also echoes the era of World War II, and Rubin alludes several times to Anne Frank (12, 61, 78). In Bryan's *A Cry in the Desert*, the violence in Nevada echoes that of both the Nazis and the Ku Klux Klan: "Crosses and swastikas were burned in lawns" (130). ERAD's "live-subject experimentation" has been "tried before" (66), though "crudely": "Those idiot Nazis. They starved and maimed and contaminated their subjects until any use for them was destroyed before it was begun" (207). Bryan explicitly compares the gay resistance movement of the "Reno ghetto" to the Warsaw Ghetto uprising of 1943 (176-77, 235). In Mains's *Gentle Warriors* and Johnson's *Plague*, though the references to Nazism are less pervasive than in the other three novels, they are still important:

> [T]onight, a people who had suffered collectively for nearly a decade (the years numbering those of the Nazi Holocaust) the death of hundreds of friends had come to realize that their own country had committed those murders, and if Ed Stevens was correct, deliberately. (Mains 133).

One of Mains's characters asks, "Are we to be the loyal citizens watching silently as the Nazis march off their victims before coming back for us?" (256). And Johnson makes explicit what all the parallels to Nazism in these novels suggest:

> I know it sounds alarmist, but I think American society is in about the same place German society was in the 1930s. And just like those people—who I'm sure were all nice people who never thought of

themselves as monsters—all ended up supporting monstrous crimes perpetrated by Adolf Hitler, it seems that Americans are being talked into committing monstrous crimes against homosexuals. (131)

The evocation of Nazi Germany and the Nazi persecution not just of Jews but of homosexuals has of course been an important strategy of the post-Stonewall lesbian and gay movement, most notably with the reclaiming of the pink triangle as a symbol of liberation. AIDS activism, particularly that of ACT UP, adding the slogan SILENCE = DEATH to the pink triangle, has made repeated use of allusions to the Holocaust: "What is Reagan's *real* policy on AIDS? Genocide of all Non-whites, Non-males, and Non-heterosexuals? . . . SILENCE = DEATH."[25] And in the broader culture, comparisons of the AIDS crisis to the Holocaust have become commonplace; in the recent words of Cornelius Baker of the National Association of People with AIDS: "We've been in this fight for 15 years now, longer than World War II, and the numbers will be greater than the Holocaust."[26] Such comparisons and appropriations can represent powerful calls to action, reminding us that, indeed, AIDS is a massive, horrific problem and that part of the problem rests in an active racism, sexism, and homophobia. As Les Wright points out, however, appeals to the Holocaust also involve certain problems—for instance, the "automatic, assumed status of [a] 'me too' victimization" that tends toward the dissolution of historical specificity.[27] Moreover, as Wright also notes, the "Nazi-as-bogeyman mythology" often serves, in the American context, an ideological agenda quite different from that of AIDS activism or the authors of the "epidemiological" novels: posing "[e]vil Nazis versus good Allies," that mythology is commonly used to bolster the image of "good Americans, good War Department, good military-industrial complex, good American wars in Vietnam, Nicaragua, Saudi Arabia."[28] Analogizing the Reagan/Bush-era United States to Nazi Germany runs afoul of a whole post-World War II ideological self-construction of American "democracy" as antithetical to "totalitarianism"— Nazism/fascism and communism both. While parallels between the United States of the AIDS crisis and Nazi Germany may be rhetorically more powerful than other conceivable appeals—since they evoke what has come in the second half of the twentieth century to typify "genocide" and "holocaust"—given the ideological positioning of American "democracy" over against Nazism, they risk being dismissed as simply outlandish.

Each of the five novelists seems to recognize something of this problematic aspect of the Nazi parallel. None develops the authentication of his political vision solely on the basis of that parallel; each supports his depiction of an American AIDS Holocaust with appeals to totalitarian, oppressive, genocidal histories in which the United States has in fact been directly implicated. The histories evoked are diverse, spanning the whole period of European presence in the Americas. Thus, Barrus recalls the genocidal basis of European colonization—"the various quarantines that were used against the American Indian where the American Indian was given blankets infected with diseases such as smallpox" (Barrus 44; also see 93)—and Mains makes one of his central characters, Marc, a Metis, who—because of his background as one of "those combination-people, Quebecois and Indian that generations of government, even today, continued to shunt around the open lands, the 'Native' lands" (55)—recognizes all the more easily "[t]he abuses of federal powers, of police powers, the same powers that had carried out the execution of Louis Riel [the Metis rebel] or beat up Indians in Williams Lake" (108; also see 87, 180-82, 255). At the other end of their historical spectrum, the novels evoke the current moment of American global politics, reminding us of active American participation in an "arms race" (Mains 67; and see Bryan 85) that might lead to "nuclear disaster" (Rubin 23) or "holocaust" (Mains 157).

American foreign policy is repeatedly critiqued in these novels not just for its cold-war, anti-communist willingness to approach nuclear apocalypse, but for its consistent support of a variety of repressive regimes and movements: the insurgent *Contras* in Nicaragua (Rubin 37, 73, 88, 89, 91-92, 125; Mains 293); the right-wing governments of Chile (Barrus 44, 46-47, 81-86; Rubin 73, 124), the Haiti of Duvalier (Rubin 125), the Philippines of Marcos (Rubin 125), Guatemala (Rubin 73, 125), the Iran of the Shah (Rubin 73, 124), Cuba (Rubin 73), Honduras (Barrus 85; Rubin 73), El Salvador (Barrus 83-85; Rubin 73). The slogan "US out of SF," used in *Gentle Warriors* in response to the CIA AIDS plot, of course recalls the common 1980s slogan "US out of El Salvador" (Mains 135). While there are some references in these novels as well to the history of communist totalitarianism—"Gulags in Mother Russia" (Barrus 44); North Korean jails (Rubin 37); Russian tanks in Prague (Mains 200-1); "East German border guards" and "Checkpoint Charlie" (Rubin 38, 41)—the relative scarcity of these supports a reading of the novels' political references as particularly intended to implicate the United States itself in a history of repressive actions that would support the novels' own depiction of American responses to AIDS as tending toward a totalitarian repression.

Each of the novels also, more or less fully, evokes the history of American intervention in Vietnam (e.g., Bryan 85)—tied to "the atrocities of our increasingly misguided war machine" (Rubin 33)—and the repression of antiwar activism, for instance, at Kent State University (Mains 181). In Mains, Gregg is a Vietnam veteran (see especially 19-22, 43-46, 173, 207-20, 283) and his lover Allan a draft resister who spent years "in Canadian exile" (78; see also 85, 245-46). In Barrus, several major figures, including the novel's narrator "Tim," are Vietnam veterans (see especially 52-55, 78, 86, 148-56). And in Johnson, Buchanan and Wilson were both in Vietnam "with one of the first groups of military advisers this country sent to help stabilize the South"

(26). Buchanan himself, the prime mover behind the plot to "spread" AIDS in *Plague*, in many ways stands in for a whole apparatus of warfare, torture, and oppression linked in these novels to American foreign policy; a consultant on weapons technologies, his personal hobby is "collect[ing] souvenirs" of "the horrors of the human heart" (219) that he stores in a closet in his office.

These novels recognize, furthermore, that the history of American repressive politics includes not only the support of regimes elsewhere but movements within the United States itself. McCarthyism—the "political holocaust of the nineteen-fifties" (Rubin 110)—is evoked as a parallel to AIDS-era politics in Rubin's novel,[29] as is the repression of the "progressive labor movement" and the "black civil rights movement" (65).[30] And Mains recalls the history of non-governmental, but sometimes governmentally-sanctioned hate groups—"Klansmen burning black homes and bombing black churches" (256); "the John Birch Society and . . . neo-Nazi, pro-Aryan groups in Idaho and Montana" (169). Barrus devotes a whole chapter, "TRESPASS," to the history of quarantine and detention, and focuses particularly on Angel Island, where Chinese immigrants were detained in a camp "very similar to . . . the camps that were eventually constructed to house the Japanese when they had their constitutional turn at containment" (48). Johnson, too, evokes the internment of Japanese-Americans during World War II (62).

Each of these novels thus works hard to make its own political constructions plausible. If the reader is tempted by the thought that "it can't happen here," the novels repeatedly emphasize that it can and has: "I wanted him to know that what happened to him in Chile (political detention/quarantine, repression, off-to-jail you go, people disappear) could happen here. And did happen here" (Barrus 47; also see 93-94, 102). Unlike these novels, we might take the view that the main failures of American responses to AIDS arise not from conspiracy or active intention, but rather from real scientific and medical difficulties and from an early and continuing government neglect and inaction— including the refusal to direct public health education to gay men, lesbians, and users of intravenous drugs, and the Church-led opposition to teaching about safer sex and condom use—that, while they express a certain homophobia, racism, and sexism, do not represent a concerted plan for genocide. But the novels remind us, not only with their historical parallels, but also through the direct citation of recent events, that their fantasies of a right-wing and specifically Christian fundamentalist backlash of homophobia in the era of AIDS are not vain imaginings, that in fact we live in a time of "fag-bashing" (Rubin 115); a time marked by the assassinations of Harvey Milk and George Moscone in San Francisco (Mains 26, 74, 78, 102, 125, 133, 227, 251); a time when sodomy laws have been upheld by the Supreme Court as constitutional (Mains 113; Rubin 94-96; and see Bryan 9, 49); a time when in fact initiatives have been proposed—for example, the LaRouche Initiative (Proposition 64) in

California (Johnson 160; Mains 113-14)—that would provide for quarantining of people with AIDS. It is clearly such events that provide much of the impetus for these "epidemiological" novels: Bryan, having put his novel aside for two years, decided to attempt again to find a publisher "when legislation was proposed in California for mandatory testing and quarantining of potential as well as confirmed AIDS victims."[31] The instances of violence against gay men and lesbians and people with AIDS that the novels depict, while sometimes luridly presented, are not hard to imagine at a moment when similar violent acts—the burning of the homes of people with AIDS;[32] murders of lesbians and gay men that are seen as somehow less serious, and more "justified," than other murders[33]—are a day-to-day reality of life in the United States. That people would be persecuted, as they are in *A Cry in the Desert*, on the basis of a panicky belief in "mucus transmission" of HIV may seem outlandish given the current emphasis, in all official sources of information, on the "proper" routes of transmission; but we should remember that people have been, and are being prosecuted for "attempted murder" based on actions (spitting, biting) that might in fact not transmit HIV: "The court . . . said it did not matter whether the virus that causes AIDS can actually be transmitted by biting as long as the prisoner believed it could."[34] While widespread mandatory testing of people for HIV has been resisted, it has also been repeatedly proposed and in fact instituted for certain populations—people in the armed forces, prospective immigrants, the inmates of certain prison systems.[35] If quarantines like those depicted in the novels seem unlikely, we should remember not only a (failed) ballot initiative like that of LaRouche but also the real, if "unofficial," imposition of quarantine in South Carolina;[36] the selective application of state "public health" quarantine laws to prostitutes;[37] and the segregation, in many states, of prisoners with HIV or AIDS.[38] HIV-positive Haitians trying to immigrate to the United States were kept quarantined at Guantánamo Bay until a court ordered them released.[39] While the novels may seem to go overboard in demonizing a homophobic, genocidal Christian fundamentalism, the stigmatizing language of certain Christian groups and individuals has not been so different from that of the fictional Reverends Stokeswood and Wickerly (in Bryan and Rubin respectively), or Ed Stevens and the New Covenant Fellowship (in Mains), or Edward Buchanan (in Johnson; on Buchanan's fundamentalism, see especially 178). A public service announcement that began airing on television in 1994 concludes with the slogan, "AIDS: it's a disease, not a sin," making clear that the concept and language of AIDS as "sin" are still very much with us. Even certain of the gestures of the Nazi Holocaust have been directly invoked in relation to AIDS, the most prominent instance being William F. Buckley's proposal that "[e]veryone detected with AIDS should be tatooed (*sic*) in the upper forearm, to protect common-needle users, and on the buttocks, to prevent the victimization of other homosexuals," a proposal reiterated in 1995 by David Duke.[40] One "San Francisco research group affiliated with the conservative Hoover Institution" suggested in 1986 that, if "AIDS could be transmitted through sweat, sneezes, and mosquito bites," "extreme public health measures"—"including 'mandatory and overt identification' of AIDS carriers, possible quarantine, and perhaps branding of HTLV-III [HIV] positive people, an option the study's authors referred to as 'a Star of David concept'"—be taken.[41]

The "epidemiological" novels present a real truth about the AIDS crisis, about the fear, violence, acts of segregation and stigma that AIDS has provoked. The novels themselves work assiduously—with their appeals to historical precedent demonstrating that real events very like what they fictionally posit can and do occur—to convince us of their own plausibility. Still, there remain real barriers to that plausibility. Perhaps this is partly due to the persistence of the very kind of denial that the novels wish to confront, a refusal to believe that the conspiracies and devastations depicted could be true of our own "here and now." But the invocation of history by these novels, their very attempt to make plausible a certain historical construction of AIDS, also works in certain ways against plausibility: the sheer mass of material cited— event after event and policy after policy marshalled in support of the novels' fictional accounts of the past, present, and future of the AIDS crisis—results in a levelling of historical specificity. In these novels, many disparate events and policies, piled up in authentication of a particular conspiratorial understanding of the history of AIDS, come to mean much the same thing. While in certain ways the novels' appeals to history do connect them to the messiness of the world, they serve as well to support narrative constructions—visions of coherent conspiracy and approaching apocalypse—neater than the stuff of history.

3. FIGHTING BACK

The "real-world" experience of a complex political and social phenomenon like the AIDS crisis tends to be fragmented rather than unified: moves to stigmatize or punish people with AIDS have been real—one can argue persuasively that certain forces have pushed toward genocide—but such forces do not present themselves in the world with anything like the inexorable narrative logic of the "epidemiological" novels. Even when repressive movements are powerful and even when they succeed with relative ease (for instance, in the series of Senate votes orchestrated by Jesse Helms that has resulted in a much different, and much less effective, program of federally funded AIDS education than might otherwise have been), they face kinds of opposition and contestation that by-and-large do not characterize the fictional worlds of these novels. While each novel does present a certain active "resistance" to the repressive events that unfold within it, in each that resistance is largely determined, and ultimately weakened, by an acceptance of the logic of a unified, conspiratorially controlled epidemic.

The "epidemiological" novels attempt to make full sense of the "course" of the AIDS epidemic. In doing so, they partly depend, despite their particularized evocations of historical material, upon an oversimplified view of history, an understanding of social and political forces as always under the more or less full control of particular, identifiable agents. Such a view tends to characterize the historical and political constructions both of the literary genres to which these novels have the closest affiliation and of conspiratorial thinking more generally. The genres of detective and spy fiction, and the political thriller, depend upon plots that, while convoluted and confusing, work out neatly—often because they uncover conspiracies, networks of intention, that, when recognized, show how what at first seems an inexplicable mystery in fact makes perfect sense. Each of the novels under consideration here performs just such an uncovering, revealing the agents responsible for AIDS, its origin (whether, as in most of the novels, an engineered origin of the virus itself, or, as in *Genocide*, an origin that is the current moment seen to hold within itself the potential unfolding of epidemic and genocide), its "spread," repressive political reactions, and a cataclysmic end. Each makes the AIDS epidemic, from origin to end, understandable as a *plot*, in the sense of a planned, intentional, even (or especially) conspiratorial narrative. These novels make all the trajectories of the epidemic and of responses to it readable as one unified and unifying motion. An intentional, engineered origin for HIV—a virus that, in its first American manifestations, affects primarily "homos" and "druggies" (Mains 39)—suggests a whole plot of biological warfare whose end would be genocide and apocalypse; conversely, a sense of approaching genocide and apocalypse implies an origin that is intentional, aimed toward just such ends. Any point in such a coherent, motivated narrative implies all other points; indeed, it is from a particular reading of the current, "real-world" situation— with its suggestive parallels to prior ominous historical moments, with its active homophobia, with its real movements of hostility against people with AIDS— that each of these novels arrives at its unified, unifying understanding of the whole epidemic in the terms of intentionality.

The structure of the unifying, "epidemiological" narratives in these novels resembles nothing so much as those homophobic understandings of the history of AIDS that the novels respond to and explicitly condemn.[42] In a homophobic "epidemiology" like that of Jesse Helms or Lawton Chiles—or indeed like that of Randy Shilts in his depiction of Gaetan Dugas as "Patient Zero"—gay men and homosexual acts stand unambiguously at the "origin" of (American) AIDS, with sexual "perversion" threatening a general "spread" to the "innocent." Lurking behind such constructions, and sometimes made explicit in them, is the belief in an intentionality operating at all points in the epidemic: AIDS originates in the "immoral" choice of homosexuality, and sometimes, as in the myth of Dugas, from the express intention of gay men to infect others ("I've got it. . . . They can get it too").[43] It also, however, is under the control of divine and natural "law," representing a judgment against "sin" or, alternatively, nature's punishment for "unnatural" sex. Apocalypse approaches either as the Last Judgment of an angry God or as the revenge of a nature too cavalierly treated, "the unexpected cost of having tampered radically with the ecological equilibria of the ages."[44]

The "epidemiological" novels take such a moralizing, homophobic narrative and rewrite the terms of responsibility within it, but without questioning its basic logic, its assumption of coherent intentionality, its reliance upon an economy of blame. In these rewritings, the (usually Christian fundamentalist) authors of homophobic histories of AIDS are themselves recast as the actual authors of the epidemic. Gay men become not victimizers of the "innocent" but themselves "innocent victims," and those who would have us believe in the culpability of gay men are themselves rendered culpable. AIDS becomes in these constructions not a divine or natural punishment for homosexuality but rather a product engineered and used by human beings to enact their own phobic judgments. An apocalypse approaches that has not been called for by God or nature but rather by those who, believing in their own access to knowledge of the divine or natural will, take the Last Judgment into their own hands. Where homophobic understandings posit as the villains of the AIDS crisis a Gaetan Dugas, "sinful" gay men more generally, and a sexual revolution at odds with traditional morality or "natural" standards of hygiene, the "epidemiological" novels propose an alternative list of villains—a Botts or Buchanan, the CIA, Christian fundamentalism—that includes especially those who would construct the AIDS crisis as the fault of gay men and then use that construction to homophobic ends.

There is a certain satisfaction in such a reversal of blame, and a real truth in the suggestion that the AIDS crisis is furthered by those who themselves level accusations of guilt while, as a matter of policy, denying information and services to those who need them. The "epidemiological" novels recognize that such accusations and policies express genocidal fantasies, and they play those fantasies out to some possible conclusions. But rather than reject homophobic views of AIDS as gay sin, as an assault on nature, as a surreptitious attack on "normal" masculinity, by challenging not just their homophobic content but also the whole logic of intentionality that would conceive an illness as authored and thus justify attacks on its ("sinful," "unnatural") authors, the "epidemiological" novels simply shift the ground of blame. Their reliance on a strategy of reversal means that they generally fail to confront or rethink important assumptions underpinning the narrative structures they adopt and rewrite. Most strikingly, the novels' replication of a logic of "us" against "them," with a simple reversal of terms—replacing the homophobic formulation of AIDS as gay men's victimization of an "innocent" "general population" with a construction in which the religious right itself is responsible for AIDS and thus for the victimization of "innocent" gay men—means that the proposition, central to homophobic accounts, that AIDS is somehow "essentially" related to gay men is maintained, even while the corollary idea that gay men are to blame for AIDS and its "spread" is rejected. Though each of the "epidemiological" novels gestures toward the idea that AIDS is not exclusively a "gay plague," that it has "spread" beyond the "risk group" of gay men, all implicitly or explicitly accept a view of AIDS as somehow originally "gay"—because, in most of these novels, "planted" in gay populations by homophobic enemies. And while these novels do sometimes depict groups other than gay men— lesbians, intellectuals, users of intravenous drugs, people of color—as objects of attack by the religious right, none of these other groups comes to play a prominent role in the novels. The action remains primarily focused on a binary confrontation between gay men and homophobes.

Even as they resist the identification of gay men as the originating force behind AIDS, these novels thus risk further reifying an identification between gayness and AIDS. Certainly, in their "epidemiologies," they ignore the worldwide situation of the AIDS pandemic, treating Africa—as it has been generally treated in American discussions—not as a place where real people are sick but as a laboratory for disease, important only as the locus where a biological agent was discovered or developed for use against American gay men. Furthermore, in their almost exclusive focus on a conflict between conservative, Christian, and (in these novels) exclusively male homophobes, on the one hand, and communities of gay men, on the other, these novels tend also largely to replicate a vision of the AIDS crisis as a battlefield of masculinity. Women are almost wholly excluded from these novels. They play only minor parts in *The Boiled Frog Syndrome*, *A Cry in the Desert*, and *Genocide*, while *Plague* and *Gentle Warriors* feature one prominent woman apiece—Lynn in *Plague*, who is in fact an important part of the novel's counter-conspiracy though she is not mentioned on the book's back jacket, which proclaims that its major characters are "FOUR VERY DIFFERENT MEN . . . all concerned with healing"; and Jo-Lyn in *Gentle Warriors*, who in fact remains separate from the novel's main action, a continent away from the events in San Francisco, until she finally inserts herself importantly into the plot against the President (292-95).

While these novels resist homophobic conceptions of AIDS, they are at the same time themselves determined by those conceptions, erecting in the place of the narratives they repudiate their own similar structures of understanding, structures largely concerned only with an American "epidemiology"; structures that exclude women and understand AIDS as primarily significant in relation to issues of masculinity; structures that continue to rely on the terms of intentionality, conspiracy, blame. And just as the novels themselves, while intervening in the politics of AIDS, remain dependent upon that which they resist, the resistance movements, the political interventions, depicted within them are represented as also largely determined by the forces they oppose. The sinister AIDS plots of these novels set in motion all of their action, including the action of resistance, and the form of those initiating plots shapes the kinds of opposition conceived, within the novels, as possible. In its convoluted, secretive, self-disguising form, conspiracy seems to demand an intervention that is similarly, conspiratorially constituted. To get to the truth of Watergate, we need a "Deep Throat." To plumb the depths of AIDS, we need, as in *Plague* and *A Cry in the Desert*, computer espionage; as in *The Boiled Frog Syndrome*, phone calls in private code (105, 111), secret meetings (105-6, 112-15), "mail drop[s] . . . for really top secret stuff" (115), and "deep-cover" informants (105). Secrecy and disinformation become as necessary to those conspiracies whose ultimate goal is the uncovering of conspiracy as they are to the original conspiracy itself. When secrecy is breached, it threatens the success of the whole countermovement. Thus, in *Plague*, because Lynn, Jon, and Mark at first speak rather openly about the belief that they have discovered the existence of an "antidote" to AIDS (150-51, 153, 164-65, 183-84, 192), Buchanan is able to anticipate and neutralize their plotting, covering over his own tracks (163-64, 192). And active resistance to the conspiracies (conspiratorially) uncovered in these novels similarly takes the form of conspiracy, demanding, as in *Genocide* and *The Boiled Frog Syndrome*, resistance movements able to escape detection, as in *Gentle Warriors*, a group of men bound to each other for a common end, the deployment of "their own conspiracy" (219). Again, the breach of secrecy represents a particularly dangerous threat to the success of these resistance movements: in *Gentle Warriors*, when one of the co-counter-conspirators, Sam, despite having been sworn to secrecy, reveals the Presidential "infection plot" to his lover Brian, that plot is deeply endangered (185-87, 201-6, 231-32, 252-57).

All the counter-conspiracies of these novels, because they are largely reactive, responding to other, already developed and deployed plots, are forced to operate in terms dictated by those prior plots. Thus, for instance, the dependence of the original AIDS conspiracies in most of these novels on computer technologies—the DIVAF program in *The Boiled Frog Syndrome*, the complex security systems designed to control the operation of ERAD in *A Cry in the Desert*, Wilson's computer-based plottings of the epidemic in *Plague*, the high-tech control of the death machines in the "Chinatown Chinatown" camp of *Genocide*—necessitates interventions themselves dependent upon computer technology: Ten Eyck uses a computer program explicitly compared to DIVAF to aid Stephen Ashcroft in ransoming his lover Troy Anderson (Rubin 119-20,

216-17); Carl, Larry, and a computer expert infiltrate the information systems at ERAD, sending to the outside world a massive amount of incriminating information about Botts's operation (Bryan 177, 231-32), and it is through computer access that Carl ultimately makes his escape from the camp (Bryan 228-30); the infiltration of Wilson's computer (Johnson 136-41, 156) gives Billy DePalma and Lynn Graves their first clear indication of the shape of Buchanan and Wilson's AIDS conspiracy; the theft of a particular computer chip from one of the "Chinatown Chinatown" rides (Barrus 37) makes possible the functioning of another high-tech machine that will destroy the camp.

Resistance is thus enabled in the novels by a familiarity with, and a coopting of, the tools of the opposition, and particularly tools, like the computer, that lend themselves to the conspiratorial through the codes and passwords that are an essential part of their operation, and that also implicitly mirror the surreptitious, coded activity of HIV. But the resistances that result from such reversals of conspiratorial power, even when successful, largely remain bound by the terms of the plots they resist, and they remain themselves always susceptible to a similar re-reversal at the hands of their opponents. The novels for the most part perpetuate an agonistic view of the epidemic in which conspiracy spawns counter-conspiracy, each hostile action demanding an appropriately hostile response. In these novels, AIDS is a war waged by homophobes against gay men (as, in the opposed, homophobic view, AIDS is a war waged by gay men against "real" masculinity, nature, and God); as war, it must be militarily resisted. Non-military options—for instance, a dependence on electoral politics or the legal system—are shown over and over again (in the assassination of Doug McKittrick in *The Boiled Frog Syndrome*; in the ways in which Allan's campaign for District Attorney in *Gentle Warriors* constrains him to expressing only "safe" opinions; in the failures of Larry's constitutional challenges to the EQA in *A Cry in the Desert*) not to present an adequate resistance to plots that are themselves, after all, often firmly supported, or put into motion, by governmentally-linked powers. The camps in *Genocide*, *The Boiled Frog Syndrome*, and *A Cry in the Desert* are set up with government sanction; the CIA, in *Gentle Warriors*, is responsible for AIDS; Buchanan and Wilson, in *Plague*, have close ties to the Defense Department and intelligence community through their consulting work. Nor is (even a quite militant) political activism seen as presenting effective opposition to these novels' genocidal plots. The demonstrations in *Genocide*—"That was the winter of civil disobedience and the mass arrests and Wall Street,[45] and you knew that they had taken your picture because you could always feel it when someone took your picture" (131)—fail to have any effect on the movement toward detention and quarantine: "It was a winter of numbed impotence" (131). The spontaneous, angry demonstrations of *Gentle Warriors*, including the bombing and burning of the Federal Building in San Francisco (140), make little difference in national policies; though a crowd can surround and stop a single tank sent into the Castro District (200-201), it cannot arrest the broader army takeover of San Francisco undertaken to secure the President's visit there.

It is for the most part only (para)military action that enjoys even limited success as resistance in these novels. Even *Plague*, the novel least dependent upon scenes of explicit battle, stages "an ambush" (203) and shows Billy preparing for a fight that never comes—"He could try to overpower Wilson, knock him out" (139). In the remaining novels, the very essence of resistance is battle. The plot to infect the President in *Gentle Warriors* takes all the forms of military action: Gregg, as he waits at his station for his chance to shoot and thus infect the President, repeatedly returns, in his mind, to the war in Vietnam (207-20). In *The Boiled Frog Syndrome*, Stephen Ashcroft's extensive past experience as a combat journalist is repeatedly evoked as having prepared him well for participation in a resistance movement whose main success is a raid on the "American diplomatic compound just outside Brussels" (100) in which two American soldiers are killed. Similarly, the counter-operation that has the most striking success in *A Cry in the Desert* is the paramilitary hijacking of a busload of prisoners headed for ERAD that enables the liberation of forty men but entails the killing of several guards (185-86). In *Genocide*, the AIDS crisis is conceived explicitly as war: "that war [Vietnam] was over and another war [the repressions attendant upon AIDS] had taken its place" (152). The resistance movement of the future world of *Genocide* is a band of hunters and warriors, and Barrus's description of that movement is self-conscious about the ways in which resistance constitutes itself in terms dictated by the oppressor:

> The hunted will often become hunters themselves. . . .
> . . .
> Anyone who was smart enough to escape the quarantine's ovens, lucky enough to be found by a warrior patrol, willing to fight back, and strong enough to survive the Sangre de Christo [mountain range], could join the resistance. . . . They were now beginning to strike at the heart of those who hunted them with unheard of savagery. Savages. Warriors. (94, 96)

Novels other than those under discussion here have depicted violent attacks as a response of last resort to the frustrations of the AIDS crisis, and particularly to the right-wing politics of AIDS. In Paul Monette's *Afterlife*, one of the three main characters, Dell, ends up killing a homophobic, fundamentalist preacher, Mother Evangeline (272).[46] In James Robert Baker's *Tim and Pete*, a band of HIV-positive men plots to assassinate Ronald Reagan (204-14, 224-27) and then decides instead to attack a conference of "the American Values Foundation" that many right-wing politicians are attending and where the effects of their action will be most far-reaching (234-41).[47] In these books, as in the "epidemiological" novels, such imagined violent interventions provide a certain kind of emotional satisfaction, substituting a sense of sudden accomplishment for the frustrating feeling that there is nothing that can be done about AIDS. But novels like Monette's and Baker's also tend to depict such violent responses as problematic. Having shot Mother Evangeline, Dell "put[s] the gun in his mouth," turning violence back upon himself (272). The guerilla actions in *Tim and Pete* are contemplated as potential suicide missions by men who have given up on their own lives, and the accomplishment of those missions entails violences not only against the right-wing "enemy" but against friends (they must forcibly confine Tim and Pete to prevent them from intervening against the plot) and neutral bystanders (in particular, Pete's mother, who, romantically involved with one of the congressmen attending the targeted convention, herself becomes a possible object of attack).

Violent resistance in these novels, as in the "epidemiological" novels themselves, is clearly "justified" by the violences being resisted, and clearly satisfying as an attack on "evil": Ten Eyck, in *The Boiled Frog Syndrome*, recalling his combat activities in World War II, comments that "never as long as I live, can I truly feel the slightest regret or sorrow, only pride, happiness and satisfaction, for every single bomb I dropped on the civilian targets!" (200), as Stephen Ashcroft himself reflects "that the lives of the two innocent boys [American soldiers killed during a resistance raid] had been a reasonable price to pay for the courage and inspiration their daring escapade would give to freedom fighters everywhere" (103). Resistant violence threatens nonetheless to become a replication of the violent oppression it resists, threatens indeed to turn back upon the resister. Barrus perhaps provides the most striking instance of such a dynamic: in *Genocide*, the fabled "hacker" Isaiah (31), using a crucial computer chip that was once itself part of the "Karnival"/"Chinatown Chinatown" camp's destructive apparatus, successfully brings about the camp's destruction:

> Sleeping humanity never knew what hit them; they just cooked. Eyes turned to putrid steam. Wires spat fire and sparks. Loudspeakers shuddered. Programs erased. And the lungs of soldiers burst into appalling molecular fleshy holocaust. (38)

The technological violence of the death camp is turned back upon itself, but, strikingly, without any real liberatory effect. The prisoners of the camp dissolve and burn along with their captors; rather than being released from their confining torture, they suffer a torturous death. Apparently only the brothers Star and Adonais escape the conflagration, and their escape entails entry into a desert made only more horrible by Isaiah's "salvific" action, made, indeed, into a replica of the camp: "The desert was Karnival" (39).

In *Gentle Warriors*, Gregg, urged on in part by his mystical roommate Marc's formulations—"Another group of potential oppressors turning against oppression" (183)—worries explicitly about how resistances tend to take the form of that which they resist:

> Was it [their own conspiracy] not just for vengeance or desire for justice, not just desire to truly prevent wrong doings, but rather from a smouldering, uncontrolled passion that was evil in itself? Were Sam and Jim and all their partners, dying like himself, just as infected with evil? Was he a prisoner of these emotions, these times, driven along by the sweep of music to present arms, as they had been in Vietnam? (219-20)

Having sworn after Vietnam "never again to wield a gun" (214), Gregg has now agreed to be the prime marksman in the plot to infect the President, swayed by the urgent need for action against a government that has conspired to eliminate its own (gay) citizens. But worried about the "evil" of his actions, Gregg wavers in his commitment to the resistance, deciding, at the last minute, not to play his part and thus causing the whole counter-conspiracy to unravel. (In a final plot twist that allows for the elimination of the President at the same time that it makes violence and "evil" return unambiguously to those associated with the original, homophobic AIDS conspiracy, Jo-Lyn, Ed Stevens's fervent fundamentalist wife and Gregg's estranged, homophobic sister, replaces her brother as the President's nemesis, moving to assassinate him because of his public disavowal of her husband [295].)

Some of the "epidemiological" novels thus explicitly recognize a danger in resistances that merely replicate the conspiratorial violence of the "oppressor." And some, less self-consciously, show the counter-plots of resistance taking forms that disturbingly reconfirm the homophobic fantasies that they ostensibly oppose. Thus, the counter-conspiracy of *Gentle Warriors*, in presenting a band of gay men dedicated to infecting the President with HIV, reinforces a certain dangerous association between gay men and the intentional infection of others,[48] even though, of course, the group of gay men in *Gentle Warriors* is depicted as acting justifiably against the government's own, much more destructive plot of intentional HIV transmission. In *Plague*, fantasies of gay men purposely infecting others are also entertained by several of the novel's characters. While these are sometimes easily dismissed, as when Lynn, in "a rush of paranoia," imagines that Billy might try to infect her—"Don't they say the homosexuals are spreading this virus on purpose!" (75)—or when Jon "dream[s] about being in the support group and having all the PWAs gang up on [him] and threaten to infect [him] with the virus by rubbing a teaspoon on [his] chest" (89), at other moments, the fantasies are granted a closer correspondence to reality:

> He worried about the possiblility that there were men who'd gotten kind of crazy from the knowledge they'd been exposed or were getting sick and were actually trying to spread the disease. Blum didn't exactly believe those people existed or, at least, that there were many of them. But the media had played up that idea so much that it bothered him.
> Most of all, he worried he'd get himself so worked up over some gorgeous number he'd forget his pledge to play safe. (101)

At a certain point Billy does imagine, though not really seriously, "infecting Lynn as a way to get even" for her having involved him in the counter-conspiracy against Buchanan and Wilson (138). And as Pat Stratford approaches his suicide, having pushed his hand through a pane of glass, he imagines "reaching out through the window and then slowly turning his hand to allow the blood to pour out—onto the sidewalk, onto the walkers below, onto the couples going home to hug and touch each other and . . . and . . ." (114).

While these novels most strikingly rewrite homophobic fantasies of intentional gay HIV transmission as accounts of intentional transmission at the hands of homophobes, they also thus preserve something of the original homophobic fantasy. Their maintenance of the idea that the "spread of AIDS" is indeed ultimately intentional enables a certain return of those homophobic constructions that they at first overturn. In a novel like *Plague*, the language of "spread"—the "spread of sexual perversion" (178) responded to by the homophobe's conscious "spread" of HIV (177); the persistent fantasies of an intentional "spread" of "disease" (101) by gay men; the "spread of th[e] antidote virus" (246)—is particularly labile, suggesting a deep interpenetration of homophobic and anti-homophobic thinking. The idea of a contagion of homosexuality linked intimately to AIDS is not banished even in a novel that would consciously challenge such an idea.

A similarly disturbing return of homophobic material characterizes the "epidemiological" novel's conception of what the category "gay man" might encompass. While gay men are consistently the heroes of these novels, valiantly confronting their homophobic, genocidal enemies, those enemies themselves are often implicated in homosexuality. In the "softer" instances of this, certain gay men—for example, the political leader Richard Wenacher in *A Cry in the Desert* or Stephen Ashcroft's conservative lover Troy Anderson in *The Boiled Frog Syndrome*—refuse at first to believe that there is a homophobic political conspiracy linked to AIDS; like the "boiled frog" of Rubin's title, they delay action that would allow early intervention against that conspiracy.[49] In *Gentle Warriors*, Allan's campaign for District Attorney is sabotaged by another gay man, Michael Fraggi, who feeds secret, damaging information to the opposing (homophobic) candidate. Allan is able to identify Fraggi as the traitor because he recognizes Fraggi's "perverse," guilt-ridden relation to his own sexuality:

> He was always into heavy humiliation, punishment of himself. . . . As you know, most of us learn to step beyond traumatic memories and come to enjoy cathartic sex for what it is. A magical moment. But Fraggi used it to wallow in self-pity. (77)

> There's some weird perversity in the man, Allan conjectured, some self-hurting guilt-ridden trip. Maybe it comes from the way he was indoctrinated as a kid. Until he died, Fraggi's father was a Mormon bishop, a crony of that notorious liberal Orrin Hatch. (127)

In *Genocide*, a repressed homosexual priest expresses a strong, punishing homophobia, beating one of a pair of gay lovers (182) and trying to force both into exile (181), before he himself, in a reversal of (sexual) power, is reduced to madness (185). Here, as in the Fraggi plot of *Gentle Warriors*, the (common) notion that homophobia is the expression of a repressed, disavowed homosexuality is invoked. And this notion is crucial in the accounts two of the novels give of the origins of the plots of gay genocide. George Wilson, in *Plague*, is "a terribly unhappy repressed homosexual" (218; also see 108-9, 174), and his sexuality, coupled with an intense dedication to Catholicism, is seen as explaining his participation in the plan to rid the world of "perversion." Edward Buchanan, too, is perhaps meant to be read as having repressed certain homoerotic impulses: though married, he shares an intimate, perhaps sexual, moment with his captive Jon Stiers (223-24). In *A Cry in the Desert*, Alfred Botts—while he occasionally expresses certain homoerotic, and simultaneously violent, impulses with his gay prisoner Carl (198-200, 225-26)—has, like Wilson (and Buchanan?), largely sublimated homoeroticism into homophobic, genocidal designs.[50] Bryan's novel makes its initial moment, dated thirty-seven years before the remainder of its action, a merging of intense homoerotic desire and violent Christian punishment as these are experienced by a twelve-year-old Alfred Botts:

> He was going to come. Sweet Jesus. Was going to shoot straight into his best friend's mouth and Jimmy was urging him on, wasn't going to stop, wasn't pushing him away to keep that white sticky stuff from pumping right into him. In all of his twelve years, he had never felt anything so terrifyingly wonderful. He was going to burst, his whole body was going to explode into a thousand million quivering fragments.

This was what it meant to die, to blend eagerly into the warmth of the universe. Then, at the last moment when blindness was just about upon him, the bedroom door burst open in a shower of wood fragments and Jimmy had pulled away cringing, arms over head[51]—had pulled away leaving him exposed to the cold and light and his father was standing over him glaring with the all-seeing wrath of God. The belt of retribution had fallen and fallen and the pain and the gushing hot/cold semen spraying his battered legs and belly, coating the belt that fell and fell. And his father, god the almighty fucking father, had dragged him to the kitchen and stretched him out on the cold metal of the table and dared him to move a fucking muscle as he grabbed his shrunken-up balls in one hand and waved a butcher knife in the other. "This is what the Almighty does to filthy fucking sodomite faggot queers!" And he felt the horror of the blade and the coldness and the sharp edge and the pain and knew that the blood was on his father's hands. And there was blood. His father was wiping it on the boy's mouth and cheeks. And then he could see nothing, hear nothing but the echo of his own shrieks in the blackness. (1)

The novel reassures us almost immediately that Botts has not in fact been castrated—"He would wake up screaming and holding his genitals. . . . They were still there, round and hard and comforting" (2)—and Botts reassures himself that he isn't gay, having learned his father's lesson that "[t]here was nothing in the world as filthy and evil as a faggot" (2). Still, at the origin of the whole complex AIDS plot of wished-for gay eradication that Botts authors—as at the origin of the very different homophobic accounts of AIDS as the fruit of gay "sin"—stands a moment of gay sex and the punishing "retribution" of an "almighty" father.

Of course, these novels present their various AIDS plots as homophobic attacks on gay men. But they also, in making (closeted, or repressed, or denying) gay men the authors of those plots, or complicit in them, reconfirm the place of gayness—even if a gayness distorted by the forces of the closet, repression, and denial—at the heart of the AIDS epidemic, of the genocidal plots manipulating AIDS, and even of homophobia itself, understood simultaneously as the force repressing the homoerotic and as an expression of that repressed, disallowed eroticism. While in many ways these novels do try to escape the traps of the homophobic conception that AIDS is a gay war against "true" masculinity, against the "innocent" and the "normal," their strategies of reversal often lead them back into not just an economy of blame and not just a language of conspiracy and warfare but, more crucially, a logic at the center of which is still inscribed the guiltiness of homosexuality—blind to the homophobia that attacks it, as with Richard Wenacher and Troy

Anderson; betraying its own, as with the "perverse" Michael Fraggi; turning self-hatred into genocidal plots, as with George Wilson and Alfred Botts. While *Gentle Warriors*—in its most sucessful attempt at leaving behind a resistance determined largely by the homophobic constructions it opposes—may envision a community of "gentle warriors" (30, 295) bound together by their exuberant expression of leathersexuality,[52] "a different army . . . that could move without destroying. . . . An army anchored in the sea of caring, touching brotherhood, of men who would rather love one another than kill" (260); while *Plague* may make a similar attempt in its new-age-inflected argument that hate needs to be countered not with more hate but with love, none of the "epidemiological" novels escapes the many ways in which resistant, anti-homophobic strategies are reincorporated into a logic of homophobic attack.

4. AVOIDING AIDS

Even when the resistance movements of these novels are well organized and enjoy a certain local success, they tend, in the final analysis, to make little overall difference in larger narrative trajectories toward genocide or apocalypse. Johnson's *Plague* presents the one exception to this rule: the course of the epidemic is turned around at the end of the novel, and at least one understanding of how this occurs would attribute agency to Jon Stiers and the others who, with him, uncover Buchanan's genocidal plot, confronting him with what they have learned in an attempt to force him to release the "viral antidote." But while Stiers's resistant intervention thus seems to have a real effect on the history of AIDS, Buchanan in fact remains largely in control: he kidnaps Stiers, effortlessly takes away, and then destroys, the evidence of a genocidal plot painstakingly and riskily obtained by Stiers and his friends in their own elaborate espionage effort. What has cost so much energy—not just to Stiers and company but also to the novel as it carefully describes the elaborate process of gathering information—and what has seemed to guarantee a certain power over Buchanan, is suddenly gone, any power dissipated. If Buchanan does in fact decide to release the "antidote" and thus stop the spread of HIV, this is his decision, influenced perhaps by Stiers, but not by any real resistant action on his part. Rather, in a move clearly intended to short-circuit a vicious cycle of hatred, but one that simultaneously sacrifices any real *resistance* to homophobia, Johnson implies that it is Stiers's forgiveness—his willingness in fact to "forgive genocide" (231)—that leads Buchanan to interrupt his own genocidal course:

> "I forgive you, Buchanan. I forgive you for whatever you're gonna do to me." Again he pointed toward the closet [Buchanan's closet of human horrors]. "I forgive all that. Why try to answer it?" (235)

In any case, control of the action in *Plague* remains firmly with Buchanan: the prime mover of the epidemic, while he may respond to pressure from others, remains, it seems, the main author of the epidemic's end.

In the other "epidemiological" novels, there is a less ambivalent sense that resistance to the hostile manipulation of AIDS is essentially futile. In Mains, the attempt of San Francisco authorities to arrest the President turns out to be an exercise in impotence, with "the City Attorney, the District Attorney, the Sheriff, the President of the Board of Supervisors, and a superior court judge" themselves detained by federal "security officials," and with "the Chief of Police" left "clutching the county/city warrant for the President's arrest" (275). The plot to infect the President fizzles out because of Gregg's decision not to go ahead with his part in it: "[I]t was too late. The Presidential party entered the building with no sign of harm" (287). In Rubin, the one striking success of Stephen Ashcroft's resistance movement is a purely symbolic one, the raising of "the rainbow-striped Lambda flag" (102) at "the American diplomatic compound just outside of Brussels" (100), which may "ma[k]e a global laughing-stock of the Reverend President Peter Joshua Wickerly's American government" (99), but which has no real influence on Wickerly's repressive policies. In *A Cry in the Desert*, all of Carl's and Larry's attempts to resist Botts are ultimately unsuccessful. The massive documentation of Botts's abuses that they gather is, like the documentation of Buchanan's actions in *Plague*, ultimately useless; no one with the power to act takes it seriously: "Everyone considered it a hoax" (233). The few successes of resistance in Bryan's novel— for instance, the hijacking and freeing of the busload of prisoners headed for ERAD—fail to challenge Botts's larger control over events; in this case, the hijackers, though they free others, themselves make no attempt to escape, and are quietly done away with by Botts. In *Genocide*, while quarantine camps may be destroyed and oppressive "enemies" captured and killed, there is no real escape from the ruined earth or universe or from the dynamic of oppression. As Barrus suggests at one point, "it was the time of fighting back. But the fighting in the final analysis was merely symbolic" (157). And even when the fighting seems to be more than symbolic, as with Isaiah's destruction of "Chinatown Chinatown," it does not necessarily lead out of "genocide" into liberation.

The stronger the conspiratorial and apocalyptic plots of these novels—the more air-tight they are as plots, in both senses of the word—the less likely resistance is to interrupt or successfully shift their course. The seamlessness of narrative trajectories in these novels, with an intentional origin and apocalyptic ending mutually implying each other, makes finding a point for efficacious intervention and resistance difficult. Of course, the novels still call on readers to "join in the fight" (Bryan, copyright page). Except perhaps for Barrus, who makes explicit in his own voice his hopelessness, his belief in an "irreversible annihilation," the authors of these novels seem to mean their fictions to puncture the denial of "it can't happen here" and push readers to resistant action. We can, indeed, read the novels as presenting worst-case scenarios that might have been avoided were action taken earlier, even if, in their fictional worlds, things have now gone too far for intervention to succeed. We can read them, in other words, as warning us not to allow things in the real world to go so far.

While the construction of the whole history of AIDS as authored, intentional, conspiratorial on the one hand makes it difficult to imagine how to intervene in that history, it also makes available a certain kind of comforting hope: that which is under human control, originating in human intention, should also somehow be subject to human interruption. The ability to unify the AIDS crisis within one particular kind of narrative understanding, to see the epidemic as fully *motivated*, and to uncover the motives that underlie it, not only provides the comfort of a coherent intellectual understanding of the epidemic but also suggests that, no matter how seamless or air-tight the conspiratorial history, some efficacious intervention should be possible. While none of the novels unambiguously shows the mounting of an effective resistance to the plots authored by their respective villains, all suggest that such resistance was at least possible at a certain point in the past: if what Botts, Buchanan, Wickerly, the CIA were intending had only been known from the beginning, if only there had been the will to discover and interrupt their plots, these—no matter how deviously conceived, still under the control of human agency—undoubtedly could have been arrested by human agency.

This kind of thinking—that an intentionally-authored epidemic could be stopped simply by an attack on the author—clearly stands in tension in these novels with the less sanguine depiction of attempted interventions against authors like Botts and Buchanan, who show themselves remarkably resistant to attack. But despite the tension, both the more and less hopeful views of how one might (not) succeed in interrupting genocidal plots depend upon conceiving the AIDS epidemic as a plot, as a narrative understandable—from origin to end—in terms of human intentionality. The more fully human beings are in control of AIDS, the more fully effective human intervention should be, but also the more difficult that intervention will be if human beings are really *in control*. The (almost paradoxical) thinking of these novels about the efficacy of possible interventions in the politics of AIDS thus simultaneously presents such interventions as easy and difficult; it assumes a world where, on the one hand, a powerful enough assertion of one's will should be able to interrupt others' evil plots but where such assertions of will are rarely powerful enough. Such a view clearly responds to a real experience of the AIDS crisis, where we wishfully desire a quick and easy "cure," a quick and easy elimination of homophobia and racism, a quick and easy restructuring of medical, scientific, and political institutions, but where, as well, action against those seemingly monolithic institutions, as against a seemingly inexorable epidemic, often seems simply futile. Of course, "real-world" politics conforms neither to the wishful ease or full futility of intervention that the novels simultaneously depict. Activist interventions have in fact proven to be possible, have had real effects on science and politics, but they remain difficult and ambiguous, never wholly efficacious. Unlike in the novels, the "agents" responsible for the AIDS epidemic are not easily identifiable in the person of an Ed Stevens or even in an institution like the CIA; indeed, "agents" like the CDC, FDA, public health officials, politicians may be, by turns, both one's "allies" and one's "enemies."

The double view of AIDS-era politics that would posit certain monolithic conspiracies that cannot be easily interrupted, though, at the same time, their authored nature makes the route to effective intervention seem clearly marked, is particularly troubling in that it enables in each novel a certain double movement toward avoiding, or even erasing, AIDS as an issue. On the one hand, the emphasis on the intentional origins of HIV allows for the fantasy that AIDS can be easily, intentionally cured, and, on the other, the implication of AIDS in larger, genocidal plots allows for a shift of attention away from AIDS itself, toward the "real" dangers of which it is shown to be only a small part.

In several of the novels, the revelation that HIV has been engineered suggests, as though inexorably, the existence of an "antidote" or "cure." When the CIA conspiracy to "spread" AIDS is revealed in *Gentle Warriors*, the immediate implication is that there must be a cure—"Surely you wouldn't release a killer virus without knowing a cure?" (Mains 39)—and the Presidential "infection plot" is imagined as the way to force a release of that cure. In the hopeful vision of *Plague*, the uncovering of the plot to "spread" HIV is simultaneous with the discovery of the existence of a "viral antidote," and almost as soon as the full conspiratorial plot becomes known, AIDS disappears as an epidemic concern. What appears at first to be oxymoronic in its full title—*Plague: A Novel about Healing*—in fact inheres in the narrative logic by which, once the real significance of "plague" is understood, its "healing" becomes possible.[53] In the less hopeful *A Cry in the Desert*, though genocide and quarantine remain realities at the end of the novel, AIDS itself—from cause to cure—has become fully known, and is no longer the source of pain and death: "AIDS isn't our only concern here [ERAD]. In fact, it isn't even a major concern" (192). And in *The Boiled Frog Syndrome*, though homosexuals continue to die in the camps, it is not because of AIDS; we witness "the waning days of the plague" (14), where AIDS can be offhandedly dismissed as "really not much of a medical problem anymore" (20). Even the most doomsaying of the novels, *Genocide*, engages in speculation about a post-AIDS world, imagining that it would in fact be possible to "burn" the virus, eliminating it from the earth (though the very process of "burning" is seen as destructive and though Barrus also imagines a different future in which the universe remains defined by "virus").

Understanding HIV as intentionally engineered and spread in one way makes AIDS more horrific, not just a "natural disaster" but a genocidal plot; at the same time, however, it allows each novel (wishfully) to imagine the disappearance of AIDS as a real threat. Only in *Gentle Warriors* does that disappearance remain simply wishful, not realized somehow in the plot of the novel. The understanding of AIDS that allows for an intensification of the sense of its hurt and horror also paradoxically allows a defusing of the epidemic's force. This is not to say that the specificity of AIDS and its ability to transform lives are completely obscured in these novels. Each novel does evoke something of the powerful effects of AIDS itself—in Barrus's depiction of the overwhelming burden of the epidemic on his narrator and in his descriptions of extreme experiences of pain and danger that can be seen to stand in for the experience of AIDS even when they do not specifically represent it; in Rubin's depiction of the intentionally induced wasting of Troy Anderson, which, while not due to AIDS, clearly evokes its symptoms; in Johnson's treatment of Pat Stratford's illness, despair, and suicide, and in the broader attention he gives to the problems of people living with AIDS as these are voiced in Jon Stiers's PWA support group; in Bryan's depiction of a gay doctor's (Carl's) first experience of an AIDS patient's death and his strong sense of self-implication in that death; in Mains's sensitive treatment of the bond among those men with AIDS who come together in the counterplot against the President, and in his often powerful evocation of a whole gay world lost through the AIDS epidemic.

But while all these novels are specifically motivated by AIDS, in each there is also a significant move to avoid AIDS and its particularity; this occurs not only in the wishful doing away with AIDS as a medical problem, but also in the very presentation of the horrific (genocidal, apocalyptic) imaginations occasioned by AIDS. As Les Wright has commented in relation to *Gentle Warriors* and *The Boiled Frog Syndrome*, "AIDS may trigger the fantasy [of gay genocide], but . . . AIDS is more nearly a redundancy than a legitimate dilemma in its own right."[54] Indeed, in each of the novels under consideration, AIDS is pushed aside to make room for broader fantasies of genocide and apocalypse. Part of this pushing aside results from the very attempt in the "epidemiological narrative" to observe the larger trajectory of a reconstructed past and projected future, an attempt that involves a certain stepping back from the contested ground of the gritty day-to-day confrontation with bodies, illness, life in the world. But beyond this, AIDS tends to get lost in the very complications of conspiratorial plotting that these novels deploy at least in part in order to call attention to the real seriousness of the AIDS crisis. In *Genocide*, AIDS fades into the background as attention shifts to the many genocidal operations of which it is only one. The quarantined, drug-laced, environmentally ruined, futuristic desert landscape of Barrus's novel is so harsh, and not only or even primarily because of AIDS, that the novel's "present," more realistic, and painful confrontation of the epidemic tends to pale by comparison. Similarly, in *The Boiled Frog Syndrome* and *A Cry in the Desert*, political upheaval, blackmail, detention, quarantine, exile, and violence become more the focus of attention than AIDS itself. As *Plague* becomes more and more concerned with uncovering Buchanan's plot, it pays less and less attention to people with AIDS. Only *Gentle Warriors* among these novels attends to the AIDS epidemic as a central reality throughout, and even here attention tends to shift from AIDS itself to the CIA's plot and the various countermovements it stimulates. In all the novels, then, to a greater or lesser degree, the focusing of attention on plots, conspiracies, impending disaster and apocalypse results in an avoidance of AIDS, people with AIDS, their lives and struggles.

All of this leads to a kind of paradoxical outcome: while only *Plague* among these novels can be thought of as having a truly positive or hopeful conclusion, with the rest signalling the more or less full success of the various genocidal plots depicted, all imaginatively neutralize the threat of AIDS itself—both by depicting it as cured or curable and by subsuming it into the larger, more threatening plots that (except in *Plague*) remain unaddressed, leaving us on a trajectory toward apocalypse. On the one hand, the dystopian fantasy of a world where AIDS is seen to be, from its beginning, intentional genocide is intimately linked with an inverse, utopian fantasy in which, the genocidal intentions behind AIDS understood, these can be simply contradicted, a cure or antidote found. The initial, motivating fear of each of the novels—that the current moment of the AIDS crisis holds within itself the potential for vast devastation—is thus, in and of itself, allayed. At the same time, however, that fear does not disappear; rather, it is displaced into other fears no longer named "AIDS." AIDS moves into the background, put aside so that we can attend to "larger" and more "basic" problems—the homophobia that stands at the root of AIDS and the various genocidal plots it employs, of which, in these novels, AIDS is one but not necessarily the most powerful or significant.

Even in confronting AIDS, then, these novels avoid it: the construction of an AIDS that is fully meaningful, arising from human intention, makes possible the diminution or even dismissal of AIDS itself as a threat. Each of the novels reveals the ways in which a particular coherent narrative of the history of AIDS carries within it the potential for obfuscating the reality of AIDS, the reality that motivates the construction of a coherent narrative account in the first place. To find the origin of HIV and AIDS in human intentions means somehow also to find a "cure," an "antidote," an easy solution to all the problems that have followed that origin; to make AIDS part of "larger" genocidal intentions enables a shifting of attention from the real bodies of people with AIDS to the "real plot" of genocide; to project an "authored" apocalyptic end to AIDS suggests, again, that there might be intervention—another end "written"—if action comes soon enough; if not, if things are so far gone that all we can imagine is "irreversible annihilation" (Barrus), then AIDS itself may disappear, be "annihilated," in the imagination of an unimaginable end transcending the "mere" epidemic that we suffer here and now.

I would suggest that such movements of avoidance inhere not just in novels like these, but more generally in the kinds of making sense to which these "epidemiological narratives" are akin: certainly, in the kind of conspiracy theory that has circled around the AIDS epidemic from the beginning and that has constructed AIDS as indeed a genocidal attack on society's "others"; also in the homophobic understandings that such conspiracy theory largely responds to, understandings in which AIDS is seen as a kind of (welcome) "conspiracy" originating in the intentions of "God" or "Nature" as punishment for "perversion" and as part of a broader movement toward ("moral") Judgment. Nor would I exempt the more respectable realm of epidemiological science from an association with the kinds of narrative effect observed in these novels. Epidemiological thinking—not just in fictions or conspiratorial fantasies but also in science—tends always to shift attention from the current moment back toward an imagined point of origin and forward into projections of the future. In such a double movement, it risks losing a needed focus on the manifestations of illness in present bodies; it risks valuing a science more concerned with pinpointing the origins of HIV (or with claiming priority for "discovering" the virus) than with studying the pathogenesis of AIDS in individuals,[55] more intent on developing vaccines than on finding treatments for opportunistic infections, ready to abandon certain "risk groups" in the drive to protect others. A narrative logic obsessed with the discovery of origins and ends risks losing the "now of now" (in Barrus's phrase), the demanding present crisis that in the first place motivates the search for beginning and end, conspiratorial origin and apocalyptic result.

NOTES

1. See Crimp, "How to Have Promiscuity in an Epidemic," on Shilts's use of "conventional novelistic" techniques and on the implication of *And the Band Played On* in traditions of "bourgeois writing" (244).

2. See the Bibliography for a (partial) list of such nonfiction narrative. Murphy, "Testimony," treats the testimonial impulse in AIDS literature.

3. For some striking and memorable examples of AIDS novels that present themselves in a first-person "autobiographical" mode, see Christopher Davis, *Valley of the Shadow* (New York: St. Martin's Press, 1988); David B. Feinberg, *Eighty-Sixed* (New York: Viking, 1989) and *Spontaneous Combustion* (New York: Viking, 1991); Hervé Guibert, *To the Friend Who Did Not Save My Life* (New York: Atheneum, 1991 [1990]) and *The Compassion Protocol* (New York: George Braziller, 1994 [1991]); and

Christopher Coe, *Such Times* (New York, San Diego, and London: Harcourt Brace & Co., 1993).

4. David Leavitt, *While England Sleeps* (New York: Viking, 1993).

5. John Rechy, *City of Night* (New York: Grove Press, 1963); *The Sexual Outlaw* (New York: Grove Press, 1977); *Marilyn's Daughter* (New York: Carroll & Graf Publishers, 1988); and *The Miraculous Day of Amalia Gómez* (New York: Arcade Publishing/Little, Brown, 1991).

6. Shaun O'Connell, "The Big One: Literature Discovers AIDS," in Padraig O'Malley, ed., *The AIDS Epidemic: Private Rights and the Public Interest* (Boston: Beacon Press, 1989) [first published as a special issue of the *New England Journal of Public Policy* 4:1 (Winter/Spring 1988)], 497.

7. Jed A. Bryan, *A Cry in the Desert* (Austin, TX: Banned Books, 1987); citations are given parenthetically in the text. Bryan discusses the writing of *A Cry in the Desert* (completed in late 1983), and his difficulties in finding a publisher for the book, in "Crying 'Wolf!': The Genesis of an AIDS Disaster Epic," in Pastore, ed., *Confronting AIDS*, 68-78. A short story by Bryan is also included in *Confronting AIDS*—"Voices," 152-56. Bryan's publishers describe his second novel, *Sacred Cows* (Austin, TX: Banned Books, 1989), as a "tongue-in-cheek satire about the world of runways, swimwear, and falsies," "an about-face" from *A Cry in the Desert*.

8. Toby Johnson [Edwin Clark Johnson], *Plague: A Novel about Healing* (Boston: Alyson, 1987); citations are given parenthetically in the text. Johnson, a psychotherapist, is also author of two autobiographical works—*The Myth of the Great Secret: A Search for Spiritual Meaning in the Face of Emptiness* (New York: Morrow, 1982) and *In Search of God in the Sexual Underworld: A Mystical Journey* (New York: Quill, 1983)—and of the "post-AIDS" science fiction novel *Secret Matter* (South Norwalk, CT: Lavender Press, 1990). Johnson's short story "Friends" appears in John Preston, ed., *Hot Living: Erotic Stories about Safer Sex* (Boston: Alyson, 1985), 24-30. See Johnson's essay "Facing the Edge: AIDS as a Source of Spiritual Wisdom," in Pastore, ed., *Confronting AIDS*, 124-41, for an exposition of some of the ideas that inform his fiction.

9. Marty Rubin, *The Boiled Frog Syndrome: A Novel of Love, Sex and Politics* (Boston: Alyson, 1987); citations are given parenthetically in the text. A story by Rubin, entitled "A Nice Jewish Boy from Toronto," appears in Preston, ed., *Hot Living*, 106-32.

10. Tim Barrus, *Genocide: The Anthology* (Stamford, CT: Knights Press, 1988); citations are given parenthetically in the text. Barrus is also author of a novel about the Vietnam War and its American aftermath, *Anywhere, Anywhere* (Stamford, CT: Knights Press, 1987), as well as such erotic/pornographic novels as *Daddy's Lover Boy* (Cleveland: Magcorp Publishing, 1985) and *My Brother, My Lover: A Novel* (San Francisco: Gay Sunshine Press, 1985).

11. Geoff Mains, *Gentle Warriors* (Stamford, CT: Knights Press, 1989); citations are given parenthetically in the text. Mains, a biochemist and environmentalist, is also author of *The Oxygen Revolution* (Newton Abbot, UK: David & Charles Publishers, 1972) and *Urban Aboriginals: A Celebration of Leathersexuality* (San Francisco: Gay Sunshine Press, 1984). He died of complications from AIDS in 1989; his panel in the NAMES Project Quilt identifies him as "author, leatherman, environmentalist." For some notes on his biography, see Mark Thompson, ed., *Leatherfolk: Radical Sex, People, Politics, and Practice* (Boston: Alyson, 1991), 37-38 and 239-42; this volume includes two pieces by Mains: "The Molecular Anatomy of Leather," 38-43, and "The View from a Sling," 233-39.

12. O'Connell, "The Big One," briefly discusses Bryan's and Johnson's novels (497-99; his discussion, however, includes some factual errors). Les Wright, "Gay Genocide as a Literary Trope," in Nelson, ed., *AIDS: The Literary Response*, 50-68, treats Mains's and Rubin's novels in relation to Paul O'M. Welles's pre-AIDS *Project Lambda* (Port Washington, NY: Ashley, 1979) and more generally in relation to gay uses of the history of Nazism and holocaust. Sander Gilman's "Plague in Germany 1939/1989"—in which

he compares Peter Zingler's German novel *Die Seuche: Roman* [*The Plague: A Novel*] (Frankfurt am Main: Eichborn, 1989) to Rudolf Heinrich Daumann's 1939 novel *Patrouille gegen den Tod: Ein utopischer Roman* [*Patrol Against Death: A Utopian Novel*] (Berlin: Schutzen-Verlag, 1939)—is also pertinent to defining an "epidemiological" subgenre of AIDS fiction.

13. O'Connell, "The Big One," 498.

14. "Apocalypse" figures importantly elsewhere in AIDS literature, most famously, of course, in Tony Kushner's *Angels in America: A Gay Fantasia on National Themes* (*Part One: Millennium Approaches*; *Part Two: Perestroika*) (New York: Theatre Communications Group, 1993 and 1994). For recent critical treatments of "apocalyptic" traditions in American and English literature, see Richard Dellamora, *Apocalyptic Overtures: Sexual Politics and the Sense of an Ending* (New Brunswick: Rutgers University Press, 1994), esp. 154-95; and Joseph Dewey, *In a Dark Time: The Apocalyptic Temper in the American Novel of the Nuclear Age* (West Lafayette, IN: Purdue University Press, 1990).

15. The panicked African opening of *Plague* calls to mind the opening of Roger Spottiswoode's film version of Shilts's *And the Band Played On* (HBO Pictures, 1993). Though, in that production, the opening scene is explicitly not about the origin of HIV (but rather about an outbreak of Ebola Fever) it nonetheless serves to figure, if in a displaced manner, just such an origin.

16. Mirko D. Grmek, *History of AIDS: Emergence and Origin of a Modern Pandemic*, Russell C. Maulitz and Jacalyn Duffin, trans. (Princeton: Princeton University Press, 1990), 147.

17. There is something illogical here, since semen as a vector for the virus would be at least as dangerous for women as for men, as is in fact the case.

18. In particular, Stevens's wife and Gregg's estranged sister, Jo-Lyn, herself a member of the New Covenant Fellowship, worries about her husband's motives (see, for one example, 112-13).

19. The plot is inaccurately described as an attempt at "Presidential assassination" on the back cover of the novel itself, a description echoed in Franklin Brooks and Timothy F. Murphy, "Annotated Bibliography of AIDS Literature, 1982-91," in Murphy and Poirier, eds., *Writing AIDS*, 326, and in Wright, "Gay Genocide," 61. Only if we identify HIV infection with death does the plot represent an assassination attempt. Within the novel, though the authors of the plot see it as "a form of pressure, to push the authorities and the CIA into revealing the cure," more angry motives are also recognized: "They weren't just acting to create pressure, they were after a form of revenge" (202-3).

20. I will treat the poetry only to note here that it often extends and develops thematic material from the prose passages to which it is linked.

21. Dante's *Inferno* is directly evoked in Barrus's description of "the great gateway to Karnival": "All who enter here enter glorious profuse religious do-as-you're-told naked extravaganza. Orgasm. Suicide" (30). See also 56: "I stopped briefly and looked back at the old felonious Auschwitz-like quarantine building, now in ruinous shadow. I could sense the angry souls once incarcerated in this place. I could hear them breathing. In the middle of the journey of our life, I came to myself within a dark wood where the straight way was lost."

22. The most extended narrative of the process of incarceration occurs in the novel's final chapter, 196-200.

23. Bryan, "Crying 'Wolf!'" 78.

24. Wright, "Gay Genocide."

25. AIDSgate poster, in Crimp and Rolston, *AIDS Demo Graphics*, 36. See Crimp's discussion of ACT UP's *Let the Record Show* . . ., "AIDS: Cultural Analysis/Cultural Activism," 7-12. And for extensive use of Holocaust allusions, see Larry Kramer's *The Normal Heart* and *Reports from the Holocaust*.

26. "Minorities Seek More Action to Halt AIDS Spread," *New York Times* 19 Sept. 1994, A14.

27. Wright, "Gay Genocide," 54.

28. Wright, "Gay Genocide," 55.

29. For a more complex evocation of McCarthyism in relation to AIDS, see Kushner's *Angels in America*.

30. Rubin is quite careful throughout his novel to suggest parallels between his own fictions and historical events. Thus, he evokes the assassinations of John F. Kennedy, Robert F. Kennedy, Medgar Evers, and Martin Luther King, Jr.—and of the conspiracy theories surrounding these, particularly skepticism about the findings of the Warren Commission—to provide historical sanction for his own reading of the conspiratorial assassination of Doug McKittrick (72-73, 139, 141-42). And he invokes the Watergate-era resignation of Agnew as Vice President, the appointment of Ford in his place, and the resignation of Nixon, as precedents for his construction of the Reverend Wickerly's route to the presidency (154-55).

31. Bryan, "Crying 'Wolf!'" 78.

32. See the account of the Ray family of Arcadia, Florida, in Kinsella, *Covering the Plague*, 193-203.

33. See, for just some of the most recent instances, "Judge Draws Protests After Cutting Sentence of Gay Man's Killer," *New York Times* 17 Aug. 1994, A15, and Sam Howe Verhovek, "With Four Gay Men Slain, Texas Revisits Issue of Hate Crime," *New York Times* 30 Aug. 1994, A15.

34. Joseph F. Sullivan, "Girl Who Thinks She Has AIDS to Stand Trial in Biting of Guard," *New York Times* 31 Aug. 1994, B6.

35. For general discussion of HIV testing and political, legal, and ethical issues, see Martin Gunderson, David J. Mayo, and Frank S. Rhame, *AIDS: Testing and Privacy* (Salt Lake City: University of Utah Press, 1989); James F. Childress, "Mandatory HIV Screening and Testing," in Frederic G. Reamer, ed., *AIDS and Ethics* (New York: Columbia University Press, 1991), 50-76; and Zoe Leonard, "HIV-Antibody Testing and Legal Issues for HIV-Positive People," in ACT UP/NY, *Women, AIDS, and Activism*, 55-67. On testing in the military, see Randy Shilts, *Conduct Unbecoming: Gays and Lesbians in the U.S. Military* (New York: Fawcett Columbine, 1994 [1993]), 477-87, 500-505, 508, 524-25, 529-30, and 548-50; and Brandt, *No Magic Bullet*, 195-96. On immigration-related testing, see Gunderson, Mayo, and Rhame, *AIDS: Testing and Privacy*, 50-51 and 196-97; Childress, "Mandatory HIV Screening and Testing," 68-69; and (for one example of Congressional debate on this issue) *Congressional Record—House*, 11 March 1993, H1203-10. On HIV testing in prisons, see Theodore M. Hammett and Saira Moini, "Update on AIDS in Prisons and Jails," *AIDS Bulletin* (National Institute of Justice, U.S. Department of Justice) Sept. 1990, 6-8.

36. DiAna DiAna, "Talking That Talk," in ACT UP/NY, *Women, AIDS, and Activism*, 220; also see the video by Ellen Spiro, "DiAna's Hair Ego: AIDS Info Up Front" (1989). On the question of whether quarantine is "a legitimate tool for protecting the public health" (Joseph) in the case of AIDS, see the exchange between Stephen C. Joseph (former New York City Commissioner of Health), "Quarantine: Sometimes a Duty," *New York Times* 10 Feb. 1990, 25, and Thomas B. Stoddard (then executive director of the Lambda Legal Defense and Education Fund), "Quarantine Is a Wrong Question on AIDS," *New York Times* 21 Feb. 1990, A24.

37. Zoe Leonard and Polly Thistlethwaite, "Prostitution and HIV Infection," in ACT UP/NY, *Women, AIDS, and Activism*, 182: "A current South Carolina AIDS law was used to prosecute a Black, mentally disabled prostitute who was placed under house arrest (quarantine) for 90 days because she was HIV positive. Under a similar law in Orlando, Florida, a sex worker was charged with manslaughter, even though she used condoms with all her customers and all her customers tested were seronegative."

38. Hammett and Moini, "Update on AIDS in Prisons and Jails," 8-9; National Commission on AIDS, "HIV Disease in Correctional Facilities," March 1991, 3-4; Zoe Leonard, "HIV-Antibody Testing," 61; and Kim Christensen, "Prison Issues and HIV: Introduction," in ACT UP/NY, *Women, AIDS, and Activism*, 139-42. For a general consideration of the history of quarantine efforts, and the implications of that history for the treatment of people with AIDS, see David F. Musto, "Quarantine and the Problem of AIDS," in Fee and Fox, eds., *AIDS: The Burdens of History*, 67-85.

39. See Tabor, "Judge Orders the Release of Haitians."

40. The citation is from William F. Buckley, Jr., "Identify All the Carriers," *New York Times* 18 March 1986, A27. David Duke's proposal is made in a recent interview—Garry Boulard, "Cover Story: The Man Behind the Mask," *The Advocate* no. 680 (2 May 1995), 32: "There needs to be some way we can protect people from sexual relations with AIDS carriers. So this may sound very draconian, but I'll tell you what I'd do: I believe in the indelible, unwashable AIDS tattoo. It would be placed in the private area, maybe even with glow-in-the-dark ink."

41. Shilts, *Conduct Unbecoming*, 547-48.

42. For one particularly perceptive reading of "right-wing conspiracy logic" (160) in the AIDS crisis, see Patton, "Tremble, Hetero Swine!"

43. Shilts, *And the Band Played On*, 200.

44. Grmek, *History of AIDS*, xi. Grmek's understanding of the epidemiology of AIDS is complex, not reducible to the blaming, homophobic logic of a Helms. Still, his reading of AIDS as ecological disaster does depend on a view of the sexual acts involved in HIV transmission as a certain unnatural interruption to natural balance, with "the homosexual community" constructed as "the ideal 'culture medium' in which, as though in a laboratory experiment, the virus could multiply during its critical phase" (170): "The current pandemic occurred because radical changes in human behavior interrupted the long-standing equilibrium between host and parasite. . . . We should not presume that humankind is done with this blood tribute once and for all. Heavy burdens still await us as the price of our actions, disturbing the dynamic equilibria between humans, their physical surroundings, and the totality of living beings" (196-97).

45. ACT UP/New York's first demonstration took place on Wall Street on March 24, 1987; see Crimp and Rolston, *AIDS Demo Graphics*, 27-29.

46. Paul Monette, *Afterlife* (New York: Crown, 1990).

47. James Robert Baker, *Tim and Pete* (New York: Simon & Schuster, 1993).

48. Intentional HIV infection is a persistent fantasy not just in homophobic constructions but in a variety of largely "gay-positive" representations. See, for instance, the screenplay of Gregg Araki's *The Living End: An Irresponsible Movie* (New York: Morrow, 1994).

49. Randy Shilts's *And the Band Played On* has been repeatedly praised for its criticism of the inaction of gay leaders and groups in the early years of the AIDS crisis, as though Shilts (or alternatively Larry Kramer) was the one gay voice willing to criticize "his own." But as the "epidemiological" novels suggest, and as diverse gay responses to AIDS from the early 1980s would confirm, there was, within the "gay community," much disagreement about the meaning of AIDS and about appropriate responses to it.

50. O'Connell, "The Big One," notes Botts and Wilson and Buchanan as "repressed homosexuals" (498) and interestingly connects them to a subplot in Reed's *Facing It* that involves "a closet homosexual man" (500). The figure of Roy Cohn in Tony Kushner's *Angels in America* stands in an interesting relation to the closeted figures of these novels.

51. The gesture here, of course, echoes traditional visual representations of the expulsion from Eden.

52. For a fine discussion of the complex functioning of leathersex in Mains's and Rubin's novels, see Wright, "Gay Genocide." For a full exposition of Mains's own ideas about leathersex, see his *Urban Aboriginals*.

53. Johnson more fully develops his vision of a "post-AIDS" reality in *Secret Matter*.

54. Wright, "Gay Genocide," 65.
55. See Mark Harrington, "Pathogenesis and Activism," *DOCUMENTS* 1:3 (Summer 1993), 4-12; printed in a somewhat different form as "Bodies on the Line," *QW* no. 43 (30 Aug. 1992), 43-44 and 70-71.

CHAPTER 7

"But Then What?": Sarah Schulman's *People in Trouble*

1. THE BEGINNING OF THE END

Sarah Schulman's *People in Trouble* has strong affinities with the "epidemiological" novels just discussed: explicitly apocalyptic, it makes AIDS part of a bleak, urban landscape, and it projects a certain repressive future connected to HIV and AIDS.[1] At the same time, however, it diverges significantly from the "epidemiological" subgenre of AIDS fiction, challenging many of that subgenre's basic assumptions. Schulman's apocalypticism functions less within a temporal narrative of conspiratorial origins and cataclysmic ends than it does within what we might call a narrative of proximity, an account of growing familiarity with AIDS, people with AIDS, the politics of the AIDS crisis. Schulman does not move, as do Mains and Johnson in *Gentle Warriors* and *Plague*, to imagine a single, intentional origin for HIV that would suggest the existence of an easy medical intervention, a "cure" or "antidote." Nor does she, as in *Genocide, A Cry in the Desert*, or *The Boiled Frog Syndrome*, dissolve AIDS into a projected future in which political repressions and genocidal plots finally exceed and obfuscate the very epidemic that occasions them. Her narrative serves, on the contrary, to focus attention on a *present* apocalyptic scene where drug addiction, homelessness, and AIDS all maintain the force of compelling presence, where the process of apocalyptic uncovering involves not so much a vision of the future as a bringing into close focus of present, urgent problems. As Schulman has one character, Molly, suggest to her lover Kate, a genocidal apocalypse is already here and now: "New York is a death camp for thousands of people" (113). But as Molly further suggests, the structures of everyday life allow a too easy disguising of suffering: the inmates of the death camp that is New York "don't have to be contained for us to avoid them": "[O]ur city is so stratified that people can occupy the same physical space and never confront one another. . . . The same streets I have fun on are someone else's hell" (113). Rather than project a future calamity, the apocalyptic narrative of *People in Trouble* urgently works to reveal the "hell" of the present, the "trouble" that, like AIDS, stands too often unconfronted—distanced, ignored, denied. Kate places the moment "when the shit comes down," "when people are dying in the streets," in some indefinite future, but Molly points out that "[t]he shit is already down," that "people are dying in the streets" (165). Where the "epidemiological" novels often avoid the present reality of AIDS, shifting their attention (like Kate) to the future, Schulman's apocalyptic narrative (like Molly) redirects attention to the present, bringing the now of AIDS into vivid focus.

Throughout, *People in Trouble* makes it clear that calamity is to be discovered in the everyday, and that the largest political trajectories are intimately connected to the most "private" details of life. In part the story of a love triangle, "a run-of-the-mill illicit lesbian love affair" (113) between Molly and Kate that intersects with Kate's marriage to Peter, Schulman's novel opens with a scene in which Kate buys two sexy bras for Molly, imagining how they will look "on Molly's body before she touched them in place" (2). But this intimate scene itself begins with a sweeping statement, the novel's opening statement, that carves out a space grander than that occupied by three individuals, setting the action of the love affair and triangle directly within a narrative of apocalypse: "It was the beginning of the end of the world" (1). A negotiation back and forth between the "private" realm of romantic concerns and the broad "public"—societal, political, historical—scene of "the beginning of the end" is crucial to the novel's structure and meaning, and Schulman makes explicit her concern with such a negotiation both in the novel's epigraph from Karl Marx, "It is not the consciousness of men that determines their being, but their social being that determines their consciousness" (ix), and in her later comments about the writing of the novel:

> I . . . made a decision for myself personally that I was not writing a novel documenting the life and death of a single individual. Instead I wanted to use the examples of people's lives to express a precise political idea—namely, how personal homophobia becomes societal neglect. That there is a direct relationship between the two and that this nation needs to confront this configuration in order to adequately address th[e AIDS] crisis.[2]

Schulman's novel consistently navigates between the details of Molly's, Kate's, and Peter's lives and the broader urban scene of which they are a part. The city within which these individual lives unfold is the landscape of apocalypse, a landscape that repeatedly evokes waste, ruin, an impending "end," a landscape that decays even through the processes of "development" that promise to "renew" it. Emphasizing the city's intimate connection to its inhabitants, Schulman anthropomorphizes it as an "organic" body that closely mirrors the misery of those human bodies it contains. While working as a lighting designer on "*The Malling of America,* a musical about urban sprawl," Peter observes that "[p]utting highways through the middle of cities was the urban equivalent of strip-mining. It bored a hole in something organic that could never be repaired" (130). And Peter directly observes such disturbances in the changing landscape of New York. Running "along the Hudson River where developers were demolishing the piers," he encounters the industrial waste of "ditches, then pipes and strips of metal," and then, more disturbingly, "an incongruous addition to the island of Manhattan," a piece of "invented real estate" that deforms the whole shape of the city: "It was stuck on like some clumsy extension or unsightly tumor that had grown where the borough was once sleek and symmetrical" (27).

The irreparable injury and illness that the city thus suffers is reflected in both the natural world that surrounds it and the human world it encompasses:

> Peter ran on through Battery Park past all the signs warning of rat poison and past all the homeless people avoiding the lines of tourists waiting to see the Statue of Liberty. . . . The river smelled of abandoned cars, old fish and stale beer. . . . That morning everything had been white; his T-shirt, his jock, shorts, socks and running shoes. Now they were soaked in his sweat and covered in the city's filth. (28-29)

As Molly observes, "Here we are trying to have a run-of-the-mill illicit lesbian love affair. . . . And all around us people are dying and asking for money" (113). The novel's love story is constantly impinged upon by homelessness, desperation, and death: "People were sleeping everywhere and because it was warm, their corpses lay with outstretched bare limbs making small sounds, head protected by a newspaper or a hand" (193). As Kate walks by the graffiti message "Arm the Homeless," she shudders with the fear of someone who lives a privileged life in the midst of suffering: "If the homeless were armed, people like her and Peter would be killed immediately. They would slash the throats of everyone who had a nice place to live and gave only fifty cents" (68).

The novel's "private" narratives and the "people in trouble" whom its main characters repeatedly encounter are placed consistently within a larger—"dirty," "polluted" (44)—landscape of danger and decay. A "reddish industrial-waste sunset" presides over the "garbage"-filled Hudson and the "mess" of New Jersey (44). The very climate seems ruined. The normal brutality of a New York summer, with the city "smell[ing] of baking garbage and decomposing bodies," gives way to "a suffocating brutality that seemed brand-new": "This year Peter noticed that the air had stayed so warm there was a creeping sensation of melting polar ice caps and a lot of speculation about the greenhouse effect as seasons came to an end as a concept" (26). Everyday natural process is no longer everyday: "The sun is coming up and there are birds everywhere. How unusual" (128). Even the novel's one foray into "the country"—to one of the "not too many places left with mountainsides and here and there between the corn, a horse, a white one that looks right at you in your passing car and flares its nostrils" (183)—fails to escape either a commodifying, industrial culture ("Oh, no, I'm thinking like a postcard" [183]) or the larger apocalyptic scene: "The sun then set in a fiery red uranium sky" (184).

Peter decides to light *The Malling of America* with "everything under a huge shadow" (130), and from her opening sentence, Schulman sets *People in Trouble* in a similarly ominous light. Her characters recognize that "it is the end of the empire" (13), and the AIDS crisis is a crucial part of that "end," impinging on individual lives and, at the same time, defining the broader landscape. The novel's first reference to AIDS explicitly positions it within a narrative of apocalypse: "It had been a hallucinatorily hot summer with AIDS wastes and other signs of the Apocalypse washing up on the beaches" (12). By the time of the novel's action, the late 1980s, illness and death related to AIDS have become commonplace: Robert, a younger co-worker of Peter's, "was growing up accustomed to being with dying people" (62). Once-unusual experiences—"wristwatch alarms going off with little beeps . . . to remind [people] to take their AZT" (157); "another one of those times when you call up an old friend and get that damn tape announcing that his number has been disconnected" (92)—come to define life. As the epidemic develops, it becomes increasingly familiar and present:

> To a certain extent [Molly] had gotten used to hearing about people dying. She hadn't gotten used to seeing it, but now when someone said, "I couldn't call you back because a friend of mine died," it was said calmly.
> This dying had been going on for a long time already. So long, in fact, that there were people alive who didn't remember life before AIDS. (44)

Deaths become more and more frequent—"Another friend of Molly's died" (72)—and "think[ing] of something else, something calming" (73), is more and more impossible: "[T]here was nothing else. It wasn't like turning to another channel on the TV because AIDS was on all of them" (73).

As the broader apocalyptic landscape of Schulman's novel suggests, the "something else" that surrounds the AIDS epidemic—turf wars, the Tompkins Square Riot, homeless people and crack smokers, to cite only examples from the novel's opening pages—is equally bleak and disturbing. As Molly waits in the "Bellevue emergency room" with her friend Fabian, who has just brought in another friend, Scott, with a case of *Pneumocystis* pneumonia, "many events occurred" (211):

> There were a number of street people sleeping, crying, with gangrene, with large infections, with snot covering their faces, with blood everywhere, unable to speak, unable to move, all unattended and with no place to go. There were a few gunshots brought in by the police. A man had been beaten up. His friend had one arm around him and another arm holding the stack of records that they had been on their way to spin. Mothers worried they had waited too long. A man urinated in his pants. Many were drinking. Some were talking very loudly about very little. The police brought in a few cases from Riker's Island—pale men in bright orange jumpsuits with manacles, leg and ankle chains. There were many, many drug overdoses. A man sat behind Molly masturbating for the entire four hours. He never got off. There were terrible smells. (211-12)

Like the "epidemiological" novels, *People in Trouble* sketches a certain progressive narrative of the "spread" of AIDS, of its widening effects on people's lives, and of its interimplication with other pressing societal problems. The novel also emphasizes the pervasiveness of AIDS in its repeated consideration of the possibility of HIV transmission, its depiction of people's reasonable and not-so-reasonable fears of their own susceptibility to infection. In part this serves to further a recognition that AIDS does not affect only gay men, calling attention in particular to AIDS among women and to the transmission of HIV through the sharing of needles. Thus, among the novel's minor characters are two lesbians, Daisy, who is living with AIDS, having "shot drugs for a couple of years, quit for ten and then went back. . . . only for a few months . . . but she'd picked the wrong months" (175), and Sam, who has "share[d] needles" with a roommate who had AIDS (181). In part, however, the novel's treatment of HIV transmission may also serve to reinforce a certain identification of AIDS with gay men and users of intravenous drugs. Molly states confidently that "I'm not going to get AIDS" (113), and when Kate wonders if she "could have AIDS," Molly answers, baldly, "No" (153). Authoritative voices in the novel like Molly's suggest several times that public attention to the "new threat from AIDS" for heterosexuals (224) represents a panicked response not necessarily consonant with the evidence about transmission. Schulman's characters insist, in particular, that the likelihood of female-to-male transmission is small: "[T]he amount of men claiming to have gotten AIDS from women is so minute that they are probably just guys who don't want to admit they've been getting fucked in the ass or shooting drugs" (74). While, on the one hand, such a claim works against the stigmatizing of women as vectors of disease, on the other, it reconfirms the "homosexuality" and maleness of AIDS. Further, the advice given to a man that "[y]ou probably can't get AIDS from women. . . . Unless you swallow their menstrual blood" (74) is echoed in information Molly gives Sam about "[h]ow lesbians keep from giving each other AIDS": "Don't eat her when she has her period if you're not sure. That's all. It's easy" (181). Schulman continues (perhaps wrongly) to deny lesbian sexual transmission of HIV in her recent nonfictional *My American History*:

> Although sexual transmission of HIV through oral sex between women has never been anecdotally or medically confirmed, there are many lesbians who have contracted AIDS through needles, blood transfusions, sex with men and direct blood-to-blood contact with HIV.[3]

As Schulman recognizes, these are controversial, perhaps even dangerous, suggestions:

> AIDS educators and activists have long debated the social issues involved in a fuller discussion of female-to-male transmission. On one hand, some feel that if heterosexual men did not perceive themselves to be at risk, they would never use condoms. So, maintaining the myth saves women's lives. On the other hand, others point out that the widespread but distorted belief in easy and frequent female-to-male transmission results in anti-prostitution hysteria and increased government harassment of sex workers. In some cases, HIV-positive prostitutes have been charged with attempted murder—a crime that might actually be impossible to commit.[4]

Whether or not Schulman is right in thus minimizing the risk of female-to-male or female-to-female sexual transmission of HIV—and my own position would be that unprotected heterosexual intercourse in fact poses a significant risk to both female and male partners, and that HIV may, if rarely, be transmitted through lesbian sex—in the economy of her novel, the material on transmission clearly operates to identify and intervene against a certain hysterical response to the AIDS epidemic particularly focused on the possibility of "heterosexual AIDS" and operating through the demonization of those others—"women, IV drug users, and homosexuals"[5]—feared as promoting the "spread" of HIV. In the novel, the police refuse to break up a demonstration by people they believe to have AIDS until supplied with rubber gloves (125-26), an episode that directly echoes a June 1, 1987, ACT UP action at the White House, with protesters in both fictional and real-life demonstrations chanting, once the police have been supplied with "Playtex Living Gloves" that are "an unfortunate lemon yellow" (126), "Your gloves don't match your shoes" (126-27).[6] In an alternative model of "casual contact," Molly does not hesitate to share a drink with Don, a gay man whose lover has died and who has not himself been tested for HIV; as she explains to Sam, "It's a rite of passage. People who may be HIV positive inevitably offer you a drink out of their glass. It's a test of loyalty to see if you're prejudiced or not, to see if you're informed enough to know that you can't get it that way" (201).[7]

Like the "epidemiological" novels, *People in Trouble* thus recognizes in the AIDS crisis a potential for the operations of stigma, and it develops, as part of its own "epidemiological narrative," a homophobic conspiracy that exploits the AIDS crisis to attack gay men. The force behind this conspiracy is "[r]eal-estate magnate Ronald Horne" (209), a figure clearly modeled after Donald Trump. Horne's properties and projects are many and varied: "Downtown City" (27), "a huge barracks for investment bankers," "advanced capitalism's version of the company town" (28); "Ronald Horne's Castle . . . the biggest, lushest, most ostentatious and expensive hotel from the Eastern Seaboard to Rodeo Drive" (119); "the Taj McHorne, a new office and condominium complex on the site of the old public library" (210); "Embalming Fluid . . . part of a chain of wine bars that Horne Realty had opened up around town" (96); "the Cineplex Odeon Horne Quad Movie Center (formerly the Waverly Theater)" (106); a "musical opening on Broadway, *Ronald's Dream*" (63). Horne plans to run for mayor, but also works assiduously to privatize the public sector: "I'd love to buy the prison system and show New York how to treat its criminals" (30). Standing as a figure of a postmodern capitalism gone wild and as a crucial architect of the crisis of homelessness, having "warehoused thousands of empty apartments while ninety thousand people live in the subways and stairwells and public bathrooms of this city" (118), Horne, behind the scenes, has begun to use the AIDS crisis and its attendant homophobia for his own economic benefit. First taking a census to determine how many "families," "single people," "blacks," "homosexuals," "single men," and "narcotics abusers" live in particular buildings (51), Horne sends eviction notices to "all the gay men in [Kate's] building" and "every other gay man in the neighborhood" (111). As is later revealed, Horne "has purposely bought buildings with more than fifty percent gay tenants in the hope that we will drop dead and leave him with empty apartments" (118). He expects that "some . . . will be too ill to contest" (118) the evictions and that his scheme will thus provide an easy real-estate windfall. But while Horne's plot is motivated by greed, it also clearly expresses homophobia and AIDSphobia. After AIDS activists occupy the restaurant of Horne's Castle, his spokesman, responding to hotel guests who have "angrily demand[ed] refunds and immediate AIDS tests," promises "all future guests . . . that all glassware and eating utensils will be replaced as soon as we clear the lobby" (123). Horne himself, announcing his plan to run for mayor, "advocate[s] barge internment camps for all those infected with the deadly AIDS virus" (209):

> Horne said he would personally finance and administer this quarantine program to show his love for the people of New York. He added that any apartments in Horne-owned buildings that might be left vacant due to internment would immediately be converted to luxury co-ops for intact nuclear families, which statistics show are the least likely to spread AIDS. (209-10)

Though the Horne plot in Schulman's novel is comically overstated, verging on the burlesque, it still expresses a serious concern that AIDS might be turned to genocidal ends: in a wholly serious moment, Scott's lover James compares AIDS to such other "catastrophic human disasters" (146-47) as "the plague . . . the Holocaust . . . Hiroshima, slavery, apartheid" (147).

While the construction of AIDS as part of an apocalyptic movement linked to intentional plots against gay men clearly connects *People in Trouble* to the "epidemiological" subgenre of AIDS fiction, the novel also stands apart from that subgenre. The comedy of the Horne material, its introduction of an exaggerated caricature into what Schulman herself calls "a social realist novel,"[8] differentiates the anti-gay, AIDS-related conspiratorial plot of *People in Trouble* from the deadly serious genocidal conspiracies of the "epidemiological" novels themselves. While those novels attempt to present *plausible* constructions of the AIDS epidemic and crisis in which the "truth" about the past, present, and future of AIDS is revealed, Schulman makes the Horne plot, unlike the bulk of what surrounds it in the novel, patently *implausible*, though at the same time clearly connected to the real-world excesses of 1980s "free enterprise," with a fiction like Horne's Castle echoing but exceeding the pretensions of the real Trump Tower:

> Ronald Horne's Castle was the biggest, lushest, most ostentatious and expensive hotel from the Eastern Seaboard to Rodeo Drive. And it was located right in the middle of midtown redevelopment, so the guests could have a clear view of their power and riches at work. It was renowned, not only for its lavishness, but also for the transplanted tropical rain forest that had been re-created inside the lobby to serve as a symbolic moat with actual crocodiles. The guests could feel like authentic aristocracy instead of the robber barons that they really were. From the moment they checked in they were treated like royalty from the middle ages. The motif was Early Modern Colonialism and the staff was required to dress in loincloths with chains hanging from their wrists and ankles. The men's room didn't say Men on the door. It said

Bwana. The bathrooms were designed to look like diamond mines with black attendants wearing lanterns and pulling paper towels out with pickaxes. Chicken salad on rye cost twelve dollars. (119)

Schulman has no stake in the reader's literal belief in Horne and his imperialist projects. Rather, she develops the exaggerated, implausible Horne empire as part of a political satire that depends not on the "truth" of the depiction or its believability but rather on its power to body forth, as the object of ridicule, a particular constellation of capitalist enterprise, political ambition, racist, sexist, and homophobic animus, and a "*Lifestyles of the Rich and Famous*" (63) media culture eager to glorify all these. Schulman's use of such satiric exaggeration does not make her treatment of the politics of AIDS less serious than that of the more earnest "epidemiological" novels. But it does make for a very different understanding of the political. Novels like *A Cry in the Desert* and *Plague* present villainous figures like Botts and Buchanan as "really" at the center of and responsible for the complex societal and political manipulations and effects of AIDS. Such men may make use of forces larger than themselves, but their individual intentions are in fact seen to govern the largest narrative trajectories of the AIDS crisis. The partly similar figure of Horne, on the other hand, in his "unrealness" clearly becomes a figure for a whole matrix of (economic, political, societal) processes lying beyond the intentional control of any one individual. While Horne provides a focus for Schulman's satiric political critique, the excessive, caricaturing depiction of him prevents *People in Trouble* from developing a political construction like that of the "epidemiological" novels, in which the whole history of AIDS is made understandable as the effect of individual intentions.

Schulman steps back in certain ways from the "epidemiological narrative." Though, as I have suggested, her novel does display a strong apocalypticism, a firm placement of AIDS within a narrative movement toward cataclysm—a placement that stresses the urgency of AIDS—the novel resists the impulse to construct the AIDS epidemic as one coherent narrative, moving from a moment of "origin," through a process of "spread," to a definitive "end." *People in Trouble* does engage, like the "epidemiological" novels, in certain projections of the future—Horne's proposed "barge internment camps" (209)—but for the most part Schulman's novel remains in the current moment. Its apocalypticism does not depend upon the projection of a distant or even not-so-distant future but is instead contained in what is occurring now:

It was the beginning of the end of the world but not everyone noticed right away. Some people were dying. Some people were busy. Some people were cleaning their houses while the war movie played on television. (1)

"The beginning of the end" is the now of death and the ignoring of death, the now of "private" triviality played out against the background of war. Schulman eschews detailed projections of the future; she also chooses not to extrapolate the narrative of AIDS back to a past, originary moment. There is no attempt in the novel to find a single cause for AIDS, a discrete event, agent, or plot responsible for the apocalyptic movement within which AIDS is implicated. Indeed, the novel's only gesture toward an origin is an oblique one that makes clear the inaccessibility of origins. At the end of their friend Jeffrey's funeral, Molly and others leave the chapel to stand together "in a light flurry of snow":

> They held hands quietly and let the snow fall on their faces. It clung to some beards and a few long eyelashes and gave each person the chance to look up into swirling endless activity coming toward them with no visible beginnings. That's when Molly finally cried. Then that was that. (94)

Apocalyptic movements in Schulman, unlike those in the "epidemiological" novels, are overwhelming precisely in their failure to cohere into a clear narrative with "visible" end and beginning. The "swirling endless activity" of the AIDS crisis, of homelessness, of illness, poverty, and death, is without recognizable origin or conclusion. The novel's own originary, apocalyptic sentence signals "the beginning of the end," a moment of *both* origin and conclusion, but also a moment that is *neither* clear beginning or unambiguous end.

The "epidemiological narrative" Schulman constructs is not so much a temporally extended, retrospective and prospective account of the AIDS epidemic as a narrative of differential *proximity*, an account of how, at "the beginning of the end," some people may be dying while others are simply busy, some deeply implicated in crises while others are ignorant of these, and of how, with time, crisis may become more urgent and present for those aware of it at first only as a "war movie" playing in the background. Though *People in Trouble* comes to be centrally concerned with AIDS and AIDS activism, its first references to the epidemic are distanced and distancing ones: the mention of "AIDS wastes and other signs of the Apocalypse" (12) is followed by a more extended, but still remote encounter, in which Peter observes a group of men in a coffee shop preparing for a funeral and then sees them gathering "at the church across the way" (31). Peter only slowly draws a connection between the funeral and AIDS, a connection that operates through an unexamined identification of AIDS with gayness. Peter concludes from his observations of the crowd first that "*[s]omething is not right here*," then that "*[t]his is gay. . . . This is a homosexual church*," and finally that "it was not a homosexual church, but a Catholic one, filled with homosexuals" (31). "[D]ecid[ing] that he want[s] to be around gay people more" (32)—since "Kate was probably spending more time with them . . . he wanted to, too" (32)—Peter enters the church. His interest in the funeral is motivated not by any real engagement with the mourners or with their experience of AIDS but by the feeling that, through Kate, homosexuality has begun to impinge on his own life: "Ever since Kate had begun her gay affair Peter had been slapped in the face by homosexuality practically every day. How ironic that her affair had coincided with this AIDS thing" (31). AIDS and homosexuality are meaningful here only as they remind Peter of his own situation and history; the funeral evokes, in addition to thoughts of Kate, memories of Peter's one "gay affair" (31). Keeping his distance from the gay mourners, "stay[ing] in the back because he [is] a tourist" (33), Peter flees the church when the impact of the funeral threatens to become more than the impact of "another culture" on a distanced observer (33). He is overcome by the literal "closeness" of the air and by the figurative "closeness" of realities—homosexuality, AIDS—he finds threatening:

> He inhaled the incense and felt again how still the air was. It barely circulated. The smell was beginning to be overpowering, stifling actually. Peter felt faint and sat down abruptly in the nearest pew. Even though he tried repeatedly to relax, he just couldn't breathe. His lungs would not fill with air, so he left as quietly and respectfully as he had come, stepping back into an almost oppressive heat, only able to take a full deep breath a few blocks away. (33)

All of the chapters in Schulman's novel are assigned to Kate, Peter, or Molly, depending upon whose perspective they express, and the novel's initial distancing of AIDS partly reflects the assignment of its opening eight chapters to Kate and Peter, neither of whom (yet) has personal experience with AIDS or people with AIDS. Only when Molly's perspective is introduced does AIDS begin to become a central concern. A memorial vigil Molly attends explicitly echoes the funeral observed earlier by Peter: Peter notes that "[m]any of the men were wearing suits but some were more relaxed, in tasteful white slacks or light prints," thinking, "*I would never wear white to a funeral*" (31), while, at Molly's vigil, "[t]here was a lot of white. There were white balloons on strings, one for every friend who had died" (43). But while Peter remains separate from the funeral, Molly is part of the vigil:

> At the beginning of the route people handed out magic markers and passed them along, so each one could write the names of their friends on the balloons. Some people had one balloon. Some people had eight. Some had more. A few were carefully inscribed with detailed information like "Thomas Ho 1957-1987." Others just said "Ray." . . . Molly

looked over the balloons and read the names. She carried two of her own. She saw the name of someone she had known peripherally and hadn't even realized was sick. (43-44)

As the balloons are released, as the group sings "somewhere over the rainbow," "[e]ach [person] had a very private thought about a person who had died or about themself or about New Jersey or why they weren't feeling anything right then" (44), and Molly reflects first on her own experience of the AIDS crisis:

> This dying had been going on for a long time already. . . . And for Molly it had made all her relations with men more deliberate and detailed. First, the men changed. They were more vulnerable and open and needed to talk. So she changed. Passing acquaintances became friends. And when her friends actually did get sick there was a lot of shopping to do, picking up laundry and looking into each other's eyes. She had never held so many crying men before in her life. (44-45)

Molly then thinks more specifically of the two men whom she has come to the vigil to commemorate, "Joseph DeCarlo 1960-1982" (46) and "Ronnie Lavallee 1954-1987" (45), retrospectively reconstructing, in a short version of the "personal narrative," Ronnie's illness and death. Molly remembers his discovery of a Kaposi's sarcoma lesion (46), his struggle to gain access to drugs that the FDA "wouldn't approve" (45), the "progress" of his illness, and his death:

> He got old very fast. He said the telephone was on fire. His skin broke open. His mother came in from Saint Louis and kissed his face when it was covered with sores. He went to the hospital and then he went home. Then he went to the hospital. Then he went home. Then he went to the hospital. Then he died in the hospital. (45)

Molly brings into the novel the intimate experience of AIDS lacking in the earlier funeral scene. In her thoughts, we move from the position of distant observer of others' grief into the position of mourner, and then, in retrospect, into a close if brief experience of one person's illness.

Schulman notes that, when she began writing *People in Trouble*, most of the "very few books about AIDS" were "about facing one's own illness or the death of a lover": "I knew that I was not writing from either of these perspectives and so identified for myself the category of 'witness fiction,' so that I could understand the position of my words in this event."[9] While, as she claims, Schulman "resolutely refused to produce a book principally concerned with watching one or more characters slowly deteriorate and die over the course of three hundred pages,"[10] she also refuses in *People in Trouble* to avoid the realities of "deterioration and death." Molly serves, within the book, as (intimate) "witness" to the epidemic made central to her life:

> Another friend of Molly's died.
> "That's the problem with having friends," she said. "You have to watch them suffer and die."
> Jeffrey Rechtschaffen 1960-1988. She was in a great rage. (72)

With this death, the movement into greater proximity with AIDS continues for both the characters and readers of Schulman's novel. Unlike Joseph and Ronnie, Jeffrey dies in the novel's present moment. Molly's angry response to his death, her inability to talk with Kate about what has happened "because they had just seen each other and she was supposed to wait for Kate to call her" (72), her finding some comfort with her ex-lover Pearl, who returns to New York for the funeral—all stand within the novel's main narrative. As with Ronnie, Molly retrospectively reconstructs the narrative of Jeffrey's illness, and she now does so in fuller detail, recalling "[w]hen Jeffrey was first diagnosed" (73), noting his dedication to "alternative" treatments (73), sketching the vicissitudes of his attitude (73-74), remembering his work "at the AIDS Hotline" (73), his participation in "the Gay March on Washington" in 1987 (73), and his denial of impending death:

> [A]t the end, of course, being human, he panicked. He got mad at his buddy when Jeffrey was moved to intensive care. Then he refused to sign the release form saying he didn't need to be kept on life supports.
> "I won't need it," he said.
> Three days before he died Jeffrey got a letter from some people in San Francisco who were doing an anthology of journalists with AIDS. Did he want to submit a piece?
> "No," he said, emaciated. "It wouldn't be fair. I mean, I'll be the only one in the whole book who is still alive and for the rest of my career I'll have to shake the stigma, you know, the AIDS thing." (75)

The funeral for Jeffrey occupies a whole chapter of the novel, and it stands, like the earlier memorial vigil, in contrast to the funeral that Peter distantly observes. Jeffrey has planned his own funeral, and it expresses much about him: "The whole service was just like Jeff, sentimental, deliberate and goofy" (93). While "[d]ifferent people respond differently" (92) to the service, most "g[e]t caught up in watching and listening" (94), responding with involvement rather than with Peter's detached and then panicked narcissism. Molly here is clearly part of a community, and a community defined specifically by its experience of grief:

> When a friend finally dies of AIDS there usually is not much surprise and often some kind of relief for everyone involved because the man they loved was suffering too much. Also, the people around him need to go on. These funerals were frequent ghastly habits that crept into the structure of everyone's personal life. In fact, for Molly, at this point, there were a number of people that she only or mostly saw at funerals. (91)

The community at the funeral, however, is a limited one; Peter and Kate still stand outside it, though Kate is Molly's lover. Kate observes the beginning of the funeral from outside the church, watching the gathering of mourners in a distanced way explicitly like Peter's earlier experience:

> "I spied on Molly from across the street, watching her going into a funeral. The mourners greeted each other very warmly. Peter was right, these are unusual funerals. There is a sincere but familiar grief, a practiced one."
> "You don't mean to tell me that both you and Peter voyeur on AIDS funerals?"
> "Yes, we're ambulance chasers." (97)

Unlike Peter, however, Kate does not flee the funeral in a panic; in fact, she returns to witness its conclusion:

> Kate thought she was going straight home from the restaurant but then decided on the studio but ended up back at the funeral instead. She stood across the street, watching what seemed to be the end of the service. There were Molly and Pearl in the front and a lot of gay men all around. *These people at the funeral* came into her mind like a sentence. The family stuck out. They looked miserable, crunched together shrinking from the community of mourning friends, not understanding any of it. They were denying themselves the comfort within arms' reach. They hadn't asked enough questions to be of use. (99-100)

Though Kate here remains separate from the goings-on, she also recognizes both a community of grief and support formed in response to AIDS and a willful separation from that community:

That family. They didn't find out who their son was, so when he died they couldn't understand his funeral. They couldn't find solace with his friends who had stood united before them. There was a deprivation that accompanies this kind of ignorance. She couldn't get them out of her mind. (100)

In the recognition voiced here, Kate herself begins to move beyond the family's "ignorance"; her observations leave a lasting impression—"She couldn't get them out of her mind"—and she, unlike Peter, begins to move toward the community she has watched from a distance.

Kate's relationship with Molly has earlier brought her into a certain proximity with AIDS; as the last stop on "a guided tour of all the lesbian bars below Fourteenth Street" (81), Molly takes Kate into "a vintage gay porn store" (84):

The first thing that she noticed about the guy behind the counter was that he had Kaposi's lesions on his face. She knew that's what they were from pictures she had seen and some sideways glances at deteriorating men on the street, but never on the face of someone she had to interact with in an equal way. *How great,* she thought. *How great of this place to let him keep working like that.* Then she remembered that this was a gay place, so that particular brand of compassion could probably be expected. She wondered how many other people in the store had AIDS. (85)

Experiencing something she has so far only seen from a distance and obliquely, Kate here responds with a certain amount of fear, overcompensating for that fear in the enthusiasm of her response ("How great"), and with a certain too easy identification of AIDS as gay. Unlike Peter, however, Kate works to overcome the distance that separates her from "people in trouble." Following the porn store encounter and her voyeuristic experience of the funeral, when given the chance "to go to a meeting" that "has to do with AIDS" (110), Kate does not hesitate to do so.

It is at the meeting Kate attends with Molly that the culminating movement of the novel's "narrative of proximity" begins. The character of Scott, who has appeared several times previously in the novel, is here for the first time identified (by his lover James) as a person with AIDS:

When you are diagnosed with AIDS or ARC, or you find out that you are HIV-positive, the normal question is "How long will I live?" Remember, no one on earth knows the answer to that question, *whether they have AIDS or not.* The fact that you have AIDS, that my lover Scott has AIDS, cannot be changed. (118)

The movement begun by placing Jeffrey's death in the present moment of the novel, thus shifting the "personal narrative" of illness and death from its retrospective position in Molly's thoughts into the novel's main narrative, here continues. From this point, the novel follows Scott through both healthy periods and bouts of illness, charting his experience of AIDS until he dies. For a character like Molly, Scott's illness reiterates familiar movements. For Kate, however, it presents a wholly new kind of knowledge, and paralleling Scott's "personal narrative" is an account of Kate's increasing familiarity with AIDS, a familiarity mirrored by the reader's increasing immersion in the details of illness. If Molly's retrospective accounts of Ronnie's and Jeffrey's lives and deaths make sense of these from the point of view of someone experienced in the AIDS crisis, the account of Scott's illness, extending throughout the second half of Schulman's novel and proceeding along with its other major storylines, shows the process by which one (Kate, the possibly inexperienced reader) becomes experienced.

In the scene where James reveals that "Scott has AIDS," Schulman focuses attention on Kate's reaction: "Kate felt her eyes shifting toward Scott" (118); "Kate looked over at Scott again" (118). When Scott enters the hospital—not for the "first time" and not with "his first complication" (145)—it is again Kate's inexperienced gaining of experience that Schulman foregrounds:

[Scott] was propped up in bed with his hair brushed out loose around his shoulders. He looked like a Madonna, even though his skin was coming apart.
  For Kate there was no more sun, there was no more closeness. There was only this other world with two distinct smells: ammonia clean and filthy, stinking dirty. It was hard to believe this raw, bleeding skin was Scott and not just something laid on top of him. She had known, intellectually, that once someone's immune system was shot, every little thing became something enormous. But she had breezed into the hospital room without having accepted that she was going to visit the first friend of hers who would probably die of AIDS. (145-46)

Kate's inexperience stands here in explicit contrast to Scott's experience: he is her "first friend" with AIDS, but "[i]t wasn't his first time there" in the hospital (145). While Kate feels overwhelmed—"This man was dying. The more she focused on it, the more out of control she felt" (147)—Scott responds to his own situation with a certain matter-of-factness: "[H]e was smiling and turning his head. He was talking to her" (147). When Scott comments that "it's much easier having visitors who are used to seeing their friends sickly and weak, because there's no expression of shock on their faces when they walk in and see me" (148), this at least obliquely comments on what has been Kate's own shocked reaction. Her inexperience in this scene stands in contrast to the experience of visitors like Molly; Molly touches Scott casually, "reach[ing] over and brush[ing] his hair off his forehead with her hand," but Kate cannot respond with equal casualness to the gesture: "Kate thought about touching that kind of skin" (147). By the end of the hospital visit, however, Kate has "finally relaxed enough to talk": "'What kind of treatment are you going with?' Kate asked" (148). At the same time, she still feels what she is encountering as wholly new: "She had never seen anyone so young dying before" (148). Later, when Scott is back in the hospital for "the third time . . . since the beginning of spring"—"It wasn't his skin this month. This month it was pneumocystis"— the sense of newness will be gone from Kate's reaction: "She had been prepared that time, walking into the hospital room to see silvery blue oxygen tubes going into his nose" (165). And when Scott dies, becoming part of Molly's (and the novel's) growing list of dead young men, "Scott Yarrow 1958-1988" (211), Kate attends the funeral as part of Scott's community. "[D]iscover[ing] that [the site of the funeral] was the same church where she had watched Molly and Pearl months before" (219), "[n]ow," rather than observe from a distance, "she too was a mourner" (219):

> Six men emerged carrying Scott's coffin. It seemed to be as light as air. They began passing the box over the heads of the crowd as each one reached out to touch the wood like it was the Torah. His encased body passed through the hands of his people on its way to burial. It was placed in the hearse without eulogy or speeches.
> As the car inched away the crowd parted and then, like one person, began walking silently to Fifth Avenue, turning up it toward the library. They walked in the street against traffic. Kate could feel the exhaust of idling cars against her calves. Her lungs were filled with it. She climbed over cars, disregarded them. When there are that many people the traffic can't move. When that many people walk together the traffic has to stop. (220)

Kate participates fully in the funeral and the angry demonstration that the funeral becomes; she participates in the movement of a "people" larger than herself, a people brought together by its intimate and intense experiences in the AIDS crisis.

Kate's radical changes in the course of the novel, including her increasing proximity to AIDS, are consistently contrasted to Peter's stasis, his continued avoidance of any close encounter with AIDS and his simultaneous reading of everything about the AIDS crisis only in relation to his own needs. When a story about AIDS appears on the television news, Peter, unable to "help himself," exclaims, "Oooh, I'm so sick of AIDS," explaining his reaction by appealing to Kate's affair: "I'm sorry. It's just that my wife is going gay, you see. And all I hear about nowadays is gay this and gay that" (123). Looking on at an AIDS demonstration at St. Patrick's Cathedral—another voyeuristic moment taking place in church—Peter objectifies the demonstrators, making them other than himself. The less "familiar," "masculine," and white the men seem to him, the less able Peter is to "sympathize":

> *These are men with AIDS*, Peter realized. *Forty of them. But that one doesn't look like he has it. He looks like he works out. The thin one has definitely got it.*
>
> He took another look at the familiar one and decided that he had definitely seen him somewhere before and that that guy probably didn't have it.
>
> *That black man*, thought Peter. *I wonder if he's gay or if he got it from drugs.*
>
> Then the black man spoke.
>
> "The church is the world's most powerful hypocrite," he said. Peter noted that the man's voice and gestures were campy.
>
> *They shouldn't have let him be the spokesman*, Peter thought. *They should have picked somebody more masculine, so people would be more sympathetic.* (58)

Peter's insistence on discerning who "has it" or not reflects his own anxious segregation of self and other. He finds it particularly disturbing that one might not be able to determine susceptibility to AIDS (or gayness) on sight, observing nervously, when the demonstrators have covered their matching t-shirts, that "they stopped looking like gay men with AIDS. They looked just like everyone else": "*That . . . is their most effective trick*" (59). Rather than an immediate or proximate problem demanding Peter's own immediate or proximate response, AIDS continues, for Peter, to belong to a "them"; it is threatening not because it affects real human beings in devastating ways, but because, despite all of Peter's confident separation of those who "have it" from those who don't, AIDS lurks in the guise of normality, hiding its difference by means of a "trick," perhaps even a conspiracy, that Peter homophobically attributes to the intentionality of "gay men with AIDS" themselves.

Peter's repeated identification of AIDS with gayness is part of his insistent distancing of himself from it. After a "panicked" moment when he thinks that his co-worker Robert might have AIDS, Peter "looked at him again and decided that Robert was not a homosexual" (62). When Robert, after Peter asks him if he "know[s] anyone with AIDS," responds by asking if Peter himself has AIDS, Peter's revealing answer is "No, I'm straight" (62). And when Robert reveals in the same scene that his "father's lover has AIDS" (62), Peter, though he is the one who has introduced AIDS into the conversation, quickly changes the subject. In a later scene, when Robert announces that his father's lover has died, Peter feels "very uncomfortable" (131), experiencing a panic attack very like the one he earlier has while watching the funeral:

> There was something so threatening in Robert's voice that Peter felt terrified. He felt his throat constrict. When he intended to answer with a typically jovial response, there was no sound. He saw white. He felt cold. Kate was ruining everything. Things were so nice between them today, why did she have to stay with that little bitch? . . .
> Peter felt afraid from being so out of control. Then he felt furious. Something in what Robert had said reminded him of his loneliness. It reminded him of his helplessness. It told him he was alone. He was sad. He had no friends and no one to take care of him. He had no one to take care of him because he had been abandoned. He was abandoned and overprotected. He was given everything and nothing. It had ruined him. (132-33)

While Kate responds to her own "out of control" (147) feelings in the hospital scene by remaining in contact with Scott, overcoming her panic, Peter retreats, moving to stifle his feelings of "abandonment," backing away from a consideration of how his response connects to the talk of AIDS, finding refuge in generalities: "It's not as easy to be a man as it once was. . . . People blame you for everything. But all along you have to keep your perspective. You have to keep your balance" (133). For Peter, "perspective" and "balance" mean distance: "This is New York City. . . . The best thing is to focus on the big picture. Just take the long view and don't get dragged down in temporary details" (133). The "long view" of "objectivity" implies a lack of connection to others that may be safe but is also "lonely," an impediment to collective action; as Peter's new girlfriend Shelley suggests to him late in the novel, "You know, Peter . . . it must be very lonely for you because you think you're the only one watching" (171).

2. THE STORY OF JUSTICE

Peter's insistent maintenance of distance through "perspective" and "balance" is ultimately self-centered and self-serving, despite its claim to "objectivity." It allows him to stand apart from the "death camp" all around him, to see it, if at all, as something foreign, as those "temporary details" ultimately to be filtered out of "the big picture" through a persistent denial of their pertinence to the self. Schulman counters such a view with the narrative of proximity, bringing Molly, Kate, and the reader into touch with the "hell" that surrounds them, placing those extreme experiences of suffering that Peter would consign to the margins, to otherness, to distance, at the center of our field of vision, in close focus. Schulman, however, sees neither the revelation of the "death camp" and "hell" that inhere in New York nor her characters' movement out of privileged positions into greater proximity with a painful existence as sufficient responses to current crises. Early in the novel, reacting to another woman's reflections on how she "avoid[s] people who need money and people who need raincoats" to "keep them away from" her own, and yet how she "feel[s] bad being dry on the street when [her] brothers and sisters have nowhere to sleep," Kate comments that such "contradictions are what let us know that we are fully human" (13); the woman, however, counters with a question that pushes toward a fuller thinking through of issues of inequity: "But then what?" (13). Later, as Molly participates in the AIDS memorial vigil, even as she is included in a community of mourning, she wonders about the significance and adequacy of her actions:

> What does it mean to sing "somewhere over the rainbow" and release balloons? It made her feel something very human; a kind of nostalgia with public sadness and the sharing of emotions. But then what? (44)

The repeated, insistent question urges toward an action that would exceed the simple recognition of societal problems, the nostalgic memorializing of the vigil with its public "sharing of emotions," the "human" experience of self-protection, guilt, and sadness. Schulman's novel pushes not just toward a recognition of the stratifications of life in New York, not just toward observations about life's "contradictions," nor even only toward a movement into proximity with a community of suffering. It urges us further, toward a particular kind of political activism that would not only confront but try to change the "hell" of the current moment, that would provide "something substantial to do in the face of all these funerals," an alternative to "feeling helpless in hospital rooms" (94).

Peter serves again as a counter to the kind of activism that the novel advocates. His "personal homophobia" is part and parcel of the "societal neglect" that the novel's activists must confront and try to change; as Schulman elsewhere suggests, Peter is "someone unaware of how other people are living and unaware of how much power he wields."[11] Unable to see the crisis within which he lives as a crisis, denying its proximity and its seriousness, Peter suggests to Kate that her involvement with AIDS activism is "narrow": "You don't care about anything unless it's gay" (217). Expressing his willingness to become politically involved, but in "something less exclusive"—"I mean, I care more about Nicaragua than I do about a group of rich white gay men" (217)—Peter shows himself able to consider a problem that already stands comfortably at a distance but not to respond to a proximate crisis that is more directly threatening. Rather than come to terms with that crisis, he denies its significance, insisting that it remain "foreign" to him.

Beyond this, Schulman shows, in Peter, the political failure of movements into proximity that remain simply sympathetic, that fail to push past proximity and sympathy into effective action. In a scene that echoes his earlier voyeuristic experiences of the funeral and demonstration, Peter ends up, during a rainstorm, in "a soup kitchen set up by a local synagogue" (134). Standing "against the back wall watching everything" (135), he remains, as at other times, a voyeur, separate from the others particularly in his ability to remain safe and comfortable: "Everyone else's clothes were soaked through, but his were dry" (137). But in this scene Peter does allow himself a certain closeness avoided when AIDS is involved. He feels "a deep, deep compassion" for those he sees outside the soup kitchen: "It drew him closer to them, this sense of injustice that they had been treated so badly. He crossed the street and was practically next to them, watching everyone file inside. Then he followed" (135). And he allows himself a certain imagined identification with those he observes, even as stands away from them: "*How can you relieve suffering for even one moment?* he thought. *Here we are, the homeless, the old, the artists*" (137). In the very emotionality of his identification with suffering, however, Peter is mired in stasis, unable to address a question like "But then what?": "*The sadness is so overwhelming I can't imagine what to do. Nothing in my life has prepared me for this*" (137).

When Peter does try to help a man on the street—again in the midst of a rainstorm, and again with Peter "well protected from the weather" (138)—his actions point up problems with a response to others' distress based *solely* on proximity and sympathy. The man, whose hand has been injured and who needs to fill a prescription for medicine, approaches Peter directly, "look[ing] him straight in the eye" (139), and Peter agrees to help, responding to the man's vivid presence—the physicality of his hand, "so huge and scarred and dry that it had cracked open many times over a few years" (139); his pants "so thin Peter could see every muscle twitch underneath them" (139). Peter's responses in this scene vacillate between a self-congratulatory satisfaction with his own altruism and a certain suspicion: "*It's really important that two men from different circumstances can communicate like this*, Peter thought. Then he wondered if the guy was just laying it on thick, trying to get some money out of him" (139). But when the two are unable to find an open drug store, Peter feels "trapped" (140), knowing neither how to help nor how to escape. Ultimately, he must rely upon the more street-smart Molly, who happens to pass by. Seeing that the prescription is for a painkiller, she buys the man "a bottle of Tylenol, a pack of Marlboros and two quarts of Budweiser" (141), and insists he "go back in the hospital tomorrow morning and tell them to look at it again" (141). As she explains to Peter:

> You can only do so much for people you don't love. . . . There are a lot of deprived people in this city. You have to know where they stop and you begin. . . .
>
>   . . .
>
>   . . . [A]t some point you would have to say *stop*. You weren't going to take him home with you and give him a pair of your pajamas, were you? (141)

Unlike Peter, Molly has worked out for herself both a certain commitment to helping those who approach her on the street and certain limits to that commitment. These are demonstrated most fully in her relationship with Charlie, who "used to be [her] friend but now [is] on the street" (113) because of his drug habit. Though Molly helps him out with money and food when she can, she refuses to get too close to him:

> She also knew that while drug addicts are real people in that they get hungry and cold and sick and die, there is a big hunk missing from them somehow. And for that reason, they couldn't be treated as fully human because they would just rip you off and exploit you every chance they got. (172-73)

While Peter sees Molly's brusque, businesslike approach to helping out those in need as lacking in compassion, "*You'd think she'd have a little more heart for a guy in trouble*" (141), the self-protective limits she sets allow her to provide effective help in a way Peter's stance—either wholly distanced or wholly, impractically taken in—does not allow.

Molly's is one attempt at developing an urban "ethos" that will allow both a certain engagement with people in need and the autonomy necessary for living one's own life. As Molly herself perceives, the actions prescribed by such an "ethos" are never enough; there are too many "deprived people" in the city for any one person's acts of involvement to suffice. But the novel does suggest that, dependent upon a movement into proximity with the crises that surround one and upon the impulse to help out those one encounters, but also exceeding such responses, there is possible a political organizing, resistance, activism that might effect real changes in structures of neglect and oppression. Such a political movement, in Schulman's vision, *begins* with intense, proximate experience, but it must also move beyond this, placing "personal" encounters into a broader, "public" context. Watching the balloons she has released in memory of Joseph DeCarlo 1960-1982 and Ronnie Lavallee 1954-1987, Molly realizes that "[s]he could only really see the sea of them after losing sight of her own" (44). From the starting point of her own losses, Molly begins to see connections to a larger crisis. From "personal" traumas, needs, sympathies, one might, with others, begin to forge a political movement.

Alongside its narrative of apocalypse and proximity, alongside its consideration of the ethics of day-to-day urban life, and as part of its central action, *People in Trouble* presents the history of the activist group "Justice," clearly modeled after the direct action group ACT UP/New York.[12] The narrative of political resistance in Schulman's novel, like the corresponding narratives in the "epidemiological" novels, shows AIDS activism emerging in reaction to oppressive structures by which it is itself partly shaped. Thus, in countering Horne's real-estate conspiracy, Justice pursues a course of action at first also conspiratorial in form. The meaning of Molly's first assignment for the group is temporarily kept secret even from her:

"He asked me if I would collect papers for him on Wednesday. He said that all I have to do is stay in the ticket booth at Cinema Village and men will come by to drop them off."
"What kind of papers? How double-oh-seven can you get?"
"I don't know, Pearl. Then he wants me to go over later that evening to an address he wrote down on this matchbook."
"To make the drop?"
Pearl had a *Twilight Zone-Untouchables* hush in her voice.
"Yeah."
"Where is it, Molly, some abandoned warehouse in Red Hook?" (95)

In a scene that continues the spy-novel atmosphere,[13] Molly collects the papers at her cinema box-office job:

Every once in a while a thin nervous man would approach the window and not ask for a ticket. He would not reach for his wallet.
"Justice?" she'd ask, with the same inflection she used to say "*Night Porter?*" Then he'd slip a yellow piece of paper through the money slot and she'd say, "Thank you. Have a nice day." (109-10)

When Molly arrives at a meeting of Justice to deliver the slips of paper, which turn out to be Horne's eviction notices, she finds the meeting taking place in the basement of Kate's building, which James and Scott have "broken into" and converted into "a cross between a meeting hall for the Kiwanis Club and an underground bunker" (115). "[T]wo men stand guard duty outside the cellar door entrance, posing nonchalantly, watching for trouble" (115). One of Horne's own buildings has been surreptitiously turned into the site of a conspiratorial resistance to his real-estate scheme.

Inside the meeting, Justice provides a way of circumventing "the boobs at the FDA" (116) with a "handy recipe" for turning lecithin into the (unapproved) drug AL721. It also offers "fake documents"—"birth certificates and passports"—so people "can get Medicaid to pay for [their] anti-AIDS drugs . . . and . . . welfare if [they]'re too sick to work" (116-17). The "Get Real Committee," "formed to face reality when everyone else chooses not to," has set up "daily drop-offs of free condoms and clean needles for the fellas and gals inside" Riker's Island; people with "friends on the inside, either inmates or staff," are urged to "pass their names on" so that they can be "plugged" into this "unofficial activity" (117). Later in the novel, Justice legally and illegally collects credit card numbers to "pay for the . . . revolution" (164), a scheme in which Kate participates. Overhearing and memorizing one man's phone card number, she calls it in to Justice: "Her skin was tingling. She had never done anything like this before" (164). At a still later point, Justice gains access to the next day's news when "the front page of tomorrow's newspaper" is "smuggled" in "by a lesbian working at the printing plant" (209). And Justice continues to guard against conspiratorial infiltration of its own meetings, beginning "every session" (156) with the announcement, "If there is anyone here from the Federal Bureau of Investigation or the New York City Police Department, you are required by law to identify yourself now" (157).

But Justice also repeatedly moves beyond such covert, secretive actions. Its emblem—"the word *Justice* inside stencils of pink triangles" (27); "black T-shirts" with "large pink triangles" and "the word *Justice* scrawled, graffiti style" (47)—speaks out strongly if somewhat obliquely: "The shirts were angry" (47). The leaflet through which Molly first begins to learn about Justice is similarly confrontational, and more explicit about its goals:

DO YOU THINK IT'S RIGHT?
That people are dying and the government does nothing? If you do not think that this is right then do something about it. (47)

While most of the men approaching Molly's ticket booth with their eviction notices act "mysterious," some "saunter by" more casually, and "[o]ne guy got into the full spirit of things by saying 'Thank you, sister,' flashing a victory sign with two fingers on his right hand followed by a fisted salute" (110). The Justice demonstration witnessed by Peter in St. Patrick's, the first in the novel, makes a bold, public statement, and one that is explicitly set against Peter's "privacy"—"As he was reciting his own private liturgy, about forty men stood up together from among the worshipers and turned to face them" (58):

The church is the world's most powerful hypocrite. . . . Why don't all you gay priests and nuns come out and get the church off the backs of your brothers and sisters? Stop spending poor people's money trying to take away everyone's sexuality. Spend it on affirmative care for people with AIDS. (58-59)

(Though the action echoes what has been perhaps ACT UP's most controversial action, the December 10, 1989, Stop the Church demonstration at St. Patrick's,[14] co-sponsored with WHAM! [Women's Health Action and Mobilization], as Schulman suggests, her account predates the actual protest and depicts an event much smaller in scope than what was ultimately to occur: "Two-and-a-half years ago I imagined forty nervous men cautiously standing up to disrupt a religious service. By the time the book was published, there had been a real-life demonstration of seven thousand angry men and women confronting the Cathedral. In this case, the community I was writing for and about made the boundaries of my imagination obsolete."[15])

Each of Justice's conspiratorial movements in fact prepares for a larger public action that, rather than imitate and perpetuate Horne's covert machinations, breaks silence, brings conspiracy out into the open for public confrontation. The outcome of the secret process of collecting eviction notices is a revelation of Horne's plan to the membership of Justice followed by an open debate on how to respond to that plan: "Men's voices filled the room. Some had constructive ideas. Some just wanted to talk. Some had bad suggestions or feeble ones like 'Let's call a lawyer.' But almost everyone wanted a chance to speak" (119). The demonstration the group finally agrees upon in part presents itself as just retribution for, and imitation of, Horne's eviction plan: "'I say an eye for an eye,' called out Cardinal Spellman, a short bald man with a tiny mustache. 'Let's take away his house'" (119). But Justice's action ends up being not just "an eye for an eye": "'I have a better idea,' called out Bob. 'Let's take away his Castle'" (119). Choosing Horne's Castle as the point of pressure broadens the group's agenda from a personal attack on Horne; it allows for a challenge to what the Castle, in its lavish postmodern imperialist chic (119), stands for. The demonstration gives Justice the opportunity not only to make Horne's real-estate plan public and "demand that the superstar developer rescind eviction notices sent to homosexual men in Horne-owned buildings" (123) but also to introduce people with AIDS and gay men into an arena that would normally attempt to exclude them: "In the background Peter could see crowds of gay men laughing, dancing and popping champagne corks" (124). (Again, Peter observes the action from a distance, this time on television.) Justice claims an exclusive space and challenges its right to exclusivity: when asked by a reporter, "who is going to pay for all this damage?" James responds, "The hotel was built on tax rebates. . . . We've already paid" (124).

Justice's covert collection of credit cards also eventuates in a big, flamboyant, public action—"credit card day" (195). Members of Justice "leaflet the welfare hotels and the Third Street men's shelter" (196) to announce that "free food" (197) will be available at "the big twenty-four-register Pathmark . . . by the waterfront on Cherry Street near the projects" (196). Then, using credit cards whose owners "are unable to be with us today because they are in the hospital" (198), members of Justice let anyone who arrives at the supermarket buy "meat, fish, chicken, all protein, cheese, eggs, dairy, beans, flour, rice, fresh fruit, vegetables, good bread, real juice, nuts, peanut butter, spice, oils and other whole foods" (197). When "everything of nutritional value" runs out and "[a]ll that's left is junk" (198), "[t]here are still people coming in the door" (198), and the group decides to "[l]et people take whatever they want, even if it is Fritos and Diet Coke" (199). With its frenetic activity reminiscent of "Supermarket Sweep" and its definition of "politically correct" foods, the scene is, like many of those that involve Justice, partly a comic one, partaking of the exaggerated, "unreal" quality of the Horne plot it counters. Schulman does not hesitate to poke fun at her activists:

> "People who only got fresh meat and good vegetables are complaining," [Fabian] said. "Because they really wanted Twinkies."
> After an emergency consultation the crew decided they had no right to tell people what to eat. They could only make suggestions and immediate happiness was not a negligible goal, so they let the first-timers go through again for their sugar fix. Bob couldn't let go completely though, so he sat by the freezer section yelling out "Haagen-Dazs, Haagen-Dazs!" hoping to have some influence.
> "This is an issue we have to seriously consider in the future," Mario said. "This cannot be denied." (199)

But as with the depiction of Horne, the comic exaggeration of Justice's actions suggests that these be read not as literal representations of activist interventions but rather as broad gestures toward how AIDS activism might constitute itself as a real resistance movement. Credit card day is comic, but it also reveals certain important features of Justice's political commitments. It shows the group bringing its energies to bear not just on the AIDS crisis, which is its primary concern, but also on other crucial urban problems—homelessness, hunger, poverty. Justice thus begins to build a certain kind of coalition. The group is also shown staging an outrageous, "fabulous" (199, 208), camp coopting of capitalist consumerism to benefit those disenfranchised by capitalism:

[T]here was this frantic food buyout at Pathmark, then a number of fur coats were purchased at Bergdorf's and distributed to residents of the women's shelter. Plumbing, electrical and construction supplies for the Lower East Side squatters were charged at Broadway Lumber until the raised letters on the Visa card got rubbed off from too many charge slips. James was stationed at Liberty Travel where many one-way tickets were issued for people wanting to go home or even better places. (207-8)

As in the intervention against Horne at his Castle, Justice's actions here mimic consumerism while opposing its capitalist foundations, insisting that money, credit, and (especially) food be available to all. In the wake of credit card day, Daisy "dreams" of "the military-industrial complex . . . reduced to rubble" (208).

In the course of *People in Trouble*, Justice becomes a large organization, its meetings moving from one venue to another in order to accommodate its growing membership: "Almost three hundred people were packed into the windowless space" (115); "The membership had simply grown too large for anybody's basement. Now they gathered in the abandoned Saint Mark's bathhouse" (156); "Justice had gotten too large for the bathhouse so they crashed the Saint, a three-story nightclub" (206). The group experiences a kind of success not imagined for any of the resistance movements in the "epidemiological" novels. In part this success reflects Schulman's different vision of the "epidemiological" narrative itself. The incoherence of the epidemic she depicts—its lack of both a clear point of origin and, despite the novel's apocalypticism, a clearly-projected endpoint—allows for a variety of effective political interventions. None of these can bring an immediate end to AIDS (or homelessness, poverty, oppression); none is the "cure" or "antidote" wishfully imagined by the "epidemiological" novels. But a resistance conceived, as in Schulman's depiction of Justice, not as a unitary solution to a monolithic, unified problem—not as one simple force opposing another—has the advantage of allowing for partial, provisional victories. As we have seen, in the models of resistance put forward by the "epidemiological" novels, despite the theoretical possibility that one resistant intentionality might neatly intervene against another, oppressive one, the practical outcome of such attempted interventions is almost universally failure. Rather than conceive resistance as war against a monolithic state apparatus that fully controls the ground upon which the war occurs, as the "epidemiological" novels tend to do, Schulman shows an active resistance movement confronting a multi-faceted, if still daunting, complex of forces—the church, government, capitalist enterprise, drug companies, the media—in strategic actions that, on the one hand, work toward building the movement itself and, on the other, call attention to, oppose, and attempt to dismantle repressive structures.

Molly suggests to Kate, in a discussion of political action, that "[i]t's not the movies, where the world divides into freedom fighters and brownshirts," and she posits instead a different kind of division: "Here in New York City there are people who take action and people who do nothing. Doing nothing is a position. It means giving approval without having to actively say so" (165). The novel's narrative of resistance depicts not a simple division into "good" and "bad"; Schulman largely eschews depicting Justice as one half of a two-sided war. While the group's actions are consistently grounded in anger, "aggressive" (158) and confrontative, their strength comes not from military might or from clout within the established political system but from their ability to move many people out of "doing nothing" into action:

> No one can ever be as angry when it's hopeless as they can be when there's something to be done about it. People work for change when they think there's a chance of getting it. Otherwise they say, "Why bother?" (119)

Justice does not simply make itself into the mirror-image of its conspiratorial opposition; it moves out of conspiracy into open, confrontational, public action. Neither does it simply echo the violence of Horne and company, though it does not wholly disown violent responses. In the final political encounter of the novel, at the Taj McHorne, Justice moves into "chaotic," angry action: "The black T-shirts with pink triangles swarmed over the equipment, smashing it. They trampled the press section, throwing cameras into the street and stomping on them. There would be no observers this time. Everyone would participate or run" (221). The crowd from Justice confronts Horne and his armed bodyguards (220); Horne himself wields a gun (221). But though something like a military engagement occurs here, Justice wins out not through military preparedness or sophistication but through the sheer force of numbers: "five guns couldn't kill a thousand people" (220). The movement succeeds insofar as it is a real, *popular* movement able to confront that power concentrated in the figure of Horne. Reflecting on the "we" of Justice—"I don't know if I can honestly say 'we' because I didn't do the most. I just do a little bit every now and then. But that makes me part of it"—Molly concludes that "a little bit now and then is okay. . . . But only because there are a lot of people in Justice, so a lot of little bits is a lot. If there were only a few, then even doing it all the time wouldn't be enough" (196). An organization like Justice provides a context within which individual action becomes meaningful, where, if it were to remain simply individual, it would be lost in the immensity of the problems it confronts.

Political resistance in Schulman's novel is conceived not as warfare but as a movement of previously disenfranchised individuals toward collective action: "Imagining what they deserve and then fighting for it . . . is something that anyone with nothing to lose can easily learn" (158). On credit card day, the homeless people "hanging out" in front of the supermarket are transformed by their "expectations": "They weren't loitering. They appeared to be gathering" (196). Refusing to see the AIDS crisis as situated on a neatly bifurcated battlefield where all the power of resources and political muscle lies with the opposition, Schulman instead depicts a complex field of forces where, though certain kinds of power may be concentrated in the government-supported, capitalist projects of Horne, other kinds of power can be mobilized and brought to bear through a politics of grassroots organizing and direct action. Militancy is part of the movement, but the novel consistently eschews the bifurcation of "brownshirts" and "freedom fighters" suggested in an understanding of the AIDS crisis as war; it refuses to conceive AIDS activism only as a battle taking place in the streets: "They folded, stuffed and stamped sheets of newsprint that might save some lives and would definitely increase the quality of others" (173).

People in Trouble also challenges the gender exclusions that tend to operate within the militarized understanding of AIDS as a battlefield of masculinity. From the beginning, Justice presents a public face that is complex in its gender, racial, class, and sexual implications, a face that might indeed best be described as queer. Molly's first view of Justice, her encounter with James and Scott handing out leaflets after the memorial vigil, includes "an older black gay man" and one who is "younger and taller and white" (47). While the t-shirts they wear are "angry," the men themselves are "smiling" (47). James in particular evokes a militant activist past, the past of sixties Black radicalism: "He wore his hair in a large natural like Angela Davis used to do, which made him look distinctly old-fashioned. . . . [T]his guy reminded Molly immediately of those posters of Huey P. Newton sitting on a throne holding machine guns" (47). But as the double comparison to Huey Newton *and* Angela Davis begins to suggest, James, who later wears "a full-length sweater dress and a white fur hat" (117) while facilitating one of Justice's meetings, also clearly distinguishes himself from the masculinist postures of most military resistance movements:

> [T]his man wasn't wearing a black beret and leather jacket. Instead he had on effeminate floral-print three-quarter pants like girls buy on Fourteenth Street. He had a gold loop and a ruby stud in one ear and a feather in the other. He was swish. He was an older black gay man who called other men "darling" and "girlfriend." On the center of each flower printed on his pants was the word *love*. (47)

The complex image that Justice thus at first projects continues throughout the novel. When "two men in black T-shirts with pink triangles on them over which was scrawled *Justice*" rob a bank to get money for "sick people who have no health insurance," they do not behave like "typical" bank robbers: "They did not wear masks. They had no guns" (74). The robbery is successful because the bank teller they confront "g[i]ve[s] them fifteen thousand dollars without setting off the alarm": "'My brother died of AIDS,' she told reporters as she was led away in handcuffs. 'So why should I send the police after those poor brave men?'" (74). Justice adopts certain militant, radical postures, but gives them a new, queer spin. When one of the men handing in his eviction notice flashes "a victory sign" and "a fisted salute," Molly concludes that "[e]ither he was an old radical or he was showing off the manual technique he'd picked up at the Mineshaft" (110). Justice meetings mix political action and sexual cruising:

[T]here were lots and lots of handsome young men who intended to live to be handsome old men or even just aging queens. They were the organization's best recruitment force, since Justice's favorite activity after raising hell was the boyfriend parade. (159)

Schulman is not uncritical of racist, sexist, and classist exclusions within Justice. The earliest meetings of the group are largely white and male, and the gay men who attend display a clear sense of class privilege:

[Scott] had a combined air of enthusiasm and serious determination: like a middle-class boy who one day discovered injustice and then proceeded to do something about it with both sincere conviction and class arrogance about getting things done his way. (116)

When the group spontaneously decides to go to Horne's Castle, "a clean-shaven young man in a black leather jacket, who looked like he had a lot of discretionary income," asks, "But how are we going to get cabs for three hundred?" (119). Still, Schulman sees the growing movement as a site where gender, race, and class assumptions can be challenged and changed. Ultimately, Justice grows to include "all kinds" (158). Only "straight men" remain unrepresented, even among the "old-time radicals of various stripes who had rioted in the sixties at Stonewall, in Newark, with the Young Lords, the SDS, and hadn't done a goddamn thing since" and who form one "contingent" in Justice (158-59): as Daisy explains, "[s]traight men don't know how to take care of other people. . . . And they don't work well in groups" (159).

Particularly invigorating for Justice is its merger with "Fury, the women-with-AIDS group"; "[n]ow Daisy, an older Puerto Rican woman with long gray hair, co-facilitated the meetings with James" (156):

> The presence of the Furies changed the Justice guys just a bit. It made for a coed institution, one in which, except for a few indiscretions, the sexes rarely mixed intimately.
> "That puts us in a special category," Molly said after one particularly lively meeting, "with other famous fag/dyke teams like the Catholic Church, Hollywood and the Olympics." (157)

The women bring extensive political experience to Justice that is otherwise lacking:

> There was a band of veterans from the now defunct women's liberation movement who were the only ones who had been consistently politically active for the last decade, and so knew better than anyone else how to make flyers, how to do phone trees, the quickest way to wheat-paste, and who weren't afraid of getting arrested.
> "Being a woman in Justice means being in leadership," Daisy once said. "As soon as you walk in the room all the guys turn around and say, 'Now what?'"
> "We like dykes," the guys would chant every once in a while when the women did something really great. (159)

Along with the change in the gender structure of Justice comes a new class constititution that leads to certain conflicts:

> There were the tough street Furies who had all been around the block a couple of times. There were distinguished homosexuals with white-boy jobs, who had forgotten that they were *queer* until AIDS came along and everyone else reminded them. At first the white collars had wanted to bring lawsuits and carry out polite picket lines, while the Furies had been willing to bash in a few heads at the expense of getting bashed themselves. (158)

But these different visions of political action do not remain in irremediable conflict with each other; instead Schulman suggests that they come to strengthen each other:

> [S]oon the two factions were able to unite in anger and a commitment to direct action[16] when the homos found out what a lifetime of anger

could create and the Furies discovered that nothing raises the level of outrage as efficiently as the level of expectation. (158)

In a way that none of the "epidemiological" novels does, *People in Trouble* thus consistently links its depiction of political activism to the politics of identity and of coalition building. Justice is particularly powerful in providing a site both for political solidarity based upon common, marginalized identifications as person with AIDS, lesbian, gay man, and for renegotiation of gender, class, and race differences. Like the feminism that particularly informs it, the AIDS activism of Justice consistently links the "private" to the "public," the "personal" to the "political," as does Schulman in structuring her novel around intricately interwoven political and personal narratives. The novel constantly rethinks gender and sexual identity categories,[17] both in the narrative of political action and in the central love triangle. Within Justice, the tough, street-smart feminism of the Furies comes together with a variety of gay male styles, from Scott's shy earnestness to Bob's "half put-on, half deep cowboy roots" (92) to the sex-positive stance of the "longtime leather queen" Fabian (117) to the outrageous camp of Cardinal Spellman:

> A number of scantily clad teenagers appeared in loincloths, hoisted her excellency up on a huge Plexiglas cross and hauled her away in a sea of kisses.
> "Oh Father," cooed Miss Spellman. "Oh Son. Oh Holy Holy Ghost." (208)

And in the story of the love triangle, gender flexibility and ambiguity are repeatedly evoked. Kate remarks that "Peter's such a girl," explaining that "[h]e's a baby. He's passive. He whines and can't take care of himself. He never carries the heaviest thing"; Molly counters that "[t]hat's not like a girl. . . . That sounds exactly like a man to me" (23). Later, Molly thinks of Kate as "a feminine tomboy" (38), "a boy," "effeminate, like a beautiful faggot" (41). And Kate herself consistently negotiates between straight and lesbian, and male and female, identities; she begins "dress[ing] as a man" (89): "she was a better man than most because she was so strikingly handsome in her black suit. She strode powerful and erect like a well-bred charming man. A male model perhaps. A movie star" (90).

Schulman repeatedly insists on an intimate linkage between the lives and identities of individual characters and their political engagements: "Even with that huge crowd [at one of Justice's meetings] everyone got to speak his name" (116). At the end of the occupation of Horne's Castle, "Justice's name rang throughout the land and Kate came back and took Molly to bed" (127). Justice may become "larger" than the people who compose it, but it never transcends them to leave behind their identities and bodies, their individual histories of life within particular communities. The convocation of one of Justice's meetings in the old Saint Mark's bathhouse connects the present of AIDS activism to a pleasurable past recalled in complicated ways by many of Justice's members:

> The baths had seemed musty to Kate at first, but the men oohed and aahed, remembering what it was like *before*, remembering with some nervousness the last time each of them had been there. They were warm and joking with one another, like adults returning to the sandlot.
> "I feel like Judas Maccabaeus returning to the trashed-out temple," Bob said. He clapped his long, sleek hands together and reached up to the cobwebbed archway. "Oh Lord, let those glory days be with us once again. Oh unknown dick, oh joy, oh most angelic thought." (157)

And Justice's actions consistently reforge connections to people with AIDS, their real bodies, their real lives and deaths. The larger movement to make experimental drugs like Ampligen available to women arises from Daisy's at first lonely efforts to gain access to the drug for herself (175-77). Justice's final, large demonstration at the Taj McHorne grows directly out of Scott's funeral, the mourners identical with the angry crowd that, "like one person," "walk[s] silently" up Fifth Avenue (220). Molly's first encounter with Justice immediately follows her commemoration of two friends; she has wondered, during the memorial vigil, what can meaningfully come from the act of commemoration, and on her way out she meets James and Scott as they distribute information that will perhaps provide an answer to her question:

> The flyer went on to invite people to a weekly meeting. Molly folded it four times and pushed it into her pocket. She missed Kate very much. She wished Kate were there. Molly walked home feeling open and vulnerable and then very angry with an energy that had nowhere to go. (47)

Molly's angry energy here is related both to the problems in her relationship with Kate, Kate's absence at the important moments in her life, and to her experience of loss:

> Molly felt enormous anger. These were her friends. These were her dead friends. She saw their faces. Were their lives worth less than the lives of heterosexuals? Where was Kate? She should be there at a time like this. (46)

Justice provides a place where such complex individual reactions of grief and anger can be transformed into political work without the reactions themselves being forgotten or erased.

The political narrative of *People in Trouble* is in certain ways utopian, wishfully depicting a movement that overcomes many obstacles. But Justice is also modeled on the real-world activism of ACT UP, and Schulman, even in presenting a certain utopian vision, does not cover over the real difficulties that attend the formation and sustenance of a group like Justice, difficulties that have in fact attended the development of an effective AIDS activism. As credit card day draws to a close, Don concludes that "[w]e're doing something real important. . . . We're making a difference today and it's not as hard as I thought it would be" (199). But Mario responds less enthusiastically: "'Yeah, well,' Mario said. 'It seems like a big deal right now but tomorrow it will be over. I've been in politics a long time and little actions like this only work if they inspire people on to bigger ones'" (199-200). At the Justice meeting that follows, a similar dynamic is enacted, with Daisy and James presenting contrasting, but also perhaps complementary visions of the group's success. Daisy begins:

> "There are times when you have to dream," Daisy said. "And then speak those dreams. Here are mine."
>
> Molly remembered where she was. She was with her people. She couldn't let Kate take her out of herself ever again.
>
> "I dream," Daisy continued, "that by tomorrow at three in the afternoon, American Express, Visa and Mastercard's stocks will have tumbled so low, they will fall off the charts. Then the entire board of directors of each company will be forced to resign with a large majority taking the easy way out via cyanide pills. The Dow Jones will close early so all the brokers can rush home and smoke crack while the banks repossess their BMWs and their health club memberships and foreclose on their condominiums which used to be your rent-controlled apartments. By Wednesday, noon, the military-industrial complex will be reduced to rubble. There will be homes for the homeless, food for the hungry, care for the ill, permission for the imagination and no weapons. Then I'll go home, light a joint, open a beer and make love for the rest of my life. How does that sound to you?"
>
> There was an explosion then of shared joy. There were many expectations in that room that night in the occupied, air-conditioned disco. (208)

But James, knowing that the newspapers will distort Justice's actions—"AIDS Victims Riot in City" (209)—and that they will also announce Horne's advocacy of "barge internment camps for all those infected with the deadly AIDS virus" (209), counters Daisy's vision with a more pessimistic view:

> "Remember that feeling," Daisy said. "Hold on to that dream while James shares a few words."
> James came to the front of the room. He was very tired. His clothes were dirty. He looked unkempt. His spirit was failing him, everyone could see that. They were very, very quiet then. You could hear a thousand people holding their collective breath.
> "Please listen to me critically," he said. He didn't start by saying "brothers and sisters," which was what he usually said. He started by saying "Please." He seemed frightened. Molly had never seen this emotion in his face before. Like someone looking out over a sea of faces knowing that each one of them had an expectation he had to live up to. There was more trust than one person could bear.
> "There is a euphoria in taking control of your own life. There is something crippling that occurs when the response to that act distorts it. As long as the people fighting for change are smaller than the institutions that control information, their activities will be misrepresented, their impact minimized and their humanity questioned. The only way to overcome the machinery is to become bigger than it is. So that, one day, more people will be participating in the event than watching it on television. That is called a revolution. In the meantime we are placated with a condition of free speech in a nation of no ideas." (209)

James tempers the "euphoria" of success, tempers the "expectations" that grow out of that success, but still pushes toward "a revolution." And Schulman tempers her euphoric, utopian depiction of Justice by ending the novel not with the massive action at the Taj McHorne, but with an account of exhaustion. Molly and Kate's relationship ends (225), and Molly spends "a long winter" largely "alone" (226). Fabian and Daisy die:

> Fabian had wanted a drug called M-Reg One. But the FDA killed it in phase-three trials. Daisy ended up on AZT, which she couldn't really tolerate and her legs went so numb that she could barely walk. They both died angry. . . . When Daisy had started dying, [her lover] Trudy became more and more belligerent, finally getting beaten by a cop with his nightstick at a demonstration at Macy's and then getting kicked in the back a few months later at the Stock Exchange. (226)

Justice continues to act, but the novel's final scene is not the demonstration at "Saint Vincent's Hospital, where a man dying of AIDS was called a 'fucking faggot' by a security guard in the emergency room" (227), that will occur later in the day, nor the "demo at the Meadowlands" scheduled "for the next Jets game" "to give women support for asking men to wear condoms" (227). Rather, it is a small planning meeting in James's apartment, a meeting where the lack of energy is most striking:

> Molly sat back into the cushions on the couch. She was very tired. She held a warm cup of tea in her hands and brought it to her face. The radiators knocked. The winds rattled the shaky windowpanes.
> "I'm tired," she said.
> "I'm tired too," James said.
> "So many people are so self-satisfied," Molly said. "They sit around, they don't do anything."
> "Suffering can be stopped," James said. "But it can never be avenged, so survivors watch television. Men die, their lovers wait to get sick. People eat garbage or worry about their careers. Some lives are more important than others. Some deaths are shocking, some invisible. We are a people in trouble. We do not act." (227-28)

In some sense the novel here returns to its apocalyptic beginning: "Some people were dying. Some people were busy" (1). But though a movement like Justice that largely depends upon individuals acting out of grief and anger runs the risk of losing momentum as personal energies wane, it remains, at the end of Schulman's novel, a viable political force. In the novel's final sentence, James and Molly overcome their "tiredness" to "act" once again: "Then everyone went to Saint Vincent's because there was nothing more to say" (228).

3. TOWARD AN ACTIVIST AESTHETIC?

Throughout *People in Trouble*, questions about art are intimately tied up with the political narrative. Both Kate and Peter are artists, and their differing artistic positions are related closely to their differing stances in the AIDS crisis. In his art as in his politics, Peter is a figure of stasis and distance. Having worked consistently in the theater, he nonetheless views art as a solitary pursuit in which the artist is ultimately fully separable from the work he creates and from his audience: "You and I go quietly into rooms, close the doors and once all alone, begin to work. When we finish there is something that exists apart from us, whether a solid object or an event. But we walk away from it while others are having the experience" (49). Kate, on the other hand, as in the novel's political and romantic narratives, is a figure of change, movement, experimentation. She abandons work in the theater to embark on a "solo" career (15) that involves several "major stylistic shift[s]" (15): "Kate had been making artwork long enough to recognize the patterns of frustration and breakthrough, denial and breakthrough, passion and frustration and breakthrough and change" (14). As she herself suggests to Peter, in art as in other aspects of their lives, while she is immersed in change, he stands still:

> I'm changing, and do you know what? I'm glad. Do you want to be the same person with the same opinions and the same habits for the rest of your life? Give in, Pete. . . . I'm changing my life. Why don't you stop wishing I wouldn't and do something about yours? (154)

Peter's aesthetic, which he himself "want[s] to proclaim a metaphor for human relations" (10), remains always distanced and perspectival: "It was just as in nature, where one could more easily see what was brightly lit from a distance than when the viewer was illuminated on the spot" (10). Kate's aesthetic, on the other hand, moves more and more away from distance and perspective, rejecting "the big picture" (133) that Peter so values in favor of "fragments," "shreds of ideas," and "partial phrases" (14). Where Peter remains committed to modernism, Kate moves into the postmodern. Looking at "a stack of old paintings," she "want[s] to smash them" (16):

> She was tired of standing too far away from a person's face. She wanted to show what she saw making love or in a fight. It was a flash of lip, a pimpled cheek, sweat between the breasts, an unidentified slope or shadow that seemed suddenly more important. Sex and violence were sensual experiences, not visual ones, although they did have a visual component. In order to bring out the touch in the visual she had to get closer, as though her eye was on his chest looking up the side of his neck. That was where she wanted the image to be. (16)

Like the narrative of AIDS in *People in Trouble,* the account of Kate's artistic movements is concerned particularly with proximity. Kate's decision to "stop designing for theater . . . and start designing for herself" is motivated by a desire "to confront directly" (49).

In her art, Kate also works, through fragmentation, to rethink questions of sequence and movement; at one point, she tears a sketch of a woman's face in half and "h[o]ld[s] both pieces next to each other as though they followed in sequence instead of being two components of the same movement" (48):

> By taking her depiction of those lips and placing them next to, instead of underneath the eyes, Kate was forced to confront the mouth first, to make a relationship with it before discovering those oil-cured black things. The order changed the effect because, after seeing the obscenity

in that mouth, one experienced a monstrously seductive face. Then the greasy eyes came as a quiet surprise. The viewer learned from this sequence that the mouth was actually all that the face had to offer. If it was viewed at once in its entirety, there would have been no expectation. No movement. (48-49)

Her various stylistic changes lead to a wholly new stage in Kate's art: in the present moment of the novel, she works on a large installation made up of fragments—"photos and some collage," "a lot of underpainting," "scraping with a razor blade" (101). This project, called "People in Trouble," emphasizes political themes and it represents Kate's gathering together of "resonant images" that express "the variety of violence she had both lived and missed" (16):

> There were black-and-whites of young Negro men being bitten by American police dogs. There were colored images of acknowledged heroes lying in swamps of their own blood. She searched each one for the particles of physicality that captured the fear, the pain and especially the willingness of some individual to enter into it. . . .
> On the side table by the single bed in her studio, Kate propped up a twenty-five-year-old photo from *Life* magazine. It showed a Buddhist monk who had set himself on fire in Saigon. The photo was one frame but it was all in motion. It caught the man at the point where he was so completely burned that his body crumpled over into the flame and flesh fell off his bones.
> *Does destroying yourself purposefully make a tangible impact?*
> What Kate retained from the photo of a collapsing human flame was a flash of light that put its faith in smoke and ashes. (16-17)

Kate's installation, incorporating images of suffering and resistance garnered "from magazines, anything—*True Detective, People, National Geographic, Personal Management, Heavy Metal*" (104), also incorporates the materials by which suffering is imaged. She paints on "[t]wo kinds of X rays":

> These in my hand are plain films. For a tumor to be seen on plain film it must be big enough and it must be more dense than the surrounding normal tissue. . . . Those are contrast films. That's when they inject dye into you. The contrast film relates to the paint differently than the plain film. It practically rejects it. (143)

Thus making the disturbances, the violence, the fragmented images and imagings of life lived under duress into the stuff of her art, Kate also attempts to mirror the frenetic disorientations of life in the way she envisions the viewing of "People in Trouble." She intends her installation to be seen in quick motion: "[Y]ou don't walk through this piece. You run. You start at one end and run turning your head to the mural so that the images fly by quickly as though it were a movie, only there's no technology" (185). When her art dealer Spiros criticizes "People in Trouble" for its lack of "compositional restraint," "pictorial entrapment," and "archetonic space" (187), Kate responds by rejecting all of these constraining and ordering concepts: "[W]ho wants to entrap photographs? Who cares about archetonic space when people are so sad?" (188). Clearly Kate intends her piece somehow as an intervention in the world's "sadness," and Schulman perhaps suggests, in her depiction of Kate's work, the development of a certain activist aesthetic. Kate's artistic movement parallels the novel's political movement: it confronts the fragmentary and proximate, and it brings fragments together to speak to each other, to work together, even if, in the absence of constrained, constraining principles of order, these never form a unified "whole."

Kate's installation in fact participates directly in one of the novel's most striking political interventions, the "murder" of Ronald Horne. When Justice confronts Horne at the Taj McHorne, behind which "People in Trouble" has been installed, and Horne "retreat[s]" into "her collage," "wrapped by her images" (221), Kate acts:

> Kate pushed harder than she had ever pushed and clawed her way to the front of the stage, catching and tearing her flesh on the splintered police sawhorses that lay mangled everywhere. Then she climbed under it, crawling on the dirt and garbage over wires, rags, cans of paint and turpentine. She watched her own hands turn black and her arms cake with dirt and blood surrounded by the moving spikes of pants legs bobbing around her. Dragging the cans and power lines to the base of the collage's wooden frames, she looked back at the chaos behind her. Each gesture was too large and so unusual that the action passed before her like a high-speed silent film. Only there was no silence. (221-22)

Horne is "enveloped" (224) in the fire that Kate sets, and the sequence of events that includes the fire, at the same time that it participates in the angry Justice demonstration, also clearly evokes Kate's new aesthetic: the image of the Buddhist monk set on fire, the "chaos" that Kate both fears and incorporates into her work (14, 16) (and that Justice itself chooses to "instigate" [221] at the demonstration), the experience of the rush of images as in a movie.

Kate's aesthetic (in "People in Trouble") reflects Schulman's own aesthetic (in *People in Trouble*). Both value proximity and fragmentation; in one of Schulman's typical descriptions, "Molly looked at Sam's green eyes, the way they twinkled. She looked at iron muscles and little pieces of flesh" (195). Both also crucially involve the navigation from an intense personal experience of the fragmentary to a certain collectivity, a bringing together of the fragmentary and disparate. At one point in Schulman's novel, James comments, that, "hav[ing] read every novel about AIDS that the publishers can get into the stores," he finds it "all unsatisfactory in the same way":

> When a person faces death . . . especially a deliberate, uncalled-for and avoidable death, they only seem to have two reactions. *Why me? and I don't want to die.*
>
> . . .
>
> . . . The only reaction we can really have is a banal one because death is the last experience of life. It's not like love. There is no retrospect. The challenge is to turn it from an overwhelming personal void into a group effort, to try to help others avoid the same fate. But this kind of extraordinary response means agitating against the grain of the habit of human reaction. (147)

Schulman's novel itself clearly tries to move in a different direction from other novels about AIDS; it repeatedly agitates in just the way James prescribes, depending upon an aesthetic that brings the "personal" and the "group" into intimacy in ways similar to those embodied in Kate's artistic work. Schulman, like Kate, perhaps develops an activist aesthetic.

People in Trouble nonetheless remains deeply suspicious of the artist's claim that art in and of itself does political work. When Kate calls to Molly's attention that "more and more artists are doing work about AIDS," Molly responds simply, "What does that do?" (113). Though Kate at first argues that "[her] artwork is [her] political work"—"artwork . . . teaches people to see things in a new way. . . . Form is content. New forms are revolutionary" (113)—and though Peter stubbornly holds onto such a claim—"We have always agreed that our artwork is our political work. We have always agreed that challenging form is more revolutionary than any political organization ever can be" (217)—Kate ultimately rethinks such a position:

> Peter and Kate had often prided themselves on how radical they were. They were artists, after all, and not stockbrokers. . . . Their lifestyle was their politics in action. But, standing in a sea-foam-green bus station in rural New York, that all seemed rather superficial. She realized, waiting for the operator to complete the call, that there was something repulsive at the base of this kind of thinking. (164-65)

As Kate concludes, "Sometimes a person has to stop talking about art for a moment and take a look around" (166). Though Kate's gathered images do mirror something of the "chaos" of the world—"At times the sum of her collection drew such a repulsive conclusion that she couldn't imagine anything worse" (16)—the world still exceeds her art: "looking out her window at the unprotected bodies, she considered that this worse thing was somehow present there" (16-17). "People in Trouble" does political work in the novel but only within the context of the Justice demonstration that forces Horne into "retreat" and only when Kate steps outside the strict role of artist to become saboteur. Despite its radical aesthetic and its political themes, Kate's installation is not necessarily a force for political change. Indeed, Schulman depicts it as deeply compromised from its beginning, funded as part of "a token gesture to the arts" that participates in just the sort of political initiative Justice opposes:

> They have promised real-estate developers millions in tax rebates if they provide funding for public artwork on their properties. There are a number of projects under way to convert former public buildings, long in disrepair, into refurbished private space, relocating the public facilities onto barges. The mayor's office will be promoting and publicizing the efforts in a bus card campaign called "Privacy Is Golden." Now, I know that there are large areas of park and sidewalk space available that would be suitable for the piece you have in mind. I think I can help you get into this granting program. Frankly, it is your only financial option and the work would be seen by people on the streets going to work, et cetera. It would not be shut up in some exclusive, out-of-the-way gallery. (99)

Arranged by Spiros, "who pulls strings and spares [Kate] the details" (184), thus allowing her, in Pearl's words, to "reap the benefits and remain morally pure at the same time" (185), the show is physically set up, without Kate's knowledge, almost as an homage to Ronald Horne: "people can begin at the front of the piece and walk a long straight line until they've seen the whole thing, which will lead them right to Horne's feet" (185).

Schulman shows even Kate's impulsive setting of her work on fire, a political act that represents at the same time the culmination of Kate's aesthetic transformation, to be subject to cooptation and commodification:

> Kate developed a high profile as a result of Horne's death and could be read about it an essay by Gary Indiana in the *Village Voice* and one by Barbara Kruger in *ArtForum*. In fact, Kate began working extensively in burning installations and quickly got commissions from a number of Northern European countries to come start fires there. She had been in

Amsterdam for six months working on a blazing sculpture in honor of the people of Cambodia . . . (225-26)

The final judgment of Schulman's novel may be that all Kate's artistic changes, including the decision to use her installation to stop Horne, ultimately mean more for her career than for the political movement. The novel suggests, in fact, that Horne's power continues on under different auspices and despite continued resistance: "After his death the bulk of Horne's holdings had been purchased by the president of a major chemical company who was himself assassinated by a man dying of cancer" (226). Schulman's novel itself, like the "epidemiological" novels, presents a call to action, and unlike them, it provides a detailed model of a possible AIDS activism; but despite its own political intentions, the novel remains deeply skeptical of the political efficacy of art except when art stands in intimate connection to a vital political movement. As Schulman elsewhere suggests:

> Reading a book may help someone decide to take action, but it is not the same thing as taking action. The responsibility of every writer is to take their place in the vibrant, activist movements along with everybody else. The image created by the male intellectual model of an enlightened elite who claim that its artwork *is* its political work is parasitic and useless for us. At the same time I don't think that any writer must write about any specific topic or in any specific way. . . . But, when they're finished with their work, they need to be at demonstrations, licking envelopes and putting their bodies on the line with everybody else.[18]

Schulman herself has followed such advice, in work with ACT UP and more recently in the formation of the direct-action group the Lesbian Avengers.[19]

But I would suggest that *People in Trouble* also does political work, and not just in helping its readers "decide to take action." As Schulman's novel itself repeatedly suggests, language, representation, and narrative do matter: as the book ends, after all, Justice is preparing to demonstrate at Saint Vincent's, because a man with AIDS has been called "fucking faggot" (227). Representations can reconfirm societal exclusions and oppressions, and representations can question, rewrite, oppose these. While the political work of a novel like *People in Trouble* is not the same as the activist work of demonstrations, licking envelopes, putting one's body on the line, and while, as Schulman suggests, novelists should not be exempted from such work, novels like Schulman's or like John Weir's can move toward a real reconception of how "we" as a culture and society think about, represent, and treat AIDS and people with AIDS. Thus, Schulman's novel begins from a widely-accepted cultural narrative that makes the "spread" of AIDS part of a world-threatening movement toward apocalypse, and goes on to challenge both the usually homophobic form of that narrative, where the goal is to "contain" AIDS by isolating people with AIDS, and its anti-homophobic form as deployed in the "epidemiological" novels, where there is a certain reconfirmation of the identification between gayness and disease even as the homophobia of such an identification is resisted. Schulman rewrites the "epidemiological" narrative as a narrative not of isolation but of proximity, and she develops out of that narrative an account of an effective, if difficult and not always successful, resistance movement. Schulman's main goal here may be recruiting for that movement, but her novel does not work just to recruit: it provides alternative representations of the politics of AIDS, representations that stand counter to the simplifying and often offensive media representations that Schulman satirizes: "In the news tonight, Ronald Horne murdered in Forty-Second Street melee. Congress approves new Contra aid plan. Mayor goes to bat for the peanut butter bagel and Masters and Johnson warn heterosexuals: new threat from AIDS" (224). Novels like Schulman's intervene in the broader discourses of AIDS, suggest how such discourses often do discredit to the realities of people's lives, and find other language, other narratives that might allow those realities to be differently represented and understood. Such work in rethinking AIDS, while it does not stand in for other, more direct political work, is a necessary way of responding to a health crisis still largely understood in (homophobic, racist, sexist) terms that continue to block an honest and open public discourse on sex and safer sex; a real commitment to the health not just of the uninfected but of those living now with HIV and AIDS; and effective health care and education for all.

NOTES

1. Sarah Schulman, *People in Trouble* (New York: E. P. Dutton, 1990); citations are given parenthetically in the text. Schulman's more recent novel *Empathy* (New York: E. P. Dutton, 1992) also concerns AIDS, though less centrally than *People in Trouble*, and it continues to develop a certain kind of apocalyptic thinking; see, for instance, 15, 31, 58, 63, 81, 142, and 169. For a discussion of *People in Trouble* in relation to Schulman's earlier fiction, see Sally Munt, "'Somewhere over the Rainbow . . .': Postmodernism and the Fiction of Sarah Schulman," in Sally Munt, ed., *New Lesbian Criticism: Literary and Cultural Readings* (New York: Columbia University Press, 1992), 33-50, esp. 47-49.

2. Sarah Schulman, "AIDS and the Responsibility of the Writer," *My American History: Lesbian and Gay Life During the Reagan/Bush Years* (New York: Routledge, 1994), 195. Also see Schulman's "Preface" to *My American History*, "My Life as an American Artist," xviii.

3. Sarah Schulman, "Wake-Up, AIDS Hysteria Will Change Your Life: Commentary," *My American History*, 172. For more on the complex issues involved in discussions of female-to-female HIV transmission, see Patton, *Last Served?* 65-75 and 138-39.

4. Sarah Schulman, "Laying the Blame: What Magic Johnson Really Means," *My American History*, 225.

5. Sarah Schulman, "Laying the Blame," *My American History*, 225.

6. On the ACT UP action, see Crimp and Rolston, *AIDS Demo Graphics*, 33.

7. Such a "test of loyalty" has been widely depicted in representations of HIV and AIDS—for just one instance, in an episode of the television series *21 Jump Street*.

8. Sarah Schulman, "Preface," *My American History*, xviii.

9. Sarah Schulman, "AIDS and the Responsibility of the Writer," *My American History*, 194.

10. Sarah Schulman, "Literature in the Age of AIDS," in Amy Scholder, ed., "AIDS, Cultural Life, and the Arts: A Forum," *City Lights Review* 2 (1988), 34.

11. Sarah Schulman, "AIDS and the Responsibility of the Writer," *My American History*, 195.

12. Other novels have depicted a developing AIDS activism as one of their narrative centers. See, for instance, David B. Feinberg's *Spontaneous Combustion* and Patrick Moore's *This Every Night* (New York: Amethyst Press, 1990). In the title story of her collection *Bodies of Water* (New York: E. P. Dutton, 1990), Michelle Cliff develops a different sort of political narrative of AIDS, with the central figure of the story drawing connections between her brother Bill, who has survived attempts to "cure" his homosexuality and who now has AIDS, and a variety of political movements: "She tacks postcards to the white wall above the desk: Billie Holiday; Chief's robe from the Third Phase; The Second Bible Quilt of Harriet Powers; ANC women. / See, Bill—also the resisters—and the artists. People like you" (146).

13. Two of Schulman's earlier novels—*The Sophie Horowitz Story* (Tallahassee, FL: Naiad Press, 1984) and *After Delores* (New York: E. P. Dutton, 1988)—have strong affinities with detective fiction.

14. On the demonstration, see Crimp and Rolston, *AIDS Demo Graphics*, 130-40, and Robert Hilferty's 1991 video *Stop the Church!*, originally scheduled to be shown on the PBS series *P.O.V.* but then cancelled amid controversy over its "appropriateness"; some PBS affiliate stations nonetheless still broadcast the video.

15. Sarah Schulman, "AIDS and the Responsibility of the Writer," *My American History*, 194.

16. Schulman here directly evokes ACT UP's self-description as "a diverse, non-partisan group of individuals united in anger and committed to direct action to end the AIDS crisis."

17. Schulman's *Empathy* continues an intensive exploration of the categories of gender.

18. Sarah Schulman, "AIDS and the Responsibility of the Writer," *My American History*, 196-97.

19. See Part Two of Schulman's *My American History*, "The Lesbian Avengers," 279-319.

APPENDIX

Bibliography of AIDS Literature

The following bibliography attempts to list, as fully as possible, literature in which HIV and AIDS play important roles. I have divided the bibliography into five categories: multi-genre anthologies, fiction, poetry, drama/performance, and nonfiction narrative.

Deciding which material to include in each category has not always been easy. Nonfictional works are included only when they have a significant *narrative* component. Certain works of fiction, drama, and poetry (like Craig Lucas's *Prelude to a Kiss*) do not explicitly concern AIDS but have nonetheless been widely read as implicitly (even allegorically) about AIDS. I have included in the bibliography some such works (like Lucas's play) but not others (for instance, David Leavitt's *While England Sleeps*, which might be read as somehow about AIDS activism, but where Leavitt seems concerned to steer us to a historical rather than allegorical reading of the novel). In certain other works (like Paul Russell's *The Salt Point* and *Boys of Life*), HIV and AIDS appear explicitly but in largely tangential ways. When I feel that AIDS nonetheless is crucial to a particular work, providing an important grounding for its central actions (as in Russell's novels), I have included it in my listing. Generally, here, I have erred on the side of inclusion rather than exclusion.

I have attempted to be as comprehensive as possible in listing booklength material published through the end of 1994 (some works published in 1995 are also included), but the bibliography is certainly marked by omissions. I have had access almost exclusively to material published in English, though, when other material has come to my attention, I have listed it here. In addition, much writing on AIDS, particularly memoirs, but also poetry and fiction, has been published by small or regional presses, and (I am sure) some of this has escaped my notice. Drama and performance art present problems of their own, given that much material remains unpublished after being performed. I have tried to include such unpublished work, and have presented, when possible, information about the history of its performance. When bibliographic information in any entry is incomplete, it is because I have relied for the listing on a review or announcement in which full bibliographic information was not provided; I have tried in each case to supply that information from other sources, but have not always succeeded.

I have not attempted here to present a full bibliography of material published in periodicals, though some such material is listed. Much more can be easily found in journals that frequently present fiction, poetry, drama, and nonfiction about AIDS: newspapers and magazines like *The Advocate*, *Gay Community News*, *The New York Native*, *NYQ* (later *QW*; no longer publishing), *Out*, *Out/Look* (no longer publishing), *Outweek* (no longer publishing), *Poz* (devoted wholly to coverage of HIV and AIDS), *RFD*, and *The Village Voice*; literary journals like *Art and Understanding* ("The International Magazine of Literature and Art About AIDS"), *Christopher Street*, and *The James White Review*; newsletters like *The Body Positive* and *PWA Newsline*; and 'zines like *Diseased Pariah News* and *Infected Faggot Perspectives*.

In compiling my own bibliography, I have consulted the important earlier work of Emmanuel S. Nelson ("Selected Bibliography," in Nelson, ed., *AIDS: The Literary Response*, 219-24), Judith Laurence Pastore ("Annotated Bibliography," in Pastore, ed., *Confronting AIDS*, 249-64), and Franklin Brooks and Timothy F. Murphy ("Annotated Bibliography of AIDS Literature, 1982-91," in Murphy and Poirier, eds., *Writing AIDS*, 321-39).

MULTI-GENRE ANTHOLOGIES

Avena, Thomas, ed. *Life Sentences: Writers, Artists, and AIDS*. San Francisco: Mercury House, 1994.

Beam, Joseph, ed. *In the Life: A Black Gay Anthology*. Boston: Alyson, 1986.

Blackman, Marci, and Trebor Healey, eds. *Beyond Definition: New Writing from Gay and Lesbian San Francisco*. San Francisco: Manic D Press, 1994.

Boffin, Tessa, and Sunil Gupta, eds. *Ecstatic Antibodies: Resisting the AIDS Mythology*. London: Rivers Oram Press, 1990.

Cook, Jim, ed. *Common Voices: An Anthology of Gay and Lesbian Writings and Art from Santa Barbara and Ventura Counties*. Gay and Lesbian Resource Center of Santa Barbara. Santa Barbara: Fithian Press, 1994.

Cooper, Dennis, ed. *Discontents: New Queer Writers*. New York: Amethyst Press, 1992.

Gott, Ted, ed. *Don't Leave Me This Way: Art in the Age of AIDS*. Canberra: National Gallery of Australia, 1994.

Hemphill, Essex, ed. *Brother to Brother: New Writings by Black Gay Men*. Boston: Alyson, 1991. A second volume in the project begun by Joseph Beam in *In the Life*.

Howe, Marie, and Michael Klein, eds. *In the Company of My Solitude: American Writing from the AIDS Pandemic*. New York: Persea, 1995.

Hunter, B. Michael, ed. *Sojourner: Black Gay Voices in the Age of AIDS*. Other Countries: Vol. 2. New York: Other Countries Press, 1993.

Klusacek, Allan, and Ken Morrison, eds. *A Leap in the Dark: AIDS, Art and Contemporary Cultures*. Montreal: Véhicule Press/An Artextes Edition, 1992.

Luczak, Raymond, ed. *Eyes of Desire: A Deaf Gay and Lesbian Reader*. Boston: Alyson, 1993.

Other Countries. *Other Countries: Black Gay Voices*. New York: Other Countries Press, 1988.

Pastore, Judith Laurence, ed. *Confronting AIDS Through Literature: The Responsibilities of Representation*. Urbana and Chicago: University of Illinois Press, 1993.

Scholder, Amy, ed. "AIDS, Cultural Life and the Arts: A Forum." *City Lights Review* 2 (1988), 7-56.

Scholder, Amy, and Ira Silverberg, eds. *High Risk: An Anthology of Forbidden Writings*. New York: Plume, 1991.

Scholder, Amy, and Ira Silverberg, eds. *High Risk 2: Writings on Sex, Death, and Subversion*. New York: Plume, 1994.

Witness: An Exquisite Corpse. Premiere Issue. *X-X-X Fruit* (Summer 1995).

Wolverton, Terry, ed. *Blood Whispers: L.A. Writers on AIDS*. Los Angeles: Silverton Books and the Gay and Lesbian Community Services Center, 1991.

Wolverton, Terry, ed. *Blood Whispers: Vol. 2: L.A. Writers on AIDS*. Los Angeles: Silverton Books, 1994.

FICTION

Aiello, Barbara, and Jeffrey Schulman. *Friends for Life: Featuring Amy Wilson*. The Kids on the Block Book Series. Frederick, MD: Twenty-first Century Books, 1988.

Aldridge, Sarah. *Michaela*. Tallahassee, FL: Naiad Press, 1994.

Ames, Jonathan. *I Pass Like Night*. New York: Morrow, 1989.

Anastos, Peter. *The Swan Prince: A Fairy Tale*. Arthur Elgort, photographs. Project conceived by Mikhail Baryshnikov. Toronto and New York: Bantam, 1987. See Miller, "AIDS in the Novel," 267-68.

Arrick, Fran. *What You Don't Know Can Kill You*. New York: Bantam, 1992.

Baer, Judy. *The Discovery*. Minneapolis: Bethany House Publishers, 1993.

Baker, James Robert. *Tim and Pete*. New York: Simon & Schuster, 1993.

Balizet, Carol. *Plague*. Grand Rapids, MI: Chosen Books, 1994.

Bantle, Lea F. *Diving for the Moon*. New York: Macmillan Books for Young Readers, 1995.

Barnes, Linda. *Steel Guitar*. New York: Delacorte Press, 1991.
Barnett, Allen. *The Body and Its Dangers and Other Stories*. New York: St. Martin's Press, 1990.
Barrow, John. "Killing the Pope." *Christopher Street* no. 110 (1987), 51-57.
Barrus, Tim. *Genocide: The Anthology*. Stamford, CT: Knights Press, 1988.
Bartlett, Neil. *Ready to Catch Him Should He Fall*. London: Serpent's Tail, 1990; New York: E. P. Dutton, 1990.
Beattie, Ann. "Second Question." *The New Yorker* 10 June 1991, 38-44.
Beaumont, Sebastian. *Heroes Are Hard to Find*. Brighton: Millivres, 1993.
Beaumont, Sebastian. *On the Edge*. Brighton: Millivres, 1991.
Beavers, David Patrick. *The Jackal Awakens*. Brighton: Millivres, 1995.
Begley, Louis. *As Max Saw It*. New York: Knopf, 1994.
Belloc, Denis. *Slow Death in Paris*. William Rodarmor, trans. London: Quartet Books, 1992. [*Képas*. Paris: Lieu Commun, 1989.]
Benderson, Bruce. *Pretending To Say No*. New York: Penguin, 1990.
Benderson, Bruce. *User*. New York: E. P. Dutton, 1994.
Berger, John. *To the Wedding*. New York: Pantheon Books, 1995.
Bergman, David, ed. *Men on Men 5*. New York: Plume, 1994. This volume continues the series edited by Stambolian.
Bergman, David, ed. *The Violet Quill Reader: The Emergence of Gay Writing After Stonewall*. New York: St. Martin's Press, 1994.
Berthelot, Francis. *Rivage des intouchables*. Paris: Denoël, 1990.
Birman, David. *The Book of Billy*. New York: Plutonia Press, 1993.
Bishop, Michael. "Icicle Music." *The Magazine of Fantasy and Science Fiction* March 1989, 6-19.
Bishop, Michael. *Unicorn Mountain*. New York: Arbor House/Morrow, 1988.
Black, Jeff. *Gardy and Erin*. Stamford, CT: Knights Press, 1989.
Borgman, C. F. *River Road*. New York: New American Library, 1988.
Bosse, Malcolm J. *Mister Touch*. New York: Ticknor & Fields, 1991.
Bouldrey, Brian. *The Genius of Desire*. New York: Ballantine, 1993.
Bouldrey, Brian. "Whipped Cream and Other Delights." *Christopher Street* no. 140 (1989), 33-36.
Bourjaily, Vance. *Old Soldier*. New York: Donald I. Fine, 1990.
Bram, Christopher. *In Memory of Angel Clare*. New York: Donald I. Fine, 1989.
Brass, Perry. *Albert or The Book of Man*. Bronx: Belhue Press, 1995.
Brass, Perry. *Works and Other "Smoky George" Stories*. Ridgefield, CT: Belhue Press, 1992.
Brown, Rebecca. *Annie Oakley's Girl*. San Francisco: City Lights, 1993.
Brown, Rebecca. *The Gifts of the Body*. New York: HarperCollins, 1994.
Bryan, Jed A. *A Cry in the Desert*. Austin, TX: Banned Books, 1987.
Bryant, Dorothy. *A Day in San Francisco*. Berkeley: Ata Books, 1982.

Buck, Charles H. [= Hugh Culik]. *The Master Cure*. New York: Jove, 1989.
Burgess, Clay. *On My Way to You: The Apprenticeship of a Lover*. North Augusta, SC: The Writers Block Publishing Company, 1994.
Busby, F. M. *The Breeds of Man*. New York: Bantam, 1988.
Caldwell, Joseph. *The Uncle from Rome*. New York: Viking, 1992.
Calhoun, Jackie. *Friends and Lovers: A Romance*. Tallahassee, FL: Naiad Press, 1993.
Calhoun, Jackie. *Lifestyles*. Tallahassee, FL: Naiad Press, 1990.
Cameron, Lindsley. *The Prospect of Detachment*. New York: St. Martin's Press, 1988.
Cameron, Peter. *The Weekend*. New York: Farrar, Straus and Giroux, 1994. On AIDS and Cameron's earlier fiction, see Myles Weber, "When a Risk Group Is Not a Risk Group: The Absence of AIDS Panic in Peter Cameron's Fiction," in Nelson, ed., *AIDS: The Literary Response*, 69-75.
Canin, Ethan. *The Palace Thief*. New York: Random House, 1994.
Carpenter, William. *A Keeper of Sheep*. Minneapolis: Milkweed Editions, 1994.
Carter, Steven, ed. *OutRage: 1993: Australian Gay & Lesbian Short Story Anthology*. Fitzroy, Victoria: Designer Publications, 1992.
Champagne, John. *The Blue Lady's Hands*. Secaucus, NJ: Lyle Stuart, 1988.
Champagne, John. *When the Parrot Boy Sings*. Secaucus, NJ: Meadowlands, 1990.
Chapman, James. *Our Plague: A Film from New York*. New York: Fugue State Press, 1993.
Chappell, Helen. *Acts of Love*. New York: Pocket Books, 1989.
Chapsal, Madeleine. *Adieu l'amour*. Paris: Fayard, 1987.
Cherry, Kelly. "Not the Phil Donahue Show." *The Virginia Quarterly Review* 69 (Summer 1993), 408-23.
Chiodo, Andrew. "Autumn Chill." *Christopher Street* no. 116 (1987), 54-59.
Chiodo, Andrew. "Blaze." *Christopher Street* no. 103 (1986), 42-46.
Claiborne, Sybil. *In the Garden of Dead Cars*. San Francisco and Pittsburgh: Cleis Press, 1993.
Clendenen, Phil. *Sex and the Single Camel*. San Francisco: GLB Publishers, 1994.
Cliff, Michelle. *Bodies of Water*. New York: E. P. Dutton, 1990. See in particular the title story, "Bodies of Water."
Coben, Harlan. *Miracle Cure*. Latham, NY: British American Pub., 1991.
Coe, Christopher. *I Look Divine*. New York: Ticknor & Fields, 1987.
Coe, Christopher. *Such Times*. New York, San Diego, and London: Harcourt Brace & Co., 1993.
Cohen, Elizabeth. "Poison." *Christopher Street* no. 155 (1991), 35-36.

Cohen, Jaffe. "Just Got Off the Phone with Charlie." *The James White Review* 7 (1990), 14, 15, 7.

Cohen, Miriam. *Laura Leonora's 1st Amendment.* New York: Lodestar Books/ Dutton Child Books, 1990.

Collard, Cyril. *Savage Nights.* William Rodarmor, trans. Woodstock, NY: The Overlook Press, 1994 [London: Quartet Books, 1993]. [*Les Nuits fauves.* Paris: Flammarion, 1989.]

Cook, Robin. *Godplayer.* New York: G. P. Putnam's Sons, 1983.

Cook, Robin. *Outbreak.* New York: G. P. Putnam's Sons, 1987.

Cooper, Dennis. *Try.* New York: Grove Press, 1994. As Earl Jackson, Jr., "Death Drives Across Pornotopia: Dennis Cooper on the Extremities of Being," *GLQ* 1 (1994), 143-61, suggests, "the AIDS epidemic is often a non-explicit horizon of Cooper's writing" (143); that "horizon" becomes more explicit in Cooper's most recent novel, *Try.*

Corbin, Steven. *Fragments That Remain.* Boston: Alyson, 1993.

Corbin, Steven. *A Hundred Days from Now.* Boston: Alyson, 1994.

Coupland, Douglas. *Life After God.* New York: Pocket Books, 1994.

Crown, Judston. *The Search for Sebastian.* San Diego: Los Hombres Press, 1991.

Cuadros, Gil. *City of God.* San Francisco: City Lights, 1994.

Cunningham, Michael. *Flesh and Blood.* New York: Farrar, Straus and Giroux, 1995.

Cunningham, Michael. *A Home at the End of the World.* New York: Farrar, Straus and Giroux, 1990.

Currier, Jameson. *Dancing on the Moon: Short Stories About AIDS.* New York: Viking, 1993.

Curzon, Daniel. *The World Can Break Your Heart.* Stamford, CT: Knights Press, 1984.

D'Allesandro, Sam. *The Zombie Pit.* Freedom, CA: The Crossing Press, 1989.

Davis, Christopher. *The Boys in the Bars.* Stamford, CT: Knights Press, 1989.

Davis, Christopher. *Philadelphia.* New York: Bantam, 1993. Based on the screenplay by Ron Nyswaner.

Davis, Christopher. *Valley of the Shadow.* New York: St. Martin's Press, 1988.

Davis, Deborah. *My Brother Has AIDS.* New York: Atheneum, 1994.

Dawson, David Laing. *Double Blind.* New York: St. Martin's Press, 1991.

Dedrick, Lucas. "The Beach." *The James White Review* 7 (1990), 14.

Define, M. A. "You Can Say What You Want I'm Not Walking Out." *Christopher Street* no. 113 (1987), 56-59.

de la Pena, Terri. *Latin Satins.* Seattle: Seal Press, 1994.

Delany, Samuel R. *Flight from Neveryon*. New York: Bantam, 1985 [reissued Hanover, NH: Wesleyan University Press/University Press of New England, 1994]. See especially "The Tale of Plagues and Carnivals."

Delany, Samuel R. *The Mad Man*. New York: Richard Kasak Book/ Masquerade Books, 1994.

DeLuca, Virginia. "A Sister's Story." *Iowa Review* 21:2 (1991), 161-84.

Denisoff, Dennis. *Dog Years*. Vancouver, BC: Pulp Press, 1991.

Denisoff, Dennis, ed. *Queeries: An Anthology of Gay Male Prose*. Vancouver, BC: Arsenal Pulp Press, 1993.

Denneny, Michael, Charles Ortleb, and Thomas Steele, eds. *First Love/Last Love: New Fiction from Christopher Street*. New York: G. P. Putnam's Sons, 1985.

de Saint Phalle, Niki. *AIDS: You Can't Catch It Holding Hands*. San Francisco: Lapis Press, 1987.

Devore, Cynthia DiLaura. *A Week Past Forever*. Edina, MN: Abdo & Daughters, 1993.

D'Hondt, John. *The Bunny Book: A Novel for Anyone Who Believes Life & Death Are, After All, a Wonder*. San Francisco: GLB Publishers, 1991.

Diaman, N. A. *Castro Street Memories*. San Francisco: Persona Press, 1988.

Donnelly, Nisa. *The Love Songs of Phoenix Bay*. New York: St. Martin's Press, 1994.

Doumbi-Fakoly. *Certificat de contrôle anti-sida*. Paris: Editions Publisud, 1988.

Drake, Robert, ed., with Terry Wolverton. *His: Brilliant New Fiction by Gay Writers*. Boston: Faber & Faber, 1995.

Dunne, Dominick. *People Like Us*. New York: Crown, 1988.

Dunne, Gary. *As If Overnight*. Sydney: BlackWattle Press, 1990.

Dunne, Gary, ed. *A New Anthology of Fruit: Contemporary Australian Gay Writing*. Sydney: BlackWattle Press, 1994.

Dunne, Gary. *Shadows on the Dance Floor*. Sydney: BlackWattle Press, 1992.

Dunne, Gary, ed. *Traveling on Love in a Time of Uncertainty: Contemporary Australian Gay Fiction*. Sydney: BlackWattle Press, 1991.

Duplechan, Larry. *Captain Swing: A Love Story*. Boston: Alyson, 1993.

Duplechan, Larry. *Tangled Up in Blue*. New York: St. Martin's Press, 1989.

Durant, Penny Raife. *When Heroes Die*. New York: Atheneum, 1992.

Eidus, Janice. *Vito Loves Geraldine: A Collection of Stories*. San Francisco: City Lights, 1990 [1989].

Ennis, Catherine. *Chautauqua: A Romance*. Tallahassee, FL: Naiad Press, 1993.

Everett, Rupert. *Hello Darling, Are You Working?* New York: Morrow, 1992.

Exander, Max [= Paul Reed]. *Leathersex*. New York: Badboy/Masquerade Books, 1994.

Exander, Max [= Paul Reed]. *LoveSex*. Boston: Alyson, 1986.
Exander, Max [= Paul Reed]. *ManSex*. San Francisco: Gay Sunshine Press, 1985.
Exander, Max [= Paul Reed]. *SafeStud*. Boston: Alyson, 1985.
Fast, Howard. *The Dinner Party*. New York: Houghton Mifflin, 1987.
Feinberg, David B. *Eighty-Sixed*. New York: Viking, 1989.
Feinberg, David B. *Spontaneous Combustion*. New York: Viking, 1991.
Fernandez, Dominique. *La Gloire du paria*. Paris: B. Grasset, 1987.
Ferrell, Anderson. *Home for the Day*. New York: Knopf, 1994.
Ferro, Robert. *Second Son*. New York: Crown, 1988.
Fisher, Carrie. *Delusions of Grandma*. New York: Simon & Schuster, 1994.
Forrest, Katherine V. *Flashpoint*. Tallahassee, FL: Naiad Press, 1994.
Fox, Paula. *The Eagle Kite*. New York: Orchard Books, 1995.
Gambone, Philip. *The Language We Use Up Here and Other Stories*. New York: E. P. Dutton, 1991.
Gervais, Paul. *Extraordinary People*. New York: HarperCollins, 1991.
Gifford, Barry. *Night People*. New York: Grove Press, 1992. Continued in *Arise and Walk* (New York: Hyperion, 1994).
Gilligan, Sharon. *Danger in High Places: An Alix Nicholson Mystery*. Huntington Station, NY: Rising Tide, 1993. The sequel to this novel is *Danger!—Cross Currents: An Alix Nicholson Mystery* (Huntington Station, NY: Rising Tide, 1994).
Girard, Linda Walvoord. *Alex, The Kid with AIDS*. Morton Grove, IL: Albert Whitman, 1991.
Gleitzman, Morris. *Two Weeks with the Queen*. New York: G. P. Putnam's Sons, 1991.
Glück, Robert. *Jack the Modernist*. New York: A Sea Horse Book/Gay Presses of New York, 1985.
Glück, Robert. *Margery Kempe*. New York and London: High Risk Books/Serpent's Tail, 1994.
Goldstein, ed. *More Like Minds*. London: GMP, 1991.
Graham, Clayton R. [= Larry Ebmeier]. *Tweeds*. Stamford, CT: Knights Press, 1987.
Granit, Robert. *Another Runner in the Night*. New York: A & W Publishers, 1981. A novel about a sexually transmitted cancer.
Greene, Harlan. *What the Dead Remember*. New York: E. P. Dutton, 1991.
Greyson, John. *Urinal and Other Stories*. Art Metropole.
Groff, David. "Labor Day." *Christopher Street* no. 119 (1988), 36-43.
Guibert, Hervé. *The Compassion Protocol*. James Kirkup, trans. New York: George Braziller, 1994. [*Le Protocole compassionnel*. Paris: Gallimard, 1991.]

Guibert, Hervé. *The Gangsters* [*Les Gangsters*]. Iain White, trans. London: Serpent's Tail, 1991 [1988].

Guibert, Hervé. *The Man in the Red Hat*. James Kirkup, trans. London: Quartet Books, 1993. [*L'Homme au chapeau rouge*. Paris: Gallimard, 1992.]

Guibert, Hervé. *To the Friend Who Did Not Save My Life*. Linda Coverdale, trans. New York: Atheneum, 1991 [New York: High Risk Books/Serpent's Tail, 1994]. [*A l'ami qui ne m'a pas sauvé la vie*. Paris: Gallimard, 1990.]

Hall, Brian. *The Dreamers*. New York: Harper & Row, 1989.

Hall, Richard. *Fidelities: A Book of Stories*. New York: Viking, 1992.

Hallasy, Paul. *New York Trilogy*. New York: Downtown Press, 1990.

Hallasy, Paul. *Nostalgia*. New York: Downtown Press, 1993.

Halliday, Mikey. *Daisychain: A Collection of Short Stories*. Washington, DC: Queer Associated Press, 1995.

Hansen, Joseph. *A Country of Old Men: The Last Dave Brandstetter Mystery*. New York: Viking, 1991.

Hansen, Joseph. *Early Graves: A Dave Brandstetter Mystery*. New York: The Mysterious Press, 1987.

Hardy, James Earl. *B-Boy Blues*. Boston: Alyson, 1994.

Harris, E. Lynn. *Invisible Life*. Atlanta: Consortium Press, 1991; New York: Anchor Books/Doubleday, 1994.

Harris, E. Lynn. *Just As I Am*. New York: Doubleday, 1994.

Harvey, Andrew. *Burning Houses*. Boston: Houghton Mifflin, 1986.

Hayes, Mary-Rose. *Amethyst*. New York: E. P. Dutton, 1989.

Heim, Scott. *Mysterious Skin*. New York: HarperCollins, 1995.

Hershman, Marcie. *Safe in America*. New York: HarperCollins, 1995.

Highwater, Jamake. *Kill Hole*. New York: Grove Press, 1992.

Hite, Molly. *Breach of Immunity*. New York: St. Martin's Press, 1992.

Hoban, Gordan. *Excaibo*. Kukuihaele, HI: Omniun Publishing, 1992.

Hocquenghem, Guy. *Eve*. Paris: Albin Michel, 1987.

Hoctel, Patrick. "Slave of Babylon." *The James White Review* 4 (1986), 12-13.

Hoffman, Alice. *At Risk*. New York: G. P. Putnam's Sons, 1988.

Holleran, Andrew. "Homosexuality, Part Two." *Christopher Street* no. 119 (1988), 4-7.

Holleran, Andrew. "How to Cruise Outer Space." *Christopher Street* no. 100 (1986), 13-16.

Holleran, Andrew. *Nights in Aruba*. New York: Morrow, 1983 [New York: Plume, 1984].

Hollinghurst, Alan. *The Folding Star*. New York: Pantheon Books, 1994.

Hollinghurst, Alan. *The Swimming Pool Library*. New York: Random House, 1988. For a discussion of this novel in the context of the AIDS crisis, see Dellamora, *Apocalyptic Overtures*, 173-91.

Holloway, Michael B. *Empath*. San Diego: Paradigm, 1993.
Home, Steward. *Red London*. Edinburgh: AK Press, 1994.
Homes, A. M. *The Safety of Objects*. New York and London: W. W. Norton, 1990. "The 'I' of It" is the one story in the collection that concerns AIDS.
Humphreys, Martha. *Until Whatever*. New York: Clarion Books, 1991.
Hunt, Angela Elwell. *A Dream to Cherish*. Wheaton, IL: Tyndale House, 1992.
Huston, Bo. *The Dream Life*. New York: St. Martin's Press, 1992.
Huston, Bo. *Horse and Other Stories*. New York: Amethyst Press, 1989.
Huston, Bo. *The Listener: A Novella and Other Stories*. New York: St. Martin's Press, 1993.
Huston, Bo. *Remember Me*. New York: Amethyst Press, 1991.
Indiana, Gary. *Gone Tomorrow*. New York: Pantheon Books, 1993.
Indiana, Gary. *Horse Crazy*. New York: Grove Press, 1989.
Indiana, Gary. *Rent Boy*. New York and London: High Risk Books/Serpent's Tail, 1994.
Ireland, Timothy. *The Novice*. London: GMP, 1988.
Ireland, Timothy. *A Time to Burn*. London: GMP, 1992.
Jacobson, Erika Antigone. *The Unknown*. Leicester, MA: Dytiscid Press, 1994.
Jaffe, Harold. *Eros: Anti-Eros*. San Francisco: City Lights, 1990.
Jennings, Bud. "Eric Back in Boston." *Christopher Street* no. 129 (1988), 22-36.
Johnson, Fenton. *Scissors, Paper, Rock*. New York: Pocket Books, 1993.
Johnson, Greg. *A Friendly Deceit*. Baltimore and London: Johns Hopkins University Press, 1992.
Johnson, Greg. *Pagan Babies*. New York: Plume, 1994 [New York: E. P. Dutton, 1993].
Johnson, Toby [= Edwin Clark Johnson]. *Plague: A Novel about Healing*. Boston: Alyson, 1987.
Johnson, Toby [= Edwin Clark Johnson]. *Secret Matter*. South Norwalk, CT: Lavender Press, 1990.
Jordan, MaryKate. *Losing Uncle Tim*. Illustrated by Judith Friedman. Morton Grove, IL: Albert Whitman, 1989.
Joseph, Bertram H. *One-Way Passage*. Jerusalem: Good Times, 1988.
Jurrist, Charles, ed. *Shadows of Love: American Gay Fiction*. Boston: Alyson, 1988.
Katz, Illana. *Uncle Jimmy*. Northridge, CA: Real Life Storybooks, 1993.
Kaye, Marilyn. *Real Heroes*. San Diego, New York, and London: Harcourt Brace Jovanovich, 1993.
Kellendonk, Frans. *Mystiek lichaam* [*The Mystical Body*]. Amsterdam: Meulenhoff, 1986. On Kellendonk's novel, see Gert Hekma, "*The Mystical

Body: Frans Kellendonk and the Dutch Literary Response to AIDS," in Nelson, ed., *AIDS: The Literary Response*, 88-94. A book about Kellendonk's novel has also been published (though I have not been able to examine it): P. Kralt. *Frans Kellendonk, Mystiek lichaam*. Laren, Netherlands: Walva-Boek, 1988.

Kerr, M. E. *Night Kites*. New York: Harper & Row, 1986.

Kertess, Klaus. Nan Goldin, photographs. *Desire by Numbers*. San Francisco: Artspace Books, 1994.

Killian, Kevin. *Bedrooms Have Windows*. New York: Amethyst Press, 1989.

Kirkup, James. *Queens Have Died Young and Fair: A Fable of the Immediate Future*. London: Peter Owen, 1993.

Klass, Perri. *Other Women's Children*. New York: Random House, 1990.

Koertge, Ron. *The Arizona Kid*. Boston: Joy Street/Little, Brown, 1988.

Kondolean, Harry. *Diary of a Lost Boy*. New York: Knopf, 1994.

Krauth, Nigel. *JF Was Here*. Sydney: Allen & Unwin, 1990.

Kringle, Karen. *Vital Ties*. Minneapolis: Spinsters Ink, 1992.

Kyle, Garland Richard. *Whatever Happened to Passion? Writings from the Epidemic Years*. San Francisco: Modern Words, 1992.

Kyle, Stephen. *Fine Lines and Other Stories*. Spectrum Press, 1995. Book on disk.

Labelle, Maurice. *Noah's Ark II: Mankind's Last Chance*. Miami: Magic City Pub., 1994.

Lassell, Michael. *The Hard Way*. New York: Richard Kasak Book/Masquerade Books, 1995.

Latzky, Eric. *Three Views from Vertical Cliffs*. New York: Amethyst Press, 1991.

Lawrence, Sean. "The New York Chronicle." *Christopher Street* no. 123 (1988), 48-51.

Leavitt, David. *Equal Affections*. New York: Weidenfeld & Nicolson, 1989. See Brooks and Murphy, "Annotated Bibliography," 325, for one rationale for including this novel in a listing of AIDS fiction.

Leavitt, David. *A Place I've Never Been*. New York: Viking, 1990.

Leavitt, David, and Mark Mitchell, eds. *The Penguin Book of Short Stories*. New York: Viking, 1994.

Lee, Johann S. *Peculiar Chris*. Singapore: Cannon International, 1992.

Lemon, Brendan. "Female Trouble." *Christopher Street* no. 116 (1987), 48-52.

Lemon, Brendan. "Positive Results." *Christopher Street* no. 114 (1987), 22-24.

Leventhal, Stan. *Candy Holidays and Other Short Fictions*. Austin, TX: Banned Books, 1991.

Leventhal, Stan. *Mountain Climbing in Sheridan Square*. Austin, TX: Banned Books, 1988.

Leventhal, Stan. *Skydiving on Christopher Street*. New York: Hard Candy/ Masquerade Books, 1995.
Levy, Marilyn. *Rumors and Whispers*. New York: Fawcett, 1990.
Lindau, Joan [= Joan Alden]. *Letting in the Night*. Ithaca: Firebrand, 1989.
Magida, Daniel L. *The Rules of Seduction*. Boston: Houghton Mifflin, 1992.
Mains, Geoff. *Gentle Warriors*. Stamford, CT: Knights Press, 1989.
Manley, Joey. *The Death of Donna-May Dean*. New York: St. Martin's Press, 1991.
Manrique, Jaime. *Latin Moon in Manhattan*. New York: St. Martin's Press, 1992.
Mars-Jones, Adam, ed. *Mae West Is Dead: Recent Lesbian and Gay Fiction*, revised ed. London: Faber & Faber, 1987 [1983]. The revised edition adds Mars-Jones's story about AIDS, "Slim."
Mars-Jones, Adam. *Monopolies of Loss*. New York: Knopf, 1993 [London: Faber & Faber, 1992].
Mars-Jones, Adam. *The Waters of Thirst*. New York: Knopf, 1994 [London: Faber & Faber, 1993].
Martin, Herbert Woodward. "The Last Days of William Short." *The James White Review* 6 (1988), 8-9.
Martin, Kenneth. *Billy's Brother*. London: GMP, 1989; Boston: Alyson, 1989.
Martinac, Paula. *Home Movies*. Seattle: Seal Press, 1993.
Maso, Carole. *The Art Lover*. San Francisco: North Point Press, 1990.
Matousek, Mark. "The Last Song." *Christopher Street* no. 112 (1987), 30-34.
Maupin, Armistead. *Babycakes*. New York: Harper & Row, 1984.
Maupin, Armistead. *Significant Others*. New York: Harper & Row, 1987.
Maupin, Armistead. *Sure of You*. New York: Harper & Row, 1989.
Mayes, James Russell. *Small Favors*. Boston: Alyson, 1994.
Mayes, Sharon. *Immune*. St. Paul, MN: New Rivers Press, 1988.
McBain, Ed. *The House That Jack Built*. New York: The Mysterious Press, 1988.
McCauley, Stephen. *The Easy Way Out*. New York: Simon & Schuster, 1992.
McCourt, James. *Time Remaining*. New York: Knopf, 1993.
McDaniel, Lurlane. *Baby Alicia Is Dying*. New York: Bantam, 1993.
McFarland, Dennis. "Nothing to Ask For." *The New Yorker* 25 Sept. 1989, 55-62.
McGehee, Peter. *Boys Like Us*. New York: St. Martin's Press, 1991. On McGehee's and Doug Wilson's fiction, see the review essay by Greg Bartholomew, "Homage to a Pair of Dead Boys," in *The James White Review* 11:4 (Summer 1994), 16-17.
McGehee, Peter. *The I.Q. Zoo*. Regina, Saskatchewan: Coteau Books, 1991.
McGehee, Peter. *Sweetheart*. New York: St. Martin's Press, 1992.
McKague, Thomas R. "Testimony." *The James White Review* 4 (1987), 6.

McMullan, Margaret. *When Warhol Was Still Alive*. Freedom, CA: The Crossing Press, 1994.

McWilliam, Candia. *A Case of Knives*. London: Bloomsbury, 1988; New York: Beech Tree Books, 1988. See the discussion in Mandy Merck, "A Case of AIDS."

Miklowitz, Gloria. *Good-bye Tomorrow*. New York: Delacorte Press, 1987.

Mills, Joe. "Long to Go." *Oranges and Lemons*. Exeter: Third House, 1987.

Mitchell, Larry. *Acid Snow: A Novel*. East Haven, CT: Calamus Books/Inland Book Co., 1993.

Mitchell, Larry. *My Life as a Mole and Five Other Stories*. New York: Calamus Books, 1988.

Mitchell, Mark, ed. *The Penguin Book of International Gay Writing*. New York: Viking, 1995.

Moffett, Judith. "Tiny Tango." *Isaac Asimov: Science Fiction* (Feb. 1989), 16-65. Rpt. in Gardner Dozois, ed. *The Year's Best Science Fiction: Seventh Annual Collection*. New York: St. Martin's Press, 1990. 2-39.

Monette, Paul. *Afterlife*. New York: Crown, 1990.

Monette, Paul. *Halfway Home*. New York: Crown, 1991.

Moore, Oscar. *A Matter of Life and Sex*. New York: E. P. Dutton, 1992 [London: Paper Drum, 1991].

Moore, Patrick. *This Every Night*. New York: Amethyst Press, 1990.

Mooser, Ron, ed. *Dit verval. Verhalen rond een grote ziekte met een kleine naam* [*This Decay: Stories of a Big Disease with a Small Name*]. Amsterdam: De Woelrat, 1988.

Morales, Alejandro. *The Rag Doll Plagues*. Houston: Arte Publico Press, 1992.

Mordden, Ethan. *Everybody Loves You: Further Adventures in Gay Manhattan*. New York: St. Martin's Press, 1988.

Mordden, Ethan. *How Long Has This Been Going On?* New York: Villard Books, 1995.

Mordden, Ethan, ed. *Waves: An Anthology of New Gay Fiction*. New York: Vintage/Random House, 1994.

Muñoz, Elias Miguel. *The Greatest Performance*. Houston: Arte Publico Press, 1991.

Murphy, Haughton. *Murder Keeps a Secret: A Reuben Frost Mystery*. New York: Simon & Schuster, 1989.

Musto, Michael. *Manhattan on the Rocks*. New York: Henry Holt and Company, 1989.

Nava, Michael, ed. *Finale: Short Stories of Mystery and Suspense*. Boston: Alyson, 1989.

Nava, Michael. *Goldenboy*. Boston: Alyson, 1988.

Nava, Michael. *The Hidden Law*. New York: HarperCollins, 1992.

Nava, Micahel. *How Town: A Novel of Suspense*. New York: Harper & Row, 1990.

Navarre, Yves. *Ce sont amis que vent emporte*. Paris: Flammarion, 1991.

Navarre, Yves. *La Terrasse des audiences au moment de l'adieu*. Montreal: Leméac, 1990.

Neale, Jonathan. *The Laughter of Heroes*. London and New York: Serpent's Tail, 1993.

Nelson, Theresa. *Earthshine*. New York: Orchard Books, 1994.

Nestle, Joan, and Naomi Holoch, eds. *Women on Women 2*. New York: Plume, 1993. See in particular the stories by Brown and Moraga.

Nevai, Lucia. "Close." *The New Yorker* 7 Nov. 1988, 36-39.

Newman, Lesléa. *Every Woman's Dream*. Norwich, VT: New Victoria Publishers, 1994.

Newman, Lesléa. *Too Far Away to Touch*. New York: Clarion Books, 1995.

Nonas, Elisabeth. *A Room Full of Women*. Tallahassee, FL: Naiad Press, 1990.

Obejas, Achy. *We Came All the Way from Cuba So You Could Dress Like This?* San Francisco and Pittsburgh: Cleis Press, 1994.

Oliver, Jim. *Closing Distance*. New York: G. P. Putnam's Sons, 1992.

Olshan, Joseph. *Nightswimmer*. New York: Simon & Schuster, 1994.

Olshan, Joseph. *The Sound of Heaven*. London: Bloomsbury, 1992.

Olson, Donald S. *Paradise Gardens*. Stamford, CT: Knights Press, 1988.

Osborn, Christopher. *A Sense of Touch*. New York: Harper & Row, 1989.

Pancrazi, Jean-Noël. *Vagabond Winter*. James Kirkup, trans. London: Quartet Books, 1992. [*Les Quartiers d'hiver*. Paris: Gallimard, 1990.]

Peck, Dale. *Martin and John*. New York: Farrar, Straus and Giroux, 1993.

Persky, Stan. *Buddy's: Meditations on Desire*. Vancouver, BC: New Star Books, 1989.

Picano, Felice. *Like People in History*. New York: Viking, 1995.

Pilcher, Darryl, ed. *Certain Voices: Short Stories about Gay Men*. Boston: Alyson, 1991.

Platt, Richard, and Orah Platt. *Letting Blood*. New York: St. Martin's Press, 1989.

Plunket, Robert. *Love Junkie*. New York: HarperCollins, 1992.

Pollack, Eileen. *Whisper Whisper Jesse, Whisper Whisper Josh: A Story about AIDS*. Cambridge, MA: Advantage/Aurora, 1992.

Porte, Barbara Ann. *Something Terrible Happened*. New York: Orchard Books, 1994.

Powell, Patricia. *A Small Gathering of Bones*. Caribbean Writers Series. Oxford and Portsmouth, NH: Heinemann, 1994.

Preston, John, ed. *Flesh and the Word: An Anthology of Erotic Writing*. New York: Plume, 1992.

Preston, John, ed. *Flesh and the Word 2: An Anthology of Erotic Writing.* New York: Plume, 1993.
Preston, John, ed., with Michael Lowenthal. *Flesh and the Word 3: An Anthology of Gay Erotic Writing.* New York: Plume, 1995.
Preston, John, ed. *Hot Living: Erotic Stories About Safer Sex.* Boston: Alyson, 1985.
Price, Reynolds. *The Promise of Rest.* New York: Scribner, 1995.
Publicover, Robert. *My Unicorn Has Gone Away: Life, Death, Grief and Living in the Years of AIDS.* Somerville, MA: Powder House Publishing, 1993.
Puccia, Joseph. *The Holy Spirit Dance Club.* N.p.: Liberty Press, 1988.
Puckett, Andrew. *Bloodstains.* Garden City, NY: Doubleday/Crime Club, 1989 [1987].
Purdy, James. *Garments the Living Wear.* San Francisco: City Lights, 1989.
Quinlan, Patricia. *Tiger Flowers.* New York: Dial Books for Young Readers, 1994.
Raphael, Lev. *Dancing on Tisha B'Av.* New York: St. Martin's Press, 1990.
Real, Philip. "Stronger and Stronger." *The James White Review* 5 (1988), 1.
Redon, Joel. *Bloodstream.* Stamford, CT: Knights Press, 1988.
Reed, Paul. *Facing It: A Novel of A.I.D.S.* San Francisco: Gay Sunshine Press, 1984.
Reed, Paul. *Longing.* Berkeley: Celestial Arts, 1988.
Rees, David. *The Colour of His Hair.* Exeter: Third House, 1989.
Rees, David. *Flux.* London: Third House, 1988.
Rees, David. *Letters to Dorothy.* Exeter: Third House, 1990.
Rees, David. *The Wrong Apple.* Stamford, CT: Knights Press, 1987.
Rees, David, and Peter Robins, eds. *The Freezer Counter: Stories by Gay Men.* Exeter: Third House, 1989.
Rees, David, Peter Robins, and Dave Royle, eds. *Fabulous Tricks: Stories by Gay Men.* Exeter: Third House, 1992.
Rees, Geoffrey. *Sex with Strangers.* New York: Farrar, Straus and Giroux, 1993.
Reidinger, Paul. *Good Boys.* New York: E. P. Dutton, 1993.
Rickets, Wendell, "Wasps." *The James White Review* 7 (1989), 14-15.
Rinaldi, Angelo. *La Confession dans les collines.* Paris: Gallimard, 1990.
Roper, Gayle G. *The Puzzle of the Poison Pen.* Elgin, IL: Chariot Books, 1994.
Rosario, John. "Lovers Anonymous." *The James White Review* 7 (1989), 8-9.
Royle, Dave. *Pleasing the Punters.* Exeter: Third House, 1990.
Rubin, Marty. *The Boiled Frog Syndrome: A Novel of Love, Sex and Politics.* Boston: Alyson, 1987.
Rudy, Sam. "Sheet Music." *The James White Review* 6 (1989), 8-9.

Rule, Jane. *Memory Board*. Tallahassee, FL: Naiad Press, 1987.
Rumaker, Michael. *To Kill a Cardinal*. N.p.: Arthur Mann Kaye, 1992.
Russell, Paul. *Boys of Life*. New York: E. P. Dutton, 1991.
Russell, Paul. *The Salt Point*. New York: E. P. Dutton, 1990.
Russell, Paul. *Sea of Tranquillity*. New York: E. P. Dutton, 1994.
Ryman, Geoff. *The Child Garden*. New York: St. Martin's Press, 1990. Depicts a world in which knowledge is transmitted virally.
Ryman, Geoff. *Was*. New York: Knopf, 1992.
Sadownick, Douglas. *Sacred Lips of the Bronx*. New York: St. Martin's Press, 1994.
Sanford, Doris. *David Has AIDS*. Portland, OR: Multnomah, 1989.
Schmidt, Mary M. *Persephone's Song*. San Diego: Los Hombres Press, 1992.
Schulman, Sarah. *Empathy*. New York: E. P. Dutton, 1992.
Schulman, Sarah. *People in Trouble*. New York: E. P. Dutton, 1990.
Schulman, Sarah. *Rat Bohemia*. New York: E. P. Dutton, 1995.
Scott, Darieck. *Traitor to the Race*. New York: E. P. Dutton, 1995.
Scott, Tom. *The Devil in Men's Dreams*. San Francisco: GLB Publishers, 1992.
Scott, Whitney. *Dancing to the End of the Shining Bar: A Novel of Love and Courage in a Time of AIDS*. Crete, IL: Outrider Press, 1994.
Searle, Elizabeth. *My Body to You*. Iowa City: University of Iowa Press, 1993.
Sher, Antony. *The Indoor Boy*. New York: Viking, 1992 [1991].
Soles, Caro, ed. *Meltdown! An Anthology of Erotic Science Fiction and Dark Fantasy for Gay Men*. New York: Richard Kasak Book/Masquerade Books, 1994.
Sontag, Susan. "The Way We Live Now." *The New Yorker* 24 Nov. 1986, 42-51. Published also as a separate volume: New York: Noonday Press, 1991, with etchings by Howard Hodgkin.
Spinrad, Norman. "Journals of the Plague Years." In Lou Aronica and Shawna McCarthy, eds. *Full Spectrum*. New York: Bantam Spectra, 1988.
Sprecher, Lorrie. *Sister Safety Pin*. Ithaca: Firebrand, 1994.
Srivastava, Atima. *Transmission*. London: Serpent's Tail, 1992 [1991].
Stambolian, George, ed. *Men on Men: Best New Gay Fiction, Men on Men 2: Best New Gay Fiction, Men on Men 3: Best New Gay Fiction, Men on Men 4: Best New Gay Fiction*. New York: Plume, 1986, 1988, 1990, 1992. The series has continued under the editorship of David Bergman.
Starkman, Neal. *I Used to Be Afraid*. Seattle: Comprehensive Health Education Foundation, 1995.
Starkman, Neal. *Z's Gift*. Seattle: Comprehensive Health Education Foundation, 1991.

Steinke, Darcey. *Suicide Blonde.* New York: Washington Square Press/Simon & Schuster, 1992. This novel is interesting in particular for its depiction of bisexuality.
Stephens, Jack. *Triangulation.* New York: Crown, 1989.
Sweet, Robert Burdette. *White Sambo: A Novel in Stories.* San Francisco: GLB Publishers, 1993.
Thomson, Robert. *Secret Things: A Collection of Shorter Stories.* Toronto: Immediate Press, 1994.
Tondelli, Pier Vittorio. *Separate Rooms.* London and New York: Serpent's Tail, 1992. [*Camere separate.* Milan: Bompiani, 1989.]
Trachtenberg, Paul. *Ben's Exit.* Cherry Valley, NY: Cherry Valley Editions, 1994.
Turnbull, Peter. *Two Way Cut.* New York: St. Martin's Press, 1988.
Updike, John. *Rabbit at Rest.* New York: Knopf, 1990.
Uyemoto, Holly. *Rebel Without a Clue.* New York: Crown, 1989.
Vallejos, Tomás. *Our Man of Earth and Sea: The Collected Works of Tomás Vallejos.* N.p.: House of Coleman, 1991.
Verghese, Abraham. "Lilacs." *The New Yorker* 14 Oct. 1991, 53-58.
Verniero, Joan. *You Can Call Me Willy: A Story for Children about AIDS.* New York: Magination Press, 1995.
Vilmure, Daniel. *Toby's Lie.* New York: Simon & Schuster, 1995.
Wakefield, Tom, ed. *Ten Commandments.* London and New York: Serpent's Tail, 1992.
Wakefield, Tom, Patrick Gale, and Francis King. *Secret Lives: Three Novellas.* London and New York: Serpent's Tail, 1992 [1991].
Warburton, Richard. "Disappearances." *Christopher Street* no. 132 (1989), 35-42.
Warmbold, Jean. *June Mail.* Sag Harbor, NY: Permanent Press, 1986; New York: Jove, 1988.
Warner, Sharon Oard. *Learning to Dance and Other Stories.* Minneapolis: New Rivers Press, 1992.
Warner, Sharon Oard, ed. *The Way We Write Now: Short Stories from the AIDS Crisis.* Secaucus, NJ: Carol Pub. Group, 1995.
Warren, Patricia Nell. *Harlan's Race.* Beverly Hills: Wildcat Press, 1994.
Weeks, Sarah. *Red Ribbon.* New York: Laura Geringer Book, 1995.
Weir, John. *The Irreversible Decline of Eddie Socket.* New York: Harper & Row, 1989.
Weir, John. "What I Did Wrong." *Word: The Literary Magazine* no. 1 (June 1995), 39-42. Excerpt from a novel in progress.
Wells, Peter. *Dangerous Desires.* New York: Viking, 1994 [Birkenhead, Auckland: Reed Books, 1991].

Weltner, Peter. *Beachside Entries/Specific Ghosts*. San Francisco: Five Fingers Press, 1989.

Weltner, Peter. *In a Time of Combat for the Angel: Three Short Novels*. San Francisco: Five Fingers Press, 1991. Though not directly about AIDS, the fiction in this volume addresses death and illness in ways clearly informed by the AIDS crisis.

White, Edmund, ed. *The Faber Book of Gay Short Fiction*. London and Boston: Faber & Faber, 1991.

White, Edmund. *Skinned Alive: Stories*. New York: Knopf, 1995.

White, Edmund, and Adam Mars-Jones. *The Darker Proof: Stories from a Crisis*. New York: Plume, 1988.

White, Michael. *Gangsters by Day, Girls by Night*. Sydney: BlackWattle Press, 1990.

Whitlock, Dean. "On the Death of Daniel." *The Magazine of Fantasy and Science Fiction* March 1991, 26-42.

Wiley, Christopher. "Slippers." *The James White Review* 7 (1987), 12.

Willkie, Phil, and Greg Baysans, eds. *The Gay Nineties: An Anthology of Contemporary Gay Fiction*. Freedom, CA: The Crossing Press, 1991.

Willocks, Tim. *Green River Rising*. New York: Morrow, 1994.

Wilson, Doug. *Labour of Love*. New York: St. Martin's Press, 1993. This completes the trilogy of Peter McGehee's novels begun with *Boys Like Us* and *Sweetheart*.

Wolfe, Tom. *The Bonfire of the Vanities*. New York: Farrar, Straus and Giroux, 1987 [New York: Bantam, 1988].

Wolverton, Terry, and Robert Drake, eds. *Indivisible: New Short Fiction by Gay and Lesbian West Coast Writers*. New York: Plume, 1991.

Woolaston, Graeme. *The Learning of Paul O'Neill*. Brighton: Millivres, 1993. The death of the title character's lover (from a heart ailment) is placed in explicit relation to AIDS.

Wydra, Frank. *The Cure*. New York: Dell, 1992.

Zahava, Irene, ed. *Lavender Mansions: 40 Contemporary Lesbian and Gay Short Stories*. Boulder, CO, and Oxford: Westview Press, 1994.

POETRY

Aaab-Richards, Dirg, Craig G. Harris, Essex Hemphill, Isaac Jackson, and Assotto Saint. *Tongues Untied*. London: GMP, 1987.

Abbott, Steve. *The Lives of the Poets*. San Francisco: Black Star Press, 1987.

Alarcón, Francisco X. *Body in Flames/Cuerpo en Llamas*. Francisco Aragon, trans. San Francisco: Chronicle Books, 1990.

Alarcón, Francisco X. *No Golden Gate for Us*. Santa Fe: Pennywhistle Press, 1993.

Alargin, Miguel, and Bob Holman, eds. *Aloud: Voices from the Nuyorican Poets Cafe*. New York: A John Macrae Book/Henry Holt and Company, 1994.

Almond, Marc. *The Angel of Death in the Adonis Lounge*. London: GMP, 1988.

Ambler, Sam. *After the Howl and Other Poems*. Berkeley: Wingfinger Press, 1989.

Ameen, Mark. *The Buried Body: A Trilogy*. New York: Amethyst Press, 1990.

Ameen, Mark, Carl Morse, and Charles Ortleb. *Three New York Poets*. London: GMP, 1987.

Anderson, Jack. *Field Trips on the Rapid Transit*. Brooklyn: Hanging Loose Press, 1990.

Anderson, Lori. *Cultivating Excess*. Portland, OR: The Eighth Mountain Press, 1992.

Anthony, Steve, ed. *Of Eros and of Dust*. London: The Oscars Press, 1992.

Ash, John. *The Burnt Pages*. New York: Random House, 1991.

Baker, Rob. *The Art of AIDS: From Stigma to Conscience*. New York: Continuum, 1994.

Bawer, Bruce. *Coast to Coast*. Brownsville, OR: Story Line Press, 1993.

Beatty, Christine. *Misery Loves Company*. San Francisco: Glamazon Press, 1993.

Becker, Bill. *An Intimate Desire to Survive*. Bryn Mawr, PA: Dorrance, 1985.

Bergman, David. *The Care and Treatment of Pain*. Lawrence, KS: Kairos Editions, 1994.

Blaser, Robin. *The Holy Forest*. Toronto: Coach House Press, 1993.

Blaski, Steven. *Keep the Killer Asleep*. Durham: Carolina Wren Press, 1994.

Bolduc, David. *Shards*. Toth Press, 1995.

Borawski, Walta. *Lingering in a Silk Shirt*. Boston: Fag Rag Books, 1994.

Bory, William. *Orpheus in His Underwear*. New York: Cythoera Press, 1993.

Boucheron, Robert. *Epitaphs for the Plague Dead*. New York: Ursus Press, 1985.

Bradstock, Margaret. *Flight of Koalas*. Sydney: BlackWattle Press, 1992.

Brass, Perry. *Sex-Charge*. Ridgefield, CT: Belhue Press, 1991.

Brock, Craig. *Everything Is Dirt and Dirt Is Very Heavy*. No publication information is provided in this chapbook.

Broumas, Olga. *Perpetua*. Port Townsend, WA: Copper Canyon Press, 1989.

Campo, Rafael. "AIDS and the Poetry of Healing." *Kenyon Review* n.s. 15:4 (Fall 1993), 93-105. A narrative essay followed by six poems.

Campo, Rafael. *The Other Man Was Me: A Voyage to the New World*. Houston: Arte Publico Press, 1994.

Carroll, Jim. *Fear of Dreaming: The Selected Poems of Jim Carroll*. New York: Penguin, 1993.

Cassells, Cyrus. *Soul Make a Path through Shouting*. Port Townsend, WA: Copper Canyon Press, 1994.
Ciscel, Dennis. *Tiny Stories*. Austin, TX: Plain View Press, 1992.
Claire, Thomas. *Songs of Surrender*. Santa Barbara: Fithian Press, 1991.
Cook, Carl. *Postscripts*. Sicklerville, NJ: Vega Press, 1994.
Cook, Carl. *The Tranquil Lake of Love*. Sicklerville, NJ: Vega Press, 1993.
Cooper, Dennis. *Dream Police: Selected Poems, 1969-1993*. New York: Grove Press, 1995.
Corn, Alfred. *Autobiographies*. New York: Penguin, 1992.
Cory, Jim. *Wife*. Philadelphia: Insight to Riot Press, 1993.
Cranfield, Steve, and Martin Humphries. *Salt and Honey*. London: GMP, 1989.
Cuadros, Gil. *City of God*. San Francisco: City Lights, 1994.
Daniels, Peter. *Be Prepared*. Huddersfield, UK: Smith/Doorstop, 1994.
Daniels, Peter, ed. *Take Any Train: A Book of Gay Men's Poetry*. London: The Oscars Press, 1990.
Daniels, Peter, and Steve Anthony, eds. *Jugular Defences: An AIDS Anthology*. London: The Oscars Press, 1994.
Daniels, Peter, Kieron Devlin, and Kenneth King. *Breakfast in Bed*. London: The Oscars Press, 1987.
Denisoff, Dennis. *Tender Agencies*. Vancouver, BC: Arsenal Pulp Press, 1994.
Dent, Tory. *What Silence Equals*. New York: Persea, 1993.
Detrez, Conrad. *William Cliff*. Paris: Le Dilettante, 1990.
Dillard, Gavin Geoffrey. *The Naked Poet: Poems from 1970 to 1985*. Beverly Hills: Bhakti Books, 1989.
Dillard, Gavin Geoffrey. *Pagan Love Songs*. Beverly Hills: Bhakti Books, 1987.
Dillard, Gavin Geoffrey. *Yellow Snow and Other Poems*. Beverly Hills: Bhakti Books, 1993.
Dixon, Melvin. *Love's Instruments*. Elizabeth Alexander, ed. Announced as forthcoming.
Dlugos, Tim. *Powerless*. Announced as forthcoming.
Dlugos, Tim. *Strong Place*. New York: Amethyst Press, 1992.
Doty, Mark. *Bethlehem in Broad Daylight*. Boston: David R. Godine, 1991.
Doty, Mark. *My Alexandria*. Urbana and Chicago: University of Illinois Press, 1993.
Doty, Mark. *Turtle, Swan*. Boston: David R. Godine, 1987.
Eggan, Ferd. *Your LIFE Story By Someone Else*. Chicago: Editorial Coqui, 1989.
Field, Edward. *Counting Myself Lucky: Selected Poems 1963-1992*. Santa Rosa, CA: Black Sparrow, 1992.

Freistadt, Berta, and Pat O'Brien, eds. *Language of Water, Language of Fire: A Celebration of Lesbian and Gay Poetry*. London: The Oscars Press, 1992.
Fries, Kenny. *Anesthesia*. Announced as forthcoming.
Fries, Kenny. *The Healing Notebooks*. Berkeley: Open Books, 1990.
Gallagher, Denis. *These Tattoos*. Sydney: BlackWattle Press, 1990.
Gibbons, William G. *In the Face of Fire*. New York: William G. Gibbons, 1995.
Gil de Biedma, Jaime. *Longing: Selected Poems*. James Nolan, trans. San Francisco: City Lights, 1993.
Gilgun, John. *From the Inside Out*. Three Phase Publishing, 1991.
Ginsberg, Allen. *Cosmopolitan Greetings: Poems, 1986-1992*. New York: HarperCollins, 1994.
Giorno, John. *You Got to Burn to Shine: New and Selected Writings*. New York and London: High Risk Books/Serpent's Tail, 1994.
Godrej, Dinyar, Pat O'Brien, and Tim Neave. Martin Humphries, ed. *Twentysomething*. London: GMP, 1992.
Gonsalves, Roy. *Perversion*. New York: Renaissance, 1990.
Gunn, Thom. *Collected Poems*. New York: Farrar, Straus and Giroux, 1994.
Gunn, Thom. *Death's Door*. N.p.: Red Hydra Press, 1989.
Gunn, Thom. *Lament*. Champaign, IL: Doe Press, 1985. For Allan Noseworthy, died 21 June 1984.
Gunn, Thom. *The Man with Night Sweats*. New York: Farrar, Straus and Giroux, 1992.
Gunn, Thom. *Night Sweats*. Florence, KY: R. L. Barth, 1987.
Gunn, Thom. *Undesirables*. Durham: Pig Press, 1988.
Hacker, Marilyn. *Going Back to the River*. New York: Vintage/Random House, 1990.
Hacker, Marilyn. *Selected Poems, 1965-1990*. New York and London: W. W. Norton, 1994.
Hacker, Marilyn. *Winter Numbers*. New York and London: W. W. Norton, 1994.
Hadas, Rachel. *Unending Dialogue: Voices from an AIDS Poetry Workshop*. Boston and London: Faber & Faber, 1991.
Hahn, Kimiko. *Earshot*. Brooklyn: Hanging Loose Press, 1992.
Harold, John, ed. *How Can You Write a Poem When You're Dying of AIDS?* London: Cassell, 1993.
Harper, Michael, and Anthony Walton, eds. *Every Shut Eye Ain't Asleep: An Anthology of Poetry by African Americans Since 1945*. Boston: Little, Brown, 1994.
Harrison, D. I., Adam Johnson, and Gerry Pinkney. *Not Another Threesome*. London: The Oscars Press, 1990.

Heartpieces: Wisconsin Poets for AIDS, An Anthology. Milwaukee: NAMRON Press.

Hemphill, Essex. *Ceremonies: Prose and Poetry*. New York: Plume, 1992.

Henry, Gerrit. *The Mirrored Clubs of Hell*. New York: Arcade Publishing/Little, Brown, 1991.

Hickman, Craig. *Rituals: Poetry and Prose*. Cambridge, MA: Parfait de Cocoa Press, 1994.

Hickman, Leland. *Lee Sr Falls to the Floor*. Los Angeles: Jahbone Press, 1991.

Holland, Walter. *A Journal of the Plague Years: Poems 1979-1992*. New York: Magic City Press, 1992.

Howard, Richard. *Like Most Revelations*. New York: Pantheon Books, 1994.

Humphries, Martin, ed. *Not Love Alone: A Modern Gay Anthology*. London: GMP, 1985.

Jacobson, Erika Antigone. *The Unknown*. Leicester, MA: Dytiscid Press, 1994.

Johnson, Greg. *Aid and Comfort*. Gainesville: University Press of Florida, 1993.

Jones, Chris. *The Times of Zenia Gold: A Verse Novel*. Sydney: BlackWattle Press, 1992.

Kikel, Rudy, ed. *Gents, Bad Boys, and Barbarians*. Boston: Alyson, 1995.

Kikel, Rudy. *Long Division*. North Augusta, SC: The Writers Block Publishing Co., 1993.

Kirkup, James, and John McRae. *So Long Desired*. London: GMP, 1986.

Klein, Michael. *1990*. Provincetown, MA: Provincetown Arts Press, 1993.

Klein, Michael, ed. *Poets for Life: Seventy-Six Poets Respond to AIDS*. New York: Crown, 1989.

Koestenbaum, Wayne. *Ode to Anna Moffo and Other Poems*. New York: Persea, 1990.

Koestenbaum, Wayne. *Rhapsodies of a Repeat Offender*. New York: Persea, 1994.

Kushner, Tony. *Thinking about the Longstanding Problems of Virtue and Happiness*. New York: Theatre Communications Group, 1995.

Lassell, Michael. *Decade Dance*. Boston: Alyson, 1990.

Lassell, Michael. *The Hard Way*. New York: Richard Kasak Book/Masquerade Books, 1995.

Lassell, Michael, ed. *The Name of Love: Classic Gay Love Poems*. New York: St. Martin's Press, 1995.

Lassell, Michael. *Poems for Lost and Unlost Boys*. Bakersfield, CA: Amelia, 1985.

Lindahl, David. *Voices over the River*. Minneapolis: Daisy Publications, 1993.

Liu, Timothy. *Vox Angelica*. Cambridge, MA: Alice James Books, 1992.

Lynch, Michael. *These Waves of Dying Friends*. New York: Contact II Publications, 1989.

Masini, Donna. *That Kind of Danger*. Boston: Beacon Press, 1994.

McCann, Richard. *Ghost Letters*. Cambridge, MA: Alice James Books, 1994.

McCann, Richard. *Nights of 1990*. Hummelstown, PA: Warm Spring Press, 1994.

McClatchy, J. D. *The Rest of the Way*. New York: Knopf, 1992.

Melville, David, Andy Archibald, and Timothy Gallagher. *Carnal Ignorance*. London: The Oscars Press, 1987.

Merrill, James. *The Inner Room*. New York: Knopf, 1988.

Merrill, James. *A Scattering of Salts*. New York: Knopf, 1995.

Messerli, Douglas. *Along Without: A Fiction in Film for Poetry*. Part I of *The Structure of Destruction*. Los Angeles: Littoral Books, 1993.

Miller, Alan. *At the Club*. N.p.: Grand Entrances Press, 1988.

Miller, Andrew, ed. *Don't Hang Up*. Vermillion: University of South Dakota Press, 1992.

Monette, Paul. *Love Alone: Eighteen Elegies for Rog*. New York: St. Martin's Press, 1988.

Monette, Paul. *West of Yesterday, East of Summer: New and Selected Poems (1973-1993)*. New York: St. Martin's Press, 1994.

Moore, Honor. *Memoir*. Goshen, CT: Chicory Blue Press, 1988.

Morse, Carl, and Joan Larkin, eds. *Gay and Lesbian Poetry in Our Time: An Anthology*. New York: St. Martin's Press, 1988.

Nersesian, Arthur. *Tompkins Square & Other Ill-Fated Riots*. New York: Portable Press, 1990.

O'Brien, Pat. *I'm Afraid This Time Love, It's Positive*. London: The Oscars Press, 1989.

O'Neil, Thomas. *Sex with God*, revised ed. [expanded to include a new Book II, *The Ashes of Eden*]. New York: Wexford Press, 1994 [first ed., New York: Indulgence Press, 1989].

Peters, Andrew. *Poems of Love and Death*. 1993. Self-published.

Peters, Robert. *Good Night, Paul*. San Francisco: GLB Publishers, 1992.

Phillips, Carl. *In the Blood*. Boston: Northeastern University Press, 1992.

Powell, Jim. *It Was Fever That Made the World*. Chicago: University of Chicago Press, 1990.

Powell, Neil. *The Stones on Thorpeness Beach*. Manchester, UK: Carcanet, 1994.

Publicover, Robert. *My Unicorn Has Gone Away: Life, Death, Grief and Living in the Years of AIDS*. Somerville, MA: Powder House Publishing, 1993.

Rashid, Ian Iqbal. *Black Markets, White Boyfriends, and Other Acts of Elision*. Toronto: TSAR, 1991.

Reed, Jeremy. *Kicks*. London: Creation Books, 1994 [1993]. Includes prose.

Reed, Jeremy. *Red-Haired Android*. London: Grafton, 1992; San Francisco: City Lights, 1992.

Rich, Adrienne. *Time's Power: Poems 1985-1988*. New York and London: W. W. Norton, 1989.

Rickel, Boyer. *Arreboles*. Hanover, NH, and London: Wesleyan University Press/University Press of New England, 1991.

Riel, Steven. *How to Dream*. Amherst, MA: Amherst Writers and Artists Press, 1992.

Robilliard, David. *Life Isn't Good It's Excellent*. Gilbert & George, 1993. Produced in Stuttgart: Uwe Kraus.

Saint, Assotto, ed. *Here to Dare: 10 Gay Black Poets*. New York: Galiens Press, 1992.

Saint, Assotto, ed. *The Road Before Us: 100 Gay Black Poets*. New York: Galiens Press, 1991.

Saint, Assotto. *Stations*. New York: Galiens Press, 1989.

Saint, Assotto. *Wishing for Wings*. New York: Galiens Press, 1994.

Sarton, May. *Collected Poems (1930-1993)*. New York and London: W. W. Norton, 1993.

Sarton, May. *Coming into Eighty*. New York and London: W. W. Norton, 1994.

Schreiber, Ron. *John*. New York: Hanging Loose Press/Calamus Books, 1989.

Schwab, Arnold T. *Elegy for a Gay Giraffe*. Long Beach, CA: Applezaba, 1987.

Schwartz, Lloyd. *Goodnight, Gracie*. Chicago and London: The University of Chicago Press, 1992.

Schwartz, Ruth, coordinator. *The Singing Bridge: A National AIDS Poetry Archive*. For selections, see *Art and Understanding* 1:1 (Fall 1991), 15, and 1:2 (Winter 1992), 15-17.

Seaton, Maureen. *Fear of Subways*. Portland, OR: The Eighth Mountain Press, 1991.

Sedgwick, Eve Kosofsky. *Fat Art, Thin Art*. Durham and London: Duke University Press, 1994.

Sherrill, Jan-Mitchell. *Friend of the Groom*. Baltimore: Stonewall Series/New Poets Series, 1993.

Shurin, Aaron. *Mortal Purposes: A Poetics of AIDS*. Forthcoming.

Smith, Patricia. *Close to Death*. Cambridge, MA: Zoland Books, 1993.

Stephens, Ian. *Diary of a Trademark: Poetry and Prose*. Quebec: The Muses' Company/La Compagnie des Muses, 1994.

Sugar and Snails: An Oscars Mixture. London: The Oscars Press, 1990.

Treby, Ivor C. *Foreign Parts*. London: De Blackland Press, 1989.

Treby, Ivor C. *Warm Bodies*. London: De Blackland Press, 1988.

Trinidad, David. *Answer Song*. New York and London: High Risk Books/ Serpent's Tail, 1994.
Trinidad, David. *Hand over Heart: Poems 1981-1988*. New York: Amethyst Press, 1991.
Vallejos, Tomás. *Our Man of Earth and Sea: The Collected Works of Tomás Vallejos*. N.p.: House of Coleman, 1991.
Vega. *Phoenix Rising*. Sicklerville, NJ: Vega Press, 1995.
Vega Press. Conceived by Assotto Saint. *Milking Black Bull: 11 Gay Black Poets*. Sicklerville, NJ: Vega Press, 1995.
Vega Studios. *A Warm December*. Sicklerville, NJ: Vega Press, 1992.
Vinograd, Julia. *Styrofoam Ghosts*. Oakland, CA: Zeitgeist Press, 1993.
Vreeland, Sandra Isham, ed. *Listening to Young Voices*. The Poetry Society of America.
Wolverton, Terry. *Black Slip*. San Diego: Clothespin Fever Press, 1992.
Woods, Gregory. *We Have the Melon*. Manchester, UK: Carcanet, 1992.
Ziggy, Alec Bell, and Greyum Pyper. *Cottage Cream*. London: The Oscars Press, 1988.
Zizik, Joel. *Hypoglycemia and the Need to Practice It*. Baltimore: New Poets Series, 1993.

DRAMA/PERFORMANCE

AIDS Crisis Anthology. Barnsdall Art Park. May 1990.
The AIDS Quilt Songbook. Alice Tully Hall, New York. 4 June 1992. Score published by Boosey & Hawkes (London and New York, 1993).
Araki, Gregg. *The Living End: An Irresponsible Movie/Totally F***ed Up*. New York: Morrow, 1994. Screenplays of Araki's two movies.
Arcade, Penny. *Bitch! Dyke! Faghag! Whore!* 1990.
Artists Confronting AIDS. *AIDS/US* (1986) and *AIDS/US II* (1990). Los Angeles.
Athey, Ron. *Four Scenes in a Harsh Life*. 60 minute performance piece. Available on video from New Queer Cinema.
Athey, Ron. *Martyrs and Saints*. Performance piece.
Aude, Richard. *Inconnu dans notre bande/Unknown in Our Comic*. Quebec City, 1989.
Berry, Kevin. *Eastside Clinic*. Dallas: Dialogus Play Service, 1985. Set in a VD clinic.
Blessing, Lee. *Patient A*. New York: Dramatists' Play Service, 1993. Also in Blessing, *Patient A and Other Plays* (Portsmouth, NH: Heinemann, 1995). This is a play about Kimberly Bergalis.
Booth, Eric Stephen. *Steeplechase*. 1992.
Bowne, Alan. *Beirut*. New York: Broadway Play Publishing, 1988.

Bowne, Alan. *A Snake in the Vein.* New York: Theatre Communications Group, 1993.

Branner, Bernard Djola, Brian Freeman, and Eric Gupton. *Pomo Afro Homos. Dark Fruit.* 1993.

Branner, Bernard Djola, Brian Freeman, and Eric Gupton. *Pomo Afro Homos. Fierce Love: Stories from Black Gay Life.* 1991.

Bumbalo, Victor. *Adam and the Experts.* New York: Broadway Play Publishing, 1990 [1989].

Bumbalo, Victor. *Show.* 1991. In Noreen C. Barnes and Nicholas Deutsch, eds. *Tough Acts to Follow: One-Act Plays on the Gay/Lesbian Experience.* San Francisco: Alamo Square Press, 1992. 59-68.

Bumbalo, Victor. *Tell: A Play for Voices.* In Helbing, ed. *Gay and Lesbian Plays Today.*

Bumbalo, Victor. *What Are Tuesdays Like?* In Jones, ed. *Sharing the Delirium.*

Butler, Dan. *The Only Thing Worse You Could Have Told Me.* 1995.

Cachianes, Ed. *Everybody Knows Your Name.*

Caron, Jean-François. *Aux hommes de bonne volonté.* Montreal: Leméac, 1994.

Chapman, James. *Our Young Black Men Are Dying and Nobody Seems to Care.* 1990.

Chesley, Robert. *Dog Plays [(Wild) Person, Tense (Dog); The Deploration of Rover; Hold].* 1990. In *Hard Plays/Stiff Parts.*

Chesley, Robert. *Hard Plays/Stiff Parts: The Homoerotic Plays of Robert Chesley.* San Francisco: Alamo Square Press, 1990.

Chesley, Robert. *Jerker; or, the Helping Hand: A Pornographic Elegy with Redeeming Social Value and a Hymn to the Queer Men of San Francisco in Twenty Telephone Calls, Many of Them Dirty.* 1986. In *Hard Plays/Stiff Parts.* Also in Shewey, ed. *Out Front.*

Chesley, Robert. *Night Sweat: A Romantic Comedy in Two Acts.* 1984. In *Hard Plays/Stiff Parts.* John M. Clum, *Acting Gay: Male Homosexuality in Modern Drama*, revised ed. (New York: Columbia University Press, 1994), calls this "the first full-length AIDS play" (43).

Clarke, Bruce. *The Inner Web.* 1990.

Club Cabaret, Boston. *Alive with AIDS: A Musical Exploration.* 1-26 March 1989.

Cofell, Elizabeth. *At Risk: A Readers' Theatre Drama.* A Project of the South Dakota Department of Education and Cultural Affairs, the Office of Educational Services, AIDS Prevention Education, 1992.

Congdon, Constance. *Dog Opera.* 1995. The Public Theater.

Copi [Raul Damonte]. *Grand finale.* 1987. In Temerson and Kourilsky, eds. *Gay Plays: An International Anthology.*

Copi [Raul Damonte]. *Une Visite inopportune*. Paris: Christian Bourgeois, 1988.
Delgado, Louis, Jr. *A Better Life*. 1993.
Dietz, Steven. *Lonely Planet*. 1994. The Barrow Group. Revived, 1995, Circle Repertory Company.
Drake, David. *The Night Larry Kramer Kissed Me*. New York: Anchor Books/Doubleday, 1994 [1992].
Dresher, Paul. *Power Failure*. 1989.
Dungate, Ron. *Playing by the Rules*. 1992. In Wilcox, ed. *Gay Plays: Volume Five*.
Durang, Christopher. *Baby with the Bathwater* and *Laughing Wild*. New York: Grove Press, 1988.
Edelstein, Lisa. *Positive Me*. 1989.
Elmslie, Kenward. Music by Steven Taylor. *Postcards on Parade: A Musical Play*. Flint, MI: Bamberger Books, 1993.
Elovich, Richard. *If Men Could Talk, The Stories They Could Tell*. 1990.
Elovich, Richard. *Someone Else from Queens Is Queer*. 1992.
Feinberg, David B. *The Pathological Flirt*. Read at the Theater for the New City, 12 Sept. 1994.
Fierstein, Harvey. *Safe Sex*. New York: Atheneum, 1988 [1987]. Three one-act plays: *Manny and Jake*, *Safe Sex*, and *On Tidy Endings*.
Finley, Karen. *A Certain Level of Denial*. 1992.
Finley, Karen. *Shock Treatment*. San Francisco: City Lights, 1990.
Finn, William, and James Lapine. *Falsettos* [*March of the Falsettos* (1981) and *Falsettoland* (1989)] and *In Trousers*. New York: Plume, 1993.
Fraser, Brad. *Poor Superman*. 1995. Produced in Toronto and Cincinnati.
Fratti, Mario. "AIDS: A One-Act Play." 1987. In *Differentia* 2 (Spring 1988), 227-36.
Friedman, Gary. *Puppets Against AIDS*. This show toured Namibia in 1990.
Galás, Diamanda. *Plague Mass*. Includes *The Masque of the Red Death* trilogy—*The Divine Punishment, Saint of the Pit, You Must Be Certain of the Devil*.
Galás, Diamanda. *Vena Cava*. 1992.
Garnhum, Ken. *Beuys Buoys Boys: A Monologue*. In Wallace, ed. *Making, Out*.
Glines, John. *Men of Manhattan*. 1990. Scene 2 published in *Christopher Street* no. 146 (1990), 17-19.
Grant, David Marshall. *Snakebit*. 1995. Circle Repertory Company.
Gray, Spalding. *Monster in a Box*. New York: Vintage Books, 1992 [1990].
Greenberg, Richard. *Eastern Standard*. New York: Grove Press, 1989; New York: Dramatists' Play Service, 1989.
Greenspan, David. *Jack*. In Osborn, ed. *The Way We Live Now*.

Greig, Noël. *Plague of Innocence*. 1988. In Wilcox, ed. *Gay Plays: Volume Five*.
Gunter, Gregory. *What's So Big About AIDS*. Health Works Theatre. Chicago Plays. For children.
Gurney, A. R. *The Old Boy*. New York: Dramatists' Play Service, 1992 [1991].
Hagedorn, Jeff. *One*.
Hampton, Aubrey. *Mixed Blood*. 1992.
Health Works Theatre. *Wizard of AIDS*. Chicago Plays.
Helbing, Terry, ed. *Gay and Lesbian Plays Today*. Portsmouth, NH: Heinemann, 1993.
Hoffman, William M. *As Is*. New York: Vintage/Random House, 1985. Also in Shewey, ed. *Out Front*.
Holsclaw, Doug. *The Baddest of Boys*. In Jones, ed. *Sharing the Delirium*.
Holsclaw, Doug. *Get Real*. New Conservatory Theatre, San Francisco. AIDS education drama for children.
Holsclaw, Doug. *The Life of the Party*. 1987. A spin-off of Theatre Rhinoceros's *The AIDS Show*.
Horne, Charles. *The Smoking Room*. Syracuse.
Housing Works. The Theater Project. *In Limbo*. 1995.
Howie Gaw'nit Players. *Snapshots*. Vancouver, BC, 1989.
Jones, Therese. *Sharing the Delirium: Second Generation AIDS Plays and Performances*. Portsmouth, NH: Heinemann, 1994.
Jones, Wendell. *Damaged Goods*. Full-length solo piece.
Jones, Wendell, and David Stanley. Music by Robert Berg. *AIDS! The Musical!* 1991. In Jones, ed. *Sharing the Delirium*. See the discussion in David Román, "'It's My Party and I'll Die If I Want To!': Gay Men, AIDS, and the Circulation of Camp in U.S. Theatre," *Theatre Journal* 44 (1992), 319-27.
Kearns, Michael. *An Actor Confronts AIDS*.
Kearns, Michael. *intimacies* (1989) and *more intimacies* (1990). In Helbing, ed. *Gay and Lesbian Plays Today*.
Kearns, Michael. *Myron: A Fairy Tale in Black and White*. In Jones, ed. *Sharing the Delirium*.
Kearns, Michael. *Rock*.
Kearns, Michael. *T-Cells and Sympathy: Monologues in the Age of AIDS*. Portsmouth, NH: Heinemann, 1995.
Kearns, Michael. *The Truth Is Bad Enough*.
Kelley, Louise Parker. *Anti Body*.
Kelly, John. *Akin*. 1992.
Kirby, Andy. *Compromised Immunity*. In Philip Osment, ed. *Gay Sweatshop: Four Plays and a Company*. London: Methuen, 1989.

Kondolean, Harry. *Love Diatribe*. New York: Dramatists' Play Service, 1991 [1990].
Kondolean, Harry. *Zero Positive*. New York: Dramatists' Play Service, 1989.
Kramer, Larry. *The Destiny of Me*. New York: Plume, 1993.
Kramer, Larry. *Just Say No: A Play About a Farce*. New York: St. Martin's Press, 1989.
Kramer, Larry. *The Normal Heart*. New York: Plume, 1985.
Kushner, Tony. *Angels in America: A Gay Fantasia on National Themes: Part One: Millennium Approaches*. New York: Theatre Communications Group, 1993.
Kushner, Tony. *Angels in America: A Gay Fantasia on National Themes: Part Two: Perestroika*. New York: Theatre Communications Group, 1994.
Kushner, Tony. *Slavs!* In *Thinking about the Longstanding Problems of Virtue and Happiness*. New York: Theatre Communications Group, 1995. Not about AIDS, this play nonetheless contains material connected to Kushner's *Angels in America*.
Larson, Jonathan. *Rent*. 1995. New York Theater Workshop.
Lipsky, Jon. *Dreaming with an AIDS Patient*. 1989. Adapted from Robert Bosnak's book; see Nonfiction Narrative below.
Loughrey, Patricia. *The Inner Circle: One-Act Version*. Boston: Baker's Plays, 1989.
Lucas, Craig. *Prelude to a Kiss*. New York: Plume, 1991 [1990].
Lypsinka [= John Epperson]. *I Could Go On Lip-Synching*. For a discussion of the play in the context of AIDS, see Román, "'It's My Party and I'll Die If I Want To!'" 311-19.
MacLean, David. *Quarantine of the Mind*. 1990.
Manbites Dog Theatre Company, Durham, NC. *Indecent Materials* and *Reports from the Holocaust*. 1990. Based on material from Jesse Helms and Larry Kramer.
McArdle, Michael. *Anonymous*. 1994. Albany Civic Theater. Printed in *Art and Understanding* 4:2 (April 1995), 10-15.
McNally, Terrence. *Andre's Mother*. In Osborn, ed. *The Way We Live Now*.
McNally, Terrence. *Lips Together, Teeth Apart*. New York: Plume, 1992; New York: Dramatists' Play Service, 1992.
McNally, Terrence. *The Lisbon Traviata*. New York: Dramatists' Play Service, 1992 [1985, 1989]. Also in McNally, *Three Plays* (New York: Plume, 1990). An earlier version of the play appears in Shewey, ed. *Out Front*.
McNally, Terrence. *Love! Valour! Compassion!* [1994] and *A Perfect Ganesh* [1993]. New York: Plume, 1995.
McNally, Terrence. *A Perfect Ganesh*. New York: Dramatists' Play Service, 1994 [1993].
McPherson, Scott. *Marvin's Room*. New York: Plume, 1992 [1990].

Mellon, James J. *An Unfinished Song*. 1992.
Miller, Tim. *My Queer Body*. In Jones, ed. *Sharing the Delirium*.
Miller, Tim. *Naked Breath*. 1994.
Miller, Tim. *Sex Love Stories*. 1991.
New York People with AIDS Theatre Workshop. *AIDS Alive*. 1988.
Osborn, M. Elizabeth, ed. *The Way We Live Now: American Plays & the AIDS Crisis*. New York: Theatre Communications Group, 1990.
Panych, Morris. *Other Schools of Thought. Life Science, 2B WUT UR*, and *Cost of Living*. Vancouver, BC: Talonbooks, 1994.
Parker, James Edwin. *Two Boys in a Bed on a Cold Winter's Night*. 1995. Rattlestick Productions and Theater Off Park, New York.
Patrick, Robert. *Pouf Positive*. In Patrick. *Untold Decades: Seven Comedies of Gay Romance*. New York: St. Martin's Press, 1989.
Pendleton, Austin. *Uncle Bob*. 1995. Mint Theater Co.
Peyton, Bruce. *Live Wire*. New York: Plays for Living, 1989.
Pickett, James Carroll. *Queen of Angels*. In Jones, ed. *Sharing the Delirium*.
Pintauro, Joe. *Plays* [especially "Rosen's Son"]. New York: Broadway Play Publishing, 1989.
Pintauro, Joe. *Raft of the Medusa*. 1991.
Planet Q. *Homo Alone: Lost in Colorado*. 1993.
PREGONES. *The Embrace*.
Principal Parts, Swansea. *We All Fall Down*. Available on video from Albany Video, London. Discussed in Sue Ellis and Paul Heritage, "AIDS and the Cultural Response: *The Normal Heart* and *We All Fall Down*," in Simon Shepherd and Mick Wallis, eds., *Coming on Strong: Gay Politics and Culture* (London: Unwin Hyman, 1989), 39-53.
Ranson, Rebecca. *Higher Ground*. Atlanta, 1988. See William Alexander, "Clearing Space: AIDS Theatre in Atlanta," *TDR* 34:3 (1990), 109-28.
Ranson, Rebecca. *Warren*. Atlanta, 1984. Seven Stages Theater.
Red Earth Ensemble. *And My Friend: Short Plays on AIDS*. Plays by Ellen Adamson, Catherine Dudley, Janet Girardeau, Jed Stiles, John Gillick, Will Schaffer, and David Simpatico. New York, October 1993.
Reinhart, Robert C. *Telling Moments: Fifteen Gay Monologues*. New York and London: Applause Theatre Books, 1994.
Rintoul, Harry. *Brave Hearts*. In Wallace, ed. *Making, Out*.
Roach, Lois P. *Living On*. Boston: Baker's Plays, 1992.
Ross, Joe. *Guards of the Heart: Four Plays*. Los Angeles: A Blue Corner Drama/Corner Books, 1990.
Roy, Camille. *Sometimes Dead Is Better*. In Roy. *Cold Heaven*. N.p.: O Books, 1993.
Rudnick, Paul. *Jeffrey*. New York: Plume, 1994.

Russell, Bill. *Elegies for Angels, Punks and Raging Queens (An AIDS Anthology)*. 1990. RAPP Arts Center.
Saar, David P. *The Yellow Boat*. 1993. Childsplay, Tempe, AZ.
Sealy, Godfrey. *AIDA, The Wicked Wench of the World!* Trinidad, 1988 [1987].
Selig, Paul. *Terminal Bar*. 1983. In Wilcox, ed. *Gay Plays: Volume Three*.
Sheppard, David. *Heartstrings*. 1986.
Shewey, Don, ed. *Out Front: Contemporary Gay and Lesbian Plays*. New York: Grove Press, 1988.
Silver, Nicky. *Pterodactyls*. New York: Dramatists' Play Service, 1994 [1993].
Silver, Nicky. *Raised in Captivity*. 1995. The Vineyard Theater.
Sister Nunsex. MIEL-Quebec, 1989/1990.
Sod, Ted. *Satan and Simon DeSoto*. In Jones, ed. *Sharing the Delirium*.
Sontag, Susan, and Edward Parone. "The Way We Live Now." In Osborn, ed. *The Way We Live Now*.
Spencer, Stuart. *Last Outpost at the End of the World*. 1987.
Stetson, Kent. *Warm Wind in China*. Montreal: Nu-Age Editions, 1989 [1988].
Stevens, David. *The Sum of Us*. 1990.
Stokes, Sandford. *Shelter*. 1994. The Chain Lightnight Theater, New York.
The Story of Hibiscus. 1992. La MaMa ETC.
Swados, Robin. *A Quiet End*. 1986. In Helbing, ed. *Gay and Lesbian Plays Today*.
Temerson, Catherine, and Françoise Kourilsky, eds. *Gay Plays: An International Anthology*. New York: Ubu Repertory Theater Publications, 1989.
Theatre Rhinoceros, San Francisco. *The AIDS Show: Artists Involved with Death and Survival*.
Theatre Rhinoceros, San Francisco. *Unfinished Business*. Sequel to *The AIDS Show*.
Thomas, Colin. *Flesh and Blood*. In Wallace, ed. *Making, Out*.
Trinity Theatre, Toronto. *AIDS in the Workplace*. For adults.
Trinity Theatre, Toronto. *Face to Face*. For children.
Trinity Theatre, Toronto. *Teaching to Learn*. For educators.
Vallejos, Tomás. *Our Man of Earth and Sea: The Collected Works of Tomás Vallejos*. N.p.: House of Coleman, 1991.
Van Itallie, Jean-Claude. *Ancient Boys*. In Temerson and Kourilsky, eds. *Gay Plays: An International Anthology*.
Vance, Danitra. *Live and in Color!* 1991. In Sydné Mahone, ed. *Moon Marked and Touched by Sun: Plays by African-American Women*. New York: Theatre Communications Group, 1994.
Vawter, Ron. *Roy Cohn/Jack Smith*. 1992. The text of the "Roy Cohn" section of this performance piece is by Gary Indiana. The "Jack Smith" section is based on Smith's 1981 play *What's Underground about Marshmallows?*

Vogel, Paula. *The Baltimore Waltz*. New York: Dramatists' Play Service; New York: The Fireside Theatre, 1992. Excerpt in Osborn, ed. *The Way We Live Now*.
Wallace, Robert, ed. *Making, Out: Plays by Gay Men*. Toronto: Coach House Press, 1992.
Wasserstein, Wendy. *The Heidi Chronicles and Other Plays*. San Diego, New York, and London: Harcourt Brace Jovanovich, 1990.
Weinberg, Tom Wilson. *Ten Percent Revue*. New York and Kansas City: New Musical Theatre Library, 1990.
Weinmann, Heinz. *Don Juan 2003: Eros et SIDA: Theatre*. Montreal: VLB, 1993.
Weiss, Jeff. *Hot Keys*. 1992.
West, Cheryl L. *Before It Hits Home*. New York: Dramatists' Play Service, 1993 [1991].
Wilcox, Michael, ed. *Gay Plays*. 5 vols. London: Methuen, 1984-1994.
Willett, Richard. *Boys Will Be Boys*. Produced in New York. Published in *Art and Understanding* 4:3 (June/July 1995), 10-12.
Wilson, Lanford. *A Poster of the Cosmos*. In Osborn, ed. *The Way We Live Now*.
Yew, Chay. *A Language of Their Own*. 1995. The Public Theater.
Young, William Baldwin. *Making the Rounds: AIDS in the Community*. New York: Plays for Living, 1993.

NONFICTION NARRATIVE

Abbott, Steve. *View Askew: Postmodern Investigation(s)*. San Francisco: Androgyne Books, 1989.
ACT UP/New York. Women and AIDS Book Group. *Women, AIDS, and Activism*. Boston: South End Press, 1990.
"AIDS and Academe, a Special Section." *The Chronicle of Higher Education* 41:8 (19 Oct. 1994), A10-A23, A67.
Althen, Michael. *Rock Hudson: Seine Film, Sein Leben*. Munich: W. Heyne, 1986.
Altman, Dennis. *AIDS in the Mind of America: The Social, Political, and Psychological Impact of a New Epidemic*. New York: Anchor Books/ Doubleday, 1986. [= *AIDS and the New Puritanism*. London: Pluto Press, 1986.]
Alyson, Sasha, ed. *You Can Do Something About AIDS*. Boston: The Stop AIDS Project, 1988 [revised ed., 1990].
Amos, William E. *When AIDS Comes to Church*. Philadelphia: Westminster Press, 1988.
Andrews, Nancy. *Family: A Portrait of Gay and Lesbian America*. San Francisco: HarperSanFrancisco, 1994.

Angier, Natalie. *The Beauty of the Beast: New Views of the Nature of Life.* New York: Houghton Mifflin, 1995.

Antoniou, Laura, ed. *Looking for Mr. Preston: A Celebration of the Writer's Life.* New York: Richard Kasak Book/Masquerade Books, 1995.

Arenas, Reinaldo. *Before Nightfall: A Memoir.* New York: Penguin, 1993.

Arno, Peter S., and Karyn L. Feiden. *Against the Odds: The Story of AIDS Drug Development, Politics and Profits.* New York: HarperPerennial, 1992.

Arpin, Robert L. *Wonderfully, Fearfully Made: Letters on Living with Hope, Teaching Understanding, and Ministering with Love, from a Gay Catholic Priest with AIDS.* San Francisco: HarperSanFrancisco, 1993.

Arterburn, Jerry, with Steve Arterburn. *How Will I Tell My Mother?* revised and expanded ed. Nashville: Oliver-Nelson, 1990 [1988].

Ascher, Barbara Lazear. *Landscape Without Gravity: A Memoir of Grief.* New York: Penguin, 1993.

Ashe, Arthur, and Arnold Rampersad. *Days of Grace: A Memoir.* New York: Knopf, 1993.

Asistent, Niro Markoff, with Paul Duffy. *Why I Survive AIDS.* New York: Simon & Schuster, 1991.

Baggett, James A., compiler. Bill Bytsura, photographer. *United in Anger.* A selection from this project was presented in *NYQ* no. 7 (8 Dec. 1991), 26-31.

Baker, Rob. *The Art of AIDS: From Stigma to Conscience.* New York: Continuum, 1994.

Barbo, Beverly. *The Walking Wounded: A Mother's True Story of Her Son's Homosexuality and His Eventual AIDS-Related Death.* Lindsborg, KS: Carlsons' Publishing, 1987.

Barouh, Gail. *Support Groups: The Human Face of the HIV/AIDS Epidemic.* Huntington Station, NY: LIAAC, 1992.

Bartlett, John, and Ann Finkbeiner. *Guide to Living with HIV Infection,* revised ed. Baltimore and London: Johns Hopkins University Press, 1994 [1991].

Bartlett, Neil. *Who Was That Man? A Present for Mr Oscar Wilde.* London: Serpent's Tail, 1988.

Bawer, Bruce. *A Place at the Table: The Gay Individual in American Society.* New York: Touchstone/Simon & Schuster, 1994 [1993].

Beachy, Stephen. "AIDS and the Apocalyptic Imagination." In Eric Liu, ed. *Next: Young American Writers on the New Generation.* New York: W. W. Norton, 1994. 17-37.

Bellamy, Dodie, and Sam D'Allesandro. *Real: The Letters of Mina Harker and Sam D'Allesandro.* Hoboken, NJ: Talisman House, 1994.

Bentley, Robert. *Dangerous Games: The True Story of a Convicted Murderer on Death Row Who Changed His Sex and Won Her Freedom*. Secaucus, NJ: Carol Pub. Group/A Birch Lane Press Book, 1993.

Berer, Marge, ed., with Sunandra Ray. *Women and HIV/AIDS: An International Resource Book*. London: Pandora/HarperCollins, 1993.

Bergman, Susan. *Anonymity: The Secret Life of an American Family*. New York: Farrar, Straus and Giroux, 1994.

Berrigan, Daniel. *Sorrow Built a Bridge: Friendship and AIDS*. Baltimore: Fortkamp Publishing, 1989.

Black, David. *The Plague Years: A Chronicle of AIDS, The Epidemic of Our Time*. New York: Simon & Schuster, 1986.

Blasius, Mark, and Shane Phelan, eds. *We Are Everywhere: An Historical Sourcebook in Gay and Lesbian Politics*. New York: Routledge, 1994.

Bosnak, Robert. *Dreaming with an AIDS Patient*. Boston and Shaftesbury, UK: Shambhala, 1989.

Bouldrey, Brian, ed. *Wrestling with the Angel: Faith and Religion in the Lives of Gay Men*. New York: Riverhead, 1995.

Bovet, Joan M. *Sida, impuls de vida?: experiencia de Joan Ferrer i Sisquella*. Barcelona: Editorial Claret, 1993.

Boyd, Terry. *Living with AIDS: One Christian's Struggle*. Lima, OH: C.S.S. Pub., 1990.

Brandt, Allan M. *No Magic Bullet: A Social History of Venereal Disease in the United States Since 1880*, expanded ed. [with a new chapter on AIDS]. New York and Oxford: Oxford University Press, 1987.

Brown, Joe, ed. *A Promise to Remember: The Names Project Book of Letters*. New York: Avon, 1992.

Browning, Frank. *The Culture of Desire: Paradox and Perversity in Gay Lives Today*. New York: Crown, 1993 [New York: Vintage/Random House, 1994].

Buckingham, Robert W. *Among Friends: Hospice Care for the Person with AIDS*. Buffalo: Prometheus, 1992.

Burns, Janice A. *Sarah's Song: A True Story of Love and Courage*. New York: Warner Books, 1995.

Buttino, Frank, with Lou Buttino. *A Special Agent: Gay and Inside the FBI*. New York: Morrow, 1993.

Califia, Pat. *Public Sex: The Culture of Radical Sex*. San Francisco and Pittsburgh: Cleis Press, 1994.

Callen, Michael, ed. *AIDS Forum: Diverse Views About Acquired Immune Deficiency Syndrome*. 1989- .

Callen, Michael. *Surviving AIDS*. New York: HarperCollins, 1990.

Callen, Michael, ed. *Surviving and Thriving with AIDS: Hints for the Newly Diagnosed*. Vol. 1. New York: PWA Coalition, 1987. Vol. 2: *Surviving and Thriving with AIDS: Collected Wisdom*. New York: PWA Coalition, 1990.

Cantacuzino, Marina. *Till Break of Day: Meeting the Challenge of HIV and AIDS at London Lighthouse*. London: Heinemann, 1993.

Cantwell, Alan, Jr. *AIDS and the Doctors of Death: An Inquiry into the Origin of the AIDS Epidemic*. Los Angeles: Aries Rising Press, 1988.

Cantwell, Alan, Jr. *AIDS: The Mystery and the Solution: The New Epidemic of Acquired Immune Deficiency Syndrome*. Los Angeles: Aries Rising Press, 1986 [1983].

Chaitow, Leon, and James Strohecker, with the Burton Goldberg Group. *You Don't Have to Die: Unraveling the AIDS Myth*. Puyallup, WA: Future Medicine Publishing, 1994.

Chase, Clifford. *The Hurry-Up Song: A Memoir of Losing My Brother*. San Francisco: HarperSanFrancisco, 1995.

Christensen, Michael J. *The Samaritan's Imperative: Compassionate Ministry to People Living with AIDS*. Nashville: Abingdon Press, 1991.

Clark, J. Michael. *Diary of a Southern Queen: An HIV+ Vision Quest*. Dallas: Monument, 1990.

Clark, Tom, and Dick Kleiner. *Rock Hudson, Friend of Mine*. New York: Pharos, 1989.

Clarke, Loren, and Malcolm Potts, eds. *The AIDS Reader: A Documentary History of a Modern Epidemic*. Boston: Branden Publishing, 1988.

Collard, Cyril. *L'Ange sauvage*. Paris: Flammarion, 1993. Diaries.

Collins, David R. *Arthur Ashe: Against the Wind*. New York: Dillon Press, 1994.

Connor, Steve, and Sharon Kingman. *The Search for the Virus*. London: Penguin, 1988.

Corea, Gena. *The Invisible Epidemic: The Story of Women and AIDS*. New York: HarperCollins, 1992.

Corless, Inge B., and Mary Pittman-Lindeman, eds. *AIDS: Principles, Practices, & Politics*. New York: Hemisphere Publishing, 1988.

Cox, Elizabeth. *Thanksgiving: An AIDS Journal*. New York: Harper & Row, 1990.

Craig, Eleanor. *The Moon Is Broken: A Mother's True Story*. New York: E. P. Dutton, 1992.

Crimp, Douglas, ed. *AIDS: Cultural Analysis/Cultural Activism*. Cambridge, MA, and London: The MIT Press, 1988 [*October* 43 (Winter 1987)].

Crimp, Douglas, with Adam Rolston. *AIDS Demo Graphics*. Seattle: Bay Press, 1990.

Daniel, Herbert. *Vida antes da morte/Life Before Death*. Rio de Janeiro: Jaboti, 1989.

Daniel, Herbert, and Richard Parker. *AIDS, a terceira epidemia: ensaios e tentativas*. São Paulo: IGLU Editora, 1991.

Daniel, Herbert, and Richard Parker. *Sexuality, Politics, and AIDS in Brazil: In Another World?* London and Washington, DC: Falmer Press, 1993.

Dansky, Steven F. *Now Dare Everything: Tales of HIV-Related Psychotherapy*. Binghamton, NY: Harrington Park Press/Haworth Press, 1994.

Delany, Samuel R. *Silent Interviews: On Language, Race, Sex, Science Fiction, and Some Comics: A Collection of Written Interviews*. Hanover, NH: Wesleyan University Press/University Press of New England, 1994.

D'Emilio, John. *Making Trouble: Essays on Gay History, Politics, and the University*. New York and London: Routledge, 1992.

Dexter, Robin. *Young Arthur Ashe: Brave Champion*. Mahwah, NJ: Troll Associates, 1995.

Dickerson, Neal. *The Promise and the Power: Public Policy Analysis and the AIDS Movement*. Las Colinas, TX: Monument Press, 1993.

Differences: A Journal of Feminist Cultural Studies 3:2 (Summer 1991). Teresa de Lauretis, ed. Special Issue on *Queer Theory: Lesbian and Gay Sexualities*. See especially the essay by Samuel R. Delany.

Dobbels, William J. *An Epistle of Comfort: Scriptural Meditations and Passages for Persons Suffering with AIDS*. Kansas City: Sheed & Ward, 1990.

Dolan, Sean. *Magic Johnson*. New York: Chelsea House, 1993.

Donnelly, Katherine Fair. *Recovering from the Loss of a Loved One to AIDS*. New York: St. Martin's Press, 1994.

Dorenkamp, Monica, and Richard Henke, eds. *Negotiating Lesbian and Gay Subjects*. New York and London: Routledge, 1994 [London], 1995 [New York].

Dreuilhe, [Alain] Emmanuel. *Mortal Embrace: Living with AIDS*. Linda Coverdale, trans. New York: Hill and Wang, 1988. [*Corps à corps: journal du sida*. Paris: Gallimard, 1987.]

Eidson, Ted, ed. *AIDS Caregiver's Handbook*, revised ed. New York: St. Martin's Press, 1993 [1988]. Several chapters report "Stories from the Front."

Eighner, Lars. *Travels with Lizbeth: Three Years on the Road and on the Streets*. New York: St. Martin's Press, 1993.

Faris, Jocelyn. *Liberace: A Bio-Bibliography*. Westport, CT: Greenwood Press, 1995.

Farmer, Paul. *AIDS and Accusation: Haiti and the Geography of Blame*. Berkeley, Los Angeles, and Oxford: University of California Press, 1992.

Faust, Wolfgang Max. *Dies alles gibt es also: Alltag, Kunst, AIDS: ein autobiographischer Bericht*. Stuttgart: Edition Cantz, 1993.

Favereau, Eric. *Chambres ouvertes: 90 jours avec 5 malades du SIDA*. Paris: Balland, 1988.

Fee, Elizabeth, and Daniel M. Fox, eds. *AIDS: The Making of a Chronic Disease*. Berkeley, Los Angeles, and Oxford: University of California Press, 1992.

Feinberg, David B. *Queer and Loathing: Rants and Raves of a Raging AIDS Clone*. New York: Viking, 1994.

Feldschuh, Joseph, with Doron Weber. *Safe Blood: Purifying the Nation's Blood Supply in the Age of AIDS*. New York: Free Press/Macmillan, 1990.

Fettner, Ann Giudici, and William Check. *The Truth about AIDS: Evolution of an Epidemic*, revised ed. New York: Owl Book/Henry Holt and Company, 1985 [1984].

Fisher, Mary. *Sleep with the Angels: A Mother Challenges AIDS*. Wakefield, RI, and London: Moyer Bell, 1994.

FitzGerald, Frances. *Cities on a Hill: A Journey Through Contemporary American Cultures*. New York: Simon & Schuster, 1986.

For Those We Love: A Spiritual Perspective on AIDS, 2nd ed. AIDS Ministry Program, The Archdiocese of Saint Paul and Minneapolis. Cleveland: The Pilgrim Press, 1991 [1990].

Francis, Myriam. *Tiempos del SIDA: Relatos de la vida real*. San Jose, Costa Rica: Euroamericana de Ediciones, 1990.

Frank, Steven. *Magic Johnson*. New York: Chelsea House, 1994.

Fried, Stephen. *Thing of Beauty: The Tragedy of Supermodel Gia*. New York: Pocket Books, 1993.

Fritscher, Jack. *Mapplethorpe: Assault with a Deadly Camera*. Mamaroneck, NY: Hastings House, 1994.

Fumento, Michael. *The Myth of Heterosexual AIDS: How a Tragedy Has Been Distorted by the Media and Partisan Politics*. New York: Basic Books, 1990.

Gaines, Steven, and Sharon Churcher. *Obsession: The Lives and Times of Calvin Klein*. New York: Avon, 1994.

Gallo, Robert. *Virus Hunting: AIDS, Cancer, and the Human Retrovirus: A Story of Scientific Discovery*. New York: New Republic Books/Basic Books, 1991.

Garrett, Laurie. *The Coming Plague: Newly Emerging Diseases in a World out of Balance*. New York: Farrar, Straus and Giroux, 1994.

Gaspar, Tomás Rodriguez. *Ginger's Book: An AIDS Primer/El Primer Libro del SIDA para niños*. New York: Into the Light Press, 1995.

Gates, Phyllis, and Bob Thomas. *My Husband, Rock Hudson: The Real Story of Rock Hudson's Marriage to Phyllis Gates*. Garden City, NY: Doubleday, 1987.

Gawthrop, Daniel. *Affirmation: The AIDS Odyssey of Dr. Peter*. Vancouver, BC: New Star Books, 1994.

Geballe, Shelley, Janice Gruendel, and Warren Andiman, eds. *Forgotten Children of the AIDS Epidemic*. New Haven: Yale University Press, 1995.

Gever, Martha, John Greyson, and Pratibha Parmar, eds. *Queer Looks: Perspectives on Lesbian and Gay Film and Video*. New York and London: Routledge, 1993.

Gevisser, Mark, and Edwin Cameron. *Defiant Desire: Gay and Lesbian Lives in South Africa*. Johannesburg: Ravan Press, 1994 [New York: Routledge, 1995].

Giorno, John. *You Got to Burn to Shine: New and Selected Writings*. New York and London: High Risk Books/Serpent's Tail, 1994.

Glaser, Elizabeth, and Laura Palmer. *In the Absence of Angels: A Hollywood Family's Courageous Story*. New York: G. P. Putnam's, 1991.

Goldstaub, Sylvia. *Unconditional Love: "Mom! Dad! Love Me! Please."* Boca Raton: Cool Hand Communications, 1993.

Goss, Robert. *Jesus Acted Up: A Gay and Lesbian Manifesto*. San Francisco: HarperSanFrancisco, 1993.

Gould, Peter. *The Slow Plague: A Geography of the AIDS Pandemic*. Oxford and Cambridge, MA: Blackwell, 1993.

Grant, Robert J. *Love and Roses from David: A Legacy of Living and Dying*. Virginia Beach: A.R.E. Press, 1994.

Grant-White, Carole. *Our Neighbors as Ourselves: A Guide for Neighbors Helping Neighbors Who Live with HIV/AIDS and "The Ripple Effect."* Herndon, VA: Acropolis Books, 1993.

Graubard, Stephen R., ed. *Living with AIDS*. Cambridge, MA, and London: The MIT Press, 1990. [*Daedalus* 118:2-3 (1989).]

Greaser, Frances Bontrager. *And a Time to Die*. Scottdale, PA: Herald Press, 1995.

Greenberg, Keith Elliot. *Magic Johnson: Champion with a Cause*. Minneapolis: Lerner Publications, 1992.

Greenly, Mike. *Chronicle: The Human Side of AIDS*. New York: Irvington, 1986.

Gregory, Scott, and Bianca Leonardo. *They Conquered AIDS: True Life Adventures from Self-Reliance, thru Inspiration, into Transformation*. Palm Springs, CA: Tree of Life Publications, 1989.

Grmek, Mirko D. *History of AIDS: Emergence and Origin of a Modern Pandemic*. Russell C. Maulitz and Jacalyn Duffin, trans. Princeton: Princeton University Press, 1990. [*Histoire du sida: Début et origine d'une pandémie actuelle*. Editions Payot, 1989.]

Gross, Larry. *Contested Closets: The Politics and Ethics of Outing*. Minneapolis and London: University of Minnesota Press, 1993.

Gruen, John. *Keith Haring: The Authorized Biography*. New York: Prentice Hall, 1991.

Gruen, John. *Keith Haring*. Mankato, MN: Creative Education, 1994.

Grumbach, Doris. *Coming into the End Zone: A Memoir*. New York and London: W. W. Norton, 1993 [1991].

Guibert, Hervé. *Cytomégalovirus: Journal d'hospitalisation*. Paris: Editions de Seuil, 1992.

Guibert, Hervé. *Photographien*. Schirmer/Mosel.

Gunn, Jacky, and Jim Jenkins. *Queen: As It Began*. New York: Hyperion, 1992.

Gunn, Thom. *Shelf Life: Essays, Memoirs, and an Interview*. Ann Arbor: University of Michigan Press, 1993.

Gutman, Bill. *Magic Johnson: Hero on and off Court*. Brookfield, CT: Millbrook Press, 1992.

Gutman, Bill. *Magic, More than a Legend: A Biography*. New York: HarperCollins, 1992.

Hall Carpenter Archives. Gay Men's Oral History Group. *Walking After Midnight: Gay Men's Life Stories*. London and New York: Routledge, 1989.

Hallman, David G. *AIDS Issues: Confronting the Challenge*. New York: The Pilgrim Press, 1989.

Halperin, David M. *Saint = Foucault: Towards a Gay Hagiography*. New York and Oxford: Oxford University Press, 1995.

Harlow, Kim, and Bettina Rheims. *Kim*. Paul Gould, trans. Munich: Gina Kehayoff, 1994.

Haskins, James. *Sports Great Magic Johnson*, revised and expanded ed. Hillside, NJ: Enslow Publishers, 1992 [1989, 1982].

Hemphill, Essex. *Ceremonies: Prose and Poetry*. New York: Plume, 1992.

Hendrikson, Peter A. *Alive and Well: A Path for Living in a Time of HIV*. New York: Irvington, 1991.

Henig, Robin Marantz. *A Dancing Matrix: How Science Confronts Emerging Viruses*. New York: Vintage/Random House, 1994. First published as *A Dancing Matrix: Voyages Along the Viral Frontier* (New York: Knopf, 1993).

Hickman, Craig. *Rituals: Poetry and Prose*. Cambridge, MA: Parfait de Cocoa Press, 1994.

Hippler, Mike. *Matlovich: The Good Soldier*. Boston: Alyson, 1989.

Hippler, Mike. *So Little Time: Essays on Gay Life*. Berkeley: Celestial Arts, 1990.

Hitchens, Neal. *Voices that Care: Stories and Encouragements for People with AIDS/HIV and Those Who Love Them*. New York: Fireside Book/Simon &

Schuster, 1994 [Los Angeles: Lowell House; Chicago: Contemporary Books, 1992].

Holleran, Andrew. *Ground Zero*. New York: Morrow, 1988.

Hooven, F. Valentine, III. *Tom of Finland: His Life and Times*. New York: St. Martin's Press, 1993.

Hostetler, Helen M. *A Time to Love*. Scottdale, PA: Herald Press, 1989.

Howard, Billy. *Epitaphs for the Living: Words and Images in the Time of AIDS*. Dallas: Southern Methodist University Press, 1989.

Hoyle, Jay. *Mark: How a Boy's Courage in Facing AIDS Inspired a Town and the Town's Compassion Lit Up a Nation*. South Bend: Langford/Diamond Communications, 1988.

Hudson, Rock, and Sara Davison. *Rock Hudson: His Story*. New York: Morrow, 1986.

Hyde, Margaret O., and Elizabeth H. Forsyth. *Know About AIDS*, 3rd ed. New York: Walker & Co., 1994 [1987, 1990].

It Happened to Nancy, by an Anonymous Teenager: A True Story from Her Diary. New York: Avon, 1994.

Italia, Bob. *Earvin "Magic" Johnson*. Edina, MN: Abdo & Daughters, 1992.

Jarman, Derek. *At Your Own Risk: A Saint's Testament*. Woodstock, NY: The Overlook Press, 1993 [London: Hutchinson, 1992].

Jarman, Derek. *Blue: Text of a Film*. Woodstock, NY: The Overlook Press, 1994.

Jarman, Derek. *Chroma*. Woodstock, NY: The Overlook Press, 1995.

Jarman, Derek. *Modern Nature*. Woodstock, NY: The Overlook Press, 1994 [1991].

Jarman, Derek. *Queer*. Exhibition Catalogue. Manchester, UK: Manchester City Art Galleries, 1992.

Jarman, Derek. *Queer Edward II*. London: British Film Institute, 1991.

Johnson, Anthony Godby. *A Rock and a Hard Place: One Boy's Triumphant Story*. New York: Crown, 1993.

Johnson, Earvin "Magic," with William Novak. *My Life*. New York: Random House, 1992.

Johnson, Earvin "Magic." *What You Can Do to Avoid AIDS* [*Como Protegerse contra el SIDA*]. New York: Times Books, 1992. Another Spanish version is available as: *Tu Puedes evitarlo*. Enric Tremps, trans. Barcelona: Planeta, 1992.

Johnson, Rick L. *Magic Johnson: Basketball's Smiling Superstar*. New York: Dillon Press, 1992.

Johnston, William I. *HIV-Negative: How the Uninfected Are Affected by AIDS*. New York and London: Insight Books/Plenum Press, 1995.

Jones, Bill T. *Last Night on Earth*. New York: Pantheon Books, 1995.

Jones, Carolyn. *Living Proof: Courage in the Face of AIDS*. New York: Abbeville Press, 1994.

Jong, Erica. *Fear of Fifty: A Midlife Memoir*. New York: HarperCollins, 1994.

Jonsson, Gustav, and Britt Jonsson. *Smittad*. Stockholm: Tiden, 1988.

Joseph, Stephen C. *Dragon Within the Gates: The Once and Future AIDS Epidemic*. New York: Carroll & Graf Publishers, 1992.

Josephs, Larry. "The Harrowing Plunge." *New York Times Magazine* 11 Nov. 1990, 38-46.

Juhasz, Alexandra. *AIDS TV: Identity, Community, and Alternative Video*. Durham: Duke University Press, 1995.

Julien, Isaac, and Colin MacCabe. *Diary of a Young Soul Rebel*. London: British Film Institute, 1991.

Juliette. *Pourquoi moi?: Confession d'une jeune femme d'aujourd'hui*. Paris: R. Laffont, 1987.

Juritzen, Arve. *Henki: å leve med AIDS-viruset*. Oslo: J. W. Cappelen, 1987.

Kaiser, Jon D. *Immune Power: A Comprehensive Treatment Program for HIV*. New York: St. Martin's Press, 1993.

Kaleeba, Noerine, with Sunanda Ray and Brigid Willmore. *We Miss You All: Noerine Kaleeba—AIDS in the Family*. Harare, Zimbabwe: Women and AIDS Support Network, 1991.

Kallen, Stuart A. *Arthur Ashe: Champion of Dreams and Motion*. Edina, MN: Abdo & Daughters, 1993.

Kavar, Louis F. *Families Re-Membered: Pastoral Support for Friends and Families Living with HIV/AIDS*. Chi Rho Press.

Kavar, Louis F. *Pastoral Ministry in the AIDS Era: Focus on Families and Friends of Persons with AIDS*. Wayzata, MN: Woodland Pub., 1988.

Kavar, Louis F. *To Celebrate and Mourn: Liturgical Resources for Worshipping Communities Living with AIDS*. Chi Rho Press.

Kelly, Kevin. *One Singular Sensation: The Michael Bennett Story*. New York: Doubleday, 1990.

King, Edward. *Safety in Numbers*. London: Cassell, 1993; New York: Routledge, 1994.

Kinsella, James. *Covering the Plague: AIDS and the American Media*. New Brunswick and London: Rutgers University Press, 1989.

Kirp, David. *Learning By Heart: AIDS and Schoolchildren in America's Communities*. New Brunswick: Rutgers University Press, 1989.

Kirp, David L., and Ronald Bayer, eds. *AIDS in the Industrialized Democracies: Passions, Politics, and Policies*. New Brunswick: Rutgers University Press, 1992.

Kittredge, Mary. *Teens with AIDS Speak Out*. Englewood Cliffs, NJ: Julian Messner/Simon & Schuster, 1991.

Kopkind, Andrew. *The Thirty Years' War: Dispatches and Diversions of a Radical Journalist, 1965-1994*. London and New York: Verso, 1995.

Kramer, Larry. *Reports from the Holocaust: The Making of an AIDS Activist*. New York: St. Martin's Press, 1989. Updated and expanded, as *Reports from the Holocaust: The Story of an AIDS Activist* (New York: St. Martin's Press, 1994).

Kraut, Alan M. *Silent Travelers: Germs, Genes, and the "Immigrant Menace"*. New York: Basic Books/HarperCollins, 1994.

Kübler-Ross, Elisabeth. *AIDS: The Ultimate Challenge*. New York: Macmillan, 1987.

Kurth, Ann, ed. *Until the Cure: Caring for Women with HIV*. New Haven: Yale University Press, 1993.

Kushi, Michio, and Martha C. Cottrell, with Mark N. Mead. *AIDS, Macrobiotics, and Natural Immunity*. Tokyo and New York: Japan Publications, 1990.

Kushner, Tony. *Thinking about the Longstanding Problems of Virtue and Happiness*. New York: Theatre Communications Group, 1995.

Kwitny, Jonathan. *Acceptable Risks*. New York: Poseidon Press/Simon & Schuster, 1992.

Landau, Elaine. *We Have AiDS*. New York: Franklin Watts, 1990.

LaPierre, Dominique. *Beyond Love [Plus grands que l'amour]*. Kathryn Spink, trans. New York: Warner Books, 1991.

Lassell, Michael. *The Hard Way*. New York: Richard Kasak Book/Masquerade Books, 1995.

Lauren, Joan. *Portraits of Life: With Love: An Intimate Collection of Exclusive Celebrities' Photographs with their Personal Reflections on Life and Love*. Los Angeles: General Pub. Group, 1994.

Lauritsen, John. *The AIDS War: Propaganda, Profiteering and Genocide from the Medical-Industrial Complex*. New York: Asklepios, 1993.

Lauritsen, John. *Poison by Prescription: The AZT Story*. New York: Asklepios, 1990.

Laygues, Helène. *SIDA, temoignage sur la vie et la mort de Martin*. Paris: Hachette Littérature, 1985.

Leibowitch, Jacques. *A Strange Virus of Unknown Origin*. Richard Howard, trans. New York: Available Press/Ballantine, 1985. [*Un Virus étrange venu d'ailleurs*. Paris: Grasset et Fasquelle, 1984.]

Leinen, Stephen. *Gay Cops*. New Brunswick: Rutgers University Press, 1993.

Leiner, Marvin. *Sexual Politics in Cuba: Machismo, Homosexuality, and AIDS*. Boulder, CO, San Francisco, and Oxford: Westview Press, 1994.

Leslie, Mark. *Dying with AIDS/Living with AIDS, 1991-1992*. Donon, Quebec: The Muses' Company/La Compagnie des Muses, 1992.

Likosky, Stephan. *Coming Out: An Anthology of International Gay and Lesbian Writings*. New York: Pantheon Books, 1992.

Locke, Richard. *Locke Out: The Collected Writings of Richard Locke*. Teaneck, NJ: Firsthand Books, 1993. Incorporates material from Locke's safer sex manual, *In the Heat of Passion: How to Have Hotter, Safer Sex* (Leyland Publications, 1987).

Lopes, Sal. *Living with AIDS: A Photographic Journal: Three Stories*. Boston: Bulfinch Press/Little, Brown, 1994.

Louganis, Greg, with Eric Marcus. *Breaking the Surface*. New York: Random House, 1995.

Lucas, Ian. *Impertinent Decorum: Gay Theatrical Manoeuvres*. London and New York: Cassell, 1994.

Lupton, Deborah. *Moral Threats and Dangerous Desires: AIDS in the News Media*. London and Bristol, PA: Taylor & Francis, 1994.

Lynch, Michael. "Last Onsets: Teaching with AIDS." *Profession 90*. New York: The Modern Language Association of America, 1990. 32-36.

Macey, David. *The Lives of Michel Foucault: A Biography*. New York: Pantheon Books, 1993.

Macher, Abe M. *AIDS: An Atlas of Cases for Diagnosis*. Baltimore: Williams & Wilkins, 1988.

Mandelbaum, Ken. *A Chorus Line and the Musicals of Michael Bennett*. New York: St. Martin's Press, 1989.

Manthorne, Jacquie, ed. *Canadian Women and AIDS: Beyond the Statistics/Les femmes canadiennes et le SIDA: au-delà des statistiques*. Montreal: Les Editions Communiqu'Elles, 1990.

Marcus, Eric. *Making History: The Struggle for Gay and Lesbian Equal Rights, 1945-1990: An Oral History*. New York: HarperCollins, 1992.

Martelli, Leonard J., Fran D. Peltz, and William Messina. *When Someone You Know Has AIDS: A Practical Guide*. New York: Crown, 1987. The revised edition of 1993 adds Steven Petrow as co-author and incorporates material from Petrow's *Dancing Against the Darkness*.

Mass, Lawrence D. *Dialogues of the Sexual Revolution*. New York: Harrington Park Press/Haworth Press, 1990.

Mass, Lawrence D. *Confessions of a Jewish Wagnerite*. London and New York: Cassell, 1994.

Mayes, Stephen, and Lyndall Stein, eds. *Positive Lives: Responses to HIV—A Photodocumentary*. London and New York: Cassell, 1993.

McCarroll, Tolbert. *Morning Glory Babies: Children with AIDS and the Celebration of Life*. New York: St. Martin's Press, 1988.

McDarrah, Fred W., and Timothy S. McDarrah. *Gay Pride: Photographs from Stonewall to Today*. Chicago: a cappella books/Chicago Review Press, 1994.

McGarrahan, Peggy. *Transcending AIDS: Nurses and HIV Patients in New York City*. Philadelphia: University of Pennsylvania Press, 1994.

McKenzie, Nancy F. *The AIDS Reader: Social, Political, and Ethical Issues*. New York: Meridian, 1991.

McKenzie, Nancy F. *Beyond Crisis: Confronting Health Care in the United States*. New York: Meridian, 1994.

McManus, Irene. *Dreamscapes: The Art of Juan Gonzalez*. New York: Hudson Hills Press, 1994.

McNamara, Robert P. *The Times Square Hustler: Male Prostitution in New York City*. Westport, CT: Praeger, 1994.

Melson, James Kenneth. *The Golden Boy*. Binghamton, NY: Harrington Park Press/Haworth Press, 1992.

Miller, James, ed. *Fluid Exchanges: Artists and Critics in the AIDS Crisis*. Toronto: University of Toronto Press, 1992.

Miller, James. *The Passion of Michel Foucault*. New York: Simon & Schuster, 1993.

Miller, Neil. *In Search of Gay America: Women and Men in a Time of Change*. New York: Atlantic Monthly Press, 1989.

Miller, Neil. *Out in the World: Gay and Lesbian Life from Buenos Aires to Bangkok*. New York: Random House, 1992.

Miller, Neil. *Out of the Past: Gay and Lesbian History from 1869 to the Present*. New York: Vintage/Random House, 1995.

Moffatt, Betty Clare. *When Someone You Love Has AIDS: A Book of Hope for Family and Friends*. New York: Plume, 1986.

Monette, Paul. *Becoming a Man: Half a Life Story*. New York, San Diego, and London: Harcourt Brace Jovanovich, 1992.

Monette, Paul. *Borrowed Time: An AIDS Memoir*. San Diego, New York, and London: Harcourt Brace Jovanovich, 1988.

Monette, Paul. *Last Watch of the Night: Essays Too Personal and Otherwise*. New York, San Diego, and London: Harcourt Brace & Co., 1994.

Monette, Paul. *The Politics of Silence*. The National Book Week Lectures. Washington, DC: Library of Congress, 1993.

Money, J. W. *To All the Girls I've Loved Before*. Boston: Alyson, 1987.

Montoussamy-Ashe, Jeanne. *Daddy and Me: A Photo Story of Arthur Ashe and His Daughter, Camera*. New York: Knopf, 1993.

Moor, Jonathan. *Perry Ellis: A Biography*. New York: St. Martin's Press, 1988.

Mordaunt, John, as told to John Masterson. *Facing up to AIDS*. Dublin: The O'Brien Press, 1989.

Morrisroe, Patricia. *Mapplethorpe*. New York: Random House, 1995.

Morrissey, Paul. *Let Someone Hold You: The Journey of a Hospice Priest*. New York: Crossroad, 1994.

Mungo, Raymond. *Liberace*. New York: Chelsea House, 1994.

Murphy, Timothy F. *Ethics in an Epidemic: AIDS, Morality, and Culture*. Berkeley, Los Angeles, and London: University of California Press, 1994.

Murray, Nicholas. *Bruce Chatwin*. Border Lines Series. Mid Glamorgan: Seren Books/Poetry Wales Press, 1993.

Nassaney, Louie, and Glenn Kolb. *I Am Not a Victim: One Man's Triumph over Fear and AIDS*. Santa Monica: Hay House, 1990.

National Lesbian and Gay Survey. *Proust, Cole Porter, Michelangelo, Marc Almond and Me: Writings by Gay Men on Their Lives and Lifestyles*. London and New York: Routledge, 1993.

Nestle, Joan, and John Preston, eds. *Sister & Brother: Lesbians and Gay Men Write about Their Lives Together*. San Francisco: HarperSanFrancisco, 1994.

Newman, Lesléa. *A Loving Testimony: Remembering Loved Ones Lost to AIDS*. Freedom, CA: The Crossing Press, 1995. Includes some poetry.

Newton, Esther. *Cherry Grove, Fire Island: Sixty Years in America's First Gay and Lesbian Town*. Boston: Beacon Press, 1993.

Nixon, Nicholas, photographs. Bebe Nixon, text. *People with AIDS*. Boston: David R. Godine, 1991.

Nungesser, Lon G. *Epidemic of Courage: Facing AIDS in America*. New York: St. Martin's Press, 1986.

Nussbaum, Bruce. *Good Intentions: How Big Business and the Medical Establishment Are Corrupting the Fight Against AIDS*. New York: Atlantic Monthly Press, 1990.

O'Brien, Mary Elizabeth. *Living with HIV: Experiment in Courage*. New York, Westport, CT, and London: Auburn House/Greenwood Press, 1992.

Odets, Walt. *In the Shadow of the Epidemic: Being HIV-Negative in the Age of AIDS*. Durham: Duke University Press, 1995.

Oikawa, Mona. "Safer Sex in Santa Cruz" and "Stork Cools Wings." In Tamai Kobayashi and Mona Oikawa. *All Names Spoken*. Toronto: Sister Vision, Black Women and Women of Colour Press, 1992. 86-99.

O'Malley, Padraig, ed. *The AIDS Epidemic: Private Rights and the Public Interest*. Boston: Beacon Press, 1989 [*New England Journal of Public Policy* 4:1 (Winter/Spring 1988)].

Oppenheimer, Jerry, and Jack Vitek. *Idol Rock Hudson: The True Story of an American Hero*. New York: Villard Books, 1986.

O'Sullivan, Sue, and Pratibha Parmar. *Lesbians Talk (Safer) Sex*. London: Scarlet Press, 1992.

Owen, Bob. *Roger's Recovery from AIDS*. Malibu: DAVAR, 1987.

Paglia, Camille. *Vamps and Tramps*. New York: Vintage/Random House, 1994.

Pallotta-Chiarolli, Maria. *Someone You Know: A Friend's Farewell*. Kent Town, South Australia: Wakefield Press, 1991.

Panem, Sandra. *The AIDS Bureaucracy: Why Society Failed to Meet the AIDS Crisis and How We Might Improve Our Response*. Cambridge, MA, and London: Harvard University Press, 1988.

Pascarelli, Peter. *The Courage of Magic Johnson: From Boyhood Dreams to Superstar to His Toughest Challenge*. New York: Bantam, 1992.

Peabody, Barbara. *The Screaming Room: A Mother's Journal of Her Son's Struggle with AIDS: A True Story of Love, Dedication and Courage*. San Diego: Oak Tree Publications, 1986 [New York: Avon, 1987].

Pearson, Carol Lynn. *Good-Bye, I Love You*. New York: Random House, 1986.

Peavey, Fran. *A Shallow Pool of Time: An HIV+ Woman Grapples with the AIDS Epidemic*. Philadelphia and Santa Cruz: New Society Publishers, 1990.

Perrow, Charles, and Mauro F. Guillen. *The AIDS Disaster: The Failure of Organizations in New York and the Nation*. New Haven and London: Yale University Press, 1990.

Perry, Shireen, with Gregg Lewis. *In Sickness and in Health: A Story of Love in the Shadow of AIDS*. Downers Grove, IL: InterVarsity Press, 1989.

Perry, Troy D., with Thomas L. P. Swicegood. *Don't Be Afraid Anymore: The Story of Reverend Troy D. Perry and the Metropolitan Community Churches*. New York: Saint Martin's Press, 1990.

Perry, Troy D., and Thomas L. P. Swicegood. *Profiles in Gay and Lesbian Courage*. New York: St. Martin's Press, 1991.

Petrow, Steven. *Dancing Against the Darkness: A Journey Through America in the Age of AIDS*. Lexington, MA: Lexington Books/Macmillan, 1990.

Pieters, A. Stephen. *I'm Still Dancing: A Gay Man's Health Experience*. Chi Rho Press.

Plummer, Ken, ed. *Modern Homosexualities: Fragments of Lesbian and Gay Experience*. London and New York: Routledge, 1992.

Plummer, Ken. *Telling Sexual Stories: Power, Change, and Social Worlds*. London and New York: Routledge, 1995.

Pogash, Carol. *As Real As It Gets: The Life of a Hospital at the Center of the AIDS Epidemic*. New York: Plume, 1994 [1992].

Preston, John, ed. *Hometowns: Gay Men Write about Where They Belong*. New York: E. P. Dutton, 1991.

Preston, John, ed. *A Member of the Family: Gay Men Write about Their Families*. New York: E. P. Dutton, 1992.

Preston, John. *My Life as a Pornographer and Other Indecent Acts*. New York: Richard Kasak Book/Masquerade Books, 1993.

Preston, John, ed. *Personal Dispatches: Writers Confront AIDS*. New York: St. Martin's Press, 1989.

Preston, John. *Winter's Light: Reflections of a Yankee Queer*. Michael Lowenthal, ed. Hanover, NH: University Press of New England, 1995.

Preston, John, ed., with Michael Lowenthal. *Friends and Lovers: Gay Men Write about Families They Create*. New York: E. P. Dutton, 1995.

Preston, Richard. *The Hot Zone: A Terrifying True Story*. New York: Random House, 1994.

Quackenbush, Robert M. *Arthur Ashe and His Match with History*. New York: Simon & Schuster Books for Young Readers, 1994.

Radical America 20:6 (1987). Facing AIDS: A Special Issue.

Ramsland, Katherine. *Prison of the Night: A Biography of Anne Rice*. New York: Plume, 1992 [1991].

Randall, R. C. *Marijuana and AIDS: Pot, Politics and PWAs in America*. Washington, DC: Galen Press, 1991.

Reed, Jeremy. *Lipstick, Sex, and Poetry: An Autobiography*. London and Chester Springs, PA: Peter Owen, 1991.

Reed, Paul. *The Q Journal: A Treatment Diary*. Berkeley: Celestial Arts, 1991.

Reed, Paul. *Savage Garden: A Journal*. San Francisco: House of Lillian, 1994.

Reed, Paul. *Serenity: Support and Guidance for People with HIV, Their Families, Friends, and Caregivers*, 2nd ed. Berkeley: Celestial Arts, 1990 [1st ed. published as *Serenity: Challenging the Fear of AIDS, from Despair to Hope*, 1987].

Rees, David. *Dog Days, White Nights*. Exeter: Third House, 1991.

Rees, David. *Not for Your Hands: An Autobiography*. Exeter: Third House, 1992.

Rees, David. *Packing It In*. Brighton: Millivres, 1992.

Richardson, Tony. *The Long-Distance Runner: An Autobiography*. New York: Morrow, 1993.

Rieder, Ines, and Patricia Ruppelt, eds. *AIDS: The Women*. San Francisco and Pittsburgh: Cleis Press, 1988.

Rist, Darrell Yates. *Heartlands: A Gay Man's Odyssey Across America*. New York: E. P. Dutton, 1992.

Rodriguez, Richard. *Days of Obligation: An Argument with My Mexican Father*. New York: Penguin, 1992.

Rose, Patti Renee. *In Search of Serenity: A Black Family's Struggle with the Threat of AIDS*. Chicago: Third World Press, 1993.

Royce, Brenda Scott. *Rock Hudson: A Bio-Bibliography*. Westport, CT: Greenwood Press, 1995.

Rozakis, Laurie. *Magic Johnson: Basketball Immortal*. Vero Beach, FL: Rourke, 1993.

Rozar, G. Edward, Jr., with David B. Biebel. *Laughing in the Face of AIDS: A Surgeon's Personal Battle.* Grand Rapids, MI: Baker Book House, 1992.

Rudd, Andrea, and Darien Taylor, eds. *Positive Women: Voices of Women Living with AIDS.* Toronto: Second Story Press, 1992.

Runnells, Robert R. *AIDS in the Dental Office? The Story of Kimberly Bergalis and Dr. David Acer.* Fruit Heights, UT: I.C. Publications, 1993.

Ruskin, Cindy, Matt Herron, and Deborah Zemke. *The Quilt: Stories from the NAMES Project.* New York: Pocket Books, 1988.

Ryan, Frank. *The Forgotten Plague: How the Battle Against Tuberculosis Was Won—And Lost.* Boston: Little, Brown, 1992.

Ryan, Michael. *Secret Life: An Autobiography.* New York: Pantheon Books, 1995. AIDS is an important part of the frame of Ryan's autobiography.

Sabatier, Renée. *Blaming Others: Prejudice, Race, and Worldwide AIDS.* Washington, DC: The Panos Institute; Philadelphia: New Society Publishers, 1988.

Santis, Jose Vicente de. *La condenación, o, Jeremias aún no ha muerte de SIDA.* Caracas, Venezuela: Watseka Publicaciones Alternativas, 1993.

Schecter, Stephen. *The AIDS Notebooks.* Albany: State University of New York Press, 1990.

Schmalz, Jeffrey. "Whatever Happened to AIDS?" *New York Times Magazine* 28 Nov. 1993, 56-61.

Schneider, Beth E., and Nancy E. Stoller. *Women Resisting AIDS: Feminist Strategies of Empowerment.* Philadelphia: Temple University Press, 1995.

Schneider, David. *Street Zen: The Life and Work of Issan Dorsey.* Boston and London: Shambhala, 1993.

Schow, Wayne. *Remembering Brad: On the Loss of a Son to AIDS.* Salt Lake City: Signature Books, 1995. With journal entries by Brad Schow.

Schulman, Sarah. *My American History: Lesbian and Gay Life During the Reagan/Bush Years.* New York: Routledge, 1994.

Schwabacher, Martin. *Magic Johnson.* New York: Chelsea House, 1993.

Sears, James T., ed. *Bound By Diversity.* Sebastian Press.

Sedgwick, Eve Kosofsky. "Memorial for Craig Owens" and "White Glasses." *Tendencies.* Durham: Duke University Press, 1993.

Sergios, Paul A. *One Boy at War: My Life in the AIDS Underground.* New York: Knopf, 1993.

Shands, Nancy. *AIDS: The Lonely Voyage.* San Carlos, CA: Wide World Publishing, 1988.

Shelby, R. Dennis. *If a Partner Has AIDS: Guide to Clinical Intervention for Relationships in Crisis.* Binghamton, NY: Harrington Park Press/Haworth Press, 1992.

Shelp, Earl E., Ronald H. Sunderland, and Peter W. A. Mansell. *AIDS: Personal Stories in Pastoral Perspective*. New York: The Pilgrim Press, 1986.

Sherman, Phillip, executive ed. *Uncommon Heroes: A Celebration of Heroes and Role Models for Lesbian and Gay Americans*. New York: Fletcher Press, 1994.

Shernoff, Michael, ed. *Counseling Chemically Dependent People with HIV Illness*. Binghamton, NY: Harrington Park Press/Haworth Press, 1991.

Sherwood, Zalmon O. *Kairos: Confessions of a Gay Priest*. Boston: Alyson, 1987.

Shilts, Randy. *And the Band Played On: Politics, People, and the AIDS Epidemic*. New York: St. Martin's Press, 1987 [New York: Penguin, 1988; with a new "Afterword"].

Shilts, Randy. *Conduct Unbecoming: Gays and Lesbians in the U.S. Military*. New York: Fawcett Columbine, 1994 [New York: St. Martin's Press, 1993].

Shokeid, Moshe. *A Gay Synagogue in New York*. New York: Columbia University Press, 1995.

Shoumatoff, Alex. *African Madness*. New York: Knopf, 1988.

Signorile, Michelangelo. *Queer in America: Sex, The Media, and the Closets of Power*. New York: Random House, 1993.

Silin, Jonathan. *Sex, Death, and the Education of Children: Our Passion for Ignorance in the Age of AIDS*. New York: Teachers College Press (Columbia University), 1995.

Silin, Jonathan. "Standing for Michael." *Kerem* (Winter 1994), 88-94.

Simeone, Regina. *Wer der Kopf hangen lasst, sieht weniger: Gedanken einer jungen aids-kranken Frau*. Basel: F. Reinhardt, 1988.

Sky, Rick. *The Show Must Go On: The Life of Freddie Mercury*. Secaucus, NJ: Carol Pub. Group, 1994 [1992].

Smith, Richard L. *AIDS, Gays, and the American Catholic Church*. Cleveland: The Pilgrim Press, 1994.

Smith, Walter J. *AIDS: Living and Dying with Hope: Issues in Pastoral Care*. Mahwah, NJ: Paulist Press, 1988.

Solomon, Rosalind. *Portraits in the Time of AIDS*. New York: Grey Art Gallery and Study Center, NYU, 1988. Catalogue of exhibition, May 17-July 2, 1988.

Solway, Diane. *A Dance Against Time: The Triumphant Life of a Young Joffrey Artist*. New York: Pocket Books, 1994. Biography of Edward Stierle.

Spence, Jim. *Arthur Ashe: Tennis Legend*. Vero Beach, FL: Rourke, 1995.

Spender, Stephen, ed. *Hockney's Alphabet*. London: Faber & Faber; New York: Random House, 1991.

Stasey, Bobbie. *Just Hold Me While I Cry*. Albuquerque: Elysian Hills, 1993.

Stasey, Bobbie, with Ed Dziczek. *Running with the Angels: The Gifts of AIDS*. Albuquerque: Elysian Hills, 1994.

Steffan, Joseph. *Honor Bound: A Gay Naval Midshipman Fights to Serve His Country*. New York: Avon, 1992.

Stein, F. *Een half jaar AZT*. Amsterdam: Dekker, 1990.

Stephens, Ian. *Diary of a Trademark: Poetry and Prose*. Quebec: The Muses' Company/La Compagnie des Muses, 1994.

Stoddard, Sandol. *The Hospice Movement: A Better Way of Caring for the Dying*, updated and expanded ed. New York: Vintage/Random House, 1992 [1978].

Strauss, Larry. *Magic Man*. Los Angeles: Lowell House Juvenile; Chicago: Contemporary Books, 1992. Biography of Earvin "Magic" Johnson.

Stribling, Thomas B., with Verne Becker. *Love Broke Through: A Husband, Father, and Minister Tells His Own Story*. Grand Rapids, MI: Zondervan Books, 1990.

Stuart, Otis. *Perpetual Motion: The Public and Private Lives of Rudolf Nureyev*. New York: Simon & Schuster, 1995.

Sunderland, Ronald H., and Earl E. Shelp. *Handle with Care: A Handbook for Care Teams Serving People with AIDS*. Nashville: Abingdon Press, 1990.

Thomas, Bob. *Liberace: The True Story*. New York: St. Martin's Press, 1987.

Thompson, Mark, ed. *Gay Soul: Finding the Heart of Gay Spirit and Nature*. San Francisco: HarperSanFrancisco, 1994.

Thompson, Mark, ed. *Gay Spirit: Myth and Meaning*. New York: St. Martin's Press, 1987.

Thompson, Mark, ed. *Leatherfolk: Radical Sex, People, Politics, and Practice*. Boston: Alyson, 1991.

Thompson, Mark, ed. *Long Road to Freedom: The Advocate History of the Gay and Lesbian Movement*. New York: St. Martin's Press, 1994.

Thomson, K. *Positively Women: Living with AIDS*. London: Sheba, 1992.

Thorson, Scott, with Alex Thorliefson. *Behind the Candelabra: My Life with Liberace*. New York: E. P. Dutton, 1990.

Tierney, Pat. *The Moon on My Back: Autobiography*. Dublin: Seven Towers, 1993.

Tilleraas, Perry. *Circle of Hope: Our Stories of AIDS, Addiction, and Recovery*. San Francisco: Hazelden/Harper & Row, 1990.

Timmons, Stuart. *The Trouble with Harry Hay, Founder of the Modern Gay Movement*. Boston: Alyson, 1990.

Trebay, Guy. *In the Place to Be: Guy Trebay's New York*. Philadelphia: Temple University Press, 1994.

Trillin, Calvin. *Remembering Denny*. New York: Warner Books, 1993.

Valdiserri, Ronald O. *Gardening in Clay: Reflections on AIDS*. Ithaca: Cornell University Press, 1994.

van den Bergen, Ineke, and Reijer Breed. *Is het waar dat Lefert aids heeft?* Amsterdam: Van Gennep, 1985.
Vaucher, Andréa R. *Muses from Chaos and Ash: AIDS, Artists, and Art*. New York: Grove Press, 1993.
Verghese, Abraham. *My Own Country: A Doctor's Story of a Town and Its People in the Age of AIDS*. New York: Simon & Schuster, 1994.
Voeller, Bruce, June Machover Reinisch, and Michael Gottlieb. *AIDS and Sex: An Integrated Biomedical and Biobehavioral Approach*. New York and Oxford: Oxford University Press, 1990. This volume includes an historical essay by John Boswell and the narrative essay, "Thoughts on AIDS," by Joseph F. Lovett.
Vogel, Christina. *Es ist wunderbar: der Lebensweg einer jungen aids-kranken Mütter*. Basel: F. Reinhardt, 1989.
Wachter, Robert M. *The Fragile Connection: Scientists, Activists, and AIDS*. New York: St. Martin's Press, 1991.
Watney, Simon. *Practices of Freedom: Selected Writings on HIV/AIDS*. Durham: Duke University Press, 1994.
Weeks, Ann E. *'. . . And Then There Were Nine'*. Louisville, KY: Passages Publishing, 1994.
Weil, Brian. *Every 17 Seconds: A Global Perspective on the AIDS Crisis*. New York: Aperture, 1992.
Weissberg, Ted. *Arthur Ashe*. Los Angeles: Melrose Square Pub., 1993.
Weitz, Rose. *Life with AIDS*. New Brunswick: Rutgers University Press, 1991.
White, Edmund. *The Burning Library*. David Bergman, ed. New York: Knopf, 1994.
White, Edmund, and Hubert Sorin. *Our Paris: Sketches from Memory*. New York: Knopf, 1995.
White, Evelyn C., ed. *The Black Women's Health Book: Speaking for Ourselves*. Seattle: Seal Press, 1990.
White, Mel. *Stranger at the Gate: To Be Gay and Christian in America*. New York: Plume, 1995 [1994].
White, Ryan, and Ann Marie Cunningham. *Ryan White: My Own Story*. New York: Dial Books, 1991.
Whitmore, George. *Someone Was Here: Profiles in the AIDS Epidemic*. New York: New American Library, 1988.
Wiener, Lori S., Aprille Best, and Philip A. Pizzo. *Be a Friend: Children Who Live with HIV Speak*. Morton Grove, IL: Albert Whitman, 1994.
Williams, Glen. *From Fear to Hope: AIDS Care and Prevention at Chikankata Hospital, Zambia*. Strategies for Hope, Vol. 1. London: ActionAID; Nairobi, Kenya: AMREF, 1990.
Wilson, Carter. *Hidden in the Blood: A Personal Investigation of AIDS in the Yucatán*. New York: Columbia University Press, 1995.

Wiltshire, Susan Ford. *Seasons of Grief and Grace: A Sister's Story of AIDS.* Nashville: Vanderbilt University Press, 1994.
Winer, Mike. *Bienvenue dans le monde du SIDA.* Monaco: Rocher, 1988.
Wojnarowicz, David. *Close to the Knives: A Memoir of Disintegration.* New York: Vintage/Random House, 1991.
Wojnarowicz, David. *Memories That Smell Like Gasoline.* San Francisco: Artspace Books, 1992.
Wojnarowicz, David. *Tongues of Flame.* Barry Blinderman, ed. Normal, IL: University Galleries of Illinois State University, 1990.
Zuger, Abigail. *Strong Shadows: Scenes from an Inner City AIDS Clinic.* New York: W. H. Freeman and Company, 1995.
Zuniga, Jose. *Soldier of the Year: The Story of a Gay American Patriot.* New York: Pocket Books, 1994.

Works Cited

Abelove, Henry, Michèle Aina Barale, and David M. Halperin, eds. *The Lesbian and Gay Studies Reader*. New York and London: Routledge, 1993.

ACT UP/New York. *AIDS Research Agenda 1991*. June 1991.

ACT UP/New York. *A National AIDS Treatment Research Agenda*. V International Conference on AIDS, Montreal. June 1989. Revised Sept. 1989.

ACT UP/New York. The McClintock Project Working Group. *The Barbara McClintock Project to Cure AIDS*. Undated.

ACT UP/New York. Treatment & Data Committee. *The Countdown 18 Months Plan*. Nov. 1990.

ACT UP/New York. Women and AIDS Book Group. *Women, AIDS, and Activism*. Boston: South End Press, 1990.

The AIDS Quarterly with Peter Jennings. Winter 1989. WGBH Educational Foundation, 1989.

AIDS: The State Response. Proceedings of a Conference for the Illinois General Assembly. April 1986.

Alexander, William. "Clearing Space: AIDS Theatre in Atlanta." *TDR* 34:3 (1990), 109-28.

Allison, Alexander W., Herbert Barrows, Caesar R. Blake, Arthur J. Carr, Arthur M. Eastman, and Hubert M. English, Jr., eds. *The Norton Anthology of Poetry*, 3rd ed. New York and London: W. W. Norton, 1983.

Alonso, Ana Maria, and Maria Teresa Koreck. "Silences: 'Hispanics,' AIDS, and Sexual Practices." In Abelove, Barale, and Halperin, eds. *The Lesbian and Gay Studies Reader*. 110-26. [Originally published in *Differences: A Journal of Feminist Cultural Studies* 1:1 (1989), 101-24.]

Altman, Dennis. *AIDS and the New Puritanism* [= *AIDS in the Mind of America*]. London: Pluto Press, 1986.

Altman, Lawrence K. "AIDS and a Dentist's Secrets." *New York Times* 6 June 1993, Section 4, 1, 3.

Altman, Lawrence K. "Decision Disappoints AIDS Experts." *New York Times* 3 Nov. 1992, B11.

Altman, Lawrence K. "Federal Health Officials Propose an Expanded Definition of AIDS." *New York Times* 28 Oct. 1992, B9.

Altman, Lawrence K. "Rare Cancer Seen in 41 Homosexuals." *New York Times* 3 July 1981, A20.

Altman, Lawrence K. "Widened Definition of AIDS Leads to More Reports of It." *New York Times* 30 April 1993, A18.

Anderson, Dave. "Sorry, But Magic Isn't a Hero." *New York Times* 14 Nov. 1991, B19.

Anderson, Laurie. *Home of the Brave*. A Talk Normal Production, 1986. Warner Reprise Video.

Angier, Natalie. "Biologists Seek the Words in DNA's Unbroken Text." *New York Times* 9 July 1991, C1, C11.

Angier, Natalie. "Blueprint for a Human." *New York Times* 6 Oct. 1992, C6.

Angier, Natalie. "A First Step in Putting Genes into Action: Bend the DNA." *New York Times* 4 Aug. 1992, C1, C7.

Angier, Natalie. "Gains Made in Effort to Map the Human Genetic Makeup." *New York Times* 1 Oct. 1992, A1, A22.

Angier, Natalie. "Keys Emerge to Mystery of 'Junk' DNA." *New York Times* 28 June 1994, C1, C3.

Angier, Natalie. "Odor Receptors Discovered in Sperm Cells." *New York Times* 30 Jan. 1992, A19.

Angier, Natalie. "U.S. Clears Use of Gene Therapy Against a Form of Lung Cancer." *New York Times* 16 Sept. 1992, A20.

Angier, Natalie. "Viruses Said to Pirate Host's Genetic Material in Invasion Strategies." *New York Times* 3 July 1990, C3.

Anonymous Queers. "It Is Too Late for Heroes." *NYQ* no. 5 (24 Nov. 1991), 30-31.

Antonio, Gene. "AIDS: The Real Dangers of Casual Transmission" (interview with David Kupelian). *New Dimensions* (1989).

Araki, Gregg. *The Living End: An Irresponsible Movie* [screenplay]. New York: Morrow, 1994.

Araton, Harvey. "Johnson Goes from Dream Ride to the Rat Race." *New York Times* 30 Sept. 1992, B9.

Araton, Harvey. "Keep Magic in the Mainstream." *New York Times* 13 Nov. 1991, B7.

Araton, Harvey. "N.B.A. Finds It Can't Overleap Reality." *New York Times* 3 Nov. 1992, B11.

Araton, Harvey. "A Worthy Bird Has an Unlikely Night." *New York Times* 5 Feb. 1993, B7-8.

Aristotle. *Generation of Animals*. A. L. Peck, ed. and trans. Loeb Classical Library. Cambridge, MA: Harvard University Press; London: Heinemann, 1953.

Aristotle. *Poetics*. Gerald F. Else, trans. Ann Arbor: University of Michigan Press, 1967.

Ashe, Arthur, and Arnold Rampersad. *Days of Grace: A Memoir*. New York: Knopf, 1993.

Auerbach, D. M., W. W. Darrow, W. W. Jaffe, and J. W. Curran. "Cluster of Cases of the Acquired Immune Deficiency Syndrome." *American Journal of Medicine* 76 (1984), 487-92.

Bahder, Paul, and Teresa Bahder. "The Spiritual Significance of Viral Infection." *New Dimensions* (1989).

Baker, James Robert. *Tim and Pete*. New York: Simon & Schuster, 1993.

Bandon, Alexandra. "Crimes Against Nature." *New York Times Magazine* 24 July 1994, 30-31.

Barrus, Tim. *Anywhere, Anywhere*. Stamford, CT: Knights Press, 1987.

Barrus, Tim. *Daddy's Lover Boy*. Cleveland: Magcorp Publishing, 1985.

Barrus, Tim. *Genocide: The Anthology*. Stamford, CT: Knights Press, 1988.

Barrus, Tim. *My Brother, My Lover: A Novel*. San Francisco: Gay Sunshine Press, 1985.

Bartholomew, Greg. "Homage to a Pair of Dead Boys." Review of Doug Wilson, *Labour of Love*, and Peter McGehee, *Beyond Happiness*, *The I.Q. Zoo*, *Boys Like Us*, and *Sweetheart*. *James White Review* 11:4 (Summer 1994), 16-17.

Beaty, Bert. "The Syndrome Is the System: A Political Reading of *Longtime Companion*." In Miller, ed. *Fluid Exchanges*. 111-21.

Berke, Richard L. "President Backs a Gay Compromise." *New York Times* 28 May 1993, A2, A14.

Berkow, Ira. "All-Stars to Give Magic a Nervous Embrace." *New York Times* 7 Feb. 1992, B9, B11.

Berkow, Ira. "Magic Johnson's Legacy." *New York Times* 8 Nov. 1991, B11.

Berkow, Ira. "Magic's Collision Course." *New York Times* 3 Nov. 1992, B9.

Bersani, Leo. "Is the Rectum a Grave?" In Crimp, ed. *AIDS: Cultural Analysis/Cultural Activism*. 197-222.

"Best Wishes from Bird." *New York Times* 30 Sept. 1992, B14.

The Biology and Gender Study Group [Athena Beldecos, Sarah Bailey, Scott Gilbert, Karen Hicks, Lori Kenschaft, Nancy Niemczyk, Rebecca Rosenberg, Stephanie Schaettel, and Andrew Wedel]. "The Importance of Feminist Critique for Contemporary Cell Biology." In Tuana, ed. *Feminism and Science*. 172-87.

Bishop, Elizabeth. *The Complete Poems 1927-1979*. New York: The Noonday Press/Farrar, Straus and Giroux, 1983.

Bleier, Ruth, ed. *Feminist Approaches to Science.* New York: Pergamon, 1986.

Bleier, Ruth. *Science and Gender: A Critique of Biology and Its Theories on Women.* New York: Pergamon, 1984.

Boffin, Tessa, and Sunil Gupta, eds. *Ecstatic Antibodies: Resisting the AIDS Mythology.* London: Rivers Oram Press, 1990.

Bordo, Susan. "The Cartesian Masculinization of Thought." *Signs* 11:3 (1986), 439-55.

Boulard, Garry. "Cover Story: The Man Behind the Mask." *The Advocate* no. 680 (2 May 1995), 28-35.

Bourjaily, Vance. *Old Soldier.* New York: Donald I. Fine, 1990.

Bowen, Peter M. "AIDS 101." In Murphy and Poirier, eds. *Writing AIDS.* 140-60.

Brandt, Allan M. *No Magic Bullet: A Social History of Venereal Disease in the United States Since 1880*, expanded ed. New York and Oxford: Oxford University Press, 1987.

Breitman, Patti, Kim Knutson, and Paul Reed. *How to Persuade Your Lover to Use a Condom . . . And Why You Should.* Rocklin, CA: Prima Publishing, 1987.

Brooks, Franklin, and Timothy F. Murphy. "Annotated Bibliography of AIDS Literature, 1982-91." In Murphy and Poirier, eds. *Writing AIDS.* 321-29.

Brothers, M. H. "Computer Virus Protection Procedures." In Denning, ed. *Computers Under Attack.* 356-80.

Brown, Clifton. "A Career of Impact, A Player with Heart." *New York Times* 8 Nov. 1991, B11, B13.

Brown, Clifton. "Decision Shocks Riley and Players." *New York Times* 3 Nov. 1992, B11.

Brown, Clifton. "For One Stirring Afternoon, Magic Johnson Dazzles Again." *New York Times* 10 Feb. 1992, A1, C4.

Brown, Clifton. "Johnson Delights and Earns a Night Off." *New York Times* 22 Oct. 1992, B20.

Brown, Clifton. "Johnson, Unbowed by H.I.V., Will Return to Pro Basketball." *New York Times* 30 Sept. 1992, A1, B14.

Browne, Malcolm W. "Lively Computer Creation Blurs Definition of Life." *New York Times* 27 Aug. 1991, C1, C8.

Browne, Malcolm W. "Quest to Mimic Life Began in 1940's." *New York Times* 27 Aug. 1991, C8.

Bruning, Fred, and Laurie Garrett. "Stunned Nation Reacts to Hero's Illness." *New York Newsday* 9 Nov. 1991, 6, 12.

Bryan, Jed A. *A Cry in the Desert.* Austin, TX: Banned Books, 1987.

Bryan, Jed A. "Crying 'Wolf!': The Genesis of an AIDS Disaster Epic." In Pastore, ed. *Confronting AIDS.* 68-78.

Bryan, Jed A. *Sacred Cows*. Austin, TX: Banned Books, 1989.
Bryan, Jed A. "Voices." In Pastore, ed. *Confronting AIDS*. 152-56.
Bryant, Dorothy. *A Day in San Francisco*. Berkeley: Ata Books, 1982.
Buckley, William F., Jr. "Identify All the Carriers." *New York Times* 18 March 1986, A27.
Bunn, Curtis G. "Courage Praised By Riley." *New York Newsday* 9 Nov. 1991, 158.
Burroughs, William S. "Ten Years and a Billion Dollars." *The Adding Machine: Selected Essays*. New York: Seaver Books, 1986. 48-52.
Butler, Judith. *Bodies That Matter: On the Discursive Limits of "Sex."* New York and London: Routledge, 1993.
Butler, Judith. *Gender Trouble: Feminism and the Subversion of Identity*. New York and London: Routledge, 1990.
Butler, Judith. "Sexual Inversions." In Stanton, ed. *Discourses of Sexuality*. 344-61.
Byrne, Melinda J. "Don't Give Up" (letter). *New York Times* 10 June 1993, A26.
Cady, Joseph. "Immersive and Counterimmersive Writing About AIDS: The Achievement of Paul Monette's *Love Alone*." In Murphy and Poirier, eds. *Writing AIDS*. 244-64.
Cady, Joseph. "Teaching About AIDS through Literature in a Medical School Curriculum." In Pastore, ed. *Confronting AIDS*. 233-48.
Cairns, John, Gunther S. Stent, and James D. Watson, eds. *Phage and the Origins of Molecular Biology*. Cold Spring Harbor, NY: Cold Spring Harbor Laboratory of Quantitative Biology, 1966.
Callen, Michael. *Surviving AIDS*. New York: HarperCollins, 1990.
Carlomusto, Jean. "Focusing on Women: Video as Activism." In ACT UP/NY. *Women, AIDS, and Activism*. 215-18.
Carroll, Mark. *Organelles*. New York and London: The Guilford Press, 1989.
Carter, Erica, and Simon Watney, eds. *Taking Liberties: AIDS and Cultural Politics*. London: Serpent's Tail, 1989.
Carvajal, Doreen. "Cardinal to Be Marshal for St. Patrick's Parade." *New York Times* 15 Dec. 1994, B3.
"Case Records of the Massachusetts General Hospital: Weekly Clinicopathological Exercises: Case 46-1984." *NEJM* 311:20 (15 Nov. 1984), 1303-10.
"Case Records of the Massachusetts General Hospital: Weekly Clinicopathological Exercises: Case 9-1986." *NEJM* 314:10 (6 March 1986), 629-40.
"Case Records of the Massachusetts General Hospital: Weekly Clinicopathological Exercises: Case 51-1986." *NEJM* 315:26 (25 Dec. 1986), 1660-68.
Castle, Terry. *The Apparitional Lesbian: Female Homosexuality and Modern Culture*. New York: Columbia University Press, 1993.

Childress, James F. "Mandatory HIV Screening and Testing." In Frederic G. Reamer, ed. *AIDS and Ethics*. New York: Columbia University Press, 1991. 50-76.

Christensen, Kim. "Prison Issues and HIV: Introduction." In ACT UP/NY. *Women, AIDS, and Activism*. 139-42.

Cliff, Michelle. *Bodies of Water*. New York: E. P. Dutton, 1990.

Clines, Francis X. "To Be Irish, Gay and on the Outside, Once Again." *New York Times* 13 March 1993, 23, 26.

Clum, John M. *Acting Gay: Male Homosexuality in Modern Drama*, revised ed. New York: Columbia University Press, 1994.

Clum, John M. "'And Once I Had It All': AIDS Narratives and Memories of an American Dream." In Murphy and Poirier, eds. *Writing AIDS*. 200-224.

Coe, Christopher. *Such Times*. New York, San Diego, and London: Harcourt Brace & Co., 1993.

Cohen, Fred. "Implications of Computer Viruses and Current Methods of Defense." In Denning, ed. *Computers Under Attack*. 381-406.

Cohen, Jon. "How Can HIV Replication Be Controlled?" *Science* 260 (28 May 1993), 1257.

Colen, B. D. "CDC Wants to Broaden the Definition of AIDS." *New York Newsday* 15 Nov. 1991, 17.

Colen, B. D. "What Magic Might Say Now." *New York Newsday* 3 Dec. 1991, 67.

Collins, Glenn. "Brad Davis, 41, a Leading Actor in 'Normal Heart' and 'Querelle.'" *New York Times* 10 Sept. 1991, B5.

Collins, Glenn. "On Helms and Grants with Poison Pills." *New York Times* 7 Aug. 1989, C11, C14.

Congressional Record—House [Debate on Immigration Provisions] 11 March 1993, H1203-1210.

Congressional Record—Senate [Debate on Helms Amendments] 14 Oct. 1987, S14202-12, S14215-20.

Coppola, Vincent, Richard West, and Janet Huck. "The AIDS Epidemic: The Change in Gay Life-Style." *Newsweek* 18 April 1983, 80.

Corea, Gena. *The Invisible Epidemic: The Story of Women and AIDS*. New York: HarperCollins, 1992.

"Courage." *New York Post* 8 Nov. 1991, 1.

Cox, Elizabeth. *Thanksgiving: An AIDS Journal*. New York: Harper & Row, 1990.

Crick, Francis. *Life Itself: Its Origin and Nature*. New York: Simon & Schuster, 1981.

Crick, F. H. C. "On Protein Synthesis." *Symposium of the Society for Experimental Biology* 12 (1958), 138-63.

Crick, Francis. *What Mad Pursuit: A Personal View of Scientific Discovery.* New York: Basic Books, 1988.
Crimp, Douglas, ed. *AIDS: Cultural Analysis/Cultural Activism.* Cambridge, MA, and London: The MIT Press, 1988. [Volume originally published as *October* 43 (Winter 1987).]
Crimp, Douglas. "AIDS: Cultural Analysis/Cultural Activism." In Crimp, ed. *AIDS: Cultural Analysis/Cultural Activism.* 3-16.
Crimp, Douglas. "How to Have Promiscuity in an Epidemic." In Crimp, ed. *AIDS: Cultural Analysis/Cultural Activism.* 237-71.
Crimp, Douglas. "Portraits of People with AIDS." In Stanton, ed. *Discourses of Sexuality.* 362-88.
Crimp, Douglas, with Adam Rolston. *AIDS Demo Graphics.* Seattle: Bay Press, 1990.
Currier, Jameson. *Dancing on the Moon: Short Stories About AIDS.* New York: Viking, 1993.
"Dallas Police Discount AIDS Revenge Tale." *New York Times* 23 Oct. 1991, A14.
Dalton, Harlon. "AIDS in Blackface." In Graubard, ed. *Living with AIDS.* 237-59.
Damian, Peter. *Liber Gomorrhianus.* In J.-P. Migne, ed. *Patrologiae cursus completus, Series latina.* Paris, 1841-79. Vol. 145. Cols. 159-90.
Daumann, Rudolf Heinrich. *Patrouille gegen den Tod: Ein utopischer Roman* [*Patrol Against Death: A Utopian Novel*]. Berlin: Schutzen-Verlag, 1939.
Davis, Christopher. *Valley of the Shadow.* New York: St. Martin's Press, 1988.
Dawkins, Richard. *The Selfish Gene.* New York: Oxford University Press, 1976.
Dellamora, Richard. *Apocalyptic Overtures: Sexual Politics and the Sense of an Ending.* New Brunswick: Rutgers University Press, 1994.
Denenberg, Risa. "Treatment and Trials." In ACT UP/NY. *Women, AIDS, and Activism.* 69-79.
Denenberg, Risa. "Unique Aspects of HIV Infection in Women." In ACT UP/NY. *Women, AIDS, and Activism.* 31-43.
Denenberg, Risa. "What the Numbers Mean." In ACT UP/NY. *Women, AIDS, and Activism.* 1-4.
Denning, Peter J. "Computer Viruses." In Denning, ed. *Computers Under Attack.* 285-92.
Denning, Peter J., ed. *Computers Under Attack: Intruders, Worms, and Viruses.* New York: ACM Press, 1990. Reprinted with corrections, New York: ACM Press; Reading, MA: Addison-Wesley Publishing Company, 1991.

Denning, Peter J. "The Internet Worm." In Denning, ed. *Computers Under Attack*. 193-200.

Derrida, Jacques. "The Rhetoric of Drugs. *An Interview.*" Michael Israel, trans. *Differences: A Journal of Feminist Cultural Studies* 5:1 (1993), 1-25.

Dewey, Joseph. *In a Dark Time: The Apocalyptic Temper in the American Novel of the Nuclear Age*. West Lafayette, IN: Purdue University Press, 1990.

Dewey, Joseph. "Music for a Closing: Responses to AIDS in Three American Novels." In Nelson, ed. *AIDS: The Literary Response*. 23-38.

de Zalduondo, Barbara O., Gernard I. Msamanga, and Lincoln C. Chen. "AIDS in Africa: Diversity in the Global Pandemic." In Graubard, ed. *Living with AIDS*. 423-63.

D'Hondt, John. *The Bunny Book: A Novel for Anyone Who Believes Life & Death Are, After All, a Wonder*. San Francisco: GLB Publishers, 1991.

DiAna, DiAna. "Talking That Talk." In ACT UP/NY. *Women, AIDS, and Activism*. 219-22.

Dickey, James. *Deliverance*. New York: Dell, 1971 [1970].

Dollimore, Jonathan. *Sexual Dissidence: Augustine to Wilde, Freud to Foucault*. Oxford: Clarendon Press, 1991.

Donne, John. *Poetry and Prose*. Frank J. Warnke, ed. New York: Modern Library, 1967.

Doyal, Leslie, Jennie Naidoo, and Tamsin Wilson, eds. *AIDS: Setting a Feminist Agenda*. London: Taylor & Francis, 1994.

Dreuilhe, Emmaneul. *Mortal Embrace: Living with AIDS*. Linda Coverdale, trans. New York: Hill and Wang, 1988.

Duplechan, Larry. *Blackbird*. New York: St. Martin's Press, 1986.

Duplechan, Larry. *Captain Swing: A Love Story*. Boston: Alyson, 1993.

Duplechan, Larry. *Eight Days a Week*. Boston: Alyson, 1985.

Duplechan, Larry. *Tangled Up in Blue*. New York: St. Martin's Press, 1989.

Edelman, Lee. "The Mirror and the Tank: 'AIDS,' Subjectivity, and the Rhetoric of Activism." In Murphy and Poirier, eds. *Writing AIDS*. 9-38.

Edelman, Lee. "The Plague of Discourse: Politics, Literary Theory, and AIDS." In Ronald R. Butters, John M. Clum, and Michael Moon, eds. *Displacing Homophobia: Gay Male Perspectives in Literature and Culture*. Durham and London: Duke University Press, 1989. 289-305. [Volume originally published as *South Atlantic Quarterly* 88:1].

Edelman, Lee. "Seeing Things: Representation, the Scene of Surveillance, and the Spectacle of Gay Male Sex." In Fuss, ed. *Inside/Out*. 93-116.

Ellis, Sue, and Paul Heritage. "AIDS and the Cultural Response: *The Normal Heart* and *We All Fall Down*." In Simon Shepherd and Mick Wallis, eds. *Coming on Strong: Gay Politics and Culture*. London: Unwin Hyman, 1989. 39-53.

Epstein, Julia. "AIDS, Stigma, and Narratives of Containment." *American Imago* 49:3 (1992), 293-310.

Erlanger, Steven. "A Plague Awaits." *New York Times Magazine* 14 July 1991, 24, 26, 49, 53.

Erni, John Nguyet. *Unstable Frontiers: Technomedicine and the Cultural Politics of "Curing" AIDS*. Minneapolis and London: University of Minnesota Press, 1994.

Essex, Max, and Phyllis J. Kanki. "The Origins of the AIDS Virus." In *The Science of AIDS*. 26-37.

Exander, Max [= Paul Reed]. *LoveSex*. Boston: Alyson, 1986.

Exander, Max [= Paul Reed]. *Leathersex*. New York: Badboy/Masquerade Books, 1994.

Exander, Max [= Paul Reed]. *ManSex*. San Francisco: Gay Sunshine Press, 1985.

Exander, Max [= Paul Reed]. *SafeStud*. Boston: Alyson, 1985.

Farmer, Paul. *AIDS and Accusation: Haiti and the Geography of Blame*. Berkeley, Los Angeles, and Oxford: University of California Press, 1992.

Fauci, Anthony S. "The Acquired Immune Deficiency Syndrome: The Ever-Broadening Clinical Spectrum." *JAMA* 249:17 (6 May 1983), 2375-76.

Fausto-Sterling, Anne. *Myths of Gender: Biological Theories About Women and Men*. New York: Basic Books, 1985.

Fee, Elizabeth, and Daniel M. Fox, eds. *AIDS: The Burdens of History*. Berkeley, Los Angeles, and London: University of California Press, 1988.

Fee, Elizabeth, and Daniel M. Fox, eds. *AIDS: The Making of a Chronic Disease*. Berkeley, Los Angeles, and Oxford: University of California Press, 1992.

Fee, Elizabeth, and Daniel M. Fox. "Introduction: The Contemporary Historiography of AIDS." In Fee and Fox, eds. *AIDS: The Making of a Chronic Disease*. 1-19.

Feinberg, David B. *Eighty-Sixed*. New York: Viking, 1989.

Feinberg, David B. *Queer and Loathing: Rants and Raves of a Raging AIDS Clone*. New York: Viking, 1994.

Feinberg, David B. *Spontaneous Combustion*. New York: Viking, 1991.

Feldman, Jamie. "Gallo, Montagnier, and the Debate over HIV: A Narrative Analysis." *Camera Obscura: A Journal of Feminism and Film Theory* 28 (1992), 100-33.

"Fellow Players Stunned." *New York Newsday* 8 Nov. 1991, 158, 157.

Ferro, Robert. *Second Son*. New York: Crown, 1988.

Fettner, Ann Giudici. *Viruses: Agents of Change*. New York: McGraw-Hill Publishing Company, 1990.

Fettner, Ann Giudici, and William A. Check. *The Truth About AIDS: Evolution of an Epidemic*, revised ed. New York: Owl Book/Henry Holt and Company, 1985.

Fields, Bernard N., and David M. Knipe. "Introduction." In Fields, et al. *Fundamental Virology*. 3-7.

Fields, Bernard N., David M. Knipe, Robert M. Chanock, Martin S. Hirsch, Joseph L. Melnick, Thomas P. Monath, and Bernard Roizman. *Fundamental Virology*, 2nd ed. New York: Raven Press, 1991 [1986].

Finkelstein, Avram. "It Has Been a Week of Magic." *NYQ* no. 5 (24 Nov. 1991), 27.

Fisher, Lawrence M. "Search Advances for 'Antisense' Drugs." *New York Times* 8 June 1993, C3.

Fried, Joseph P. "O'Connor Says Catholic Groups May Shun St. Patrick's Parade." *New York Times* 16 Feb. 1993, B5.

Friend, Tom. "Just Like Starting over for Lakers." *New York Times* 3 Nov. 1992, B11.

Friend, Tom. "No Anger by Johnson on Malone's Remarks." *New York Times* 4 Nov. 1992, B22.

Fuss, Diana, ed. *Inside/Out: Lesbian Theories, Gay Theories*. New York and London: Routledge, 1991.

Gagnon, Monika. "A Convergence of Stakes: Photography, Feminism, and AIDS." In Miller, ed. *Fluid Exchanges*. 53-64.

Gallo, Robert C. "The AIDS Virus." *Scientific American* 256 (Jan. 1987), 47-56.

George, Nelson. "The Magic Touch." *Village Voice* 19 Nov. 1991, 37, 156.

Gergen, Joe. "'See? I'm Not Sick.'" *New York Newsday* 12 Dec. 1991, 157.

Gever, Martha. "Pictures of Sickness: Stuart Marshall's *Bright Eyes*." In Crimp, ed. *AIDS: Cultural Analysis/Cultural Activism*. 108-26.

Gilman, Sander L. "AIDS and Syphilis: The Iconography of Disease." In Crimp, ed. *AIDS: Cultural Analysis/Cultural Activism*. 87-107.

Gilman, Sander L. "Plague in Germany, 1939/1989: Cultural Images of Race, Space, and Disease." In Murphy and Poirier, eds. *Writing AIDS*. 54-82.

Glueck, Grace. "Border Skirmish: Art and Politics." *New York Times* 19 Nov. 1989, Section 2, 1, 5.

Glueck, Grace. "Senate Vote Prompts Anger, But Some Approval in the Art World." *New York Times* 28 July 1989, B6.

Goldstein, Marianne, and Florence Anthony. "Magic is HIV Positive." *New York Post* 8 Nov. 1991, 5.

Goleman, Daniel. "Scientists Pinpoint Brain Irregularities In Drug Addicts." *New York Times* 26 June 1990, C1, C7.

Gordon, Michael R. "Hints of Gay-Ban Compromise in Senate." *New York Times* 30 March 1993, A18.

Graubard, Stephen R., ed. *Living with AIDS*. Cambridge, MA, and London: The MIT Press, 1990. [Volume originally published as *Daedalus* 118:2-3 (1989).]

Gray, Jerry. "Gay Group Rebuffed in Bid to Join St. Patrick's Parade." *New York Times* 8 March 1991, B3.

Gray, Jerry. "Longer St. Patrick's Parade May Allow Gay Irish Group." *New York Times* 9 March 1991, A27.

Grmek, Mirko D. *History of AIDS: Emergence and Origin of a Modern Pandemic*. Russell C. Maulitz and Jacalyn Duffin, trans. Princeton: Princeton University Press, 1990.

Gross, Jane. "At AIDS Epicenter, Seeking Swift, Sure Death." *New York Times* 20 June 1993, 16.

Grover, Jan Zita. "AIDS: Keywords." In Crimp, ed. *AIDS: Cultural Analysis/Cultural Criticism*. 17-30.

Grover, Jan Zita. "Constitutional Symptoms." In Carter and Watney, eds. *Taking Liberties*. 147-59.

Grover, Jan Zita. "Visible Lesions: Images of the PWA in America." In Miller, ed. *Fluid Exchanges*. 23-51 (illustrations following 51).

Guibert, Hervé. *The Compassion Protocol*. New York: George Braziller, 1994 [1991].

Guibert, Hervé. *To the Friend Who Did Not Save My Life*. New York: Atheneum, 1991 [1990].

Gunderson, Martin, David J. Mayo, and Frank S. Rhame. *AIDS: Testing and Privacy*. Salt Lake City: University of Utah Press, 1989.

Hall, Richard. "From the Guest Prose Editor: The High-Tech Gay Novel." *The James White Review* 8:3 (Spring 1991), 3.

Hammett, Theodore M., and Saira Moini. "Update on AIDS in Prisons and Jails." *AIDS Bulletin* (National Institute of Justice, U.S. Department of Justice) Sept. 1990, 6-8.

Hanson, Ellis. "Undead." In Fuss, ed. *Inside/Out*. 324-40.

Haraway, Donna J. *Primate Visions: Gender, Race, and Nature in the World of Modern Science*. New York: Routledge, 1989.

Haraway, Donna J. *Simians, Cyborgs, and Women: The Reinvention of Nature*. New York: Routledge, 1991.

Harding, Sandra. *The Science Question in Feminism*. Ithaca: Cornell University Press, 1986.

Harding, Sandra, and Merrill B. Hintikka, eds. *Discovering Reality: Feminist Perspectives on Epistemology, Metaphysics, Methodology, and Philosophy of Science*. Dordrecht: D. Reidel, 1983.

Harper, Phillip Brian. "Eloquence and Epitaph: Black Nationalism and the Homophobic Impulse in Responses to the Death of Max Robinson." In

Murphy and Poirier, eds. *Writing AIDS*. 117-39. [Also printed in Abelove, Barale, and Halperin, eds. *The Lesbian and Gay Studies Reader*. 159-75.]

Harper, Phillip Brian. "Private Affairs: Race, Sex, Property, and Persons." *GLQ* 1:2 (1994), 111-33.

Harrington, Mark. "Bodies on the Line." *QW* no. 43 (30 Aug. 1992), 43-44 and 70-71.

Harrington, Mark. "Pathogenesis and Activism." *DOCUMENTS* 1:3 (Summer 1993), 4-12.

Harris, Daniel. "Making Kitsch from AIDS: A Disease with a Gift Shop of Its Own." *Harper's* 289:1730 (July 1994), 55-60.

Harrison, Stephen C. "Principles of Virus Structure." In Fields, et al., eds. *Fundamental Virology*. 37-61.

Harty, Kevin J. "'All the Elements of a Good Movie': Cinematic Responses to the AIDS Pandemic." In Nelson, ed. *AIDS: The Literary Response*. 114-30.

Haseltine, William A., and Flossie Wong-Staal. "The Molecular Biology of the AIDS Virus." In *The Science of AIDS*. 12-25.

HEAL [Health Education AIDS Liaison]. "Information Packet." Spring 1991, updated Spring 1992.

Hekma, Gert. "*The Mystical Body*: Frans Kellendonk and the Dutch Literary Response to AIDS." In Nelson, ed. *AIDS: The Literary Response*, 88-94.

Hemingway, Ernest. *Death in the Afternoon*. New York: P. F. Collier & Son, 1932.

Herzog, Bob. "Hall of Fame Says Magic Must Wait." *New York Newsday* 9 Nov. 1991, 86.

Hevesi, Dennis. "Gay Irish Win Right to March in a Parade That Might Die." *New York Times* 29 Oct. 1992, B1, B4.

Heyward, William L., and James W. Curran. "The Epidemiology of AIDS in the U.S." In *The Science of AIDS*. 38-49.

Highland, Harold Joseph. "The BRAIN Virus: Fact and Fantasy." In Denning, ed. *Computers Under Attack*. 293-98.

Highland, Harold Joseph. "Computer Viruses—A Post Mortem." In Denning, ed. *Computers Under Attack*. 299-315.

Hilchey, Tim. "How a Flu Molecule Stands on Its Head to Infect Human Cells." *New York Times* 6 Sept. 1994, C3.

Hilferty, Robert, director. *Stop the Church!* 1991.

Hilts, Philip J. "U.S. Agency Is Criticized for Dropping AIDS Ads." *New York Times* 1 July 1992, A10.

Hoffman, Alice. *At Risk*. New York: G. P. Putnam's Sons, 1988. [Paperback edition: New York: Berkley Books, 1989.]

Hoffman, William M. *As Is*. New York: Vintage/Random House, 1985.

Holleran, Andrew. *Nights in Aruba*. New York: Plume, 1984 [1983].

hooks, bell. "Reconstructing Black Masculinity." *Black Looks: Race and Representation*. Boston: South End Press, 1992. 87-113.

Howard, Ted, and Jeremy Rifkin. *Who Should Play God? The Artificial Creation of Life and What It Means for the Future of the Human Race*. New York: Delacorte Press, 1977.

Hruska, Jan. *Computer Viruses and Anti-Virus Warfare*. New York: Ellis Horwood, 1990.

Hubbard, Jan. "A Strange Homecoming." *New York Newsday* 11 Nov. 1991, 92, 80.

Hughes, Holly, and Richard Elovich. "Homophobia at the N.E.A." *New York Times* 28 July 1990, 21.

Ifill, Gwen. "Senate Votes to Limit Arts Grants." *New York Times* 20 Sept. 1991, C3.

Irigaray, Luce. "'I Won't Get AIDS.'" *Je, Tu, Nous: Toward a Culture of Difference*. Alison Martin, trans. New York and London: Routledge, 1993. 61-65.

Jackson, Earl, Jr. "Death Drives Across Pornotopia: Dennis Cooper on the Extremities of Being." *GLQ* 1 (1994), 143-61.

James, John S. "Berlin Conference Overview." *AIDS Treatment News* 177 (18 June 1993), 1-3.

Jasny, Barbara R. "Editorial: AIDS 1993: Unanswered Questions." *Science* 260 (28 May 1993), 1219. [Special issue: "AIDS: The Unanswered Questions."]

Johnson, Earvin. Roy S. Johnson, ed. "I'll Deal with It." *Sports Illustrated* 78 (18 Nov. 1991), 16-27.

Johnson, Toby [Edwin Clark Johnson]. "Facing the Edge: AIDS as a Source of Spiritual Wisdom." In Pastore, ed. *Confronting AIDS*. 124-41.

Johnson, Toby [Edwin Clark Johnson]. "Friends." In Preston, ed. *Hot Living*. 24-30.

Johnson, Toby [Edwin Clark Johnson]. *In Search of God in the Sexual Underworld: A Mystical Journey*. New York: Quill, 1983.

Johnson, Toby [Edwin Clark Johnson]. *The Myth of the Great Secret: A Search for Spiritual Meaning in the Face of Emptiness*. New York: Morrow, 1982.

Johnson, Toby [Edwin Clark Johnson]. *Plague: A Novel about Healing*. Boston: Alyson, 1987.

Johnson, Toby [Edwin Clark Johnson]. *Secret Matter*. South Norwalk, CT: Lavender Press, 1990.

Jones, James W. "Refusing the Name: The Absence of AIDS in Recent American Gay Fiction." In Murphy and Poirier, eds. *Writing AIDS*. 225-43.

Jordanova, Ludmilla. *Sexual Visions: Images of Gender in Science and Medicine between the Eighteenth and Twentieth Centuries.* Madison: University of Wisconsin Press, 1989.

Joseph, Stephen C. "Quarantine: Sometimes a Duty." *New York Times* 10 Feb. 1990, 25.

Joslin, Tom, and Peter Friedman. *Silverlake Life: The View from Here.* Zeitgeist Films, 1993.

"Judge Draws Protests After Cutting Sentence of Gay Man's Killer." *New York Times* 17 Aug. 1994, A15.

Kakutani, Michiko. "On the 'Datasphere' and a Generation Absorbed in It." *New York Times* 6 Dec. 1994, C19.

Kantrowitz, Barbara, with Mary Hager, Geoffrey Cowley, Lucille Beachy, Melissa Rossi, Brynn Craffey, Peter Annin, and Rebecca Crandall. "Teenagers and AIDS." *Newsweek* 3 Aug. 1992, 44-49.

"Kaposi's Sarcoma and *Pneumocystis* Pneumonia Among Homosexual Men—New York City and California." *MMWR* 30:25 (3 July 1981), 305-7.

Keller, Evelyn Fox. "Feminism and Science." *Signs* 7:3 (1982), 589-602.

Keller, Evelyn Fox. *Reflections on Gender and Science.* New Haven: Yale University Press, 1985.

Kennedy, Shawn G. "Israel Parade to Include a Gay Group." *New York Times* 21 April 1993, B3.

Kerber, Fred. "Magic Slam Dunks Story." *New York Post* 22 Oct. 1992, 69.

Kinsella, James. *Covering the Plague: AIDS and the American Media.* New Brunswick and London: Rutgers University Press, 1989.

Kolata, Gina. "Coincidence or Link Between Cancer and Hereditary Diseases?" *New York Times* 11 May 1993, C3.

Kolata, Gina. "N.I.H. Neglects Women, Study Says." *New York Times* 19 June 1990, C6.

Kolata, Gina. "Novel Kind of Computing: Calculation with DNA." *New York Times* 22 Nov. 1994, C1, C13.

Kolata, Gina. "Scientist at Work: Leonard Adleman: Hitting the High Spots of Computer Theory." *New York Times* 13 Dec. 1994, C1, C10.

Kolins, Jerry. "On Trojan Horses and Surrogate Mothers" (letter). *NEJM* 311:1 (5 July 1984), 53.

Koop, C. Everett. "Surgeon General's Report on Acquired Immune Deficiency Syndrome." U.S. Department of Health and Human Services. [1987].

Kramer, Larry. *The Normal Heart.* New York: Plume, 1985.

Kramer, Larry. *Reports from the Holocaust: The Making of an AIDS Activist.* New York: St. Martin's Press, 1989.

Krauss, Clifford. "Housing Nominee Is Attacked." *New York Times* 21 May 1993, A12.

Kushner, Tony. *Angels in America: A Gay Fantasia on National Themes: Part One: Millennium Approaches.* New York: Theatre Communications Group, 1993.

Kushner, Tony. *Angels in America: A Gay Fantasia on National Themes: Part Two: Perestroika.* New York: Theatre Communications Group, 1994.

Labaton, Stephen. "U.S. Drops Effort to Oust a Gay Sailor." *New York Times* 29 Nov. 1994, A20.

Lambert, Bruce. "Unlikely AIDS Sufferer's Message: Even You Can Get It." *New York Times* 11 March 1989, 29, 32.

Leary, Warren E. "A Key to Flu Virus Infection Is Identified." *New York Times* 21 May 1993, A18.

Leary, Warren E. "New Techniques Hold Promise in Fighting AIDS." *New York Times* 8 Nov. 1994, C5.

Leavitt, David. "The Way I Live Now." *New York Times Magazine* 9 July 1989, 28.

Leavitt, David. *While England Sleeps.* New York: Viking, 1993.

Lehmann-Haupt, Christopher. "The Art of Going Gentle into That Good Night." *New York Times* 10 June 1993, C17.

Leonard, Zoe. "HIV-Antibody Testing and Legal Issues for HIV-Positive People." In ACT UP/NY. *Women, AIDS, and Activism.* 55-67.

Leonard, Zoe, and Polly Thistlethwaite. "Prostitution and HIV Infection." In ACT UP/NY. *Women, AIDS, and Activism.* 177-85.

LeVay, Simon. "A Difference in Hypothalamic Structure Between Heterosexual and Homosexual Men." *Science* 253 (30 Aug. 1991), 1034-37.

LeVay, Simon. *The Sexual Brain.* Cambridge, MA: The MIT Press, 1993.

Lewis, Peter H. "Personal Computers: The Virus: Threat or Menace?" *New York Times* 15 June 1993, C7.

Lewis, Peter H. "The Executive Computer: Medicine, and Common Sense, for Virus Problems." *New York Times* 21 June 1992, F9.

Lewontin, R. C., Steven Rose, and Leon J. Kamin. *Not in Our Genes: Biology, Ideology, and Human Nature.* New York: Pantheon Books, 1984.

Lii, Jane H. "Judge Says Gay Group Can't March." *New York Times* 16 March 1995, B3.

"The Long Road from HIV to AIDS." *New York Times* 17 Nov. 1991, Section 4, 1.

Longino, Helen E., and Evelynn Hammonds. "Conflicts and Tensions in the Feminist Study of Gender and Science." In Marianne Hirsch and Evelyn Fox Keller, eds. *Conflicts in Feminism.* New York and London: Routledge, 1990. 164-83.

"Magic Starts New Chapter: Teacher: On 'Arsenio' Touts Safe Sex." *New York Newsday* 9 Nov. 1991, 5.

"Magic's Brave New World." *New York Newsday* 9 Nov. 1991, 1.

Mains, Geoff. *Gentle Warriors*. Stamford, CT: Knights Press, 1989.
Mains, Geoff. *The Oxygen Revolution*. Newton Abbot, UK: David & Charles Publishers, 1972.
Mains, Geoff. *Urban Aboriginals: A Celebration of Leathersexuality*. San Francisco: Gay Sunshine Press, 1984.
Mains, Geoff. "The Molecular Anatomy of Leather." In Thompson, ed. *Leatherfolk*. 38-43.
Mains, Geoff. "The View from a Sling." In Thompson, ed. *Leatherfolk*. 233-39.
Mann, Jonathan M., James Chin, Peter Piot, and Thomas Quinn. "The International Epidemiology of AIDS." In *The Science of AIDS*. 50-61.
Markoff, John. "Beyond Artificial Intelligence, A Search for Artificial Life." *New York Times* 25 Feb. 1990, E5.
Marshall, Stuart. "Picturing Deviancy." In Boffin and Gupta, eds. *Ecstatic Antibodies*. 19-36.
Mars-Jones, Adam. *Monopolies of Loss*. New York: Knopf, 1993.
Martin, Emily. *Flexible Bodies: Tracking Immunity in American Culture—From the Days of Polio to the Age of AIDS*. Boston: Beacon Press, 1994.
Martin, Emily. *The Woman in the Body: A Cultural Analysis of Reproduction*. Boston: Beacon Press, 1992 [1987].
Martinez, Michael. "Citing 'Controversies,' Johnson Retires Again." *New York Times* 3 Nov. 1992, B9.
Massa, Robert. "The Way We Wear Our Genes." *Village Voice* 24 Dec. 1991, 49.
Maupin, Armistead. *Babycakes*. New York: Harper & Row, 1984.
Maupin, Armistead. *Further Tales of the City*. New York: Harper & Row, 1982.
Maupin, Armistead. *More Tales of the City*. New York: Harper & Row, 1980.
Maupin, Armistead. *Significant Others*. New York: Harper & Row, 1987.
Maupin, Armistead. *Sure of You*. New York: Harper & Row, 1989.
Maupin, Armistead. *Tales of the City*. New York: Harper & Row, 1978.
McCarthy, Sheryl. "Magic Conjures Up What's Real." *New York Newsday* 11 Nov. 1991, 14.
McDonald, Malcolm I., John D. Hamilton, and David T. Durack. "Hypothesis: Hepatitis B Surface Antigen Could Harbour the Infective Agent of AIDS." *Lancet* no. 8355 (13 Oct. 1983), 882-84.
McKinley, James C., Jr. "Parade Permit Will Benefit Gay Marchers." *New York Times* 9 Jan. 1993, 25, 28.
McKinley, James C., Jr. "St. Patrick's Standoff: Gay Issue Still Unresolved." *New York Times* 12 Feb. 1993, 25.
Merck, Mandy. "A Case of AIDS." In Boffin and Gupta, eds. *Ecstatic Antibodies*. 44-53.

Miller, D. A. "Anal Rope." In Fuss, ed. *Inside/Out*. 119-41.
Miller, James. "AIDS in the Novel: Getting It Straight." In Miller, ed. *Fluid Exchanges*. 257-71.
Miller, James. "Dante on Fire Island: Reinventing Heaven in the AIDS Elegy." In Murphy and Poirier, eds. *Writing AIDS*. 265-305.
Miller, James, ed. *Fluid Exchanges: Artists and Critics in the AIDS Crisis*. Toronto, Buffalo, and London: University of Toronto Press, 1992.
Mills, John, and Henry Masur. "AIDS-Related Infections." *Scientific American* 263 (Aug. 1990), 50-57.
"Minorities Seek More Action to Halt AIDS Spread." *New York Times* 19 Sept. 1994, A14.
Mohr, Richard D. "On Some Words from ACT UP: Doing and Being Done." *Gay Ideas: Outing and Other Controversies*. Boston: Beacon Press, 1992. 49-52.
Monette, Paul. *Afterlife*. New York: Crown, 1990.
Monette, Paul. *Borrowed Time: An AIDS Memoir*. San Diego, New York, and London: Harcourt Brace Jovanovich, 1988.
Monette, Paul. *Love Alone: Eighteen Elegies for Rog*. New York: St. Martin's Press, 1988.
Moore, Patrick. *This Every Night*. New York: Amethyst Press, 1990.
Morrison, James. "The Repression of the Returned: AIDS and Allegory." In Nelson, ed. *AIDS: The Literary Response*. 167-74.
Morrison, Paul. "End Pleasure." *GLQ* 1:1 (1993), 53-78.
Mosher, Howard Frank. "Adventures in the Maine Woods." *New York Times Book Review* 28 Oct. 1990, 15.
Munk, Erika. "The Arts Act Up: Can We Save the National Endowment?" *Village Voice* 3 April 1990, 57-59.
Munt, Sally. "'Somewhere over the Rainbow . . .': Postmodernism and the Fiction of Sarah Schulman." In Sally Munt, ed. *New Lesbian Criticism: Literary and Cultural Readings*. New York: Columbia University Press, 1992. 33-50.
"Murderous Mischief on AIDS." *New York Times* 23 Oct. 1989, A18.
Murphy, Frederick A., and David W. Kingsbury. "Virus Taxonomy." In Fields, et al., eds. *Fundamental Virology*. 9-35.
Murphy, Timothy F. "Testimony." In Murphy and Poirier, eds. *Writing AIDS*. 306-20.
Murphy, Timothy F., and Suzanne Poirier, eds. *Writing AIDS: Gay Literature, Language, and Analysis*. New York: Columbia University Press, 1993.
Musto, David F. "Quarantine and the Problem of AIDS." In Fee and Fox, eds. *AIDS: The Burdens of History*. 67-85.

Nanney, David L. "The Role of the Cytoplasm in Heredity." In William D. McElroy and Bentley Glass, eds. *A Symposium on the Chemical Basis of Heredity*. Baltimore: Johns Hopkins University Press, 1957. 134-66.

National Commission on AIDS. "HIV Disease in Correctional Facilities." March 1991.

Navarro, Mireya. "Agencies Slowed in Effort to Widen Definitions of AIDS." *New York Times* 10 Feb. 1992, A1, B11.

Navarro, Mireya. "AIDS Numbers Increase Under New Federal Rules." *New York Times* 22 March 1993, B3.

Navarro, Mireya. "Dated AIDS Definition Keeps Benefits from Many Patients." *New York Times* 8 July 1991, A1, B5.

Navarro, Mireya. "More Cases, Costs and Fears Under Wider AIDS Umbrella." *New York Times* 29 Oct. 1992, A1, B2.

Navarro, Mireya. "New Definition for AIDS Arrives, Bringing New Concerns." *New York Times* 6 Jan. 1993, B3.

Nelson, Emmanuel S. "AIDS and the American Novel." *Journal of American Culture* 13:1 (1990), 47-53.

Nelson, Emmanuel S., ed. *AIDS: The Literary Response*. New York: Twayne Publishers, 1992.

Nelson, Emmanuel S. "Selected Bibliography." In Nelson, ed. *AIDS: The Literary Response*. 219-24.

"'Not the Same As No Risk.'" *New York Times* 3 Nov. 1992, B11.

Nungesser, Lon G. *Epidemic of Courage: Facing AIDS in America*. New York: St. Martin's Press, 1986.

Nunokawa, Jeff. "'All the Sad Young Men': AIDS and the Work of Mourning." In Fuss, ed. *Inside/Out*. 311-23.

O'Connell, Shaun. "The Big One: Literature Discovers AIDS." In Padraig O'Malley, ed. *The AIDS Epidemic: Private Rights and the Public Interest*. Boston: Beacon Press, 1989. 485-506. [Volume originally published as *New England Journal of Public Policy* 4:1 (Winter/Spring 1988).]

O'Connor, Flannery. *Three by Flannery O'Connor*. New York: Signet, 1962.

O'Connor, Flannery. "The Fiction Writer and His Country." *Mystery and Manners: Occasional Prose*. Sally Fitzgerald and Robert Fitzgerald, eds. New York: Farrar, Straus and Giroux, 1969. 25-35.

Oleske, James, Anthony Minnefor, Roger Cooper, Jr., Kathleen Thomas, Antonio dela Cruz, Houman Ahdieh, Isabel Guerrero, Vijay J. Joshi, and Franklin Desposito. "Immune Deficiency Syndrome in Children." *JAMA* 249:17 (6 May 1983), 2345-49.

O'Malley, Jeff. "The Representation of AIDS in Third World Development Discourse." In Miller, ed. *Fluid Exchanges*. 169-76.

Oreskes, Michael. "Senate Votes to Bar U.S. Support of 'Obscene or Indecent' Artwork." *New York Times* 27 July 1989, A1, C18.

Oxford English Dictionary, 2nd ed. J. A. Simpson and E. S. C. Weiner, eds. Oxford: Clarendon Press, 1989.

Packard, Randall M., and Paul Epstein. "Medical Research on AIDS in Africa: A Historical Perspective." In Fee and Fox, eds. *AIDS: The Making of a Chronic Disease*. 346-76.

Pastore, Judith Laurence. "Annotated Bibliography." In Pastore, ed. *Confronting AIDS*. 249-64.

Pastore, Judith Laurence, ed. *Confronting AIDS through Literature: The Responsibilities of Representation*. Urbana and Chicago: University of Illinois Press, 1993.

Pastore, Judith Laurence. "Suburban AIDS: Alice Hoffman's *At Risk*." In Nelson, ed. *AIDS: The Literary Response*. 39-49.

Patton, Brian. "Cell Wars: Military Metaphors and the Crisis of Authority in the AIDS Epidemic." In Miller, ed. *Fluid Exchanges*. 272-86.

Patton, Cindy. "Containing 'African AIDS': The Bourgeois Family as Safe Sex." In Andrew Parker, Mary Russo, Doris Sommer, and Patricia Yaeger, eds. *Nationalisms and Sexualities*. New York and London: Routledge, 1992. 265-84.

Patton, Cindy. "From Nation to Family: Containing African AIDS." In Abelove, Barale, and Halperin, eds. *The Lesbian and Gay Studies Reader*. 127-38.

Patton, Cindy. *Inventing AIDS*. New York and London: Routledge, 1990.

Patton, Cindy. *Last Served? Gendering the HIV Pandemic*. Social Aspects of AIDS Series. London: Taylor & Francis, 1994.

Patton, Cindy. *Sex and Germs: The Politics of AIDS*. Boston: South End Press, 1985.

Patton, Cindy. "Tremble, Hetero Swine!" In Michael Warner, ed. (for the Social Text Collective). *Fear of a Queer Planet: Queer Politics and Social Theory*. Minneapolis and London: University of Minnesota Press, 1993. 143-77.

Patton, Cindy. "Visualizing Safe Sex: When Pedagogy and Pornography Collide." In Fuss, ed. *Inside/Out*. 373-86.

Pear, Robert. "U.S. Alters Rules on People with H.I.V." *New York Times* 17 Dec. 1991, A16.

People With AIDS Coalition. "Founding Statement of People with AIDS/ARC (The Denver Principles)." In Crimp, ed. *AIDS: Cultural Analysis/Cultural Activism*. 148-49.

Pérez-Peña, Richard. "Irish Groups Expect Unity on Parade." *New York Times* 30 Jan. 1993, 25.

Pérez-Peña, Richard. "Judge Allows Group to Bar Gay Marchers." *New York Times* 27 Feb. 1993, 21, 25.

Piel, Jonathan. "Foreword." In *The Science of AIDS*. vii.

"*Pneumocystis* Pneumonia—Los Angeles." *MMWR* 30:21 (5 June 1981), 250-52.

"A Pneumonia That Strikes Gay Males." *San Francisco Chronicle* 6 June 1981, 4.

Preston, John, ed. *Hot Living: Erotic Stories About Safer Sex*. Boston: Alyson, 1985.

Preston, John, ed. *Personal Dispatches: Writers Confront AIDS*. New York: St. Martin's Press, 1989.

Purdum, Todd S. "New York Sets Out on Legal Path to Allow Gay Irish Unit in Parade." *New York Times* 25 Jan. 1992, 1, 26.

Rechy, John. *City of Night*. New York: Grove Press, 1963.

Rechy, John. *Marilyn's Daughter*. New York: Carroll & Graf Publishers, 1988.

Rechy, John. *The Miraculous Day of Amalia Gómez*. New York: Arcade Publishing/Little, Brown, 1991.

Rechy, John. *The Sexual Outlaw*. New York: Grove Press, 1977.

Redfield, Robert R., and Donald S. Burke. "HIV Infection: The Clinical Picture." In *The Science of AIDS*. 62-73.

Redfield, Robert R., D. Craig Wright, William D. James, T. Stephen Jones, Charles Brown, and Donald S. Burke. "Medical Intelligence: Disseminated Vaccinia in a Military Recruit with Human Immunodeficiency Virus (HIV) Disease." *NEJM* 316:11 (12 March 1987), 673-76.

Redfield, Robert R., D. Craig Wright, and Edmund C. Tramont. "The Walter Reed Staging Classification for HTLV-III/LAV Infection." *NEJM* 314:2 (9 Jan. 1986), 131-32.

Reed, Paul. "Early AIDS Fiction." In Pastore, ed. *Confronting AIDS*. 91-94.

Reed, Paul. *Facing It: A Novel of A.I.D.S.* San Francisco: Gay Sunshine Press, 1984.

Reed, Paul. *Longing*. Berkeley: Celestial Arts, 1988.

Reed, Paul. *The Q Journal: A Treatment Diary*. Berkeley: Celestial Arts, 1991.

Reed, Paul. *Savage Garden: A Journal*. San Francisco: House of Lillian, 1994.

Reed, Paul. *Serenity: Support and Guidance for People with HIV, Their Families, Friends, and Caregivers*, 2nd ed. Berkeley: Celestial Arts, 1990 [1987].

Reel, Bill. "What Magic Did Isn't Really So Heroic." *New York Newsday* 13 Nov. 1991. [Letters in response to this article appeared in *New York Newsday* 23 Nov. 1991, 16.]

René, Norman, director. Craig Lucas, writer. *Longtime Companion*. American Playhouse for PBS, 1990.

Rhodes, William C. "Magic, Not AIDS, Leaves Stage." *New York Times* 4 Nov. 1992, B21.

Richardson, Diane. *Women and AIDS*. New York: Routledge, 1989 [1988].

Richardson, Justin. "Uncle Sam Wants You to Live a Lie" (letter). *New York Times* 10 June 1993, A26.

Rieder, Ines, and Patricia Ruppelt, eds. *AIDS: The Women*. San Francisco and Pittsburgh: Cleis Press, 1988.

Rifkin, Jeremy. *Declaration of a Heretic*. Boston and London: Routledge and Kegan Paul, 1985.

Rifkin, Jeremy, and Nicanor Perlas. *Algeny*. New York: Viking, 1983.

Rist, Darrell Yates. "Are Homosexuals Born That Way?" *The Nation* 19 Oct. 1992, 424-29.

Robinson, David. "An Open Letter to Newscasters." *NYQ* no. 5 (24 Nov. 1991), 27-31.

Roizman, Bernard. "Multiplication of Viruses: An Overview." In Fields, et al., eds. *Fundamental Virology*. 87-94.

Román, David. "'It's My Party and I'll Die If I Want To!': Gay Men, AIDS, and the Circulation of Camp in U.S. Theatre." *Theatre Journal* 44 (1992), 305-27.

Roommates [made-for-television movie]. NBC. 30 May 1994.

Rotello, Gabriel. "Do Gays Really Have a Nerve?" *New York Newsday* 13 Aug. 1992, 48, 90.

Rubin, Marty. *The Boiled Frog Syndrome: A Novel of Love, Sex and Politics*. Boston: Alyson, 1987.

Rubin, Marty. "A Nice Jewish Boy from Toronto." In Preston, ed. *Hot Living*. 106-32.

Rubinstein, Arye, Marc Sicklick, Asha Gupta, Larry Bernstein, Norman Klein, Ethan Rubinstein, Ilya Spigland, Lazar Fruchter, Nathan Litman, Haesoon Lee, and Melvin Hollander. "Acquired Immunodeficiency with Reversed T4/T6 Ratios in Infants Born to Promiscuous and Drug-Addicted Mothers." *JAMA* 249:17 (6 May 1983), 2350-56.

Rudd, Andrea, and Darien Taylor. *Positive Women: Voices of Women Living with AIDS*. Toronto: Second Story Press, 1992.

Rumsey, Sunny. "AIDS Issues for African-American and African-Caribbean Women." In ACT UP/NY. *Women, AIDS, and Activism*. 103-6.

Rushkoff, Douglas. *Media Virus! Hidden Agendas in Popular Culture*. New York: Ballantine, 1994.

Ryman, Geoff. *Was*. New York: Penguin, 1993 [1992].

Sabatier, Renée. *Blaming Others: Prejudice, Race and Worldwide AIDS*. Washington, DC: The Panos Institute; Philadelphia: New Society Publishers, 1988.

Saffo, Paul. "Consensual Realities in Cyberspace." In Denning, ed. *Computers Under Attack*. 416-20.

Schmalz, Jeffrey. "Call Him Earvin: 'I Can't Be Magic.'" *New York Times* 19 Nov. 1992, C1, C10.

Schmalz, Jeffrey. "Split on Gay Tactics for Military Ban." *New York Times* 23 May 1993, 18.

Schmitt, Eric. "Compromise on Military Ban Gaining Support Among Senators." *New York Times* 12 May 1993, A1, A16.

Schmitt, Eric. "Gay Congressman Offers a Plan on Homosexuals in the Military." *New York Times* 19 May 1993, A14.

Schmitt, Eric. "Joint Chiefs to Get 2 Options on Homosexuals." *New York Times* 29 May 1993, 8.

Schulman, Sarah. *After Delores*. New York: E. P. Dutton, 1988.

Schulman, Sarah. *Empathy*. New York: E. P. Dutton, 1992.

Schulman, Sarah. "Literature in the Age of AIDS." In Amy Scholder, ed. "AIDS, Cultural Life, and the Arts: A Forum." *City Lights Review* 2 (1988), 34.

Schulman, Sarah. *My American History: Lesbian and Gay Life During the Reagan/Bush Years*. New York: Routledge, 1994.

Schulman, Sarah. *People in Trouble*. New York: E. P. Dutton, 1990.

Schulman, Sarah. *The Sophie Horowitz Story*. Tallahassee, FL: Naiad Press, 1984.

The Science of AIDS: Readings from Scientific American Magazine. New York: W. H. Freeman and Company, 1989 [1988].

Sedgwick, Eve Kosofsky. *Between Men: English Literature and Male Homosocial Desire*. New York: Columbia University Press, 1985.

Sedgwick, Eve Kosofsky. *Epistemology of the Closet*. Berkeley and Los Angeles: University of California Press, 1990.

Sedgwick, Eve Kosofsky. "Gender Criticism." In Stephen Greenblatt and Giles Gunn, eds. *Redrawing the Boundaries: The Transformation of English and American Literary Studies*. New York: The Modern Language Association of America, 1992. 271-302.

Shakespeare, William. *The Complete Works of Shakespeare*, 3rd ed. David Bevington, ed. Glenview, IL: Scott, Foresman & Co., 1980.

Shatzky, Joel. "AIDS Enters the American Theater: *As Is* and *The Normal Heart*." In Nelson, ed. *AIDS: The Literary Response*. 131-39.

Sherry, Michael S. "The Language of War in AIDS Discourse." In Murphy and Poirier, eds. *Writing AIDS*. 39-53.

Shilts, Randy. *And the Band Played On: Politics, People, and the AIDS Epidemic*. New York: Penguin, 1988 [1987].

Shilts, Randy. *Conduct Unbecoming: Gays and Lesbians in the U.S. Military*. New York: Fawcett Columbine, 1994 [1993]).

"A Side Trip into AIDS Theory." *New York Times* 13 Dec. 1984, C11.

Silverstein, Arthur M. *A History of Immunology*. San Diego: Academic Press, Inc., 1989.

Simmons, Doug. "Magic's Manhood." *Village Voice* 19 Nov. 1991, 37, 156.

Simmons, Sara. "A Community Responds." *NYQ* no. 5 (24 Nov. 1991), 28-29.

Slaff, James I., and John K. Brubaker. *The AIDS Epidemic: How You Can Protect Yourself and Your Family—Why You Must.* New York: Warner Books, 1985.

Sontag, Susan. *AIDS and Its Metaphors.* New York: Farrar, Straus and Giroux, 1989.

Sontag, Susan. *Illness as Metaphor.* New York: Farrar, Straus and Giroux, 1978.

Sontag, Susan. *Illness as Metaphor* and *AIDS and Its Metaphors.* New York: Anchor Books/Doubleday, 1990.

Sontag, Susan. "Spiritual Style in the Films of Robert Bresson." *Against Interpretation and Other Essays.* New York: Anchor Books/Doubleday, 1990 [1966]. 177-95.

Spafford, Eugene H., Kathleen A. Heaphy, and David J. Ferbrache. "A Computer Virus Primer." In Denning, ed. *Computers Under Attack.* 316-55.

Specter, Michael. "When AIDS Taps Hero, His 'Children' Feel Pain." *New York Times* 9 Nov. 1991, 1, 32.

Spiro, Ellen. "DiAna's Hair Ego: AIDS Info Up Front." 1989. Video Data Bank, distributor.

Spottiswoode, Roger, director. *And the Band Played On.* HBO Pictures, 1993.

Stanley, Wendell M., and Evans G. Valens. *Viruses and the Nature of Life.* New York: E. P. Dutton, 1961.

Stanton, Domna C., ed. *Discourses of Sexuality: From Aristotle to AIDS.* Ann Arbor: The University of Michigan Press, 1992.

Steinberg, Jacques. "Gay Dispute Fails to Disrupt Israel Day March." *New York Times* 10 May 1993, B1, B3.

Stent, Gunther S., and Richard Calendar. *Molecular Genetics: An Introductory Narrative*, 2nd ed. San Francisco: W. H. Freeman and Company, 1978.

Stevenson, Richard W. "Johnson's Frankness Continues." *New York Times* 9 Nov. 1991, 33.

Stoddard, Thomas B. "Quarantine Is a Wrong Question on AIDS." *New York Times* 21 Feb. 1990, A24.

Sullivan, Joseph F. "Girl Who Thinks She Has AIDS to Stand Trial in Biting of Guard." *New York Times* 31 Aug. 1994, B6.

Sullivan, Joseph J., Jr. "St. Patrick's Parade Organizers Don't Bar Gays from Marching" (letter). *New York Times* 15 March 1993, A18.

Tabor, Mary B. W. "Judge Orders the Release of Haitians." *New York Times* 9 June 1993, B4.

"The Talk About Magic." *New York Times* 3 Nov. 1992, B11.

Thomas, Lewis. "Epilogue: AIDS: An Unknown Distance Still to Go." In *The Science of AIDS.* 123-24.

Thompson, Ken. "Reflections on Trusting Trust." In Denning, ed. *Computers Under Attack*. 97-104.

Thompson, Mark, ed. *Leatherfolk: Radical Sex, People, Politics, and Practice*. Boston: Alyson, 1991.

Treichler, Paula A. "AIDS and HIV Infection in the Third World: A First World Chronicle." In Fee and Fox, eds. *AIDS: The Making of a Chronic Disease*. 377-412.

Treichler, Paula A. "AIDS, Gender, and Biomedical Discourse: Current Contests for Meaning." In Fee and Fox, eds. *AIDS: The Burdens of History*. 190-266.

Treichler, Paula A. "AIDS, Homophobia, and Biomedical Discourse: An Epidemic of Signification." In Crimp, ed. *AIDS: Cultural Analysis/Cultural Activism*. 31-70.

Treichler, Paula A. "Beyond *Cosmo*: AIDS, Identity, and Inscriptions of Gender." *Camera Obscura: A Journal of Feminism and Film Theory* 28 (1992), 20-77.

Treichler, Paula A., and Lisa Cartwright, eds. *Imaging Technologies, Inscribing Science*. Special issue of *Camera Obscura: A Journal of Feminism and Film Theory* 28 (January 1992).

"'Trojan Horse' Infects and Destroys Personal Computer Systems: AIDS Information Affected." *AIDS & Society: International Research and Policy Bulletin* 1:2 (Jan. 1990), 13.

"'True Love Waits' for Some Teen-Agers." *New York Times* 21 June 1993, A12.

Tuana, Nancy, ed. *Feminism and Science*. Bloomington: Indiana University Press, 1989.

Tyler, Carole-Anne. "Boys Will Be Girls: The Politics of Gay Drag." In Fuss, ed. *Inside/Out*. 32-70.

"U.S. to Weigh Female Illness in Defining AIDS." *New York Times* 3 Sept. 1992, A16.

Vecsey, George. "Magic Makes Highlights for His Tape." *New York Times* 10 Feb. 1992, C1, C4.

Vecsey, George. "Magic Words for Earvin: 'Go for It,'" *New York Times* 30 Sept. 1992, B9.

Verhovek, Sam Howe. "With Four Gay Men Slain, Texas Revisits Issue of Hate Crime." *New York Times* 30 Aug. 1994, A15.

VerMeulen, Michael. "The Gay Plague." *New York* 31 May 1982, 52-62.

Warren, Robert Penn. *All the King's Men*. San Diego, New York, and London: Harcourt Brace Jovanovich, 1982 [1946].

Watney, Simon. *Policing Desire: Pornography, AIDS and the Media*, 2nd ed. Minneapolis: University of Minnesota Press, 1989.

Watney, Simon. "The Possibilities of Permutation: Pleasure, Proliferation, and the Politics of Gay Identity in the Age of AIDS." In Miller, ed. *Fluid Exchanges*. 329-67.
Watney, Simon. *Practices of Freedom: Selected Writings on HIV/AIDS*. Durham: Duke University Press, 1994.
Watney, Simon. "The Spectacle of AIDS." In Crimp, ed. *AIDS: Cultural Analysis/Cultural Activism*. 71-86.
Watson, James D., Nancy H. Hopkins, Jeffrey W. Roberts, Joan Argetsinger Steitz, and Alan W. Weiner. *Molecular Biology of the Gene*, 4th ed. 2 vols. Menlo Park, CA: The Benjamin/Cummings Publishing Company, Inc., 1987.
Watson, James D., John Tooze, and David T. Kurtz. *Recombinant DNA: A Short Course*. Scientific American Books. New York: W. H. Freeman and Company, 1983.
Weber, Bruce. "Gay Irish Group Sues to March in Parade." *New York Times* 3 March 1992, B3.
Weber, Bruce. "Judge Permits Parade Ban of Gay Group." *New York Times* 14 March 1992, 27-28.
Weber, Bruce. "Judge Refuses to Order Gay Group Admitted to St. Patrick's Parade." *New York Times* 17 March 1992, A1, B2.
Weber, Myles. "When a Risk Group Is Not a Risk Group: The Absence of AIDS Panic in Peter Cameron's Fiction." In Nelson, ed. *AIDS: The Literary Response*. 69-75.
Weir, John. "After You've Gone: Rage, Rage." *New Republic* 13 Feb. 1995, 11-12.
Weir, John. "AIDS Stories." *Harper's* 273:1636 (Sept. 1986), 22, 24, 26.
Weir, John. "Bent out of Shape." [Review of *Philadelphia*, *Savage Nights*, and *Totally F***ed Up*.] *Details* 12:9 (Feb. 1994), 131-33.
Weir, John. "Death Becomes Him (Not)." *QW* no. 44 (6 Sept. 1992), 38-39.
Weir, John. "Getting a Life." *Details* 11:8 (Jan. 1993), 20-21, 23, 25-28.
Weir, John. "Homo in Heteroland." *QW* no. 41 (16 Aug. 1992), 22-25. [Reprinted in Ethan Mordden, ed. *Waves: An Anthology of New Gay Fiction*. New York: Vintage/Random House, 1994. 3-12.]
Weir, John. "In God's Country." *Details* 12:12 (May 1994), 116-21, 175-76.
Weir, John. *The Irreversible Decline of Eddie Socket*. New York: Harper-Collins, 1991 [1989].
Weir, John. "NWA's [Novels with AIDS]." [Review of Jim Oliver, *Closing Distance*.] *QW* no. 50 (18 Oct. 1992), 42-43.
Weir, John. "There Goes the Neighborhood . . ." *VOX* (Winter 1991), 16-19.
Welles, Paul O'M. *Project Lambda*. Port Washington, NY: Ashley, 1979.

Wetsel, David. "The Best of Times, The Worst of Times: The Emerging Literature of AIDS in France." In Nelson, ed. *AIDS: The Literary Response*. 95-113.

Williams, Tennessee. *Summer and Smoke. Four Plays*. New York: Signet, 1976 [1948].

Williams, William Carlos. *Selected Poems*. New York: New Directions, 1968.

Williamson, Judith. "Every Virus Tells a Story." In Carter and Watney, eds. *Taking Liberties*. 69-80.

Witten, Ian H. "Computer (In)security: Infiltrating Open Systems." In Denning, ed. *Computers Under Attack*. 105-42.

Wong-Staal, Flossie. "Human Immunodeficiency Viruses and Their Replication." In Fields, et al., eds. *Fundamental Virology*. 709-23.

Woods, Gregory, "AIDS to Remembrance: The Uses of Elegy." In Nelson, ed. *AIDS: The Literary Response*. 155-66.

Wright, Les. "Gay Genocide as a Literary Trope." In Nelson, ed. *AIDS: The Literary Response*. 50-68.

Yeats, William Butler. *Selected Poems and Two Plays of William Butler Yeats*, updated edition. M. L. Rosenthal, ed. New York: Collier, 1966.

Zingler, Peter. *Die Seuche: Roman [The Plague: A Novel]*. Frankfurt am Main: Eichborn, 1989.

Index

Abelove, Henry, 63, 69, 70
abstinence, sexual, 69, 115-17, 155
Achtenberg, Roberta, 67
ACLU National Prison Project, 69-70
ACT UP (AIDS Coalition to Unleash Power), 69, 70, 71, 80, 102, 105, 107, 203, 230, 254, 255, 256, 264, 281, 283, 292, 300, 302
activism, AIDS, 24, 31, 45, 56, 61, 69, 71, 102, 184, 203, 227, 230, 239-40, 249, 254, 256, 264, 265, 268, 275, 276, 278-301, 302, 303. *See also* resistance
  anti-Vietnam War, 231
  in the 1960s, 287-88
activist aesthetic, 294-301
activity and passivity, 33-36, 39, 41-42, 45, 62, 73, 77, 79, 130, 290
addiction, 21, 57, 259. *See also* drug use
Adleman, Leonard, 16, 29
Africa, 19, 63, 75, 80, 106, 208, 209, 210, 211, 214-15, 237, 254

African Americans, 40, 47-48, 56, 57, 70, 76, 83, 109, 195-96, 214, 224, 232, 255, 265, 267, 276, 287, 296, 302
African origin of HIV and AIDS, theories of, 41, 63, 75, 80, 105, 208-12, 214-15, 237, 254. *See also* engineering of HIV, origin of HIV and AIDS
African National Congress (ANC), 302
African swine flu virus, 184
Agnew, Spiro T., 255
Ahdieh, Houman, 106
AIDS Counseling and Education (ACE), Bedford Hills Correctional Facility (NY), 70
AIDS Quarterly (television show), 105
"AIDS victim," 45, 46, 89, 124, 201, 227, 233, 292
"AIDS virus," misnomer for HIV, 12, 14, 27-28, 36, 38, 40, 44, 45, 50, 59, 63, 105, 107, 112, 143, 209, 211, 212, 214, 266, 293
AIDS-Related Complex (ARC), 64, 75, 93-95, 111-12, 121, 273

AIDSphobia, 143, 147, 158, 224, 265
AL721 (experimental drug), 282
Albrecht, Thomas, 14
All About Eve (movie), 187
Allison, Alexander W., 204
Alonso, Ana Maria, 56, 70
Altman, Dennis, 108
Altman, Lawrence K., 66, 70, 71
"America Responds to AIDS" (television ad campaign), 55
American Journal of Medicine, 78, 106
Ampligen (experimental drug), 291
Amsterdam, 229, 300
anal sex, 39, 41-42, 64, 115, 119
Anderson, Dave, 65
Anderson, Laurie, 15-16, 28-29
Angel Island, CA, 232
Angier, Natalie, 25, 26, 27, 28, 29, 62, 63
Angola, 215
Annin, Peter, 160
Anonymous Queers, 65
Anthony, Florence, 65
antidote (fictional), for HIV, 210-11, 238, 243, 246, 249, 251, 259, 285
antisense drugs, 7, 26
Antonio, Gene, 63
anus, 62, 152-53, 178, 193
apartheid, 266
apocalypse, 19, 76, 80, 82, 207, 208-9, 211, 213, 218, 223, 226, 227, 231, 234, 235, 236, 246, 247, 250, 251, 252, 254, 259, 260, 262, 266, 267, 268, 281, 285, 294, 301. *See also* Last Judgment
Araki, Gregg, 202, 256
Araton, Harvey, 65, 66

Archie comics, 188
Argentina, 195
Aristotle, 34, 61, 204
art and politics, 54, 68, 294-301
ArtForum (magazine), 299
"artificial intelligence," 16, 29
"artificial life," 16, 29
Ashe, Arthur, 55, 65
Asia, 19
assassination, 217, 220, 222, 232, 239, 240-41, 242, 254, 255, 300
Associated Press (AP), 77
Atlanta, 216
Auerbach, D. M., 106
Auschwitz, 229, 254
Australia, 225
AZT, 24, 74, 97, 98, 262, 293
B Cells, 43
Bahder, Paul, 63
Bahder, Teresa, 63
Bailey, Sarah, 62
Baker, Cornelius, 230
Baker, James Robert, 206, 240-41, 256
balloons, as memorial, 269-70, 278, 280-81
Baltimore, 211
Bandon, Alexandra, 70
Barale, Michèle Aina, 63, 69, 70
Barbara McClintock Project to Cure AIDS, 105, 107
Barrows, Herbert, 204
Barrus, Tim, 206-8, 222-40, 241-42, 244, 245-46, 247-52, 253, 254, 259
bathhouses, 78, 212, 217, 285, 291
Baum, L. Frank, 82
Bay of Fundy, 157-58
Beachy, Lucille, 160
The Beatles, 187
Beaty, Bert, 107

beepers and alarms (as reminders for taking medication), 97, 98, 104, 262
Beldecos, Athena, 62
Belgium, 215, 240, 247
Bellevue Hospital (NYC), 262
Belmondo, Jean-Paul, 189
benefits, fundraising, 102-3, 109
Bergalis, Kimberly, 60
Bergen, Candice, 194
Bergen-Belsen, 229
Bergman, Ingmar, 190
Berke, Richard L., 69
Berkow, Ira, 65, 66
Bernstein, Larry, 106
Bersani, Leo, 64
Bevington, David, 203, 204
Bible, 183, 187, 220, 291, 302
biological metaphors, 16-23, 29
Biology and Gender Study Group, 33, 34-35, 62
Bird, Larry, 48, 66
bisexuality, 46, 51, 59, 111-12, 113, 114, 129, 209
Bishop, Elizabeth, 186-87, 203
biting, as presumed mode of HIV transmission, 233, 255
Blake, Caesar R., 204
Bleier, Ruth, 61-62
blood, 21, 43, 44, 47, 51, 59, 60, 65, 73, 76-77, 79, 115, 116, 118, 121, 126, 128, 129, 130, 133, 142-43, 146, 154, 158, 166, 168, 169, 174, 175, 193, 209, 211, 216, 218, 243, 245, 263, 264, 296, 297
blood transfusions, and HIV transmission, 47, 51, 60, 65, 73, 76-77, 126, 128, 211, 216, 264
"blueprint," DNA as, 5, 10, 27

body, 3, 7, 16-18, 33, 40, 42-45, 57, 58, 61, 77, 79, 84, 86, 94-97, 100, 116, 118, 119, 121, 125, 129, 138, 140, 141, 152-54, 164, 167, 168, 176, 177-82, 191, 193, 200-202, 203, 224, 244, 250, 252, 260-61, 275, 279, 291, 296, 299, 300
Boffin, Tessa, 64, 105
Bordo, Susan, 62
Boston, 48, 129, 141, 148, 203
Boulard, Garry, 256
Bourjaily, Vance, 141-60, 161, 166, 170, 177, 206
Bowen, Peter M., 67, 107
Bowers v. Hardwick (Georgia sodomy case), 219, 232
Bowie, Sam, 49
brain, 50, 57, 66-67, 70, 124
Brandt, Allan M., 71, 255
Breathless (movie), 189
Brecht, Bertolt, 204
Breitman, Patti, 108
Bresson, Robert, 204
Brooks, Franklin, 254, 304
Brothers, M. H., 29, 30, 31
Brown, Charles, 107
Brown, Clifton, 65, 66
Browne, Malcolm W., 29
Brubaker, John K., 43-44, 64
Bruning, Fred, 65
Bryan, Jed A., 206-7, 214, 215-19, 222, 226, 227, 228-40, 243, 244-46, 247-52, 253, 254, 255, 259, 267
Bryant, Dorothy, 108
bubonic plague, 113, 148, 266
Buchanan, Pat, 4, 47
Buckley, William F., Jr., 233, 256
Bunn, Curtis G., 64-65
Burk family, 71

Burke, Donald S., 64, 71, 75, 105, 107
"Burn Cycle" (computer videogame), 15
Burroughs, William S., 15, 29
Bush, George, 230
Butler, Judith, 50, 53, 66, 68, 194-95, 198, 204
Butters, Ronald R., 24
Byrne, Melinda J., 69
Cady, Joseph, 202
CAIDS (Community Acquired Immune Deficiency Syndrome), early name for AIDS, 108
Cairns, John, 25
Calendar, Richard, 5, 25, 26, 28
California, 108, 130, 171, 172, 173, 184, 185, 203, 213, 215, 221, 233
Callen, Michael, 74-75, 105
Cambodia, 300
camp humor and style, 149, 186, 203, 276, 284, 290
Canada, 78, 231
cancers and neoplasms, 5, 7, 28, 45, 74, 85, 86, 96, 108, 133, 218, 300. *See also* Kaposi's sarcoma
cancer model, of AIDS, 74
capitalism, 34, 47, 265, 266, 267, 283-85, 287, 292
Caribbean people, 70, 76
Carlomusto, Jean, 70
Carr, Arthur J., 204
"carriers" of illness, 18-19, 29, 41, 58, 75, 234, 256
Carroll, Mark, 25
Carter, Erica, 24, 105
Carter, Jimmy, 109
Cartwright, Lisa, 24
Carvajal, Doreen, 69

Castle, Terry, 71
Castro District (San Francisco), 115, 240
"casual contact," and HIV transmission, 76-77, 106, 216-17, 233-34, 265
cell biology, 5, 33-34, 62
censorship, 220, 222
Centers for Disease Control (CDC), 57, 61, 70, 76, 78, 108, 216, 249
definition of AIDS, 57-58, 61, 70
Central America, 219
"central dogma," of molecular genetics, 8-9, 15, 26-27, 34, 37, 38, 62
Chanock, Robert M., 26
Chaplin, Charlie, 189
Check, William A., 26
chemotherapy, 74, 85
Chen, Lincoln C., 63
Chicago, 213, 215
children, and HIV/AIDS, 52, 59, 76-77, 106, 125-41, 216. *See also* infants
Childress, James F., 255
Chile, 224, 231, 232
Chiles, Lawton, 51-53, 56, 67, 111, 125, 128, 235
Chin, James, 105
China, 214
Chinatown Health Clinic (NYC), 69
Chinese immigrants, to the United States, 232
Christensen, Kim, 256
Christianity, 54, 68, 101, 168, 170, 174, 183, 200, 220, 222, 226, 232, 233, 236-37, 244, 285

Catholicism, 68-69, 213, 244, 268, 276, 282-83, 289, 290, 302
  fundamentalism, 211, 213, 214, 217, 219, 226, 232, 233, 236, 240, 242, 254
  the religious right, 68, 81, 219-21, 237
  Southern Baptist Convention, 69, 221
Christological traditions, 188
"chronic disease," redefinition of AIDS as, 74, 163
CIA (Central Intelligence Agency), 211-12, 226, 231, 236, 239, 248, 249, 251, 254
citationality, 186-202, 204
civil rights movement, 232
"C.J.," figure in HIV transmission hoax (Dallas), 59
Clancy, Tom, 206-7
Clark, Eugene, 51, 67
class, socioeconomic, 24, 40, 56, 57, 60, 61, 69, 124, 132, 196, 199, 287-90
Cliff, Michelle, 302
Clift, Montgomery, 198, 200
Clines, Francis X., 68
Clinton, Bill, 40
cloning, 9, 25, 29
the closet, 50, 53, 67, 69, 154, 221, 245, 256
closet of horrors, in Toby Johnson's *Plague*, 232, 246
Clum, John M., 24, 71, 107, 186, 203
coalition politics, 284, 290
codons, 6-8, 25, 26, 27
Coe, Christopher, 253
Cohen, Fred, 20, 30, 31
Cohen, Jon, 105
Cohn, Roy, 68, 256

cold war, 64, 231
Colen, B. D., 65, 70
Collins, Glenn, 68, 70
Collins, Judy, 187
colonization, European, of the Americas, 231
Colson, Charles, 50-51, 67
"coming out," 48, 69, 193, 283
communism, 230, 231
compound Q (experimental drug), 100
computer and information science, 3, 4, 15-17, 22-24, 27, 29, 32
computer technology, in fictional accounts, 209, 218, 221-22, 238-39, 241
computer viruses, 16-24, 29-32
  "AIDS" and "cyberaids," 21
computer worms, 29
concentration camps, 213, 214, 218, 219, 222, 224-26, 228-29, 232, 238-39, 241-42, 247, 249, 259, 266, 267, 277, 278, 293
condoms, 21, 108, 115, 117, 165, 232, 255, 264, 282, 294
Congress and Congressmen, United States, 40, 55, 63, 213, 221, 241, 255, 301. *See also* Senate and Senators
Congressional Record, 4, 53, 63, 67-69, 160, 161, 255
Connecticut, 52, 143
conspiracies and conspiracy theory, 32, 79, 208-26, 228, 231, 232, 234-52, 254, 255, 256, 259, 265, 266, 268, 276, 281-83, 286
Cooper, Roger, Jr., 106
Coppola, Vincent, 107
Cops (television series), 70

Corea, Gena, 70
COSSMHO, The National Coalition of Hispanic Health and Human Services Organizations, 69
Cowley, Geoffrey, 160
Cox, Elizabeth, 71
Craffey, Brynn, 160
Crandall, Rebecca, 160
CRIA (Community Research Initiative on AIDS), 80
Crick, Francis, 8, 26, 28, 29
crime, and HIV "risk groups," 56-57
  and viral action, 14, 23, 29, 38-39
Crimp, Douglas, 24, 27, 31, 64, 67, 71, 106, 252, 254, 256, 302
cryptanalysis, 6, 26
Cryptosporidium, 133
Cuba, 231
Cunningham, Representative, of California, 63
"cure," for AIDS, 74, 89, 96, 105, 117, 137, 171, 212, 215, 248, 249, 251, 254, 259, 285
  for computer viruses, 18, 19
  for homosexuality, 302
Curran, James W., 106
Currier, Jameson, 90, 109
Cyril, Saint, 168, 170, 202
cytoplasm, cell, 7, 13, 33-39, 62
Dachau, 229
Dade County, FL, 219
Dallas, 59, 71
Dalton, Harlon, 56, 70
Damian, Peter, 28
Dannemeyer, William E., 213
Dante, 187, 225, 254
Dark Victory (movie), 173

Darrow, William W., 78, 106
Daumann, Rudolf Heinrich, 254
Davis, Angela, 287
Davis, Bette, 191
Davis, Brad, 55, 56, 70
Davis, Christopher, 252
Dawkins, Richard, 27
Day, Doris, 188, 191, 198
ddC, 74
ddI, 74
Dead End Kids, 199
Dean, James, 192
death and dying, 3, 4, 27-28, 36, 40, 41, 44, 45-46, 50, 56, 60, 61, 66, 69, 71, 73, 74-75, 77-79, 80-88, 90-95, 97, 98, 99, 101, 102, 103, 104, 107, 109, 111, 112, 113, 114, 122, 123, 124, 130, 131-33, 135-39, 140-41, 148-49, 155-60, 161, 163, 164, 168, 170, 171-77, 178, 179-86, 187, 188, 189, 191-93, 197, 202, 203, 205, 208, 212, 214, 216, 217, 218, 219, 222-24, 225, 226, 229, 230, 238, 241, 242, 244, 245, 249, 250, 253, 254, 259-62, 265, 266, 267, 268, 269-71, 272, 273, 274, 275, 277, 278, 280, 282, 288, 291, 293, 294, 296, 298, 299-300
"Deep Throat" (Watergate), 238
Defense Department, United States, 239
de Havilland, Olivia, 199
dela Cruz, Antonio, 106
Dellamora, Richard, 254
"dementia," associated with AIDS, 45, 85-86, 100-101, 102
Denenberg, Risa, 70

denial, 82-83, 137-38, 167, 171, 234, 245, 248, 271, 277-78
Denning, Peter J., 20, 23, 29-32
dentists, 71, 126, 130, 137
Derrida, Jacques, 29, 194
Desposito, Franklin, 106
detective fiction, 206, 208, 211, 228, 235, 302
Dewey, Joseph, 160, 161, 254
dextran sulfate (experimental drug), 100
de Zalduondo, Barbara O., 63
D'Hondt, John, 82, 107
DiAna, DiAna, 255
Dickey, James, 144, 161
A Different World (television series), 47
"directed panspermia" (theory of the origin of life), 29
DNA, 5-17, 25-27, 29, 33, 34, 36-39, 41, 62
"selfish," 10, 27
Dollimore, Jonathan, 53, 67
Donne, John, 190, 203
Doyal, Leslie, 70
drag, 64, 171, 194, 196, 198, 199-200
drama, 68, 108, 254, 303, 304
Dreuilhe, Emmanuel, 21-22, 31
drug companies, 285
drug use, and the AIDS crisis, 20, 21, 37, 40, 51-52, 56-57, 59, 60, 61, 67, 70, 73, 76, 79, 81, 114, 125-27, 128, 129, 130, 209, 212, 215, 232, 233, 235, 237, 259, 262, 263, 264, 265, 276, 280
Duesberg, Peter, 24
Dugas, Gaetan (so-called "Patient Zero"), 78, 80, 81, 106, 235-36

Duke, David, 234, 256
Duplechan, Larry, 89-90, 91, 92-97, 109, 111-13, 114, 117-21, 123, 124, 132-33, 163, 166, 167, 177, 206
Durack, David T., 31
Duvalier, Jean-Claude, 231
Dylan, Bob, 188
dysentery, 222
dystopian fiction, 206, 214, 216, 226, 251
Eastman, Arthur M., 204
Ebola fever, 254
ecological process, and HIV/AIDS, 57, 225-26, 236, 256
Edelman, Lee, 24, 62, 67, 71
Eden, expulsion from, 256
education, AIDS, 50-53, 55-56, 57, 67, 76, 80, 81, 142-43, 144, 211, 227, 232, 234, 236, 264, 301
"effeminacy," 50, 57, 287, 290
egg (ovum), 34-36
elegy, 58
Eliot, T. S., 187
Ellis, Perry, 194
Elovich, Richard, 68
El Salvador, 224, 231
Else, Gerald F., 204
engineering of HIV, theories of 22-23, 208-15, 235, 236, 249-50. *See also* African origin of HIV and AIDS, origin of HIV and AIDS
England, 59
English, Hubert M., Jr., 204
enzymes, 7, 8, 9, 12, 13, 14, 28, 37, 210
"epicenter," used in describing the AIDS epidemic, 50, 66
epidemic "spread," 3-4, 18, 19, 21, 22, 23, 30, 32, 50-52, 57,

epidemic "spread" (cont'd)
    59, 61, 62, 67, 75-83, 88,
    92, 106-9, 111, 112, 113,
    127, 135, 165, 193, 206-16,
    222, 224, 227-28, 232, 235,
    236, 237, 238, 239, 242-43,
    245-52, 256, 259, 262, 263,
    264, 266-68, 271, 285, 301
epidemiology, 67, 88, 105-6, 206,
    207, 235, 236, 237, 252,
    256
Epstein, Julia, 105
Epstein, Paul, 63
Epstein-Barr virus, 14
Erie, PA, 195
Erlanger, Steven, 71
Erni, John Nguyet, 105
erotica, 108, 206, 228, 253
espionage, 21, 36, 79, 106, 209,
    238, 246, 281-82
Essex, Max, 63, 105
Europe and Europeans, 185, 214,
    230-31, 299
Evers, Medgar, 255
Exander, Max, 108. *See also* Reed,
    Paul
exons, 9, 27
factory, cell as, 7, 10, 18, 27, 44
false diagnosis, of AIDS, 91, 92,
    94, 97, 98
family, and the AIDS crisis, 34, 57,
    60, 71, 76-77, 92, 97, 101,
    112, 113-14, 118-21, 123-
    27, 129-30, 132, 135, 136,
    141, 148, 150-51, 159-60,
    171, 189, 193-94, 205, 217,
    222, 255, 265, 266, 272-73
Family Matters (television series),
    47
Farmer, Paul, 63
fascism, 206, 230. *See also* Nazism
Fauci, Anthony S., 76, 106

Faulkner, William, 187
Fausto-Sterling, Anne, 61
FBI (Federal Bureau of Investigation), 282
FDA (Food and Drug Administration), 249, 270, 282, 293
Fee, Elizabeth, 24, 63, 74, 105, 256
Feinberg, David B., xii, xiii, 24-25, 252, 302
Feldman, Jamie, 105
Felson, Arthur, 108
femaleness, 33, 34, 35, 37, 43, 45, 47, 52, 54, 57, 58, 59, 62, 64, 67, 70, 76, 151-54, 160, 195, 197, 230, 264, 290
female-to-female transmission of HIV, 264, 301
female-to-male transmission of HIV, 263-64
"femininity," 33, 35, 37-38, 45, 62, 154, 177-78, 198, 290
feminism, 33, 40, 58, 61-62, 290
Ferbrache, David J., 29, 30, 31
Ferro, Robert, 82, 107
Fettner, Ann Giudici, 26, 27, 28
Fields, Bernard N., 26, 28
    et al., *Fundamental Virology* (*FV*), 26, 27, 28, 30
Finkelstein, Avram, 65
Fire Island, NY, 115
Fisher, Lawrence M., 26
Fisher, Mary, 60
Fitzgerald, Robert, 202
Fitzgerald, Sally, 202
Flemington, NJ, 166, 170, 189
Florida, 51, 52, 63, 101, 149, 195, 215, 219, 255
flu virus, 14, 31, 36, 62, 116, 135, 222
Follett, Ken, 206
football metaphors, 43

Ford, Gerald, 255
foreignness, 7, 13-15, 38, 39, 40, 43, 45, 80
foscarnet, 74
Fox, Daniel M., 24, 63, 74, 105, 256
France, 31, 40, 78, 209, 224
Frank, Anne, 229
Fried, Joseph P., 68
Friedman, Peter, 203
Friend, Tom, 66
Fruchter, Lazar, 106
funerals and memorial services, 101, 164-65, 185, 202, 204, 268-73, 275, 277, 278, 279, 287, 291. *See also* memorializing, mourning
Fuss, Diana, 27, 62, 64, 106, 161
Gagnon, Monika, 64
Gallo, Robert C., 105, 107
Garbers, David L., 35
Garrett, Laurie, 65
gayness, 3, 21, 24, 28, 38-42, 45, 46-61, 62, 64, 65, 66, 67, 68, 69, 76, 78-84, 86, 88-89, 92, 99, 102-3, 107, 108, 109, 111-26, 128-30, 132, 141-42, 144, 147-55, 159-60, 163-65, 170, 177, 183, 184, 186, 187, 192-99, 201, 203, 205-24, 226, 227, 228-30, 232, 233, 235-37, 239, 242-45, 249, 250, 253, 255, 256, 263-64, 265-66, 268-69, 271-73, 276-77, 278-79, 283, 287-91, 300-301, 302
Gay Men's Health Crisis (GMHC), 54, 68, 124
"gay plague," AIDS called, 42, 64, 105, 111, 123, 193, 214, 216, 227, 237
Gay Sunshine Press, 108

gender, 4, 24, 28, 33-35, 36-38, 39, 40, 42, 43, 45, 54, 56-61, 62, 70, 115, 116, 144, 149, 152, 194-95, 196-97, 199, 230, 287-90, 302
gene "library," 9
"general population," 40, 52-53, 61, 63, 67, 76, 80, 125, 212, 237
genes, 5-7, 9-14, 25, 27, 37, 38, 39
genetic engineering, 5, 9, 10, 22, 25, 212, 218
genocide, 193, 211, 213, 214, 215, 218, 222, 226, 228-31, 232, 233, 234, 235, 239, 243, 244, 245, 246, 247, 248, 249-52, 259, 266
genre and subgenres, of AIDS fiction, 4, 83, 88-89, 108, 144, 163, 206-8, 214, 228, 235, 252-53, 254, 259, 266, 270-71
genres, of mainstream American fiction, 205
George, Nelson, 65
Georgia, 219
Gergen, Joe, 65
Germany, 71, 228-30, 231, 253-54
Gerrold, David, 31
Gertz, Alison, 60
Gever, Martha, 64
Gilbert, Scott, 62
Gilman, Sander L., 64, 71, 253
Glaser, Elizabeth, 60
Glass, Bentley, 62
Glueck, Grace, 68
God, 81, 107, 142, 183, 212, 213, 216, 220, 236, 239, 245, 252
Goldstein, Marianne, 65
Goleman, Daniel, 70
Gordon, Michael R., 69

INDEX 389

Graubard, Stephen R., 63, 70
Gray, Jerry, 68
Greenblatt, Stephen, 64
greenhouse effect, 261-62
GRID (Gay Related Immune Deficiency), early name for AIDS, 92, 108
Grmek, Mirko D., 209, 254, 256
Gross, Jane, 66
"ground zero," 80
Grover, Jan Zita, 24, 27, 63, 64
Guantánamo Bay, "HIV prison camp" at, 40, 63, 233
Guatemala, 231
Guerrero, Isabel, 106
Guibert, Hervé, 252
"guilt" and "innocence," 19, 30, 39, 41, 47, 52, 61, 73, 112, 114-15, 120, 122, 125-28, 131, 132, 165, 197, 210, 211, 212, 235-38, 241, 244, 245, 278
Gulag, 231
Gunderson, Martin, 255
Gunn, Giles, 64
Gupta, Asha, 106
Gupta, Sunil, 64, 105
Hager, Mary, 160
Haiti, 40-41, 63, 122, 183, 215, 231, 233, 256
Haitian Coalition on AIDS (Brooklyn), 69
Hall, Arsenio, 47, 65
Hall, Radclyffe, *The Well of Loneliness*, 192
Hall, Richard, 185, 203
Halperin, David M., 63, 69, 70
Hamilton, John D., 31
Hammett, Theodore M., 255, 256
Hammonds, Evelynn, 62
Hanson, Ellis, 106

Haraway, Donna J., 16, 25, 29, 33, 36, 40, 61, 62, 63, 64, 106
Harding, Sandra, 61
Harper, Phillip Brian, 46-47, 48, 65, 66, 69
Harrington, Mark, 257
Harris, Daniel, 203
Harrison, Stephen C., 27, 62
Hart, Lorenz, 186, 187, 198, 200
Harty, Kevin J., 107
Haseltine, William A., 28, 62, 64
Hatch, Orrin, 244
Hay, Louise, 96
HEAL (Health Education AIDS Liaison), 24
"health," as a category, 53, 79-80, 123
health care workers, and HIV transmission, 80, 209-10
health insurance, 168, 175-76, 288
Heaphy, Kathleen A., 29, 30, 31
The Heiress (movie), 199
Helms, Jesse, 4, 24, 50-54, 55, 59, 67-68, 81, 111, 112, 214, 234, 235, 256
Hemingway, Ernest, 203
hemophilia, 51, 76, 122
hepatitis B, 21, 31, 84, 209
Herzog, Bob, 65
heterosexism, 4, 54-56, 199, 203
"heterosexual AIDS," 41, 111-23, 124, 147, 263-64, 301
heterosexuality, 37, 41, 42, 47-49, 51-54, 56, 58-59, 60-61, 65, 66, 67, 80, 102-3, 111-24, 147, 150-54, 160, 192-93, 195, 196-97, 230, 263-64, 288, 291, 301
Hevesi, Dennis, 68
Heyward, William L., 106
Hicks, Karen, 62
hierarchy, 34, 39, 42, 45

Highland, Harold Joseph, 30, 31
Hilchey, Tim, 62
Hilferty, Robert, 302
Hilts, Philip J., 69
Hintikka, Merrill B., 61
Hiroshima, 208, 266
Hirsch, Marianne, 62
Hirsch, Martin S., 26
Hitler, Adolf, 184, 203, 229, 230
HIV (Human Immunodeficiency Virus), 3, 4, 5, 8, 11, 12, 15, 19-24, 26-28, 30, 36-49, 55-61, 62, 63, 65, 66, 67, 69-70, 71, 73-75, 77-80, 83, 88, 90, 91, 93, 97, 98, 104-8, 111-17, 119-28, 130, 133, 142, 143, 146, 147, 154, 155, 174, 177, 202, 207, 209-15, 216, 222, 228, 233, 234, 235, 239, 240, 242, 243, 246, 249-52, 254, 255, 256, 259, 263, 264, 265, 266, 273, 293, 301, 302, 303, 304
Hoffman, Alice, 125-41, 144, 160, 161, 163, 166, 170, 177, 179, 206
Hoffman, William M., 108
Holiday, Billie, 302
Hollander, Melvin, 106
Holleran, Andrew, 108
Holocaust, 203, 228-33, 241, 253, 254, 266
homelessness, 56, 61, 69, 83, 125, 259, 261, 262-63, 265, 268, 278, 279-80, 284, 285, 287, 292
homophobia, 4, 24, 41-42, 45, 48-50, 52-57, 64, 67, 68, 78, 79, 81, 86, 92, 102, 111, 112, 114, 123-25, 142, 147, 149, 150, 152, 153, 154, 169, 170, 182, 184, 187, 192-93, 198, 213, 216, 217, 221, 222, 224, 230, 232, 233, 235-37, 239, 240, 242-46, 248, 251, 252, 256, 260, 265, 267, 276, 278, 301
"homosexual body," 125
"homosexual panic," 68
homosociality, 37, 48, 57, 69, 115, 146, 148, 149, 154, 160
Honduras, 195, 231
hooks, bell, 47, 65, 70
Hoover Institution, 234
Hopkins, Nancy H., 26
hospitals, 58, 83, 85, 87, 120, 124, 139, 140, 164, 170, 173-76, 177-79, 182, 185, 193, 200, 202, 203, 209, 218, 223, 270, 274-75, 277, 278, 280, 284, 293
hotlines, AIDS, 129-31, 271
Housing Works (NYC), 69
Houston, 215
Howard, Ted, 32
Hruska, Jan, 19, 20, 29, 30, 31, 32
Hubbard, Jan, 65
Huck, Janet, 107
Hudson, Rock, 55, 60, 89, 92, 191
Hudson River, 181, 261
Hughes, Holly, 68
human genome project, 5, 25
Idaho, 232
Ifill, Gwen, 68
Ilebo, Zaire, 208-10
Illinois, 105
immigration, 40, 63, 80, 232, 233, 255
immune system, 5, 14, 20, 22, 36, 40, 42-45, 64, 73-74, 77, 79, 93, 95, 96, 209, 274
immunology, 5, 20, 25, 43, 106
India, 220

Indiana, Gary, 299
Indonesia, 224
infants, and HIV/AIDS, 76-77, 106, 118. *See also* children
intentionality, of biological process, ideas of, 3, 10, 11, 15, 16, 22-24, 27, 28, 32, 33
  in understandings of the AIDS epidemic, 79, 81, 112, 130, 210-15, 216, 222, 232, 235-38, 240, 242-43, 247-49, 250, 251, 256, 259, 266, 267, 276, 285
International Conferences on AIDS, 106
introns, or intervening sequences, 9, 27
Iran, 231
Irigaray, Luce, 40, 63
Irish Lesbian and Gay Organization, 55
Israel Day Parade (NYC), 54, 69
Jackson, Jesse, 184
Jackson, Michael, 194
Jaffe, W. W., 106
JAMA (Journal of the American Medical Association), 106, 216
James, John S., 106
James, William D., 107
Japanese Americans, internment during World War II, 213, 232
Jasny, Barbara R., 105, 106
Jennings, Peter, 105
John Birch Society, 232
Johnson, Earvin "Magic," 45-49, 53, 65, 66
Johnson, Roy S., 65
Johnson, Sterling, Jr., 63
Johnson, Toby [Edwin Clark], 206-11, 212, 213, 214, 215, 226, 227-40, 242-43, 244, 245-52, 253, 256, 259, 267
Jones, James Earl, 199
Jones, James W., 107
Jones, T. Stephen, 107
Jordanova, Ludmilla, 62
Joseph, Stephen C., 255
Joshi, Vijay J., 106
Joslin, Tom, 203
journalism, 3, 14, 61, 73, 75, 78, 84, 87, 92, 202, 221, 240, 271, 292-93. *See also* media
Judaism, 54-55, 196, 197, 204, 229, 230, 234, 279
Julius II, Pope, 198
"jumping genes," 9
Kafka, Franz, 175
Kakutani, Michiko, 28
Kamin, Leon J., 26
Kanki, Phyllis J., 63, 105
Kansas, 166
Kantrowitz, Barbara, 160
Kaposi's Sarcoma (KS), 73, 78, 84, 85, 86, 87, 90, 91, 93, 94, 97, 104, 108, 118, 132, 166-67, 169, 270, 273
Karolyi, Bela, 138
Keats, John, 133
Keller, Evelyn Fox, 34, 61, 62
Kennedy, John F., 255
Kennedy, Robert F., 255
Kennedy, Shawn G., 69
Kenschaft, Lori, 62
Kent State University, 231
Kerber, Fred, 66
Kim, Peter S., 36
King, Martin Luther, Jr., 255
King, Stephen, 95
Kingsbury, David W., 30
Kinsella, James, 106, 255
Kinshasa, Zaire, 208
Kitt, Eartha, 194

Klein, Norman, 106
Knipe, David M., 26, 28
Knutson, Kim, 108
Kolata, Gina, 26, 29, 70
Kolins, Jerry, 31
Koop, C. Everett, 75, 105
Koreck, Maria Teresa, 56, 70
Kramer, Larry, 108, 203, 254, 256
Krauss, Clifford, 67
Kristallnacht, 221
Kruger, Barbara, 299
Ku Klux Klan, 214, 229, 232
Kupelian, David, 63
Kurtz, David T., 25
Kushner, Tony, xii, 68, 254, 255, 256
Labaton, Stephen, 69
labor movement, 232
Lambda Legal Defense and Education Fund, 255
Lambert, Bruce, 71
"language is a virus," 15-16, 28-29
Larouche Initiative, 232-33
Las Vegas, 215, 216
Last Judgment, 211, 213, 236. *See also* apocalypse
latency period, in viral infection, 18-19, 30, 74, 77
Latina/os, 40, 56, 57, 70, 76, 83, 148, 195
Lawrence, D. H., 190
Leary, Warren E., 31, 62, 63
leathersexuality, 246, 253, 256, 290
Leavitt, David, 125-28, 132, 160, 161, 205, 253, 303
Lee, Haesoon, 106
Lehmann-Haupt, Christopher, 65
Lennon, John, 109
Leonard, Zoe, 255, 256
leprosy, 220
Lesbian Avengers, 300, 302

lesbians, 50, 52, 54-55, 59-60, 61, 66, 67, 71, 149, 199, 203, 214, 217, 219, 220, 221, 222, 226, 230, 232, 233, 237, 260, 261, 263, 264, 273, 282, 289, 290, 300, 301, 302
LeVay, Simon, 50, 66, 70
Lewis, Peter H., 30
Lewontin, R. C., 26
Liberace, 55, 60
Life (magazine), 296
Lifestyles of the Rich and Famous (television series), 267
Lii, Jane H., 69
linguistic metaphors, 5-13, 15-17, 21, 22, 23, 25, 26, 27, 33, 36-37, 38, 39, 40, 42, 45
Litman, Nathan, 106
long-term survivors, of AIDS, 74-75
Longino, Helen E., 62
Longtime Companion (movie), 82, 107, 108
Los Angeles, 48, 78, 102, 108, 112-13, 218
Lost in Space (television series), 190
Lucas, Craig, 82, 107, 303
Ludlum, Robert, 206
Madonna, 137
Magnificent Obsession (movie), 191
Maine, 141, 144, 221
Mains, Geoff, 107, 206-8, 211-14, 215, 226, 228-40, 242, 243-44, 245-46, 247-52, 253, 256, 259
maleness, 33-39, 43, 45, 48-49, 51-52, 54, 56-59, 61, 67, 69, 144, 146, 148-50, 152-55, 160, 178, 194-95, 197, 198,

maleness (cont'd)
    199, 209, 230, 237, 264,
    277, 288, 290, 300
Manchester Union Leader (newspaper), 67
Mann, Jonathan M., 105
March on Washington (1987), 51,
    67, 271
    (1993), 50
Marcos, Ferdinand, 231
Markoff, John, 29, 31
Marlowe, Christopher, 203
marriage, 33-34, 37, 48, 51, 65,
    102-3, 109, 111, 113, 119-
    20, 123, 129, 144, 150-51,
    153-54, 165, 185, 189, 194,
    196-97, 244, 260
Mars-Jones, Adam, 81-82, 107
Marshall, Stuart, 64, 105
Martin, Emily, 27, 43, 62, 64
Martinez, Michael, 66
Marx, Karl, 260
masculinity, 3, 28, 33, 35-39, 42-
    45, 47-50, 53-61, 65, 66,
    70, 119, 144-55, 160, 178,
    192, 198, 236-39, 245, 276,
    287
Massa, Robert, 66
Masters and Johnson, 301
Masur, Henry, 74, 105
maternal, or cytoplasmic, inheritance, 25, 35
Maupin, Armistead, 90-92, 97-104,
    108, 109, 111, 113-17, 119,
    121, 122-23, 124, 132, 160,
    163, 166, 167, 177, 185,
    206
Mayo, David J., 255
McCarthy, Sheryl, 65
McCarthyism, 232, 255
McDonald, Malcolm I., 31
McElroy, William D., 62

McKinley, James C., Jr., 68
McKinney, Steward, 55
The McLaughlin Report (television series), 47
The Meadowlands (NJ), 294
media, 3, 4, 15, 16, 24, 27, 28, 45-
    49, 53, 57, 60, 64, 66, 77,
    81, 87, 89, 105, 106, 108,
    125, 217, 219, 243, 267,
    285, 286, 292-93, 301. *See also* journalism
Medicaid, 176, 282
Meinhold, Keith, 55
Mellman, Michael, 66
Melnick, Joseph L., 26
Melville, Herman, 173
memorializing, 65, 140, 159, 177,
    205, 278. *See also* funerals and memorial services, mourning
Merck, Mandy, 105
metaphor, 3, 4, 5-23, 26, 27, 28,
    29, 30, 31, 32, 33-34, 36-
    37, 38, 39, 40, 42, 43, 58,
    66, 69, 71, 79, 81, 106,
    107, 148, 295. *See also* biological metaphors, linguistic metaphors, military language
Metis, 231
Michelangelo, 198
The Midwest, 213
military, United States, 219, 231-32
    HIV testing in, 233, 255
    service of gay men and lesbians in, 55, 66, 69
    service of women in, 58
military depictions, in representing the AIDS crisis, 21, 62, 79,
    80, 148, 149, 155, 208, 214,
    235, 239-42, 245, 246, 247,
    267-68, 285-87

military-industrial complex, 220, 230, 285, 292
military language, 3, 13-14, 23, 28, 31, 35, 36-38, 40, 42-45, 58, 64, 70, 71, 106
Milk, Harvey, 232
Miller, D. A., 152-53, 161
Miller, James, 31, 63, 64, 67, 106, 107, 108, 109
Mills, John, 74, 105
Mineo, Sal, 192
The Mineshaft, 212, 288
Minnefor, Anthony, 106
Minnesota American Indian AIDS Task Force (Minneapolis), 69
Minority Task Force on AIDS (NYC), 69
misogyny, 45, 64, 151-53, 203
modernism, 184, 295
Mohr, Richard D., 71
Moini, Saira, 255, 256
molecular genetics and molecular biology, 4, 5-12, 15, 16, 21, 23, 25-27, 33, 34, 42
Monath, Thomas P., 26
Monette, Paul, 58, 71, 202, 206, 240, 241, 256
Montagnier, Luc, 105
Montana, 232
Moon, Michael, 24
Moore, Patrick, 302
Morbidity and Mortality Weekly Report (*MMWR*), 84, 108
Mordden, Ethan, 202
Mormonism, 244
Morrison, James, 67
Morrison, Paul, 81, 105, 106, 107
Moscone, George, 232
Mosher, Howard Frank, 161
mosquito bites, as presumed mode of HIV transmission, 234

mourning, 159, 269, 270, 272, 275, 278, 291. *See also* funerals and memorial services, memorializing
movies, 15-16, 32, 82, 105, 107, 108, 123-24, 190, 191, 192, 199, 254, 256, 267, 268, 286
Moynihan, Daniel Patrick, 50
M-Reg One (experimental drug), 293
Msamanga, Gernard I., 63
Munk, Erika, 68
Munt, Sally, 301
murder, 44, 59, 128, 130, 131, 158, 209, 229, 233, 255, 297, 301. *See also* assassination
  attempted, 233, 264
Murphy, Frederick A., 30
Murphy, Timothy F., 67, 69, 71, 107, 202, 252, 254, 304
Musto, David F., 256
Naidoo, Jennie, 70
NAMES Project Quilt, 253
naming, 173, 198-99, 204
Nanney, David L., 62
narrative, in cell biology, 34-42
  of epidemic "spread" (the population or epidemiological narrative), 3-4, 67, 75-81, 83, 88-89, 92, 105-7, 111-14, 120, 205-28, 234-52, 254, 259-77, 281, 285-86, 300-301
  of individual illness (the personal narrative), 3-4, 73-75, 76, 77-104, 105, 106-7, 111, 132-41, 155-60, 163-86, 187, 188, 189, 190-94, 202, 205-8, 250, 270-75, 290

narrative (cont'd)
 of political activism, 278-94, 301, 302
 of proximity, 259-81, 295, 301
National Association of People with AIDS, 230
National Commission on AIDS, 256
National Endowment for the Arts (NEA), 54, 67, 68
National Geographic (magazine), 36, 296
National Institutes of Health (NIH), 70, 76
National Native American AIDS Prevention Center (Oakland and Minneapolis), 69
Native Americans, 69, 222, 224, 231, 302
natural and artificial, the boundary of, 3, 15-16, 22-24, 28, 29, 33
nature, ideas of, and the AIDS epidemic, 57, 236, 239, 256
Navarro, Mireya, 70
Nazism, 175, 206, 228-30, 232, 233, 253, 286, 287. *See also* fascism
Nebraska, 166-67, 171
needles, 21, 51-52, 76, 143, 233, 264
 exchange of, in HIV prevention, 67, 282
 sharing of, 20, 57, 130, 263
needle-sticks, accidental, 210
Nelson, Emmanuel S., 31, 67, 107, 108, 109, 160, 253, 304
Nevada, 216, 219, 229
Newark, NJ, 288
New Dimensions (magazine), 39-40, 63
New England, 125, 151

New England Journal of Medicine (NEJM), 50
Newfoundland, 158
New Hampshire, 132
New Haven, 152
New Jersey, 170, 182, 185, 187, 198, 203, 261, 270
New Orleans, 149, 155, 215
Newton, Huey P., 287
New York City, 54, 59, 60, 68, 69, 70, 78, 83, 108, 143, 144, 149, 163, 172-74, 184, 188, 189, 190, 195, 197, 204, 210, 212, 215, 216, 255, 256, 259, 261, 265, 266, 271, 273, 275, 277, 278, 282, 284, 286, 287, 291, 301
New York City Commission on Human Rights, AIDS Discrimination Unit, 69
New York Newsday (newspaper), 64, 65
New York Post (newspaper), 64, 66
New York State, 298
New York Times (newspaper), 59, 68, 108
Nicaragua, 230, 231, 279
Nicaraguan *Contras*, 231, 301
Niemczyk, Nancy, 62
Night Porter (movie), 281
Nirenberg, Marshall, 6
Nixon, Richard M., 255
nonfiction narrative, 205, 223, 252, 303
North Carolina, 214
North Korea, 231
nuclear arms, 32, 64, 113, 208, 209, 218, 231
nucleotides, 6-8, 12, 13, 25
nucleus, cell, 7, 13, 25, 33-39
Nungesser, Lon G., 108

Nunokawa, Jeff, 81, 106, 107
Nureyev, Rudolf, 55, 60
NYQ (magazine), 65
Oberlin, 183, 184
obituaries, 45, 102
O'Connell, Shaun, 206-7, 253, 254, 256
O'Connor, Flannery, 187, 202
O'Connor, John Cardinal, 68-69
Oleske, James, 106
Oliver, Jim, 202
O'Malley, Jeff, 63
O'Malley, Padraig, 253
opportunistic infections, 28, 45, 73, 74, 84, 133, 213, 215, 252
oral sex, 118, 264
Orange County, CA, 213
Oreskes, Michael, 68
Orgel, Leslie, 29
origin of HIV and AIDS, theories of, 22, 41, 63, 75, 78, 80, 105, 111, 207, 208-15, 222, 235, 237, 244, 245, 247, 248, 249, 251, 252, 254, 259, 267, 268, 285. *See also* African origin of HIV and AIDS, engineering of HIV
Orwell, George, *1984*, 206
"outing," 55
ovens, concentration-camp, 224, 225, 229, 240
Packard, Randall M., 63
palindromes, molecular, 9, 27
pandemic. *See* epidemic "spread"
"paranoia," 22, 211, 228, 242
Parker, Andrew, 63
Pasteur Institute, 29
Pastore, Judith Laurence, 108, 132, 160, 161, 202, 253, 304
pathogenesis, of HIV illness, 24, 252, 257
"Patient Zero." *See* Dugas, Gaetan

Patton, Brian, 31, 64, 71
Patton, Cindy, 24, 27, 28, 39, 41, 43, 49, 63, 64, 70, 71, 106, 256, 301
PBS (Public Broadcasting System), 220, 302
Pear, Robert, 70
penis, 21, 147, 169, 177-79, 190, 197, 204, 245, 291
pentamidine, 74, 90, 99
people of color, 61, 237
People With AIDS (PWA) Coalition, 64
Pérez-Peña, Richard, 68
performance art, 15-16, 28, 303
Perlas, Nicanor, 32
phallus, 21, 36, 37, 47
Philadelphia (movie), 202
The Philippines, 231
Piel, Jonathan, 79, 106, 107
The Pièta, 188
pink triangle, 102, 230, 282, 286, 288
Piot, Peter, 105
Pneumocystis carinii pneumonia (PCP), 78, 84, 87, 90, 99, 108-9, 124, 131, 136, 139, 156, 161, 174, 263, 275
poetry, 222, 254, 303, 304
Poirier, Suzanne, 67, 69, 71, 107, 202, 254, 304
police, 59, 70, 143, 144, 192, 217, 220, 231, 247, 263, 264, 282, 288, 293, 296, 297
popular fiction, 205, 206
pornography, 206, 228, 253, 273
Portland, ME, 221
positionality, 34, 38-39, 41-42, 49, 62
"post-AIDS" world, 225, 249, 253, 256

postmodernism, 9, 28, 36, 64, 106, 195, 265, 283, 295, 301
Pound, Ezra, 185
P.O.V. (television series), 302
poverty, 60, 61, 76, 83, 195, 214, 268, 283, 284, 285
Powers, Harriet, 302
Prague, 231
pregnancy, 58, 111-13, 120
Preston, John, 105, 253
prisons and prisoners, 40, 56, 63, 69-70, 125, 222, 229, 233, 239, 240, 241, 244, 247, 255, 256, 263, 265, 282
"private" and "public," distinction of, 33, 88, 103, 205-6, 260-61, 268, 278, 280-81, 282, 290-91, 294, 298, 299
promiscuity, 19, 47, 58-60, 80, 81, 106, 169, 192
proofreading, molecular, 8
prostitution, 35, 40, 51, 59-60, 76, 215, 216, 233, 255, 264
proteins, 6-14, 25, 26, 27, 36-39
Puerto Rico, 289
Purdum, Todd S., 68
Quaid, Randy, 124
quarantine, 20, 80, 213-17, 221-26, 229, 232-34, 239-40, 247, 249, 251, 254, 255, 256, 266
queerness, 39-40, 41, 45, 47, 49, 53, 55, 57-59, 65, 78, 103, 123, 144, 153, 160, 170, 192-93, 220, 224, 229, 247, 287-89
"queer paradigm," 39-40, 41, 47, 49
queer theory, 192
Quinn, Thomas, 105
rabies, 208

race, 24, 40, 45, 48, 56, 57, 60-61, 63, 65, 69-70, 76, 109, 124, 165, 195-96, 198, 199, 230, 265, 267, 276, 278, 287-88, 290
racism, 4, 40, 42, 47, 56, 67, 148, 195, 196, 199, 204, 224, 230, 232, 248, 267, 288, 301
radiation therapy, 74
Ralegh, Sir Walter, 203
rape, 35, 36, 39, 42, 45
Ray family, 255
Reagan, Nancy, 102, 142, 196
Reagan, Ronald, 54, 142, 184, 203, 230, 240
Reamer, Frederic G., 255
Rebel without a Cause (movie), 192-93
Rechy, John, 205, 253
Redfield, Robert R., 64, 71, 75, 105, 107
Reed, Paul, 83-89, 91-92, 108, 132, 163, 166, 170, 177, 206, 256. *See also* Exander, Max
Reed, Robert, 60
Reel, Bill, 65
René, Norman, 82, 107
Reno, 229
replication, biological, 5
  of DNA, 8, 10, 25
  of viruses, 11-13, 17-18, 29, 37, 38, 44, 77, 210
reproduction, sexual, 34-36, 41, 58, 67
research, scientific, and the AIDS crisis, 24, 56-58, 81, 86, 92, 107, 208, 210, 211, 216-18, 229
resistance, political, in the AIDS crisis, 61, 207, 214, 222, 225, 226, 229, 234, 238-42,

246-49, 280-82, 284-87, 296, 300, 301, 302. *See also* activism
retroviruses, 6, 8, 11, 15, 37-38, 210
reverse transcriptase, 8-9, 15, 28
Rhame, Frank S., 255
Rhodes, William C., 66
Richardson, Diane, 70, 71
Richardson, Justin, 69
Rieder, Ines, 70
Riel, Louis, 231
Rifkin, Jeremy, 32
Riker's Island (NY), 263, 282
Riley, Pat, 48
risk, 19, 21, 30, 40, 51-52, 55-57, 59, 60, 63, 64, 66, 76, 80, 88, 111, 112, 114, 115, 120, 121, 123, 125, 126, 128, 130, 132, 133, 146, 207, 209, 212, 216, 228, 237, 252, 263-65
Rist, Darrell Yates, 66
RNA, 5-13, 15, 17, 25, 27, 37, 38
Roberts, Jeffrey W., 26
Robinson, David, 65
Robinson, Max, 55, 69
Rodgers and Hart, 187, 200
Roizman, Bernard, 26, 27, 30
The Rolling Stones, 187
Rolston, Adam, 71, 254, 256, 302
Roommates (made-for-television movie), 123-24, 160
Rose, Steven, 26
Rosenberg, Rebecca, 62
Rosenthal, M. L., 203
Rosetta Stone, 6, 26
Ross, Diana, 194
Rossi, Melissa, 160
Rotello, Gabriel, 66
Rubin, Marty, 206-7, 214-16, 219-22, 226, 228-40, 241, 243, 245-46, 247-52, 253, 255, 256, 259
Rubinstein, Arye, 106
Rubinstein, Ethan, 106
Rudd, Andrea, 70
Rumsey, Sunny, 70
Ruppelt, Patricia, 70
Rushkoff, Douglas, *Media Virus!*, 15, 16, 28
Russell, Paul, 303
Russia, 80, 112-13, 231
Russian River (CA), 115, 116
Russo, Mary, 63
Ryman, Geoff, 82, 107
Sabatier, Renée, 63, 105
safe(r) sex, 19-20, 21, 53, 55, 68, 80, 108, 109, 165, 211, 232, 243, 301
Saffo, Paul, 31
Sahara, 209
Saigon, 296
The Saint (nightclub), 285
Saint Mark's Bathhouse, 212, 285, 291
Saint Vincent's Hospital (NYC), 293-94, 300
Salt Lake City, 213
San Diego, 221
San Francisco, 50, 59, 78, 86, 101, 108, 149, 172, 212-14, 231, 232, 234, 237, 239, 240, 247, 271
Sarton, May, 84
Saudi Arabia, 230
Savage Nights (movie), 202
Schaettel, Stephanie, 62
Schmalz, Jeffrey, 66, 69
Schmitt, Eric, 69
Scholder, Amy, 302
Schulman, Sarah, xii, 4, 206, 259-302
Science (journal), 14, 106

science fiction, 31, 206, 222, 228, 253
Scientific American (journal), 79
Scott, Byron, 46
Scottishness, 148-49, 157, 159
Sedgwick, Eve Kosofsky, 53, 64, 67, 68, 69
semen, 169, 183, 198, 209, 244-45, 254
Senate and Senators, United States, 50-54, 56, 67-68, 111, 125, 128, 160, 161, 213, 214, 221, 234. *See also* Congress and Congressmen
sexism, 4, 42, 230, 232, 267, 288, 301
"sexual revolution," 21, 236
sexuality, 4, 24, 34, 35, 38-42, 45-57, 59-61, 62, 64, 65, 66, 67, 69, 113, 115-19, 123, 124, 145, 147, 150-55, 159-60, 161, 192-200, 210, 213, 222, 230, 243-46, 276-77, 283, 287-88, 289-91
sexually transmitted diseases, 58
Shah of Iran, 231
Shakespeare, William, 187, 189, 203, 204
Shatzky, Joel, 108
Sherry, Michael S., 71
Shilts, Randy, 78, 80, 81, 83, 106, 205, 235, 252, 254, 255, 256
Sicklick, Marc, 106
silence and unspeakability, 53-55, 61, 68, 95, 101, 283
SILENCE = DEATH, 61, 71, 230
Silverlake Life: The View from Here (movie), 203
Silverstein, Arthur M., 5, 25
Simmons, Doug, 65
Simmons, Sara, 65

Since You Went Away (movie), 187, 188
Slaff, James I., 43-44, 64
slavery, 109, 226, 266
smallpox, 29, 231
sneezing, as presumed mode of viral transmission, 23, 234
social realist novel, 266
Social Security benefits, 58
sodomy, 51, 142, 170, 219, 220, 232, 245
"Somewhere over the Rainbow," 270, 278, 301
Sommer, Doris, 63
Sondheim, Stephen, 186, 187
Sontag, Susan, 32, 71, 204
The South, 130, 213
South Carolina, 233, 255
South Carolina AIDS Education Network (SCAEN), 69
Soviet Union, 212, 213
Spafford, Eugene H., 29, 30, 31
Specter, Michael, 65
speech act theory, 194-95
sperm, 21, 25, 34-36, 62
Spigland, Ilya, 106
Spiro, Ellen, 255
spitting and saliva, presumed role in HIV transmission, 126, 233
splicing, molecular, 10, 37-39
The Sporting News (magazine), 49
Sports Illustrated (magazine), 47, 65
Spottiswoode, Roger, 254
"spread" of HIV. *See* epidemic "spread"
spy fiction, 205, 206, 228, 235, 281
St. Louis, 195, 215
St. Patrick's Cathedral (NYC), 276, 282-83, 302
St. Patrick's Day Parade (NYC), 54-55, 68-69

Stalin, Joseph, 198
Stanley, Wendell M., 28
Stanton, Domna C., 64, 66
Staten Island, 171, 198, 199
Stearns, Representative, of Florida, 63
Stein, Gertrude, 189
Steinberg, Jacques, 69
Steitz, Joan Argetsinger, 26
Stent, Gunther S., 5, 25, 26, 28
Stevenson, Richard W., 65
stigmatization, and HIV/AIDS, 4, 20, 56, 57, 61, 80, 125, 126-28, 130, 132, 135, 141, 144, 182, 203, 206, 213, 233, 234, 263, 265, 271
Stirnglass, Ernest, 209
Stoddard, Thomas B., 255
Stoltz, Eric, 123-24
Stonewall, 230, 288
Stop the Church (demonstration), 283, 302
"strategies," viral, 11, 13-14, 18, 27, 28, 38-39
suicide, 50, 59, 94-95, 158-60, 168, 170, 208, 222, 241, 243, 250, 254, 292
Sullivan, Joseph F., 255
Sullivan, Joseph J., Jr., 69
support groups, for people with AIDS, 208, 242, 250
Supreme Court, United States, 219, 232
suspense fiction, 206-7, 228
sweat, as presumed mode of HIV transmission, 234
sympathy, and its limits, 125, 132, 133, 141, 276, 279
symptoms, physical, associated with HIV illness, 45, 73-75, 83, 93-94, 116, 127, 132-33, 139, 142, 156, 166, 170-73, 250
 bedsores, 178
 blindness, 90
 brain tumors, 124
 chills, 133
 colds, 93, 133
 diarrhea, 90, 93, 139, 224
 fatigue and weakness, 83, 87, 89, 123, 124, 138, 139, 156, 172
 fever, 116, 133, 139, 172
 headache, 116, 123, 124, 170, 171
 kidney disease, 78
 lesions, 73, 86-87, 89-90, 94, 104, 118, 166-69, 178, 270, 273
 lymphadenopathy, 73, 83, 89, 93, 133
 nausea and vomiting, 133, 139, 170
 night sweats, 73, 116-17, 122-23, 133, 139
 pallor, 83, 85, 86, 172
 shingles, 174
 shortness of breath, 142, 156-57, 171
 skin disorders, 270, 274, 275
 sore throat, 133, 170
 spleen disorders, 174, 176, 194
 staph infections, 83, 86
 stomach ache, 116, 170
 strep throat, 98
 swollen joints, 133
 thrush, 73, 74, 174, 178
 weight-loss and "wasting," 73, 83, 89, 92-93, 109, 133, 139, 178-79, 271
Tabor, Mary B. W., 63, 256
TAG (Treatment Action Group), 80

tattooing and branding, for identification of people with HIV/AIDS, 225, 228-29, 233-34, 256
Taylor, Darien, 70
Taylor, Elizabeth, 200-201
T Cells, 43-44, 73-74, 98-99, 194
Teagle, Terry, 46
television, 15, 47, 55, 70, 77, 123-24, 175, 190, 213, 219, 220, 222, 233, 262, 267, 276, 283, 293, 294, 302
testing, and HIV, 20, 30, 41, 49, 73, 80, 94, 112, 113, 115-19, 121-23, 133, 142, 147, 149, 155-56, 167, 169, 213, 216-18, 233, 255, 265
Thailand, 59
Thistlethwaite, Polly, 255
Thomas, Isaiah, 46-47
Thomas, Kathleen, 106
Thomas, Lewis, 107
Thompson, Mark, 253
Thompson, Ken, 30
Time (magazine), 27, 62
Tolstoy, Leo, *War and Peace*, 169
Tompkins Square Riot, 262
Tooze, John, 25
Traherne, Judith, 173
Tramont, Edmund C., 75, 105
transcription, molecular, 8-13, 25, 27, 36
translation, molecular, 8, 10, 11, 13, 25, 36
transposons and transposable elements, 9, 10, 27
treatment and health care, for HIV/AIDS, 20, 45, 56, 57, 74, 76, 80, 81, 85, 90, 95-97, 98-99, 100, 106-7, 123, 130, 174-76, 180, 213, 228, 252, 270, 271, 275, 282, 283, 291, 292, 301
Treblinka, 229
Treichler, Paula A., 23, 24, 31, 32, 36, 37, 62, 63, 70, 71, 105, 106
Trifonov, Edward, 7
Trojan Horses, 21, 31
Trump, Donald, 265, 266
Tuana, Nancy, 62
21 Jump Street (television series), 302
Twilight Zone (television series), 281
Tyler, Carole-Anne, 64
Tyrone, Mary, 186
United Press International (UPI), 77
"universal precautions," 80
Untouchables (television series), 281
Upper Manhattan Task Force on AIDS, 69
urethra, 62
U.S. News and World Report (magazine), 105
uterus, 35, 62
utopian fiction, 206, 251, 254, 292, 293
vaccine, against HIV, 76, 215, 252
vagina, 62, 153
vaginal sex, 41, 117-18, 264
Valens, Evans G., 28
Valentino, Rudolph, 174
Vecsey, George, 66
Verhovek, Sam Howe, 255
VerMeulen, Michael, 64, 105
vertical transmission, of HIV, 77, 106
"victim," 35, 39, 45, 46, 49, 53, 60-61, 64, 77, 78, 79, 87, 89, 114, 124-26, 128, 201,

212, 215, 227, 229, 230, 233, 236, 237, 292
Vidal, Gore, 187, 192
Vietnam, 195, 230, 231, 240, 242, 253, 296, 297
Village Voice (newspaper), 299
violence, 14, 28, 36-37, 47, 112-13, 124, 144, 151, 153, 154, 219, 221, 225, 228, 229, 232-34, 240-42, 244, 251, 286, 295, 296
virginity, 69, 193
viroids, 27
virology, 5, 25, 26
viruses and viral action, 3, 5, 7, 8, 11-24, 25, 26, 27-29, 30, 31, 32, 36-41, 44, 75, 77, 209, 214-15, 218, 223, 225-26, 249-50, 256. *See also* computer viruses, HIV
voice, 92, 129-31, 140, 164, 170, 180, 182-84
von Sydow, Max, 190
wake-up calls, 164-65, 172
Wall Street, 239, 256, 292, 293
Walter Reed Staging Classification for HTLV-III/LAV Infection, 73-74, 75, 105
War Games (movie), 32
Warner, Michael, 63
Warnke, Frank J., 203
Warren, Robert Penn, 202
Warren Commission, 255
Warsaw Ghetto, 229
Watergate, 238, 255
Watney, Simon, 24, 63, 64, 67, 105, 106, 107, 160
Watson, James D., 8, 25, 26
    et al., *Molecular Biology of the Gene* (*MBG*), 26-28
Weber, Bruce, 68
Webster (television series), 47

Wedel, Andrew, 62
Weicker, Lowell, 50, 69
Weiner, Alan W., 26
Weir, John, xii, 4, 68, 163-204, 206, 300
Welles, Paul O'M., 253
West, Richard, 107
Wetsel, David, 31
WHAM! (Women's Health Action and Mobilization), 283
White House, 220-21, 264
Wilde, Oscar, *The Picture of Dorian Gray*, 81
Williams, Tennessee, 175, 186, 199, 202
Williams, William Carlos, 187, 203
Williamson, Judith, 105, 106, 107
Wilson, Tamsin, 70
witness fiction, 270-71
Witten, Ian H., 30, 31
women, and the AIDS crisis, 3, 33, 45, 46, 49, 50, 57-61, 62, 67, 70, 71, 76, 118, 122, 170, 186, 217, 221, 237-38, 254, 255, 263-64, 289-90, 291, 294
Wong-Staal, Flossie, 26, 27, 28, 62, 63, 64
Wood, Natalie, 192
Woodlawn Cemetery, 173
Woods, Gregory, 107
Wordsworth, William, 204
World War II, 213, 214, 220, 229, 230, 232, 241
Worthy, James, 46
Wright, D. Craig, 75, 105, 107
Wright, Les, 228, 230, 250, 253, 254, 255, 256, 257
Wyman, Jane, 191
xenophobia, 40
Yaeger, Patricia, 63

Yeats, William Butler, 183, 187, 203
Yerkes, Robert M., 25
Yonkers, 181, 195
Yosemite National Park, 57
Zaire, 208-10, 212
Zingler, Peter, 71, 254

DATE DUE